Like Christ, the Christian ⟨...⟩ ⟨...⟩on is
like chewing your food we⟨...⟩ ⟨...⟩e to
help you to cut your meat, ⟨...⟩ ⟨...⟩ spiritual nutrition of
the Bible.

—Dr. Joel R. Beeke, President
Puritan Reformed Theological Seminary
Grand Rapids, MI

I am thankful for the writing ministry of Dr. J. D. Watson and the rich insights he gives us into the Word of God. In yet another installment of his excellent word studies, this new book provides us with a greater understanding of key words used throughout the Old and New Testaments. These studies are written with a pastor's heart and a scholar's mind. I am certain that your knowledge of Scripture will be greatly enhanced by this book, as well as your ability to live out its essential truths.

—Dr. Steven J. Lawson
Founder and President, OnePassion Ministries
Author, *A Long Line of Godly Men* series

Seek Him Early is a wonderful daily devotional resource that will actually get you into the text of Scripture. If you are looking for a way to make your devotional life more fruitful, this book offers precisely the kind of day-to-day spiritual discipline I recommend, with instructive daily Bible readings that will edify, equip, and encourage you in your daily walk.

—Phil Johnson
Executive Director, *Grace to You*
Founder, *The Spurgeon Archive* (www.spurgeon.org/)

Seek Him Early is not trite, silly, or man-centered—it is God-exalting—and it is so meaty that it will keep your brain from wandering when you should be focusing. Don't delay. Get this book. Read it, apply it, and you will love Jesus more.

—Todd Friel
Author and host of nationally syndicated
Wretched TV and *Wretched Radio* programs

Seek Him Early is a great combination of linguistic care, theological depth, and devotional application. My wife, Margaret, and I are always on the lookout for edifying material we can read together that does our souls good and shows us the greatness of the Lord in his redemptive work. We look forward to reading and contemplating this book together.

—Dr. Thomas J. Nettles
Professor of Historical Theology, The Southern Baptist Theological Seminary
Author, *By His Grace and For His Glory*

Doc Watson's third devotional book is a blessing to me, and I would recommend it to other readers. Its Bible studies are accurate and deep. They glorify God, and they edify the reader. I pray that God will use them in the hearts and minds of many.

—Dr. John M. Frame
Reformed Theological Seminary; Orlando, FL
Author, *A Theology of Lordship* series

A paramount need in the lives of most believers is the discovery of a way to sweeten the devotional walk with God and pour fresh flavor into a daily meeting with God. Dr. Watson, informed by years of tending to the sheep under his care, has opened both his heart and the Scriptures, inviting the larger flock of God to walk with him in the Heavenlies. Doctrinal truth placed on a level where none can miss it, this book will encourage your heart even as it builds your strength. Walk with Doc day-by-day.

—Dr. Paige Patterson, President
Southwestern Baptist Theological Seminary; Fort Worth, TX

These devotional readings prove to be profoundly biblical and life-changing. I recommend a daily dose for everyone.

—Dr. Richard Mayhue
Research Professor of Theology Emeritus, The Master's Seminary

In these devotional studies, Dr. Watson seeks to help Christians with the perennial challenge of getting deeply and usefully into the Word of God. Nothing is more important than knowing, loving, and serving the Lord Jesus Christ. These studies seek to take the believer to Christ in all these ways. May God grant them great usefulness!

—Dr. Samuel E. Waldron, Professor of Systematic Theology
Covenant Baptist Theological Seminary; Owensboro, KY
Author, *A Modern Exposition of the 1689 Baptist Confession of Faith*

What a joy it is to commend to you *Seek Him Early*. In a day and age in which devotionals are characterized by emotions, feelings, and claims of direct messages from God, Dr. Watson gives a thoroughly exegetical and intensely practical devotional book for believers who take seriously the study of God's sufficient Word. This devotional book will deepen your knowledge of God and will, in turn, deepen your love for Him. I will be using *Seek Him Early* in my own personal times of study and hope that you will as well.

—Justin Peters, M.Div, Th.M.
Clouds Without Water Seminar (http://JustinPeters.org/)
Author, *Do Not Hinder Them: A Biblical Examination of Childhood Conversion*

Seek Him Early is a meat-eaters devotional, not milk but daily solid food for those who wish to have their powers of discernment trained by constant practice to distinguish good from evil (Heb 5:14). Doc Watson builds on his earlier, excellent

Greek and Hebrew word study works to present a daily immersion in the unfathomable riches of God's Word. The finite can never grasp the infinite, but we are called to pursue the mind of God in so much as He has revealed to us. God willing, *Seek Him Early* will sanctify the pursuit.

—JD Wetterling
Author, *"No one . . ."* and *No Time To Waste*

I have not read Dr. Watson's first two devotional books, but if their content can be judged by the theological scholarship of *Seek Him Early: Daily Devotional Studies on Knowing, Loving, and Serving Our Lord Jesus Christ*, the loss has been mine. Most devotional books tend to give encouragement for Christian living but offer little in teaching you the character of God and knowing Him in a deeper and more personal way. This devotional will guide you to loving Him more fully, obeying Him more faithfully, and serving Him better. It is, indeed, a pleasure to commend this theologically challenging and thought provoking book.

—Dr. Allen Monroe
Equipping Leaders International
Former Professor, Cedarville University

It's with great joy that I recommend Doc Watson's latest devotional book, *Seek Him Early*. Each day you use this tool, you will be drawn into close communion with the living God through succinct, exegetical, pungent, doctrinal, experiential, and very applicable instructions from Scripture. In addition, it's also shot through with many sound homiletical insights, accurate word studies, helpful illustrations, and God-centered directives to begin your day. An excellent gift for the maturing teen, and extremely edifying for the faithful disciple, and senior saint alike. May God use this gift to bless His people!

—Pastor Jerry Marcellino
Audubon Drive Bible Church; Laurel, MS
Co-founder, Fellowship of Independent Reformed Evangelicals (FIRE)

Fans of J. Sidlow Baxter are sure to enjoy the elegance and eloquence of Doc Watson's *Seek Him Early*. The similarity of style and depth of spiritual understanding and application are a fitting tribute to Baxter's work *Awake My Heart*. In one year, the reader will progress from the basics of knowing God, to the beauty of loving God, and then be led into the brilliance of serving our Lord and Savior. *Seek Him Early* is as motivating and inspirational as it is theologically solid. As a daily devotional guide, it is unsurpassed in quality and content.

—Dr. James Bearss, President
On Target Ministry, Teaching Faithful Men through International Education

"Doc" Watson has once again given the Church a precious gift. In this easy to read, yet substantive, daily devotional, the reader will be blessed and instructed. I enjoyed the enumeration, keeping it to the point. The Greek and Hebrew words give the reading some meat rather than just some nice stories. Each daily reading is a well thought out commentary of the selected text with practical application. Important questions are asked throughout and answered by the text of Scripture. Many important areas of the Christian Life are covered. Instead of a "Daily Devotional," this is a "Daily Mini Sermon" for the soul. As a pastor in the ministry approaching 40 years, I can whole heartedly recommend *Seek Him Early*!

—Dr. Richard C. Piatt II
23-year pastor, Fellowship Baptist Church; Lakeland, FL

The Scriptures make it clear that the people of God need teachers, teachers who are gifted at not only understanding the Bible, but also in explaining it and drawing appropriate application. J. D. "Doc" Watson is one of these gifted teachers, whether through the spoken or written forum. It is a privilege to endorse his newest devotional book because it is biblical, insightful, and helpful to those desiring to dig into the resources of God's Word.

—Dr. Gary E. Gilley, 41-year Senior Pastor
Southern View Chapel; Springfield, IL
Author/Director, *Think on These Things Ministries*

I have loved using devotionals for most of my Christian life, yet finding many to be heavy on devotional thoughts and light on textual depth or vice versa. I love what Doc Watson has done in marrying the two nicely. Here is food to chew on from the text of Scripture that always lands you communing with the Living God. I highly recommend this devotional.

Pastor Ken Murphy, M.Div
Southside Bible Church; Centennial, CO

Doc Watson has done it again! Here you are offered a devotional guide of benefit to both your study and soul. Doc is a wordsmith who takes you beyond a mere definition of a Bible term. He shows you how all doctrine is practical to life. Nothing will serve you as a devotional aid more than one geared toward stimulating mind and heart in knowing, loving and serving Christ. Few devotionals offer the meat of the Word page-by-page as does this one. You will be blessed from the growth available through the insights offered from someone who has labored hard in knowing Him.

—Pastor Kevin Kottke, M.Div
37-year pastor, Plainfield Bible Church; Plainfield, IN

Each of these devotions seeks first and foremost to show us God. Each passage is exegetically and accurately explained in its context, leading the reader in a powerful study. Although short, each daily reading is not a snack but a banquet. This is an exceptional work.

—Pastor Jim Bryant, MBS
27-year pastor, Grace Bible Chapel; San Antonio, TX
Author, *Presumed Faith: A Verse-By-Verse Study of 1 John*

Dr. Watson draws from a breadth of knowledge and experience in these daily readings. They were not written in haste, nor are they to be read in haste. Pastoral and sermonic, they are a substantial blend of keen scholarship and warm devotion, a welcome alternative to the spiritual dime-store fluff common today. A year with this volume will be time well spent!

— Pastor Daniel Chamberlain
16-year pastor, Covenant Baptist Church; Broken Arrow, OK
Author, *A Portrait of God: Stephen Charnock's "Discourses Upon the Existence and Attributes of God" Summarized for the 21st Century*

It is the desire of every born again Christian to gain a deeper understanding of our great God and Savior through His Word. I have always admired Doc Watson for his giftedness in bringing clarity to controversial doctrines of Scripture in his book, *Truth On Tough Texts*. Now in his new devotional book, he masterfully draws his readers to a closer walk with God through profound insights into His inspired Word. I highly recommend this book for those who seek to re-ignite their passion for serving the King of kings with a thankful heart.

—Mike Gendron, MABS
Director, Proclaiming the Gospel Ministry

The vast majority of daily devotionals available today are shallow in content and light in practical application. By comparison, Dr. Watson has created a masterpiece of biblical literature. Readers are treated to devotional readings that are exegetically sound, show a fervent love for the Savior, and illuminate and encourage a path to faithful obedience to Christ. I know of no devotional that is more insightful in helping readers to better know, love, and serve Christ than this one. You will be immensely blessed to have this in your possession.

—Pastor Jack Jenkins, BS, MA
Pastor, Faith Baptist Church; Orlando, FL

I am excited about this new devotional from our friend Doc Watson. This will be a breath of fresh air for those who desire "a little more" for their devotional readings. These readings are interesting and thought provoking; doctrinal, but not stuffy. What I appreciate most about *Seek Him Early* is that it goes someplace: it takes the reader on a one year journey to reach the goal of knowing, loving, and serving our Lord. This is a goal worth pursuing, and this book can greatly aid in achieving it.

—Pastor Dan Aldrich
40-year pastor, Fremont Street Baptist Church; Crawfordsville, IN

Many devotional books today take a cute story and then try to find a Scripture to match. It comes off as shallow fluff. Not so this book! It brings to light spiritual truths using biblical examples as illustrations. His insights are offered in an orderly fashion using both every day examples and biblical characters as a means of conveying timeless truths. You will be blessed by his concise and thoughtful comments. It is spiritual meat to nourish and depth that draws us nearer to the Lord.

—Pastor Mark Smeltzer (see Jan. 2)
Glenwood Community Church; Glenwood, IA

This daily devotional by Dr. J. D. Watson immediately satisfied my desire to engage with a daily "teaching" devotional. Having enjoyed a daily fellowship with my Lord from a young age, I have used many quality devotional guides—certainly Spurgeon's and Chambers' are perennial classics. But it was the thematic sections of Watson's devotional that intrigued me. Upon working through the three sections on, *Knowing, Loving,* and *Serving* the Lord Jesus Christ, I found them to be a seamless progression of daily teaching thoughts. Having enjoyed Dr. Watson's *A Word for the Day* (Greek) and *Hebrew Word for the Day*, I was pleased how he incorporated his word studies knowledge along with very interesting anecdotes to produce a thoroughly lively daily drink in the Scripture. I can recommend this devotional series to a range of Christians, both to those who are newer in the faith and desire some doctrinally sound thoughts to start or finish the day, or to the mature believer who enjoys some prayerful impressions from God's Word.

—Russell H. Spees, Christian Businessman
President, Rapid-Packaging Corporation; Grand Rapids, MI

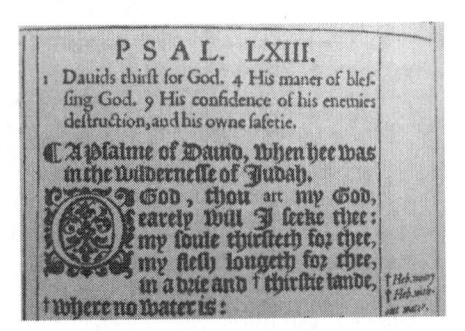

Psalm 63:1 in the original 1611 King James Version

Seek Him Early

Daily Devotional Studies on Knowing, Loving, and Serving Our Lord Jesus Christ

Dr. J. D. Watson

Sola Scriptura
Publications

Seek Him Early: Daily Devotional Studies on Knowing, Loving, and Serving Our Lord Jesus Christ

Copyright © 2017 Dr. J. D. Watson

Fourth printing: June 2018

Published by Sola Scriptura Publications
P. O. Box 235
Meeker, CO 81641
dwatson@thescripturealone.com

www.TheScriptureAlone.com
This website includes a podcast based on this book.

All rights reserved. Except for brief quotations in printed reviews, no part of this publication may be reproduced, stored in a retrieval system, or transmitted in any form or by any means (printed, written, photocopied, visual electronic, audio, or otherwise) without the prior written permission of the copyright holder.

Unless otherwise noted, all Scripture quotations and word references are from our beloved *The Authorized King James Version* (KJV).

Scripture quotations marked YLT are from *Young's Literal Translation* (Public Domain, 1862, 1898)

Scripture quotations marked NKJV are from the *New King James Version* (Nashville: Thomas Nelson, Inc. Publishers, 1979, 1980, 1982, 1990)

Scripture quotations marked NIV are from the *New International Version* (Colorado Springs: International bible Society. 1978, 1984)

Scripture quotations marked NASB are from the *New American Standard Bible* (La Habra, CA: The Lockman Foundation, 1995).

Scripture quotations marked ESV are from the *English Standard Version* (Crossway Bible, A Division of Good News Publishers, 2001)

Cover picture: © Michaeljung | Dreamstime.com
www.dreamstime.com/stock-photos-sky-image6034193#res4830540 Sky Photo

Library of Congress Cataloging-in-Publication Data

ISBN–13: 978-1544123011
ISBN–10: 1544123019

Dedication

This work is dedicated first to my dear
Savior and Lord, Jesus Christ,
and also to the memory of

Dr. J. Sidlow Baxter

whose books helped *mold* my
theology, *mend* some errors, and
magnify my love for our Lord and His Word.

Acknowledgements

My heartfelt thanks goes out to many who in one way or another have significantly supported the ministry of Sola Scriptura Publications (alphabetically): Dr. James Bearss; the late Joe Bruce; Eric Duncan; Faye Goggin; Grace Bible Church members; Dave and Linda Olson; Rico Patterson; Mark Phillippo, Jr.; Jim Spees; Russ Spees; Debbie Watson; Celeste Watson; and Paul Watson.

Deep thanks also goes to the dear men of God who endorsed this book. Such encouragement and confirmation means more than they can know.

Special thanks also go out to every dear believer who has supported this ministry by purchasing this book and other titles we publish.

My bottomless appreciation also goes to those who call and email with their kind comments on this writing ministry.

Soli Deo Gloria

Contents

Introduction	13
Part I: Knowing Our Lord January – February – March – April	15
Part II: Loving Our Lord May – June – July – August	139
Part III: Serving Our Lord September – October – November – December	265
Selected Bibliography	391
Main Text Index	393
About the Author	395
Greek Pronunciation Guide	397
Hebrew Pronunciation Guide	399
Notes	401

Early Will I Seek Thee

Lord, I endeavor early to seek Thee,
Before venturing out into the way.
It is Thy face I first desire to see,
And there is no better time of the day.
As the hart pants after the water brooks,
So panteth my soul after thee, O Lord.
It is upon Thee that I first must look,
So I am armed for the day with Thy Sword.
My soul thirsts for Thee and for Thee alone
Before the sun even begins to rise.
To be with Thee I would give all I own,
For just being there is the greatest prize.
    I arise to meet Thee in the morning,
    To enjoy a time that's all-absorbing.

Introduction

WHAT a wonderful blessing it was to begin my Christian publishing endeavors with two daily devotional books (which also double as reference books)—*A Word for the Day: Key Words from the New Testament* (2006) and *A Hebrew Word for the Day: Key Words from the Old Testament* (2010)—both graciously published by AMG Publishers.

Having published several titles since, the present work returns to those roots. While it is, like the other two, thematic, word studies are not the foundation this time, although such studies still appear often. Instead, the overarching emphasis is on *knowing*, *loving*, and *serving* our Lord and Savior Jesus Christ. In three distinct parts, each encompassing four months of devotional/theological studies, the reader is first encouraged to know the Lord in a personal way, then to love Him like never before, and finally to be driven to more passionately serve Him.

In a very literal sense, this book is the final realization of a desire that began some 37 years ago. It was then I began pondering the idea of penning a devotional book, even writing two months worth of meditations. But for several reasons—not the least of which was my own need to grow deeper, both as a Christian and a penman—I set the project aside. Now, all these years later—having grown at least a little deeper—I would like to share with you that passion, even including a few of the original thoughts, though greatly (and thankfully) reworked.

A Tribute

That brings me to my tribute to a dear saint whose books actually ignited that original zeal, **Dr. J. Sidlow Baxter** (1903–1999).[1] Having read every book of his that I know of, there are three that have had the most influence on my inward life and outward ministry: the most dear of all, *Going Deeper*, followed next by his own daily devotional, *Awake My Heart*, and finally *Christian Holiness Restudied and Restated*.[2] I would also interject, in light of the virtual stylelessness of much writing today,[3] reading Baxter is as refreshing as breathing mountain air. Read him once and you will be wholly hooked.

At this point, it is time for honest confession: this present work has a few clear earmarks of the first two Baxter books above. No one, in my humble opinion, blends together doctrine, devotion, and duty better than Baxter. He was scrupulously theological while at the same time thoroughly practical. Those qualities have profoundly affected me through the years, and I have tried with great effort to reflect them.

Going Deeper is my ultimate example.[4] It is not only my favorite of Baxter's works, but it's also my favorite "devotional/Christian living" book of all time. That is saying much, as I have read many wonderful books through the years. But this one ascends to its own level of magnificence—it is very special. Its sub-title—*A Series of Devotional Studies in Knowing, Loving, and Serving Our Lord Jesus*

Christ—demonstrates the impact it has had on this present work. I have dared to adopt a similar sub-title and even organize the book in that three-fold emphasis.

As for *Awake My Heart* (subtitled *Daily Devotional and Expository Studies-in-brief Based on a Variety of Bible Truths, and Covering One Complete Year*), it is also my humble opinion that nothing in the annals of Christian history equals it as a daily devotional. One can read it through and then at the end of the year immediately start over and gain new insights as he strolls through it again. That book has also affected this present one, as both vary from the norm, being more *expository* and even *homiletical* than daily devotionals typically are.

Using This Book

Like the two predecessors mentioned earlier, the present work also includes an important section at the end of each daily study, "Scriptures for Study," which lists other related verses for you to explore. I would also encourage you to use each day's study to generate "promptings for prayer." Meditate on each day's study and allow the Holy Spirit to prompt you in the three basic aspects of prayer: thanksgiving, praise, and petition. All this is also conducive to journaling; organize your studies and reflections by date in a separate notebook.

Finally, cross references to other readings often appear in parentheses to point you to related subjects or verses. Other conventions and abbreviations include:

- **Bold text** – used for the main text for each day's study and for the words of that text within the devotional reading.
- **OT** – Abbreviation for the Old Testament.
- **NT** – Abbreviation for the New Testament.
- **Classical (ancient or secular) Greek** – Greek prior to NT times. References to that include, for example, the Greek used by Plato (ca. 435–427 BC) and the Greek of the poet Homer (8th-century BC), who is famous for his epic poems, *The Illiad* and *The Odyssey*.
- **Septuagint** – the Greek translation of the Hebrew OT; translated in the 3rd- and 2nd-centuries BC, probably in Alexandria, for the Library of Ptolemy Philadelphus, king of Egypt, by a delegation of 70 Jewish scholars; hence the name Septuagint (70), and the abbreviation LXX.
- **Strong's Number** – For easy cross-referencing to many language tools, Hebrew and Greek Words include the universally used Strong's number enclosed in parentheses. Numbers for Greek words appear alone, while numbers for Hebrew words end with the letter "H."

So, while the present work—37 years in the making and two years in the writing—will most certainly not equal the masterpieces mentioned earlier, I pray it will perhaps be moderately comparable. If it fails even in that, I pray it will at least be of small profit to a few of God's people scattered about, for what is written here comes from the very depths of my heart.

The Author
January 2017

PART I
Knowing Our Lord

January
February
March
April

Knowing My Lord

Knowing my Lord is my greatest desire
Ever pressing forward to that high call.
With each new day more knowledge to acquire,
And to that single task giving my all.
It's not my Lord I want to know *about*,
But to really know Him personally.
Such sweet communion erases all doubt
That I will enjoy Him eternally.
So I keep on pressing toward the prize
Of the upward calling of God in Him.
For only there do I learn what is wise,
And gaze on the Light that will never dim.
    Knowing my Lord is my greatest desire;
    To that final goal I ever aspire.

JANUARY 1

Seek Him Early

... early will I seek thee ... (Ps. 63:1)

IN keeping with the title of our book of meditations, we first consider David's deep desire as he wrote while in the wilderness of Judah. Not only was he acutely aware of his need to commune with God, but he also recognized the need to do so **early**. How important it is to seek God's face before we face the day! Before we go out into the *world* alone, we need to get with *God* alone. Before we encounter the difficulties of life, we need an encounter with our Lord. The Hebrew (*sāḥar*, 7836H) includes not only the idea of "early" but also diligent search (Is. 26:9; Prov. 8:17).

First, we note David's *problem*. Verse 1 goes on to declare: **my soul thirsteth for thee**. That metaphor is rooted in reality. Israel is a very arid land, so as an outdoorsman and soldier, David well understood thirst. It is estimated that a person can live only about three days without water. Severe thirst causes the lips to crack, the stomach to cramp, and the body to ache. As dehydration continues, results include increased heart and respiration rates, spastic muscles, shriveled and wrinkled skin, and renal problems.

Far worse, David therefore tells us, is *spiritual* thirst. An aching *soul* is a much more severe condition than an aching *body*. This picture was so graphic for David that he wrote elsewhere: "My soul thirsteth for God, for the living God" (Ps. 42:2).[5] Can we each say that we thirst for communion with God? Can we say with David, my soul thirsts for God?

Second, we see God's *provision* in verse 5: **My soul shall be satisfied**. To be in God's presence is food and drink to a dying man. The Hebrew behind **satisfied** (*śābaʻ*, 7646H) means to have enough of something, or even more than enough, as Israel had more than enough to eat in the wilderness (Ex. 16:8, 12). Further, the expression **marrow and fatness** pictures the finest foods one would expect to savor at a feast. Likewise, when we come before the Lord through His Word and prayer, we will feast on enticing entrées, savory side dishes, and delicious desserts we have never tasted before. We will eat to our fullest but will not be able to take it all in.

Third, we finally note David's *praising*. No host or hostess wants to hear the expression, "I hate to eat and run, but I have to be going." Well, David wasn't going anywhere. **My mouth shall praise thee with joyful lips** he writes in verse 5 and then adds in verse 7: **Because thou hast been my help, therefore in the shadow of thy wings will I rejoice**. As baby birds hide under their mother's wings for safety and solace, David could **rejoice** under God's **wings**. He knew that nourishment was nothing to be rushed, so he lingered there to praise the Host and rejoice in the bounty.

Scriptures for Study: What did Job testify in Job 23:12? 📖 What does Amos 8:11 declare about thirst? (Reminder: you could keep a journal for these studies.)

January 2

Let us Linger Longer

... thou shalt eat bread at my table continually. (2 Sam. 9:7)

DURING an extensive traveling ministry many years ago, I had the joy of ministering several times at a particular church in Iowa, then pastored by a dear brother, Mark Smeltzer. Like many churches, a time of food and fellowship followed each service. What made this one special, however, was the term used for it. Those dear folks called it "A Linger Longer," and I have never forgotten either the clever sentiment or the sweet fellowship.

One of the most beautiful stories in all Scripture appears in 2 Samuel 9. It is about David, who for the sake of his dear friend Jonathan, wanted to show kindness to his family. He found such a recipient in Jonathan's crippled son Mephibosheth. In several staggering parallels, David's kindness pictures the grace and love God has shown to man for the sake of His son Jesus Christ. Just a few include: mercy to one who was crippled by a fall, grace to the undeserving, adoption into the king's family, and the bestowing of riches.[6]

One blessing, however, is particularly striking. Having been brought into the palace and made a king's son, David declared that Mephibosheth would now **eat** at the king's table **continually**. And that is exactly what happened, as verse 13 verifies: "So Mephibosheth dwelt in Jerusalem: for he did eat continually at the king's table." Both instances of **continually** translate the Hebrew *tāmiyḏ* (8548H), which speaks of continuity. One notable occurrence of this word is in Numbers 4:7, where it refers to "the continual bread" (or "bread of continuity") that was always "upon the table of shewbread."

What a blessing Mephibosheth enjoyed for the rest of his life! Hunger was a thing of the past. No longer did he live in Lodebar, which literally means "pastureless," for he now lived in the security and bounty of the palace. Food was continually available, and he could linger at the table as long as he liked.

We too have access to such a table, one that is always lavishly set and awaiting our arrival. That table is the Word of God. Sadly, however, we are often simply too busy to sit down and feast. We either "skip breakfast" altogether or hurriedly walk by and snatch a bite or two and then rush out into the world. Our present day is, indeed, one of rapid travel, rapid communication, and rapid reading (when we read at all). One of our truly great needs is to take the time to sit down at the King's Table and there to linger longer.

> From my crippled state He did enable,
> Even in weakness making me stronger.
> Daily lavishing at the King's table,
> It is there with Him I linger longer.

Scriptures for Study: What do Luke 22:30 and Revelation 19:9 teach us about the future?

JANUARY 3

Be Still

Be still, and know that I am God. I will be exalted among the heathen, I will be exalted in the earth. (Ps. 46:10)

WITH our loss of the sense of majesty has come the further loss of religious awe and consciousness of the divine Presence," wrote A. W. Tozer in the preface to his wonderful classic, *The Knowledge of the Holy*. "We have lost our spirit of worship and our ability to withdraw inwardly to meet God in adoring silence. Modern Christianity is simply not producing the kind of Christian who can appreciate or experience the life in the Spirit. The words, 'Be still, and know that I am God,' mean next to nothing to the self-confident, bustling worshiper in this middle period of the twentieth century."[7] While that was written in 1961, consider again where we are today. Much of the Church is a blur of activity, but spiritual depth is sorely missing.

First, then, note the *command*: **Be still**. The Hebrew behind **still** (*rāpāh*, 7503H) has a wide range of meanings and connotations. Here it includes ideas such as to relax, to cease striving, or to desist. In legal parlance, a "cease and desist order" is an order to stop an activity (cease) and not take it up again later (desist) or else face legal action. Obviously, God does not advocate laziness, rather He is telling us to "cease and desist" from our anxiety, fear, and impatience, to stop striving for things that don't matter, to relax so we can contemplate Him.

Second, consider the promise of *confidence*: **and know that I am God**. When we stop long enough to meditate on God's Word, He assures us that we will really get to **know** Him. **Know** is *yāda'* (3045H), which has a broad array of meanings concerning knowledge acquired by the senses, to know relationally and experientially. Once we are **still**, we will then have time for a truly deeper relationship with God. Of that we can have full confidence.

Third, we will be driven to *contemplation*. As we will see in studies to come, there can be no greater exercise of the mind than contemplating God. If I may humbly add a stanza to that old hymn, *Be Still My Soul*, originally penned in the 17th-century and the favorite of Eric Liddell, a gold medallist in the 1924 Olympics and later a missionary to China (the movie *Chariots of Fire* told his story):

> Be still, my soul, and know that He is God,
> To contemplate the wonders that are His.
> Whatever I face or path I may trod
> My only confidence is that He is.
> > Be still, my soul, and know He's on His Throne.
> > My rest is knowing I'm never alone.

Scriptures for Study: What do the following verses tell us about knowing God: Exodus 18:11; Psalms 83:18; 100:3?

JANUARY 4

A Still Small Voice

. . . a still small voice. (1 Kings 19:12)

THE setting of this verse is a dramatic scene indeed. *First*, there is the *confrontation*. In verse 9, God appears to his usually faithful prophet and asks him, "What doest thou here, Elijah?" What prompted such a question? While this courageous and powerful prophet of God had stood boldly before the prophets of Baal on Mount Carmel and had humiliated, defeated, and destroyed them, he ran in terror from a single woman, Jezebel. Instead of repenting of her wickedness, she was enraged by what Elijah had done and sent him a message declaring he would be dead within 24 hours (v. 2). In response, Elijah fled some 100 miles south to Beersheba and hid in a cave (vv. 3, 9). The word **here** (*pōh*, 6311H, "present, in this place") is pivotal. It underscores that Elijah was *here* where he should *not* be instead of *there* where he *ought* to be. That challenges each of us to consider how often we run and hide when we should stay and stand. While we might, like Elijah, look upon our withdrawal as "going on a retreat" to get closer to God, such might simply be masking our attempt to escape.

Second, we note Elijah's *confession*: "I have been very jealous for the LORD God of hosts . . . I, even I only, am left" (v. 10). What was certainly a sincere confession also exposes some self-pity. Was Elijah really the only one left in Israel who hadn't turned against God? Besides, if he was truly as faithful as he claimed, why was he 100 miles from his place of ministry?

Third, there is the *comfort*. What did Elijah need? He just needed a reminder, a "refresher course" in God's power and glory. The following display was staggering: gale force winds tore rocks and even mountains apart, an earthquake shook the very foundations of those mountains, and fire roared around it all. But as dramatic as all that was, there was not a single word from God in any of it (vv. 11–12).

Why? Sadly, many think God speaks in such things and so are looking for dramatic and colossal happenings in the Church. But our text tells us the exact opposite: He speaks in **a still small voice**, or "a still and soft voice" (*The Geneva Bible*), or even more literally, "a sound of soft stillness," which we might simply call "a whisper." Just as it is impossible to hear a pin drop in a factory, it is impossible to hear God in all the noise of our day. So where do we hear God's whisper? In His Word and our silence before it.

> Here is a great truth in which to rejoice:
> Look not for some great vision to appear;
> God speaks through His Word in a still small voice,
> And He will whisper it in your heart's ear.

Scriptures for Study: What assignment did God go on to give Elijah in verses 15–21? 📖 How does this encourage you?

JANUARY 5

Elements of Meditation (1)

My meditation of him shall be sweet . . . (Ps. 104:34)

PURITAN Thomas Watson observed, "The reason we come away so cold from reading the Word is because we do not warm ourselves at the fire of meditation."[8] But what is *meditation* and how does it relate to us? While it is a much misunderstood concept, it is an essential element in our growth.

First, we must understand the *definition* of meditation. The famous Zen *kōan*[9]—"What is the sound of one hand clapping?"—is often equated with meditation. But such things are not true meditation at all, rather meaningless contradiction that do not "enlighten" the practitioner, as it is claimed, but rather serve only to deepen the darkness in which he wanders aimlessly.

The word **meditation** (along with "meditate") appears about 20 times in Scripture. The most common Hebrew word (*higgāyôn*, 1902H, from the verb *hāgâ*, 1897H, "to growl, groan, sigh, mutter") refers to the murmur or dull sound of a harp and therefore the subdued or soft playing of a musical instrument (it's also used for the coos of a dove [Is. 38:14] and the moans of grief [16:7]). Hence, the idea is quiet and concentrated thought (we will note another meaning tomorrow).

Another Hebrew word (*śiyaḥ*, 7879H)—which appears in our text and is also sometimes translated "prayer" in other occurrences—denotes contemplation. Interestingly, its primary meaning is actually "complaint," which strikes us as odd at first. The idea, however, is not complaining in the sense of blaming God, rather deep meditation brought on by distress and urgent need. Job, for example, used this very word in the midst of his suffering (Job 7:13; 9:27; 10:1; 21:4; 23:2), as did David in his distress when he hid from Saul in a cave (Ps. 142:2).[10]

There is a profound appearance of the word "meditate" in 1 Timothy 4. Paul first exhorts Timothy on several issues: false teachers (vv. 1–5), teaching doctrine (v. 6), avoiding myths and legends (v. 7), godliness (vv. 7–8), and exposition (v. 13). Paul then urges his "son in the faith" (1:2): "Meditate upon these things; give thyself wholly to them; that thy profiting may appear to all" (v. 15). While modern translations prefer "be diligent" (NIV), "take pains" (NASB), or "practice" (ESV), "meditate" is not only accurate but more appropriate. The Greek *meletaō* (3191) means, "To consider, weigh, or ponder over something so as to be able to perform well."[11] Attitude precedes action. We must think, ponder, and consider things before we act. We cannot *practice* (ESV) correctly until first we *ponder* rightly.

So, meditation is not mind*less*ness, as it is often viewed, but mind*ful*ness. It is not *emptying* the mind, rather *filling* the mind. It is also a "talking within the mind,"[12] as we will also note in our next study. The question, of course, is: with *what* do we fill our mind? What should we talk about in the mind? And it is there that we will continue tomorrow.

Scriptures for Study: What do the following verses declare about meditation: Psalm 119:97 and 99?[13]

JANUARY 6

Elements of Meditation (2)

My meditation of him shall be sweet ... (Ps. 104:34)

CONTINUING our contemplation of **meditation**, *second*, we must choose its *direction*. To what or whom do we direct our thoughts? Should we "turn inward" and direct it at ourselves or think that other men are worthy of such reflection? God forbid!

The Psalmist, therefore, answers our question: **My meditation of him**. While modern translations, and therefore some commentators, tend to view this as our meditation being pleasing to God, we are compelled to stay with older expositors.[14] As the context indicates, God is the object of our meditation because of the glory of His person and works. No one has said it better than that great 18th-century expositor John Gill: we should meditate on "the glories, excellencies, and perfections of his person; of his offices, as Mediator, King, Priest, and Prophet, the Savior and Redeemer; of his works of creation, providence, and redemption; of his word, the blessed truths and comfortable doctrines of it; of his providential dispensations, and gracious dealings with his people in the present state."[15]

And where do we find these (and other) objects of our meditation? In God's Word. We should quietly ponder the Word, concentrate on its precepts, turn it over and over in our thoughts. The Hebrew *higgāyôn* (1902H), in fact, pictures a soft muttering, as we might quietly repeat a verse over and over to help assimilate and even memorize it, and the Greek *meletaō*, as noted yesterday, indicates "talking within the mind." Or, as Thomas Watson put it, "Meditation is chewing the cud."[16]

Third, we should enjoy the *drive* of our meditation. A driving motive for such meditation is simply how **sweet** it is to do so. The Hebrew (*'ārab*, 6149H) refers to something pleasant, acceptable, desired, or satisfying. Again, modern interpretation of this verse is that our meditation should be sweet to *God*, which certainly should be true, but the primary focus here seems to be how sweet it should be to *us*. As Gill goes on to add, when we "meditate upon [these things], when grace is in exercise, [it] is very sweet, delightful, and comfortable."

Is there any doubt, then, as Charles Spurgeon submits, that "meditation is the soul of religion"?[17] As we continue our studies through the remainder of the year, there will be much to consider and ponder, much on which to meditate. Each day provides a new opportunity to "consider the wondrous works of God" (Job 37:14).

> My meditation of Him shall be sweet
> As I contemplate hour-by-hour.
> Opening the Word my Savior I meet,
> And there finding pleasure, peace, and power.

Scriptures for Study: According to the following verses, on what should we meditate: Psalm 119:15, 23, 148; 143:5? 📖 What "things" does Philippians 4:8 tell us to "think on"?[18]

JANUARY 7

Knowing God (1)

... that ye might be filled with the knowledge of his will in all wisdom and spiritual understanding; ... and increasing in the knowledge of God. (Col. 1:9–10)

IT is probably safe to say that few Christian believers in our day have ever heard a series of messages on the doctrine of God preached from the pulpit of their local church. It's simply not a "popular" subject. Even on the rare occasion that some particular aspect of His nature *is* mentioned, it is often done so with little more than syrupy sentimentality.

In his classic, *The Knowledge of the Holy*, A. W. Tozer profoundly wrote: "A right conception of God is basic not only to systematic theology but to practical Christian living as well."[19] Indeed, while it is certainly critical to be *orthodox* in our thinking, it is far more vital that we are *obedient* in our living.

We, therefore, begin our meditations on knowing God using the present text for good reason. These verses comprise a portion of Paul's prayer for the Colossian believers (vv. 9–14). These first three requests are not mutually exclusive, rather they are dependent upon one another.

First, Paul prays that we will be *plenteous* in our *wisdom*. **Filled** (*plēroō*, 4137) pictures filling a container and means to influence fully, to control. The key word **knowledge**, then, is *epignōsis* (1922), the root of which (*gnōsis*, 1108) refers to knowledge gained by experience. With the added prefix *epi* (motion upon or toward), the word takes on the even fuller meaning of an experiential, personal knowledge that is full, thorough, precise, and correct. How crucial it is that we have such knowledge of God! Why?

Paul here answers the claim of the Gnostics of his day. Gnosticism boasted of a deeper, superior knowledge that only certain people could attain. (The New Age Movement, in fact, is the modern version of Gnosticism.) Paul contends that *full* knowledge, that is, true and complete knowledge, can be found only in God. This knowledge is not just knowing *about* God, but knowing *God*. It is one thing to know *theology*—to know such things as salvation doctrine, prophecy, and other subjects—but it is quite another to know *Theos* (God). "A man may be theologically knowing and spiritually ignorant," wrote Puritan Stephen Charnock.[20]

As Paul goes on to say in verse 10, this knowledge is to be **increasing** (*auxanō*, 837), which speaks of the growth that occurs in something because it is alive. It is precisely because we were once dead in sin (Eph. 2:1–3) but now alive in Christ (Rom. 6:11; 1 Cor. 15:22), that we are ever growing and increasing in fruitfulness (Jn. 15:1–5). And no matter how far we advance in our knowledge, there are still more heights to ascend and more depths to explore. We will continue climbing higher and plunging deeper tomorrow.

Scriptures for Study: What does Peter say about our knowledge and growth in 1 Peter 2:2 and 2 Peter 3:18?

JANUARY 8

Knowing God (2)

... That ye might walk worthy of the Lord unto all pleasing, being fruitful in every good work, and increasing in the knowledge of God. (Col. 1:9–10)

CONTINUING our thoughts on the first of Paul's prayer requests here, knowing God is not some abstract concept. It is not theoretical; it is, in fact, most practical. That is why Paul not only prays for God's people to desire general **knowledge**, but also **wisdom** (*sophia*, 4678), which speaks specifically of deep "knowledge of the most precious things," "implying cultivation of mind and enlightened understanding."[21] What are the most precious things? The things of God. These things should cultivate, captivate, and concentrate our minds.

Not satisfied, Paul makes sure there will be no ambiguity by adding the word **understanding** (*sunesis*, 4907). This simply refers to the ability of the mind to grasp concepts and see the proper relationship between them. Does Paul mean to refer to just *any* concept? Indeed not. He qualifies it with the word **spiritual**. It is not philosophy, psychology, sociology, science, or any other subject that should be our *primary* focus. Spiritual things should occupy our minds.

Even more specifically, Paul prays that we will have an ever increasing, continually deepening knowledge of God's **will**. The reason many are not filled with the knowledge of *God's* will is because they are occupied with the knowledge of *their* will. And where do we discover God's *will*; it is, of course, in His *Word*.

Second, to demonstrate further how all this is practical, and to stress that it is not just theoretical, Paul prays that we will be *pleasing* in our *walk*. Right knowledge promotes right behavior. Our **walk** (*peripateō*, 4043), that is, our conduct and manner of life as we "walk about" [detailed on Oct. 12] is to be **pleasing** unto God. While the unbeliever can please God in *nothing*, the believer should please Him in *everything*. How can we do this? By walking **worthy**. This fascinating word (*axios*, 516) originally carried the idea of balancing scales, of one side of the scale counterbalancing the other. How do we walk worthy? By weighing ourselves against the standard **of the Lord**.

Third, Paul prays that we will be *productive* in our *work*. Again, how practical! Not only will right knowledge *promote* proper *behavior*, but it will also *produce* proper *labor*. Think of it! With the right knowledge, whatever **work** (*ergon*, 2041, act, deed, labor, or even employment) we perform will be **good** (*agathos*, 18, benevolent, profitable, useful, beneficial, excellent, virtuous, and suitable). Every good work, in fact, will be **fruitful** (cf. Jn. 15:1–5). Anyone can count the seeds in the apple, as the adage goes, but no one can count the apples in the seed. Right *knowing*, right *living*, right *producing*—that is the progression.

Equally critical is the sequence of *wisdom*, *walk*, and *work*. Wisdom from God's word makes our walk *straight* and our work *strong*.

Scriptures for Study: What else does Paul pray for in Colossians 1:11–14? What observations can you make in John 15:1–5?

JANUARY 9

Finding the Knowledge of God

...find the knowledge of God. (Prov. 2:5)

OUR text presents the goal of verses 1–4. Solomon encouraged his son Rehoboam to pursue wisdom and **the knowledge of God**. Although Rehoboam rejected this counsel (1 Kings 12:1–6)—no doubt, at least in part, part, because his father ultimately failed to live up to it (11:1, 4, 6, 7–11)—it nonetheless instructs us that our attitude toward the Word of God determines whether or not we attain the goal.

First, we must *receive* the Word: **My son, if thou wilt receive my words** (v. 1a). So much had *God's* words permeated Solomon's thinking, that they had actually become his *own* **words**. To **receive** (Hebrew *lāqaḥ*, 3947H) God's Word, then, simply means that we take hold of it so firmly that it becomes ours and no one can wrench it from our grasp.

Second, we must *regard* the Word: **hide my commandments with thee** (v. 1b; cf. Ps. 119:11). To **hide** (*ṣāpan*, 6845H) God's Word is to conceal it as we would priceless treasure. Verse 2 goes on: **incline thine ear . . . and apply thine heart**. To **incline** (*qāšaḇ*, 7181H) our **ear** means to listen carefully, pay attention, and obey what we hear. Likewise, the Hebrew behind **apply** (*nāṭāh*, 5186H) is used figuratively here to mean leaning toward something. We lean neither on the world nor ourselves; we lean on the Word.

Third, we must *request* the Word: **Yea, if thou criest after knowledge, and liftest up thy voice for understanding** (v. 3). **Criest** (*qārā'*, 7121H) means to call or summon. "We must cry, as new-born babes after the sincere milk of the word (1 Pet. 2:2)," wrote Puritan Matthew Henry. This, along with **[lift] up thy voice**, underscores the need for prayer. "If any of you lack wisdom, let him ask of God" (Jas. 1:5), a prayer He answers using His Word.

Fourth, we must *respect* the Word: **If thou seekest her as silver, and searchest for her as for hid treasures** (v. 4). In other words, we do all we can to obtain God's Word and search for it as we would hunt for buried treasure.

That brings us back to the goal. We do all this so we can **find the knowledge of God**. In a day when there is a "made easy" book on virtually every subject known to man, we need to be reminded that to **find the knowledge of God** demands dedication, diligence, and discernment. Solomon, in fact, includes another key word of the OT that this process yields: he says we will also **understand**. This important word (*biyn*, 995H) has a wide range of meanings, including not only to understand but also to discern, observe, pay attention, and perceive. Our goal, then, is not just to get knowledge, but to **understand** that knowledge and how it applies. The truths of God's Word are not *abstract*, rather they are *absolute*, and we ignore them at our peril.

Scriptures for Study: What does Proverbs 2:6–12 go on to tell us about knowledge and understanding? 📖 What does 1 John 5:20 add?

January 10

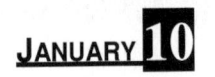

Your Wisdom House

Through wisdom is an house builded; and by understanding it is established: And by knowledge shall the chambers be filled with all precious and pleasant riches. (Prov. 24:3–4)

HERE we encounter a fascinating passage. Solomon records one of the sayings of an unnamed sage ("words of the wise," 22:17) who describes **wisdom, understanding,** and **knowledge** as the materials for building, establishing, and furnishing a house. While **house** (*bayit,* 1004H) can also refer to a family (Josh. 24:15), or even a royal dynasty (1 Kings 11:38), a literal house seems to be in view, thereby creating for us a wonderful image.

First, we note the *erecting* of the house: **through wisdom is an house builded.** The first three OT occurrences of the Hebrew *bānāh* (**builded,** 1129H) are extremely significant: God built Eve from Adam's rib (Gen. 2:22); Cain built a city (4:17); and Noah built an ark (8:20). In each case, and many others, building materials were used for construction. There are likewise many different materials used in building a physical house: concrete, steel, wood, glass, gypsum, and others.

The sage, however, mentions only a single material for *this* house: **wisdom.** The Hebrew (*ḥokmāh,* 2451H) refers to the skill, experience, shrewdness, and ability to make the right choices at the right times. We would submit this simple definition: *Wisdom is the skill for living in the fear of the Only True and Living God.* If we build the footer, foundation, and structure of our house with wisdom, it will stand no matter what storm might come.

Second, we see the *establishing* of the house: **by understanding it is established. Established** (*kûn,* 3559H) simply means "to set up," as in founding a city (Hab. 2:12). Once the *house* is built, a *home* is then established. A family moves in and transforms an empty building into a warm residence. And what is it that transforms *this* house?—**understanding** (*tebûnāh,* 8394H), that is, insight and discernment. A home that is led by such qualities will be a warm place indeed.

Third, there is the *equipping* of the house: **by knowledge shall the chambers be filled.** Furnishings also contribute much to transforming a house into a home. Every home is unique because of the personal likes and dislikes of the inhabitants. But while physical décor varies according to taste—there is cottage, contemporary, rustic, traditional, eclectic, and a plethora of others—*this* house has but a single choice: it is furnished, filled, and flourishing with **knowledge.** Every **chamber** (that is, every room) is dominated by this singular décor, and all the residents are in complete agreement and perfect harmony in their love for it. Here is a house that is indeed **filled with all precious and pleasant riches.** All physical riches can lose their value, but these daily incur more wealth.

Scriptures for Study: Proverbs is filled with references to the theme we explored today. Read each of the following and note its significance: Proverbs 2:6; 9:1; 15:6, 21; 20:15; 21:20.

JANUARY 11

Oh, the Depth! (1)

O the depth of the riches both of the wisdom and knowledge of God! how unsearchable are his judgments, and his ways past finding out! (Rom. 11:33)

LOCATED in the western Pacific, the Mariana Trench is the deepest part of the world's oceans. Its known depth is nearly seven miles (more than a mile deeper than Mt. Everest is high). Amazingly, despite the staggering pressure at this depth (almost eight tons per square inch, or more than 1,000 times the standard atmospheric pressure at sea level), as well as the numbing cold (just above freezing), living creatures have been discovered. Darkness, however, is total for no light can penetrate such a depth. Compare this to our text for a moment.

First, the *depths* of God. **Depth** translates *bathos* (899, English "bath" and "bathysphere"). It is used in the literal sense only in the Synoptic Gospels to indicate not only the depth of the sea (Lk. 5:4)[22] but also the depth of soil (Matt. 13:5; Mk. 4:5). Its other six occurrences are figurative and mean greatness, immensity, profoundness, inscrutability, and complexity. Significantly, it is closely connected to another word, *abussos* (12, English "abyss"), meaning bottomless or unfathomable (e.g., Rev. 20:2, 10).

What wondrous truth, then, is Paul telling us? Simply that the **depth** of God and the spiritual **riches** found in Him are bottomless and unfathomable. Additionally, in marvelous contrast to the pressure, cold, and darkness of the abyss, the deeper we go into the depth of God the less life's pressures affect us, the warmer we feel, and the more light we see.

(1) We marvel at the depth of His *person*. As we meditate on God's attributes in the studies to come, His depth will become evident. Indeed, traits of His nature—such as omniscience, omnipotence, and omnipresence—are unfathomable; they are "bottomless" in that we can never reach their limits because there are none. Further, aspects of His character—such as holiness, justice, mercy, love, and grace—are inscrutable, beyond our capacity to grasp in their fullness.

(2) We are awed by the depth of His *power*. In Genesis 1, we read "And God said" ten times as He brought into being what had never existed before: light, atmosphere, land, plants, heavenly bodies, animals, man, and procreation.

(3) We stand amazed by the depth of His *preservation*. He not only *created* all things, but He also *carries* them along, "upholding all things by the word of His power" (Heb. 1:3). What holds an atom together? It is "nuclear force" or "atomic glue," the scientist confidently asserts. Ah, but who made the glue? As Colossians 1:17 declares, "by him all things consist."

(4) We are struck speechless by the depth of His *providence*. He reigns "over all" (1 Chron. 29:11, 12), bringing every event into servitude to His sovereign preference, purpose, and plan. *Soli deo Gloria!*

Scriptures for Study: Read the following verses, noting what God is controlling in each one: Job 9:5–7; Psalms 22:28; 147:9.

JANUARY 12

Oh, the Depth! (2)

O the depth of the riches both of the wisdom and knowledge of God! how unsearchable are his judgments, and his ways past finding out! (Rom. 11:33)

IN addition to our text, 1 Corinthians 2:9–10 declares: "But as it is written [Isa. 64:4], Eye hath not seen, nor ear heard, neither have entered into the heart of man, the things which God hath prepared for them that love him. But God hath revealed them unto us by his Spirit: for the Spirit searcheth all things, yea, the deep things of God." Both texts lead us to two other observations.

Second, we note the *dilemma* of the task. Paul uses two words here that further demonstrate the depths of God. One is **unsearchable** (*anexereunētos*, 419), that is, not able to search out. The other is even more graphic: **past finding out** translates a single Greek word (*anexichniastos*, 421), the root of which means "a track or a trail." The only other place this word appears in the NT is in Ephesians 3:8: "That I should preach among the Gentiles the unsearchable riches of Christ." According to the Septuagint, it was also one of Job's favorite thoughts, as he declared of God, "Who doeth great things and unsearchable, marvelous things without number (Job 5:9; 9:10).

But Paul adds something else: God's **ways** are **past finding out**. **Ways** is *hodos* (3598), which literally refers to a path, road, or street and so figuratively to one's manner of life, the way he does things, his morals, doctrine, teaching, and so forth. So, what picture does Paul paint? That the depths of God, all that He is and does, are incapable of being traced out, as impossible to search out as is the expert mountain man who leaves no trail or trace in the wilderness.

What a dilemma, indeed! But never has there been a *sweeter* dilemma! No, we cannot discover all that God is because it is undiscoverable. We cannot learn everything because it is unlearnable. But does that discourage the search? Certainly not! Why? Because a single hint leads to a clue, the clue guides us to the next discovery, and the discovery spurs us on to look for a breakthrough. Yes, it is **past finding out**, but it is not past *looking for*. The search will never be in vain.

Third, the above also encourages us in the *dedication* of our search. Men have invested millions of dollars and even years of their lives searching the ocean's depths. Some have done so simply for the treasure, but others have had a nobler motive—they just wanted to solve a mystery, such as the discovery of the *Titanic* in 1985, which rests more than 12,000 feet beneath the waves.

Should we be any less dedicated to searching out the things of God? While those who are of the world usually search for things with a motive of money or other gain or advantage, the Christian searches for *true* **riches**, real wealth. What could possibly be of more value than the **riches** of God's **wisdom and knowledge**, for, "In [Him] are hid all the treasures of wisdom and knowledge" (Col. 2:3).

Scriptures for Study: What does Matthew 6:19–21 say about riches? 📖 What are "the riches of [God's] grace" in Ephesians 1:3–14?

JANUARY 13

There Are No Atheists in Foxholes

The fool hath said in his heart, There is no God . . . (Ps. 14:1)

WHILE the adage, "There are no atheists in foxholes," has most often been attributed to the famous World War II journalist Ernie Pyle, it has also been ascribed to U.S. Military Chaplain William T. Cummings in a field sermon during the Battle of Bataan in 1942.[23] Indeed, it is hard to imagine anyone experiencing the terrors of combat or coping with the horrors of war while at the same time denying, or even doubting, the lasting comfort that only a knowledge of God can provide.

Whoever first coined that phrase, however, actually missed a key truth of Scripture, namely: not only are there are no atheists in *foxholes*, there are no true atheists *anywhere*.

Does that sound odd? After all, we often hear someone claim to be an atheist or agnostic. From ancients such as Democritus and Epicurus, to the "closet atheists" of the Renaissance, to outspoken and proud moderns such as Ernest Hemingway, Madalyn Murray O'Hair, and Carl Sagan, countless individuals throughout history claimed (or do claim) a complete rejection of the notion of God's existence. "All thinking men are atheists," Hemingway wrote. But we could ask in response: is it really clear thinking to say that no one made everything out of nothing?

The simple truth is that such a claim is just that, a *claim*, an empty one, in fact. While they can *evade* the truth, they cannot *escape* it because this knowledge is resident within them. Romans 1:18–20 is clear: "For the wrath of God is revealed from heaven against all ungodliness and unrighteousness of men, who hold the truth in unrighteousness; Because that which may be known of God is manifest in them; for God hath showed it unto them. For the invisible things of him from the creation of the world are clearly seen, being understood by the things that are made, even his eternal power and Godhead; so that they are without excuse."

The knowledge of God is inherent. A man might *say* he doesn't believe, but he is deceiving himself, for his soul knows better. What, then, is a person who calls (or even thinks) himself an atheist?—sadly, a **fool** (Ps. 14:1; see also Jan. 18). "No better title than that of a fool is afforded to the atheist," wrote Puritan Stephen Charnock; "every atheist is a grand fool. If he were not a fool, he would not imagine a thing so contrary to the stream of the universal reason of the world, contrary to the rational dictates of his own soul, and contrary to the testimony of every creature, and link in the chain of creation: if he were not a fool, he would not strip himself of humanity, and degrade himself lower than the most despicable brute."[24] In contrast, as noted yesterday, the believer rejoices with Paul, "O the depth of the riches both of the wisdom and knowledge of God!" (Rom. 11:33).

Scriptures for Study: Read Psalm 14 (and its twin, Ps. 53). What do these say about the moral foolishness and corruption of the human race?

JANUARY 14

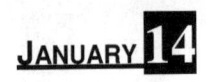

God Is

In the beginning God . . . (Gen. 1:1)

THE Bible begins with God, not with philosophical inferences, logical arguments, or scientific evidences for His existence.

First, we note God's identity in the single word **God**. As we each have a signature that we put on important documents, God has signed His name on this document called the Bible. And just so there would be no question as to this identity, He signs this document with His name more than 2,600 times, 32 of which occur in Genesis 1 alone.

So what is His name? While He actually has *many* names in the OT,[25] this one is primary, His signature. It is the Hebrew *Elōhiym* (430H). Probably derived from both a root that means the "Strong One" and another that denotes fear (which therefore creates the idea of reverence), *Elōhiym* means: *the Strong One who is to be feared and revered because of who He is*. This is the name of the One and Only True God. It identifies Him as Creator (Gen. 1:1; 5:1), King (Ps. 47:7), Judge (Ps. 50:6), Lord (Ps. 86:12), and Savior (Hosea 13:4). And as noted yesterday, it is only the fool who denies or doubts this God of the universe.

Second, consider God's self-existence. Since He was there *in the beginning*, it is a self-evident truth that He was there *before* the beginning. Think of it! There was a time—although time didn't even exist—when there was nothing, absolutely nothing. We, of course, cannot comprehend "nothing" because for us everything is something, and no thing is "nothing." Since we are created beings, we are part of space-time and therefore cannot comprehend existence apart from space-time. For us to speak *of* (or even think *about*) "eternity" is itself a time reference (as in "time without end"). We, therefore, cannot say, "God has always been," or, "God is timeless," or even "God is eternal," for all these are time references. Rather, the best we can do is say: *God Is*. He exists in an ever present *now* (ah, but that too is a time reference). What does God say of Himself, in fact? "I AM THAT I AM" (Ex. 3:14). *Hāyāh* (1961H, "I AM") is a simple verb meaning "to be or exist" and therefore emphasizes God's self-existence and unchangeableness.

Third, ponder also God's triune nature. Because of the ending *–iym*, *'Elōhiym* is plural. While plural doesn't in itself mean "trinity," this seems a clear allusion to the Trinity. While this doctrine is not as prevalent in the OT as in the NT, it is still noticeably there. The three persons of the Godhead, in fact, are seen in the first three chapters of Genesis: 1:1 and 2 allude to two members of the Trinity ("the Spirit of God moved upon the face of the waters"), and 3:15 points directly to the Son who would come in the flesh (Jn. 1:14).

Take some time today to meditate on the fact that *God Is* and then how that applies to His working throughout the universe and in you.

Scriptures for Study: Who was "in the beginning" according to John 1:1–3?

January 15

Our All-Knowing God (1)

... God is greater than our heart, and knoweth all things. (1 Jn. 3:20)

GOD'S "natural attributes" speak of His basic essence, His nature. These are what are in view when we say, as noted yesterday, *God Is*. The first characteristic that "*God Is*" has been dubbed *omniscience*, which is comprised of two Latin words: *omni* ("all") and *sciens* ("knowledge," English "science"). This provides us with a definition: *God knows all things and is absolutely perfect in knowledge*. John Calvin is perhaps better: "God knows Himself and all other things in one Eternal and most simple act." Simple act? Indeed, as easily as we might pick up a dropped pencil, God knows all things as though it were all one act.

First, God's knowledge is comprehensive. **God knoweth all things**, our text declares, so there is "no thing" that He doesn't know. **Knoweth** is *ginoskō* (1097), knowledge gained by experience. John couldn't use *oida* (1492), a knowledge gained by outside learning, as a teacher to a student, for there's nothing for God to learn and no one who could teach Him. Because *God Is*, His "experience" is always "now," while we are shackled by space-time: past, present, and future. This is doubly emphasized by **knoweth** being in the present tense (continues knowing).

Second, God's knowledge is all-inclusive, that is, it includes *all* knowledge of *every* subject. *All* and *every* obviously encompass much. Regardless of how well any of us might know a particular subject, our knowledge is neither perfect nor beyond the possibility of learning something new. Not so with God. He is not the God of Open Theism, which views Him (like the Greek mythological Zeus) as ever learning and changing His plans according to His new knowledge.

(1) He has perfect knowledge concerning the *wonders* of nature. "He telleth the number of the stars; he calleth them all by their names" (Ps. 147:4). While one of the stars we know well has been called by several names—such as Cynosūra, Lodestar, North Star, and Polaris—we should look forward to one day learning its *real* name.

(2) He has perfect knowledge concerning the *works* and *words* of men. Of the former the psalmist declares, "Thou knowest my downsitting ... mine uprising ... my thought ... my path ... my lying down ... [and] all my ways" (Ps. 139:2–3). The very next verse then addresses the latter: "For there is not a word in my tongue, but, lo, O LORD, thou knowest it altogether."

(3) He has perfect knowledge concerning the *workings* of history. What a staggering thought we read in Isaiah 46:9–10: "I am God, and there is none else; I am God, and there is none like me, Declaring the end from the beginning, and from ancient times the things that are not yet done, saying, My counsel shall stand, and I will do all my pleasure." God sees into the future more easily than we see in the present moment.

Scriptures for Study: Read the following verses, noting God's omniscience in each: Matthew 10:29; Exodus 3:7; 1 Chronicles 28:9; Psalm 139:1–4.

JANUARY 16

Our All-Knowing God (2)

Known unto God are all his works from the beginning of the world. (Acts 15:18)

GOD'S knowledge is both comprehensive and all-inclusive. It's from everlasting to everlasting, comprehending all things in a "simple act" and in the minutest detail. While for us it is often the "little things" of a matter that trip us—those pesky details—not so with God. But there is still something else.

Third, God's knowledge is unchanging. As our text declares, God knows exactly what He will do, how He will do it, and when He will do it. Our usual procedure is to sit down and formulate a certain plan. We try to look ahead and try to see every angle of a situation and try to think of every ramification of the action we contemplate. But God has no such limitation. He instantaneously knew His program for the ages. When did God formulate His plans? The only answer to such a question is, He didn't "formulate" anything—He always knew what He was going to do! Nothing surprises God or "sneaks up" on Him.

A pastor friend of mine, a very good chess player, one day came upon a chess exhibition being held by a world class grand master at a shopping mall. The grand master was playing 50 games simultaneously against all comers, so my friend took a seat. In the endgame, he came to what he thought was a crucial move and sat intensely for about 30 minutes considering it. When the grand master came to his board, my friend made his move. The grand master then reached to make his planned move, which he worked out many moves before, but stopped abruptly and said, "Oh, no, I don't want to do that." He had to reevaluate his move because he did not expect an amateur to make the one move that would force the game to a draw. He then made the proper move, and they both agreed to a draw, the only one of the day, in fact.

In spite of his ability and mastery of the game, in spite of having worked out his moves far in advance, that grand master was forced to reevaluate because something unexpected came along. But such can never occur with God. Nothing catches Him by surprise. He knows everything from start to finish, and nothing is unforeseen. "The counsel of the LORD standeth for ever, the thoughts of his heart to all generations" (Ps. 33:11). I once heard a certain preacher put it well: "You know, it often occurs to me that nothing ever occurs to God."

We would also humbly submit that the term God's "plan" of salvation is a misnomer. Does it not picture God sitting down and trying to think of a plan on how to save His fallen people? "Oh, what shall I do now?" it implies. What a dreadful picture! God didn't have to formulate a *plan*, for He knew His *purpose* and *provision* from eternity past. God never needs a "Plan B."

Scriptures for Study: Read the following verses, noting God's omniscience in each: Proverbs 5: 21; 15:3; 2 Chronicles 16:9; Job 31:4; 34:21.

JANUARY 17

Our All-Knowing God (3)

Elect according to the foreknowledge of God . . . (1 Pet. 1:2)

WHILE *knowing* truth and *applying* truth are two different things, they are not mutually exclusive, rather two sides of the same coin. *Doctrine* leads to *duty*; *principles* lead to *practice*. What bearing, then, does God's omniscience have on our daily living?

First, regarding our *conversion*, God knew us and chose us before the foundation of the world (Eph. 1:4). As Peter assures us in today's text, **Elect according to the foreknowledge of God**. "Foreknowledge" is *proginōskō* (4268). This does *not* mean precognition, as some insist. The root is *ginōskō* (1097), which is knowledge gained by experience and is practically synonymous with love and intimacy. What a truth! Christ personally knew us in the *elective* and *saving* sense before we even existed.[26] He also foreordained us to "adoption" (Eph. 1:5) and foreordained us to complete and final conformity to the image of Christ (Rom. 8:28–30).

Second, regarding our *comfort*, God knows all our burdens and needs. David lamented in Psalm 38:9, "Lord, all my desire is before thee; and my groaning is not hid from thee." Again he cried in Psalm 56:8, "Put thou my tears into thy bottle." That expression had its roots in the Eastern custom of catching tears in water bags and placing them in the tombs of loved ones. We then read the words of our Savior to the church at Smyrna, "I know [understand] thy . . . tribulation, and poverty" (Rev. 2:9). What more comforting words could we read?

Third, regarding our *conduct*, God's omniscience drives us to holiness. It has a transforming effect over our conduct, for He sees everything (Job 34:21) and nothing can be hid from Him (Is. 29:15). God knows our inward thoughts, attitudes, values, priorities, desires, and goals, and He knows our outward words and actions. How often do we deceive ourselves into thinking that since we can hide such things from other people we can also hide them from God? Let us not forget: God *knows* us, inside and out.

In previous studies we have quoted Puritan Stephen Charnock. Another great Puritan was Thomas Watson. Amazingly, Watson and Charnock co-pastored a church for five years before Charnock's death (1680).[27] In his wonderful work, *A Body of Divinity* (sermons on doctrine), Watson challenges us: "The consideration of God's omniscience would be preventive of much sin. . . . Will we sin when our judge looks on? Would men speak so vainly, if they considered God overheard them? . . . Would men go after strange flesh if they believed God was a spectator of their wickedness? . . . Viewing ourselves as under the eye of God's omniscience, would cause reverence in the worship of God."[28]

Oh, if we *really* believe God is omniscient, we will live a life that is holy before Him!

Scriptures for Study: What is God's promise in 1 Corinthians 10:13? 📖 What encouragement do we read in Romans 8:26 and Psalm 126:5–6?

JANUARY 18

Our All-Powerful God (1)

God hath spoken once ... power belongeth unto God. (Ps. 62:11)

VOLCANOES are among the most powerful forces on earth. One of the most famous eruptions was Krakatoa in 1883, which destroyed more than two-thirds of the island on which it stood and caused massive tsunamis, more than 100 feet high, that killed thousands of people. Considered to be the loudest sound ever heard in modern times, the explosion was heard 3,000 miles away, and its shock waves registered on barographs around the globe.

Such power is certainly awe-inspiring and humbling, but in the shadow of our present subject it is no more significant than a firecracker. The second natural attribute of God is "omnipotence" (*omni*, "all," and *potens*, "power or energy," English "potency" and "potential"). Its meaning, then is: *God can bring to pass anything and everything He wills*. Here is power beyond limit or comprehension.

God hath spoken once. What a captivating phrase! This doesn't mean God spoke only once throughout time—He spoke many times, such as at creation, when giving the Law, when revealing truth to the prophets, and so forth. Rather it means that *when* God *speaks*, it *stands*; it is firm and irrevocable. While we can speak a thousand times and accomplish *nothing*, God speaks once and accomplishes *everything*. Our speech is just hollow *sound*; His is immeasurable *strength*.

Neither is it even necessary for God to "speak." The Hebrew behind **spoken** (*dabar*, 1696H) not only means to say or speak but also to *think*, as when Solomon spoke in his heart (Ecc. 2:15). God need only think **once**, and a matter is settled.

First, then, we see God's power in His *creation* of all things. We again come face-to-face with Genesis 1:1: "In the beginning God created the heaven and the earth." "Created" (*bārā'*, 1254H) refers to initiating something new and creating it from nothing. We often compliment a poet, sculptor, painter, or composer by saying he has *created* a work of art, but such is not true in the *bārā'* sense, for he still had to start with physical materials, not to mention his own mind, all of which God created from nothing. As has been noted often, the humble sculptor Michelangelo took credit for nothing, reportedly saying that the statue was always there, requiring him simply to chip away the excess.[29] He said something else, however, that we read less often: "The true work of art is but a shadow of the divine perfection."

We read the same truth in Psalm 33:6–9, where the psalmist says of creation, "For he spake, and it was done; he commanded, and it stood fast." "Spake" is *'amar* (559H), which again means not only "to say or speak," but also "to say to one's self," that is, to *think*. It is also used for "said" in the ten "God said" statements in Genesis 1 (Jan. 11), as well as in Psalm 14:1, "The fool hath said in His heart [or, thinks] there is no God" (Jan. 13). We need *tools*; God needs only His *thoughts*.

Scriptures for Study: What do Psalm 148:1–6 and Revelation 4:11 both declare and command?

JANUARY 19

Our All-Powerful God (2)

... upholding all things by the word of his power ... (Heb. 1:3)

ALL three basic elements of the physical universe—space ("heaven"), matter ("heaven and earth"), and time ("beginning")—were brought into existence by the Word of God (Gen. 1:1). But that is not all. While volcanoes and other forces of nature are certainly graphic examples of power, they illustrate destructive, uncontrolled power, while God's is quite different.

Second, we see God's power in His *continuation* of all things. The above forces tend to *crush* things, while God's power *continues* them. **Upholding** (*pherō*, 5342) means "to bring, bear, or carry" with the added picture of carrying something that is in motion to another place. This word appears in Acts 27:15–17 to describe how a ship is carried along by the wind. What a picture, indeed! God continually preserves and maintains the entire universe, which is in constant motion and ever changing.

Colossians 1:17 provides another amazing image: "He is before all things, and by him all things consist." "Consist" (*sunistēmi*, 4921) means to join parts together into a whole. "The world is not a chaos but a cosmos," writes William Hendriksen. "It is an orderly universe, a *system*."[30] We could translate this phrase: "By him everything sticks together."

Third, we see God's power in His *control* of all things. Again, the forces mentioned earlier cannot be controlled, but God's power is controlled by the perfections of His will and purpose. In other words, omnipotence not only describes God's power but also His power over His power. For this reason He controls everything.

(1) God controls men. His power brought the plagues upon Egypt (Ex. 7–12), gave Moses the exact words to say to Pharaoh (Ex. 4:11), protected Daniel in the lion's den (Dan. 6), as well as Shadrach, Meshach, and Abed-nego in the furnace (Dan. 3), and struck down and blinded Saul on his way to Damascus (Acts 9).

(2) God controls angels. "He doeth according to His will in the army of heaven" (Dan. 4:35). These are also "ministering spirits, sent forth to minister for them who shall be heirs of salvation" (Heb. 1:14).

(3) God controls Satan and the fallen angels. Satan is limited by what God allows, as when he could do to Job only what God allowed (Job 1:12; 2:6). The Lord Jesus ordered demons out of a man at Gadara and permitted them to enter a herd of pigs (Mk. 5:1–20). God will also chain Satan for a thousand years (Rev. 20:2) and will finally cast him into the Lake of Fire forever (20:10).

While chaos, confusion, and calamity do, indeed, seem to rule the day, God *is* in control. Dear Christian Friend, we can forsake all doubt and fully trust that God's power is in control.

Scriptures for Study: Read the following verses, noting God's omnipotence in each: Psalms 107:24–29; Daniel 4:35; Nahum 1:3–6.

JANUARY 20

Our All-Powerful God (3)

...preserved in Jesus Christ... (Jude 1)

ANTIGONUS (c.382–301 BC) was a Macedonian nobleman and general who ultimately declared himself king over all Macedonia. At the beginning of one particular battle, the pilot of his ship cried that an enemy armada outnumbered their own in ships, to which Antigonus replied, "But how many ships do you reckon my presence to be worth?"[31] Infinitely greater, what worth is God's omnipotence to us?

First, God's power gives us *preservation*, that is, security in our salvation. Sadly, there are many Christians who doubt the security of the believer, never stopping to realize that they are actually denying God's power. To think one can "lose their salvation" is to say that God can't keep what belongs to Him. **Preserved**, in fact, is *tēreō* (5083), derived from *tēros* (a warden or guard) and, therefore, means to keep an eye on, watch over, observe attentively, and guard protectively. A similar word appears in 1 Peter 1:5, where Peter assures us that we are "kept by the power of God through faith unto salvation." So God's power guards and cherishes us. Absolutely nothing can pluck us from His grasp (Jn. 10:28–30), and absolutely nothing can separate us from His love (Rom. 8:38–39). Satan can't touch us, the Law can't condemn us, and sin can't destroy us.

Second, God's power gives us *provision*. Realizing God's omnipotence gives new understanding of Philippians 4:19: "My God shall supply all your need according to His riches in glory by Christ Jesus" (cf. Matt. 6:25–34). What good would God's provision be if He were not omnipotent, if He instead had certain limits? God could barely be even *a* provider, much less *The* Provider if He were not all-powerful. Indeed, we must work for a living (2 Thes. 3:10), but it is God who provides the work. Further, God's omnipotence is not limited to whether there is even work. He is not limited by an earthly vocation. Why worry about paying the light bill when He who said "let there be light" has promised to care for us?

Third, God's power gives us *protection*. As the Lord Jesus had victory over Satan's temptation (Matt. 4), we too can resist Satan and all temptation to sin. While Jesus, of course, could not sin because He is *God*, He faced temptation *in His humanity*. He was "in all points tempted like as we are [the lust of the flesh, the lust of eyes, and the pride of life, 1 Jn. 2;16; cf. Matt. 4:1–10], yet without sin" (Heb. 4:15). He therefore had victory, not because He was God, but because as a man He claimed *the power of God* through His Word—He quoted Scripture in response to each of Satan's three temptations. As James tells us, "Resist the Devil and he will flee from you" (Jas. 4:7). That is power, and to ensure protection, we are to "put on the whole armor of God" (Eph. 6:10–20).

Scriptures for Study: Read Matthew 6:25–34. How does God exhort us concerning earthly needs? 📖 What comprises "the whole armor of God" (Eph. 6:10–20)?

JANUARY 21

Our Sovereign God (1)

Thine, O LORD, is the greatness, and the power, and the glory, and the victory, and the majesty: for all that is in the heaven and in the earth is thine; thine is the kingdom, O LORD, and thou art exalted as head above all. Both riches and honour come of thee, and thou reignest over all; and in thine hand is power and might; and in thine hand it is to make great, and to give strength unto all. (1 Chron. 29:11–12)

PERHAPS with the exception of His wrath, no other teaching about God has been as subtly diluted as has the doctrine of His sovereignty. Shamefully, some doctrine books omit it entirely. But to misunderstand God's sovereignty is to forfeit knowing who God really is. To say God is sovereign, in fact, is to say: God *is* God! The words are practically synonymous. If this is ignored, however, and we view Him as less than absolutely sovereign in all things, it is the equivalent of saying He is not really God—and that is unthinkable.

Our text defines God's sovereignty. These verses are actually part of David's prayer of praise and thanksgiving and are a "mini-course" in theology extolling, exalting, and exulting in the sovereignty of God. My Dear Christian Friend, have you ever prayed like this?

First, David *designates* God's *identity*. The name **LORD** (*Yāhweh* or *Yehōwāh*, 3068H) actually surpasses "God" (*'Elōhiym*, Jan. 14) in significance. This was originally only the Hebrew consonants *YHWH* (the Tetragrammaton), vowels being added during the Renaissance with the hope of recovering the pronunciation, which most likely is *Yāhweh* (Jehovah).[32] (Traditional English translations signify this by using the word **LORD** in small initial capital letters.) It was this name that God chose as His personal name by which He related specifically to and most dramatically with His chosen people. It was also His "covenant name," which He used when making covenants and giving promises to His people. *Yāhweh* shows us much about God.

(1) God's *revelation* of Himself. Because *Yāhweh* appears 5,321 times in the OT, it reveals more about God's character and work than any of the other names used for Him. Just one example is *Jehovah-Ṣābā'ôt* (LORD of Hosts), that is, Ruler Over the Heavenly Hosts, the God of the Universe who governs all the powers of heaven and earth (Gen. 2:1; Pss. 103:21; 148:2; cf. Rom. 9:29; Jas. 5:4).

(2) God's *regard* for His people. One example here is *Jehovah-jireh* ("the LORD Will Provide" or "the LORD Will See to It," Gen. 22:14). Oh, how God takes care of His people!

(3) God's *redemption* of His people. A chief use of *Yāhweh*, in fact, relates to His work of redemption, as when He brought His people out of Egyptian bondage (Lev. 26:45), and the reminder in Psalm 19:14: "Let the words of my mouth, and the meditation of my heart, be acceptable in thy sight, O LORD, my strength, and my redeemer."

Scriptures for Study: Read the verses cited today and rejoice in *Yāhweh*.

JANUARY 22

Our Sovereign God (2)

Thine, O LORD, is the greatness, and the power, and the glory, and the victory, and the majesty: for all that is in the heaven and in the earth is thine; thine is the kingdom, O LORD, and thou art exalted as head above all. Both riches and honour come of thee, and thou reignest over all; and in thine hand is power and might; and in thine hand it is to make great, and to give strength unto all. (1 Chron. 29:11–12)

NOTHING humbles our heart, rebukes our pride, or casts aside all thoughts of our so-called self-esteem than does concentrated meditation upon the sovereignty of God. Not only does David *designate* God's *identity* here in our text, but he tells us more.

Second, he *details* God's *integrity*. After underscoring who God is using His great covenant name, *Yāhweh* (**LORD**), David builds on that by listing five characteristics in rapid succession that highlight God's sovereignty.

(1) God's **greatness** (*gedûllāh*, 1420H) depicts His surpassing deeds and acts: "men shall speak of the might of thy terrible [fearful] acts: and I will declare thy greatness" (Ps. 145:6).

(2) God's **power** (*gebbûrāh*, 1369H) describes his strength and might: "O Lord GOD [*yehowih*, 3069H], thou hast begun to shew thy servant thy greatness, and thy mighty hand: for what God is there in heaven or in earth, that can do according to thy works, and according to thy might?" (Deut 3:24).

(3) God's **glory** (*tiph'ārāh*, 8597H) also speaks of beauty. This is vivid in Isaiah's vision of the New Jerusalem: "The sun shall be no more thy light by day; neither for brightness shall the moon give light unto thee: but the LORD shall be unto thee an everlasting light, and thy God thy glory" (Is. 60:19).

(4) God's **victory** (*neṣaḥ*, 5331H) literally means "ever, always, perpetual": "Why leap ye, ye high hills? this is the hill which God desireth to dwell in; yea, the LORD will dwell in it *for ever*" (Ps. 68:16, emphasis added).

(5) God's **majesty** (*hôd*, 1935H) also refers to His vigor and authority, as the psalmist declared: "I will speak of the glorious honour of thy majesty, and of thy wondrous works" (Ps. 145:5).

Third, David *describes* God's *influence*. The remainder of these verses go on to proclaim with crystal clarity God's sovereign rule. He is **head above all**, He **reignest over all**, has **power** and **strength** over all, and will **make great** what He desires. So, what does sovereignty mean? It means that since God is the *Creator* of all things, He then *owns* all things and therefore *rules* all things. It has been well said: "If the God you believe in is not a sovereign God, then you really don't believe in God."[33] Indeed, so axiomatic is this doctrine that to deny it is the equivalent of practical atheism, which is folly (Jan. 13).

Scriptures for Study: Read all of David's prayer of praise in 1 Chronicles 29:10–19. What principles can you observe in this glorious prayer?

JANUARY 23

Our Sovereign God (3)

... according to the purpose of him who worketh all things after the counsel of his own will. (Eph. 1:11)

WHILE there is a certain overlapping of God's omnipotence and sovereignty, they are not the same thing. God's omnipotence has to do with His nature, what He *is*. Sovereignty has to do with His purposes and work, what He *does*. In fact, as one theologian submits, "The sovereignty of God is not an attribute, but a prerogative of God arising out of the perfections of His nature."[34] This draws our attention to three basic theological truths. While we have already noted one ("preservation," Jan. 19), consider two others.

First, the *decrees* of God. While the two greatest historical confessions of faith—*The Westminster Confession* (1646) and *The London Baptist Confession* (1689) are virtually identical on this point and state it wonderfully,[35] preceding both of those was *The London Baptist Confession of 1646* (Article V): "God in His infinite power and wisdom, doth dispose all things to the end for which they were created; that neither good nor evil befalls any by chance, or without His providence; and that whatsoever befalls the elect, is by His appointment, for His glory, and their good (Job 38:11; Is. 46:10,11; Ecc. 3:14; Ex. 21:13; Prov. 16:33; Rom. 8:28)."

Our text is wondrous: God does all that He does according to the **counsel of his own will**. While **will** (which Paul uses back in v. 5) is *thelēma* (2307), a desire that proceeds from one's heart or emotions, **counsel** is *boulē* (1012), which speaks more of conscious deliberation and consideration that is free from emotion. God does not act arbitrarily or according to whim. He acts with deliberate purpose to the praise of His glory (v. 14).

So, mark it down: whatever happens in the world, no matter how insignificant it appears to be, happens for a reason and happens at God's decree. Whether He *decreed* that something would happen or whether He *decreed to allow* it to happen, all events occur as a result of God's sovereign purpose.

Second, the *providence* of God. Providence simply means that God continuously fulfills His original plan, purpose, and design through the events that occur in the universe. In short, providence is God's decrees in action.

Most Christians believe in the providence of God though they might not know it. How often have each of us looked back on something that happened years ago and realized that it happened for a reason? At the time we did not understand, but we do now. That is God working providentially. Think now of all the things you will encounter in your Christian walk. Why will they occur? To lead you to the ultimate purpose God has for you.

Scriptures for Study: Read each of the verses in the *London Confession* above, noting what each declares about God's decrees. 📖 What does Proverbs 16:9 assure us of concerning the providence of God?

JANUARY 24

Our Sovereign God (4)

... the counsel of his own will. (Eph. 1:11)

OH, the staggering applications there are for us when we meditate on the sovereignty of God! *First*, it deepens our view of God, which is certainly the most important. Who of us could possibly ponder this and not be changed? Does it not magnify His will, His plans, His purposes, His grace, and all else concerning His nature and work? This leads directly to a contrasting truth.

Second, it lessens our view of self. Man has dethroned God and enthroned himself (Rom. 1:25), but all the "self-sins" that are part of human nature and culture are rebuked by this doctrine.

Third, it gives us a new view of security. What a future we have! We have been "sealed [by the Holy Spirit] unto the day of redemption" (Eph. 4:30; cf. 1:13), "predestine[d] to be conformed to the image of [Christ]" (Rom. 8:29), can never be "separate[d] from the love of Christ" (v. 35), and have "an inheritance incorruptible, and undefiled, and that fadeth not away, reserved in heaven for [us]" (1 Pet. 1:4). How could we ever feel insecure?

Fourth, it gives us a new view of trust. We would dare conjecture that there has never been a Christian who has not at some point wondered what God was doing or wondered why He was doing something a certain way. That was certainly Habakkuk's experience—he just could not understand how God could possibly use a wicked nation to bring about His purpose. Abram, however, was just the opposite. With no explanation or details, he simply trusted God. No one puts it better than beloved Bible teacher Warren Wiersbe: "We do not live by *explanations*; we live by *promises*."[36] That principle will transform our lives.

Fifth, it gives us a new view of comfort and peace. When we fully realize that God is working all things for our good (Rom. 8:28) and that prayer brings the peace of God in our hearts (Phil. 4:6–7), we will also be able to say with the psalmist: "I will both lie down in peace, and sleep; for Thou, Lord, only makest me dwell in safety" (Psalm 4:8). How can we not feel comfort and peace knowing that God is sovereign? It doesn't matter what turmoil rages around us, for we know that God is in control.

Sixth, it gives us a new view of provision. As the Apostle Paul assured a poor little church in Macedonia: "But my God shall supply all your need according to his riches in glory by Christ Jesus" (Phil. 4:19). Our Lord made the same promise: "Seek ye first the kingdom of God, and his righteousness; and all these things [physical needs] shall be added unto you" (Matt. 6:33). How can we not believe in the sovereignty of God when He makes promises like that? How can we not rejoice in His sovereignty when we see evidence of His provision every day of our lives?

Scriptures for Study: Read Matthew 6:25–34. What observations can you make from our Lord's promise and illustrations?

JANUARY 25

Are You a "Big-Godder"?

For the LORD is a great God, and a great King above all gods. (Ps. 95:3)

SOVEREIGNTY characterizes the whole being of God," wrote Arthur W. Pink. "He is sovereign in all his attributes."[37] We, therefore, simply cannot leave this grand subject without sharing one other thought. The great expositor Donald Gray Barnhouse tells of how he realized the fact of a **great** God:

"Men are always in difficulty with their faith because their God is too small. If they can once see the true God, and get the perspective that sees Him as filling all in all, then the difficulties will rapidly diminish to their proper proportions. I learned of the idea of a great God and a little god from my old professor of Hebrew, Robert Dick Wilson, who was one of the intellectual glories of Princeton Theological Seminary in the great days of Warfield, Davis, Machen, and others. After I had been away from the seminary for about 12 years, I was invited back to preach to the students. Old Dr. Wilson came into Miller Chapel and sat down near the front while I set forth the Word of God. At the close of the meeting the old gentleman came up to me, cocked his head to one side in his characteristic manner, extended his hand, and said, 'I am glad you are a big-godder. When my boys come back, I come to see if they are big-godders or little-godders, and then I know what their ministry will be.' I asked him to explain, and he replied: 'Well, some men have a little god, and they are always in trouble with Him. He can't do any miracles. He can't take care of the inspiration of the Scripture to us. He doesn't intervene on behalf of His people. They have a little god and I call them little-godders. Then there are those who have a great God. He speaks and it is done. He commands and it stands fast. He knows how to show Himself strong on behalf of them that fear Him. You have a great God; and He will bless your ministry.' He paused a moment and smiled, and said, 'God bless you,' and turned and walked out. I am certainly glad that I do have a great God. I have the God who knows all, is all-powerful, unchanging, eternal, never-failing. My God has never made a mistake. He has never been surprised by anything that happened, for He has always known and decreed all things."[38]

How sad it is that many today are, in fact, "little-godders," and because of that they will never fully understand either their **great God** or their great salvation. As Jonathan Edwards wrote: "The absolute, universal, and unlimited sovereignty of God requires that we should adore Him with all possible humility and reverence. It is impossible that we should go to excess in lowliness and reverence of that Being who may dispose of us to all eternity as He pleases."[39] Indeed, how can we possibly reverence Him *too* much? How can we think Him *too* sovereign?

My Dear Christian Friend, are you a "big-godder" or just a "little-godder"?

Scriptures for Study: How big is God in the following verses: Nehemiah 1:5; 9:32; Psalm 47:2; Jeremiah 10:10; Malachi 1:14; Matthew 5:34–35?

JANUARY 26

Our Immutable God (1)

For I am the LORD, I change not. (Mal. 3:6)

HAVE you ever read or heard the word *contemporaneity*? Probably not, but don't despair; it is a rarely used word. Meaning "living or occurring during the same period of time, contemporary," we don't use it because our entire culture is so "contemporary," so "in the moment," that the word is rendered irrelevant. This word goes far deeper, however, than its sterile dictionary definition. Contemporaneity is actually a philosophy, a value system, in fact, that considers the past as passé, obsolete, unrelated, worthless, and even contemptible. We see it even in the Church in regard to theology, music, and even Bible translations. What is ignored, however, is the fact that everything is in a constant state of change with no continuity or consistency.

All that, however, is not new to humanity. It has always been true. The last OT message to Israel, for example, was an important one. Its basic thrust was a rebuke of the Jews for their neglect of true worship and a call to repentance. The book records several dreadful developments: Israel's disrespect for God (Mal. 1:6–14), unfaithfulness and failure of the priests (2:1–9), intermarriage with pagans (2:10–12), unlawful divorce (2:13–16), the robbing of God by the lack of giving tithes and offerings (3:7–12), and outright blasphemy and rebellion (3:13—4:3). All this is summarized in 3:7: "Even from the days of your fathers ye are gone away from mine ordinances, and have not kept them." Israel's history was one of a continual cycle of disobedience, ever up and down and back and forth in their fellowship. In short, Israel was constantly changing.

Gloriously, such is not true of God (or His revelation, for that matter). "Immutability" means "unchangeableness," and God is absolutely unchangeable in His person, purpose, and plan. While *changelessness* is impossible with man, *change* is impossible for God. Man changes according to his age, moods, motives, attitudes, and cravings, but God remains constant, unchangeable, always the same.

I am the LORD, I change not, Malachi wrote. **Change** (*sānāh*, 8138H) means to disguise or to become something different, indicating a change in attitude or character. **Not** (*loh*, 3808H), then, is the word for factual negation, which makes this the polar opposite. God *cannot*, in any way or manner whatsoever, change in His character, attitudes, actions, or any other aspect of His being. Unlike Satan, who "is transformed into an angel of light" (2 Cor. 11:4) and who specializes in deception, God is always "the same" (Ps. 102:27). As we have noted (Jan. 14), God's "I AM THAT I AM" statement (Ex. 3:14) underscores His self-existence and unchangeableness. As **change** essentially indicates imperfection, **not** to change fundamentally indicates perfection. In a culture where contemporaneity rules, it is a comfort to know that God (and His revelation) is always the same.

Scriptures for Study: What do the following verses declare about God's immutability: Psalm 102:27; Hebrews 13:8; James 1:17?

JANUARY 27

Our Immutable God (2)

*The Father of lights, with whom is no variableness,
neither shadow of turning. (Jas. 1:17)*

WRITING about God's immutable nature, Puritan Thomas Watson put it beautifully: "There is no eclipse of His brightness. His essence shines with a fixed luster."[40] The pictorial text before us reveals much about this aspect of God's nature.

First, God is *controlling*. He is **The Father of lights**. **Father** is *patēr* (3962, English "paternal"), which speaks of a progenitor, ancestor, father, mentor, or model. God is, indeed, *the* Progenitor, *the* Father, *the* Controller of all things. **Lights**, then, is a clear allusion to the heavenly bodies He hung in space.

Second, God is *constant*. **Variableness** translates *parallagē* (3883), a compound comprised of *para*, "from, beside," and *allassō*, "to change," and so to change from one form or condition to another. **No** is a tiny word in the Greek (*ou*, 3756) but one with huge meaning. It is "a negative particle," expressing full and absolute negation. God, therefore, *never* changes from the condition in which He has been for all eternity—*perfection*.

Third, God is *consistent*. Most graphic of all, **neither** is there with God a **shadow of turning**. **Shadow** (*aposkiasma*, 644) literally means "to shade" and metaphorically means "the slightest degree or trace." The light from our sun gives off approximately one half million candlepower per square inch. Now consider how many square inches there are in the sun, as it is about 110 times larger in diameter than the earth. We might also add, our sun (called Sol) is actually a quite average, even mundane, star. But all this light is but a flicker in comparison with the light of God. Further, the sun, like God, casts no shadow. "Oh, but the sun *does* cast shadows," someone might object. We submit, however, that is only so from *our* perspective, not the sun's; we or another object cause the shadow. The same is even truer with God. When we are tempted to question God and what He does, let us realize that any "shadows" we see are only from our perspective. God knows what He is doing whether we understand it or not.

Further still, **turning** is *tropē* (5157), which was used often by Classical Greek writers to refer to the heavenly bodies (stars, planets, and moon) as they were in constant motion in their courses. So, while those, and everything else in the universe, is in constant motion and change, God never changes, never varies, never has the minutest waver in His character or conduct. "He cannot change for the worse because He is holy," Warren Wiersbe observes, and "He cannot change for the better because He is already perfect."[41]

Again, in a universe that does nothing but change, let us rejoice in the knowledge that God never does.

Scriptures for Study: What do the following verses declare about God's immutability: Hebrews 1:12; 6:17; 13:8; Revelation 1:4?

JANUARY 28

Our Immutable God (3)

*The Father of lights, with whom is no variableness,
neither shadow of turning. (Jas. 1:17)*

UNDERSTANDING God's immutability produces some profound results in our thinking and living. *First*, it deepens our *adoration of* God. What is there in the world to really adore? In our world, in our society today, there are no absolutes; in men's minds all things are relative and constantly changing. But we can truly adore the God who never changes. In fact, this should be one of the major reasons we *do* worship God—He *never* changes. While the world has the relativism of the age, Christians have the Reality of the Ages.

Second, it deepens our *assurance in* God. What assurance is there in the world? As the adage goes, "Nothing is a 'sure thing.'" But because God never changes, there *are* some "sure things."

(1) We can be sure of His Truth. Psalm 117:2 declares: "The truth of the LORD endureth for ever." God's Word does not change from generation to generation, from year to year, from situation to situation, or from person to person. We can stand on it knowing that it will *never* change.

(2) We can be sure of our security in Christ. "The foundation of God standeth sure, having this seal, The Lord knoweth them that are his" (2 Tim. 2:19). Think of it! Our security of salvation actually stands in the immutable character of God!

(3) We can be sure of strength and comfort. "Trust ye in the Lord forever; for in the Lord God is everlasting strength" (Is. 26:4). Human relationships can destabilize and waver, but in God there is stability.

(4) We can be sure of answered prayer. Would not prayer be absolutely worthless if God were not immutable? In the words of Stephen Charnock: "Prayer is an acknowledgement of our dependence upon God; which dependence could have no firm foundation without unchangeableness."[42] Does this mean prayer "changes God's mind?" While that is a popular thought, it is incorrect. *Prayer works with God's mind as He works out His purpose.* Again, Charnock puts the matter beautifully: "Prayer doth not desire any change in God, but is offered to God that He would confer those things which He hath immutably willed to communicate; but He willed them not without prayer as the means of bestowing them."[43]

Third, it deepens our *attitude toward* God. As we will see, God is unchangeable in His holiness, that is, His attitude toward sin. Therefore, our attitude toward God should be to emulate His unchanging holiness. Consider Charnock once again: "This doctrine will teach us to imitate God in this perfection, by striving to be immovable in goodness. God never goes back from Himself; He finds nothing better than Himself for which He should change; and can we find anything better than God to allure our hearts to a change from Him?"[44] Can we be perfect? No, but we should ever be striving for perfection, striving to be holy in our living.

Scriptures for Study: What does Hebrews 13:5 promise? Why is that possible?

JANUARY 29

God Repented?

*It repented the LORD that he had made man on the earth,
and it grieved him at his heart. (Gen. 6:6)*

ANY study of God's immutability inevitably leads to a very old question: "If God never changes, what then does Scripture mean when it says 'God repented'?" The issue is seemingly made worse by verses such as 1 Samuel 15:29: "the Strength of Israel will not lie nor repent: for he is not a man, that he should repent" (cf. Num. 23:19).

A seeming contradiction, however, is actually quite easily answered when we understand the language. **Repented** translates the Hebrew word for the name of the prophet Nahum (*naḥam*, 5162H) and essentially means "to draw a deep breath" and pictures the "physical mode of giving expression to a deep feeling, either relief or sorrow."[45] Interestingly, in fact, most of the some 100 occurrences of this word actually refer to God.

Our "troubling text," therefore, simply means God was deeply sorry and grieved because of man's sin and therefore changed His dealing with man by bringing judgment. "Similarly, God was sorrowful that He had set up Saul as king (1 Sam. 15:11), but a few verses later we read that 'the Strength of Israel [God] will not lie nor repent: for he is not a man, that he should repent' (v. 29). While the first speaks of God's *conduct* in being sorrowful, the second addresses His *character* as being unchangeable. On the other hand, God also declared that if the people would 'turn from their evil, I will repent of the evil that I thought to do unto them' (Jer. 18:8), that is, if they would turn from evil, He would (*from the human perspective*) change His course of action without violating His sovereign purpose."[46]

Likewise, speaking of the wicked population of Ninevah, the prophet Jonah wrote, "God saw their works, that they turned from their evil way; and God repented of the evil, that he had said that he would do unto them; and he did it not" (Jon. 3:10). Here we see the reverse of the above; because men turned from ungodliness to godliness, God changed in His dealing with them and withheld judgment.

So, while God might change His dealings with us, He will never change in His nature. Puritan Thomas Watson well states the principle: "There may be a change in God's work, but not in His will. He may will a change, but not change His will. God [as Judge] may change His sentence, but not His decree."[47] Theologian Emory H. Bancroft well adds: "The sun is not fickle or partial because it melts the wax but hardens the clay—the change is not in the sun but in the objects it shines upon."[48]

What great comfort this is! We can be assured that God will never "change horses in the middle of the stream." He will always deal with us according to the dictates of His perfect character and purposeful conduct.

Scriptures for Study: What does God promise in Isaiah 54:10 and Romans 11:29?

JANUARY 30

Our Omnipresent God (1)

Whither shall I go from thy spirit? or whither shall I flee from thy presence? . . . (Ps. 139:7–12)

AN ungodly philosopher once asked a Christian, "Where is God?" The Christian's wise reply was: "Let me first ask you, Where is He not?" There is one other "omni" concerning God's absolute, unchanging character: *omnipresence*. It declares the incomprehensible truth that God is present everywhere, and there is no place in the universe where He is not. He is present everywhere not in the physical or bodily sense (as the Pantheist believes), rather in the spiritual sense. "God is everywhere and in every place; His center is everywhere; His circumference nowhere."[49]

Psalm 139 is a thoroughly theological psalm. Verses 1–6 speak of God's *omniscience*, and verses 13–18 speak of God's *omnipotence*. But right in the middle of the passage are the words concerning God's *omnipresence* (vv. 7–12). Is this order of presentation significant? Indeed it is. On the one side there is God's complete knowledge of all history and all men. On the other side there is God's complete power over all He knows. But right in the middle is God's ever-presentness, which makes His knowledge and power personal to His creation. So, the "natural attribute" that actually makes God a personal God is His omnipresence.

David, therefore, asks rhetorically: "Where can I go that You are not there?" It is not that He is trying to get away from God, rather he merely proclaims that God's **presence** is, in fact, inescapable. While many do try to escape God, even denying His existence (Jan. 13), their efforts are folly. **Presence** (*pāniym*, 6440) literally means "face" so figuratively refers to one's presence, even their whole being (Ex. 33:14–15). So, where is God present? Everywhere.

First, He is present regardless of our *location*. Whether **I ascend up into heaven**, David says, or **make my bed in hell, behold, thou art there** (v. 8) **Heaven** is *sāmayim* (8064H), which is plural. Scripture, in fact, indicates at least a fourfold "heaven": (1) There is the lower sky, that is, where the birds fly (Gen. 1:20). (2) There is the upper sky, from whence come clouds (1 Kings 18:45), rain (Gen. 8:2; Is. 55:10), snow (Is. 55:10), and hail (Josh. 10:11). (3) There is "outer space," where the sun, moon, and stars are (Gen. 1:14; Ps. 104:2 cf. 15:5). (4) There is the heaven that is the dwelling place of God (Ps. 2:4; Deut. 4:39; cf. 10:14; 26:15). Further, **hell** (*še'ôl*, 7585H) can refer to a pit but usually means death or the grave.

So, whether we are ascending Mt. Everest, flying in an airplane, standing on the moon, exploring a cave, or buried in the grave, God is there. He is in every place simultaneously, but His essence is not diminished in any location. God cannot "spread Himself too thin."

Scriptures for Study: Read Psalm 139. What strikes you the most profoundly in this wonderfully theological psalm?

JANUARY 31

Our Omnipresent God (2)

Whither shall I go from thy spirit? or whither shall I flee from thy presence? . . . (Ps. 139:7–12)

IF a man owes a debt to another, he may make his escape and flee into another land where the creditor cannot find him," wrote Puritan Thomas Watson, "but 'whither shall I flee from thy presence?' God is infinite, He is in all places; so that He will find out His enemies and punish them."[50] Our text tells us more.

Second, God is present in any *situation*. His presence is in **the wings of the morning** (v. 9). Here is a beautiful metaphor of the morning light. Think of it! If we could fly at the speed of light (approximately 186,000 miles per second), we still could never escape God's presence. David then adds that God's presence is in **the uttermost parts of the sea**. According to ancient geography, this describes the far western side of the Mediterranean Sea. So a deserted island isn't really deserted at all.

Speaking of **the sea**, does not Jonah come to mind? He tried to run away from God's command and away from his responsibilities, and we all remember what happened to him. This should challenge each of us when we are tempted to shirk the responsibilities God has given us. What will God have to do to bring us back to where we should be?

Third, God is present regardless of our *disposition* (vv. 11–12). Men in their rebellion try to hide in **darkness**, for they "[love] darkness rather than light because their deeds [are] evil" (Jn. 3:19), but God "will bring to light the hidden things of darkness" (1 Cor. 4:5). But ponder David's deeper thought: when the believer is oppressed by darkness (anxiety, depression, discouragement, and the like), then **the night shineth as the day** because of God's presence.

Consider also Jeremiah 23:23–24: "Am I a God at hand . . . and not a God afar off? Can any hide himself in secret places that I shall not see him? . . . Do not I fill heaven and earth?" The surrounding context speaks of certain false prophets who opposed Jeremiah's prophecies of coming judgment, proclaiming peace and that no harm would come to Judah. But Jeremiah declares that these prophets deluded themselves into thinking that God could not see their deceit.

Of those words "fill heaven and earth," Puritan Stephen Charnock well said: "God is essentially everywhere present in heaven and earth. If God be, He must be somewhere; that which is nowhere is nothing. Since God is, He is in the world; not in one part of it, for then He [would be] circumscribed by it: if in the world, and only there, though it be a great space, [He would still] be limited. . . . He is everywhere, because no creature, either body or spirit, can exclude the presence of His essence."[51]

Scriptures for Study: What observations can you make concerning God's omnipresence in Acts 17:24–28?

FEBRUARY 1

Our Omnipresent God (3)

Whither shall I go from thy spirit? or whither shall I flee from thy presence? . . . (Ps. 139:7–12)

DOCTRINE always leads to practice, and this doctrine is no exception, achieving two sweeping results in our Christian experience.

First, it is a *grand comfort*. Is not the knowledge that God is ever-present a wondrous comfort to the heart? Think a moment. How can we ever feel *deserted*? Why would we ever be *despondent*? Who could ever make us *discouraged*? When should we ever feel *destitute*? What could ever make us *depressed*?

Further along in Psalm 139 we read: "How precious also are thy thoughts unto me, O God! how great is the sum of them! If I should count them, they are more in number than the sand: when I awake, I am still with thee" (vv. 17–18). How sublime! When it seems that everyone else has forsaken us, we can be assured that God is still there. David tells us that even if our parents forsake us, God will lift us up (Ps. 27:10). When trial and temptations press upon us, God is there (1 Cor. 10:13). When our daily witness becomes difficult because of the world's attack, God is there to give us the words to say, just as He did with Moses (Ex. 4:12). When persecution for Christ's sake comes upon us, God is there and will "comfort us in all our tribulation," and the more "sufferings" we have, the more "consolation" will come (2 Cor. 1:3–5). Even when physical infirmity touches us, God is there to give us His strength, which is "made perfect in weakness" (2 Cor. 12:9). Oh, what grand comfort indeed! But there is something else.

Second, God's omnipresence is also a *grave challenge*. How so?

(1) It challenges us to *deepen* our worship. Reverence and true worship are lacking in much of today's Church. Levity, frivolity, and outright entertainment are common. We would submit that the reason for this is a failure to grasp the fact that God is actually present. If we *truly* believe the omniscient, omnipotent, sovereign God is present, we will reverently and quietly approach Him in worship. (We will return to worship in deeper detail in our June 1–8 studies.)

(2) It challenges us to *defeat* sin. "Doth not he see my ways?" (Job 31:4), another rhetorical question. "This makes it dreadful work to sin," Charles Spurgeon wrote, "for we offend the Almighty to His face, and commit acts of treason at the very foot of His throne."[52]

(3) It challenges us to *desire* to serve. Does not our knowing that God is present make us more aware of our responsibility to be a witness of our Savior to those around us? Since He is our constant companion, should we not introduce Him to others on the spot? This is also an encouragement: since God is with us, we have more courage to do the job.

Scriptures for Study: In the verses cited today, what struck you the most profoundly? Why?

FEBRUARY 2

Our Holy God (1)

Holy, holy, holy, is the LORD of hosts: the whole earth is full of his glory. (Is. 6:3)

"HOLINESS is the most sparkling jewel of His crown," wrote Puritan Thomas Watson, "it is the name by which God is known."[53] While many think *love* is the great shining jewel of God's nature, the angels around His throne indicate otherwise. They exalt Him not by shouting, "Loving, loving, loving," rather, **Holy, holy, holy**. While He is certainly loving, that attribute is not the "crown jewel" of His character. More than all else, *God is holy.*

First, then, we see the *magnitude* of God's holiness. The three-fold repetition of an idea is one of the ways of indicating the superlative in Hebrew (as we would add "-est" to a word). So, God is not just *holy*, or *holier* than anyone else, rather He is the *holiest* that is possible. There is "a continuous and unbroken antiphonal song"[54] of God's holiness around His throne. This is the only attribute of God, in fact, that is presented in this way. God is not just righteous, rather He is *"plus-righteous,"* not just pure but *"beyond* pure."

Second, we see the *mightiness* of God's holiness. He **is the LORD of hosts** (*Jehovah-Ṣābā'ôt*, Jan. 21), that is, Ruling Jehovah of the Universe (Gen. 2:1). He governs everything according to His sovereign will.

Third, we see the *manifestation* of God's holiness. **The whole earth is full of his glory**. Think of it! Everything that exists—mountains, oceans, rivers, trees, animals, people, the planets, the stars—gives Him glory and lay the foundation for praise. Giving God glory is the immediate response to understanding His holiness, for holiness deserves glory. There is nothing else in the universe worthy of praise than is God in His perfections. His holiness is everywhere we look and is demonstrated in all He does. "The LORD is righteous in all his ways," the psalmist declares, "and holy in all his works" (Ps. 145:17).

Fourth, we also see the *majesty* of God's holiness in that final word **glory**. The Hebrew here (*kābôd*, 3519H) is derived from the verb *kābēd* (3515H), "to be heavy or weighty," so to speak of God's glory is to speak of His "weight," His quality, and therefore His majesty and splendor.

> Holy, Holy, Holy, His greatest name,
> The name by which God's glory is best known.
> From beginning to end always the same,
> He's seated upon His heavenly throne.
>   Holy, holy, holy, is Jehovah,
>   Giving praise to His holy name. Selah.

Scriptures for Study: Read Psalm 148:1–14, listing all the ways God is to be praised.

FEBRUARY 3

Our Holy God (2)

Holy, holy, holy, is the LORD of hosts. (Is. 6:3)

OUR finite minds often tend to think of holiness as "the absence of evil." While that is certainty true, it puts the matter in the negative when it should, in fact, be stated in the positive. If I say, "I am healthy," those words mean more than "not sick." Being healthy is a positive state. God's holiness is likewise a positive state; He is absolutely pure. Again, as noted yesterday, His righteousness is "plus-righteousness."[55] Consider two broad principles.

First, we see the *prominence* of God's holiness, which can be explained in three words.

(1) God is holy *intrinsically*. His holiness is part of His very nature. While man is sinful because of his *inherited* nature, God is holy by his *intrinsic* nature. God is not holy because He *wills* to be holy, rather because He *is* holy. This is seen with further clarity by the Hebrew for **holy** (*qāḏôš*, 6918H), which not only is the polar opposite of wicked, but also of just *ordinary*. In other words, it denotes something that is sacred and set apart not only from anything evil, but also anything common. Isaiah 5:16 declares, "But the LORD of hosts shall be exalted in judgment, and God that is holy shall be sanctified in righteousness."

(2) God is holy *surpassingly*. "This attribute hath excellence above His other perfections," wrote Stephen Charnock. "None is sounded out so loftily, with such solemnity, and so frequently by angels that stand before His throne, as this . . . [and] it is the glory of all the rest."[56] Further, His holiness surpasses the holiness of *anyone* else, whether men or angels, and *everyone* else combined. Moses asks rhetorically, "Who is like unto thee, O LORD, among the gods? who is like thee, glorious in holiness" (Ex. 15:11)?. The prophet Samuel then declares: "There is none holy as the LORD" (1 Sam. 2:2). Angels are holy, but not in themselves. Men can be holy, but not by themselves. That, in fact, leads to a third word.

(3) God is holy *effectively*. He actually imparts holiness to his creatures. He made the angels holy. He made His Word holy. He makes us holy through Christ. His holiness is not a theoretical principle, rather an active reality. He doesn't "keep it all to Himself"; He actively uses it in His creation.

If I may, I would humbly offer another stanza to that great hymn, "Holy, Holy, Holy":

> Holy, Holy, Holy, only Thou art worthy!
>   Lifting up your holy name above all else we pray;
> Holy is Your Presence, Holy is Your Essence,
>   May we in all things praise Your name each day.

Scriptures for Study: Read the following verses, noting what each says about God's holiness: Psalms 99:5, 99:9; 111:9; Revelation 4:8–9; 15:3–4.

FEBRUARY 4

Our Holy God (3)

Holy, holy, holy, is the LORD of hosts. (Is. 6:3)

WHILE God's "natural attributes" describe His basic essence (what He *is*), His "moral attributes" delineate His character and actions (what He *does*). So prominent is this first aspect of God's character, in fact, that all His other moral attributes flow from and are guided by it. All that God does in His dealings with man operate according to His holy character.

Many people, for example, are fond of saying, "A God who is love would never send anyone to hell." This is saying, therefore, that love is God's *primary* attribute and that His dealings with man flow exclusively from love. But Scripture is not ambiguous on this point. First and foremost, God is holy and therefore cannot violate His holiness by allowing sin to come into His presence. Such false notions also ignore strong statements such as God "hatest all workers of iniquity" (Ps. 5:5) and "the wicked and him that loveth violence [God's] soul hateth" (11:5).

Another example is that God's righteousness and justice (which we shall explore in other studies) are both an outworking of His holiness. Both have to do with God imposing His laws and executing penalties for breaking them. What is the foundation of such laws?—His holiness. So, based upon the *prominence* of God's holiness, there is something else.

Second, we observe the *particulars* of God's holiness. Scripture reveals several ways in which God's holiness is manifested.

(1) In His *detesting* of sin. Oh, how God hates sin! It is a vile and abhorrent thing. Proverbs 15:9 and 26 tell us that not only is "the way [acts] of the wicked an abomination unto the LORD," but even their "thoughts" are an abomination. "Abomination" translates the strong Hebrew word *tô'ēḇāh* (8441H), which refers to something loathsome, detestable, repugnant, repulsive, revolting, vile, villainous, and vain. Do you get the picture? That is why Habakkuk declared, "Thou art of purer eyes than to behold evil, and canst not look upon evil" (Hab. 1:13).

Those who place God's love over His holiness, therefore, violently rip away the very attribute that forms the foundation of His moral character. Moreover, this is not only a wrong view of God's holiness and love, but it's also a wrong view of *sin*. Sin is the breaking of God's law, law that is based upon His holiness. A wrong view of holiness, then, produces a wrong view of sin, and vice-versa. While love is certainly one aspect of God's nature (1 Jn 4:8, 16), so are holiness and justice. He abhors and judges evil.

What is the practical application of all this? This principle challenges us that to love God we must, like Him, hate evil (Ps. 97:10).

Scriptures for Study: Read the following passages, noting in each what God abhors: Leviticus 18:22–30; 20:13; Deuteronomy 7:25–26; 18:9–14; 23:18; 25:13–16; Proverbs 6:16–19.

FEBRUARY 5

Our Holy God (4)

Holy, holy, holy, is the LORD of hosts. (Is. 6:3)

THE *prominence* of God's holiness is a stunning feature of Scripture. He is called "the Holy One" some 50 times, and we read of His "holy name" another 20 times. The *particulars* of His holiness are equally sobering. It is manifested first in His *detesting* of sin.

(2) In His *delight* of righteousness. "The way of the wicked is an abomination unto the Lord; but *he loveth him that followeth after righteousness* (Prov. 15:9, emphasis added). Think of this truth in light of John 3:16, of which William Evans beautifully writes: "Here God's holiness is seen in that He loves righteousness in the life of His children to such a degree that He gave His only begotten Son to secure it. The cross shows how much God loves holiness. *The cross stands for God's holiness before even His love.* For Christ died not merely for our sins, but in order that He might provide us with that righteousness of life which God loves."[57] Yes, Christ died for us because He loved us, but He died first and foremost because God is holy and wants us to be holy.

(3) In His *doing* of nothing wicked. After all we have seen, this is obvious. "Far be it from God, that he should do wickedness; and from the Almighty, that he should commit iniquity" (Job 34:10). "Far be it" is a single word in the Hebrew (*ḥaliylāh*, 2486H), an adversative interjection of strong emotion: "let it never be!"

(4) In His *distinguishing* Himself apart from sinful man. A vivid manifestation of God's holiness is that it demands He be separate from sinful humanity. This is first evident in the OT (e.g., 2 Sam. 6:6–7; Is. 59:1–2). The entire Mosaic system, in fact, taught this primary truth of God's unapproachable holiness because of man's abominable sinfulness. It all underscored the fact that God is holy while man is defiled. This principle is also evident in the NT (e.g., Jn. 14:6; Eph. 2:13; Heb. 9:22). All approach to God is on the ground of shed blood. Why? Because God is holy and sin must be removed before we can come into His presence.

(5) In His *destruction* of sinful men. "The wages of sin is death" (Rom 6:23). Why? Again, because God is holy. If He does not destroy sin and those who commit it, He would violate His character. John 3:16 comes into focus again. Why do we perish? Because we are sinners who are in violation of God's holiness. The cross was a symbol of God's holiness, and if we reject that, we perish.

(6) In His *deliverance* of man from his own sinfulness. Let us ponder one last time: God's holiness demands holiness from man. So holy is He that He must see holiness in others. Therefore, this holiness demands that He impart holiness to those who have none. And where did he impart that needed holiness?—at the glorious cross of Jesus Christ.

Scriptures for Study: What is the purpose of salvation, according to verses such as Ephesians 1:4, 2:10, and Titus 2:11–12?

FEBRUARY 6

Our Holy God (5)

Ye shall be holy: for I the LORD your God am holy. (Lev. 19:2)

BECAUSE God is holy and has imparted holiness to us through Christ, we are to live a holy life. Holy living is not an option; it is a command. Leviticus 18–20 outlines laws regulating personal standards and relationships, including: marriages, sexual relationships, idolatry, spiritism, and various immoralities. Right in the heart of this dissertation we find our text. Here is God's demand for holiness from His people; He demands holiness because He is holy. A virtually identical command in 11:44–45, and its context (chs. 11–15), again concerns practical matters of holiness, including purity in relation to: food, child bearing, leprosy, and personal hygiene. So, in every aspect of life the Jew was to be pure because God is pure.

Turning to the NT, we encounter 1 Peter 1:15–16, which is actually a quotation of Leviticus 11:44–45. Does this imply a tying together of the OT and NT in regard to the area of practical holiness? Indeed it does! While this does *not* mean we today are to live under the Mosaic Law, it does mean that pure living has not really changed much over the centuries as far as God's viewpoint is concerned. We, therefore, again see two broad principles.

First, applying God's holiness creates a *solemnity* in our approach to Him. A popular approach to God typical of our day is He is our "buddy" and "pal." This comes partly from a misunderstanding of the term "Abba Father."[58] Such overfamiliarity, however, is improper. While God is certainly our Father, and while it is true that Jesus is our "elder brother" (Rom. 8:29), we must still come before God in awe of His holiness. We must never bring Him down to our level with our flippant, earthly, irreverent attitudes.

What then is the correct approach? We approach God with reverence and awe. In Exodus 3:3–5, we read that God *called* Moses to draw near, but He also *cautioned* Him to neither come *too* near lest he violate God's holiness nor come *rashly* lest he be irreverent.

We should also consider again the six-winged cherubims ("burning ones") before God's throne (Is. 6:1–3). With one set of wings they cover their feet, a less honourable member of the body than any other. With another set they cover their faces "because they cannot bear the dazzling lustre of the Divine glory, and because, being conscious of an infinite distance from the Divine perfection, they are ashamed to show their faces before the holy God."[59]

Should our approach to God be any less reverent? Sadly, as A. W. Tozer lamented in the mid 20th-century, there is in much of the Church "little sense of the divine Presence, no moment of stillness, no solemnity, no wonder, no holy fear."[60]

Scriptures for Study: What do the following verses declare about worship: Psalm 89:7; 95:6; Hebrew 12:28; Ephesians 3:14; Philippians 2:10?

February 7

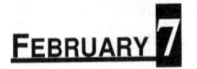

Our Holy God (6)

Ye shall be holy: for I the LORD your God am holy. (Lev. 19:2)

APPLYING God's holiness creates a *solemnity* in our approach to Him, but it also accomplishes something else. *Second*, it creates a *sanctity* in every area of life. As noted back on January 28, our attitude toward God should be to emulate His unchanging holiness. How, then, do we manifest holiness?

(1) Purity in sexual relationships. Leviticus 18–20 is a terrible catalog of impure sexual relationships. Not only does this stress that sexual relations must be *within* marriage, but it also dictates the right *kind* of marriage. These basic morals continue to be ignored in our ever degenerating culture.

(2) Purity in worship. Leviticus 19 also declares that *only* God is to be worshipped. No idol was ever to be worshipped, nor was *any* image of God to be made. Moreover, no type of divination was ever to be sought or any occult practice observed. All this is still true in this age.

(3) Purity in our dealings with men. Again in Leviticus 19 we read how God expects his people to deal with one another. They should provide for the needy (v. 10), not steal, deal falsely, or cheat one another (v. 11), not oppress one another (v. 13), show partiality (v. 15), slander or gossip (v. 16), be vengeful or bear a grudge (v. 18), and in general, just love one another (v. 18). Every one of these is, of course, a NT principle of conduct.

(4) Purity in our diet. It is troubling how many Christians will listen to the latest "diet guru" but will not open their Bible and read what *God* says on this subject. (Is not God's Word sufficient?) Many have the mistaken idea that the dietary guidelines God gave were strictly for arbitrary religious reasons—or at best just for ceremonial (not literal) cleansing—when they were, in point of fact, given primarily for *health* reasons. In Leviticus 11, God forbids eating certain animals because they are "unclean" (*ṭāmēʼ*, 2931H, impure). Note also that animals were considered either clean or unclean even *before the Mosaic Law* (Gen. 7:2). Why? Because every unclean animal, without exception, is either a scavenger or has a crude digestive system that does not filter out the impurities in what the animal eats (both are true, in fact, of pigs). Many insist, "God has now cleansed all animals for food," but that denies physical reality. Is a modern pig less filthy than an ancient one? It will eat literally anything, and whatever it eats will be in the meat within four hours, which means you will eat it, too.[61] (Who would eat a vulture?)

No, we are *not* under the Mosaic Law; we are at liberty. But did not Paul also write: "All things are lawful unto me, but all things are not expedient [*sumpherō*, 4851, to be to advantage, to be profitable]" (1 Cor. 6:12; 10:23)? While we are at liberty to eat certain foods, is it advantageous? Is it not odd that we think smoking tobacco is harmful (cf. 1 Cor. 6:19–20) but eating certain foods is not? We cannot help but ask: how much physical illness is related to eating unclean meats?[62]

Scriptures for Study: Prayerfully consider the passages cited today.

FEBRUARY 8

Our Righteous and Just God (1)

The Lord is righteous in all His ways, and holy in all His works. (Ps. 145:17)
Justice and judgment are the habitation of thy throne . . . (Ps. 89:14)

TODAY we consider two of God's attributes because they are actually inseparable. In fact, some say these are the same. "Justice and righteousness are scarcely to be distinguished from each other," writes one author. "The same word in the original becomes in English *justice* or *righteous*, almost, one would expect, at the whim of the translator." While we would agree with this as far as the language is concerned, we cannot agree that righteousness and justice are synonymous. They are related but not identical; there is a subtle difference between them in Scripture. And, as noted in a previous study, both are an outworking of God's holiness. Holiness has to do with God's character while righteousness and justice demonstrate how He deals with men.

First, then, the righteousness of God is the imposing of laws and demands that are based on His holiness. In theological terms, this is called "legislative holiness." Think of what our society would be today if all the legislation made by governments was based on holiness. But this is exactly what we see with God. Notice our first text (Ps. 145:17). **Righteous** is the Hebrew *ṣaddiyq* (6662H), the root of which means "to be straight" and stands for "a norm," yielding the idea of a moral, ethical standard.[63] In other words, someone is considered to be just or righteous because of conformity to a given standard. This word is used of Noah, for example, who was a "just [righteous] man" because he "walked with God" (Gen 6:9). Think of it! The moral, ethical standard is not some university course in ethics, man's legislation, a Supreme Court decision, or the world's view of morality. *God Himself is the moral, ethical standard.* So, when we speak of God's righteousness, we are speaking of Him making laws that are based on His own perfect holiness, the moral, ethical standard of conduct.

Second, the justice of God is the executing of penalties for breaking God's laws and rewards for keeping them. Again, in theological terms, while righteousness speaks of God's "*legislative* holiness," justice speaks of God's "*judicial* holiness." As emphasized in our study of holiness, God hates sin and cannot allow it in His presence; therefore, God's nature demands justice. This brings us to our second text (Ps. 89:14). **Justice** (or "righteousness") translates the related word *ṣedeq*, (6664H), which in turn is frequently connected with the term **judgment** (or "justice"). The Hebrew here (*mišpāṭ*, 4941H) not only refers to a binding judicial decision that establishes a precedent but also indicates ruling.[64] God, therefore, judges and rules in perfect agreement with His holy character and the standards that are founded upon it. It is our responsibility, then, to live in accordance with that.

Scriptures for Study: According to the following verses, how should leaders carry out their duties: Deuteronomy 1:16; Proverbs 8:15; Isaiah. 32:1?

FEBRUARY 9

Our Righteous and Just God (2)

Upon the wicked he shall rain snares, fire and brimstone, and an horrible tempest. (Ps. 11:6)

HAVING noted yesterday the subtle difference between the righteousness and justice of God, we now focus on their inseparable relationship. God's righteousness and justice are revealed in two basic ways.

First, we must observe God's *wrath* upon the *wicked.* "What can the righteous do? The LORD is in his holy temple, the LORD'S throne is in heaven: his eyes behold, his eyelids try, the children of men. The LORD trieth the righteous: but the wicked and him that loveth violence his soul hateth. Upon the wicked he shall rain snares, fire and brimstone, and an horrible tempest: this shall be the portion of their cup. For the righteous LORD loveth righteousness; his countenance doth behold the upright" (Ps. 11:3–7).

Another example is found in the fact that even Pharaoh admitted God's righteousness and justice. Recall that after the plague of hail Pharaoh said to Moses and Aaron, "I have sinned this time: The Lord is righteous and I and my people are wicked" (Ex. 9:27). Pharaoh knew in his heart that he deserved what he got.

An ages-old question arises here: If God is just, why does it appear that the wicked prosper? Jeremiah asked this question (Jer. 12:1); Job asked this question (Job 21:7); Habakkuk asked this question (as mentioned in our study of sovereignty). And countless other godly people have asked this question. One reason is that God allows men to continue in sin so they will be that much more inexcusable when they stand before Him. Another reason—and this is helpful indeed—is that the wicked only *appear* to prosper; they only prosper in the things of the world. But such is not true prosperity; earthly things mean nothing. Thomas Watson put it beautifully:

"If God lets men prosper a while in their sin, His vial of wrath is all this while filling; His sword is all this time [sharpening]. . . . The longer God is in taking His blow, the heavier it will be at last. . . . Justice may be as a lion asleep, but at last the lion will awake, and roar upon the sinner."[65]

We might look at the ungodly and think they prosper, but they are far from true prosperity. They are going to suffer God's wrath. As a lover of history, I often think of the words reportedly spoken by Admiral Isoruku Yamamoto, the commander of the Japanese Combined Fleet in World War II, after the attack on the U.S. fleet in Pearl Harbor on December 7, 1941: "I fear all we have done is to awaken a sleeping giant and fill him with a terrible resolve."[66]

How infinitely greater God's wrath will be on the ungodly, a warning we must share with those who know not our Lord and His righteousness.

Scriptures for Study: What does Psalm 73:3–20 say about those who seem to prosper?

FEBRUARY 10

Our Righteous and Just God (3)

For thou, LORD, wilt bless the righteous ... (Ps. 5:12)

AS we observed yesterday, there is an inseparable relationship between God's righteousness and justice, which are revealed in two basic ways. First, we noted God's *wrath* upon the *wicked*.

Second, however, we are struck by God's *reward* upon the *righteous*, as our text declares. A wondrous truth is that God says much more in His Word about His righteousness and justice in relation to His people than He does in relation to the wicked. There are at least three ways in which God rewards the righteous.

(1) He forgives us of sin when we confess it. First John 1:9 declares: "If we confess our sins, he is faithful and just to forgive us our sins, and to cleanse us from all unrighteousness." The Greek behind the NT words "righteousness" and "justice" is *dikaios* (1342). This is usually the word used in the Septuagint to translate the Hebrew *ṣaddîq*, which we studied earlier; there is, therefore, a great similarity between the two.[67] When used of men, this word speaks of "uprightness, observing Divine and human laws, virtuousness." However, when the word is used of God, it speaks of His "rendering to each his due" and is used in "a judicial sense of passing judgment on others."[68] So, God is just in that He forgives us when we meet His law by confessing our sins.

(2) He rewards our faithfulness. "For God is not unrighteous to forget your work and labour of love, which ye have shewed toward his name, in that ye have ministered to the saints, and do minister" (Heb. 6:10). This assures us that God is just and will reward us for obeying His command to minister to one another. We also read: "Henceforth there is laid up for me a crown of righteousness, which the Lord, the Righteous Judge, will give me at that day: and not to me only, but unto all them that love His appearing" (2 Tim. 4:8). What wondrous words! Paul is about to go to his death and reminds Timothy that God's command is that we look for Christ's second coming. As we obey this command, God is just in rewarding us with a crown of righteousness.

(3) He protects and delivers us from adversaries. Part of Psalm 129:1–4 reads: "Many a time have they afflicted me . . . yet they have not prevailed against me . . . The Lord is righteous: He hath cut asunder the cords of the wicked." Just as David triumphed over Saul, all believers will triumph over their adversaries because God is just. When we allow Him to work, He brings vindication in His own *way* and in His own *time*.

Dear Christian, be assured that God will bring justice. *He* will repay those who afflict His people. Let us never take matters into our own hands, rather let us allow God to bring about His purposes.

Scriptures for Study: What does 2 Thessalonians 1:6–7 declare concerning God's working?

FEBRUARY 11

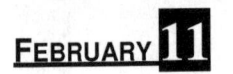

Our Righteous and Just God (4)

For thou, LORD, wilt bless the righteous . . . (Ps. 5:12)

THERE are four wonderful applications to this doctrine. The *first* is God's *wrath* upon the *wicked*, and the *second* is His reward upon the righteous. Today we discover the other two.

Third, there is a *comfort* to the *Christian*. We find, in fact, three comforting thoughts when we quietly meditate on the righteousness and justice of God.

(1) Is it not comforting to know we have been forgiven? Some might ask, "Is there not a contradiction between God's justice and His forgiveness? If He is truly just, and gives man what he deserves, how then can He forgive?" But recall, God is holy, so holy, in fact, that His holiness demands that He impart holiness to those who do not have it. To satisfy His holiness, then, God sent His Son as payment for the just penalty of sin—death. Therefore, when Christ died, justice was served. If Christ had not died for us, the only way justice could have been served would have been for each of us to die an eternal death.

(2) Is it not also comforting to know we have continued forgiveness through confession of sin? As noted yesterday, 1 John 1:9 declares the forgiveness we have through confession. Christ not only died for our *sin* (the one and only sin that sends us to hell, the rejection of God), but Christ also died for our *sins* (the individual transgressions we commit along the way).

(3) Is it not comforting finally to know that God will take care of our adversaries? As we have seen, God will take care of those who afflict His people; we need not and must not try to do it ourselves. Let us also observe that God allows trials, tribulations, and suffering to come into our lives. Why? To aid our growth. James is clear about this (Jas. 1:2–3).

Fourth, there is a *challenge* to the *Christian*. God's justice challenges us to be just in our dealings with men. Picture in your mind today's courtroom judge. He puts on his robe, a symbol of justice, and goes into his courtroom. Later, upon leaving his courtroom, he removes the robe. But the believer is never to take off the "robe of righteousness and justice." Job's words were, "I put on righteousness, and it clothed me; my justice was like a robe and a diadem" (Job 29:14). A "robe" (*me'iyl*, 4598H) was an outer garment and the most elegant of one's dress. Job's justice, then, was the most elegant aspect of his character and how he was best known. He dealt justly and fairly with everyone around him.

This being true of one in the OT economy, how much more so should it be true of NT believers? We are in Christ, clothed in His righteousness and justice. Oh, let us act like it! As Thomas Watson put it: "Imitate God in justice. Let Christ's golden maxim be observed, 'What you would have men to do to you, do ye even so to them' (Matt. 7:12)."[69]

Scriptures for Study: What does Romans 3:21–26 declare? 📖 What does James 1:2–3 teach us about trials?

FEBRUARY 12

Our Merciful God (1)

The Lord is merciful and gracious, slow to anger, and plenteous in mercy. (Ps. 103:8)

"MERCY—what music in those two syllables!" one commentator writes. "There is no term of richer import in any language. It is sweeter than sympathy, more tender than charity, and lies deeper than the fountain of tears."[70] Mercy is the withholding of deserved punishment and relieving distress. The words "compassion," "pity," and "loving-kindness" are all used in Scripture to convey this truth.

Our text uses the Hebrew word *ḥesed* (2617H), which speaks of kindness, loving-kindness, mercy, goodness, faithfulness, loyal love, and acts of kindness.[71] No word better summarizes God's dealing with men than *mercy*. Our text goes deeper, in fact, than just saying God has mercy; it says that God is **plenteous** in mercy, which intensifies mercy all the more.

Consider also Titus 3:5: " Not by works of righteousness which we have done, but according to his mercy he saved us, by the washing of regeneration, and renewing of the Holy Spirit." The Greek behind mercy here (*eleos*, 1656) is the word used in the Septuagint to translate the Hebrew *ḥesed*. The Greek means "compassion, pity, mercy." One Greek authority gives us this wonderful definition: "Kindness or good will towards the miserable and the afflicted, joined with a desire to relieve them."[72]

Mercy, then, is always to the helpless. You see, we actually deserve the affliction, whatever it might be. Why? Because we are sinful. But God, because He is merciful, comes to our aid and relieves the affliction. When we get to our study of God's love, we will see how John 3:16 speaks of mercy. That great text implies that we deserve to perish, but flowing out from God's love is His mercy.

What is the contrast between "mercy" and "grace"? We will meditate on the riches of grace in later studies, but we should take a moment here to note this difference. While some view these terms as essentially synonymous, there is a crucial contrast between them. Briefly, "mercy" is the *withholding* of what *is* deserved. We deserve wrath, punishment, even death, but God has relieved us from it all. "Grace," then, is the *bestowing* of what is *not* deserved. In other words, in addition to relieving us from what *is* deserved, God gives us added blessings such as life and inheritance that we could *never* deserve.

A visitor who was attempting to console the dying Puritan preacher (and "Father of Connecticut") Thomas Hooker said, "Sir, you are going to receive the reward of your labor." Hooker replied, "Brother, I am going to receive mercy."[73]

Amen!

Scriptures for Study: How is mercy described in each of the following verses: Nehemiah 9:19; Psalms 25:6; 86:13; 106:45; 1 Peter 1:3?

FEBRUARY 13

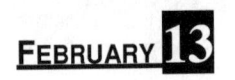

Our Merciful God (2)

The Lord is merciful and gracious, slow to anger, and plenteous in mercy. (Ps. 103:8)

"THE mercies of God make a sinner proud, but a saint humble," wrote Thomas Watson.[74] How true we discover that statement to be the more we meditate upon it.

First, we consider the *depth* of God's mercy. Mercy is an aspect of God's character that is deeply rooted in Him and its depth is seen in at least three ways.

1. Mercy is a foundational truth of Scripture. God's mercy is referred to some 240 times in the OT, not including about 27 references to the "mercy-seat." God's mercy is then referred to some 40 times in the NT. An interesting comparison is that "mercy" is spoken of more often in the OT than in the NT, while "grace" is spoken of more often in the NT than in the OT. The reason, as will become evident in our study of grace, is because the greatest manifestation of God's grace was in the person and work of Christ.

2. God actually prefers to show mercy rather than execute wrath. The gods of pagan religions are always angry and demand constant appeasement. But the true God "delights in mercy" (Mic. 7:18) and "does not afflict willingly" (Lam. 3:33). God only brings wrath when He can no longer endure the sin of man (Jer. 44:22).

3. Mercy tempers God's other attributes. God's holiness, righteousness, and justice would be numbingly terrible without His mercy. Why? Because we would have absolutely no hope without the mercy of God. Thomas Watson again puts the matter beautifully: "God's mercy is one of the most orient pearls of His crown; it makes His Godhead appear amiable and lovely. . . . God's mercy is His glory. His holiness makes Him *illustrious*; His mercy makes Him *propitious*."[75]

Second, consider the *manifestations* of God's mercy.

1. His pardoning of sin when confessed and forsaken. Perhaps the best illustration of this is David's confession of sin in Psalm 51:1–4. In this great Psalm of penitence David confesses his great sin and God shows mercy. We are reminded again of 1 John 1:9, and it is God's mercy that makes that verse possible.

2. His patience with man even when he hardens his heart. We read in Nehemiah 9 that as revival broke out among the Israelites, the Levites recalled the people's rebellion and general sin, but God showed mercy.

3. His delivering man from sickness, sorrow, and suffering. God had mercy on Epaphroditus' life-threatening illness (Phil. 2:27), and He still manifests such mercy today.

4. His being a refuge and protector. David again comes to mind, as he called God his "defense and refuge in the day of my trouble" (Ps. 59:16).

Scriptures for Study: Read Psalm 136 over the next two days. First, how many times does the psalmist declare: "His mercy endureth for ever"?

FEBRUARY 14

Our Merciful God (3)

The Lord is merciful and gracious, slow to anger, and plenteous in mercy. (Ps. 103:8)

THE *depth* and *manifestations* of God's mercy lead us to another consideration. Third, we note the *recipients* of God's mercy. To whom does God show mercy? In general, writes Thomas Watson, "God pours the golden oil of mercy into empty vessels."[76] More specifically:

1. God shows mercy to whom He wills. Do we not all tend to think we deserve something, that we deserve "a little consideration," as the expression goes? But God declares, "I will have mercy on whom I will have mercy and I will have compassion on whom I will have compassion" (Rom. 9:15). Verse 18 goes on to add, as illustrated by Pharoah, He has "mercy on whom he will have mercy, and whom he will he hardeneth." Let us not forget God is sovereign and does not have to show mercy to anyone because all have sinned against Him. Thankfully, however, there is another principle.

2. God shows mercy to all men. In light of our previous thought, in His sovereign will, God has chosen to show mercy to all men. This is manifested in many ways, the most important of which is even allowing them to live another day and giving them one more opportunity to repent of their sin and believe the Gospel.

3. God shows mercy *especially* to those who love and obey Him. God is "the faithful God, which keepeth covenant and mercy with them that love him and keep his commandments" (Deut. 7:9).

4. God shows mercy *especially* to those who confess and forsake their sin. "He that covereth his sins shall not prosper, but whoso confesseth and forsaketh them shall have mercy" (Prov. 28:13).

5. God shows mercy *especially* to those who trust in Him. This is perhaps the grandest of all. "Many sorrows shall be to the wicked; but he that trusteth in the Lord, mercy shall compass him about" (Ps. 32:10). "Compass" translates the wonderfully graphic word *sāḇaḇ* (5437H), which carries the literal idea "to surround or encircle." It is used, for example, in Ecclesiastes 1:6: "The wind goeth toward the south, and turneth about [*sāḇaḇ*] unto the north; it whirleth about continually, and the wind returneth again according to his circuits." Think of it! When we trust in the Lord, when we lean upon Him, He surrounds us, He encircles us with His mercy. What assurance that is! "God keeps the best wine until last," Thomas Watson again assures us. "Here he gives us mercies only in small quantities; the greatest things are laid up. Here there are some honey drops and foretastes of God's love; the rivers of pleasure are reserved for paradise. . . . Who can tread upon these hot coals of God's love and his heart not burn in thankfulness?"[77]

Scriptures for Study: Continue your mediation on Psalm 136. What observations can you make about mercy in this humbling Psalm?

FEBRUARY 15

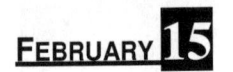

Our Merciful God (4)

The Lord is merciful and gracious, slow to anger, and plenteous in mercy. (Ps. 103:8)

WE close our mediations on God's mercy today by considering the *application* it has to our daily living.

First, God's mercy *crushes* us into humility. By this we do not mean we must now grovel as some vile creature, but neither are we to become proud as though we deserve God's mercy. We need to realize that even as we did not deserve mercy while in a lost condition, neither do we deserve it in a saved condition. In ourselves, "that is, in [our] flesh, dwelleth no good thing" (Rom. 7:18) and are wholly undeserving of *any* consideration of God, much less actual mercy. Oh, if this doesn't humble us, nothing will!

Second, God's mercy *causes* us to love God more. Oh, Dear Christian Friend, do you *really* love the Lord? Think again: God is merciful when we deserve only wrath; He pardons sin when we deserve only condemnation; He is patient even when we are in rebellion; He delivers us from sickness, sorrow, and suffering even though we deserve whatever comes our way; He protects us and continuously provides for us even though we deserve to be abandoned. Does this not inspire a love we never before considered? How the following words from Thomas Watson should bless our hearts: "God's justice may make us fear Him, His mercy makes us love Him. . . . Sure that heart is made of marble, which the mercy of God will not dissolve in love."[78] Indeed, one who is not moved by the thought of God's mercy is without doubt unmovable.

Third, God's mercy *challenges* us to imitate Him in mercy. "Be ye, therefore, merciful, as your Father also is merciful," our Lord Himself commanded (Lk. 6:36). "This [verse] explains Matthew 5:48—'Be perfect, as our Father is perfect,'" wrote Matthew Henry. "Imitate your Father in those things that are his brightest perfections." The NT Epistles likewise repeat that refrain. "Be ye kind one to another, tenderhearted, forgiving one another, even as God, for Christ's sake, hath forgiven you" (Eph. 4:32). "Forgiving" is *charizomai* (5483), which is derived from *charis* (5485, "grace") and therefore speaks of showing favor, graciously giving to someone. God demands that we show *unconditional* mercy and forgiveness just as He did. It matters not whether someone asks for our forgiveness, we give it. It matters not whether we think the person who wronged us deserves our forgiveness, we give it. Why? Because we didn't deserve God's forgiveness, but He gave it anyway. We are to do the same. How dreadful it is if we do not. Puritan Thomas Adams well said: "He that demands mercy, and shows none, ruins the bridge over which he himself is to pass."[79]

Scriptures for Study: What do the following verses declare about showing mercy and forgiveness: Colossians 3:12–13 and 1 Peter 3:8–9?

FEBRUARY 16

Our Gracious God (1)

Noah found grace in the eyes of the Lord. (Gen. 6:8)

TODAY we step with great deference onto hallowed ground. While this moral attribute of God is, of course, no more important than any other, there is something especially captivating about the concept of **grace**. No other word, in fact, more epitomizes the Christian faith than does this simple word.

It is amazingly significant that neither the Hebrew nor Greek word behind **grace** is all that extraordinary in its original usage.[80] Most of the occurrences of the Hebrew *ḥēn* (2580H), for example, are actually secular, not theological, and simply refer to a superior person showing favor to an inferior person, such as a king to his subjects.[81] Likewise, in secular Greek, *charis* (5485) simply meant "that which affords joy, pleasure, delight,"[82] and from there several meanings developed: grace, favor, thankfulness, gratitude, delight, kindness, and so on.[83]

It is the biblical usage of these words, however, that transforms them from the mundane to the marvelous, from the secular to the sublime, from the ordinary to the extraordinary. They both raise the meaning to something that is entirely undeserved, what has accurately been dubbed "unmerited favor." That principle, in fact, is absolutely paramount in understanding biblical grace. In the OT, "[*ḥēn*] tends to carry with it . . . the idea of unmerited favor, or of supreme graciousness and condescension on the part of the giver, who is the superior. . . . It is all His generosity."[84] While a secular king's "generosity" is usually just a reward for his subjects' obedience to him, God's grace is entirely undeserved and is bestowed upon those who live in total rebellion against Him. Our text, for example, is the very first OT occurrence of *ḥēn* and declares this great theological truth. Noah did not deserve God's grace any more than those who perished in the deluge.

The transforming of the NT *charis* (5485) is even more dramatic. Because secular Greek philosophy believed in human merit and self-sufficiency, grace was no more than "getting a little help" from the gods once in awhile in the form of favors or gifts. In the NT, however, *charis* is inseparably linked to the person and work of Jesus Christ. "For the law was given by Moses, but grace and truth came by Jesus Christ" (Jn. 1:17). Removing grace from the NT also removes Christ; conversely, any weakening of the doctrine of Christ returns grace to its former commonness.

We, therefore, humbly offer this definition: *Grace is the unmerited favor of God toward man, manifested primarily through the person and work of Jesus Christ, apart from any merit or works of man.* As Richard Sibbes wonderfully observes, "For what is grace but the beams of Christ, the Sun of Righteousness."[85]

Scriptures for Study: Spend some time in the following passages, carefully observing what they teach us about grace: Romans 11:6; 2 Corinthians 9:13–15; 2 Thessalonians 1:12.

FEBRUARY 17

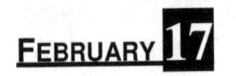

Our Gracious God (2)

For the grace of God that bringeth salvation hath appeared to all men. (Titus 2:11)

THERE are three major emphases concerning grace in the NT. *First*, there is *salvation by* grace. Our text can also be rendered: "For the saving grace of God was manifested to all men" (*YLT*). The words "was manifested" translate *epiphainō* (2014), which means "to make to appear, to be revealed" and appears here in the past tense. We could even render this: "The grace of God was revealed once-for-all." Here is, indeed, a direct reference to the incarnation of Christ, which again couples Him with God's grace. The words "that bringeth salvation" (AV) are one word in the Greek that qualifies grace. What does God's grace do? It brings salvation. Salvation does not come by works; it comes only by grace, as manifested in Christ.

Second, there is *security through* grace. What good is grace if it is not permanent? Some sincere Christians believe we can lose our salvation, that we can "fall from grace." But how can we fall from that which was not deserved in the first place? How can we fall from favor that was unmerited? You see, the grace that *saved* us is the same grace that *keeps* us. "Therefore, being justified by faith," Paul declares, "we have peace with God through our Lord Jesus Christ, By Whom we also have access by faith into this grace in which we stand, and rejoice in hope of the glory of God" (Rom. 5:1–2).

"We stand" is a single Greek word (*histēmi*, 2476) that means "to make to stand, to establish." More importantly, it is in the perfect tense, which refers to past action with an emphasis on the result. Getting married, for example, is a past action but the result is that the couple is still married. Paul is saying that we were placed in Christ through God's grace with the result that we are still there. Once established *in* Christ, we will never be *out* of Him. Why? Because of grace!

Returning to our text, Paul utilizes what is called "paraphrasic construction," which was used when the writer could not describe all the action that was taking place with a single verb and so used two verbs. The first verb, "saved," is again in the perfect tense. Therefore, "By grace you have been completely saved in the past with the present result that you are in a saved state of being right now." But Paul is still not satisfied with showing the *reality in* the present time; he wants to show the *result through* the present time. So he adds the words "ye are," which are from the Greek verb that means "to be" and are in the present tense, indicating continuous duration of the resulting state of being.

Putting all this together, an expanded translation of this verse is: "By grace you were completely saved in the past with the result that you are in the state of salvation now and which now continues through the present time." And how did all this come about? *Grace!*

Scriptures for Study: Spend some time in Ephesians 2:5–9, observing what it teaches us about grace.

FEBRUARY 18

Our Gracious God (3)

... by the law is the knowledge of sin. (Rom. 3:20)

WE noted yesterday two of three major emphases concerning grace in the NT: *salvation by* grace and *security through* grace. *Third*, then, there is *spirituality* as the way of life *in* grace. The Christian is to live by grace, which is synonymous with what we call "spirituality." To see exactly how grace applies to Christian living, ponder four possible ways a Christian can live.

1. Living according to *law*. There is no better illustration of this attitude than the Pharisees. Not only did they adhere to the OT Law (the Torah), but through the centuries they added thousands of traditions, which they considered "applications" of the Law and therefore just as binding. They believed that adhering to all this made them acceptable to God. Sadly, some Christians have similar ideas, thinking that following OT laws is somehow more sacred, spiritual, and superior. But, as our text declares, the Law can only *expose sin*; it cannot *express spirituality*.

So, as noted in our study of holiness, we are not to live under the Mosaic Law. We do not keep the Law in order to be blessed. On the other hand, does this also mean that there are no laws today? Of course not. The word "law" can be defined as "a system of rules for conduct," and we do indeed have rules for living. As we will see, there is today "the law of liberty."

What then is the contrast? The main difference between OT law and NT grace is one of *motive*. The Law says, "Obey *in order* to be blessed; obey because you *have* to." But grace says, "Obey *because* you have been blessed; obey because you *want* to." (We will explore God's Moral Law starting June 14.)

This contrast is vividly seen in an illustration from Harry Ironside. He told of an old Navaho Indian who explained the difference between law and grace this way. The Indian recalled his first long train trip from the southwest to Oakland, California. During the trip the train stopped at a beautiful railroad station. As he walked along he saw a sign that said, "Do not spit here." But as he looked at the sign and then looked at the floor, he saw that many people had spit on the floor. And, before he even realized what he was doing, he too spit on the floor. When he arrived in Oakland he was invited to some people's home for dinner. As he sat in the beautiful home he noticed the beautiful pictures, furniture, grand piano, and plush carpet. He then thought that it was rather odd that there was no sign saying, 'Do not spit here.' But still, as he looked around, he saw no spit on the floor. With great insight he said, 'Now I understand. That sign is law, but inside the home it is grace. They love their home and want to keep it clean.'"[86]

What a simple picture. We do not obey the Lord because He says to do so. We obey Him because we love Him and love whatever He says. Spirituality is not the result of obedience, rather obedience is the result of spirituality.

Scriptures for Study: What does Galatians 2:19–21 say about the Law and Christian living?

FEBRUARY 19

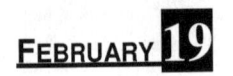

Our Gracious God (4)

O foolish Galatians . . . (Gal. 3:1a)

CONTINUING our look at four possible ways a Christian can live, akin to the first way (*law*), there is another.

2. Living according to *legalism*. Legalism can be defined as, "A fleshly attitude that obeys rules, but does so with a motive of self-glorification." Legalism is an attitude that is divorced from objective truth and truly biblical rules for conduct. It is entirely subjective, being based upon personal opinions and motives.

I am sure of all this because in my earlier ministry I was guilty of legalism, although I preferred to call it "spirituality." Typical to legalism is someone's own list of "dos and don'ts," that is, the conduct *they* think is either spiritual or unspiritual. But, if I may be lovingly blunt, at the heart of legalism is self-righteousness. Indeed, such Christians obey rules and laws (and impose it on all others), but in so doing they build themselves up in the sight of others.

Consider Paul's words to the churches in Galatia (Gal. 3:1–3; 5:6–7). The Judaizers had infiltrated those churches and were undermining justification by faith alone, a doctrine that is at the very core of Christianity. In their self-righteousness and self-appointed superiority, they insisted that Gentiles had to become Jewish proselytes and obey the Mosaic Law. But Paul was absolutely horrified (and quite disgusted) that the Galatian believers would be deceived by such apostasy.

Later in his letter, Paul goes on to deal with what it means to "walk in the Spirit" (5:16–18), emphasizing in verse 18, "if ye be led of the Spirit, ye are not under the law." In verses 19–21, he goes on to list the works of the flesh that should no longer characterize the Christian and then adds in verses 22 and 23 the "fruit of the Spirit" that characterizes those who walk in the Spirit. So, as the Law was never a means of *salvation*, neither is it a means of *spirituality*. Nothing we do or refrain from doing *makes* us spiritual. To say it does is to be trapped in the snare of legalism. Rather, when we *are* spiritual (that is, when our minds, goals, desires, values, and all else are set on spiritual things), the right conduct will then flow out from that spirituality. (We will study "spirituality" in more depth on Apr. 3.)

Legalistic Christianity is tragic because it never builds a Christian up; it only tears him down. Yes, there are rules of conduct in God's Word, things we should and should not do. But legalism *creates* rules that God's Word does not *confirm*. Instead, let us simply obey the "rules" God's Word actually lists, such as those in Ephesians 4:25–32, for example. But even then, let us remember that our motive is to glorify God not ourselves. Let us never think we are better than someone else just because we have come a little farther than they in growth and conduct, for we all still have a long way to go. *That* is grace living.

Scriptures for Study: Read the passages cited today and write down your observations. How does all this affect your attitudes before and after?

FEBRUARY 20

Our Gracious God (5)

For, brethren, ye have been called unto liberty . . . (Gal. 5:13)

HAVING considered two of four possible ways a Christian can live (*law* and *legalism*), we come to two others.

3. Living according to *license*. We look again at those "foolish Galatians." As the remainder of our text declares, "also use not liberty for an occasion to the flesh, but by love serve one another" (5:13b). Paul's point here is that *liberty* is not *license*. There are those who insist, "Eternal security gives a person freedom (or license) to go out and do whatever he wants to do." That is totally false! Liberty is not license to indulge the flesh. In fact, a true Christian will not indulge, that is, give himself over to the flesh. Further, we must seriously doubt the salvation of anyone who thinks that liberty *does* mean license. This leads us to one other way the Christian can live, the way God intends for the Christian to live.

4. Living according to *liberty*. In addition to our text, note also verse 1: "Stand fast, therefore, in the liberty with which Christ hath made us free, and be not entangled again with the yoke of bondage." What is "Christian liberty"? Based on that verse, we submit this: *Christian liberty is the freedom from the bondage of sin, the flesh, and religious ritual that we have been given in Christ.* Think of it! Liberty means freedom. We are free from the shackles of sin, the chains of the flesh, and even the bondage of the Law's rituals.

But we must go deeper. What is the guiding principle of liberty? If liberty is *unrestricted*, it turns into *license*, while if liberty is *over-restricted*, it turns into *legalism*. What is the balance? We would submit simply this: When liberty is correctly restricted, it is controlled by *love*.

First, because our liberty is controlled by love for the Lord, all we do displays the Lord (1 Cor. 10:31). Second, such control means we will never be enslaved by anything else. "All things are lawful unto me, but all things are not expedient [i.e. profitable]: all things are lawful for me, but I will not be brought under the power of any" (Heb. 6:12). Third, this controlling love means we will not be encumbered by a "weight" that will slow us down as we run the Christian race (Heb. 12:1; Nov. 8). Fourth, such control means we will do nothing to offend another believer, that is, cause him to sin (1 Cor. 8:13). Fifth, this controlling love produces a desire to do all things so as to draw men closer to Christ. Paul once again encourages the Corinthians to become all things to all men so that some of them will come to Christ (1 Cor. 9:19–22; Sept. 11). You see, the lost are watching us and are doing so when we least expect it. All we do and say should manifest Christ and draw the lost to Him.

So, God's grace is not just in *Him*, but now in *us*, not just His nature, but ours. That does not mean we are *God*, but it does mean we are *godly*.

Scriptures for Study: Read the passages cited today and write down your observations. How does all this affect your attitudes before and after?

February 21

Our Loving God (1)

. . . God is love. (1 Jn. 4:8a)

BY the love of God," writes J. Sidlow Baxter, "we mean the purest, strongest, wisest, most thoughtful and self-abnegating love which ever flowed in the heart of the noblest father or mother on earth—only a myriad times purer and sublimer—a mighty, tender, boundlessly outreaching compassion that has no parallel."[87]

Many good definitions of God's love have been offered over the years. Just one such example is: "God's love is an exercise of His goodness towards individual sinners whereby, having identified Himself with their welfare, He has given His Son to be their Savior, and now brings them to know and enjoy Him in a covenant relation."[88] That is excellent because it emphasizes sacrifice, which is critical in understanding love: *there is no love where there is no sacrifice.*

To have even a chance of grasping God's love, we must first understand the Greek *agapē* (26). While *philos* (5384) means "a tender affection," this word speaks of willful sacrifice and can be defined as "a self-emptying self-sacrifice." Like *charis* (5485, grace), *agapē* is rather colorless in secular Greek. While it carried an element of sympathy, described the love of a person of higher rank for one of a lower rank, and even spoke of a love that was not self-seeking, it never carried the depth of meaning we now know until our Lord transformed it. When He used *agapē*, it took on the meaning of being *totally sacrificial*, and it "thus creates a new people who will tread the way of self-sacrificing love that [He] took."[89]

So, I would offer this definition: *God's love is a self-emptying self-sacrifice in which God gave of Himself in the form of His only begotten Son who gave His life for us.* No, God did not "empty" himself of any aspect of His nature, but sacrificially offered up His Son as the price for our sin. That thought gives new understanding to verses such as Romans 5:8: "But God commendeth his [self-emptying self-sacrifice] toward us, in that while we were yet sinners, Christ died for us."

Sadly, many misunderstand our text. Some insist, "Love is God's primary essence," or worse yet, "God and Love are equal; they are the same." A. W. Tozer well answers such skewed notions: "Had the Apostle declared that love is what God is, we would be forced to infer that God is what love is. If literally God is love, then literally love is God, and we are in all duty bound to worship love as the only true God there is."[90] The Apostle's obvious meaning is that love is *part* of God's nature. In other words, this statement describes God's character, as do all of His other attributes. And, what's more, as we pointed out in our study of holiness, God never violates one attribute for the sake of manifesting another. So, to repeat, the words "God is love" mean that love is a distinct attribute of God; it is one aspect of His nature and character.

Scriptures for Study: In preparation for tomorrow's study, meditate on John 3:16 in light of the meaning of *agapē* love.

FEBRUARY 22

Our Loving God (2)

For God so loved the world ... (Jn. 3:16)

OUR text has been called by many, "The greatest text of the Bible." Whether that is true or not, I do not presume to say, but without doubt this *is* the greatest text on God's love, revealing at least eight truths about such love.

First, the *origin* of love (**God**). It is significant indeed that Christianity is the only faith that presents "a god" as being loving. The gods of the heathen are always angry and must constantly be pacified. But such is not so with the one true and living God. He is not some Task-Master who demands blind obedience from those who cower before Him. Rather, He is a loving, caring Father.

Second, the *magnitude* of love (**so loved**). Note that **loved** is past tense. Think of it! God loved us even before we believed. That is the magnitude of His love; He loved us "while we were yet sinners" (Rom. 5:8). We were, in fact, "elect according to [His] foreknowledge" (1 Pet 1:2). Again, the Greek *proginōskō* (4268, "foreknowledge") does not simply mean knowing something before it happens (Jan. 17) but rather also denotes foreordination (cf. v. 20, where the same word is translated "foreordained"). Further, the root *ginōskō* (1097) means "to know by experience" and often is practically synonymous with love and intimacy. What Peter declares here is that we were foreknown and foreordained by *a loving, intimate relationship before the foundation of the world*. Note also the word *so* (*houtō*, 3779), which is often used to express magnitude or quantity. What a thought! God loved us **so** much, with such magnitude, with such quantity, that we cannot possibly comprehend it. How could God actually love us who are sinful and lack any lovable quality? That is unknown.

Third, the *object* of love (**the world**). John uses *kosmos* (2889) in his Gospel in no less than nine ways: the whole universe (Jn. 1:10; 17:5); the physical earth (13:1; 16:33; 21:25); the world system or order (12:31; 14:30); unbelieving humanity (7:7; 15:18); an undefined group. (12:19); the general public (7:4; 14:22); general humanity (1:10); the non-elect (17:9); and finally the elect, as here in our text. Because Psalm 5:5 declares that God "hatest all workers of iniquity," it is clearly incorrect to say that God loves every single person on the earth (cf. Ps. 10:3; 11:5; Hos. 9:15). The words **whosoever believeth in Him** narrows down the meaning of **world** only to those who believe, that is, the elect, the objects of God's special love. Our Lord goes on, in fact, to clarify in verse 17: "For God sent not his Son into the world to condemn the world; but that the world [of believers] through him might be saved." There can be absolutely no doubt here as to whom **world** refers. Christ's death gave life only to the believers of this world.[91]

What a staggering truth it is to know that God's special love was upon those whom He knew before the foundation of the world (Eph. 1:4).

Scriptures for Study: What do the following verses say about God's love for His people: Romans 5:8; Titus 3:4–6; 1 John 4:9–10?

FEBRUARY 23

Our Loving God (3)

For God so loved the world ... (Jn. 3:16)

"THE only ground for God's love is God's love," wrote Thomas Brooks. "The ground of God's love is only and wholly in Himself."[92] Turning again to our great text, we see something else about God's love.

Fourth, the *proof* of love (**gave his only begotten Son**). **Gave** is, of course, in the past tense in the Greek. God **gave his only begotten Son** in one decisive, once-for-all act. This brings us right back to our definition of love—"a self-emptying self-sacrifice." As Martin Luther observed: "When God gives His Son, what does He retain and what does He not give? Yea, He gives Himself entirely."[93] If I may say it again: *love is sacrifice*. We *hear* much talk of love in society today, but we *see* little sacrifice. That is why John declared: "In this was manifested the love of God toward us, because that God sent his only begotten Son into the world, that we might live through him. Herein is love, not that we loved God, but that he loved us, and sent his Son [to be] the propitiation for our sins" (1 Jn. 4:9–10).

Fifth, the *recipients* of God's love (**whosoever**). This goes one step deeper than the object of love (**the world**). There is a fine distinction here. Not only did God love all His people *collectively* (**the world** of believers), but He also loved each one *individually* (**whosoever**). Is it not more personal and more meaningful when, instead of saying, "I love all my people," God says, "I love *you*?"

Sixth, the *requirement* of love (**believeth on Him**). This does not mean God loves us only if we believe, for God loved us in eternity past before we even existed. It means rather that we are required to believe in order to have eternal life. God indeed loves us, but His love and holiness demand our belief in the blood of Christ.

Seventh, the *mercy* of love (**shall not perish**). Please take special notice of these two final observations. Recall that in our study of mercy we saw that mercy is the *withholding* of what *is* deserved. Each and every one of us deserves eternal death for our sin. But God's love bestows mercy so that when we trust Christ, we **shall not perish**. What great mercy indeed!

Eighth, the *grace* of love (**everlasting life**). We also recall that grace is the *bestowing* of what is *not* deserved. Since we deserved death, then we certainly did not deserve any blessing or reward. But not only did God *withhold death*, He also *bestows life*.

"Of the several wonders of the magnet," wrote Thomas Watson, "it is not the least that it will not draw gold or pearl, but despising these, it draws the iron to it, one of the most inferior metals: thus Christ leaves angels, those noble spirits, the gold and pearl, and comes to poor sinful man, and draws him into His embraces."[94]

Oh, what an amazing love God had for us! Will we ever comprehend it?

Scriptures for Study: What do the following verses declare about God's love: Romans 5:8–10; 8:32; 1 John 3:16?

FEBRUARY 24

Our Loving God (4)

For God so loved the world . . . (Jn. 3:16)

As is true for all the attributes of God, His love has direct application to our own practical living.

First, God's love *cherishes* us. "For no man ever hated his own flesh, but nourisheth and cherisheth it, even as the Lord the Church" (Eph. 5:29). The context says that the husband is to love his wife "as Christ also loved the church, and gave himself for it" (v. 25). So, as we cherish our own body (i.e., take care of it, don't abuse it), we also cherish our wives. Does this not bring us right back to the definition of love?—a self-emptying self-sacrifice. This is the picture of God's love: He *prizes* us, He *protects* us, and He *provides* for us.

Second, God's love *chastises* us. Here is a principle we do not like to face, but as Hebrews 12:6 declares, "For whom the Lord loveth He chasteneth, and scourgeth every son he receiveth." The rest of this passage is truly fascinating, for it goes on to say that a father *must* chasten a child. Why? What purpose does this serve? The answer is in verse 10, "That we might be partakers of his holiness." A father chastens a child to make him do right. Why should we make him do right? Because, as we have studied, God commands us, "Be ye holy as I am holy" (1 Pet. 1:16). Your motive for disciplining a child is love. Likewise, God disciplines us because He loves us and wants us to do right.

Third, God's love *constrains* us. I am drawn often to Paul's words: "The love of Christ constraineth us" (2 Cor. 5:14). Those first four words refer, of course, to Christ's sacrificial death on Calvary. Paul is saying, "Motivated by Christ's love for us, we now go out and point others to Him." "Constrains" is *sunechō* (4912), which figuratively means "to compel or press on. In this context, then, it means that 'the love of Christ 'controls' or 'dominates' Paul so that he has to live for Christ and not self."[95] Dear Christian, is that true of you? Is the controlling desire of your life to grow in Christ? Is the dominating compulsion of your life to be a faithful witness of Christ to the unbelievers you meet each day? Are you constrained to live for self or live for Christ?

We close our study of God's attributes with this thought from Stephen Charnock: "[God's] love *to* His people is as great as His sovereignty *over* them."[96] Unlike many today—who end up denying one or the other—the Puritans saw how God's *sovereignty* is complemented by His *love*. He not only brings about His sovereign plans and purposes, which are far beyond human understanding, but He also, while doing so, takes a personal interest in each of us and loves us dearly.

Oh, what a God we serve!

Scriptures for Study: Read the story of Peter and John's arrest and address to the Sanhedrin (Acts 4:1–22). What can you observe from this incident?

FEBRUARY 25

Knowing Christ (1)

That I may know him . . . (Phil. 3:10)

MOST of us hold certain verses of God's Word especially close to our hearts, verses we particularly cherish for some personal reason. Our text is one of mine: "That I may know him, and the power of his resurrection, and the fellowship of his sufferings, being made conformable unto his death."

How men pride themselves in knowledge, often considering it an end in itself! Socrates postulated, "There is only one good, knowledge, and one evil, ignorance." Hippocrates believed that "science begets knowledge." The "renowned" John Henry Newman, former Anglican turned Roman Catholic Cardinal, wrote, "There is a knowledge which is desirable, though nothing come of it, as being of itself a treasure, and a sufficient remuneration of years of labor." Others are convinced that knowledge is basically subjective. "No man's knowledge can go beyond his experience," John Locke insisted. In muddled rhetoric, Confucius taught, "When you know a thing, to hold that you know it; and when you do not know a thing, to allow that you do not know it—that is knowledge."

On the other hand, English philosopher, statesman, scientist, and author Francis Bacon, whose writings seem to indicate he was a Christian, wrote the famous proverb, "Knowledge is power," which is, in fact, a biblical truth: "A wise man is strong; yea, a man of knowledge increaseth strength" (Prov. 24:5). Less well known, however, is another of Bacon's statements: "Knowledge is the rich storehouse for the glory of the Creator and the relief of man's estate."

As useful and beneficial as knowledge of science, history, mathematics, and other disciplines is, all of them combined pale to insignificance when compared with the knowledge of God in general (see Jan. 7–9) and Christ in particular, as Paul emphasizes here. What should amaze us first about Paul's statement is the point in his life when he utters it. He was not a new convert or even new to ministry. He penned this statement after 30 years of service. Think of it! He had spent three years with Christ in Nabatean Arabia being trained (Gal. 1:16–18), and then for three decades he grew in spiritual depth, preached throughout most of the known world, founded numerous churches, and penned half of the NT. But *still* he writes, **That I may know him.** What does that say about our small, shallow, and superficial knowledge? I would offer the following as a prayer:

> More about my Lord I desire to know,
>> More knowledge of His person and glory;
> More understanding so that I may grow
>> More passionate in telling His story.

Scriptures for Study: What do the following verses teach about knowing Christ: Philippians 3:8 and 2 Peter 3:18?

FEBRUARY 26

Knowing Christ (2)

That I may know him . . . (Phil. 3:10)

THERE are four ways in which we can know someone. First, we can know someone merely *historically*, as one might know Abraham Lincoln through historical record. Second, we can also know someone *contemporaneously*, that is, know of them because we live in the same time period, but still we do not know them personally. Third, we can know someone *contactually* in that we have met them briefly, but once again we still do not know them. All these touch only the head, not the heart. The fourth way we can know someone, however, is far deeper, and it is also the first of four ways we should know Christ.

First, we must know Him *personally*. To know someone personally is to know them not only by *name*, but by *nature*. We know their mind, thinking, feelings, reactions, disposition, temperament, habits, and even idiosyncrasies. That is how we should know our Lord, not just know *about* Him, but know *Him*!

The word "know" in our text is *ginōskō* (1097). Another word for "know" is *oida* (1492), which speaks of head knowledge, but *ginōskō* speaks of experiential knowledge. In an attempt to bring out the full force of this verse, I would humbly offer this expanded "translation": "For my unwavering goal is that I might know Him—that I might become increasingly, intensely, and intimately more familiar with Him, that I might observe, identify, and comprehend Him (through the wonders of His person and works of His passion) more clearly and completely."

So, Paul's unwavering, focused desire was to have a progressively deeper, intimate, "hands-on" knowledge of the things that are unique about the Lord, His nature, His character, and His work. But how can we do this? How can we know Him personally? Well, there are no "shortcuts" here.

(1) Such knowledge comes first by *immersion in the Word of God*. People immerse themselves in all kinds of things: pleasure, popularity, making money, and so on. But to immerse oneself in the Word is to begin knowing its author, "the Word [who] was made flesh" (Jn. 1:14). Such knowledge commences in reading the Gospels. It is there we read of Him *demonstrably*; it is there we *see* Him, read the evidence *of* Him, and have our encounters *with* Him.[97] Such knowledge continues, deepens, and grows by then reading the Epistles, where we read of Him *doctrinally*. While the Gospels *introduce* Him, the Epistles *interpret* Him. It is here we learn the great theological truths that His life, death, and resurrection instituted.

(2) Such personal knowledge of our Lord comes by *intimate times of prayer*. He cannot be known by "minuteman" prayers at breakfast, or by "give me" prayers that express our wants, or by our "emergency prayers" in times of crisis. We must get unhurriedly alone with Him and there, and always in conjunction with His Word, "linger longer" (Jan. 2).

Scriptures for Study: As an example of today's study, read John 4:1–42, listing things you learn *about* Christ and then things you learn *of* Christ.

FEBRUARY 27

Knowing Christ (3)

That I may know him . . . (Phil. 3:10)

"LET us not satisfy ourselves with a knowledge of God in the mass," Stephen Charnock submits; "a glance upon a picture never directs you to the discerning the worth and art of it."[98] As we meditated yesterday, knowing Christ *personally* cannot be attained by quick snatches of Bible reading and hurried prayer. Such knowledge comes only by *immersion* in the Word and *intimate* prayer.

Second, and going deeper, we must know Him *progressively*. Such personal, experiential knowledge of Christ is to be ever increasing and deepening. As every happily married couple knows, even after years of marriage, each partner is still learning about the other and there are still new things to share and enjoy together. While it is sad that many marriages lack this, it is even more tragic that many Christians do not have this with their Lord. There is little growth, little maturity, and little increase in their knowledge of Christ and His Word. In his classic, *The Pursuit of God*, A. W. Tozer writes of our text: "Paul confessed the mainspring of his life to be his burning desire after Christ. 'That I may know Him,' was the goal of his heart, and to this he sacrificed everything."[99]

Such personal, experiential knowledge is an ongoing "maturing process." "Perfect" (*teleios*, 5046) appears often in the NT and means full grown or mature. As Colossians 4:12 declares, "That we may stand [mature] and complete in the will of God." Paul also wrote, "May we all come into the unity of the faith and the knowledge of the Son of God, unto a [mature] man" (Eph. 1:13). What is the road to maturity? Know the Lord and His Word—again, not just know *about* Him, but know *Him*, to "grow in grace and knowledge" of Him (2 Pet. 3:18).

Third, we must know Christ *powerfully*. Oh, what depth there is in the words "the power of His resurrection"! Think of it! Paul wanted to experientially know the very power of Christ's resurrection. Likewise, we are meant to know that power and should progressively desire to know it more and more. What does knowing this power provide us? It *provides victory* over self, sin, and Satan, and then *produces vitality* for service.

Fourth and finally, we must know Christ *painfully*. Once again, what depth we see here as Paul wanted to know experientially the fellowship of Christ's sufferings. This is less "glamorous" than knowing Him personally, progressively, and powerfully, but it is no less essential. What is this fellowship of His suffering? While it is certainly not a mystical participation in His past death or some reenacting of His suffering in our own present experience, it is a contemplation of what He did suffer for us, as well as our willingness to suffer for Him.

Scriptures for Study: What does the power of Christ's resurrection provide for us in John 11:25 and Colossians 3:1? 📖 What do 2 Timothy 2:12 and 3:12 teach us about suffering?

FEBRUARY 28

Pursuing Christ

I count all things but loss . . . (Phil. 3:8)

PHILIPPIANS 3:10 is not an isolated example of this truth of pursuing our Lord. In verse 8 Paul writes: "Yea doubtless, and I count all things but loss for the excellency of the knowledge of Christ Jesus my Lord: for whom I have suffered the loss of all things, and do count them but dung, that I may win Christ." Paul was willing to give up anything, even everything, which he ultimately did, to increase in his personal knowledge of Christ. In fact, he considered everything else in life as nothing but "dung" in comparison.[100]

Paul continues in verses 13–14: "Brethren, I count not myself to have apprehended: but this one thing I do, forgetting those things which are behind, and reaching forth unto those things which are before, I press toward the mark for the prize of the high calling of God in Christ Jesus." It is not enough to read about God and try to *comprehend* Him, for we never can; rather, we get alone with God and *commune* with Him. That is Paul's point. In this context "apprehended" (*katalambanō*, 2638) means "to lay hold of with the mind, to understand, perceive, learn, comprehend." In other words, Paul says, in effect, "Even though I do not fully comprehend God, or ever can for that matter, I continue to pursue knowing Him, I continue to look to the things of heaven as my all-consuming desire."

Further, Hebrews 3:1 declares: "Wherefore, holy brethren, partakers of the heavenly calling, consider the Apostle and High Priest of our profession, Christ Jesus." "Consider" (*katanoeō*, 2657) implies attention and continuous observation. The idea is, "Put your mind on Jesus and keep it there, continue to concentrate upon Him, that you might understand who He is and what He wills." The situation here was that some Christian Jews were trying to hold on to many rituals and ceremonies of Judaism for fear of being ostracized from family and the synagogue because of their Christianity. The challenge here, however, is that we no longer need *ritual* because we have *Reality*; we no longer look at the *shadow* because we have the *Substance*; we no longer need the *pictures* because we have the *Person*.

In much the same way, many Christians today hold on to various externals, such as: a certain place and way of worship, assorted symbols and acts, even observing a form of the Passover during Easter. But I lovingly submit, there is simply no place in biblical Christianity for such externalism. As the Epistle to the Hebrews makes clear, Christ is better than all those externals.

Our Lord Himself also made this clear in John 4:24: "God is a Spirit: and they that worship him must worship him in spirit and in truth." All our worship is to be in spirit and in truth, not in ritual and ceremony. A true pursuit of God is internal, not any particular external.

Scriptures for Study: What else did Paul say about his sufferings for Christ in Acts 20:24 and Romans 8:18? 📖 What is the promise of 1 John 5:20?

FEBRUARY 29

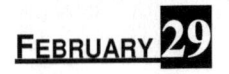

A Prayer of Thanksgiving

... abounding therein with thanksgiving. (Col. 2:7)

ON this "odd" day that comes once every four years, let us pause from our series and just reflect on thanksgiving. Of the seven Greek words used in the NT for various aspects of prayer, one is *eucharistia* (2169) at the root of which is *charis* (grace) with the prefix *eu* (good or well). The idea, then, is to "give good grace," that is, be thankful, give thanks.[101] What are you thankful for?

> I thank You, Father, for so many things,
>   The blessings you bestow, the gifts You bring.
> Thank You for Your great love, mercy, and grace,
>   For even considering this dead race.
> Thank You for salvation, its tranquil joy,
>   Satan's power You came down to destroy.
> Thank You for provision and daily care,
>   Heavenly riches You lavishly share.
> Thank you for the charm and love of my wife
>   And for our son who's the joy of our life.
> Thank You for music, the praises we sing,
>   And for Your promises to which we cling.
> Thank you for victory over the flesh,
>   The Spirit's indwelling makes each day fresh.
> Thank You for the love of a Christian home,
>   I am never tempted to stray or roam.
> Thank You, Lord, for the greatest Book of all,
>   Specially dear are those letters of Paul.
> Thank You for the wonderful gift of prayer,
>   Your presence anytime and anywhere.
> Thank You for opportunities to serve,
>   A privilege I could never deserve.
> Thank You for the fellowship of others,
>   The love of Christian sisters and brothers.
> Thank You, Father, for the Church of Your Son,
>   All that He's doing and already done.
> Thank You for language we can use to write
>   Sonnets that will praise you both day and night.
> Thank You, Dear Father, for everything,
>   For being my God, my Savior, my King.

Scriptures for Study: Read the following verses, noting what each says about prayer: Philippians 4:6; Colossians 4:2; 1 Timothy 2:1 (*eucharistia* is rendered in each as "thanksgiving" or "thanks").

MARCH 1

Seeking Jesus

What seek ye? (Jn. 1:38)

THE setting of our text is the Apostle John's account of Jesus' call of His first disciples to salvation. As they were following Him, He turned and asked, **What seek ye?** In His omniscience, our Lord already knew what they wanted, but He asked them so they would examine their own motives.

That question, in fact, is a profound one in light of our own day. Notice that our Lord did not ask them *whom* they were seeking, rather He asked *what* they were seeking. Multitudes of people seek all kinds of things, and many churches gear their entire ministry to such so-called seekers. They give them entertainment, a particular style of music, a coffee bar, and whatever else will please them. The multitudes in Jesus' day, in fact, sought Him for the same reason—they followed along just to get what they wanted (e.g., Jn. 2:23–25). Such people, however, are not seeking Christ at all; they are seeking only the *what*, not the *who*.

I do not say this lightly or out of mere opinion, for the word **seek** (*zēteō*, 2212) is very clear; it is "a technical term for striving after knowledge, especially philosophical investigation"[102] and strongly involves the will. While before conversion no man "seeketh [*ekzēteō*, 1567, 'to seek out'] after God" (Rom. 3:11)—it is God who does the seeking (Lk. 19:10)—the honest, sincere seeker, whom God is already drawing to Himself (Jn. 6:44), is seeking not the *what* but the *who* and will always find Him (Deut. 4:29; 1 Chron. 28:9; Jer. 29:13).

This is further verified by the question Andrew and John asked—"where dwellest thou?"—and Jesus' answer: "Come and see" (v. 39). They were not just asking where He was residing but were seeking to spend time with Him and, in fact, to become His disciples. The word "see" means more than just physical sight. Used metaphorically the Greek (*eidō*, 1492) speaks of perception with the mind and senses, to understand. So, they didn't want to just meet Jesus, they didn't want some casual acquaintance. They wanted to walk with Him, learn from Him, and be committed to Him. And so they did, as verse 39 goes on to say: "they came and saw"—or as the verb tenses indicate, "they sought and found"—and not only spent many hours with Him that day but also the next three years.

This incident is not only a challenge to the multitudes today who claim to be seeking Jesus when in reality they are seeking only *what* they *want* not *who* they *need*, but it is also an encouragement to those who have, by His sovereign grace, sincerely sought and found Him. It is because we are in Him that we now "seek those things which are above [and] set [our] affection on" them (Col. 3:1–2).

As we continue our meditations on knowing Christ, let us constantly be reminded that we are not concerned about the *what*, but the *who*.

Scriptures for Study: Read Deuteronomy 4:29, 1 Chronicles 28:9, and Jeremiah 29:13, noting what each says about sincere seekers.

MARCH 2

What's In a Name?

... his name ... (Matt. 1:21)

"WHAT'S in a name?" Shakespeare asked. "That which we call a rose by any other name would smell as sweet."[103] How important is a name? In Western culture, names aren't all that important. In ancient Near Eastern thinking, however, names were very significant. A person's name, in fact, "often carried more significance than an identification mark; it was considered to be a description of character or conditions."[104] In the OT, for example, *Eve* means "the mother of all living" (Gen. 3:20), *Nabal* reflects the fact that he was a fool (1 Sam. 25:25), and *Isaac* means "he laughs," a reminder of his parents' laughter at the thought they could conceive a child in old age (Gen. 17:17, 19; 18:12). The same is true in the NT: *Peter* (from *petros*, 4074) means "small stone"; likewise, the Roman name *Paul* means "little," in contrast to his Jewish name *Saul*, which means "desired"; and *Nicodemus* means "victor among the people," reflecting his position as a ruler of the Jews and a distinguished member of the sect of the Pharisees.

This is all the more significant when we turn to the names of God, which are many: *God* (*'Elōhiym*, "the Strong One, who is to be feared and revered because of who He is"); *Jehovah* or LORD (*Yāhweh*, His covenant name emphasizing self-existence and unchangeableness); *Lord* (*'Adōnāy*, which speaks of dominion, possession, and sovereignty); and many others.[105]

In the same way, there is perhaps no better way to get to know Christ more deeply and intimately than understanding His names. While we might think that is limited to "Jesus Christ," the fact is that more than 50 names are ascribed to Him in Scripture. But why so many? Multiple names serve three purposes that could never be accomplished by any one name.

First, multiple names more fully *describe His nature—what* He is. Among the countless attacks upon Christianity through the ages, none has been more violent in its execution or critical in its importance than the exact nature of Jesus Christ. Man, philosopher, sage, revolutionary, and a god have all been used to describe Him. This question is answered, however, simply by turning to His names.

Second, Jesus' names *detail His character—who* He is. There is perhaps no better summation of Christian character than Galatians 5:22–23. The reason those nine characteristics can reign in the Christian is because they are the very character of Christ, and His names delineate that character.

Third, Jesus' names *display His work—*what He *did*. He came "to seek and to save that which was lost" (Lk. 19:10), and His names display it in vivid pictures.

So, with our desire to know and pursue Christ firmly rooted in our hearts, we turn tomorrow to that wondrous adventure.

Scriptures for Study: What Christ-likeness of character do we read in Galatians 5:22–23? What does Philippians 1:11 add?

MARCH 3

Jesus

And she shall bring forth a son, and thou shalt call his name JESUS: for he shall save his people from their sins. (Matt. 1:21)

OH, what a verse stands before us! Of all the names ascribed to our Lord, none is sweeter than **Jesus**. "There's just something about that name," as the old chorus goes. It is here, then, we begin our meditations.

First, we *recognize* the *person*. Appearing almost 900 times in the NT, the name **Jesus** translates the Greek *Iēsous* (2424), a transliteration of the Hebrew *Yehôsûa* (3091H), "He will save" or "Jehovah is salvation." While there has been (and still is) much debate about who Jesus was, this name erases all doubt in the believing heart—He was Jehovah God who came in the flesh (Jn. 1:14).

Second, we *realize* the *plight*. Why did **Jesus** come? To **save his people from their sins.** While a growing number of "preachers" today downplay, discount, or just outright deny, the reality of sin, it is central to the Gospel. If sin is not an issue, in fact, or if it is not really all that bad, there is actually no need for the Gospel. But sin is not *a* problem; it is *the* problem. Man's plight is not some vague sense of shame, a perceived guilt, an "amiable weakness," or a low self-esteem. The Greek for **sins** here (*hamartia*, 266) means "missing the mark." It was used in ancient times for a spearman missing the target and so came to be used in the ethical sense of not measuring up to a standard or falling short of a purpose or standard. Whose standard, then, have we missed? God's standard of holiness and glory (Rom. 3:23).

Third, we *relate* to the *people*. Here is a wondrous truth indeed. Jesus came not to save an unknown group or a vague, undetermined number of souls. He came to save a specific **people**, those He knew, in fact, before the foundation of the world (cf. Eph. 1:4–7). As He explicitly stated, "I am the good shepherd: the good shepherd giveth his life for the sheep" (Jn. 10:11), that is, *us*. The Shepherd's intent, His whole purpose in coming, was to die for and redeem His sheep.

Fourth, we *rejoice* in the *purpose*. We see this first in the word **save** (*sōzō*, 4982), which here means "to save, deliver, make whole, preserve safe from danger, loss, [and] destruction."[106] Jesus came, therefore, "to seek and to save that which was lost" (Lk. 19:10), "all [those] that the Father giveth [Him]" (Jn. 6:37).

Going deeper, however, this entire verse prompts our praise of the eternal purpose of God. **Jesus** coming to **save his people** was not an afterthought; this wasn't "Plan B" because the OT Mosaic system failed. **Jesus** was always the focus of God's redemptive purpose. As far back as Genesis 3:15, in the shadow of the Fall, **Jesus** is in view. While Satan would bruise Jesus' *heel* (cause Him to suffer), **Jesus** would deliver the death blow to Satan's *head* at the Cross. From that moment forward, everything pointed to when **Jesus** would **save his people from their sins.**

Scriptures for Study: What do the following verses declare about Jesus: Acts 4:10–12; 5:29–31; 13:23, 38–39?

MARCH 4

Christ

... Thou art the Christ ... (Matt. 16:16)

MATTHEW 16:13–17 records a crucial moment in redemptive history. Up to this moment, Jesus had been slowly leading His disciples to the point of true recognition of His identity. Mark's account adds (Mk. 8:27) that as He now walks along with them—oh, what a joy to walk with Jesus! (cf. Gen 3:8)—it is now the proper time.

First, our Lord asks a *summary question*. "When Jesus came into the coasts of Caesarea Philippi, he asked his disciples, saying, Whom do men say that I the Son of man am?" It was a probing question, one designed not only to underscore the varied views of men, but also to set the stage for the chief question to come.

Second, men offer a *score of opinions*. The disciples reported that some, such as Herod, viewed Him as John the Baptist risen from the dead (Matt. 14:2). Others thought He was Elijah, a forerunner of the true Messiah (Mar. 31) yet to come (cf. Matt. 17:12; Lk. 1:17). Jeremiah was another view because the Jews thought He was that prophet that should be raised up from among them (Deut. 18:15). Still others thought, as we might say today, "He's just another prophet, maybe even one raised from the dead" (Lk. 9:19).

Nothing has changed. One popular picture of the "historic Jesus" paints him as an itinerant Hellenistic Jewish sage who preached a simple "social gospel." In this way He was simply a social reformer whose "Kingdom of God" was a means for personal and egalitarian cultural transformation. He has been described variously by others as "a good man," "a wise teacher," "a moral example," a "profound thinker and sage," and even "a revolutionary." Interestingly, the disciples left out that some identified Jesus with Beelzebub (Matt. 10:25); likewise today, many think He is dangerous, His teachings destructive, and His ways dated.

Third, Jesus asks the *singular question*. It is here Jesus makes His point: "But whom say ye that I am?" This is even more pointed in the original, literally reading: "But ye, whom do ye say Me to be?" As the "ye" in our KJV indicates (which is always plural), Jesus addresses all His disciples. While Peter answers, he does so on behalf of the entire group.

Fourth, God reveals the *solitary truth*. As Jesus makes clear, Peter's answer—**Thou art the Christ**—is a divinely revealed truth (v. 17). **Christ** is *Christos* (5547), which means *anointed*, an OT term used to apply to anyone anointed with holy oil, primarily the high priesthood (Lev. 4:5; 4:16). Peter testifies, in effect: "You are the long awaited, repeatedly prophesied Anointed One, the people's Greatest Prophet (Deut. 18:15, 18; Acts 3:22; 7:37), Only High Priest (Ps. 110:4; Heb. 6:20; 7:24), and Eternal King (Ps. 2:6; Zech. 9:9; Lk. 1:33; Mar. 28–31.) As the disciples received this staggering truth, so must we all answer Jesus' question.

Scriptures for Study: In the following verses, who is speaking and what do they say: Matthew 14:33; 26:63; 27:54; John 19:7; 20:28; Acts 9:20?

MARCH 5

The Son of God

... Thou art the Christ, the Son of the living God. (Matt. 16:16)

As we reflected yesterday, Matthew 16:13–17 recounts a pivotal scene, the disciples' recognition and reception of Jesus' full identity. Speaking for the group, Peter testified: **Thou art the Christ**. But that was not his full testimony. There is something deeper here.

First, we note the *fundamental appellation*. The further divinely revealed truth Peter and the other disciples recognized was that Jesus was also **the Son of ... God**. This title, which appears 47 times in the NT, as well as many other references to "the Son," fundamentally underscores His deity. While some cults latch onto this title to "prove" He was just God's *son* but not *God*, all they actually prove is either their own ignorance at best or obstinate rebellion at worst.

This truth is undeniable in light of the Greek behind "son [of]" (*huios*, 5207) and its use in ancient times. While it certainly means "offspring of," it also means "partaking of," "connected with," or "of the order of."[107] Sons (or children) of the kingdom, for example, are partakers of it and connected with it, while sons of Satan are partakers of him (Matt. 13:38).[108] "In Jewish usage," one theologian well writes, "the term 'Son of . . .' did not generally imply any subordination, but rather equality and identity of nature. . . . Thus for Christ to say, 'I am the Son of God' (Jn. 10:36) was understood by His contemporaries as identifying Himself as God, equal with the Father, in an unqualified sense."[109] This is explicitly stated, in fact, in John 5:17–18. The Jews sought to kill Christ because He called God His Father and Himself the Son, thereby "making himself equal with God."

Second, we observe the *further amplification*. God revealed something else to His disciples: **Christ** is also **the Son of the *living* God**. Whether a god be a rock, a stick, or a philosophy, it is dead. Gods are made of fame, fortune, and fun, but not one has ever drawn a breath. God is the only God that is alive. **Living** is *zaō* (2198; noun *zōē*, 2222; English *protozoa*). "In the thinking of the ancient Greeks, life was not a thing, but *vitality*. For that reason, *zōē* can't be used in the plural. In other words, we don't possess several 'lifes' like we could possess several books or shoes; rather, life is a singular, vital, and active reality."[110] God is life and vitality Himself, and **the Son** is equal to it.

Third, we see the *final application*, which is two-fold. In John 8:24, our Lord makes it clear that to deny who He is, is to be lost: ". . . if ye believe not that I am he, ye shall die in your sins." But to receive Him as God, Savior, and Lord is to become, like Him, a child of God. While He is the "only begotten" Son (see Mar. 7), we are sons (and daughters) by adoption, with all the rights and privileges of that Son by birth.

Scriptures for Study: What do the following verses say about **the living God**: Joshua 3:10; 1Samuel 17:26, 36; Psalm 42:2; Jeremiah 10:9–10?

MARCH 6

The Son of Man

. . . the Son of man . . . (Dan. 7:13)

APPEARING more than 80 times in the Gospels, this title is used exclusively, with only one exception, by Jesus Himself and was actually His favorite title for Himself. While its meaning is difficult to discern, as many expositors and scholars agree, three basic principles are understood in this title.

First, it is a title of *authority.* As most agree, this title without doubt traces back to Daniel 7:13–14: "I saw in the night visions, and, behold, one like the Son of man came with the clouds of heaven, and came to the Ancient of days, and they brought him near before him. And there was given him dominion, and glory, and a kingdom, that all people, nations, and languages, should serve him: his dominion is an everlasting dominion, which shall not pass away, and his kingdom that which shall not be destroyed." This authority is then made clear in Mark's Gospel, in that, for example, He "hath power on earth to forgive sins" (2:10) and is "Lord also of the sabbath" (2:28). The religious leaders also recognized this reference to Daniel and knew Christ was claiming to be that heavenly ruler; they therefore shouted: "He hath spoken blasphemy . . . He is guilty of death" (Matt. 26:65–66).

In light of our understanding of the term **Son of** noted yesterday, "'Son of Man,' especially as applied to Christ in Daniel 7:13 and constantly in the [NT], essentially means 'The Representative Man.'"[111] While many would consider Michelangelo's statue *David* as "The Representative Man" (the ultimate statement) of the Renaissance and humanism, it is Christ alone who is the true **Son of man**.

Second, it is a title of *affliction.* We are not told why Jesus adopted this title, but we can observe that it did not possess the restrictions of other messianic titles. As one writer puts it, "It allowed the concept of the Suffering Servant to be integrated with that of the Messianic King."[112] This is a critical point. Nothing underscores the dual nature of Christ more than this. He is both God *and* man, fully and completely, and nothing underscores His humanity as does His suffering *for* humanity. As Mark again declares: "the Son of man . . . must suffer many things . . . they shall condemn him to death . . . and [He will] give his life a ransom for many" (9:12; 10:33, 45).

Third, it is a title of *adulation.* Because He was not only the **Son of man** but also the "Son of God," death could not hold Him (Acts 2:24). "And they shall mock him, and shall scourge him, and shall spit upon him, and shall kill him: and the third day he shall rise again" (Mk. 10:34). But also because of that dual nature, "Then shall they see the Son of man coming in the clouds with great power and glory" (13:26). What shall follow? Praise and adulation throughout eternity.

Scriptures for Study: The Gospel of John records only 13 occurrences of **Son of man**, but they are noteworthy. What do the following examples in John declare: 3:13–14; 6:27; 12:23; 13:31?

MARCH 7

The Only Begotten (1)

... only begotten ... (Jn. 1:14, 18; 3:16, 18; 1Jn. 4:9)

HERE is one of the most remarkable titles of our Lord in all Scripture. **Only begotten** translates *monogenēs* (3439), a compound word comprised of *monos* (3441; English *monograph*), "only, alone, without others," and *genos* (1085; English *gene*), "offspring, stock." The idea then is "only offspring," "only physical stock," or, as one commentator well puts it, "only born-one."[113] In ancient Greek, this word was used to refer to a unique being. To say "only son," or worse, "one and only son," as some modern translations do, is an error. Jesus is *not* the *only* Son of God, else Paul was wrong when he wrote that Christ is "the firstborn among many brethren" (Rom. 8:29). Who are those brethren? We are! We, too, are sons of God by the sovereign act of God in adoption. Jesus, however, is, as one translator renders it, "the uniquely begotten one,"[114] the only Son of God physically born as a Son. Interestingly, only John uses this term and does so five times. Examining these occurrences helps us grasp this remarkable title.

First, it is a term of *incarnation*: "The Word was made flesh, and dwelt among us, (and we beheld his glory, the glory as of the only begotten [i.e., born] of the Father,) full of grace and truth" (Jn. 1:14). No better summary of this reality is found than that in the *Westminster Confession of Faith*:

"The Son of God, the second person of the Trinity, being very and eternal God, of one substance and equal with the Father, did, when the fullness of time was come, take upon Him man's nature, with all the essential properties, and common infirmities thereof, yet without sin; being conceived by the power of the Holy Ghost, in the womb of the virgin Mary, of her substance. So that two whole, perfect, and distinct natures, the Godhead and the manhood, were inseparably joined together in one person, without conversion, composition, or confusion. Which person is very God, and very man, yet one Christ, the only Mediator between God and man."[115]

Second, it is a term of *intimacy*: "the only begotten Son, which is in the bosom of the Father" (1:18). To be in someone's bosom (*kolpos*, 2859) indicates the deepest affection, to be cherished and embraced (e.g., the English expression "bosom friend"). The expression reflects the Oriental custom of reclining at meals so that the head of one guest rested on the chest of another (cf. Jn. 13:23; Lk. 7:37–38). The imagery in our text, then, is that the Son has from all eternity been in the close fellowship, the intimate embrace, of the Father. He did not become the Son at His incarnation; He has always been the Son. The "Father-God" and "Son-God" are, in fact, one while at the same time distinct. Each knows all about the other, and it should be our desire to know both as intimately as possible.

Scriptures for Study: What do the following verses declare about today's theme: Psalm 2:7; Acts 13:33; Heb. 1:5; 5:5?

MARCH 8

The Only Begotten (2)

... only begotten ... (Jn. 1:14, 18; 3:16, 18; 1 Jn. 4:9)

CHRIST as the **only begotten** is one of the great themes of the Gospel, and it is one of the most remarkable titles of our Lord. In the first of its five occurrences in John's writings, it is a term of *incarnation* (1:14), and in the second, a term of *intimacy* (1:18).

Third, it is a term of *impetus*: "For God so loved the world, that he gave his only begotten Son, that whosoever believeth in him should not perish, but have everlasting life" (3:16). As we have noted (Feb. 22), "so loved" demonstrates the *magnitude* of God's love, but here we see that it also reveals the *motivation* for sending His only begotten Son. While love is difficult to *define*, it is much more easily *displayed*. And so it is that "greater love hath no man than this, that a man lay down his life for his friends" (Jn. 15:13).

Fourth, this is a term of *inclusion* (3:18a): "He that believeth on him is not condemned." While the modern "inclusivist" insists that other religions can be vehicles of salvation for people who never even heard of Jesus Christ,[116] our text unambiguously specifies that only those who believe on Christ escape condemnation. A few verses later, our Lord adds, "He that believeth on the Son hath everlasting life" (3:36a).

While many today view "faith" and "belief" as nebulous and mere mental assent, the Greek *pisteuō* (4100) is very specific. It not only speaks of trusting in and being firmly persuaded of something, but it also clearly carries the idea of being committed to and obedient to something; this fact is indisputable.[117]

Further, just as there is another side to every coin, *in*clusion automatically implies *ex*clusion: "he that believeth not is condemned already, because he hath not believed in the name of the only begotten Son of God" (3:18b). This exclusion is also clear in the second half of the other verse cited above: "he that believeth not the Son shall not see life; but the wrath of God abideth on him" (3:36b). It is only those who trust fully in God's **only begotten** Son and commit to Him with full intention of obedience that are saved.

Fifth, it is a term of *intent* (1 Jn. 4:9): "In this was manifested the love of God toward us, because that God sent his only begotten Son into the world, that we might live through him." What was God's intent in sending His **only begotten** Son? "That we might live through him." It was because we were "dead in trespasses and sins" (Eph. 2:1) that Christ came to give life, for only He *could* give life (Jn. 14:6). John later declares, in fact, another inclusion and exclusion: "He that hath the Son hath life; and he that hath not the Son of God hath not life" (5:12). As the **only begotten**, our Lord is especially dear to the Father, and we pray that He is also dear to us, His adopted siblings.

Scriptures for Study: Read 1 John 5:10–13. What observations can you make in this passage?

MARCH 9

"I Am"

... Before Abraham was, I am. (Jn. 8:58)

I AM is a name for the Lord Jesus that explodes off the pages of Scripture. As we will note in our next few studies, in fact, Jesus' own seven "I am" statements in the Gospel of John are the most profound declarations of His nature and work contained in Scripture.

First, we note the *man* who made the statement. We use "man" here simply because that is all the religious leaders considered Jesus to be. Just as one of the blasphemous songs in the 1971 rock opera *Jesus Christ Superstar* declared, "He's a man, He's just man," that was the view of the scribes and Pharisees. As we have noted previously, most people today agree, calling Him by one of a plethora of epithets that malign His true character.

Second, we consider the *meaning* of the statement. To our ears, the words "I am" seem quite benign. To us they are no more meaningful than saying "I exist," for that is, in fact, exactly what they mean. The Greek is *egō eimi* (1473/1510) the latter of which is the verb "to be" and is merely the usual word of existence. But that is not what the Jews heard! They heard *hāyāh* ("I AM," Ex. 3:14; Jan. 14), a simple Hebrew verb meaning "to be or exist" but one that emphasizes God's self-existence and unchangeableness. They heard "this *man*" claim equality with *God*, and that enraged them. Earlier, in fact, Jesus said that those who do not believe He is the "I am" ("he" is not in the Greek text), "shall die in [their] sins" (8:24).

Third, we observe the *manner* in which the statement was made, which is especially significant. The religious leaders loved to bring up Abraham. Earlier in this scene, and responding to Jesus' admonition—"If ye continue in my word, then are ye my disciples indeed; And ye shall know the truth, and the truth shall make you free"—they said, "We be Abraham's seed, and were never in bondage to any man: how sayest thou, Ye shall be made free?" (8:31–33). And again, when Jesus said, "I speak that which I have seen with my Father [God]: and ye do that which ye have seen with your father," they responded: "Abraham is our father" (v. 39). But Jesus' scathing rebuke was, in effect, "You think Abraham is your father, but he obeyed God, while you seek to kill me, who *am* God. I know Abraham, and you are not of Abraham at all, rather of your father the devil" (v. 44).

Still thinking Jesus was only a man, the Jews challenged Him, "Thou art not yet fifty years old, and hast thou seen Abraham?" Since Jesus was only about 33, this snide remark was meant to emphasize that fact and prevent any reply. It is then our Lord says, **Before Abraham was, I am**. "I predate the one you supposedly revere so highly," He says, in effect. "I existed long before Abraham. I am the self-existent and unchangeable God." It was a truth His hearers hated then and one that is still hated today. Let us thank God for revealing Himself through the person of Jesus Christ and praise Christ as God in His fullest.

Scriptures for Study: Read John 8. What other observations can you note?

MARCH 10

I Am the Bread of Life

Jesus said unto them, I am the bread of life: he that cometh to me shall never hunger . . . (Jn. 6:35)

JOHN 6:22–58 records our Lord's famous "Discourse on the Bread of Life," which comes on the heels of the miraculous feeding of the 5,000. Sadly, like many today, the crowds were following Him simply because of superficial desires (v. 26); again, they were seeking the *what* instead of the *who* (Mar. 1).

And so it is in verse 35 that our Lord drops all ambiguity and speaks in the first person throughout the rest of the discourse, using "I" or "Me" no less than 35 times, in fact. In this first of Jesus' seven "I am" statements recorded by John, He speaks of Himself as life-giving bread.

First, recognize the *necessity* of bread. It is no accident that bread has been called "the staff of life." It's been a food staple since the beginning of recorded history. The Egyptians were baking bread more than 2,000 years before Christ. Unleavened bread fragments have been discovered in the ruins of the Swiss Lake Dwellers, who inhabited Switzerland from 4300 to 800 B.C. Nothing is more nourishing in and of itself than bread, and when people can afford nothing else, that is what they savor.

Second, appreciate the *appeal* of bread. Does anyone ever tire of it? Its appeal is universal; king or subject, young or old, rich or poor, weak or strong, everyone loves bread. Does it not appeal, in fact, to all the senses? Consider just the *sight* of it. We don't mean the factory-made packaged bread in the local market, rather the hand-made variety where each loaf is unique. The texture inside and out is a work of art. What person on the planet is not then drawn toward the *smell* of freshly-baked bread. (Am I making you hungry?) As it then comes out of the oven, we can hardly wait to *touch* it. The warmth and texture tell us there is something substantial here. And who needs a knife to slice it? Tearing off a chunk works just fine. Even our *hearing* is captured when the crust crackles as we pull off that piece. And finally, what we have been waiting for, we *taste* it. That warm chunk doesn't need any butter or jam, though that will come later when it has cooled and we are savoring our second (or third) piece.

Third, consider the *variety* of bread. With the virtually infinite combinations of different flours and proportions of ingredients, the result is a variety of types, shapes, sizes, and textures of bread that would take one years to explore. What a journey that would be!

The application of all this to our Lord scarcely needs explanation. Our Lord is necessary for spiritual life, His appeal is to our entire being as we appreciate Him in His fullness, and the variety of the truths we discover in Him are endless.

Oh, that we would savor the Bread of Life!

Scriptures for Study: Read our Lord's entire "Discourse on the Bread of Life." What observations can you note?

MARCH 11

I Am the Light of the World

Then spake Jesus again unto them, saying, I am the light of the world: he that followeth me shall not walk in darkness, but shall have the light of life. (Jn. 8:12)

THE occasion of our Lord's second "I am" statement was when he stood on the spot in the Temple treasury where four massive candleholders were located; once ignited, "there was not a courtyard in Jerusalem which was not lit up from the light."[118] He was saying, in effect, "While these great torches light all *Jerusalem*, I light the entire *world*. Only if you know Me, will you be delivered from darkness and have light to see." The Greek for **light** (*phōs*, 5457) refers to light *itself*, not the *source* of light, such as the sun, a torch, fire, or a lamp. **Darkness** (*skotos*, 4653) in turn, is the total absence of light. Jesus, then, is the only source of light that shines in a **world** (*kosmos*, 2889) of darkness, the fallen world system that surrounds and inundates us.[119] So, just as light and darkness are polar opposites, the light of Christ delivers us from the characteristics of darkness.

First, to the darkness of falsehood He is the light of truth. "He that doeth [i.e., habitually practices] truth," our Lord declares, "cometh to the light" (Jn. 3:21). The true believer is one who loves the truth because of the One who illumines it to him.

Second, to the darkness of ignorance Christ is the light of wisdom. "I saw that wisdom excelleth folly, as far as light excelleth darkness" (Ecc. 2:13). While the fool gropes in darkness and falls into every snag and snare, the wise man walks in the perfect light of Christ and sees every danger on the path.

Third, to the darkness of sin Christ is the light of holiness. Peter challenges us here: "Ye are a chosen generation, a royal priesthood, an holy nation, a peculiar people; that ye should shew forth the praises of him who hath called you out of darkness into his marvellous light" (1 Pet. 2:9). Why did God choose us "in Christ before the foundation of the world"? So that we can be holy (Eph. 1:4).

Fourth, to the darkness of sorrow Christ is the light of joy. Having been delivered from two months of turmoil and terror, "The Jews" in Esther's day "had light, and gladness, and joy, and honour" (Esth. 8:16). As noted in the *Geneva Bible* of the Puritans, "He showed by the words that follow, what this light was." Light illumines and energizes everything.

Fifth, and most dramatic of all, to the darkness of death Christ is **the light of life**. In Christ alone is a *light* that can never be *extinguished* and a *life* that can never be *ended*.

> To this world Jesus is the only light,
> Rescuing His own from darkness and strife;
> To the blinded ones He has given sight,
> And bestowed upon them eternal life.

Scriptures for Study: What do the following verses declare about light: John 1:4–9 and 3:19?

MARCH 12

I Am the Door

Then said Jesus unto them again ... I am the door of the sheep ... by me if any man enter in, he shall be saved, and shall go in and out, and find pasture. (Jn. 10:7, 9)

LIKE the first two, our Lord's third "I am" statement uses common imagery. Everyone knows what a **door** is and make use of many every day.

First, then, consider for a few moments various types of doors in the context of how people view Jesus. Some clearly view Him as simply an open doorway with no "door" at all. I am often reminded of the motto of a well-known liberal denomination: "Open Hearts, Open Minds, Open Doors." Here is the "inclusivist" (see Mar. 8); everyone is admitted no matter who they are or what they believe. Others seem to view Him as a French Door, which is comprised of two vertical door panels. This reminds us of those who mix religion with true Christianity, who label one door "Grace" and the other door "Works." Others hang a "Dutch Door," a door divided horizontally into two halves, allowing the top half to be open while keeping the bottom half closed. This reminds us of the "cult Jesus," which permits people to look in but can never deliver what it promises.

A particularly fascinating type of door is the "Revolving Door," multiple panels that spin inside a circular frame. This term is actually used in politics as a metaphor to describe people switching jobs, such as lawmaker to lobbyist and back again; in other words, they "spin in and out" of the private and public sectors. Likewise, some people cannot commit to Christ, rather just spin in and out.

So, what kind of **door** is Jesus? As the Greek word indicates,[120] He should be viewed as a standard door, nothing pretentious or modern.

Second, there is the purpose of a door. What is its function? It is actually two-fold. A door fundamentally implies *inclusion*. It is designed to let people *in*. While John 10:2 refers to the door into the sheepfold of Israel, our text refers to Jesus Himself as the **door** that allows the elect sheep to enter the fold. Salvation comes only by Jesus Christ, which is why a door also implies *exclusion*. This reminds us of the Parable of the Great Supper (Lk. 14::15–24). Many were invited but offered various excuses for not coming. As a result, none of them could taste of the supper—the door was shut to them.

Third, consider the nature of a door. It is, of course, an opening, but how large is that opening? As our Lord made clear near the end of His great sermon, the "gate" (i.e., the large door of an edifice, *pulē*, G4439) that leads to destruction is wide, while the one that leads to life is narrow (Matt. 7:13–14).

Fourth, note the quality of a door. A door can be made of either inferior or superior materials. While Christ appears to be just a "standard door," He is the genuine article and is comprised of flawless materials.

Scriptures for Study: Read the Parable of the Ten Virgins (Matt. 25:1–13). How does it apply to today's study?

MARCH 13

I Am the Good Shepherd

... the good shepherd giveth his life for the sheep. I am the good shepherd, and know my sheep, and am known of mine. (Jn. 10:11, 14)

WHAT a beautiful picture we see in our Lord's fourth "I am" statement! The imagery immediately reminds us of Psalm 23. Shepherding was the most common occupation throughout ancient Palestine. The lowly shepherd humbly tended, fed, and protected his sheep at the risk of his own life. "What condescension is this," wrote Charles Spurgeon, "that the Infinite Lord assumes towards his people the office and character of a Shepherd!"[121] Think of it! God descended and assumed one of the lowliest occupations in the ancient world.

First, then, we see the Shepherd's *character*. He is the **good shepherd**. While the Greek *agathos* (18) is a magnificent word, having a wide range of meanings (good, benevolent, profitable, useful, beneficial, excellent, virtuous, and suitable), the word rendered **good** here is *kalos* (2570) and is even more striking. While *agathos* has an "ethical and religious emphasis, [*kalos*] stresses more the aesthetic aspect, and stands for beautiful, fine, free from defects."[122] It is used, for example, of "good ground" (Matt. 13: 8, 23) and "seed" (vv. 24, 27, 37, 38), "good pearls" (13:45), "good fruit" (7:17–19), "good wine" (Jn. 2:10), and even the "good stones" of the Temple (Lk.21:5). That is certainly true of our Lord.

Second, we should consider carefully the Shepherd's *cause*: He **giveth his life for the sheep**. While the ancient shepherd *risked* losing his life in protection of the sheep—David, for example, battled wild animals (1 Sam. 17:34–36)—our Lord came specifically to *give* His **life for the sheep**. While the first is a *potential* loss, the second is a *premeditated* loss.

Our Lord's analogy here is both glorious and crucial. One of the greatest doctrines of Scripture is that Christ gave his life not *potentially* for those who *might* believe, but *purposefully* and *particularly* for those who *would* believe, His **sheep**, who were always His sheep though not yet in their own experience. As we were the elect before the foundation of the world (Jn. 13:18; 15:16, 19; 17:9, 24; Eph. 1:4; Acts 13:48; Rom. 8:28–30; 9:15–24), we were likewise sheep (lost sheep, but sheep nonetheless), and it was for us that our Lord laid down His life.[123]

Third, we rejoice in the Shepherd's *companionship*: **[I] know my sheep, and am known of mine**. Both **know** and **known** translate *ginoskō* (1097), "to know by experience" and is practically synonymous with love and intimacy. Joseph, for example, "did not know" Mary before Jesus was born, that is, they had not yet been physically intimate (Matt. 1:25; cf. Matt. 7:23). The Shepherd knows His sheep (true disciples) and the sheep in turn know the Shepherd (acknowledging Him as their Lord). Together, then, we all experience loving fellowship.

Scriptures for Study: What do the following verses say about knowing Christ: John 17:8; Ephesians 1:17; 3:19; Philippians 3:8; 1 John 5:20?

March 14

I Am the Resurrection and the Life

Jesus said unto [Martha], I am the resurrection, and the life: he that believeth in me, though he were dead, yet shall he live . . . [and] never die. (Jn. 11:25–26)

THE setting of our Lord's fifth "I am" statement is at the scene of raising Lazarus from the dead. "Martha, as soon as she heard that Jesus was coming, went and met him" and said, "Lord, if thou hadst been here, my brother had not died" (vv. 20–21). This was not *criticism* of his delay, rather *confidence* in his ability to heal the sick. Her confidence went on to say that His arrival would certainly bring some good out of this sad situation (v. 22). When our Lord then said, "Thy brother shall rise again" (v. 23), Martha simply assumed He was comforting her with the knowledge of future resurrection, a doctrine clearly taught in the OT (e.g., Job 19:25–27; Ps. 16:10; Dan. 12:2).

First, then, we see Jesus' *announcement*: **I am the resurrection, and the life.** With this statement Jesus pulled Martha out of the *abstract* into the *actual*, from *what* was in the future to *who* was in the present. The same One who was going to raise Lazarus *then* is the same One who was going to raise him *now*. Note that He doesn't say, "A resurrection is coming *through* Me," or, "I *perform* resurrections," rather he declares, **I** *am* **the resurrection**. The definite article (**the**) further demonstrates that only He is this resurrection. So there would be no ambiguity, He adds, still further: **and the life.** Is it not, indeed, significant that we read of not a single person who died in Jesus' presence? Why? Because *life* is in His presence.

Second, there is the *application*: **he that believeth in me, though he were dead, yet shall he live.** Physical death is not "the end of the line" for those who receive Christ as Savior and Lord. While the believer might one day die physically, he is still alive spiritually, which leads to a final principle.

Third, there is the *assurance*: **never die.** Our Lord is not being redundant in these verses. The truths are related but still distinct. Physical death ushers the believer into the eternal reality where he will **never die**, no matter what. The language could not be stronger. **Never** is comprised of two "negative particles" in the Greek (*ou mē*, 3364): *ou* (3756), which not only means "not" or "no," but strongly expresses direct, full, and absolute negation; *mē* (3361) is then added to create a double negative, "not at all, no never." We could even translate it "shall never die unto eternity." Because of his belief in Christ, it is an absolute impossibility for a Christian to ever die. He cannot lose his salvation as is insisted by some teachers, for it would then be possible for him to spiritually die, and that can *never* happen. "Living believers in Christ shall never die a spiritual death; they are passed from death to life, and shall never return to death; their spiritual life cannot be lost; grace in them is an immortal seed, a well of living water springing up into everlasting life."[124] To deny that wondrous truth is to contradict our Lord Himself.

Scriptures for Study: What do the following verses declare about our salvation: John 10:28–30; 17:11–12; Romans 8:38–39; 2 Timothy 1:12?

MARCH 15

I Am the Way, the Truth, and the Life

Jesus saith unto [Thomas], I am the way, the truth, and the life: no man cometh unto the Father, but by me. (Jn. 14:6)

OUR Lord's sixth "I am" statement is among the most definitive statements about Him in the NT. We again see the "definite article" (**the**), which is the only article in Greek and is used to define, limit, and point out something in particular. "The article is associated with gesture," writes Greek grammarian A. T. Robertson, "and aids in pointing out like an index finger.... Whenever the Greek article occurs, the object is certainly definite [and] leads to exactness."[125]

First, then, as **the way**, Jesus is the only *sufficient road*. "All roads lead to Rome" (which was actually true in the ancient empire) is a very old idiom that simply means there are many different routes to the same goal. Tragically, many believe this also applies to the spiritual realm, namely: "All religions lead to God," that no matter what "religion road" one takes, He will still get to God. But our Lord declares here that He is the Only Road to the Father.

Second, as **the truth**, He is the only *suitable vehicle*. We all use different vehicles for different purposes. While one does not use a luxury sedan to go off-roading in the mountains, a virtually universal error today in spiritual matters is to use the wrong "vehicle" to get to God. One such vehicle is feelings, whatever makes one feel "comfortable with God," or having some "existential encounter with Jesus," whatever that might mean. Perhaps the most common of all vehicles in our day is "sincerity," that is, as long as one is sincere in whatever he believes, he will ultimately get to God. Again, our Lord declares something quite different. He says that He alone—the **truth** (Greek *alētheia*, 225, reliable, constant, sure, and unchanging[126])—is the only Vehicle to the Father.

Third, as **the life**, He is the only *satisfying destination*. The Greek behind "life" is extremely significant. It is *zōē* (2222), where we get English words such as *zoology* and *protozoa*. As we noted in a recent study (Mar. 5), life was not a *thing* to the ancient Greeks, rather they viewed it as *vitality*. It, therefore, cannot be used in the plural, only in the singular; life, then, is a singular, vital, and active reality. When the modifier "everlasting" is added, as our Lord does elsewhere (3:16; 4:14; 5:24; 6:27, 40, 47; 12:50), the term takes on a whole new meaning. While physical life comes to an end, "everlasting life" is just what it says—it is forever. It is a *perpetual, never-ending vitality*.

And so it is that the definite article points to Christ and only to Christ as the Road, the Vehicle, and the Destination. To put it another way: without the Way there is no *going*, without the Truth there is no *knowing*, and without the Life there is no *growing*.[127]

Scriptures for Study: Note the exclusivity of Christ in the following verses: John 3:36; Acts 4:12; 1 Peter 3:18; 1 John 5:11–12; 2 John 9.

March 16

I Am the Vine

I am the true vine. . . . I am the vine, ye are the branches: He that abideth in me, and I in him, the same bringeth forth much fruit: for without me ye can do nothing. (Jn. 15:1a, 5)

IN light of the final words of the previous chapter, "Arise, let us go hence" (14:31), the setting of these verses is Jesus leaving the Upper Room, disciples in tow, moving through Jerusalem and the Kidron Valley, and heading for the Garden of Gethsemane. Prompted either by the fruit of the vine they just drank, or by the elaborate gold-engraved vines on the massive Temple doors, or simply by vines along the path they walked (perhaps even all three), our Lord declares His seventh and final "I Am" statement recorded in John's Gospel: **I am the vine.**

First, He is the *authentic* Vine. **True** translates the common yet critically important Greek word *alēthinos* (228). The best way to understand this word in our day is its reference to "the genuine article," in contrast to that which is in any way false, fake, or forged. Oh, how many false vines there are! Dionysus—the god of the grape harvest, wine, winemaking, and ritual madness and ecstasy in Greek mythology (Bacchus to the Romans)—reminds us of the fake vine of hedonism in our own day. All religions, in fact, are such fakes, even Judaism itself. While the vine was the historic and religious symbol of Israel (Isa. 5; Ezek. 19; Ps. 80), Judaism ultimately became a forgery, a counterfeit, as it rejected the true Messiah and persecuted His apostles. Christ alone, then, is the genuine article.

Second, He is the *animated* Vine. A vine is alive and vital, imparting nutrients to the branches so they can grow **fruit**. Our Lord uses that very imagery of Himself. He is the Vine that gives and sustains our life so we can reproduce as we are designed to do. Without Him, in fact, we can do nothing and are in effect dead. Separated from the Vine, the branch is lifeless (v. 4).

Third, He is the *abiding* Vine. **Abideth** translates *menō* (3306), which in Classical Greek literally means "to remain in one place, at a given time, with someone" and metaphorically "to remain in a particular sphere of life." When used for the gods, it spoke of continuing existence.[128] Those secular meanings are actually used in the NT, as graphically demonstrated here. Both the Vine and the branches continue. This is further emphasize by this verb being in the present tense, continuous action. Further still, it appears that the Apostle John was so captivated by this word that he used it no less than 12 times in verses 4–16, where it is also translated "continue" (v. 9) and "remain" (v. 11).

And so it is in this image of the Vine that we find these three truths in Christ: reality, vitality, and fertility. He is the genuine Vine that gives life to the branches and the enduring blessing of fruit that is *rewarding* to the taste, *representative* of the Vine, and *reproduces* itself.

Scriptures for Study: What do the following verses tell us about fruit: John 15:16; Galatians 5:22–23?

MARCH 17

I Am Alpha and Omega

I am Alpha and Omega, the beginning and the end, the first and the last.
(Rev. 22:13)

AMONG the closing verses of the Bible, as well as the final recorded words spoken by our Lord, we read the words of our text. While not in John's Gospel, they are still from John's pen and include one additional "I Am" statement (*egō eimi*, Mar. 9), which is actually three-fold and comprises the summary statement in Scripture of the eternal divinity of Jesus Christ.

First, the *message* is in the idiom **Alpha and Omega**. John adapted this from the Jews, who express the whole breadth of things, or the whole of a particular matter, using the first and last letters of the Hebrew alphabet: א (*aleph*) and ת (*tau*). Rabbis would say, for example, "Adam transgressed the whole law from *aleph* to *tau*." Since he was writing in Greek, however, John used *A* (*alpha*) and *Ω* (*omega*). This expression unambiguously identifies Him as the God of the OT. Isaiah several times ascribes this aspect of Jesus' nature as part of the triune God: "I the LORD, the first, and with the last; I am he" (41:4; also 44:6; 48:12).

Second, we see the *meaning* of the above in the phrase **the beginning and the end**. The words themselves, however—as words always do—add greater significance. **Beginning** is *archē* (746), which also appears in John 1:1–3, underscoring that Christ is the beginning of Creation and therefore the beginning of everything. **End**, then, is *telos* (5056), which indicates a term, termination, or completion. All that our Lord has *created* He will bring to final *conclusion*. More than that, because He is the *beginning* and the *end*, He is also everything *in between*. Like bookends that bracket a valuable collection of rare volumes, it is the whole set that gives the bookends purpose. Like the prologue and epilog of the most valued book, they frame the whole story.

Third, we note the *majesty* in the final expression **the first and the last**. The first and the last what? The first and the last *Word*. He is the Word who *created* the universe (Jn. 1:1–3; cf. Gen. 1:1; Ps. 33:6) and the Word who will be *crowned* King of that domain (Rev. 19:11–16). And so it is that when our Lord speaks, that is the **first** and the **last** Word on the matter. There is to be no dissent, no dispute, and no disobedience. The matter "is settled in heaven" (Ps. 119:89).

We would close with one other related "first and last," namely, the first and last chapters of the Apocalypse itself. The similarities between the two are stunning. Both, in fact, "refer to God's revelation, obedience to the Word, the identity of the Lord, and the testimony to the churches" (see *Scriptures for Study*).

Scriptures for Study: Compare the following passages in Revelation 1 and 22 and note the similarities: 1:1 with 22:6; 1:3 with 22:7, 10; 1:8, 17 with 22:13; and 1:1 with 22:16.[129]

MARCH 18

The Lamb of God (1)

Behold the Lamb of God . . . (Jn. 1:29, 36)

FEW pictures of our Lord that hang in the Scripture gallery are as touching and tantalizing than is the one titled **Lamb of God**. Tracing the ten instances of the Lamb through Scripture demonstrates eight wondrous principles.

First, we see the *prefiguring* of the Lamb in Genesis 4:3–7a. The scene is Cain and Abel bringing their offerings to God (Oct. 7–9). While Cain did not bring the best he could offer, rather only what he could "get by on," Abel brought "of the firstlings," that is, one of the firstborn of his flock (Gen. 4:4, *bekôrāh*, 1062H), the best he had. Cain *personifies* the way of religion, but Abel *proves* the way of faith. He also prefigures Christ as the best and ultimate offering that was yet to come.

Second, we see the *provision* of the Lamb in Genesis 22:6–8. In one of the most heart wrenching scenes in Scripture, God tests Abraham to see if he was willing to sacrifice his "only begotten son" (cf. Mar. 7, 8). Responding to Isaac's question, "Behold the fire and the wood: but where is the lamb for a burnt offering?" Abraham answered, "God will provide himself a lamb." And He did!

The picture of Christ here is striking. In verse 2 we find the first occurrence of the word "love" in the Bible, the love of a father (Abraham) for his son (Isaac). This story, therefore, is a type of the heavenly Father and His only begotten Son, foreshadowing the coming sacrifice at Calvary.

Also remarkable is the fact that the first occurrence of "love" in each of the three synoptic Gospels (Matt. 3:17; Mk. 1:11; Lk. 3:22) records the Father calling out from heaven, "this is my beloved Son," at the baptism of Jesus (which, of course, also speaks of death and resurrection). Also significant, in contrast, in John's Gospel, where "love" occurs more often than in any other book of the Bible, its first occurrence is in John 3:16 (cf. Feb. 22–23). God loved the world so much that He, like Abraham, was willing to sacrifice His "only begotten son."

Still deeper, we should also focus on the substitute for Isaac, the ram (vv. 11–13). This illustrates the substitutionary sacrifice of the Lamb of God. As we will detail, this pointed unwaveringly at John the Baptist's declaration centuries later: **Behold the Lamb of God, which taketh away the sin of the world**.

Third, we see the *punishing* of the Lamb in Exodus 12:3–23, which describes the sacrificial lamb slain at Passover (cf. the Day of Atonement in Lev. 16). The chosen lamb was to be: "without blemish," picturing Christ's *sinlessness*; "a male of the first year," picturing Christ's *strength* in the prime of life; "[taken] . . . out from the sheep" and kept "until the fourteenth day of the same month," picturing Christ's *separation* and testing in the wilderness; "[killed] in the evening" (about 3:00 PM), picturing Christ's *sacrifice* on the Cross, which occurred at the same time of day; and its blood was applied to the door, picturing Christ's blood as the *satisfaction* of God's demand. *Soli Deo Gloria!*

Scriptures for Study: What did Paul proclaim in 1 Corinthians 5:7?

MARCH 19

The Lamb of God (2)

Behold the Lamb of God, which taketh away the sin of the world. (Jn. 1:29)

"NEVER was there a fuller testimony borne to Christ upon earth," wrote J. C. Ryle, "than that which is here borne by John the Baptist."

Fourth, then, we see the *personage* of the Lamb in Isaiah 53. Up to this point, the lamb has been an animal, certainly one that pointed to more, but still an animal. But here we discover specifically the "He" to which it all has been pointing. "*He* is brought as a lamb to the slaughter" (v. 7). Only one person in history matches the detailed description in this chapter. But who?

Fifth, we see the *presentation* of the Lamb in John 1. While Isaiah 53 tells us that the typified Lamb is a *person*, we now learn who this person *is*: Jesus Christ. The word **Behold** (*ide*, 2396) is an interjection that calls attention to its object, so we could translate the phrase, "*Look*, the Lamb of God!" And what would the Lamb do? He would **[take] away the sin of the world**. The Greek behind **taketh away** (*airō*, 142) means to lift up and carry away and indicates permanence. Every lamb that preceded could only temporarily *cover* sin; this Lamb would forever *carry* it away.

Sixth, we see the *promise* of the Lamb in Acts 8:26–39. As an Ethiopian dignitary was reading Isaiah 53, the Holy Spirit directed Philip to overtake the man's chariot so he could ask him, "Do you understand what you are reading?" "How can I," he answered, "except some man should guide me?" Philip then preached the Gospel to him, making it clear that Jesus Christ was indeed the promised Messiah Isaiah graphically described. What was the result? The man testified, "I believe that Jesus Christ is the Son of God."

Seventh, we see the *power* of the Lamb in 1 Peter 1:18–21. This passage not only declares that we were "redeemed . . . with the precious blood of Christ, as of a lamb without blemish," but goes on to confirm the resurrection of the Lamb, a truth never disclosed in the OT. By first looking *back* and then looking *forward*, Peter ties together the OT and NT lamb. And it is the resurrection of the Lamb that demonstrates His true power to redeem us from sin and deliver us from hell.

Eighth and finally, we see the *praising* of the Lamb in two passages in Revelation. In 5:6–14, we see the Lamb *ruling formidably* over His worshipping people, and in 21:1—22:5 we see Him *reigning forever* over the eternal state.

Behold the Lamb of God!

>Worthy is the Lamb of God who was slain
>To redeem from death and depravity.
>His praise and glory will be our refrain
>Now and forever through eternity.

Scriptures for Study: Read and rejoice over the above Revelation passages.

MARCH 20

The Cornerstone

And are built upon the foundation of the apostles and prophets, Jesus Christ himself being the chief cornerstone. (Eph. 2:20)

THE image of Jesus as **the chief cornerstone** is one of the more fascinating metaphors ascribed to Him. In our modern era of sophisticated measuring equipment, we do not readily appreciate the ancient cornerstone and its critical role in building construction.

First, the *purpose* of the cornerstone. The Greek here is *akrogoniaios* (204), a compound word comprised of *akron* (206), "top" or "tip," and *gōnia* (1137), "an angle or corner." The literal idea then, as one commentator puts it, is "at the tip of the angle" and refers to "the stone set at the corner of a wall so that its outer angle becomes important."[130] It provided no more support to the structure than any other stone; rather, its entire value lay in its outer angle. It set the level, angle, and outer dimensions of the building and became the basis for every measurement. It governed every line and angle and dictated the alignment of the walls vertically and horizontally.

Second, the *preparation* of the cornerstone. As one can quickly see, this stone was not just any random stone. It had to be carefully selected and painstakingly prepared. It had to be square on all sides and level on the top and bottom. In short, it had to be *perfect*.

Third, the *placement* of the cornerstone was equally critical. While today we can easily prepare a building site using machinery and pour a reinforced concrete footer and foundation, the ancients had no such luxury. Preparing the site was a monumental undertaking, and setting the cornerstone surgically meticulous.

Fourth, the *picture* all this paints of Christ is stunning. The term **cornerstone**, in fact, had for centuries been a prophetic metaphor for the coming Messiah. Isaiah declared, for example, "Therefore thus saith the LORD GOD, Behold, I lay in Zion for a foundation a stone, a tried stone, a precious cornerstone, a sure foundation; he that believeth shall not make haste" (Is. 28:16). It is also no accident that Psalm 118 is the most quoted psalm in the NT, for it is entirely messianic in character. Verse 22 declares that the stone the Jews would reject would be the very stone God would use to build all His work.

As the Cornerstone, then, our Lord's purpose was to be the measuring standard for His Church. **The apostles and prophets** were the **foundation**, but all they taught was dictated by the Cornerstone. Likewise, we too are to measure our lives and ministries by that standard. Sadly, many "stones" in today's churches are crooked, cockeyed, and even calamitous because they were not placed in line with the Cornerstone.[131] Let us always be in-line with our Lord's standard.

Scriptures for Study: Compare the following verses with their source in Psalm 118: Matthew 21:9, 42; 23:39; Mark 11:9, 10; 12:10, 11; Luke 13:35; 19:38; 20:17; John 12:13; Acts 4:11; Hebrews 13:6; 1 Peter 2:7.

MARCH 21

The Prince and Perfecter of Faith

Looking unto Jesus the author and finisher of our faith . . . (Hebrews 12:2)

THE context of our text is the "great cloud of witnesses" (v. 1) listed in chapter 11. While each of those witnesses is a "great" example of saving and serving faith, it is Jesus who is the supreme pattern to follow. In that light, the word **looking** is of very special importance. The Greek is *aphoraō* (872) which appears in the NT only here and Philippians 2:23. Comprised of *apo* (575, from) and *horaō* (3708, to perceive with the eyes), it means not just to look upon something with understanding but to look *away* from everything else. We could literally translate this, "Looking away unto Jesus." We are so consumed with gazing upon Christ, so intently focused upon Him, that we consider nothing else (such as the "weights and sin" of verse 1; Nov. 8–9) that might distract us from that singular sight. Why should we look so intently upon Him?

First, because He is the *Prince* of **faith**. **Author** translates *archēgos* (747), which is derived from the verb *agō* (71), to lead, and therefore refers to an "originator, founder, leader, chief, [or] prince, as distinguished from simply being the cause."[132] It is, in fact, rendered "Prince" in Acts 3:15, where Peter boldly declared to the religious leaders that they "killed the Prince of life, whom God hath raised from the dead." We again read in 5:31: "Him hath God exalted with his right hand to be a Prince and a Saviour." Here in our text, then, He assumes His rightful place as Prince "at the right hand of the throne of God," the place of honor. Further, as Leader, He goes before us in the battles of faith.

Second, we also look intently upon Jesus because He is the *Perfecter* of **faith**. **Finisher** is *teleiōtēs* (5051), which appears only here in the NT and means: "A completer, perfecter, particularly one who reaches a goal so as to win the prize."[133] A 1916 article in the *New York Times* reported how "a glance over his shoulder at the trio of flying runners in his rear, cost Joseph T. Higgins of Holy Cross College the victory." Looking back is, indeed, the cardinal sin a runner can commit, which is the very analogy in the passage before us (v. 1). Our Lord never looked back and neither should we. We are to be so intent upon Him in our race, our eyes so fixed upon Him who stands waiting for us at the finish line, that nothing can divert our gaze. Oh, let us not look to the world, ourselves, or any other person, but to Christ alone. In the spirit of the old song "Turn Your Eyes upon Jesus," we offer this:

> Looking away unto Jesus alone,
>   So transfixed are we on His wondrous face,
> That nothing can cause our gaze to roam,
>   In the brightness of his glory and grace.

Scriptures for Study: What do the following verses tell us about the race we are in: 1 Corinthians 9:24–27; Galatians 5:7; Philippians 2:16; and 2 Timothy 4:7?

MARCH 22

Savior (1)

God according to his promise raised unto Israel a Saviour, Jesus. (Acts 13:23)

THE Greek *sōtēr* (4990; **Savior**, deliverer, preserver, protector, and provider) occurs 24 times in the NT, 16 of which refer to the Lord Jesus (the other eight refer to God). Tracing five of these occurrences provides us with an overall picture of our Savior.

First, our text speaks of the Savior *prophesied*: **Of this man's seed hath God according to his promise raised unto Israel a Saviour, Jesus.** This verse points back to the some 300 messianic prophecies in the OT. It is actually part of Paul's first recorded sermon and illustrates, as someone has well stated, "All roads in Paul's preaching led to Christ." Its outline also demonstrates how he preached to an audience grounded in the OT: the *anticipation* of the Messiah (vv. 16–25); the *antagonism* toward Jesus Christ (13:16–25); and the *appeal* to men to believe in Jesus, the obvious Messiah (13:38–41).

Second, we see the Savior *identified* in Luke 2:11, which in the Greek literally reads: "Because was born to you this day a Savior, who is Christ [the] Lord, in [the] city of David." We must quote William Hendriksen here, who puts it so well: Luke is saying, in effect, "Long ago promised, promised, promised, now finally born: the promise has been fulfilled."[134]

A missionary named Mr. Colemeister worked among the Esquimaux (Eskimos or Inuits) for 34 years. While translating the Gospels into their language, he could not find a word for "Savior." Finally, he asked them, "Does it not happen sometimes when you are out fishing, that a storm arises, and some of you are lost and some saved?" They answered that such happened often and that "a brother or friend" would stretch out his hand to help. "Then what do you call that friend?" Colemeister asked. They understood, and he now had the needed word.[135]

Third, we see the Savior *amplified* in Acts 5:31, which we mentioned yesterday: "Him hath God exalted with his right hand to be a Prince and a Saviour, for to give repentance to Israel, and forgiveness of sins." Peter so amplifies the identity of Christ to his audience that he says, in effect, "You not only killed the Exalted Prince of God but also the Expected Savior of God's people."

Fourth, we see the Savior *typified* in Ephesians 5:23. *Sōtēr* is never used of men except here, by application, to describe the Christian husband, who through Christ is the provider for and protector of His wife. As the wife is a picture of the *Church*—for the Church is under the spiritual leadership of Christ—she is to put herself under the spiritual leadership of the husband. The husband, however, has a far greater responsibility, for he is a picture of *Christ*; as Christ loved the Church and gave Himself totally for it (or "her" as she is spoken of as being a bride), the husband is to love his wife and give himself totally for her.[136]

Scriptures for Study: Read just these few OT prophecies: Genesis 3:15; Isaiah 7:14; 9:6; Jeremiah 23:5–6; Zechariah 9:9.

MARCH 23

Savior (2)

To the only wise God our Saviour, be glory and majesty, dominion and power, both now and ever. Amen. (Jude 25)

WE have seen the Savior prophesied, identified, amplified, and typified. There is one more emphasis that culminates this wondrous progression.

Fifth, we see in our text the Savior *glorified*. *Soli Deo Gloria*, glory to God alone—that great climax of the "five solas" of the Reformation—flows right out of our text. In these final words of Jude's doxology, we see four divine attributes, all of which belong **to the only wise God our Saviour** alone.

(1) He *deserves* all **glory**. While in Secular Greek *doxa* (1391) described favorable human opinion, including an evaluation placed by others, such as fame, repute, honor, or praise, this was transformed in the NT to attribute those qualities to God alone. Also added were the ideas of "radiance" and **glory**, concepts foreign to secular Greek. It now denotes "divine and heavenly radiance, the loftiness and majesty of God, and even the being of God."[137] In contrast to the human craving for glory in every endeavor, God alone deserves glory of any kind.

(2) He *displays* all **majesty**. This is *megalōunē* (3172; *megas*, [3173], large or great) and appears in only two other places. Hebrews 1:3, interestingly enough, ties **glory** and **majesty** together: "Who being the *brightness* of his *glory*, and the express image of his person, and upholding all things by the word of his power, when he had by himself purged our sins, sat down on the right hand of the *Majesty* on high" (emphasis added). In Hebrews 8:1 we also read: "We have such an high priest, who is set on the right hand of the throne of the *Majesty* in the heavens" (emphasis added). So what does Jude put on display? God's kingly greatness!

(3) He *declares* all **dominion**. Here we encounter a magnificent word, *kratos* (2904), which means "strength, power, control, and supremacy." The most fascinating feature about this word is that it is never used of man; that is, man cannot have or gain *kratos*. While men rant and rave, fuss and fume, and scribble their theories and manifestos, Jude quietly writes the truth: God is sovereign (Jan. 21–24). Is it not wonderful to know that God?

(4) He *demands* all **[authority]**. Our beloved KJV renders the Greek *exousia* as **power**, which while correct reflects older English. Its fuller meaning in modern understanding is "unrestricted freedom of action, power, authority, and right of action."[138] These meanings are evident throughout Scripture. God's authority and right to act are evident in His absolute sovereignty. Most graphic is the picture of God in Romans 9:21: "Hath not the potter power over the clay, of the same lump to make one vessel unto honour, and another unto dishonour?" (cf., Acts 1:7).

Soli Deo Gloria indeed!

Scriptures for Study: Read the following "doxologies," noting *kratos* in each: 1 Timothy 6:15–16 ("power"); 1 Peter 4:11; 5:11 ("dominion"); Revelation 1:6.

MARCH 24

Bridegroom

Can the children of the bridechamber mourn, as long as the bridegroom is with them? (Matt. 9:15)

TODAY'S title is especially close to my heart, for I ponder it and pen these words on the heels of officiating at my son's wedding just three weeks before. What indescribable joy it was to see two godly young people—both of whom had kept themselves pure for that day in time—become one. What inexpressible delight it was to see my son (Paul) as a bridegroom standing beside his beautiful bride (Celeste). Infinitely more profound, our Savior is a Bridegroom, and the Church is His bride. This title is of special significance, for none is more dramatically tied to human experience. Not only does this imagery appear some 14 times in the NT, but it is also linked to the *Yāhweh* of the OT (Jan. 21), the Husband of Israel, His wife, and expresses His covenant relationship with His people.

First, we see the *person* of the Bridegroom. In light of the speaker in verses 1–3, it seems clear that Isaiah 61:10 is spoken by the coming Messiah (instead of Isaiah or Zion, as some insist), as He leads the praises of His redeemed remnant: "Jehovah . . . clothed me with garments of salvation; He put on me the robe of righteousness, even as a bridegroom dons as a priest his head-dress, and as a bride wears her ornaments." As the bridegroom would wear the headdress of a priest and the bride would adorn herself with jewels, so shall it be for Christ and His bride (Rev. 21:2, 9).

Second, we mark the *provision* of the Bridegroom. Isaiah 62:4–5 declares that God's people would no longer be called "Forsaken" or "Desolate" but would now "be called [My Delight is in Her], and thy land [Married]: For as a young man marrieth a virgin, so shall thy sons marry thee: and as the bridegroom rejoiceth over the bride, so shall thy God rejoice over thee." The same image appears in Ephesians 5:25–29, where Christ gave Himself for the Church, thereby cherishing it, providing for it, protecting it, and preserving it, all the things the godly husband does for his wife.

Third, we note the *presence* of the Bridegroom. Our text records our Lord's answer to the question from the self-righteous Pharisees concerning why His disciples did not observe the twice-weekly ritual fasting "required" by tradition. He said, in effect, as long as He was with them, it made no sense to fast. A wedding feast usually lasted seven days and was a time of rejoicing, not mourning. While the time would come when He would be "taken away" (*apairō* [522], violently removed) and mourning would be appropriate, it was not so then because He was present. As He promised, however, even after He was taken away He would send "another comforter," who was identical to Him in nature, to dwell with them forever (Jn. 14:6). Think of it! Even in His absence, the Bridegroom is still present.

Scriptures for Study: What does John 3:29–30 add to the imagery of the Bridegroom?

MARCH 25

The Word (1)

In the beginning was the Word ... (Jn. 1:1)

IT has been reported often that during the so-called Greek Golden Age in Athens, Plato was addressing a group of students and philosophers one day and said, "It may be that someday there will come forth from God a Word, a Logos, who will reveal all the mysteries and make everything plain." If that incident is true, we can imagine the Apostle John responding, "Well, Plato, that Logos *has* come, and His name is Jesus Christ." Here in John 1:1–3 is yet another great name stamped upon the nature and character of our Lord (this writer's favorite).[139]

First, the Word is a *person*. **Word**, of course, is *logos* (3056), which means to speak intelligently, to articulate a message, to give a discourse. It's derived from *legō*, which originally (prior to the 5th-century BC) denoted the "activity of collecting, carefully selecting, cataloguing in succession, and arranging together in an orderly sequence."[140] This developed into the meaning "to lay before, i.e., to relate, recount" and finally "to say, speak, i.e., to utter definite words, connected, and significant speech equal to discourse."[141] Our Lord, then, is "the Logos," for *He is the very intelligence of God come in the flesh to deliver His discourse, to proclaim His message to the world*. As verse 14 goes on to say, this Logos, this Discourse of God, came in the "flesh, and dwelt among us."

Second, the Word is *preeminent*. There is no doctrine concerning Christ that is denied more vehemently or attacked more violently than His deity, but that deity is definitively declared in the words **and the Word was God**. Not only is "the Word" the very intelligence of God come in the flesh to deliver His discourse, His message, but He is, in fact, God incarnate. While many have tried to twist the Greek grammar to deny the deity of Christ, the grammar *requires* this rendering. If one misses this fact, he has missed the whole point of John's Gospel!

Third, the Word is *powerful*. Nothing underscores deity and sovereignty more convincingly than does the power of creation. As verse 3 goes on to declare, **All things were made by him; and without him was not any thing made that was made.** This verse, like no other, declares that the Logos, the Word, the Speech, the Intelligence, the Discourse made the universe. He was not part of the *creation*; He is the *Creator*. Neither did He simply create some things and allow the rest to "evolve," rather He created "all things." As the psalmist declares it, "He spake, and it was done; he commanded, and it stood fast" (Ps 33:9).

Fourth, the Word is *perpetual*. The phrase **In the beginning** is a Hebraism[142] (idiom) that indicates eternity. If, therefore, **all things were made by him**, and if He was there when it all began, then He had to have existed before that beginning. Have you ever noticed that while two genealogies of our Lord appear in Matthew and Luke, there is none in John? Such would be out of place.

Scriptures for Study: What do the following verses add to today's study: Exodus 20:11; Psalm 90:2; John 20:28; Colossians 1:16–19?

MARCH 26

The Word (2)

For he spake, and it was done; he commanded, and it stood fast. (Ps. 33:9)

WE mentioned today's verse in yesterday's meditation, but we do not wish to hurry on, rather just "linger a little longer" (Jan. 2). *Logos* (3056) was by no means an exclusive concept to the Greeks; "word" was also a critical OT theme. The Hebrew *dābār* (1697H), for example, means a word or speech and is a general term for God's revelation (and is usually rendered *logos* in the Septuagint). The Ten Commandments are referred to using *dābār* (Ex. 34:28; Deut. 10:4), which we could translate as "the ten words" because they are exactly what God said (June 16). While the specific terms used in our text are different, the emphasis on what God says is the same.

First, the psalmist declares, **For he spake, and it was done**. **Spake** is again *'amar* (559H; Jan. 18), which means not only "to say or speak," but also "to say to one's self," that is, to *think*. It is also used for "said" in the ten "God said" statements in Genesis 1 (Jan. 11). Particularly fascinating is the Hebrew behind **was done**. It is *hāyāh* (1961H), the same word for "I AM" in Exodus 3:14 (Jan. 14; Mar. 9), the simple verb meaning "to be or exist." The most literal idea in our text, then, is, "God thought, and it was." The context of this verse, in fact, is creation. With a mere thought from God, all things sprang into existence. "Creation was the fruit of a word," Spurgeon wrote. Puritan Matthew Henry added, "With men saying and doing are two things, but it is not so with God." Indeed, the Lord's acts are *instantaneousness* in their *execution* and *incomprehensible* in their *ease*. For God to *say* is for Him the same as to *do*.

Second, the psalmist, apparently not satisfied with the first statement, is compelled to add, **he commanded, and it stood fast**. **Commanded** translates the Hebrew verb *ṣāwāh* (6680H), a general word that denotes a superior verbally ordering or commanding a subordinate. In its first occurrence, for example, God verbally commanded Adam that he could "freely eat" of every tree in the garden except "the tree of the knowledge of good and evil" (Gen. 2:16, 17). It is also commonly used of people commanding other people (e.g., Gen. 18:19; Ex. 1:22; Judg. 4:6; 1 Kings 5:17).

What was the result when God commanded? **It stood fast**. This is a single word in the Hebrew (*'āmad*, 5975H), which in this context refers to something enduring, continuing, and being preserved. It's used in Jeremiah 32:14, where God told the prophet to buy a field and put the title deeds "in an earthen vessel, that they may continue many days" (Jer. 32:14). And so it is that the same power that *made* all things now *maintains* all things. First it *created*, now it *continues*. First it *uplifted*, now it *upholds*.

Scriptures for Study: What do the following verses tell us about creation: Psalm 148:1–6; 119:90: Hebrews 1:3?

MARCH 27

The Carpenter

Is not this the carpenter? (Mk. 6:3)

THE setting of our text is Jesus' return to Nazareth, his home, with his disciples again in tow. Upon hearing His teaching in the synagogue, the people were astonished, but also offended, so they scornfully remarked, "Is not this the carpenter, the son of Mary, the brother of James, and Joses, and of Juda, and Simon" (v. 2)?[143] In other words, "What does he know? He's just a common laborer like us. He builds good houses and furnishings and makes excellent farm implements, but He's not qualified to teach the Law and the Prophets."

Any carpenter today would be fascinated by his ancient colleague. In light of our advanced tools, their ancient counterparts were primitive, indeed, but at the same time they teach us some lessons. The prophet Isaiah actually lists four of the tools used by the carpenter of his day: "The carpenter stretcheth out his rule; he marketh it out with a line; he fitteth it with planes, and he marketh it out with the compass" (Is. 44:13). As we today use a tape measure, he used a "rule," that is, a measuring cord. The ancient equivalent of a carpenter's pencil was a "line," a piece of chalk. While we have power tools to scrape and smooth down the wood, we still have the ancient "plane" today. We also still have the "compass" to draw circles for finer detail work. Elsewhere we also read of the hammer (Judg. 4:21), the axe and hatchet (Deut. 19:5; Ps. 74:6; Jer. 10:3), and the saw (Is. 10:15).

All these are appropriate when we again think of our Lord as "the Word." Philippians 3:16 challenges us to "walk" (*stoicheō*, 4748, march orderly) in our Christian life according to the "rule" (*kanōn*, 2583, measuring rod) of God's Word.[144] Ephesians 1:13 declares that the Holy Spirit, whom Christ sent (Jn. 14:16), has put His mark upon us ("sealed" is *sphragizō*, 4972, to mark with a seal; Apr. 15). We then read in Luke 3:5 that among many effects of the Word's coming, one would be that "the rough ways [would] be made smooth," that is, men's coarse temperaments would be smoothed and polished. The finer details are then pictured in Ephesians 2:10, where Paul says we are Christ's "workmanship," which is *poiēma* (4161; English "poem") and refers to a work of art or a masterpiece. In Jeremiah 23:29 God declares that His "word [is] like a hammer," and as for "cutting tools," there is no better image than "the word of God, [which] is quick, and powerful, and sharper than any two-edged sword" (Heb. 4:12; cf. Eph. 6:16).

How striking it is that the Carpenter would one day be nailed to a tree!

> While Creator of glorious array,
> Even also the eternal Logos,
> The Carpenter labored from day to day
> In the shortening shadow of the Cross.

Scriptures for Study: In view of the four lines above, reflect on the following verses: Acts 5:30; 10:39; 13:29; Galatians 3:13; 1 Peter 2:24.

MARCH 28

Prophet

... a Prophet from the midst of thee ... like unto me. (Deut. 18:15–18)

THE OT describes three major offices among the people of Israel—prophet, priest, and king—and the Lord Jesus fulfilled all three to the letter.

First, then, the prophet represented God to man. He was not an ambassador, negotiator, diplomat, or debater. He proclaimed God's Word to the people with absolute authority. Moses was the first major prophet, which is graphically demonstrated by his writing of the Pentateuch. While many other prophets would appear, Moses declares in our text that a prophet like him would one day arise from their own ranks and proclaim what God commanded.

It is noteworthy that Jesus is not *primarily* viewed as a prophet in the Gospels, nor is He ever called a prophet in the Epistles. This is no doubt true because He fulfilled that office and was far superior to any other prophet. That said, however, He was none-the-less a prophet—just as Moses predicted—because He spoke God's Word. He was, in fact, God's Word itself, the Ultimate Prophet.

We are here returned to the concept of *logos* (3056, "word"). Again, the crucial concept of "the word" is not only prominent in the NT, but also the OT, as the Hebrew *dāḇār* (1697H) is usually rendered as the Greek *logos* in the Septuagint. The term "word of the Lord," for example, was the expression of divine power and wisdom and appears some 241 times in the OT. It was by His word that God revealed Scripture to the prophets, as we see *logos* in the opening verses of many of the prophetic books, such as Jeremiah 1:2: "the word of the LORD came [to Jeremiah] in the days of Josiah."[145]

As significant as that is, there is another Greek word that translates *dāḇār* in the Septuagint and at times is even more striking, namely, *rhēma* (4487). While *logos* often refers to a proclamation as a whole, that is, an entire discourse or speech, *rhēma* usually relates to individual words and utterances.[146] It appears, for example, when God, by His word, introduced the Abrahamic covenant (Gen. 15:1): "After these things the word of the LORD came unto Abram." Even more noteworthy, both *logos* and *rhēma* are used in Exodus 24:3–4: "Moses came and told the people all the words [*rhēma*] of the LORD ... and all the people answered with one voice, and said, All the words [*logos*] which the LORD hath said will we do. And Moses wrote all the words [*rhēma*] of the LORD."

And so it was that Jesus was the Ultimate Prophet. Among its some 70 NT occurrences, *rhēma* appears in John 3:34 to refer to Jesus coming to "[speak] the words of God." In 5:46–47 our Lord even mentions Moses in His rebuke of the Jews: "Had ye believed Moses, ye would have believed me: for he wrote of me. But if ye believe not his writings, how shall ye believe my words [*rhēma*]?"

Scriptures for Study: In Psalm 33:6, what was accomplished by "the word of the LORD" (*dāḇār* is rendered *logos* in the Septuagint)?

MARCH 29

Priest

... a great high priest ... Jesus the Son of God. (Heb. 4:14)

YESTERDAY we considered the first major office among the people of Israel, the prophet. The prophet represented God to man, and our Lord perfectly fulfilled it.

Second, in contrast, the priest did the exact opposite; he represented man to God. He was the mediator, offering sacrifices, prayers, and praise to God on behalf of the people. Jesus, of course, was the complete and total fulfillment of this. As the **great high priest**, He did not just *make* sacrifices, He *was* the sacrifice (Heb. 9:26), not only the offer*er* but the offer*ing*. This is, of course, one of the great themes of Hebrews (cf. 7:27; 9:12, 24–28; 10:1–2, 10–14, 18; 13:12). Most important of all, while the OT priests were constantly offering sacrifices (as do Roman Catholic priests), Jesus offered Himself only once (10:12, 14).

Of special import is that Jesus is spoken of as **a great high priest**. There were many priests under the old system, but the **high priest** was the focus. Only the high priest could enter the Holy of Holies and then only once a year. On the Day of Atonement (Yom Kippur), the most sacred day in the Jewish community, the high priest selected two unblemished goats, one of which he killed and sprinkled its blood on the mercy seat in the Holy of Holies. He took the other, laid his hands on it, confessed the sins of the nation, and then sent it into the wilderness.

While all this was a graphic picture of forgiveness and the taking away of sin, it was just that, a *picture*. It was a *representation* but not a *reality*. None of this could forever take away the people's sin. It had to be repeated over and over again, ad infinitum. Only the ***great* high priest** could do that. Of all the high priests spoken of in the biblical record, not one was called **great**. Never was there a more important adjective! The Greek, of course, is *megas* (3173), which literally means large in the sense of magnitude. We use it in English words such as, megaton and megaphone. Used metaphorically, as it is here, it speaks of something great in estimation, weight, or importance, such as a "great commandment" (Matt. 22:36, 38) or a "great mystery" (Eph. 5:32). So important was He, of such great magnitude and weight was His sacrifice, that all other priests (both then and now) were rendered obsolete.

Ah, but there is still more. As the OT priest was the intercessor between God and the people, Christ is now our only mediator (1 Tim. 2:5) and is ever interceding for us in prayer (Heb. 7:25; Rom. 8:34). Besides the horrific blasphemy of the Roman Catholic Mass, its so-called priesthood makes a mockery of our **great high priest**. Neither is there a priesthood in the NT, nor were there priests in the 1st-century Church. Once the **great high priest** came, there was no need for the "lower" ones.

Scriptures for Study: Read the verses cited in Hebrews today. What observations can you make?

MARCH 30

King

... King of kings, and Lord of lords. (Rev. 19:16)

AS a prophet represented God to man, a priest did the exact opposite in representing man to God. *Third*, a king, however, is especially unique, for he represented himself to his subjects. By definition, a king is a monarch, one who rules singularly, unilaterally, and absolutely.[147] History chronicles a plethora of such monarchs. There have been benevolent rulers, such as Joseph II, the first ruler of Austrian dominions of the House of Lorraine (1765–1790), a truly unselfish ruler who wanted the best for his people, even abolishing slavery and serfdom. Others, of course, have been the opposite, such as: Genghis Khan (1162–1227), perhaps the most brutal ruler the world has ever seen. Heading a virtually endless list of monarchs, just a few include: Alexander the Great, Caesar Augustus, Charlemagne, Elizabeth I, Victoria, James I, Napoleon, Frederick II of Prussia, Peter the Great, and Louis XIV, who reigned as King of France for 72 years, longer than any other European monarch.

But the one thing that is true of every one of those, and all others we could list, is that the day came when their rule ended. This universal reality is explained in Daniel 5:1–31, when Belshazzar, king of Babylon, "saw the writing on the wall" (which has become an idiom for "imminent doom or misfortune" and "the future is predetermined"). The ominous Chaldean writing declared: "MENE [God hath numbered thy kingdom, and finished it], MENE, TEKEL [Thou art weighed in the balances, and art found wanting], UPHARSIN [Thy kingdom is divided, and given to the Medes and Persians]" (vv. 25–28). Has not *every* ruler and kingdom, in one way or another, been "found wanting"?

Not so with Christ! First, in His perfection, He is Monarch of a spiritual kingdom now (Matt. 3:2; 5:3, 10; Lk. 17:21; Acts 1:3; Rom 14:17; 1 Cor. 6:9). Second, He will also one day rule and reign as **King of kings, and Lord of lords** (cf. Rev. 17:14) over His earthly kingdom (2 Sam. 7:12-16; Ps. 89:26-29; Lk. 1:32-33; Rev. 20:1-6), vanquishing all foes in the process. Third, and most glorious of all, His reign will *never* end: "The kingdoms of this world are become the kingdoms of our Lord, and of his Christ; and he shall reign for ever and ever" (Rev. 11:15; cf. 22:5; Ex. 15:18; Ps. 146:10).

Bringing together these three offices—prophet, priest, and king—one other amazing thought encourages us: each of us imitates Christ (figuratively and in a subordinate role) in these offices. As "prophets" we proclaim the Truth, as "priests" (1 Pet. 2:9) we live sanctified lives (1:5) and "offer up spiritual sacrifices acceptable to God by Jesus Christ" (2:5), and as "kings" we shall both share in His future reign (Rev. 5:10) and even now claim victory over spiritual forces (Eph. 6:10-18; Jas. 4:7; 1 Jn. 4.4).

Scriptures for Study: What do the following verses declare about Christ's present spiritual kingdom: Luke 17:21; Acts 1:3; Romans 14:17?

MARCH 31

Messiah

We have found the Messiah ... (Jn. 1:41)

WE have noted the word **Messiah** several times in our daily meditations (e.g., Mar. 4), but we again plunge deeper. The Hebrew is *māšiyah* (4899H), which is derived from *māšah* (4886H), the most common word for anointing. The word is actually quite mundane, referring simply to smearing something, such as paint on a house (Jer. 22:14) and other such common uses.

Used theologically, however, *māšah* is a symbol of sanctification and service. Aaron and his sons, for example, were anointed to "consecrate them, and sanctify them" so they could "minister unto [God] in the priest's office" (Ex. 28:41), as were prophets (1 Kings 19:16; Is. 61:1). The word **Messiah** appears only four times in the Bible, but each occurrence is, of course, greatly significant.

First, we see the *prediction* of "Messiah the Prince" in the first two occurrences in Daniel 9:24–27. In this fascinating, and critically important, prophetic passage, 490 years (seven "weeks" of years) will pass from Persian king Artaxerxes' decree to rebuild Jerusalem in 445 BC (Neh. 2:1–8) to the reign of Messiah in His Kingdom. As Sir Robert Anderson brilliantly calculated in his classic book, *The Coming Prince*, allowing for leap years, calendar errors, and other factors, he figured that the first 69 "weeks" (483 years) ended on the very day of Jesus' triumphal entry into Jerusalem, five days before his death, at which time He was "cut off" (a common reference to death). The final week (seven years) is yet to come during the Tribulation Period. The fulfillment of such a prediction apart from omnipotent, sovereign control is beyond *any* calculation.

Second, we witness the *presentation* of **Messiah** in our text. Just five verses earlier, John the Baptist made his momentous announcement, "Behold the Lamb of God!" (Mar. 18–19), to which the Apostle John and Andrew responded. When the excited Andrew found his brother Peter, he exclaimed, **We have found the Messias, which is, being interpreted, the Christ**. Here the Hebrew *māšiyah* is simply transliterated into Greek (and English). Its actual Greek translation, of course, is *Christos* (5547, **Christ**), which means "anointed," as Peter Himself later testified in Matthew 16:16 (Mar. 4). What a moment! People had been waiting some four millennia for this presentation, and here it was! Further, each wanted to tell others, and so should we.

Third, we learn the *purpose* of Messiah's coming in John 4:25, where a woman at a Samaritan well incisively affirmed, "I know that Messias cometh, which is called Christ: when he is come, he will tell us all things." Just like our own day, most were looking for a Messiah who would solve all their problems and "meet their felt needs." But here was one who knew that He would tell us everything that pertains to sin, salvation, and service.

Scriptures for Study: What did Jesus promise His Holy Spirit would do (Jn. 14:26)? ◻ What does Peter declare Christ has given us (2 Pet. 1:3)?

April 1

The Root and the Offspring of David

I am the root and the offspring of David . . . (Rev. 22:16a)

THE words of our text were addressed to the seven churches in Asia, who were the original recipients of the book of Revelation (1:11). They state a glorious paradox: Christ was *both* a **root** *and* an **offspring**. But how can such a thing be?

First, **the root** *declares* His *divinity*. Our Lord made this clear in Mark 12:35–37. Quoting Psalm 110:1, a messianic Psalm, He declared, "For David himself said by the Holy Ghost, The LORD said to my Lord, Sit thou on my right hand, till I make thine enemies thy footstool. David therefore himself calleth him Lord; and whence is he then his son?" In the Hebrew, "LORD" is *Yāhweh*, God's covenant name (Jan. 21), while "Lord" is *'Aḏōnāy*, which Jews used instead of *Yāhweh* (sometimes out of reverence but more often out of superstition) and speaks of God's dominion, possession, and sovereignty. Jesus, therefore, told the Pharisees that since David would not call one of his human descendants *'Aḏōnāy*, then Jesus was more than "the Son of David" (v. 35); He was, in fact, the Son of *Yāhweh*.

Botanists tell us that there are four major functions of a root, all of which illustrate our Lord in His nature and work (cf. Jn. 15:1–8): (1) absorption of water and nutrients; (2) anchoring of the plant body to the ground and supporting it; (3) storage of food and nutrients; and (4) vegetative reproduction.

Second, **the offspring** *designates* His *humanity*. In other words, while in His deity Christ is David's *designer*, in His humanity He is David's *descendant*. All this is rooted in the Davidic Covenant, which is delineated in 2 Samuel 7:8–16 (cf. Ps. 132:11–12; Is. 11:1, 10; Matt. 1:1; Rom. 1:3). As God assured David in verse 12: "When thy days be fulfilled, and thou shalt sleep with thy fathers, I will set up thy seed after thee, which shall proceed out of thy bowels, and I will establish his kingdom." Not only would God give David a son to rule contemporarily (Solomon), but would also give him another who would rule eternally (Messiah). In the words of James Montgomery's beautiful hymn: "Hail to the Lord's anointed, great David's greater Son! / Hail in the time appointed, His reign on earth begun!"

Third, taken together, these terms *demonstrate* His *unity*. Theologians call this the "hypostatic union," that is, Christ's *sui generis* (unique, one of a kind) dual nature, being both God and man in totality and lacking in neither. He has always been God (Jn. 8:58; 10:30) but became human at the incarnation (Jn. 1:14). Both natures are seamlessly inseparable and perfectly unified in the one. This truth is, indeed, "in the realm of deep mystery"[148] and incomprehensible to our finite thinking, but that makes it no less comforting. Only as a *man* could He identify *with* us (Heb. 2:17; 4:15), and only as *God* could He die *for* us (Phil. 2:5–11).

Scriptures for Study: What encouragement does Hebrew 4:15 give us? How does this then apply to 1 Corinthians 10:13?

APRIL 2

The Bright and Morning Star

I am . . . the bright and morning star. (Rev. 22:16b)

YESTERDAY we considered the first half of Revelation 22:16, where Jesus declares: "I am the root and the offspring of David." But in the second half, He announces something equally stunning: **I am . . . the bright and morning star**, which echoes Numbers 24:17: "there shall come a Star out of Jacob." We also read in 2 Peter 1:19 of "a more sure word of prophecy" (the Scriptures), which lights every "dark place" until the "day star" (Christ) returns in the full revelation of His glory and the regal splendor of His kingdom.

The Greek behind "day star" is *phōsphoros* (5459; from *phōs*, 5457, light, and *pherō*, 5342, to bring), so literally "light bringer." From early in Greek history this word was used of the planet Venus, and in this we see some striking parallels.

First, its *presence* brings the light. Venus is, indeed, the **morning star**. Because it appears to the west of the sun, it consequently rises before it and ushers in the light of day. Likewise, but far more profound, our Lord is the true Light Bringer. One of our Lord's great "I am" statements was, "I am the light of the world" (Jn. 8:12; Mar. 11). That "light," in fact, is a major theme from John's pen. Using it more than any other NT writer, *phōs* appears 23 times in his gospel and four more times in his first epistle. (This also reminds us of the title of this book; what better time of the day could there be to seek the **morning star** than early?)

Second, its *position* is in the east. I shall not soon forget standing on the Mount of Olives and gazing at the East Gate. Oh, what a momentous gate! God's Shekinah glory was seen departing from the Temple by way of this gate, the main processional gate (Ezek. 10–11). It was then undoubtedly through this gate that our Lord entered Jerusalem the week He was crucified (Matt. 21:2–11), and it is through this gate He will return (Zech. 14:4). The only gate of eight that is sealed, this was done in 1530 by the Ottoman Turks and a cemetery planted in front of it to supposedly prevent the Jewish Messiah from entering it. What folly to think that will succeed. While an early American motto was, "Go West, young man," we would be far wiser to do as the magi did (Matt. 2:2): *look east*.

Third, its *prominence* is bright. Venus is the third brightest object in the sky, outshined only by the sun and the moon. Amazingly, in fact, like the other two objects, it is actually bright enough to cast shadows. Our text, therefore, declares that the morning star is **bright**. This is the Greek *lampros* (2986), which speaks of shining brilliance. Another form of this word appears in Acts 26:13, where Paul described the light that struck Him down on his way to Damascus as "above the brightness [*lamprotēs*, 2987] of the sun, shining round about me."

Oh, let us keep looking east!

Scriptures for Study: What did our Lord promise the church at Thyatira, the church that was clinging to paganism (Rev. 2:28)?

APRIL 3

Am I Spiritual?

... he that is spiritual ... (1 Cor. 2:15)

HOW often do we hear people say something like this: "I'm not really religious, but I consider myself to be a very spiritual person"? Such statements, however, invariably come from people who want little or nothing to do with Christ or His Word, which makes them far from "spiritual." On the opposite end of the spectrum, some true Christians believe that spirituality comes from *doing* certain things and/or *not* doing certain other things. But this is nothing more than a form of legalism (Feb. 19).

"Spirituality" is, indeed, a term that is used often but one that is seldom actually defined biblically. Such dictionary definitions as the following are hardly helpful: "the quality or state of being concerned with religion or religious matters." Even many Christian writers just *describe* spirituality by listing characteristics or results of Spirit-filling, but very few really *define* the term in simple, straightforward language. Some who do try to define it seem to miss the real heart of the issue. For example, one theologian's definition—"Spirituality means a mature, yet maturing relationship to God"—is certainly correct as far as it goes, but it doesn't tell us either what this maturity or relationship to God actually is or what it involves. What, then, does this term mean?

While the word "spirituality" does not itself appear in Scripture, the word "spiritual" does. Perhaps the key verse is our text, which speaks of **he that is spiritual**. The Greek is *pneumatikos* (4152), an adjective formed from the noun *pneuma* (4151). In Classical Greek, *pneuma* literally means "a dynamic movement of air [and the resulting] inherent power." When *pneuma* is used of the Holy Spirit in the NT (which it does more then 250 times), it refers to "that power which is most immediately of God as to source and nature." *Pneumatikos*, then, conveys the idea of belonging to the *realm* of the Holy Spirit and *manifesting* the Holy Spirit.[149]

So, when "spiritual" is attached to another word, it lifts that word to a new realm. A "spiritual gift" (Rom. 1:11; 1 Cor. 12:1) is a gift that manifests the Holy Spirit's power in our life. Likewise, a "spiritual song" is a song that belongs to the spiritual realm and emphasizes spiritual truth. And "spiritual things" in general (1 Cor. 9:11) are simply things that transcend temporal things and manifest holy things. A truly "spiritual person," then, is one who lives above the temporal realm and lives by the dictates of the Word of God, as illumined by the Holy Spirit.

With that in mind, we would humbly offer the following definition: *Spirituality is the ever-deepening desire to manifest the Holy Spirit and to be dominated, influenced, and controlled by His power through the Word.* So, as we begin our mediations on the Holy Spirit, let us each ask ourselves, "Am I truly spiritual?"

Scriptures for Study: What do the following verses tell us about being spiritual: 1 Corinthians 3:1; 14:37; Galatians 6:1?

APRIL 4

The Personal Presence of the Godhead

...another Comforter... (Jn. 14:16)

MUCH has been written on the Holy Spirit in the last several decades. In fact, as one writer points out, "Many people have labeled the twentieth century as the century of the Holy Spirit."[150] Sadly, however, while some of this has been good, much of it has been equally bad (some even appalling). Misunderstanding of this doctrine, as well as misleading teaching (which sometimes has even been deliberate), has done incalculable damage.

While we will not focus on controversies in these daily meditations—this is not the place for that—we do want to address a few matters that are often overlooked. While some good books have been written on the *doctrine* of the Holy Spirit, there seems to be a lack of solidly biblical studies on the *personal application* of such doctrine. In short, we will concentrate our thoughts on the practical ministry of the Holy Spirit to the believer. After a few foundational studies on the Holy Spirit Himself, we will turn our full attention to how He ministers to the believer, that is, what He is doing in us in a very personal way.

So, what is this personal ministry? We find it in the five occurrences of the Greek noun *paraklētos* (3875) in the NT, which appear only in the writings of the Apostle John: John 14:16; 14:26; 15:26; 16:7–8; and 1 John 2:1. This word is translated "Comforter" and "Advocate" in the KJV, and, as we'll discover, both translations are superbly appropriate. We'll discover the wondrous truth that these five occurrences of *paraklētos* are the provisions God has given in answer to the five basic problems of the Christian life. We will see that an understanding of this personal ministry of the Holy Spirit is essential for spiritual living.

While we will go much deeper as we journey forward, we should reemphasize the uniquely personal nature of the Holy Spirit's relationship to the believer. It is through Him that the Trinity becomes truly intimate. While God as our Father is certainly profound (Matt. 6:9; Jn. 1:14, 18; 5:20; Eph. 1:2; Phil. 4:20; etc.), and while the fact that we are actually siblings of our elder brother the Son is equally striking (Rom. 8:29; cf. Matt. 12:50), both these members of the Godhead can still feel a little remote, a little far off from our own here-and-now.

Ah, but the Holy Spirit! He is not some distant cloud of ether or some cold force of the universe. Indeed not! First, He is *alive* within us. As we will detail, Jesus sent **another Comforter** in His place—one of similar or identical nature as Himself, in fact—who will abide within us forever (Jn. 14:16, 23). Second, He is *affectionate* within us. Since He produces "love" in us (Gal. 5:22), love is part of His essential nature. Third, He is *active* within us, teaching us (Jn. 14:26), strengthening us (15:26–27), and empowering us for service (Acts 1:8).

Oh, what wondrous truths await us!

Scriptures for Study: What do the following verses say about the Holy Spirit: Job 33:4; Romans 8:9; 1 Corinthians 6:19; Galatians 5:22–23; 2 Peter 1:20–21?

APRIL 5

The Holy Spirit Is a Person

... another Comforter ... (Jn. 14:16)

ONE of the first in Church History to deny the personality of the Holy Spirit was the notorious heretic Arius (AD 256–336), a parish priest in Alexandria. Arius not only denied the eternality of Christ and viewed Him as a created being, but he also viewed the Holy Spirit as merely "the exerted energy of God." Many, in fact, from Montanus (AD 150) to present day neo-orthodox theologians and others, have denied that the Holy Spirit is actually a person. But there are, indeed, several blessed proofs of the Holy Spirit's personality. These proofs fall into three major categories.

First, many personal pronouns are used of the Holy Spirit. Even though the Greek word for "spirit" (*pneuma*, 4151) is neuter in gender and would, therefore, *grammatically* require a neuter pronoun, we still find that the Word of God uses masculine pronouns to refer to the Holy Spirit. We might also add, the personal pronoun "Him" (or "Himself") appears five times and the relative pronouns "who" and "whom" each appear once and twice respectively (see also Eph. 1:13–14, etc.). We should point out again that John 14:16, 14:26, 15:26, and 16:7–8 cannot be over-emphasized because they form the basis of the *personal ministry* of the Holy Spirit to the believer, which we will examine in later studies.

Second, the Holy Spirit possesses the three aspects of personality. Personality consists of three characteristics, and the fact that the Holy Spirit possesses these is, by far, the greatest proof of His personality. First, the Holy Spirit possesses *intellect*. He has a mind and knowledge (Rom. 8:27; 1 Cor. 2:10–11) and is capable of teaching men that knowledge (Jn. 14:26; 16:13; 1 Cor. 2:13, which can be literally rendered, "explaining spiritual things to spiritual men"). Second, the Holy Spirit has *emotion*. He can be grieved (or saddened; Eph. 4:30), insulted (Heb. 10:29), and is capable of love (Rom. 15:30). How could some "force" or "influence" *feel* such things? Third, the Holy Spirit has *will*. He distributes "spiritual gifts" according to His will (1 Cor. 12:11), and He leads and directs His servants, as stated in Romans 8:14 and illustrated in Acts 13:1–4 and 16:6–7.

Third, many other traits of the Holy Spirit can be true only if He has personality. He can be obeyed (Acts 10:19–21), lied to (Acts 5:3), resisted (Acts 7:51), and blasphemed (Matt. 12:31). He also is the One who calls and commissions God's servants (Acts 13:1–4). It is absurd, indeed, to think that such things could be true of some impersonal force, influence, or energy. "The Holy Spirit is not enthusiasm," wrote A. W. Tozer. "Neither is the Holy Spirit another name for genius. He is a Person. Put that down in capital letters."[151]

Scriptures for Study: Read the following verses in the Gospel of John: 14:16–17, 26; 15:26; 16:7–8, 13–14. How many times does the personal pronoun "He" appear in reference to the Holy Spirit?

APRIL 6

The Holy Spirit Has Power

...another Comforter... (Jn. 14:16)

WHILE the Holy Spirit must be recognized as a person, He must also be acknowledged as God, the third member of the Godhead. There are several evidences of this truth.

First, He is *called* God. He is referred to as the "Spirit of God" (1 Cor. 6:11; 1 Pet. 4:14), the "Spirit of the Lord" (Is. 11:2; Lk. 4:18), the "Spirit of Christ" (Rom. 8:9; Phil. 1:19), and the "Breath of the Almighty" (Job 32:8). We see in all this, therefore, that He is identified with the Father and the Son, which clearly demonstrates Deity. In fact, He is related by name to the other two persons of the Godhead 16 times in Scripture. Two of the most outstanding examples are in the "Baptismal Formula" (Matt. 28:19) and the "Apostolic Benediction" (2 Cor. 13:14).

Second, the Holy Spirit possesses the *characteristics* of God. But even more specific is the fact that He possesses the three basic natural attributes of Deity (Jan. 15). He possesses the Divine attribute of *omniscience*, that is, all-knowledge (Is. 11:2; Jn. 14:17, 26; 1 Cor. 2:11–12).

He also possesses *omnipotence*, that is, all power. This is demonstrated first by His being involved in creation. As we have noted before (Jan. 14), the word "God" in Genesis 1:1 is the Hebrew *'Elōhiym*. The suffix *–iym* makes this word plural showing that all the Persons of the Godhead were involved in the creation work. Verse 2 tells us that the Holy Spirit "moved upon [i.e. brooded or hovered over] the face of the waters." The Holy Spirit was also responsible for the inspiration of Scripture. Second Peter 1:21 declares that "holy men of God spoke as they were moved [carried along] by the Holy Spirit." The Holy Spirit was also involved in the conception of Jesus Christ. It was the Spirit who conceived the Lord Jesus within the virgin Mary (Matt. 1:18; Lk. 1:35).

The Holy Spirit also possesses *omnipresence*, that is, being present in all places simultaneously. This is not the same as the false teaching called "Pantheism" which says that God is *in* all things, but rather this means that God's *presence* is everywhere in the universe.[152] The Psalmist wrote, "Wither shall I go from thy Spirit, or whither shall I flee from thy presence" (Ps. 139:7). This leads us to a third principle.

Third, the Holy Spirit carries on the *conduct* of God. He is actively present in the world today. For one thing, He is a restraining force against sin and rebellion against God (2 Thes. 2:3–7). He also convicts men of sin and their need of the Savior (Jn. 16:8–11). Finally, as we will see, the Holy Spirit indwells, infills, and empowers the believer.

Scriptures for Study: Read the following passages, noting how all three members of the Godhead are present: Matthew 3:16–17; John 14:15–17; Romans 8:9, 14–17; 1 John 5:7–8.

APRIL 7

The Holy Spirit Has Purpose

... another Comforter ... (Jn. 14:16)

WE could examine many functions, offices, and duties of the Holy Spirit, but we briefly consider three basic categories here, which will help prepare us for the studies that follow.

First, to the *sinner* He *convicts* and *converts.* As we will detail, the Holy Spirit convicts men of sin and their need of the Savior (Jn. 16:8–11). He also converts men to Christ; that is, He is the one who regenerates, gives new life to those who are "dead in sin" (Eph. 2:1). It is the Word of God (Rom. 10:17; 1 Peter 1:23), energized by the Holy Spirit, that accomplishes regeneration.

Second, to the *saint* He *comforts.* It is this principle, in fact, that is really the main theme of our studies of the Holy Spirit. As we will meditate on at length, the **Comforter,** the *paraklētos* (3875) is the key to our personal relationship to God, and He **will abide with [us] forever**. He is *always* with us to comfort, aid, teach, uplift, console, and, yes, even chastise. This thought immediately reminds us of the wondrous doctrine of the indwelling of the Holy Spirit.

(1) This indwelling is first and foremost *personal,* that is, the personal presence of God living in the believer. This personal presence begins at the precise moment when one receives Christ as Savior. Romans 8:9 declares, "Now if any man have not the Spirit of Christ, he is none of His" (that is, he does not belong to Him). Later in verse 23, Paul tells us of "the firstfruits of the Spirit." What are these "firstfruits?" This can refer only to His regenerating and indwelling work.

The crux of this matter, however, appears in 1 Corinthians 6:19: "What? know ye not that your body is the temple of the Holy Spirit who is in you, whom ye have of God, and ye are not your own?" Even though the believers at Corinth were the most carnal to be found in the NT record, they were still indwelt by the Holy Spirit. In fact, Paul actually appealed to them on this very point. He says in effect, "Don't you realize that you are indwelt by the Holy Spirit! Turn away from acting like the world, for it grieves the Spirit who indwells you!"

(2) The indwelling of the Holy Spirit is also *permanent.* We are again drawn to our text, for it unambiguously declares that the Comforter will abide with each of us **forever**.

Third, to the *servant* He *commissions.* (1) The Holy Spirit commissions *every* believer to be a witness of Jesus Christ (Acts 1:8; we will go deeper in our April 22 and Sept. 26–27 studies). (2) He bestows "spiritual gifts" (divinely given abilities) for the purpose of service (Rom. 12:6–8; Eph. 4:11–12). (3) He "infills," that is, controls and empowers, us (Eph. 5:18–21).

Scriptures for Study: What do the following verses teach us about the indwelling Holy Spirit: 1 John 3:24; 4:13–16? 📖 What does Paul go on to tell us in Romans 8:9–17?

APRIL 8

The Infilling of the Holy Spirit (1)

... be filled with the Spirit ... (Eph. 5:18)

TRUE spirituality is a growing process. There is no such thing as "instant spirituality." We must never think, "I have arrived," rather our attitude must ever be, "I'm on my way." Neither is there a supposed "second blessing," or "second work of grace," as some teach without a shred of biblical support. True spirituality involves being filled (controlled, monopolized) by the Holy Spirit and is a process of growth in the knowledge and character of Christ.

Few doctrines have been as misunderstood and misinterpreted as has the infilling of the Holy Spirit.[153] Various teachers have confused it with the "sealing" of the Holy Spirit (Eph. 1:13; 4:30), the "baptism" of the Holy Spirit (1 Cor. 12:13), and even the "indwelling" of the Spirit (Rom. 8:9; etc.). Still others view this infilling as a rapturous state where you speak in ecstatic language or have visions.

Our text, however, is very specific in telling us precisely what this infilling is. **Filled** translates *plēroō* (4137), which speaks of filling a container and means "to influence fully, to control." As one Greek authority adds, "To fill up, to cause to abound, to furnish or supply liberally, to flood, to diffuse throughout."[154] It is used, for example, in Matthew 13:48 to refer to a full fishing net. The chief idea then is that we are to be permeated with, and therefore controlled by, the Spirit.

Now, all this is fine in *theory*, but what does it mean in *practice*? Preachers often say that "filling" means "control," but what exactly does that mean? In short, it's not a matter of *us* getting *more* of the Spirit, as some teachers insist, but rather the Spirit getting *all* of *us*. It means that we are influenced by Him and nothing else. To put it succinctly: *to be filled with the Spirit is to have our thoughts, desires, values, motives, goals, priorities, and all else controlled by Him through the Word and set on spiritual things and spiritual growth.* When that statement is true of a Christian's life, all other things will fall in line behind it.

Spirit-filling is not something magical or mystical, rather wondrously practical. A. B. Simpson provides us with a beautiful picture of Spirit filling: "Being filled with the fullness of God is like a bottle in the ocean. You take the cork out of the bottle and sink it in the ocean, and you have the bottle completely full of ocean. The bottle is in the ocean, and the ocean is in the bottle. The ocean contains the bottle, but the bottle contains only a little bit of the ocean. So it is with the Christian."[155] To take the analogy one step further, as the bottle in the ocean now characterizes more ocean than it does bottle, to be completely filled with the Spirit means that we now contain more Spirit than we do ourselves. He now permeates us. He now controls us. How sorely we need this today! We will continue our thoughts on this profound and essential truth tomorrow.

Scriptures for Study: Read Acts 6:1–6. What did God demand of the men chosen to serve? (Many believe this incident is the origin of the office of "deacon" [cf. 1 Tim. 3:8–13]).

APRIL 9

The Infilling of the Holy Spirit (2)

... be filled with the Spirit ... (Eph. 5:18)

CRITICALLY important to the understanding of spirit-filling is the construction of the verb behind the words **be filled** in our text. First, it is in the imperative mood, that is, it's a command. Second, it is in the present tense, indicating continuous action, something that is repeated. The most literal translation of Paul's command is: "be being filled."

The beloved expositor Harry Ironside makes an observation about Spirit-filling that is enormously significant. In the sister book to Ephesians, we read, "Let the word of Christ dwell in you richly in all wisdom; teaching and admonishing one another in psalms and hymns and spiritual songs, singing with grace in your hearts to the Lord" (Col 3:16). Note carefully the effect of the Word of God dwelling richly in the soul. When we then turn back to Ephesians, we notice that we get the exact same results when we are filled with the *Spirit* as we do when we are filled with the *Word*. What's the correlation? Ironside writes:

"It should be clear that the *Word*-filled Christian is the *Spirit*-filled Christian. As the Word of Christ dwells in us richly, controls all our ways, as we walk in obedience to the Word, the Spirit of God fills, dominates, controls to the glory of the Lord Jesus Christ."[156]

That is Spirit-filling! Notice again the definition we offered yesterday. When the *Word of God permeates* us, the *Spirit of God controls* us. Dear Christian, the Word of God is everything, the key to living the Christian life. That is why Acts 4:31 declares, "And when they had prayed, the place was shaken where they were assembled together; and they were all filled with the Holy Ghost, and they spake the word of God with boldness."

One purpose of Spirit-filling, then, is service, specifically, the empowering to proclaim the Truth of God. Spirit-filling is not some emotional high, not something by which we "better commune with God," and is certainly not to be found in the emotionalism and entertainment atmosphere of "seeker-sensitivity." Rather, we are to be *Word*-filled and, therefore, *Spirit*-filled. It is impossible for the Holy Spirit to work in us apart from the Word of God; it is always through His Word that God works. It is then, as a result of that work, that we are equipped to be more faithful and effective witnesses of Christ. Spirit-filling does not result in some "emotional rapture." On the contrary, its purpose is to make us more lucid, coherent, and in control of our faculties so we can more clearly proclaim the Truth.

You will see this happen as you witness for Christ. When someone asks you a question, the Holy Spirit will give you the answer. He won't give you some opinion, some silly cliché, or some psychobabble, rather He will give you the Word of God that you have already committed to your mind and heart.

Scriptures for Study: According to John 14:26 and 16:13–15, what is another purpose of Spirit-filling?

APRIL 10

The Infilling of the Holy Spirit (3)
... be filled with the Spirit ... (Eph. 5:18)

THE Christian life contains no "formulas." We cannot mix "a little of this" with "a little of that," throw in "a pinch of something else," and then stir it around and magically get results, whether it be prosperity, revival, or even Spirit-filling. Since God has commanded this filling, however, He has given us four commands (all through Paul) concerning our relationship to the Holy Spirit.

First, we must not grieve the Holy Spirit (Eph. 4:30). The word "grieve" there is *lupeō* (3076), "to sadden or bring pain." While all sin grieves Him, the sins listed in verse 31 are especially painful to the Holy Spirit because they are particularly inconsistent in the Holy Spirit indwelt life: bitterness, wrath, anger, clamor, evil speaking, and malice.

Second, we must not quench the Holy Spirit (1 Thes. 5:19). While this is linked to "grieving" the Holy Spirit, it is still distinct. "Quench" is *sbennumi* (4570), which in the literal sense means "to extinguish by drowning with water, as opposed to smothering"[157] (e.g., Mk. 9:44; in Eph. 6:16). Figuratively, then, *sbennumi* means "to dampen, hinder, repress, as in preventing the Holy Spirit from exerting His full influence."[158] How do we "drown" the Holy Spirit's working? By simply saying "No" to Him, by resisting His guidance, or by opposing His will.

Third, we must yield to the Holy Spirit. This is at the very heart of Spirit-filling and is what makes it possible. As Paul wrote, "Neither yield ye your members as instruments of unrighteousness unto sin: but yield yourselves unto God, as those that are alive from the dead, and your members as instruments of righteousness unto God" (Rom. 6:13; see also 12:1–2, Sept. 3–6). There is no middle ground here. The believer either yields to the Spirit or yields to sin. "Yield" (and "present" in 12:1) is *paristēmi* (3936), "to cause to stand near or before." It was used widely in secular Greek, such as, "to place at someone's disposal," "to bring [as a sacrifice]," and "bring before (the emperor or the court)."[159] Paul's point, then, is clear: the Christian is commanded to place himself before the Lord as a living sacrifice for God's glory and use, to yield to the total control of God's will, to conform not to the world's *mold* but to God's *model* as revealed in His Word.

Fourth, we must walk by the Holy Spirit (Gal. 5:16). "Walk" is *peripateō* (4043; detailed on Oct. 12), "to walk about" and figuratively refers to our "conduct of life," how we conduct ourselves as we walk through life. Our conduct is dictated and regulated by the Holy Spirit through the Word of God. We do not walk according to the world system's standards, Satan's devices, our flesh, or some legalistic method; rather, we walk by the Spirit. So, if we are walking in the Spirit, it is impossible for us to fulfill the lust of the flesh. The reverse, however, is also true; if we are fulfilling our lusts, we are not walking in the Spirit.

Scriptures for Study: Write down your reflections on this three-day study.

APRIL 11

The Provisions of the Comforter (1)

... another Comforter ... (Jn. 14:16)

THERE is a common teaching nowadays that advertises Christianity as the "cure all." In fact, more and more, the Gospel is packaged with promises such as this: "If you just 'accept Jesus,' He will fix all of your problems, wipe away all of your pain, prosper you, and destroy all your enemies."

Such teaching, however, is not only unbiblical, but it's also inexcusably misleading. Why? Because when someone comes to Christ under such pretenses, he finds that just the opposite is true: he still has problems, he still experiences pain and suffering, he doesn't get rich, and people hate him more than ever and never get punished for any abuse they dish out.

There is, however, an answer: *the **Comforter***. Through all the problems and difficulties of life, God has given us a provision—His indwelling Presence. As already mentioned, there are five (and only five) NT occurrences of the Greek noun *paraklētos* (3875), all of which appear in the writings of the Apostle John: John 14:16; 14:26; 15:26; 16:7-8; and 1 John 2:1.

It is vitally important that we understand the meaning and the amazing uniqueness of this dramatic and powerful word. The prefix *para* means "along side of" and is used in such English words as "parallel" (lines that are along side of one another). The root word *kaleō* (2564) means "to call to someone." So, in Classical Greek, *paraklētos* literally meant "one who is called along side to aid." The word was originally used in the court of justice to show legal assistance. Our English word "paraclete" carries much the same idea.

In the NT, however, *paraklētos* took on a much deeper meaning. Our Savior took this word and transformed it into a stunningly beautiful and supremely practical term. We can see the contrast between the Classical usage and the NT usage in three principles. First, in the NT the Paraclete is not *called in*, but rather He is *sent* (Jn. 14:16; 15:26; 16:7). Second, the NT Paraclete brings *active help* to those in need. He doesn't just "put in a good word" or "pat us on the shoulder." As we'll see, His comforting work involves teaching, convicting, challenging, and empowering. Third, and most blessed of all, the NT Paraclete is *personal* not *professional*. Most defense attorneys have an underlying motive of money; they must be paid to help. But the Divine Paraclete really cares; He is there with the right motive. Oh, what a beautiful term this is! As we will see:

> The Comforter has come to meet our need;
>   He's within as the Divine Paraclete.
> He is ever present our case to plead;
>   His defense and provision are complete.

Scriptures for Study: In preparation for our studies, read the five occurrences of *paraklētos* and record your reflections.

APRIL 12

The Provisions of the Comforter (2)

... another Comforter ... (Jn. 14:16)

IT is puzzling, indeed, that over the years there has been discussion concerning how *paraklētos* should be translated. Some feel that **Comforter** is inaccurate in conveying the idea of the Greek. Alternate translations that have been offered include: "counselor," "convincer," "paraclete," and "helper."

We would submit, however, that **Comforter** is by far the best translation precisely because *it holds a deep meaning of personality*. We agree with Arthur W. Pink: "Personally, we believe that no better term can be found, providing the original meaning of our English word be kept in mind."[160] What does he mean? "Comforter" comes from the Latin *comfortis*, which in turn consists of two words: the prefix *com*, "along side of," and the root *fortis*, "strong." So, what we have in this word is the thought that the **Comforter** is, "One who stands with us to keep us company and to give us strength." Does this not touch the heart as being personal? Is there not a sweetness and preciousness in this word? As another commentator sums up:

"Taking all the four passages in which the Spirit is thus spoken of in this Discourse [Jn. 14:16; 14:26; 15:26; 16:7–8], that of a Helper certainly lies at the foundation; but that of a *Comforter* seems to us to be the kind of help which suits best with the strain of the Discourse at this place. The comfort of Christ's personal presence with the Eleven had been such, that while they had it they seemed to want for nothing; and the loss of it would seem the loss of everything—utter desolation (v. 18). It is to meet this, as we think, that He says He will ask the Father to send them *another* Comforter; and in all these four passages, it is as an all-sufficient, all-satisfying *Substitute for Himself* that He holds forth this promised Gift."[161]

Indeed, we are compelled to insist that **Comforter** is the preferred term. It is personal, peaceful, and powerful. To paraphrase Pink, He give us *consolation* when we are cast down, *courage* when we are weak or timid, and *counsel* when we are perplexed.[162] With this understanding, we are now ready to look at "The Provisions of the Comforter." Dear Christian Friend, do you ever have problems and difficulties in your Christian experience? I am quite sure your answer to that question is, "Yes, indeed!" The Christian Life *is* difficult, and those who say it isn't prove that they are not truly living it according to Scripture.

On close examination we find that there are really only five basic difficulties in the Christian life; that is, whatever problem we might have, it will fall into one of five categories. But all these difficulties are provided for in the five occurrences of *paraklētos*.

Oh, how God takes care of us!

Scriptures for Study: To prepare further for the studies that follow, read the five occurrences of *paraklētos* once again. Can you recognize the greatest problem in your own Christian life and which occurrence of *paraklētos* addresses it?

APRIL 13

The Problem of Solitude (1)

And I will pray the Father, and he shall give you another Comforter, that he may abide with you forever. (Jn. 14:16)

DEAR Christian Friend, do you ever feel lonely, isolated, or even deserted? Do such feelings ever come on you when you are around relatives, friends, or coworkers when they are talking about ungodly matters? Do you ever feel that you are the only one standing for godliness?

Ponder a moment how people around you would react if you said to them on Monday morning, "What a thrilling time we had in the Word of God last evening!" No doubt those who heard would immediately remember that they needed to run an errand. One of the most serious problems today is that many Christians are afraid to stand alone. They do not want to feel "out of place"; they do not want to be isolated.

The best illustration of this difficulty appears when we contrast Adam and Christ. When we see Adam in the garden, we notice that he was lonely. Some years ago I heard one preacher put it this way, "Loneliness was the first shadow to cross the human path." Of course, loneliness was not sin; it was merely a *problem* for which God made a *provision*.

We then look thousands of years into the future and see that Jesus, too, was lonely. Practically everyone rejected Him. He hung alone on the cross, and even the Father turned away from Him because He became sin (Matt. 27:46). Why did Jesus suffer such loneliness, such isolation? *So we wouldn't have to.* Think of it! Our Savior suffered loneliness for us.

Our text, and its context, vividly demonstrate that God has made provision for our loneliness. Let us examine this provision in three ways.

First, consider this provision *practically*. The very first word we should notice here is the word **and**, for it connects verses 15 and 16. Verse 15 speaks of the *disciples'* love for Jesus; it declares that if the disciples really love the Lord, they will keep His commandments. Verse 16 then speaks of *Jesus'* love for the disciples. The evidence of His love was that when He departed He was going to send them "another Comforter." Up to this time Jesus had been their Comforter, but He is preparing to leave, so He assures them that His *departure* is not *desertion*. Verse 18 can literally be translated, "I will not leave you orphans" (*orphanos*, 3737). This thought looks back to John 13:33 where Jesus uses the term "little children." He assures His beloved disciples that He will not leave them shepherdless; He will not leave them forsaken, forgotten, and forlorn orphans. What a wondrous paradox! As we will see in more detail tomorrow, our Lord went into the *glory* of Heaven, but He is still not *gone* from the earth.

Scriptures for Study: What does God promise in the following verses: Deuteronomy 31:6, 8; Psalm 37:25, 28; Isaiah 41:10, 17?

APRIL 14

The Problem of Solitude (2)

And I will pray the Father, and he shall give you another Comforter, that he may abide with you forever. (Jn. 14:16)

CONTINUING our consideration of this provision *practically*, we discover the most blessed truth of all in the word **another**. The Greek here is not *heteros* (2087)—another of a different kind—rather *allos* (243), *another of similar or identical nature*. What a truth this is! Our Savior is saying in effect, "When I depart, I will send another in My place who is virtually identical to Me." There is, in fact, only a single difference between the Lord Jesus and the Holy Spirit: the Lord Jesus ministered from *without*, while the Holy Spirit ministers from *within*. The Lord Jesus even warned the disciples not to expect a visible person (v. 17), but assured them nonetheless that His "replacement" would minister as He always had. Indeed, while Jesus walked *beside* them, the Holy Spirit would dwell *within* them.

This truth is amplified when we notice that the entire Trinity is in view in verse 16: "I [the Son] will pray the Father [Jehovah God] and He will give you another Comforter [the Holy Spirit]." Think of it! All three persons of the Godhead are living in us!

Note also the word **forever**. Without doubt, the disciples were saddened that Jesus was departing, grief-stricken that His presence was only temporary. But He promised that His replacement would abide forever! Verse 23 elaborates: "Jesus answered and said unto him, If a man love me, he will keep my words: and my Father will love him, and we will come unto him, and make our abode with him." The Greek behind "abode" (*monē*, 3438) pictures a dwelling place and even a mansion (Jn. 14:2). The whole picture then is one of intimacy. The Holy Spirit (and therefore the entire Godhead) has come into us and is always in us. Those who reject the doctrine of the security of the believer will never in this life know the blessing of this truth.

This blessing becomes all the more precious and personal when we view it as an application of the Divine attribute of omnipresence, that is, that God is present everywhere and there is no place where He isn't present. Tragically, many Christian teachers avoid this truth, perhaps because they fear being charged with teaching pantheism. But the more time we spend with the Lord, the more we will realize that He is *here* and is *always* here. He's not floating around in the ether somewhere, but is right here within us. As David declared, "Whither shall I go from thy spirit? or whither shall I flee from thy presence?" (Ps. 139:7).

Oh, with this truth embedded in our hearts, how can we ever say we are lonely? But if we may we also ask: Are we making the most of the Spirit's abiding? Are we living perpetually in His influence and control?

Scriptures for Study: What do the following verses declare: Psalms 90:1; 91:1; 1 John 4:15–16?

APRIL 15

The Problem of Solitude (3)

And I will pray the Father, and he shall give you another Comforter, that he may abide with you forever. (Jn. 14:16)

HAVING considered this provision first *practically*, we secondly look at it *positionally*. This provision actually underscores one of the most neglected doctrines of the NT: *the sealing of the Holy Spirit*, which is spoken of three times in Scripture (Eph. 1:13; 4:30; 2 Cor. 1:22).[163]

The Greek verb (*sphragizō*) means "to set a seal, mark with a seal" and comes from a noun (*sphragis*) that refers to the signet ring that has a distinctive mark. The sealing work of the Spirit occurs at salvation. The literal translation of Ephesians 1:13 is, "Having believed [i.e. "when you believed"], ye were sealed." This sealing provides us with four pictures.

(1) Sealing pictures *acquisition*, that is, a finished transaction. The Ephesian believers understood this because Ephesus was a seaport and had a large lumber trade. A lumber merchant purchased his timber, stamped it with his seal, and left it in the harbor to be later claimed by his agent. Likewise, we have been "bought with a price" (1 Cor. 6:19–20), redeemed by the blood of Christ (Eph. 1:7), and the indwelling Holy Spirit is the seal of that finished transaction.

(2) Sealing pictures *absolute ownership*. The ancients would place their seal on animals and even on slaves to prove ownership. The branding of cattle and horses is still done today. A brand is registered with the particular state in which the owner lives and that brand shows legal ownership. The same is true of a patent or copyright. Along with the copyright symbol, date, and copyright holder, many books also include the words, "All Rights Reserved," meaning that only the copyright holder and the publisher are entitled to the benefits of the sale of that book. The Holy Spirit likewise proves we belong to Christ. "All rights are reserved" to Him; only He is entitled to the benefits of ownership (2 Tim. 2:19).

(3) Sealing pictures *authenticity*. A seal attests to the authenticity of a signature; likewise, a signature proves the genuineness of a letter. Spiritually, the indwelling Spirit proves that the believer is genuine.

(4) Sealing pictures *assurance*, that is, security. As Matthew 27:62–66 reports, the Roman seal was placed on Jesus' tomb. No one in that day would have dared break that seal, as that would have resulted in certain death; the seal protected the contents. A modern parallel is the "registered letter," which is recorded in a book and can be opened only by the addressee. The spiritual application is clear; we are sealed eternally in Christ by the Holy Spirit's indwelling. All three of the NT references to sealing are in the aorist tense, which indicates a past action. The seal has been placed and will not be "opened" until we go to heaven to be with Christ (Eph. 4:30).

Scriptures for Study: What other guarantee do we have besides sealing (2 Cor. 1:21–22)? 📖 What should we endeavor to do in light of this (Eph. 4:30)?

APRIL 16

The Problem of Solitude (4)

And I will pray the Father, and he shall give you another Comforter, that he may abide with you forever. (Jn. 14:16)

FINALLY, we contemplate this provision of the **Comforter** *progressively*. When we gaze back through the unfolding ages, we see an amazing progression. With each successive age, God has come a little closer to man.

At first, in the Garden of Eden, we do see a very special intimacy as God was *with* man. Genesis 3 tells us that in the gentle breeze of the evening, the Creator Himself would walk through the garden. This is not symbolism or anthropomorphism, but clearly implies an actual Christophany, that is, the Lord Jesus Himself in His preincarnate state as He regularly appeared in the garden for fellowship with these two who were actually one. Think of it! What anticipation it must have been! Throughout each busy day of tending the garden, *'Iysh* (Man) and *'Ishshah* (Woman) would look forward to the moment when Jesus would come walking through the garden with the express purpose of being with them. But, alas, sin destroyed that intimacy.

For the next many centuries the relationship was changed to God *to* man. God spoke to Noah, for example (Gen. 6:3; 7:1; 8:15; 9:8). He likewise spoke to many others: Cain (4:6, 9); Abram (13:14; 18:13); Rebekah (25:23); Jacob (Gen. 31:3; 46:2); Moses (Ex. 3:7; 4:2–27; etc.); and Aaron (9:8).

God then, in three phases, came a little closer during the time when the Mosaic Law was in force. Early on it was God *among* men in His sanctuary (Ex. 25:8), later it was God *through* man, as He worked through His prophets, and at the close it was God *as* man when Jesus arrived.

But now it is God *in* man. Meditate a moment on John 14:20: "At that day ye shall know that I am in my Father, and ye in me, and I in you." The words "at that day" can refer only to the Day of Pentecost when Christ's promise of sending the Spirit was fulfilled. The words "ye in me" declare that we are in Christ and in His body. And the words "I in you" proclaim the fact that He indwells us.

Oh, how dare we ever say we are lonely! How can we be lonely knowing that God lives within? Everyone else might forsake us; we might stand alone against the crowd; our beloved life-mate might go home to be with the Lord. But we are *never* alone. It is not sinful to feel the pangs of loneliness, but to wallow in that pain *is* sin because God has made the provision for it and we must not disregard it.

> Oh, gift of gifts! oh, grace of grace!
> That God should condescend
> To make my heart His dwelling place,
> And be my closest Friend.[164]

Scriptures for Study: What does Matthew 28:20 tell us about God's abiding? 📖 Read John 14:18–23. What observations can you make here?

April 17

The Problem of Shallowness (1)

But the Comforter, who is the Holy Spirit, whom the Father will send in my name, he shall teach you all things, and bring all things to your remembrance, whatever I have said unto you. (Jn. 14:26)

MORE than half a century ago, A. W. Tozer addressed most of the same issues that are diluting Christianity and undermining the Church today. "Evangelical Christianity," he wrote, "is now tragically below the New Testament standard. Worldliness is an accepted part of our way of life. Our religious mood is social instead of spiritual. We have lost the art of worship. . . . Our literature is shallow and our hymnody borders on sacrilege."[165] Shallowness is indeed a major problem in today's Church. We would submit two reasons for this.

First, a lack of knowledge. My Dear Christian Friend, have you ever said such things as, "I wish I could serve the Lord, but I lack the knowledge and education; I've never had Greek, much less Hebrew; sometimes I even have trouble with English; I've never been to seminary or had any theological courses; how can I possibly serve the Lord?"

Several years ago a fellow recounted to me the day a sheep farmer offered to show him just how dumb sheep are. They were in a barn with some sheep so the farmer put a staff across the doorway just high enough off the ground that the sheep would have to jump over it. The farmer then let a few sheep jump over the staff but then took the staff away only to watch the remaining sheep jump over a staff that wasn't there! While we certainly are not that bad, the Word of God likens us to sheep because we do tend toward ignorance and lack of discernment.

Second, and far worse, there is a lack of *desire* for knowledge. Many Christians seem to have no desire for any depth. There is a general attitude of "satisfaction." Many are content with the spiritual level they have attained, satisfied with the meager knowledge they have. Worse, much of the so-called knowledge put out today is shamefully shallow. The majority of the Christian books published today are totally experience oriented instead of doctrinal or expositional.

Added to all this is the amount of shallow preaching. Much of today's "preaching" is topical or issue oriented instead of a careful exposition and application of Scripture. This, of course, is the fault of pastors. During a pastor's breakfast back in the early 1980s, I was sharing some things about preaching and encouraged those present that the majority of a pastor's ministry time should be spent in the study of the Word so that he is adequately equipped to feed the sheep. After the meeting one pastor walked up and somewhat gruffly said to me, "I don't believe that the majority of my time must be spent studying." Is it any wonder that countless Christians, God's dear lambs, are starving to death?

Thankfully, God has made provision for our ignorance and shallowness here in our text. The Comforter came to alleviate our ignorance by teaching us the Truth.

Scriptures for Study: What observations can you make in 1 Corinthians 2:10–13?

APRIL 18

The Problem of Shallowness (2)

But the Comforter, who is the Holy Spirit, whom the Father will send in my name, he shall teach you all things, and bring all things to your remembrance, whatever I have said unto you. (Jn. 14:26)

LIKE the first provision, this one also provides us with three principles. *First*, there is the *need* for this provision. By itself head knowledge is of little value. While knowledge and education are certainly important, a string of degrees is empty without the Comforter's application. That is why the word **he** is the key word in our text. In the technical sense, no man really "teaches." A pastor can only *present* the truth of God's Word to His people; it is the Holy Spirit who does the teaching.

John 16:13 adds here: "Howbeit when he, the Spirit of truth, is come, he will guide you into all truth: for he shall not speak of himself; . . . and he will shew you things to come." The Apostle John was profoundly struck by this and adds his own thought in his first epistle: "But the anointing which ye have received of Him abideth in you, and ye need not that any man teach you; but as the same anointing teacheth you of all things, and is truth, and is no lie, and even as it hath taught you, ye shall abide in Him" (1 Jn. 2:27). These verses have been abused to teach that Christians don't need a pastor or regular attendance to a local church, that they can just read their Bibles and get all they need. But God calls certain men to be pastors so they can devote their time to study. Few Christians can spend large amounts of time in study, so that is what God calls pastors to do. God's people then, by being faithful in their attendance to the local church, benefit from the pastor's many hours of preparation. So, the Christian should *desire* preaching and teaching but must *depend* upon the Holy Spirit.

Second, we note the *nature* of this provision. What exactly will the Holy Spirit teach us? While He won't necessarily make us "Bible Dictionaries" or "apologetic encyclopedias," our text (with 16:13), reveals three things He will do.

(1) He will teach us **all things**. While this obviously doesn't mean He will make us omniscient, what it does mean is that the Holy Spirit will teach us all the things in God's Word that are needful for Spiritual living. And that is no small amount of knowledge! Think of it! While we can never learn it all, we ever strive to do just that.

A common excuse used today when one encounters a "problem text" is, "Oh well, that's one of the things we'll find out when we get to heaven." But God wants us to know and understand His Word now, even "the hard parts." Because of our finite minds, we might not *comprehend* a truth (such as the Trinity, the sovereignty of God, or even grace), but God still wants us to explore, to dig, to plunge ever deeper nonetheless. In this we honor Him and His Word.

Scriptures for Study: Read Ephesians 4:7–15. What observations can you make in this passage?

APRIL 19

The Problem of Shallowness (3)

But the Comforter, who is the Holy Spirit, whom the Father will send in my name, he shall teach you all things, and bring all things to your remembrance, whatever I have said unto you. (Jn. 14:26)

IN answer to our basic problem of shallowness, we see first the *need*, and second, the *nature* of God's provision. What will the Holy Spirit teach us? (1) He will teach us **all things**.

(2) He will **bring all things to [our] remembrance** concerning what Christ said. What an astounding promise! Consider two other verses here in John. "When, therefore, he was risen from the dead, his disciples remembered that he had said this unto them; and they believed the Scripture, and the word which Jesus had said" (2:22). Then, in reference to Jesus' entry into Jerusalem on a donkey, we read: "These things understood not his disciples at the first; but when Jesus was glorified, then remembered they that these things were written of him, and that they had done these things unto him" (12:16).

Think of it! The Holy Spirit brings to our mind, through the Scriptures, the things our Savior said and did. While many today are looking for new revelation from the Spirit, *that is not His function*. His occupation is bringing to our minds all that Christ said and did and to exalt Him alone (15:26).

(3) The Holy Spirit will show us "things to come" (16:13). Our Lord was speaking directly to His apostles and told them that the Spirit would make known to them the things concerning the Church Age, as well as all other prophetic truth that would take place after this age. For example, the Apostle John recorded the book of Revelation, which contains truth about the period *before* the Church Age (chapter 1, the vision of Christ), *during* this age (chapters 2–3, the letters to the seven churches in Asia), and then *after* this age (chapters 4–22, the Tribulation Period, Millennium, etc.). All this applies to Christians now because we possess the complete revelation of God—the Scriptures. God has given us everything we need in His Word alone. Those who seek "new revelation" are simply wrong.

Third, we see the *necessity* for understanding this provision. An understanding of God's Word is not automatic; it has a very specific prerequisite—*a spiritual mind*. "Which things also we speak, not in the words which man's wisdom teacheth, but which the Holy Spirit teacheth, comparing spiritual things with spiritual" (1 Cor. 2:13). That final phrase can *grammatically* be translated in several ways.[166] We would submit, however, that *contextually* it can be rendered: "interpreting [or explaining] spiritual things to spiritual men," since the context speaks both of men (masculine) and "things" (neuter). To grasp Holy Spirit teaching, to get the most from the Word of God, we must be spiritually minded (Apr. 3). God doesn't want us to stay in the shallows, rather to plunge into the deep.

Scriptures for Study: Read 1 Corinthians 2:1–16. What observations can you make in this passage?

APRIL 20

The Problem of Strength (1)

But when the Comforter is come, whom I will send unto you from the Father, even the Spirit of truth, who proceedeth from the Father, he shall testify of me; And ye also shall bear witness, because ye have been with me from the beginning. (Jn. 15:26–27)

"MY grace is sufficient for thee," our Lord assured Paul, "for my strength is made perfect in weakness" (2 Cor. 12:9). Dear Christian Friend, do you ever feel weak or powerless? Do you ever feel inconsistent in your daily walk or ineffective in Christian service? Do you ever lack the boldness to stand for Christ and be a witness of Him? This is, indeed, a common problem. But once again, God has made a provision for our problem.

First, the *source* of this provision. Ponder carefully: what makes Christianity powerful? The answer is not only foundational to our faith, but it is also fascinating history and helps to show us how we can have power for daily Christian living. This power is actually twofold.

(1) The literal, historical, bodily resurrection of Christ is the *foundation* of this power, without which we would still be lost in our sin (1 Cor. 15:12–19). While there are those who deny this historical reality, no one who does so is a true Christian. The resurrection is a distinctive mark of Christianity. There is something else, however, that is even more distinctive.

(2) The coming of the Holy Spirit at Pentecost is the *functioning* of this power. Like today, there were many religions in the ancient word. As someone has said, "Christianity did not grow up in a religious vacuum." Men were full of religious and philosophical ideas and concepts. In particular, there were the "mystery cults," such as Mithraism, the cult of Dionysius, and others. There were actually some parallels between those and Christianity (such as "baptism" and resurrection of their deity, although without any historical evidence, of course), so God used such things in His providence to prepare men's minds for the true Gospel. Many early Christians, in fact, came out of those cults.

So what, then, made Christianity unique? The one feature of the Christian faith that immediately and fundamentally differentiated it from all other faiths was the Christian doctrine of the Holy Spirit, that is, God indwelling the believer. Here was something that was up to this point *unprecedented*. Never had a "god" lived inside his worshipers. Here also was something truly *unique*, for nothing even remotely similar to this had ever happened before. Further still, here was something that was no less than *unimaginable*. Man could not even *conceive* of something like this. The religious man can think only of his god as an idol, but to have a god inside man was unimaginable, beyond the finite mind of man.

That is the power of Christianity. That is the power that raised Christ from the dead. That is the power Paul spoke of in Philippians 3:10 (Feb. 25–26).

Scriptures for Study: Read Acts 2:29–33. How does this relate to today's study?

April 21

The Problem of Strength (2)

But when the Comforter is come, whom I will send unto you from the Father, even the Spirit of truth, who proceedeth from the Father, he shall testify of me; And ye also shall bear witness, because ye have been with me from the beginning. (Jn. 15:26–27)

KNOWING the *source* of God's provision for our lack of strength points us to something else. *Second*, there is the *success* of this provision. We say success because we notice that the emphasis in our text is not what this power *will do* but what it *has done*.

Sadly, many today are *seeking* things that God has already given us. Can we overcome sin in our lives? Yes, because the Spirit gives us victory (Rom. 7–8). Can we manifest the character of Christ? Yes, because the Spirit gives us the capability (Gal. 5:22–25). Can we be used in service for Christ? Yes, because the Spirit bestows gifts that are used in service (Rom. 12:6–8).

But there is one thing the Holy Spirit has done that is specifically mentioned in our text: *He empowers us to be witnesses of Christ*. To prepare us for this principle, notice another first. Note carefully the words **he** and **ye**. It is crucial that we keep these words in order, that we never get the **ye** before the **he**. Many today get these reversed. All the glitz, glamour, gimmicks, and gadgets of modern "worship," and even evangelism, prove that we've gotten the **ye** before the **he**.

We can now more fully appreciate our Lord's words: **he will testify of me**. What was the main purpose of the Holy Spirit's coming to earth? *To proclaim and glorify Jesus Christ*. John 16:13–14 declare this: "Nevertheless, when He, the Spirit of truth, is come, He will guide you into all truth; for He shall not speak of Himself, but whatever He shall hear, that shall He speak; and He will show you things to come. He shall glorify Me; for He shall receive of Mine, and shall show it unto you." The Holy Spirit *never* glorifies Himself, nor is He ever to be glorified over the Lord Jesus. In blatant violation of this, however, the Holy Spirit *is* glorified at the expense of Christ alone in many circles today.

Now observe still further that not only is the Holy Spirit a witness of Christ (**he shall testify of me**), but He has also made *us* witnesses (**ye also shall bear witness**). **Witness** is the Greek *martureō* (3140); its original use was the legal sphere. A witness would give solemn testimony of what he knew and offer evidence. Likewise, the Christian is one who testifies of Christ and gives evidence through his or her life. So, it's not just that we witness for Christ with our *lips*, but rather what we also do so through our *life*. It's not so much that the Local Church evangelizes through "evangelistic programs and campaigns," but rather individual believers are the outreach. The Holy Spirit has given evidence of Christ, and **he** now gives us (**ye**) the power to give evidence of Christ in our lives.

Scriptures for Study: What do the following verses say about witnessing: Acts 4:20; 10:39–42; 18:5? 📖 What does 2 Timothy 1:7 promise?

APRIL 22

The Problem of Strength (3)

But when the Comforter is come, whom I will send unto you from the Father, even the Spirit of truth, who proceedeth from the Father, he shall testify of me; And ye also shall bear witness, because ye have been with me from the beginning. (Jn. 15:26–27)

"THERE is no such thing as an inactive church member," wrote Vance Havner. "If you are not gathering with Christ, you are scattering abroad, and either is activity. By not actively working with and for Him, you are working against Him."[167] In addition to our text, Acts 1:8 is a critical statement about evangelism: "But ye shall receive power, [when] the Holy Spirit is come upon you; and ye shall be witnesses unto me both in Jerusalem, and in all Judaea, and in Samaria, and unto the uttermost part of the earth."

While the Greek behind "witness" here is similar to that used in our text, there is a subtle difference. Our text uses the verb *martureō* (3140), which means **bear witness**, that is, we are citing evidence, reporting the events. Acts 1:8, however, uses the noun *martus* (3144, English *martyr*), which indicates that we ourselves *are* the evidence. That's what Vance Havner meant. We are either drawing people closer to Christ with our *godly* lives or driving them farther away by our *ungodly* lives. We are not only to *carry* the Gospel; we are to *illustrate* the Gospel.

Will such testimony be welcomed with open arms? Indeed not! We will not be popular when we stand for Christ. Jesus warned His disciples about this before He even uttered the words of our text (15:20–21). But we still will have the victory because the Holy Spirit has given us the power to overcome any obstacle. The word "power" in Acts 1:8 is *dunamis* (1411), which can be translated "that which overcomes resistance." Indeed, only the Holy Spirit can give this kind of power.

Third, the *supply* of this provision. While we know that the foundation of this is yieldedness (Mar. 10), how do we claim this power in practical, day-to-day living? *Prayer*. It is through "constant communion" with God in prayer (1 Thes. 5:17; cf. Lk. 18:1; Eph. 6:18) that we can be ensured of the power of the Spirit in our daily living.

Think a moment of Jesus' disciples. When Jesus was with them, oh, what power they had! But when He was gone, so was their power. We think of Peter's bravado when he was going to take on a group of professional soldiers with a sword (Jn. 18:10), but then see him shrink from the enquiries of a little girl in Jesus' absence (Lk. 22:56). But later, after the Holy Spirit came, we see Peter stand unflinchingly for Christ even before the Sanhedrin (Acts 4). Only by communing with the Lord, which itself is only possible through the indwelling Holy Spirit, can we claim the power He provides. Dear Christian, we are so very weak! But glory to God for His provision in the Comforter.

Scriptures for Study: What does John 15:20–21 warn us about being a witness for Christ?

APRIL 23

The Problem of Society (1)

... the Comforter ... will reprove the world of sin, and of righteousness, and of judgment ... (Jn. 16:7–11)

WHAT are the underlying problems of society today? We refer not to things such as world hunger, crime, political unrest, and the like. We refer rather to the *real* problems, of which the former ones are only symptoms. The real issues are *philosophical*, that is, problems that are *in* us.

One problem, of course, is rampant materialism, coupled with hedonism. To many, money and pleasure are their gods. Life is all about material gain and gratification. "Eat drink, and be merry," is their motto, but our Lord responded to that very idea with: "Thou fool, this night thy soul shall be required of thee: then whose shall those things be, which thou hast provided? So is he that layeth up treasure for himself, and is not rich toward God" (Lk. 12:19–21). Tragically, even many Christians have been lured into wrong attitudes concerning money and merriment.

Another major problem is the relativism of our postmodern world. Since rationalism leaves man stiff and machine-like and really doesn't seem to be able to fix society's problems, it is insisted that each person should believe whatever he or she wants to believe. Everything is relative, even truth, *especially* religious truth. What might be true for *you* might not be true for *me*. But Scripture, of course, is replete with statements about Truth and absolutes. The Greek *alētheia* (225, "the real state of affairs, the way things really are") appears no less than 187 times in the NT (e.g., Jn 1:14; 14:6; 16:13; 17:17, 19; etc.). Romans 1:18 and 25, in fact, declare what ungodly people do with the Truth: they *suppress* it and *change* it.

So how can Christians, in their witnessing for Christ, possibly break through these and other philosophies? Some think you have to meet such people "on their own ground" and so debate atheists and evolutionists, for example, in various open forums. But does that not simply "cast pearls before swine" (Matt. 7:6) and make Christianity just another "debatable philosophy"? Paul, in fact, refused to do that very thing in Corinth. Instead of *debating* the Greek philosophers, he simply *delivered* God's Truth (1 Cor. 2:1–5). There are also Christian leaders who preach "moral reform" to a world that doesn't want to be reformed. Man's actions will not change until his heart changes, and his heart will change only when he receives Christ as Savior and Lord.

So then, how do we break through this world? How do we reach people with the Gospel? The answer is simple: *we* don't break through this world at all! We don't reach anyone for Christ. The Holy Spirit does all this. As our text asserts, the Holy Spirit "will reprove [i.e., convict or convince] the world of sin, and of righteousness, and of judgment." As we will see, God uses us to *declare* the *Savior*, but it is the Holy Spirit who *delivers* from *sin*.

Scriptures for Study: Read 1 Corinthians 2:1–5. What observations can you make about Paul's "method" of evangelism?

APRIL 24

The Problem of Society (2)

... the Comforter ... will reprove the world of sin, and of righteousness, and of judgment ... (Jn. 16:7–11)

THIS world is steeped in godless ideas, submitted to the implications of them, and submerged in their consequences. It is not our efforts that will reach this world, rather it the Holy Spirit who will do so. Our text provides us further assurance.

First, the provision is *announced* with the words: **the Comforter ... will reprove the world**. This is an extremely powerful statement. **Reprove** is *elegchō* (1651) and is sometimes translated "convict" (Jn. 8:9) or "convince" (Titus 1:9; Jas. 2:9). The word means more than that, however. Another way to translate it would be "expose," for it paints the picture of ripping away any façade, mask, or pretense and revealing exactly what is underneath. As one Greek authority well explains, it means "to rebuke another, with such effectual wielding of the victorious arms of the truth, as to bring him, if not always to a confession, yet at least to a conviction, of his sin."[168] In his commentary on Ephesians, John Calvin adds, "It literally signifies to drag forth to the light what was formerly unknown."[169] What a picture! The Holy Spirit drags the sinner's sin kicking and screaming into the light to expose it for what it is.

To illustrate, a person might be "under conviction"; he might be angered, fearful, or even sorry, but might still not be truly convinced of his sin, fully persuaded he is a sinner. But he is nonetheless condemned by the Holy Spirit's exposing power. So, the work of the Holy Spirit is that of exposing and condemning the world for what it is. He rips away all pretenses and exposes every false philosophy.

Second, this provision is *amplified* by three specific words, which detail exactly what the Holy Spirit does. He first exposes the world's **sin**. The Greek here (*hamartia*, 266; Mar. 3) comes from a verb (*hamartanō*, 264) that means "to miss the mark." Used literally, it referred to a spearman who missed his intended target and so figuratively describes one's failure to measure up to an absolute standard. The sinner, indeed, fails to measure up to God's standard of holiness and refuses to **believe on [Christ]**. In light of that sin, the Holy Spirit then exposes the world's need of **righteousness**, which can only be found in Christ. Man has no righteousness (Is. 64:6; Rom. 3:10–12, 23; Eph. 2:1–3), so "the righteousness of God is by faith of Jesus Christ unto all them that believe" (Rom. 3:22). Finally, the Holy Spirit warns the world that it is under **judgment** if it rejects Christ's righteousness. That judgment is not just future (Rev. 20:11–15; 21:8) but is also now, for "he that believeth not is condemned already" (Jn. 3:18). How thrilling this is! It is the Holy Spirit (not us) who breaks through the attitudes of this world.

Scriptures for Study: Read John 3:18–21. What do these verses contribute to today's study?

APRIL 25

The Problem of Society (3)

... the Comforter ... will reprove the world of sin, and of righteousness, and of judgment: Of sin, because they believe not on me; Of righteousness, because I go to my Father, and ye see me no more; Of judgment, because the prince of this world is judged.
(Jn. 16:7–11)

OUR text provides us with a priceless provision for dealing with society. With the provision *announced* (**reprove the world**) and then *amplified* (**of sin, righteousness, and judgment**), we can now see one other principle.

Third, the provision *applied*. To help us see the application, ponder a moment how the Church began: Jesus went *up*, the Spirit came *down*, and the Spirit-filled witnesses went *out*. Those early Christians depended only upon the Holy Spirit. This is thrilling when we consider that those early Christians went out against *incredible resistance*.

First, they went out against the power and domination of Rome. From Rome, the Empire stretched as far west as modern day Spain, as far east as Turkey and the Holy Land, as far north as Bulgaria, Yugoslavia, and Germany, and as far south as North Africa. But Christianity aided in the final fall of that vast military empire. Second, those early Christians went out against the philosophy of the Greeks with its humanistic foundation but won many people out of pagan religion and philosophy. Third, those early Christians went out against the religious bigotry of the Old Covenant Jew. This was, without doubt, the worst obstacle, in fact. It was the "religious crowd" that crucified Christ and persecuted the Apostles. But the Holy Spirit overcame it all!

So how did the early Christians do what they did? What brought the great success they experienced? Was it because of oratory, clever sermons, emotional stories, debating, special programs, celebrities, contests, entertainment, or gimmicks? No. Success came only by Holy Spirit power. We are reminded again of Acts 1:8 (Apr. 22; Sept. 26–27), where Jesus promised that His disciples would "receive power [to] be witnesses" to the world. Recall the Greek behind "power," *dunamis* (1411), "that which overcomes resistance." Just as those early Christians overcame incredible resistance, so shall we. All the Holy Spirit demanded of them, and all He demands of us, is that we be witnesses and preach Jesus Christ.

Ah, but does that mean that everyone will believe? Indeed, not! As Paul made clear, preaching appears foolish to Gentiles (because they want philosophy and debate) and stumbles the Jews (because they want miraculous signs, which sadly has crossed over nowadays to undiscerning Gentiles). But preaching is neither one of those. It is merely the announcing of what God says in His Word and allowing the Holy Spirit to do His work (1 Cor. 3:5–8).

Scriptures for Study: In his parting words, what did Paul tell Timothy to do? What reason did Paul give for doing this (2 Tim. 4:1–4)?

APRIL 26

The Problem of Sin (1)

. . . we have an Advocate with the Father . . . (1 Jn. 2:1; cf. Rom. 6)

WE have arrived at one final major problem we face in the Christian life, one that threatens to defeat us at every turn. But once again, we have a provision in the *Paraklētos*. We will address all this beginning on April 29, but it is critical that we first understand the doctrinal foundation of *sanctification*. While most Bible teachers agree that sin is still a problem in the believer's life, there have been various deliberations and debates concerning the nature of the problem. Such issues vanish, however, when we simply understand the language.

First, in Romans 6, we *realize* our *position*. Many experience defeat in their Christian life simply because of a complete misunderstanding of this crucial chapter, especially the key verse: "Knowing this, that our old man is crucified with him, that the body of sin might be destroyed, that henceforth we should not serve sin" (v. 6). Many view this verse—and sadly many Bible teachers teach it—as something experiential, that is, something we do. It is insisted that while our "old nature" (which non-biblical and inaccurate term) cannot be eradicated, "it can be suppressed by an inward joint-crucifixion with Christ in our own experience."

That view, however, is the exact opposite of what the text says. Succinctly, Romans 6 declares that God has declared us dead to sin by His judicial act through Christ's death. This principle cannot be over-emphasized. All this is *judicial*, not *experiential*. We do none of it, for God has done all of it. This is demonstrated beyond any doubt by the verb tenses in 5:12—7:6; every Greek verb that speaks of Christ's death and our association with it is in either the aorist or perfect tense, both of which indicate *past* and *completed* action. There are, in fact, no less than 14 verses in this passage that demonstrate this (e.g., 6:2, 4).

In verse 6, then, Paul unambiguously states that sin was *positionally* "destroyed" (the past tense of *katargeō*, 2673, "to render inactive, put out of use, cancel, bring to nothing, do away with"[170]) by Christ. As J. Sidlow Baxter masterfully summarizes, here is the *positional* meaning of Romans 6:6 according to the language of the text: "'Our Old Man' (all that we were in position and relation to Adam, with all our culpability and condemnation) 'was crucified with him' (was judged and executed in the once-for-all death of Christ), 'that the body of sin' (the whole Adam humanity as guilty before God) 'might be destroyed' (completely done away in the judicial reckoning of God), 'that we should no longer be in bondage to sin' (that is, no longer in *legal* bondage through *judicial* guilt)."[171]

So, because of Christ, we are no longer under the penalty of sin because He paid the price. Neither does sin have power or dominion over us because Christ has freed us from the bondage of sin (Rom. 6:7). No longer are we shackled by sin; no longer do we *have* to sin. We can, indeed, live above sin and have victory.

Scriptures for Study: What do Romans 6:22 and Galatians 2:20 add to today's study?

APRIL 27

The Problem of Sin (2)

... we have an Advocate with the Father ... (1 Jn. 2:1; cf. Rom. 7)

YESTERDAY we learned that in Romans 6 we must *realize* our *position* in Christ. There we discovered that sin no longer has dominion over us; it no longer enslaves us. In short, we do not *have* to sin.

Second, in Romans 7, we *reflect* on the *problem*. If Romans 6 is true, then why do we still sin? Knowing this question would arise in the minds of his readers, Paul immediately addresses the reason. We can summarize this chapter thusly: the believer still possesses "the flesh," which is still a part of our humanity.

The term "flesh" has also been greatly misunderstood. Paul, in fact, uses the Greek *sarx* (4561) 89 times in his epistles (excluding five occurrences in Hebrews for those who question its Pauline authorship): 37 of these refer to the actual physical body, 25 refer to humanity (or that which is human), and 27 refer to the inherent evil within the human nature.

It is in 7:5, in fact, that we see that third meaning of flesh: "For when we were [Greek imperfect tense, 'were and continue to be'] in the flesh, the motions of sins, which were by the law, did work in our members to bring forth fruit unto death." "Motions" is an Old English term for "impulses," which is the idea in the Greek *pathēma* (3804, from *pathos*, 3806, English, "pathology"), and "describes the emotions of the soul, i.e., human feelings, and impulses which a man does not produce within himself but finds already present, and by which he can be carried away."[172]

So, what is our greatest problem? Well, it's not the devil, as much as we would like to blame him for it all. Neither is it the world, our boss, our spouse, our environment, or anything else external. The problem is *self*, that inherent evil in human nature, our selfish propensities and drives, those urges to gratify our selfishness, self-sensitiveness, self-assertiveness, self-centeredness, self-motivation, and everything else of *self*. While the concept of "self-esteem" has burrowed deep into our culture (and the Church), it is the real problem. As Martin Luther reportedly said, "I dread my own heart more than the pope and all his cardinals, for within me is the greater pope, even self."[173] This self is not some separate entity, some separate nature, which can be "cut out" by some "spiritual surgery." This is the "wretched man" Paul so graphically describes in 7:15–24. After explaining "the body of this death" (i.e. inherent evil) and the struggle with the "sin that dwelleth in me," he concludes with the question we all have asked, "Who shall deliver me?"

Oh, how thankful we are that Paul did not stop there! How discouraged and hopeless we would be! As we will study tomorrow, he went on to answer his own question in verse 25, *and* in all of chapter 8, by demonstrating that God has not only delivered us once-for-all *judicially* from *sin* but continues delivering us *experientially* from *self*.

Scriptures for Study: Read Romans 7:15–25. What observations strike you the most profoundly?

APRIL 28

The Problem of Sin (3)

... we have an Advocate with the Father ... (1 Jn. 2:1; cf. Rom. 8)

ONCE we *realize* our *position* in Christ (Rom. 6) and then *reflect* on the *problem* of the flesh (Rom. 7), there is but one more step, and this is the great encouragement.

Third, in Romans 8, we *rejoice* in the *provision*. In 7:25, Paul summarizes chapter 7 and introduces chapter 8: "I thank God through Jesus Christ our Lord. So then with the mind I myself serve the law of God; but with the flesh the law of sin." It is absolutely crucial to note that Paul does not say we have "two natures," since the term "nature" immediately implies something inbred that we can't control. Rather, we have two "states of mind," the *spirit* and the *flesh*. We are now "partakers of the *divine* nature, having escaped the corruption that is in the world through lust" (2 Pet. 1:4; emphasis added). That nature is present because the Holy Spirit regenerated our dead spirit, now making it alive and empowering it by His continuous indwelling. But at the same time, while our "spirit indeed is willing ... the flesh is weak" (Matt. 26:41). Our flesh is still unredeemed.

That is why Paul penned chapter 8! It is here that he assures us we can have victory over the flesh by the indwelling Holy Spirit. In fact, "the flesh" is never mentioned in chapter 8 without the Holy Spirit also being mentioned (vv. 1, 3–4, 5, 8–9, 12–13). Note also in verses 3–9 we again see two states of mind: "the mind of the flesh" or "the mind of the Spirit." We either desire earthly things or we desire spiritual things. God's desire, of course, is that we have the "mind of the Spirit"; that is, our minds must be continually *renewed*. Romans 12:2 declares that we must be "transformed by the renewing of the mind," and Ephesians 4:23 commands us to "be renewed in the spirit of your mind."

So, in daily practice, how do we get victory over the flesh? The answer is this, and is something we would do well to memorize: *Victory over the flesh comes, not by struggling to subdue it, but by allowing the Holy Spirit to infill, renew, and transform the mind.* It's not *will* power that gives victory, rather it is *Spirit* power.

I would encourage you, dear Christian Friend, with something else I heard many years ago and have never forgotten: *We do not have the inability to sin, but we do have the ability not to sin.* Did you get it? Have we reached sinless perfection? Have we reached the point where we no longer sin? Certainly not. But we still have the ability not to sin; we can still have victory over sin by the power of the Holy Spirit. No longer can we say, "I just couldn't help it. It's just part of my nature. It's just who I am." Yes, we *can* "help it" because of the Holy Spirit. The fact is that it is *not* part of our nature (Rom. 6; 2 Pet. 1:4). Yes, the flesh is still present (Rom. 7), but the Holy Spirit gives us power over even that. No, we are not *sinless*, but we do sin *less*.[174]

Ah, but what happens when we *do* sin? That is our study tomorrow.

Scriptures for Study: Read 1 Corinthians 10:13. Of what does this assure us?

APRIL 29

The Problem of Sin (4)

My little children, these things write I unto you, that ye sin not . . . (1 Jn. 2:1)

WITH Paul's teaching firmly imbedded in our hearts, we are prepared to see that John's teaching is the same, only worded differently. John's letters are extremely affectionate. Here in our text he uses the expression **little children**, which he uses seven times in this first epistle (2:1, 12, 28; 3:7, 18; 4:4; 5:21). Undoubtedly, he captured this word from our Lord (Jn. 13:33) and uses this personal tone because with fatherly concern he is preparing to exhort these Christians about sin in the believer's life.

Let us first consider 1:8–10. John saw two ways his words could be perverted. Based on verses 8 and 10, he saw that someone could twist the meaning and say, "If we can never be done with sin, why strive for holiness?" We have the same thought today among those who say, "The 'old nature' forces me to sin; I can't help it, so why try?" Additionally, John saw that someone could then twist verse 9 to say, "If forgiveness is so easy, why dread falling into sin?" We hear this very thought today from those who reject the security of the believer; they insist that such so-called security gives people a "license to sin."

Therefore, in 2:1 John says, in effect, "No, I am not writing these things either to discourage you about holy living or to condone sinning, but rather to encourage you not to sin." But what does that mean? The answer is in the words **if any man sin**. The tense of the Greek verb here is aorist subjunctive and so refers to a *single act* of sin, not *habitual* sin. Literally, the phrase reads, "If any man commits an act of sin." John emphasizes that sin in the believer's life *cannot* be habitual. He stresses that fact in 3:6, which uses the present tense to literally say, "Whosoever abideth in [Christ] does not habitually commit sin."

Further, an expanded rendering of 3:9 is: "Whosoever is born of God does not habitually commit sin; for his [God's] seed remains in him: and he cannot habitually commit sin, because he is born of God." "His seed" refers to the Divine life that has been placed in the believer (cf. 2 Pet. 1:4). This life makes it impossible for us to live in habitual sin and transforms us in such a way that we hate sin (as God does) and love holiness. No longer will we live in lying, stealing, corrupt speech, immorality, and the like because we have the Divine seed within us. In other words, sin is no longer the rule, rather it is the exception that proves the rule.

So, there will be times when we commit *acts* of sin, times when we allow the flesh to rule. There will be times when there will arise a wrong thought, attitude, value, goal, action, or word. *It is for those times that God has made provision!* Our text says that when we commit an *act* of sin, we have an "Advocate with the Father, Jesus Christ the Righteous."

Scriptures for Study: What do the following verses say about sin in your life: Romans 6:1–2; Titus 2:11–13; 1Peter 4:1–3?

APRIL 30

The Problem of Sin (5)

My little children, these things write I unto you, that ye sin not. And if any man sin, we have an Advocate with the Father, Jesus Christ the righteous. (1 Jn. 2:1)

JOHN'S wonderful assurance concerning the acts of sin that occur in the believer's life is that **we have an Advocate**. This glorious word **Advocate**, which we submit is the best translation here, is the final use of *paraklētos* in the NT. The picture here is that the Lord **Jesus Christ** is our "Defense Attorney" who pleads our case before the Judge. The fascinating thing here, however, is that unlike an earthly defense attorney who pleads our *innocence*, the Lord Jesus admits our *guilt*. But in His defense of us, He presents His death and resurrection as the grounds for our acquittal. *Hallelujah!*

Notice also the adjective that is used to modify **Advocate**. The Advocate, that is, the Lord Jesus, is not called "The Resurrected," or "The Ascended," or "The Glorified," or any other of His great names. Rather, He is called **the righteous**. This adjective is the exact one needed here. Why? Because only "The Righteous One" could be our **Advocate**; we are clothed in His intrinsic righteousness.

Let us never forget that we do, indeed, have a problem with our own sin. But God has already given us the victory; all we must do is claim it. We have been saved from sin's power and penalty by judicial act of God through Christ. And even though the flesh (inherent sin) remains, God gives the victory over this as well through the infilling of the Holy Spirit. My Dear Christian Friend, it is up to you whether or not you sin. Let us again remember: *We do not have the inability to sin, but we do have the ability not to sin.*

Oh, what wonder there is in the *paraklētos!* The Holy Spirit (our Comforter) is the *Earthly* Paraclete, and the Lord Jesus (our Advocate) is the *Heavenly* Paraclete. We say again, *Hallelujah*!

📖 📖 📖

This brings us to the close of the first part of these daily meditations:

> Knowing the Father's sovereign power
>   Is as sweet as knowing His love each hour.
> Knowing the Son and each wonderful name
>   Brings us the joy of His Kingdom and fame.
> Knowing the Holy Spirit's provisions
>   Gives victory in thinking and actions.
> More precious than gold or shining sapphire,
>   Knowing God is our greatest desire.

Scriptures for Study: Meditate today on Ephesians 1:3–14.

PART II
Loving Our Lord

May
June
July
August

Loving My Lord

Oh, Lord, flowing from my need to know You,
Is the deeper desire to love You more.
Not just a love of feelings to renew,
But a love that in all ways does adore.
I love you, Lord, with my heart, soul, and might,
With my intellect, emotion, and will;
It is through your Word I receive insight
Into how that love can greater instill.
Your question to Peter, "Do you love Me?"
Ever serves me as an encouragement
To ask myself the same regularly
And then answer with honest discernment.
    Lord, I desire to love you more each day
    As I walk with You always in the way.

MAY 1

Love the LORD thy God (1)

And thou shalt love the LORD thy God . . . (Deut. 6:5; Mk. 12:30)

WHILE *knowing* God is one thing, *loving* Him is quite another. But the reassuring truth is that the latter inevitably flows from the former. When we *really* know God, our love for Him is automatic. In this second part of our daily meditations, then, we turn to this deeper and even more intimate understanding. (Please pause for a word of prayer before you read on.)

First, what is the *meaning* of love? Mankind has wrestled with that question throughout time, although most answers fall abysmally short. A few years ago, for example, a Jewish author recounted speaking to a group of high school students about the Jewish idea of love. "Someone define love," she challenged. No response. She urged them again and got the same result. "Tell you what," she said, "I'll define it, and you raise your hands if you agree. Okay?" There were nods all around. "Love is that feeling you get when you meet the right person." At this every hand went up, to which the author, in characteristic Jewish fashion, thought to herself, "Oy!"[175]

That is, indeed, typical, as the author went on to explain. Most people view love as a sensation, a magical feeling based upon physical and/or emotional attraction that overtakes us when "the right person" comes along. One problem, of course (among others), is that the "magic" can go away, resulting in "falling *out* of love" as quickly as "falling *in*."

That, and many other notions about love (such as that author's dreadful alternative, in fact), are foreign to Scripture. The Greek word most often rendered **love** is *agapē* (26; Feb. 21), which while originally carrying an element of sympathy and even a love that was not self-seeking, was transformed by our Lord to mean being *totally sacrificial*. It can be defined, then, as "a self-emptying, self-sacrifice." Another Greek word used for **love** is *philos* (5384), which speaks of esteem, high regard, and tender affection and is more emotional. As we will see (beginning May 5), Peter and our Lord both used this word (along with *agapē*) in John 21:15–17.

The word used in our Hebrew text, then, is *'āhab̲* (157H), which is actually more similar to *philos* than *agapē*; it is a general word that speaks of desire, affection, or inclination, "a strong emotional attachment to and desire either to possess or to be in the presence of the object."[176] Much like the word "faith," therefore, the real crux of love in the Hebrew lies in its *object*, whether negative (such as lust, 2 Sam. 13:1) or positive (true affection, 1 Sam. 1:5).

So, is our love for God willful and sacrificial, or is it affectionate and emotional? *Yes!* It is two sides of the same coin. It is a love of both *will* and *want*, a love of both *pain* and *passion*, a love of both *sacrifice* and *satisfaction*.

Scriptures for Study: Read the following verses, noting what God requires in each: Deuteronomy 10:12; 11:13; 30:6; and 1 John 5:3.

May 2

Love the LORD thy God (2)

And thou shalt love the LORD thy God with all thine heart, and with all thy soul, and with all thy might. (Deut. 6:5)
... all thy mind, and with all thy strength. (Mk. 12:30)

FROM the outset of his restatement of the Law, Moses made clear to the people that the Law was not to be obeyed mechanically but rather observed out of heartfelt love and affection for God. First, then, the *meaning* of love.

Second, the *magnitude* of love. How much are we to love God? Our OT text says we first love Him with our **heart** (*lēbāb*, 3824H), which refers not only to the physical organ but also figuratively to the entire inner person and personality. We also love him with our **soul** (*nepeš*, 5315H), which literally refers to breathing and figuratively to the inner being with its thoughts and emotions. Added to that is loving Him with our **might** (*me'ōd*, 3966H), that is, our power, will, and abundance. All those are then intensified with the word **all** (*kōl*, 3605H), which refers to the whole of something, every part of it. So, we do not love God half-heartedly, but with undivided attention and unfailing allegiance.

When we then turn to our NT text—which is, of course, Jesus' quotation of our OT text—we plunge even deeper. First, we again love God with our **heart**, but this time the Greek (*kardia*, 2588) is an enormously significant word that figuratively refers here to loving God with our feelings, thoughts, and decisions. Second, we love God with our **soul** (*psuchē*, 5590), that is, with our very life. Third, we love God with our **mind** (*dianoia*, 1271), which speaks of our thoughts, understanding, and intellectual faculty. Fourth, we love God with our **strength** (*ischus*, 2479), which also refers to ability (especially physical) And, like the OT text, we see the **all** (*holos*, 3650) modifier, signifying the undivided whole of each of these.

So, what is the magnitude of our love for God? We would submit this: *Love for God is a willful, sacrificial affection that encompasses our entire being—intellect, emotion, and will—and completely dominates every part of our lives with our undivided attention, unfailing allegiance, and unreserved ability.*

If we may borrow from Charles Spurgeon: "In those grand old ages [of the early Christians] . . . the love which they felt towards the Lord was not a quiet emotion which they hid within themselves in the secret chamber of their souls . . . but it was a passion with them of such a vehement and all-consuming energy, that it was visible in all their actions, spoke in their common talk, and looked out of their eyes even in their commonest glances. Love to Jesus was a flame which fed upon the core and heart of their being; and, therefore, from its own force burned its way into the outer man, and shone there."[177]

Oh, that we would be thus!

Scriptures for Study: How does Deuteronomy 4:29 complement today's study? 📖 What does John 14:21 add?

MAY 3

Love the LORD thy God (3)

Thou shalt love the LORD thy God. . . . And these words, which I command thee this day, shall be in thine heart: And thou shalt teach them diligently unto thy children . . . (Deut. 6:5–7)

LOVE is not just an *attitude*, but also an *action*. It involves not only *profession*, but also *proof*. Our text, therefore, includes not only the *meaning* and *magnitude* of our love for God, but one more principle as well.

Third, the *mandate* of our love. We see here two critical directives that flow from a true love for God:

(1) We constantly remind ourselves of these truths. God again emphasizes that His **words . . . shall be in [our] heart**. As before, the Hebrew behind **heart** (*lēbāb*, 3824H) refers figuratively to the entire inner person and personality. How short memory can be sometimes! We are reminded of Shakespeare's words concerning King Hamlet's death, "The memory be green,"[178] that is, the memory is still recent, still fresh. We do, indeed, need to keep our memory green, to prevent these things from turning brown and withering away with age.

(2) We continually **teach** these truths **diligently unto [our] children**. In a way, it is sad that parents drifted away from catechizing their children. This was standard, for example, among the Puritans. Matthew Henry wrote that not only would reading Scripture and "other good books contribute very much to family instruction" but also added: "You must also catechize your children and household. Let them learn some good catechism by heart, and keep it in remembrance; and by familiar discourse with them help them to understand it, as they become capable. It is an excellent method of catechizing, which God himself directs us to do (Deut. 6:7)."[179] As verse 7 goes on to say, teaching continues throughout the day.

Whichever method we use, however, it's critical that we **teach** our children the Truth, "for the church in the house is the nursery in which the trees of righteousness are reared," Henry went on to encourage. **Thou shalt teach them diligently** translates a single word in the Hebrew (*shānan*, 8150H), "to sharpen or whet," which literally refers to sharpening swords and arrows (Deut. 32:41; Isa. 5:28) and so figuratively pictures either whetting or sharpening the words themselves as we apply them or using the words to sharpen our children, either of which is adequate. Just as words are chiseled into a stone tablet, so must God's Word be carved into the very hearts of our children. The world (and its education system), the flesh, and the Devil will do all they can to fashion our children into the image of false gods, so we must be all the more diligent in shaping them into the image of Christ.

It is also worthy of note that verses 4–9 are known as the *Shema* ("hear"), which was recited twice daily (morning and evening) as a creed by devout Jews. We would do well to imitate that with a passage such as Matthew 22:37–40.

Scriptures for Study: What do the following verses say about teaching our children: Deuteronomy 4:9; Psalm 78:4–6; Ephesians 6:4?

MAY 4

Failing Love

Peter remembered the word of Jesus, which said unto him, Before the cock crow, thou shalt deny me thrice. (Matt. 26:75)

BEFORE beginning tomorrow's thoughts on Peter's recommission to service after his denial of his Lord, it is important to consider why he failed in the first place. We, of course, recall the story of Jesus' predicting that Peter would deny Him three times (Matt. 26:31–75), but ponder why Peter's love failed.

First, he failed because of his *independence*. Knowing their fear would overwhelm them, Jesus said to His disciples, "All ye shall be offended because of me this night: for it is written [Zech. 13:7], I will smite the shepherd, and the sheep of the flock shall be scattered abroad" (v. 31). But Peter, in his independent self-sufficiency, proudly announced: "Though all men shall be offended because of thee, yet will I never be offended" (v. 33). After Jesus assured Peter of his coming denial, he compounded his autonomous attitude: "Though I should die with thee, yet will I not deny thee" (v. 35). Oh, how true it is that "pride goeth before destruction, and an haughty spirit before a fall" (Prov. 16:18)! Only true love for the Lord is the sure cure for pride.

Second, Peter failed because of his *inattentiveness*. Even after imploring His disciples to sit with Him and support Him during His agony in the Garden of Gethsemane, they were so inattentive and indifferent that they fell asleep (vv. 36–40). "Could ye not watch with me one hour?" He asked. "Watch" translates *grēgoreuō* (1127), which literally means "to watch, to refrain from sleep" but eventually took on the metaphorical and religious sense of attention, watchfulness, and vigilance. Such is the attitude of believers who truly love the Lord. They will be ever vigilant in standing for Christ.

Third, Peter failed because of his *impulsiveness*. When the soldiers came to arrest Jesus, it was Peter who "drew his sword, and struck a servant of the high priest's [Malchus], and smote off his ear" (v. 51, cf. Jn. 18:10). Such an impulsive act, however, was, as one commentator observes, unprofitable, unnecessary, and unenlightened.[180] Indeed, love is long-suffering and "not easily provoked" (1 Cor. 13:4–5).

Fourth, Peter failed because of his *insecurity*. Finally, after "the disciples forsook [Jesus], and fled" (v. 56), we at least see Peter "[following] him afar off" (v. 58), but still his love was too weak to stand with his Lord till the end. And it was that very insecurity that led ultimately to his outright denial of even knowing Jesus. "There is no fear in love," the Apostle John reminds us, for "perfect love casteth out fear" (1 Jn. 4:18).

So, as one expositor well puts it, Peter failed because he "boasted too much, prayed too little, acted too fast, and followed too far."[181] O, let us not fail likewise!

Scriptures for Study: Read the following verses, noting the use of "watch" (*grēgoreuō*): Matthew 24:42; 1 Corinthians 16:13; 1 Peter 5:8.

MAY 5

Do You Love Me? (1)

. . . lovest thou me? (Jn. 21:15–17)

ONE of the most heartwarming, humbling, and hopeful scenes in all of Scripture is that of our Lord's three-fold recommissioning of Peter after his threefold denial of his Lord (Jn. 18:15–17, 25–27). This is also among the surest tests of our own love for Him.

First, we see the *confrontation* with the *Savior*. I never read this passage without thinking of what Peter must have been going through. For three years he followed Jesus so closely that we rarely see Jesus without Peter tagging along. He dearly loved his Lord and was His "little shadow." But then Peter actually denied knowing his Lord, even to the point of calling down a whole host of curses upon himself if he was lying (Matt. 26:74). So, where do we find Peter after the resurrection? Back where Jesus originally found him, back in his old life. His momentary failure had led to his miserable defeat. Again paralleling Peter's threefold denial, we here see Jesus question Peter three times, Peter then replying three times, and finally our Lord recommissioning him three times.

(1) The first exchange (v. 15). Having dined on fish and bread with Peter and six other apostles, Jesus turned to Peter and asked, **Simon, son of Jonas, lovest thou me more than these?** That simple question is striking, again because of a threefold significance. First, it is noteworthy because our Lord used the name **Simon**, which was Peter's given name and a common one of the day. The name "Peter" was actually a nickname. It transliterates *Petros* (4074, Aramaic *Cephas*), which means "a piece of rock, a throwable stone." It appears that the name change was to remind Peter what he *should* be instead of the impatient, impetuous, and at times even impertinent fellow he was. In fact, each time he started acting like his old self, we see Jesus and the Gospel writers using the name Simon. It is also a wonderful truth that the incident here is the last time Jesus ever used the name Simon. Think of it! As a result of this meeting, that name was never needed again. We, too, have a new name, *Christian*, and we must live up to it.

That leads to a second striking feature, namely, what Jesus did *not* say to Simon. Even though a rebuke was certainly justified, it did not come. Our Lord did not even mention the denial or if Peter was sorry for what he had done. This in turn leads to the third feature, Jesus' question, which was, in effect: "do you love Me more than these other men?"[182] Jesus, of course, uses *agapaō* (25), a willful love, a self-emptying self-sacrifice. But guilt prevented Peter from using that word, so he said, in effect, "Lord, You know I have a tender affection [*phileō*, 5368] for you." Jesus' next words are startling: **Feed my lambs. Lambs** is *arnion* (721), an affectionate term for young lambs. So, our Lord is saying that even a tender affection is enough to qualify us and motivate us to serve Him. And this story just keeps getting better.

Scriptures for Study: What does John 14:15–24 tell us about loving Christ?

MAY 6

Do You Love Me? (2)

... lovest thou me? (Jn. 21:15–17)

AS Matthew Henry observes, because of his denial, Peter "might justly expect to be struck out of the roll of the disciples, and to be expelled from the sacred college." But, happily, God's love does not work that way.

(2) The second exchange (v. 16) appears to be a repeat of the first, but we see our pattern of three once again, this time in three subtle differences. First, our Lord again asks, **lovest thou me?** but omits the phrase "more than these." In other words, "If you can't say you love me more than these other disciples, do you at least have a completely selfless, all-giving love for Me?" Peter's, response, of course, is a verbatim repetition of the first exchange. Acknowledging that Jesus can read his heart, Peter says, "You *know* I have a tender affection for you."

It is then in Jesus' next words that we see the other two differences. Notice that Jesus again uses the word **feed**, but instead of *boskō* (1006), to feed or pasture sheep, He uses *poimainō* (4165), to care for and rule the sheep. Note also, instead of the word "lambs" as before, we now read **sheep** (*probaton*, 4263), which refers to full-grown sheep. And amazingly again, because of his training and tender affection, Peter is qualified to carry out this commission.

(3) The third exchange (v. 17), the truly heart wrenching one, has three differences yet again. First, Jesus asks what appears to be the same "nagging" question, but alas, it is far from identical. This time He adopts *phileō*, asking in effect: "Simon, using your own word, do you *really* have this tender affection for Me?" Second, this **grieved** Peter to the core of his being. We can envision the tears streaming down his face not only because of what he had done but also because Jesus apparently doubted his deep affection. Perhaps with a crack in his voice and pleading in his tone, Peter responds, "Lord, You know *everything*, you *know* my affection for you." What is the third difference? Jesus' final response brings the other two together: **Feed** (*boskō*) **my sheep** (*probaton*). The recommissioning is complete, the implication clear: "Okay then, Simon, so be it. Get on with the job."

It is in this incident that we see the great turning point in Peter's life. No longer the brash fellow he once was, he is now a humble servant that God is about to use in wondrous ways. But did Peter *ever* love the Lord with an *agapē* love? Indeed, he did, as he wrote in his first epistle: "Whom having not seen, ye love" (1 Pet. 1:8; May 10). Dear Christian Friend, do you need such a crisis?

> Oh, Lord, it is my chief complaint
> That my love is weak and faint.
> Yet I love Thee, and adore.
> O, for grace to love Thee more.[183]

Scriptures for Study: What do the following verses say about loving Christ: Matthew 10:37; 1 Corinthians 16:22; 1 John 4:19; 5:1?

MAY 7

Do You Love Me? (3)

... thou knowest that I love thee. (Jn. 21:15–17)

THIS incident wonderfully illustrates that our Lord is not concerned so much with *rebuking* as He is with *restoring*. While He certainly does not overlook sin, once it is dealt with, it is "remember[ed] no more" (Heb. 8:12) and is removed from us "as far as the east is from the west" (Ps. 103:12). The *confrontation* with the *Savior*, therefore, points us to something else.

Second, the *crisis* of *self-examination* comes through the words **thou knowest that I love thee.** Dear Christian, please stop for a moment and ask yourself: "How much do I really love the Lord?" Now, I do not want to abandon you there, so I will try to help you answer. *How much* we love our Lord can be determined by *how* we love Him. Ponder with me four ways we can love our Lord.

(1) We can love Him *thankfully*. First John 4:19 is the key here: "We love him, because he first loved us." Both instances of "love" are *agapaō*, the love of sacrifice. When we sit and meditate on the humbling truth that He "loved me, and gave himself for me" (Gal. 2:20), we will respond in thankful appreciation. This is a simple truth, but oh, it is mighty! We love Him first and foremost for what He has done for us. If we may humbly expand on an old chorus,[184] ponder four truths:

> His sovereignty sought me in sin;
> His blood bought me to make me kin;
> His love then brought me forever in;
> And His grace taught me how to win.

"What hast thou that thou didst not receive?" the Apostle Paul asked (1 Cor. 4:7). We thank God for all we have, all we are, all we will become, and all we will do.

(2) We can love the Lord *mutually*. A truly thankful love will inevitably grow into a mutual one. What do we mean by "mutual"? It refers to something shared between two or more people or groups. We are reminded here of the friendship of David and Jonathan: "the soul of Jonathan was knit with the soul of David, and Jonathan loved him as his own soul" (1 Sam. 18:1). The Hebrew behind "knit" (*qašar*, 7194H) depicts binding or tying one thing to another, and "loved him as his own soul" indicates loving the other as much as one's own life. The Hebrew *Mishnah* characterized this relationship thusly: "Whenever love . . . does not depend on some selfish end, it will never pass away. . . . This was the love of David and Jonathan."[185] Far greater than that, of course, is our mutual love for the Lord. We love Him not only "because he first loved us" (1 Jn. 4:19), but also because He "is a friend that sticketh closer than a brother" (Prov. 18:24). We love Him now not only because of what He *accomplished for* us but also because of what He has *become to* us.

Scriptures for Study: Review our February 29 reading. 📖 What is our relationship to Jesus according to John 15:14–15?

MAY 8

Do You Love Me? (4)

... lovest thou me? (Jn. 21:15–17)

"MANY love God because He gives them corn and wine, and not for His intrinsic excellencies," wrote Puritan Thomas Watson. "We must love God more for what He is, than for what He bestows. True love is not mercenary. You need not hire a mother to love her child: a soul deeply in love with God needs not be hired by rewards."[186] That introduces the third way we love God.

(3) We can love Him *affectionately*. As before, this grows from those that precede it. We love Him now not just because of what He *accomplished for* us or even because of what He has *become to* us, but now because of who He is *in Himself*. Who is He then? He is our Sovereign, our Savior, our Solace, our Sustenance, our Strength, and our Security. Having received in Part I of our daily studies a glimpse of God in His names, a characterization of Christ in His titles, and a sketch of the Spirit in His activities, how can we not love Him for *who* He is and *all* He is? Is there anyone greater to love? As much as I have loved and adored my wife for 43 years, my son for 28, and my daughter-in-law for three, I love my Lord more; in fact, I can love them the way I do only because I love the Lord first. So, while "we can never love God as He *deserves*,"[187] we can love Him with all our *desire*.

(4) We can love the Lord *overwhelmingly*. Ah, here is one more level, and it is the culmination of all the others. When we contemplate, meditate, and deliberate on what He accomplished for us, what He has become to us, and who He is in Himself, how can all that not overwhelm us? While a thankful love is one of *respect*, a mutual love one of *fellowship*, and an affectionate love one of *worship*, an overwhelming love is one of *control*. It is a "giving over" of ourselves to Him. It is remembering and responding to the truth of Galatians 2:20: "I [have been] crucified with Christ"—that is the *reality*—"nevertheless I live; yet not I, but Christ liveth in me"—that is the *result*—"and the life which I now live in the flesh I live by the faith of the Son of God"—that is the *response*.

Perhaps you are thinking, "How can I cultivate such love as this? How do I grow to love God more?" If I may encourage, to ask the question is to prove how much you already love Him. Further, you are growing even now by reading the studies in this book and other books dedicated to His Truth. Reading and meditating on His Word, of course, is the most important in this regard, especially the Psalms and the Gospels. And so we pray:

> Lord, I love You thankfully for what You've done;
> I love You mutually for all that we share;
> I love You affectionately for the victory You've won;
> I love You overwhelmingly, nothing of myself I spare.

Scriptures for Study: What do the following verses add to our study today: 2 Corinthians 5:15; 1 Thessalonians 5:10; 1 Peter 4:2?

MAY 9

Do You Love Me? (5)

...feed... [tend]...feed... (Jn. 21:15–17)

THE *confrontation* with the *Savior* and the subsequent *crisis of self-examination* lead us inescapably, and encouragingly, to one final principle.

Third, the *challenge* to *service* unmistakably comes to us by our Lord's threefold recommissioning of Peter to the service already sovereignly marked out for him in the years to come. Let us once more see a threefold emphasis.

(1) The *service* Peter would *execute*. Peter's commission, of course, was to be a pastor, to feed, tend, and rule the sheep. Now, not all Christians are called to and trained for such leadership ministry, but there is one thing all must do, which was at the root of Peter's ministry. While there are other aspects of Christian service, there is one overarching mandate: *being a witness for Christ*.

We will look much deeper into Christian service in Part III of these daily studies, but for now we note the key verse that records the commission Christ gives to every believer: "But ye shall receive power, [when] the Holy Spirit is come upon you; and ye shall be witnesses unto me both in Jerusalem, and in all Judaea, and in Samaria, and unto the uttermost part of the earth" (Acts 1:8; Apr. 22). "Witnesses" is *martus* (3144, English "martyr"), which was originally a legal term for one who gave solemn testimony and evidence in court. Likewise, we each *proclaim* Christ with our *lips* and *prove* our transformation with our *life*.

(2) The *success* Peter would *experience*. Peter's self-directed efforts were abysmal. Earlier in the passage, for example, his self-will is evident in the words, "I go a fishing" (v. 3). His humanistic leadership was also demonstrated in that he led others back to the old life, as seen in the group's impulsiveness when they "entered into a ship immediately." And what was the result? "That night they caught nothing." Such failure, in fact, was a repeated theme throughout Peter's three years with Jesus. But by obeying Jesus' command (v. 6), there was *security* ("ye shall find"), *success* (a full net), and *sustenance* ("come and dine," v. 12). And, oh, how God used Peter in the years to come, starting, in fact, just a few days from this incident. There are many false results in today's methods of evangelism, but when we do things God's way, He will "[give] the increase" (1 Cor. 3:6).

(3) The *suffering* Peter would *endure*. As Matthew Henry writes: "Christ, having thus appointed Peter his *doing* work, next appoints him his *suffering* work." While the typical "Gospel" presentation today promises "a wonderful plan," a "betterment of life," "happiness and problem-free living," Scripture promises the exact opposite. Every apostle (except John) died a horrific death, and every one of them (including John) suffered terribly, all for the sake of Christ. But they (and countless others since; cf. Heb. 11 and *Foxes Book of Martyrs*) all did it willingly and without a tinge of regret. Why? *Because they loved the Lord*. Do we?

Scriptures for Study: What promises do we read in John 15:19–21; 16:2, 33; 1 Corinthians 3:5–8; 2 Timothy 3:12; 1 Peter 4:12–16?

MAY 10

Uncommon Love

Whom having not seen, ye love; in whom, though now ye see him not, yet believing, ye rejoice with joy unspeakable and full of glory. (1 Pet. 1:8)

THIS wonderful verse demonstrates that after the great turning point in his life (see May 5), Peter's "tender affection" (*phileō*, 5368) for his Lord did ultimately grow into a willful self-emptying, sacrificial **love** (*agapaō*, 25). Specifically, he here commends the recipients of his first epistle for their love for Christ.

First, we notice the *Unseen Loved One*. What is Christianity? It is not a philosophy, a system of ethics, or even a religion or a structure of belief. *Christianity is Christ.* Unlike any religion or cult on earth, Christianity is about a *person*. We cannot have a personal relationship with an idea, a concept, or a teaching, but only with a person, and Christianity is the only faith in the world that rests solely upon the person of its founder. He, then, is the Unseen Loved One that the word **whom** refers to here, as the previous verses specify.

Second, the *uncommon love*. In one of the great statements in military history, Admiral Chester Nimitz characterized the Marines at Iwo Jima—which was ultimately applied to the entire Marine Corps in World War II—as: "Uncommon valor was a common virtue." Far greater than that, we see here an uncommon love that becomes a common trait. Our love for Christ is uncommon for two reasons. The first, Peter tells us, is because **having not seen** Him, we love Him. Peter had personally seen the Lord Jesus, but the Jews to whom he wrote—those of the Dispersion—had never laid eyes on Him. Moreover, Peter adds, we love Christ even though *now* **[we] see him not** (emphasis added).

"Absence makes the heart grow fonder,"[188] it has been said. Never was that truer than here. The more we learn of Him, the more *dear He* becomes, and the more we meditate upon Him, the more *dedicated we* become. Why is this so uncommon? Because it is unprecedented! Could a young man adore a girl he has never met? Could a young lady have passion for a man she has never seen? All the senses are at work in this physical realm, but none of that applies in the spiritual. We do not have to see our Lord to love Him.

Third, the *unequalled luster*: **ye rejoice with joy unspeakable and full of glory**. Oh, what a phrase! **Rejoice** (*agalliaō*, 21) means to exult or leap for joy, **unspeakable** (*aneklalētos*, 412, appears only here in the NT) means unutterable and inexpressible, and **glory** (*doxazō*, 1392) means to give someone recognition, dignity, praise, and esteem by putting him into an honorable position. The latter, in fact, comes from *doxa* (1391), which in the NT has the added ideas of radiance and glory. Putting all this together: *Through our trusting in and uncommon love for the Unseen Loved One, we exult in a joy we cannot express in words, a radiant glory we anticipate in heaven and glimpse even now.*

Scriptures for Study: What did Paul write in 2 Corinthians 9:15 and 12:4?

MAY 11

Our First Love

... thou hast left thy first love. (Rev. 2:4)

JESUS' messages to the seven churches in Asia Minor carry enormous significance. Revelation 2 and 3, in fact, comprise about one eighth of the content of the book and contain much "Church Truth" found elsewhere in the NT. Each church was in a specific spiritual state (whether good or bad) and provides us with either a *model* to emulate or a *malignancy* to evade. The Church at Ephesus (2:1–7) is especially important to our present study.[189]

First, we hear our Lord's *regard* for this church. "Ephesus" actually means "desirable," and this church seemed to fit that description perfectly. Jesus praised it for seven realities: their **labor**; **works**; **patience**; separation from sin (**cannot bear evil men**); doctrinal purity (**tried those who called themselves apostles**); endurance of persecution (**hast borne, and hast patience**); and positive attitude (**hast laboured, and hast not fainted**). But the word **Nevertheless** undoubtedly "burst their bubble" because there is still something lacking in such a church.

Second, we note our Lord's *rebuke*: they had **left [their] first love**. Notice that it does not say they "lost" their first love, as some incorrectly quote. The Greek behind **left** (*aphiēmi*, 863) literally means "to leave, desert, forsake, leave behind, send away." Simply put, then: *To leave our "first love" means to leave behind the simplicity, joy, depth, and passion of a personal relationship with Christ.*

Some 35 years earlier, these believers loved the Lord and had a passion for Him (Eph. 1:15–16). But now most were second generation, many of the first generation having gone to glory. While the new generation had the *purity*, they didn't have the *passion*. Everything had become mechanical. What tragically occurs in many marriages had happened in that church: they left behind the simplicity, joy, depth, and passion of their love. What had caused this? As we will see tomorrow, the *actions* of **labor**, **works**, and **patience** were not balanced with the *attitudes* of "faith," "hope," and "love" (1 Thes. 1:2–3).

Third, we observe our Lord's *requirement* of this church (v. 5). First, they were to **remember ... from whence** they were **fallen. Remember** is *mnēmoneuō* (3421), which refers not just to the mental capability to recall something, but "to be mindful" of it and "take [it] into account."[190] It's also in the present tense, so it is critical to "keep remembering" what we were in our lost condition and what we are now in Christ. Second, Jesus said **repent**. This is *metanoeō* (3340), to turn around, change one's mind, and involves regret and sorrow accompanied by a true change of heart toward God. Third, they were to **return** (and **do the first works**). "Get back to the basics," Jesus said in effect. Get back to the things that originally brought the joy and thrill of knowing the Lord: worship, the depth of His Word, prayer, fellowship with other believers, and proclaiming the Gospel to the lost.

Oh, let us never leave our **first love**!

Scriptures for Study: What was Jesus final *reassurance* to this church (v. 7)?

MAY 12

The Primacy of Love (1)

And now abideth faith, hope, [love], these three; but the greatest of these is [love]. (1 Cor. 13:13)

HERE we see another extremely powerful occurrence of *agapē* (26), the love that is totally sacrificial. While often called the "love chapter," the fact often missed is that it appears in the very gravity center of three chapters on spiritual gifts. The Corinthians were so obsessively enamored with the more spectacular gifts that they had lost sight of what mattered most.

First, then, we *recognize* the *passing* of the *many*. While there is debate concerning the identity of "the perfect thing" in verse 10, Paul tells us that whenever it comes (whatever it is), certain gifts will "cease" (v. 8), even naming three of them ("prophecy, tongues, and [supernatural] knowledge"). The Greek construction indicates that these would literally "cease of themselves," that is, just fade away.[191] Not only was this because such gifts were no longer needed, but also because something far more useful and universal remained.

Second, we *realize* the *permanence* of the *three*. The word **abideth** (*menō*, 3306, to remain in one place at a given time) appears here in the present tense, indicating that **faith**, **hope**, and **love** forever remain. How important are these three? The answer lies in 1 Thessalonians 1:2–3: "We give thanks to God always for you all, making mention of you in our prayers, Remembering without ceasing your *work* of **faith**, and *labor* of **love**, and *patience* of **hope** [i.e., certainty] in our Lord Jesus Christ" (emphasis added). Do you see? Works, labor, and patience are not enough in themselves. Without the controlling attitudes of faith, hope, and love, our works, labor, and patience become mere ritual and mechanical. As occurred in the Church at Ephesus noted yesterday, we can do all the right things, but still be wrong. When passion wanes, power wilts. Ponder the correlations.

(1) Our *works* are tied to our **faith**, for "faith without works is dead" (Jas. 2:17). All our works are to flow out of our faith, trust, and dependency on Christ. We do everything in the knowledge that God will use it for His purpose.

(2) Our *labor* is tied to our **love**. "God will not forget your work and labour of love" (Heb. 6:10). We do all things not because God commands it, not because the pastor requests it, not because everyone expects it, not because of the recognition it brings us, but because we love the Lord and want to serve and please Him alone.

(3) Our *patience* is tied to our **hope**. We can only be patient in trials and tribulations because our **hope** (which literally means *certainty*; Greek *elpis*, 1680) is in Christ. The only reason we can be patient in anything is that we are looking way beyond the circumstances to our position in Christ.

Let us each search our hearts: "Am I just going through the motions? Is my Christianity mechanical?" Oh, that it would be driven by faith, hope, and love!

Scriptures for Study: What does each of the following verses say about faith, hope, and love: Psalm 43:5; Luke 22:32; Galatians 5:6; 1 Peter 1:21?

MAY 13

The Primacy of Love (2)

And now abideth faith, hope, [love], these three; but the greatest of these is [love]. (1 Cor. 13:13)

THE Apostle Paul was very concerned about what was going on in the church at Corinth. Multiple problems had arisen that were causing discord and division. The foundation of the cure was first to *recognize* the *passing* of *many* of the gifts and second to *realize* the *permanence* of *three* gifts. But there was one more truth they needed to hear and embrace, as do we.

Third, we *rejoice* in the *primacy* of the *one*. As great and glorious as **faith** and **hope** are, **love** is the **greatest** of all. "Love is the queen of the graces," wrote Puritan Thomas Watson; "it outshines all the others, as the sun the lesser planets."[192] Ah, but why is this?

(1) Because love is *divine*. Perhaps the most striking principle here is that **faith** and **hope** are related to *us* while love is related to *God*. God has no reason to exercise either faith or hope, but He certainly does express **love** in the greatest ways possible, Christ being the supreme demonstration. Nowhere does Scripture say, "God is faith," or, "God is hope," but it does say, "God is love" (1 Jn. 4:8). While his love is not to be elevated over His other attributes (Feb. 21), it is nonetheless an essential, and no less significant, aspect of His nature and character.

How does all that relate to us, then? Look at the context of this verse. How can love be patient, kind, not envy, or be puffed up (v. 4)? Because of our *affection* for Christ, since all this was true of Him. How can love not behave itself in an unbecoming manner, insist on its own way, not get provoked easily, or think evil thoughts (v. 5)? Because of our *adoration* of Christ. Why does love not rejoice in unrighteousness but in truth and then bear, believe, hope, and endure all things (vv. 6–7)? Because of our *adulation* of Christ.

(2) Love is the greatest also because it is *dynamic*. While faith *saves us* and hope *satisfies us*, love *serves others*. Love is not only a noun; it is also a verb. It is not just an *attitude*; it is an *action*. This begins with what we do "to serve the living and true God" (1 Thes. 1:9; cf; Heb. 9:14), but then "by love [we will] serve one another" (Gal 5:13). Why is this dynamic love so crucial? Because "if a man say, I love God, and hateth his brother, he is a liar: for he that loveth not his brother whom he hath seen, how can he love God whom he hath not seen?" (1 Jn. 4:20).

(3) One other reason love is the greatest is because it is *diverse*. The Apostle John again brings home this principle: "We know that we have passed from death unto life, because we love the brethren" (1 Jn. 3:14). It is simply because we love the Lord Jesus, who is our Elder Brother (Rom. 8:29), that we love all our "siblings" as well. What a wonderfully diverse family!

Scriptures for Study: How does Mark 12:29–31 sum up what we have been studying? 📖 What does 1 Corinthians 16:14 add?

May 14

Will You Also Go Away?

Then said Jesus unto the twelve, Will ye also go away? Then Simon Peter answered him, Lord, to whom shall we go? thou hast the words of eternal life. (Jn. 6:67–68)

THOUSANDS of false followers (today we call them "seekers") had flocked to Jesus because He performed miracles (v. 2), gave them free food (vv. 3–13; cf. v. 26), and hoped He would deliver them from Roman oppression (vv. 14–15). But as a result of His "hard sayings" (v. 60) about being the only way to heaven, those same thousands deserted Him (v. 66). As Jesus stood there with **the twelve**, who were probably the only ones who remained, He asked, **Will ye also go away?** Ever the spokesman for the group, Peter's answer is one of the sweetest and most sublime declarations in all history.

First, he declares that there is no other *person* to *follow*. With the word **Lord**, Peter acknowledged the divinity and lordship of Jesus. While **Lord** (*kurios*, 2962) is sometimes used as simply a title of honor, such as Rabbi, Teacher, Master (Matt. 10:24; cf. Luke 16:3), or even a husband (1 Pet. 3:6), when used of Jesus in a confessional way, as Peter did here, it without question refers to His divinity. As He goes on to add in verse 69, in fact—"Thou art the Christ, the Son of the living God" (cf. Matthew 16:16; Mar. 5)—Peter proclaims the uniqueness of Jesus, that He alone is worthy of worship, obedience, and trust. To follow anyone else is to be led into the abyss.

Second, Peter declares that there is no other *place* to *flee*. **To whom shall we go?** is the only wise answer to Jesus' question. As much as men claim to be independent and self-sufficient, they still have need of someone. "No man is an island, entire of itself," wrote the poet John Donne; "every man is a piece of the continent, a part of the main." Peter understood that he could not go to the Scribes and Pharisees, who knew nothing except their legalism. Neither could he go to the Greek or Roman philosophers, who clung hopelessly to their superstition and paganism. Neither could he go to the Mosaic Law, for it only convicts, curses, and condemns, but never can it convert. All that is true today. Men flee to every sort of teacher, sage, or guru looking for what they think is Truth. But with David we pray, "I flee unto thee to hide me" (Ps. 143:9). Where else can we go?

Third, Peter declares that there is no other *precept* to *fathom*. **Thou hast the words of eternal life**, he adds. **Words** translates *rhēma* (4487), which as we have noted before (Mar. 28) usually relates to individual words and utterances instead of a discourse or speech as a whole (*logos*, 3056). Oh, how common are "the commandments and doctrines of men" (Col. 1:22)! Yes, they might stimulate our thinking, fascinate our imagination, or captivate our attention, but in the end, they are "[brought] to nothing" (1 Cor. 1:19, a quotation of Is. 29:14). There are no **words** deeper, more profound, or more critical than the doctrines of salvation, for only they are **the words of eternal life**.

Scriptures for Study: What is the psalmist's testimony in Psalm 73:25?

MAY 15

Spiritual Devotion: Level 1

And a great multitude followed him, because they saw his miracles which he did ... (Jn. 6:2)

YESTERDAY'S thoughts lead us to another. Have you ever noticed the various levels of spiritual devotion illustrated in the NT? We observe, in fact, at least five such levels from the most superficial to the more sentimental to the truly steadfast.[193]

First, there is the level of *curiosity*, which we again see in the feeding of the 5,000 (Mar. 10). The multitudes followed Jesus not because of the *man* He personified, not because of the *message* He proclaimed, but first because of the *miracles* He performed and ultimately only because of the *meals* He provided. Does this not sound familiar? Do we not see this in abundance today?

(1) We see them *seeking* (vv. 22–40). At first, it seems the people were sincere in their "seeking Jesus" (v. 24). After all, the Greek here (*zēteō*, 2212) means "look for, strive to find" (cf. Matt. 7:7–8). But actions have attitudes behind them, and Jesus knew their real motive, as the context confirms: "Ye seek me, not because ye saw the miracles, but because ye did eat of the loaves, and were filled" (v. 26).

Today's so-called seekers are exactly the same. They view Christianity as the Ultimate Give-Away Program and God as the Heavenly Genie. This is made all the worse by false teachers who propagate this false notion of prosperity. While such teaching is more prominent in our day, it's not new, as our text demonstrates. Charles Spurgeon faced it in his day, writing. "It is anti-Christian and unholy for any Christian to live with the object of accumulating wealth."[194] A. W. Tozer echoed by calling such things "religious racketeering, pure and simple!"[195]

(2) We see them *skeptical* (vv. 41–51). Jesus used the phrase "came down from heaven" five times in this chapter (vv. 38, 41, 42, 51, 58), and every time the Jews recognized it as a claim of deity. But in their hardened skepticism, they "murmured" against Him (v. 41). The Greek is *gogguzō* (1111), an onomatopoeic word that mimics the low muttering sound of complaint. The curiosity seeker is a born skeptic and his complaints against Truth will come quickly and audibly.

(3) We see them *striving* (vv. 52–59). Completely missing the point our Lord was making about His being the spiritual Bread of Life (Mar. 10), the people argued about what He meant. This, too, is typical of curiosity seekers, each arguing his own opinion, his own interpretation, his own theology.

(4) We see them *stumbling* (vv. 60–70). The Greek behind "offend" in verse 61 is *skandalizō* (4624), to scandalize or offend. Everything Jesus taught offended the Jews simply because the Truth offends. Such is always the case with those who follow Jesus just out of curiosity. And so it is that we are to love Him not for the *gifts* He can give *us* but the *glory* we can give *Him*.

Scriptures for Study: What do the following verses tell us about "seekers": Luke 9:57–62; Romans 16:17–18; Philippians 2:21?

MAY 16

Spiritual Devotion: Level 2

The Lord appointed other seventy also, and sent them two and two before his face into every city and place, whither he himself would come. (Lk. 10:1)

WHILE the first level of spiritual devotion (*curiosity*) is a sham, the others demonstrate ever increasing loyalty and depth.

Second, there is the level of *concern*, which we find well illustrated in Luke 10:1–24. There we read of Jesus' sending out the 70 witnesses[196] who would announce His coming (only Luke, in fact, records this incident).

(1) There is the *declaration* (vv. 1–12). The 70 (who were in addition to Jesus' twelve disciples) were to go into the Judean cities (Matt. 19:1) Jesus was preparing to visit and proclaim that Messiah was coming. While certain aspects of the commission Jesus gave them were clearly not meant to be repeated today (i.e., healing and miracles), there are principles here that certainly apply: we are to go out into the field and reap a harvest of souls (v. 2); there will be strong resistance (v. 3); we should not be concerned about our personal comfort (vv. 4–8); and we do not continue to witness to those who are confirmed in their unbelief (vv. 10–12). This leads to a second observation.

(2) There is the *denunciation* (vv. 13–16). These verses seem harsh, indeed, but they demonstrate the dire consequences of rejecting Christ. Tyre was a great city on the eastern coast of the Mediterranean. Because of its terrible wickedness, Ezekiel 26 declares that it would be utterly destroyed and would never again be rebuilt or even inhabited. This was dramatically fulfilled by Alexander the Great about 275 years later, and today the site is merely a flat island where fisherman dry and repair their nets. Ezekiel 28:21–23 goes on to record God's judgment upon the city of Sidon. But Jesus says here that had those two cities witnessed the miracles Jesus performed in Chorazin and Bethsaida, they would have repented in the deepest sorrow. But because they repented not, the latter two cities were to be judged severely, so much so that they were so utterly destroyed that their exact location is not definitely known today. Likewise, Capernaum, Jesus' base of operations, was plunged into judgment. Such is the fate of those who reject Him.

(3) There is the *delight* (vv. 17–24). Upon their return, those witnesses manifested their joy in a three-fold manner: their pleasure in *service* (vv. 17–19), their praising in *salvation* (v. 20), and their peace in *sovereignty* (vv. 21–24).

Now, while all this is laudable, of course, and while there were no doubt some in the group (if not all) whose concern led to continued service,[197] this was still only a one time assignment, not an ongoing project. Sadly, there are some who just "sign on" for a particular task but with no intention of any ongoing dedication. While concern is admirable, it is not enough to sustain a ministry. So, is our service *decided* by *convenience*, or is it, as we will see, *driven* by *commitment*?

Scriptures for Study: What do the following verses say about laboring in the field: John 4:35–38; 1 Corinthians 3:6–9; 1 Thessalonians 2:9?

MAY 17

Spiritual Devotion: Level 3

And he ordained twelve, that they should be with him, and that he might send them forth to preach. (Mk. 3:14)

THE *curiosity* level of devotion is not real devotion at all but rather a pretense, and the level of *concern*, while admirable, makes no promise of continued service.

Third, there is the level of *constancy*. Our text appears in one of several passages that list the twelve disciples (cf. Matt. 10:2–4; Luke 6:13–16; Acts 1:13). Luke, however, adds that Jesus called these men by another name: "apostles." The Greek (*apostolos*, 652) is a very distinctive term that indicates one who is sent as an ambassador. Jesus used this word to emphasize the uniqueness of these men. In the "official sense," only they were apostles for four reasons: each was called and commissioned by Christ personally; each received special revelation from God; each had the power to work miracles; and each had seen the resurrected Jesus.[198]

(1) Their *selection*. Mark tells us that Jesus **ordained** these men. This does not refer to the ordination of men for the ministry (Titus 1:5, where "ordain" is *kathistēmi*, 2525, to set down, to place), rather the Greek is *poieō* (4160), to make, form, or produce. Another form of the word, *poiētēs* (4163), refers to one who makes something or to a work of art. In ancient Greek this referred to an author or poet. In fact, our English word *poem* is derived from *poiēma* (4160). So, these men were, indeed, a work of art produced by the Great Artist. We too are one of His masterpieces, "for we are His workmanship [*poiēma*]" (Eph. 2:10).

(2) Their *security* is underscored by their being **with him**. **With** translates *meta* (3326), which means to be among something and implies accompaniment. The present tense of the verb indicates continuing action, so "one purpose of our Lord in forming the Twelve was that they might constantly be with Him."[199] Think of it! What better security could there be? We, too, have this, for Jesus sent His Spirit to "abide with [*meta*]" us forever (Jn. 14:16).

(3) The *service* these men were fashioned for was to **preach** the Word. **Preach** is one of the key words of the NT; it is *kērussō* (2784), to announce or to publicly herald. The noun form *kērux* (2783) refers to the imperial herald who represented the emperor or king and announced his wishes. It is formal, grave, serious, and authoritative. These men, therefore, demonstrate a day-by-day fidelity to Christ.

But again, even this level of devotion is no assurance of continued service. Judas was one of these twelve, enjoying the same presence of Christ and training as did the rest, yet he was a traitor. Demas was a commendable soldier (Col. 4:14) but ultimately was a deserter (2 Tim. 4:10; Aug. 23). Likewise, we have seen many in our day forsake the ministry. *Fruitfulness* does not ensure *faithfulness*.

Scriptures for Study: What do the following verses say about the preacher and his preaching: 1 Timothy 2:7; 2 Timothy 1:11; 4:2–4; 2 Peter 2:5?

MAY 18

Spiritual Devotion: Level 4

And he took with him Peter and the two sons of Zebedee . . . (Matt. 26:37)

WHILE *curiosity* reflects a mere pretense, *concern* the potential of faithfulness, and *constancy* the possibility of continued service, there is yet another more promising level.

Fourth, there is the level of *communion*. It is interesting, indeed, that all the disciples had the same Lord, the same training, the same opportunities, but for some reason three of them—Peter, James, and John—were chosen to be what has been called "the inner circle." They were, for example, the only ones present at three major events: the resurrection of Jairus' 12 year old daughter (Matt. 9:18–25), the transfiguration (17:1–9), and in the Garden of Gethsemane (26:36–45). It is the latter scene we again visit (May 4).

(1) We see the *fellowship* of the group (v. 37). The presence of the word **with** (*meta*, 3326) again demonstrates the ongoing communion these disciples had with the Lord. This closeness is even more strongly indicated at Jesus' transfiguration, when "Jesus taketh Peter, James, and John his brother, and bringeth them up into an high mountain apart" (Matt. 17:1). In the Greek, the definite article ("the") appears before the name "Peter," but not before the other two, which binds all three men together as a unit. As Mark and Luke both point out, in fact, no one else was allowed to accompany the Lord (Mk. 5:37; Lk. 8:51).

We, too, have such fellowship with Christ. As we observed in our mediations on the Holy Spirit (April 16), Jesus promised that on the Day of Pentecost we would be in Him and He in us (Jn. 14:20). Paul builds upon this in His analogy of every believer being a member of Christ's body, with no member superior to any other (1 Cor. 12:12–27). Oh, what communion we have in Him!

(2) We mark the *failure* of the disciples (vv. 38–44). As we recall, because of their inattentiveness and indifference, the disciples fell asleep and could not even keep "watch" for an hour as our Lord agonized over what awaited Him. This again challenges us to vigilance in our Christian walk, for true love is ever alert.

(3) We note the *fate* of the Savior (vv. 45–46). As Matthew Henry observes, our Lord speaks ironically here, saying in effect, "Now sleep if you can, sleep if you dare; I would not disturb you if Judas and his band of men would not." Rather, as the betrayer approaches, Jesus then challenges, "Rise [from sleep], let us be going." The time of our Lord's death had arrived.

So it is once again, we see weakness even at this level of devotion. Here were our Lord's closest followers, yet they vacillated. Vance Havner once observed, "Judas betrayed the Lord with a kiss, not a slap. Our Master is betrayed more often with a show of affection than any other way."[200] And even His true disciples were not without guilt. They had not yet reached the highest level of devotion.

Scriptures for Study: Read 1 Corinthians 12:12–27. What observations can you make concerning the Body of Christ?

MAY 19

Spiritual Devotion: Level 5

I am crucified with Christ: nevertheless I live; yet not I, but Christ liveth in me: and the life which I now live in the flesh I live by the faith of the Son of God, who loved me, and gave himself for me. (Gal. 2:20)

SETTING aside the emptiness of mere curiosity, what more could there be above a devotion that is concerned, constant, and communicative?

Fifth, there is the level of *commitment*. Sadly, here is a word that has lost much of its impact in our day, thanks mostly to many evangelists who speak of a vague commitment to Christ that amounts to little more than a shallow profession of faith, which in turn constitutes no change of life or intention of obedience. Webster, in contrast, defines this word as "a promise to do or give something; a promise to be loyal to someone or something." What does this entail?

(1) A life that is *sacrificed*. What did Paul mean when he wrote **I am crucified with Christ**? Yes, it was Christ who was sacrificed, but we were with Him spiritually. It, therefore, means such things as the end of a sinner's condemnation, the end of one striving to merit salvation, and the end of the law. But most of all, Paul simply meant that it was the end of *Paul*. The old man, that is, all that he was in Adam, was dead and a new man took his place (Rom. 6:6–11, Apr. 26–28; cf. Eph. 4:22–32). That leads immediately to another principle.

(2) A life that is *sanctified*. **Nevertheless I live; yet not I, but Christ liveth in me**, Paul added. It was no longer the self-righteous, legalistic Paul (Saul) who was living but rather Christ. The sanctifying resurrected life of Christ through the Holy Spirit empowered Paul to live as the new man he now was. Here is the greatest *transition*, one from death to life, the greatest *transformation*, from sin to holiness, and the greatest *translation*, from the road to hell to the gates of heaven.

(3) A life that is *steadfast*. Paul's pen was always practical, so he added finally: **the life which I now live in the flesh I live by the faith of the Son of God**. As we have noted previously (Mar. 8), the word **faith** is one that has come to mean very little nowadays. It is vague and nebulous and is reduced simply to "faith in faith" minus any object, but a verb without an object has no meaning. Scripture, however, is not ambiguous. Every time we see faith being exercised in Scripture, it always has an object, and that object, however manifested, is always in what God has said. (Hebrews 11 provides a representative list of examples; Oct 1–Nov. 10.)

In that light, then, what does Paul tell us here? He tells us that the new life he received from Christ is **now** lived by continued **faith** in Him, a life of total and complete obedience, a life of true commitment, loyalty, and fidelity, a life not *dictated* by the *law* but rather *defined* by *liberty*.

Let us each examine ourselves and discern our level of spiritual devotion.

Scriptures for Study: Read Ephesians 4:22–32. What are the characteristics of the "new man"?

MAY 20

Losing Sight of Jesus (1)

... Jesus tarried behind in Jerusalem; and Joseph and his mother knew not of it. (Lk. 2:43)

SCRIPTURE is unambiguously clear that the true Christian believer can never lose his *salvation*, but it is equally explicit that we can lose *sight* of our Lord. There are times when, like Peter, we look away from our Savior and sink into the depths, or when, like David, we look away from our responsibilities and because of sin lose that which is most precious to us, or when, like Sampson, we turn our eyes away from God's will and lose all vision for Him.

In our next few daily studies, let us prayerfully ponder two graphic illustrations of this principle, one in the NT and the other in the OT. The first incident appears in Luke 2:41–49, where our Lord is 12 years old and has accompanied his parents to the temple in Jerusalem to celebrate the Feast of the Passover. The law required all Jewish males of mature age to go to Jerusalem to attend the three great feasts, the other two being Pentecost and Tabernacles (Ex. 23:14–17; 34:22–23; Deut. 16:16). When this became impossible because of increased distances of travel after the Dispersion, a single feast per year became the requirement. While our text implies no sin on either Jesus' or his parents' part, it does demonstrate the trepidation that comes when Jesus is absent. Note four movements in this incident.

First, the *distraction.* Verse 43 recounts that when Joseph and Mary "had fulfilled the days" of the feast and began their northward journey home, "the child Jesus tarried behind in Jerusalem; and Joseph and his mother knew not of it." In the crowded hustle and bustle that surrounded the Temple, distraction could easily have occurred. It is even more possible, in light of a custom of the day, that while women and children traveled in the front of the caravan, the men and young men traveled at the rear. Each parent, therefore, might very well have supposed that young Jesus was with the other (v. 44).

Oh, how easily we can become distracted! Never has there been an era in human history that is busier than the present one. Everywhere we turn, there is a plethora of attractions, and it is invariably our spiritual life that is neglected. Further, like Joseph and Mary, we just take Jesus' presence for granted. We don't give it a second thought. "Of course, He's there," we assume, "He's always there." While that is certainly true, we take for granted what He has accomplished and forget what His presence should really mean to us. Yes, Jesus promised, "Lo, I am with you always" (Matt. 28:20), but how often do we forget to be with Him?

But let us not overlook young Jesus here. It was because of His desire to hear and discuss the Truth of God's Word that He "tarried behind" (cf. v. 46). Is this not a lesson for both youth and parents?

Scriptures for Study: What do the following verses encourage us to do: Psalms 25:15; 101:3; 119:18; 123:1–2; 141:8?

MAY 21

Losing Sight of Jesus (2)

... Jesus tarried behind in Jerusalem; and Joseph and his mother knew not of it. (Lk. 2:43)

MY wife and I shall never forget the panic that struck the day our only child wandered out of our yard at the age of two and walked several blocks from home. It took only a few seconds of *distraction* for us to lose sight of him. As serious as that was for us, there is something far worse in our text.

Second, the *detection*. Verse 43 adds another dimension to this incident—Jesus' parents went an entire day's journey before realizing He was not among them. Since Nazareth was a three-day, some 63-mile journey from Jerusalem, Jesus' parents were more than 20 miles away when they finally realized Jesus was missing. We can't help but wonder what finally brought the realization. Likewise, what will it take to snap us back to reality when we get too busy and distracted?

Third, the *diligence*. Verses 44–45 describe the parents' diligent search: "they sought him among their kinsfolk and acquaintance." The Greek behind "sought" is *anazēteō* (327). While the root *zēteō* (2212) is a common verb simply meaning to seek, the prefix *ana* (303) greatly intensifies it. When used in a compound word, as it is here, it means up or upward or even back and then back again. It is equivalent to our English prefix *re-*, denoting repetition and intensity. It appears only one other place in the NT (Acts 11:25), where Barnabas, knowing his own limitations and that Saul (Paul) was God's man for the hour, went to Tarsus "to seek" him—"to seek [him] up and down (*ana*), back and forth, hunt up, make a thorough search till success [came]."[201] Today we might say "look high and low."

So, can we not picture Jesus' parents running through the crowd, probably on the precipice of panic, asking every person they know, "Have you seen Jesus? We can't find Him anywhere!" When this was to no avail, they spent another day retracing their steps back to Jerusalem. Perhaps they asked others they met along the way if they had seen a lost boy, never realizing that they were the lost ones, not Jesus. He knew exactly where He was and why. In like manner, when we lose sight of our Lord we, too, frantically look in all the wrong places. We run in all directions, not knowing what to do. The answer lies in the last scene of the drama.

Fourth, the *discovery*. Upon returning to Jerusalem, the parents spent another day looking for Jesus, making a total of three days since they had wandered away from Him (v. 46). Finally, after all their frantic search, all their fretful worry, all their failing methods, *they found Him exactly where they lost Him*. Sadly, Mary did not even recognize her fault, as she asked, "Son, why hast thou thus dealt with us? behold, thy father and I have sought thee sorrowing" (v. 48). Ah, do we not often blame God for the anxiety we caused? *We* wander off but then wonder why *He* deserted us. Oh, let us realize that He is waiting for us where we lost him!

Scriptures for Study: What do the following verses say about seeking: Deuteronomy 4:29; Psalm 119:2, 10?

May 22

Losing Sight of Jesus (3)

... we [know] not what is become of him. (Ex. 32:1)

CONTINUING our thoughts on losing sight of Jesus, we consider an even more graphic OT illustration. While not about Jesus specifically, of course, it nonetheless pictures this crucial principle. The scene is Moses' delay in coming down from the mountain and the people's response to such lost sight.

First, we note the *initial* loss of sight. Our text graphically exhibits the impatience of the people. Because events were not progressing according to their timetable, they impetuously cried, **We [know] not what is become of him**. Before we are tempted to think it was actually Moses who "wandered off" in this case, we need to realize that all this is a *heart* issue, not an *eye* issue. We are reminded of Peter, for example, walking on the water. He didn't literally take his *eyes* off Jesus before plunging into the sea—the tossing of the waves would have periodically blocked that sight—but rather he took his *heart* off Jesus. So it is with us. Like Peter and the children of Israel, we take our spiritual eyes off Jesus and plunge headfirst into the depths and proceed headlong into disaster.

Second, we see the *idolatry* that resulted. Here is one of the most appalling scenes in all of Scripture. As many commentators rightly point out, the image that Aaron fashioned was not meant to be *another* God but rather a visible symbol of the *True* God. Verse 5, in fact, tells us that Aaron "built an altar before" the golden calf and then proclaimed, "Tomorrow is a feast to the LORD."

That distinction, however, does not lessen the condemnation one iota. On the contrary, this was just as serious a sin as worshipping a false God, as the first two commandments of the Moral Law make clear (June 17–18). While some Bible teachers insist that the second commandment merely forbids art or other images of *false* gods, that is incorrect, as the context makes clear. As many faithful theologians, expositors, and commentators maintain, the first commandment commands us to worship God alone: "Thou shalt have no other gods before me" (Ex. 20:3), while the second tells us to do so not by our own devices (images) but only by His self-disclosure (His Word). Verse 5 goes on to detail how pagans make images of heavenly and earthly objects to represent their gods, but this must *never* be so of the True God. As Thomas Watson put it: "To set up an image to represent God, is debasing Him. . . . What greater disparagement to the infinite God than to represent Him by that which is finite?"[202] Sadly, we are all idolaters at heart.[203]

That is precisely what the people did here. Why? Well, as Calvin scathingly put it: it was because of their "detestable impiety, their worse than base ingratitude, and their monstrous madness, mixed with stupidity."[204] Strong words, yes, but justified. When we take our eyes off the Lord, we will invariably either turn to a substitute for Him or look to Him in the wrong way.

Scriptures for Study: What do the following verses add to our thoughts today: Acts 17:29; Isaiah 42:8, 17?

MAY 23

Losing Sight of Jesus (4)

... we [know] not what is become of him. (Ex. 32:1)

THE incident of the golden calf is one of the most hideous in Israel's history. "To commit such an act at any time would have been gross sin," wrote H. I. Hester, but to do so "at the very place where the commandment against idols had been given, and in so short time after receiving this commandment, made their sin doubly grievous."[205]

Third, then, we see the *intolerable* excuse. As already noted, verse 5 recounts that all this was actually done in the name of "the LORD." As we recall, "LORD" translates *Yāhweh* (Jan. 21), God's personal, covenant name. We, therefore, can think of few things more reprehensible as such an "attempt to save appearances and hallow sin by writing God's name on it!"[206] How often do we see this today? How many invoke God's name when all they are doing is furthering their own agenda? As one expositor well puts it, "Strange that the wicked should like, if possible, to get the cloak of religion even for their vices. But light and darkness will not mingle."[207]

Fourth, we mark the *inferiority* of ungodly leadership. Aaron's part in all this is critical, as his frequent mention demonstrates (vv. 1, 2, 4, 5, 22). Here, indeed, is the low point of this leader's life. Instead of keeping his eyes on the Lord, he succumbed to the pressure of the people. Today's direct descendant is the "Christian leader" who insists that Church ministry consists of giving people what they *want* and thereby denying his real responsibility to give people what they *need*. In contrast, consider carefully what one preacher declared:

"Read the religious advertisements in [the] local papers. I have done this again and again, until the hideous fact has been proved up to the hilt, that 'amusement' is ousting 'the preaching of the gospel' as the great attraction. 'Concerts,' 'Entertainments,' 'Fancy Fairs,' 'Dramatic Performances,' are the words honored with biggest type and most startling colors. The Concert is fast becoming as much a recognized part of church life as the Prayer Meeting, and is already, in most places, far better attended."[208]

That vividly describes our 21st-century but was actually spoken in the 19th-century by Archibald Brown, a little known, faithful Baptist preacher who was not only one of Charles Spurgeon's students but also his successor at the Metropolitan Tabernacle in London.

Further demonstrating his weakness, Aaron blamed the people for his failure to lead: "Let not the anger of my lord wax hot: thou knowest the people, that they are set on mischief" (v. 22). So serious was Aaron's lack of leadership that God would have killed him had it not been for Moses' intercession (Deut. 9:19–20). How critical leadership is! Leaders will answer for losing sight of Jesus (Jas. 3:1).

Scriptures for Study: What does 2 Timothy 4:1–5 tell us about a pastor's leadership responsibility and its difficulty?

MAY 24

Losing Sight of Jesus (5)

... we [know] not what is become of him. (Ex. 32:1)

A note on our text in the great *Geneva Bible* of the Puritans declares, "The root of idolatry is when men think that God is not present, unless they see him physically." How faithless it is to want something that *appeals* to the senses instead of what *applies* to the heart. That leads us to another observation.

Fifth, the *insolent* disobedience of the people. While Aaron's piteous excuse for his actions was reprehensible, his words were nonetheless accurate: "the people ... are set on mischief" (v. 22). "Mischief" translates the common Hebrew word *ra'* (7451H). In light of its opposite (*tôb,* 2896H), whatever is *not* good, pleasant, beneficial, precious, delightful, right, well-pleasing, fruitful, morally correct, proper, or convenient is evil. This is further confirmed in verse 24, where Aaron said he just threw the gold into the fire "and there came out this calf," apparently by some mysterious means. (If it were not so tragic, it would be humorous.) The sin of the people was, of course, deliberate and blatant. "Stiffnecked" in verse 9 (*qāšeh,* 7186H) means being stubborn, rebellious, and obstinate. Still further, verse 3 adds that "all the people" were involved. Whether this means every individual or just all those who were actually complicit in the deed, the result is the same: sin effects everyone in one way or another (note the consequences in vv. 20, 27–28).

Sadly, this incident set a precedent of idolatry for years to come. Especially vivid are the books of Judges and 1 Kings. Over and over again we read, "And the children of Israel did evil in the sight of the LORD" (or similar words), which in "all the historical books ... is the regular phrase for falling into idolatry"[209] (Judg. 2:11; 3:7, 12; 4:1; 6:1; 10:6; 13:1; 1 Kings 14:22; 16:30). Such is the consequence when we lose sight of the Lord.

Sixth, the *intercession* of godly leadership. In contrast to Aaron's abysmal leadership, we see the exemplary character of Moses' (vv. 11–14). It is the godly leader who intercedes for God's people. It is the faithful and godly pastor who not only *preaches to* the sheep but also *prays for* them. As with Moses, such prayer is unselfish, unrestrained, and unwavering.

Seventh, the *inquiry.* In verse 26, as "Moses stood at the gate of the camp," he asked the searching question, "Who is on the LORD'S side?" This provides us with three final thoughts. First, there is the *challenge.* Indeed, who will stand with the Lord? Who will "[turn] ... from idols to serve the living and true God" (1 Thes. 1:9)? Second, every person must make the *choice.* While some made the choice to continue in their perversion, the Levites rallied to Moses and judged the unrepentant. Third, there is the *consecration:* "Consecrate yourselves to day to the LORD" (v. 29). "Consecrate" (*mālē',* 4390H) literally means "fill your hand" and pictures total dedication. Oh, let us never lose sight of that!

Scriptures for Study: What does Jesus declare in Matthew 12:30?

MAY 25

Six Absolutes from the Savior

I am . . . the truth. (Jn. 14:6)

WE live in a day of unprecedented uncertainty—it is the age of Postmodernism, a philosophy that affirms no objective or absolute truth, especially in matters of religion and spirituality. The maxim of Postmodernism regarding any truth claim about God or any religious topic is: "that might be true for you, but not for me." The danger, and ultimate disaster, of such thinking is obvious to anyone with even an ounce of discernment. For example, while one person's opinion about which make or model of car to drive is as acceptable as another's, such matters have nothing to do with Truth. Truth, in fact, is absolute by its very definition (Mar. 15), and without it there is nothing.

The term *Postmodernism* literally means "after Modernism" and is a knee-jerk response to Modernism's failures. Since Modernism believed in absolutes but also that they could be discovered only through reason, Postmodernism rejected absolutes when Modernism failed to deliver on its promise to better mankind and make a better world through reason. In other words, unbiased reason is a myth, so reality is in "the eye of the beholder." Since each person can construct his own reality however he wishes to view it, he cannot judge another person's construct of reality. Each of us, therefore, believes what he wants to believe. Postmodernism is about experience over reason, subjectivity over objectivity, spirituality over religion, images over words, and feelings over Truth.

What makes all this even more troubling is that it has spilled over into the thinking of many who call themselves Christians. In fact, a poll taken by the Barna Research Group shortly after the September 11, 2001 terrorist attacks revealed the appalling reality that "less than one out of three born again Christians adopt the notion of absolute moral truth."[210]

What all such thinking refuses to recognize, however, is that Truth, by its very nature and definition, is absolute. If it is not absolute, it is not Truth. Further, they do not recognize that Truth cannot be *deduced by reason* or *discovered by reaction,* rather it can only be *disclosed by revelation.*

Such Truth is nowhere better delineated than in six verses in the Gospel of John, all of which are spoken by the Lord Jesus Christ Himself. Our Lord does not speak in generalities or with open-minded tolerance. He speaks in very narrow terms. In all six verses, in fact, He uses the exclusive expression "no man." The Greek in every case is *oudeis* (3762), which means "not even one, not the least." Further, because the gender is masculine, it means "no man, no one, no person." There are no exceptions or loopholes. "None" means *none*! In our next few studies, then, we will consider these six absolutes: sovereignty, salvation, sacrifice, security, solidarity, and satisfaction.[211]

Scriptures for Study: To prepare for our study, read these six texts in John and write down your own observations: 6:44; 14:6; 10:18; 10:29; 15:13; 16:22.

MAY 26

The Absolute of Sovereignty

No man can come to me, except the Father which hath sent me draw him. (Jn. 6:44a)

WHILE many people resist this truth, Scripture is unambiguous in setting forth the principle that salvation is solely the result of God's sovereign action. The Doctrines of Sovereign Grace declare one basic truth: God has done *all* of it because we can do *none* of it. To put it another way, *saving* grace is *sovereign* grace; salvation, from beginning to end, and everything in between, is by God's sovereign grace, apart from any contribution from man.

First, note man's *inability*. Our text is just one of many that underscore this truth; it is among the most powerful verses in the NT concerning God's sovereignty in salvation. The word **can** is especially critical. The Greek *dunamai* (1410; English, *dynamic*) speaks of inherent power, the ability to do something. Man, therefore, does not have the inherent power or natural ability to come to God without God's intervention. In other words, Jesus didn't say "may" (a word of *permission*) but **can** (a word of *ability*). Yes, man has *permission* to come to God, but he doesn't have the *ability*. Just as Christ had to call dead, decaying Lazarus from the grave (Jn. 11:43–44; cf. Eph. 2:1–3), He must call us forth, regenerate us, and give us the faith to believe (cf. Acts 18:27; Eph. 2:8–9; Phil. 1:29). So crucial is this principle that we read it again later in the chapter, where Jesus adds: "No man can come unto me, except it were given unto him of my Father" (vv. 63a, 65).

Again, many people reject all this, as the very next verse demonstrates: "From that time many of his disciples went back, and walked no more with him" (v. 66). When people don't like what they hear, they often just shut their ears and walk away; they don't want their weakness and inability pointed out to them.

Second, we see God's *intervention*. The other crucial word here is **draw**, which is *helkuō* (1670), one of the most powerful words in the NT and means to draw, tug, or even compel and denotes an irresistible force (note its other five occurrences: Jn. 12:32; 18:10; 21:6, 11; Acts 16:19). It was used in ancient Greek literature to picture a desperately hungry man being drawn to food.[212]

So what was our Lord telling the listening crowd that day on the shore of the Sea of Galilee? What is He still declaring to us today? Simply this: **no [one]** can come to God *on* his own merit, *in* his own ability, or *under* his own power. Just as a magnet draws the powerless iron filings to itself, so God draws to Himself those He knew before the foundation of the world (Eph. 1:4). While "this act of drawing is an act of power, [it is] not of force," wrote John Gill; "God in *drawing* of the unwilling, *makes* willing . . . He enlightens the understanding, bends the will, gives a heart of flesh, sweetly allures by the power of his grace [and] draws with the bands of love." Does this not make us love Him all the more?

Scriptures for Study: Read Ephesians 2:1–10. What does this wondrous passage tells us about salvation?

MAY 27

The Absolute of Salvation

I am the way, the truth, and the life: no man cometh unto the Father, but by me. (Jn. 14:6)

AS we meditated in an earlier study (Mar. 15), this verse is among the most definitive statements about Christ in the NT. As noted there, Jesus is the only *sufficient road* (**the way**), the only *suitable vehicle* (**the truth**), and the only *satisfying destination* (**the life**).

First, note the *offense*. It is this very truth of Jesus as the absolute for salvation that offends people more than any other religious concept. The common view in our postmodern world, as one religious organization puts it, is: "each individual is different and so what works for one person might not work for another." That writer goes on to illustrate how one mountain climber might get to the top one way while another will take a different route, or that a physician would not give the same medicine to five people who have different illnesses. Likewise, it is concluded, there are as many paths to God as there are people.[213]

What is obviously ignored here, of course, is that such illustrations are about earthly, temporal matters, making the inference about God illogical. Further, we could just as easily illustrate by observing that the telephone company is narrow minded in forcing us to dial the exact number we wish to call. Or we could ask, are we not thankful that engineers build bridges and buildings to exact specifications, not some relativistic standard that they feel is close enough at the moment?

Indeed, we are not addressing such earthly matters. Salvation is an eternal, spiritual question. Our Lord, therefore, is again unambiguous. He declares boldly (and dare we add dogmatically?) that **no [one]** comes to God by any other way than by Him. Is it not amazing how many people say such things as, "Jesus was a good man" or, "Jesus was a great teacher," but completely overlook His "narrowness"? How could He possibly be good, according to modern standards, if He was that narrow in His attitudes and intolerant of the beliefs of others?

Second, we see the *object*. To build on an observation made by Calvin, **no man cometh unto the Father but by me** explains the preceding three-fold statement: He is **the way** because He is the *path* that leads to the Father, **the truth** because He is the *perception* of the Father, and **the life** because He is the *power* of the Father.[214] Or, we can put it another way: **the way** *reaches* the Father, **the truth** *reveals* the Father, and **the life** *radiates* the Father.

Third, there is the *overshadowing*. The most critical principle of all here is that the context very clearly indicates the predominate concept of Christ as **the way**. In other words, "He is **the way** *because* He is **the truth** and **the life**." Does this not again cause us to love our Lord all the more? Can love exist in relativism and ambiguity? Can we really love uncertainty? Oh, let us rejoice in **the way**!

Scriptures for Study: Review our March 15 reading, including the Scriptures for Study. What observations can you add?

MAY 28

The Absolute of Sacrifice

No man taketh it from me, but I lay [my life] down of myself. I have power to lay it down, and I have power to take it again. (Jn. 10:18a)

THE reason the absolute of *salvation* is true (as we considered yesterday) is because the absolute of *sacrifice* is true. The reason *we have* life is because Jesus *gave His*.

First, His sacrifice was *voluntary*. **No [one]** took our Lord's life, rather He gave it freely. As He said to His disciples in the Garden of Gethsemane, He could have summoned "more than twelve legions of angels" to rescue Him (Matt. 26:53), but the whole purpose of His coming was to be a sacrifice.

While others in history have given their lives for a cause, the horrific realities of crucifixion elevate our Lord's sacrifice to an incomprehensible level. Beginning in the Garden, Jesus' anguish caused Him to sweat drops of blood, a medical condition called hematidrosis. Every aspect of His trials were illegal. The scourging was done with a leather thonged whip with pieces of bone woven into the ends. He was beaten on the back, buttocks, and upper legs, which not only shredded the skin but cut into the subcutaneous tissue and skeletal muscles. All this set the stage for hypovolemic shock brought on by blood loss.[215] This was often enough to kill a victim before he even made it to the cross. Crucifixion itself was the most cruel, barbaric, and excruciating torture ever devised by depraved minds. Iron spikes (five to seven inches long and three-eighths of an inch in diameter) were driven through the wrists, which crushed or severed the median nerve, causing unimaginable bolts of pain and shriveled the hand to a claw-like appearance. The most fiendish aspect, however, was that the weight of hanging on the cross locked the intercostals muscles, hindering the ability to exhale. To breathe, the victim had to lift himself by his wrists and push with his feet, which had been nailed through the heels. Death came slowly by asphyxia, shock, dehydration, arrhythmia, and congestive heart failure. And it was all voluntary!

Second, His sacrifice was *vicarious*. Why did Jesus lay down His life? So we would not have to. He was our substitute. He was the spotless, perfect Lamb of God who died in the sinner's place. "Christ's death is the Christian's life," wrote J. C. Ryle; "Christ 'lifted up' and put to shame on Calvary is the ladder by which Christians 'enter into the holiest,' and are at length landed in glory."[216]

Third, His sacrifice was *victorious*. Our Lord not only laid down His life, but He also had the power (*exousia*, 1849, right or authority) to take it up again. He didn't stay in the grave; He rose from it. He didn't remain a *dead* sacrifice; He became a *living* sacrifice. That is, in fact, what we are commanded to be (Rom. 12:1–2), those who are alive because of Christ's resurrection and living a life of total dedication (Sept. 3–6). His love for us produces our love for Him.

Scriptures for Study: What do the following verses declare about Christ's vicarious sacrifice: Isaiah 53:4–5; Titus 2:14; 1 Peter 2:24?

MAY 29

The Absolute of Security

My Father, which gave them me, is greater than all; and no man is able to pluck them out of my Father's hand. (Jn. 10:29)

OUR text is the climax of the two preceding verses: "My sheep hear my voice, and I know them, and they follow me: And I give unto them eternal life; and they shall never perish, neither shall any man pluck them out of my hand."

First, we see the *Shepherd* and the *sheep*. As we have studied previously (Mar. 13), the Good Shepherd condescended to one of the lowliest occupations in the ancient world to purposefully give His life for the sheep that already belonged to Him from eternity.

Second, we see our *salvation*. It was the Shepherd's sacrifice that provided eternal life. The Greek behind "eternal" in verse 28, as well as many other verses in John (e.g., 3:16; 3:36; 4:14; 5:24; 6:27, etc.), is *aiōnios* (166), which simply means "indeterminate as to duration, eternal, everlasting." If life is eternal, it is *really* eternal. If you can lose something that is eternal, then it was not eternal in the first place. To argue this is self-defeating folly. That leads to our main thought.

Third, we see our *security*. Our text assures us of total, absolute security. Just as Jesus is the *Vine* and the Father the *Landowner* (15:1), He is also the *Shepherd* of the sheep, and the Father is the *Owner*, having given them to His Son. The two, therefore, are one in nature and purpose, and the sheep are doubly secure.

The crucial point here is that danger is implicitly implied. There *is* a danger of being plucked from the Father's hand and the Son's hand. **Pluck** is *harpazō* (726), to seize, snatch, carry off, rob, or plunder. It is used back in 10:24 to refer to a wolf in the fold catching some of the sheep and scattering the rest. There are, indeed, dangers everywhere. There is the danger of false doctrine, the peril of doubt, the threat of our own sin, and much more that tries to wrench us from God's grasp. But all fail to remove the authentic believer from God's hand. **No [one]** can wrench us from His sovereign grasp. The Shepherd is never surprised by the stealthy robber, rather he is ever vigilant and supremely powerful. Those who "fall away" (Heb. 6:4–6) were never true sheep.[217] True sheep *know*, *follow*, and *obey* the Shepherd, and are forever *secure* in the Shepherd, which leads us to a final principle.

Fourth, we see our *steadfastness*. While some argue that the idea of "eternal security means a license to sin," verse 27 says quite the contrary. True sheep "hear" the Shepherd's voice. This is *akouō* (191), which not only means to hear in general, hear with attention, and understand, but also to *obey*. Further, "follow" is *akoloutheō* (190), which in the NT "is always the call to decisive and intimate discipleship."[218] A true sheep follows the shepherd, and never stops following.

Scriptures for Study: What do the following verses declare about our security: Romans 8:33–39; 1 Peter 1:5; 1 John 5:13?

MAY 30

The Absolute of Solidarity

Greater love hath no man than this, that a man lay down his life for his friends. (Jn. 15:13)

FIRST, this staggering text speaks of *affection*. It captivates us because it contains both Greek words for **love** that we have noted several times: **love** is *agapē*, "a self-emptying self-sacrifice," while **friends** is *philos*, the more emotional word for esteem, high regard, and tender affection (see Feb. 21, May 1, 5–7, and 12 for more on these words). *Philos*, in fact, is used repeatedly in the NT for friendship (e.g., vv. 14–15; Lk. 11:5–6, 8; 15:6; Jn. 11:11; 3 Jn. 14; etc.). "Friendship is the marriage of affections," wrote Puritan Thomas Watson.[219] Think of it! Our Lord calls us **friends**. What solidarity that is!

Second, notice the *affirmation*. How did our Lord confirm His love for His **friends**? By **lay[ing] down His** life **for** (i.e., "in place of") them. And that is what the **no [one]** means here. Obviously, no one can love exactly as Jesus did. No one can equal the infinite *cost*, substitutionary *character*, or redemptive *consequences* of His death. But, on the other hand, there is something else here.

Third, consider the *application*. While no one can love to the extent that He did, we are still challenged to love sacrificially, as Jesus commands in the preceding verse: "love one another, as I have loved you."

I have yet to read an earthly story that better illustrates this than that of a seven-year-old boy and his infant sister in a small Midwestern town. She had been critically injured and was in desperate need of a blood transfusion, but no one could be found who had her rare blood type, except, it was finally discovered, her older brother. The doctor took him into his office, held the youngster on his knee, and said, "Son, your sister is very, very sick. Unless we can help her, I'm afraid the angels are going to take her to heaven. Are you willing to give blood to your baby sister?" The young boy's face turned pale, and his eyes widened with fright and uncertainty. He appeared to be in great mental agony, but after a minute or so he half-whispered, "Yes, I will." The physician smiled reassuringly and said, "That's a fine, boy; I knew you would." The transfusion took place, but the seven-year-old, watching the tube carrying the life-giving fluid to his sister, seemed apprehensive. The doctor said, "Don't be nervous, son. It will all be over before long." At that moment big tears welled up in the little boy's eyes. "Will I die pretty soon?" he asked. It then became apparent that he thought he was giving up his own life to save his baby sister![220]

That is love. And what is most significant here is that even *philos*, the tender affection of friendship, is powerful enough to motivate such sacrifice. The word "friend" is used very loosely nowadays, but true friendship lays down one's life for such friends. How many friends do you have?

Scriptures for Study: Read the verses cited above where *philos* is used for friendship. What observations can you make?

MAY 31

The Absolute of Satisfaction

Ye now therefore have sorrow: but I will see you again, and your heart shall rejoice, and your joy no man taketh from you. (Jn. 16:22)

"WHEN happenings happen to happen happily, you have happiness," I once heard J. Sidlow Baxter quip; "when happenings happen to happen unhappily, you have unhappiness; happiness, then, is merely circumstantial happenness. But joy is independent of circumstances." Looking for happiness "in the moment" does, indeed, describe our culture. But true **joy** (*chara*, 5479, "gladness and rejoicing") goes far beyond circumstances.

First, we note the *prompting* of joy. What prompts and encourages us to joy? It is, of course, **sorrow** itself. The preceding verse illustrates with the "anguish" of childbirth. This is *thlipsis* (2347), a graphic word that literally means "to crush, press, compress, squeeze [and] is from *thlaō*, to break."[221] It appears, in fact, many times in the NT to indicate that tribulation, hardship, affliction, distress, and other difficulties are simply an everyday part of Christian living.

Second, however, there is the *promise* of joy. Just as the anguish of childbirth is the promise of the joy that is to come, so do the difficulties of the Christian life assure us that "the new birth" we have in Christ (Jn. 3:3–8) is the source of our joy. Specifically, Jesus promises His disciples that while His departure brings sorrow now, that should just prompt them to joy because they would see Him again. But wait a moment. Does this refer to His resurrection, His sending "another Comforter" (14:16), or His bodily Second Coming? Does it really matter? Whichever it is (perhaps all three?), the result is exactly the same: *joy*.

Third, there is the *permanence* of joy. Here is the greatest truth. While happiness is fleeting, joy is fulfilling; happiness is shifting, but joy is secure; happiness is uncertain, while joy is unchanging. **No [one]**, our Lord goes on to assure us, can take our joy away from us. Yes, we can give it away, but no one can steal it; we can misplace it, but no one else can hide it from us; we can be careless with it, but no one else can capture it.

There is something seriously wrong with the sad Christian. We do not say that lightly. Puritan William Gurnall, for example, challenges: "Christ takes no more delight to dwell in a sad heart, than we do to live in a dark house."[222] Stronger still is Thomas Watson: "Let me tell you, it is a sin not to rejoice. You disparage your Husband, Christ. When a wife is always sighing and weeping, what will others say? 'This woman has a bad husband.' Is this the fruit of Christ's love to you, to reflect dishonour upon him?"[223]

Let us note finally that joy is, in fact, the culmination of all the other absolutes we have seen. When we *comprehend* God's sovereignty in our salvation, when we *contemplate* Christ's sacrifice and the security that results, and when we *consider* the solidarity we have in His friendship, how can we not have joyful satisfaction?

Scriptures for Study: What has blessed you the most in this study of "absolutes"?

JUNE 1

The Motive of Worship

Last of all he sent unto them his son, saying, They will reverence my son. (Matt. 21:37)

AT the very core of our love *for* the Lord there must be a deep sense of worship *of* Him. Sadly, however, there is much that merely passes for worship these days. While there is, in fact, a lot of *talk* about worship, there is little *true* worship as revealed in Scripture.

We do not say that lightly, so to demonstrate it, we begin our meditations on worship with an incident that is recorded in all three synoptic Gospels (Matt. 21:33–46; Mk. 12:1–12; Lk. 20:9–19). In response to Israel's rejection of Him, Jesus told a parable of a landowner who rented out his vineyard to tenement farmers who would share the profits with him at harvest. But when he sent several of his servants to collect what was rightfully his, the farmers terribly mistreated the servants one by one, beating, stoning, and even killing them. Finally, he sent his son, thinking the farmers would surely respect him. But the very opposite occurred: they reasoned that if they killed the son, they could claim the vineyard as their own. This graphically pictured the actions of Israel (described as God's vineyard in Is. 5:1–7). They mistreated and killed God's prophets and ultimately His Son.

The key word here is **reverence**. This is the Greek *entrepō* (1788), which appears only nine times in the NT. It is comprised of *en* (1722, "in") and *trepō* ("to turn") and so literally means "to turn into oneself" and therefore figuratively "to put self to shame and feel respect or deference toward someone else."

Oh, how that single word reveals the absence of respect and worship! This is true not just of the world's attitude toward God, but it's also prominent even in the Church. The typical "worship" service nowadays has far more to do with looking outward with *stipulations* than looking inward with *shame*. We often demand what type of music we want, insist on being entertained, and even specify what kind of sermons we want to hear. If I may be lovingly frank, it's simply man-centered and all about the *feelings* of the worshipper not *fidelity* to the Truth.

But we would also lovingly submit that even something as seemingly insignificant and meaningless as talking before the service is irreverent. This is a time for *silence*, not *socializing*. This is a time of preparation, a time for purging our minds and mouths of the things of self and concentrate on the things of God. This is the first and foremost reason we gather together.

What, then, is the motive of worship? What should drive it? We submit that it is as simple as John the Baptist's words: "He must increase, but I must decrease" (Jn. 3:30). Who are we thinking of during worship, God or ourselves? If He is not the single focus, the solitary consideration, we are not worshipping. Worship is not about *us*; it's about *God*.

Scriptures for Study: What does Hebrews 12:9 say about reverence?

JUNE 2

The Meaning and Magnitude of Worship

O come, let us worship and bow down: let us kneel before the LORD our maker. (Ps. 95:6)

GOING deeper in our thoughts on worship, this subject permeates the Scriptures. Our words **worship** and "worshipped" appear some 170 times in the KJV (though some refer to worshipping false gods). Additionally, there are words such as "praise" and "praised" (about 270 times), "glorify" and "glorified" (75 times), and others. But there is something truly profound about the *meaning* of the words in both the OT and NT for **worship**.

First, in the OT there is *sāḥah* (7812H), which appears about 190 times. While most often translated "worship," it's also rendered bow, bow down, obeisance, and reverence and means to bow down, to prostrate oneself as in bowing before a monarch or a superior and paying homage to him or her. While it was used of earthly monarchs, when used of God it took on a deeper sense. It appears 17 times in the Psalms and is used, for example, "to describe all the earth bowing down in worship to God as a response to His great power (Ps. 66:4)."[224] Does that not shed much light on our text? If the whole earth bows down in worship, how much more should the child of God? This is just one of many Psalms that also declare the *magnitude* of worship (Ps. 5:7; 29:2; 45:11; 66:4; 86:9; 96:9; 99:5, 9; 132:7; 138:2). Additionally, some 30 of the psalms are dedicated to praise.

God's mandate to worship is no more clearly given than it is in the first two commandments of the Moral Law (Ex. 20:2–5). Worship was the whole point of the Tabernacle and even the camp that surrounded it (Ex. 25–31), and it is graphically illustrated by the seraphim (literally, "burning ones") in Isaiah 6:1–3.

Second, the NT counterpart of the Hebrew *sāḥah* is the Greek *proskuneō* (4352), which means "to kiss toward, to kiss the hand, to bow down, to prostrate oneself." And what is the importance of worship there? It was the first *concern* of the Magi who came to visit Jesus (Matt. 2:2). It was the *crux* of the greatest spiritual battle ever fought between Jesus and Satan (Matt. 4:8–10). It was Mary of Bethany's *craving* when she anointed Jesus' feet with oil, which was probably worth a year's wage (Jn. 12:1–2). It was Jesus' *command* to the Samaritan woman immediately after telling her about salvation (Jn. 4:20–24). It was the *critical* issue that Paul emphasized to the Athenians (Acts 17:23). And it is, in fact, the defining *characteristic* of the true Christian (Phil. 3:3) and will be the *central* activity in heaven (Rev. 4:10–11).

In a day when people's "felt needs" are more important than God's glory, when "personal fulfillment" is more important than God's attributes, and when entertainment is more important than reverence, there needs to be a new emphasis on true biblical worship in the Church. Again, worship is not about us.

Scriptures for Study: Read the verses listed in Psalms (and others if you wish) and write down your own observations.

JUNE 3

The Misconception of Worship (1)

What thing soever I command you, observe to do it: thou shalt not add thereto, nor diminish from it. (Deut. 12:32)

A truth that seems to be little thought of in today's Church is that worship, even if practiced with the greatest sincerity, can actually be wrong. A common idea is that we can worship God in any way we wish and He will accept it. Such misconception, however, is grave error.

This thought introduces us to a principle that is virtually ignored in much of the Church, namely, what has been called "the regulative principle of worship." This principle simply means that all forms and aspects of worship must be expressly stated in Scripture or they are to be rejected. In other words, Scripture, both in word and by example, forbids any form of worship or observance that God Himself does not institute.

This principle, in fact, is a direct corollary to *sola scriptura* (Scripture alone), which has been called the "formal principle" of the Reformation. By "formal" is meant that this principle is the authority that *forms and shapes* the entire movement from beginning to end. Scripture alone, then, gave form to everything involved in the Reformation (although it was far from perfect).[225] Without that, there could be no form, no content, and no truth because all of those demand an authority. Without authority, there can be nothing else. The purpose of *sola scriptura*, then, was to reposition the Bible as the final authority over the Church.[226] Flowing of necessity from that, therefore, is the regulative principle of worship.

Scriptures such as Deuteronomy 12:30–32 could not be clearer on this mandate. The context of this passage addresses idolatry. God's people were instructed not even to investigate the worship practices of pagans, lest they be tempted to introduce any of it into the worship of God. Unlike our day, this principle was consistently the view of historic Christianity. The Reformers and the Puritans were passionately devoted to this truth, men such as: John Knox, Theodore Beza, David Calderwood, George Gillespie, William Ames, Thomas Vincent, Thomas Watson, and many others. The latter wrote, for example: "Let us, then, as we would show ourselves to be godly, keep close to the rule of worship, and in the things of Jehovah go no further than we can say, 'It is written.'"[227]

Equally pointed are the words of the great doctrinal statements of the Church: *The Westminster Confession* and *The London Baptist Confession*. In both we read: "The acceptable way of worshipping the true God is instituted by Himself, and so limited to His own revealed will, that He may not be worshipped according to the imaginations and devices of men, or the suggestions of Satan, under any visible representations, or any other way not prescribed in the holy Scripture (Ex. 20:4–6; Deut. 4:15–20; 12:32; Matt. 4:9–10; 15:9; Acts 17:25; Col. 2:23)."[228]

Scriptures for Study: Read the following passages, noting the wrong worship in each: Malachi 1:6–14; 3:13–15.

JUNE 4

The Misconception of Worship (2)

What thing soever I command you, observe to do it: thou shalt not add thereto, nor diminish from it. (Deut. 12:32)

CONTINUING our thoughts from yesterday, we must be very careful exactly how we worship. We should, in fact, be warned by three principles.

First, God will not tolerate the worship of a false god (Exod. 34:14, 15). He is absolutely intolerant of idolatry. The whole reason for both the Assyrian and Babylonian captivities was Israel's continued worship of pagan gods. We can do the same by elevating a job, money, fame, or anything else to "god" status.

Second, God will not accept the worship of Him in the wrong way. There is no better example than Nadab and Abihu (Lev. 10:1–2). While they had been trained for the priesthood by their father Aaron, they did something different. What did they do? Perhaps they offered the sacrifice at the wrong time of day (cf. Ex. 30:7–9), used coals in their censers that didn't come from the altar (cf. Lev. 16:12), or even went into the Holy of Holies, which only the high priest was permitted to do, and then only once a year on the Day of Atonement (cf. Lev.16:12–13). In the final analysis, however, it doesn't really matter what they did. *They did something not prescribed by God*. Whether it was an "honest mistake" or a deliberate departure because they thought it would be okay to "get creative," the result was the same. It was "strange fire." Puritan Jeremiah Burroughs comments here:

"All things in God's worship must have a warrant out of God's word, [and] must be commanded. It's not enough that it is not forbidden. . . . Now when man shall put a Religious respect upon a thing, by virtue of his own Institution when he hath not a warrant from God; Here's superstition! we must all be *willing* worshipers, but not *will*-worshipers."[229]

The application could not be clearer: *God will not accept worship that is offered in the wrong way*. Many today worship in a way that is self-defined. They add any symbol, ritual, ceremony, "crowd-pleaser," or anything else they want that is not prescribed in Scripture. And that is simply unacceptable to God.

Third, God will not accept the worship of the True God with the wrong attitude, such as ceremony, habit, and tradition. Our Lord's own words to the Pharisees underscore such errant attitudes: "Well hath Esaias prophesied of you hypocrites, as it is written, This people honoureth me with [their] lips, but their heart is far from me" (Mk. 7:6, quoting Is. 29:13;). "This was all lip labour," wrote John Gill; "there was no lifting up their hearts, with their hands, unto God; these were not united to fear his name, but were distracted in his worship, and carried away from him to other objects."[230] Our worship can likewise become just ritual, routine, and repetition with no value and in the end be hypocrisy. Let us carefully guard our attitude in worship.

Scriptures for Study: Read the following passages, noting the wrong worship in each: Isaiah 1:11–20; Amos 5:1, 21–23; Colossians 2:20–23.

JUNE 5

The Manner of Worship (1)

And they continued stedfastly in the apostles' doctrine and fellowship, and in breaking of bread, and in prayers. (Acts 2:42)

HOW, then, shall we worship? What does Scripture specifically tell us about how to worship? Our text provides us with four unmistakable features of the public gathering of the Church.

First and foremost, at the very core of the Church gathering was the preaching and teaching of **doctrine**. Unlike our day of the progressive discounting of this principle, this was the very beating heart of the Church at its birth. The Greek here is the pivotal word *didachē* (1322). While its basic meaning is *teaching*, it also stresses what is actually *taught*, that is, a body of doctrine. Another key verse here is 2 Timothy 4:2, where Paul, with no ambiguity, apology, or alternative, commands pastors to "preach the word; be instant in season, out of season; reprove, rebuke, exhort with all longsuffering and doctrine." He goes on in verses 3 and 4 to give a reason for his command, namely, that the time will come when people will not put up with this and will seek teachers who will humor them and tickle their ears to entertain them. In spite of such attitudes, however, Paul commands Timothy to preach anyway, *to change absolutely nothing in his method.*

We should also observe here that part of worship involves just the public *reading* of Scripture, which was, in fact, an integral part of the meetings of God's people throughout the biblical record (Ex. 24:7; Josh. 8:34; 2 Kings 23:1–3; Neh. 8:1–8; 9:1–3; Acts 13:15; Col. 4:16; 1 Thes. 5:27; 1 Tim. 4:13; etc.). Those who decry the importance of worship dismiss these many verses, insisting that the reason the Scriptures had to be read then was because people did not have their own copies of the Scriptures. While that has some truth in it, public reading is the biblical precedent nonetheless, and such precedents must not be ignored. There is no greater spiritual power than the spoken Word of God, both publicly read and precisely exposited (cf. July 1).

Second, worship in the Early Church consisted of **fellowship**. The Greek here (*koinōnia*, 2842) speaks of a partnership, close union, and brotherly bond. Its NT use is perhaps best expressed as a "joint participation in a common interest or activity."[231] One of the essentials of any local church, then, is a partnership, a close communion with other believers. Second only to the foundational element of doctrine and teaching, it is crucial that Christians fellowship with one another. This is why church attendance is so crucial, so that God's people can encourage one another in fellowship (cf. Heb. 10:25; June 21, Dec. 9). True fellowship is far more than a "Christian coffee klatch" or any other social gathering. It involves a real union and bond in thought, desire, and goal. Such is true corporate worship.

Scriptures for Study: What is the command of Hebrews 10:25? 📖 What observations can you make in the other verses cited today?

JUNE 6

The Manner of Worship (2)

And they continued stedfastly in the apostles' doctrine and fellowship, and in breaking of bread, and in prayers. (Acts 2:42)

WE ignore the precedents of Scripture at great peril, and one such crucial precedent is how we are to carry on worship in the Church. As noted yesterday, our text provides us with four unmistakable features.

Third, in line with our **fellowship**, our corporate worship each Lord's Day should include the **breaking of bread**. Some view this as simply eating a regular meal, but that cannot be true here. As virtually all evangelical commentators agree, used in the present context, this expression refers to the Lord's Supper being observed on the first day of the week (cf. Acts 20:7; 1 Cor. 16:2). While the common view is that there is no precedent for how often we observe the Lord's Supper, our text unambiguously indicates the opposite. Since the other three features are practiced each Lord's Day, why would this not also be the case for the Lord's Supper? While this has been the practice of the Church throughout her history, in fact, only in modern times have many challenged this precedent and drifted away from it.[232]

Fourth, **prayers** comprise the capstone of our corporate worship. The Greek here (*proseuchē*, 4335) is the most common word for prayer in the NT. It is a general word that speaks of prayer to God, underscoring the obvious principle that only the true God should receive prayer (not Mary or the saints, as in Roman Catholicism). Such prayer in our worship services includes pastoral prayer, as well as the prayers offered up by all the saints as they prepare their hearts for worship. This emphasizes again that this is a time for *silence*, not *socializing*.

My Dear Christian Friend, have you noticed the absence of something in our study of worship that is nowadays often emphasized far more than anything else? We are speaking, of course, about music. We cannot emphasize it strongly enough that while music has become the central focus of worship today, it is extremely significant that it is not even mentioned in the Book of Acts.[233] Yes, we see it referred to later in the Epistles (Eph. 5:19; Col. 3:16), but it clearly was never central either to worship or church ministry in general. Even more tragic, "style of music" is at the forefront of many churches, further obscuring the centrality of the pulpit ministry and elevating music to a place to which it has no right to be.

Now, are we saying that music has no place at all? Certainly not! But we are saying that its overemphasis has caused some serious consequences. Not only has it taken first place, but much of its style is inappropriate for worship and often its lyrics are shallow and devoid of Truth. Oh, how we should love the great hymns of the faith! "The hymnal is lyric theology," wrote A. W. Tozer. "The hymns are warm with the breath of worshipers, a breath that may still be detected fragrant upon them after the passing of a century."[234]

Scriptures for Study: Read 1 Corinthians 11:20–26. What observations can you make concerning the Lord's Supper?

JUNE 7

The Majesty of Worship

Whoso offereth praise glorifieth Me. (Ps. 50:23a)

CONSIDER finally the majesty of worship, that is, its glorious results, its wondrous blessings. We see, in fact, no less than four results of worship.

First and foremost, God is *glorified*. Our text declares, **Whoso offereth praise glorifieth Me**. Instead of the word "worship," we see here the word **praise**. This is the Hebrew *tôdāh* (8426H), which is derived from *yādāh* (3034H, "to confess publicly") and expresses the idea of an offering or sacrifice of thanksgiving, an integral ingredient of worship (Ps. 97:12; 136:1–3, 26).

Glorifieth in turn translates the fascinating word *kābēd* (3513H), which literally means "to be heavy or weighty." As the old saying goes, a person's opinion might "carry a lot of weight," indicating that he is important or influential. God, therefore, is "heavy," that is, powerful, and is worthy of honor, glory, respect, and obedience. In fact, in Proverbs 3:9 and 4:8, *kābēd* is translated "honour," and in Isaiah 30:27, it is rendered "heavy," speaking of His judgment. Praising Him—that is, admiring His attributes, adoring His works, and acquiescing to His will—brings Him glory. "This is the yearly rent we pay to the crown of heaven."[235]

Second, Christians are *purified* by worship of God. As David declared, "Who shall ascend into the hill of the LORD? or who shall stand in his holy place? He that hath clean hands, and a pure heart" (Ps. 24:3–4a). A worshipping Christian is a pure Christian. A worshipping Christian is one who, *realizing* his sinfulness, comes before God, *recognizing* His holiness, and is *renewed* in his desire to be conformed to that holy image. This reminds us again of how important the Lord's Table is in worship. As Paul teaches us about this occasion (1 Cor. 11:28–29), one must "examine" himself (*dokimazō*, 1381, "test, pronounce good, establish by trial") before partaking so that he does not partake "unworthily" (*anaxiōs*, 371, "irreverently, or in an unbecoming manner"). This is a place of worship, so there is no room here for sin. In the context of the fleshly and divisive Corinthians, there is no place for such actions and attitudes during worship.

Third, the Church is *edified* through worship. To edify means to build up, and that is what transpired in the Early Church. They not only were built up in the apostle's doctrine (Acts 2:42), but they also enjoyed unity (v. 46) and added to their number (v. 47).

Fourth, the world is *evangelized* through worship. Here is yet another by-product of the weekly observance of the Lord's Supper. It is a proclamation of Christ's death and resurrection. It is through this we "show" (*kataggellō*, 2605, declare plainly, openly, and aloud) "the Lord's death till he come" (1 Cor. 11:26). Our worship proclaims Christ to a watching world.

Scriptures for Study: What do these verses in Psalms say about worship: 50:14–15; 22:23; 27:6; 86:9, 12?

JUNE 8

The Meditations of Worship

My meditation of him shall be sweet ... (Ps. 104:34)

WE studied today's text very early in these daily readings (Jan. 5–6), but we encounter it again briefly. As noted there, **meditation** translates *śiyaḥ* (7879H), which denotes contemplation. Let us do just that as we close our all too brief study of worship. There is perhaps no better way to meditate on worship than through the musings of the "lyric theology" in our hymnal.

From *Robert Grant* (1779–1838) come the words: "O worship the King, all glorious above, / And gratefully sing His wonderful love; / Our Shield and Defender, the Ancient of Days, / Pavilioned in splendor, and girded with praise." *Reginald Heber* (1783–1826) gave us: "Holy, holy, holy! Lord God Almighty! / Early in the morning our song shall rise to Thee; / Holy, holy, holy, merciful and mighty! / God in three Persons, blessed Trinity!" And, oh, that second stanza: "Holy, holy, holy! All the saints adore Thee, / Casting down their golden crowns around the glassy sea; / Cherubim and seraphim falling down before Thee, / Who was, and is, and evermore shall be." *Frederick Faber* (1814–63) exulted: "I worship Thee, most gracious God, / And all Thy ways adore; / And every day I live, I seem / To love Thee more and more." *Edward Perronet* (1726–92) gave us: "All hail the power of Jesus' name! / Let angels prostrate fall; / Bring forth the royal diadem, / and crown Him Lord of all." And we mustn't overlook *Charles Wesley's* (1708–88): "O for a thousand tongues to sing / My great Redeemer's praise, / The glories of my God and king, / The triumphs of His grace!" Finally, I would offer the following to close:

Worship

"O come, let us worship and bow down [low],
"Let us kneel before the LORD our maker."
Thus is the command for us here below,
For there is no name anywhere greater.
Humbly do we come into His presence,
Deeply in reverent contemplation.
Meditating His nature and essence,
We raise our voices in acclamation.
We kneel and remember all He has done.
We rejoice and sing praises to His name.
We celebrate the vict'ry He has won
In His conquering of sin, death, and shame.
    We come before Him nothing to receive.
    Rather only to worship and believe.

Scriptures for Study: Read your favorite hymn. What Scriptures come to mind?

JUNE 9

Loving God's Name and Word

Look thou upon me, and be merciful unto me, as thou usest to do unto those that love thy name (Ps. 119:132)

PSALM 119 is devoted to praising the virtues, merits, and sufficiency of the Word of God and demonstrates the author's total commitment to it. Out of 176 verses, every one (except 122) speaks of God's Word. We see the writer low and lofty, discouraged and diligent, frightened and fearless, vanquished and victorious. The more we read, however, we discover his secret. While many Christians today are looking for the newest trend for their excitement, or seeking the answers to problems by reading the latest self-help book, the psalmist *always* went to the Word of God. Why? Because it is there, and there alone, that he found everything: happiness (vv. 1–8), maturity (vv. 9–16), victory (vv. 17–24), therapy (vv. 25–32), consistency (vv. 33–40), confidence (vv. 41–48), and all else.[236]

One of many fascinating features about this psalm is the author's (probably David) repeated mention of his *love* for God's Word. He emphasizes this, in fact, no less than 11 times (vv. 47, 48, 97, 113, 119, 127, 132, 159, 163, 165, 167). The Hebrew used in every occurrence is *'ahab* (157H), which speaks of "a strong emotional attachment to and desire either to possess or to be in the presence of the object."[237] Do not we all want to be in the presence of those we love? Abraham loved Isaac (Gen. 22:2), Isaac loved Rebekah (24:67), Jacob loved Joseph "more than all his children" (37:3), and Ruth loved her mother-in-law Naomi (Ruth 4:15). Likewise, God commands us to love Him: "Thou shalt love the LORD thy God with all thine heart, and with all thy soul, and with all thy might." (Deut. 6:5; May 1–3).

Our text is one of those 11 verses and is especially striking: **Look thou upon me, and be merciful unto me, as thou usest to do unto those that love thy name** (v. 132). We have been studying loving God in this second part of our daily readings, but now we learn that to love God's *Word* is to love His *name*. In other words, love for *God* and love for His *Word* are inseparable, they are synonymous, virtually identical. If we do not love *both*, we love *neither*.

In one of the most staggering verses of Scripture, in fact, David writes, "I will worship toward thy holy temple, and praise thy name for thy lovingkindness and for thy truth: for thou hast magnified thy word above all thy name" (Ps. 138:2). Think of it! We spent a great deal of time studying God's names, but now we learn there is something even greater! "The Lord lays all the rest of his name under tribute to his Word," observed Charles Spurgeon.[238] Another writer adds: "It is impossible to place the inspired, inerrant Word of God on too high a pedestal, for God Himself honors it above His name!"[239]

In our next few studies, therefore, we will note the other ten verses in this psalm that speak of love for God's Word and note the specific aspect in each one.

Scriptures for Study: What observations can you make in these 10 verses?

JUNE 10

Loving God's Commandments

And I will delight myself in thy commandments, which I have loved. My hands also will I lift up unto thy commandments, which I have loved; and I will meditate in thy statutes.
(Ps. 119:47–48)

ANOTHER fascinating feature at the very heart of Psalm 119 is its use of no less than eight synonyms that refer to God's Word, each of which carries a little different shade of meaning or emphasis: law, testimonies, precepts, statutes, commandments, judgments, and word (two different Hebrew words). It is also significant that all eight are used within the first eleven verses, setting the stage for the rest of the Psalm. Finally, we then observe that David uses four of the eight synonyms in the 11 verses about his love of God's Word.

First, he says he loves God's **commandments** (vv. 47, 48, 127). Appearing 21 times in Psalm 119, this is the Hebrew feminine noun *miṣwah* (4687H), which indicates a clear, definite, and authoritative command. Its first occurrence in the psalm is in verse 6: "Then shall I not be ashamed, when I have respect unto all thy commandments." When we keep God's Word, when we obey Him implicitly, we will never have to apologize, never need to be ashamed because we failed to keep that Word. Of our text, then, John Gill submits, we can see David "stretching out his hands, and embracing [God's commandments] with both arms."[240] What a picture! Matthew Henry agrees: "I will lay hold of them as one afraid of missing them, or letting them go."[241]

As proof of that love, David vows, **I will meditate in thy statutes**. "Meditation kindled love," observed Puritan Charles Bridges.[242] The more we meditate, the more we will love, and the more we love, the more we will meditate—and the circle continues. One meaning of the Hebrew behind **meditate** (*śiyaḥ*, 7878H) is a "silent reflection on God's works (Pss. 77:8; 9:12), and God's Word (Ps. 119:15, 23, 27, 48, 78, 148)."[243] Another Puritan, Thomas Manton, puts this into practice: "What is the reason there is so much preaching and so little practice? For want of meditation. Constant thoughts are operative, and musing makes the fire burn. Green wood is not kindled by a flash or spark, but by constant blowing."[244]

In verse 127, David adds another striking picture, "I love thy commandments above gold; yea, above fine gold." Amazingly, "gold" and "fine gold" are actually two different Hebrew words. "Gold" (*zāhāb*, 2091H) refers to gold ore, gold in its raw state, while "fine gold" ("fine" is *paz*, 6337H) refers to pure, refined gold, an extremely scarce commodity. True wealth is not in the *world*, rather in the *Word*.

What an encouragement and challenge! In what do we find joy? What do we really love? What do we desire more than anything else? What do we consider true wealth? If our answer to each of those questions is not God's Word, we are in grave error, and we will ultimately be "of all men most miserable" (1 Cor. 15:19).

Scriptures for Study: What do the following verses declare about our relationship to God's commands: Matthew 7:21; John 15:14; James 1:22–25?

JUNE 11

Loving God's Law

O how love I thy law! it is my meditation all the day. (Ps. 119:97)

THE *second* synonym for God's Word David attaches to his love for that Word is **law**. Not only is this the most frequent synonym in the psalm (25 times) but also the one David uses most often as the object of his love.

The Hebrew, of course, is *tôrah* (8451H), a feminine noun meaning "instruction or direction." It most often refers to a body of teaching, and that is precisely what all Scripture is. *Tôrah* "must be understood to mean all Divine revelation as the guide of life," writes one commentator. "This it is which kindles the Psalmist's enthusiasm and demands his allegiance. It is no rigid code of commands and prohibitions, but a body of teaching, the full meaning of which can only be realized gradually and by the help of Divine instruction."[245]

The first occurrence of *tôrah* is in verse 1: "Blessed are the undefiled in the way, who walk in the law of the LORD." How significant that the Psalm begins with God's promise to those who love and obey the body of revealed truth He has given! If we obey God's body of revealed truth, we will be blessed. The opposite, however, is also true; if we do not obey that body of truth, we will be cursed.

Here in our text, then, David tells us that because he loved God's Word, it was his **meditation all the day**. No matter where he was, what he was doing, or who he was with, the Word permeated his thoughts. "How can a soul prosper," asked C. H. Mackintosh, 19th-century Plymouth Brethren preacher and writer, "how can there be growth in the divine life where there is no real love for the Bible or for books which unfold the precious contents of the Bible to our souls?"[246]

We are compelled to ask, and we believe it is a valid question: can anyone truthfully be called a Christian who does not love God's Word? Our Lord made it clear, "If ye love me, keep my commandments" (Jn. 14:15). The Apostle John echoed: "But whoso keepeth his word, in him verily is the love of God perfected: hereby know we that we are *in him* [i.e., true believers]" (1 Jn. 2:5; emphasis added). We cannot *keep* God's Word unless we *know* it, and we cannot know it unless we *love* it.

David adds in verse 113 that there is only one alternative, the "vain thoughts" of men, and only one remedy for it: the absolute truth of God's law that he loves. Likewise, in verse 163, he declares that he loved God's law so much, it motivated him to "hate and abhor lying." Indeed, love of Truth automatically demands that we hate untruth. This is all the more critical in a world that justifies lying "in certain circumstances" at best or condones it wholesale to achieve a desired end at worst. How much, then, do we love truth? Do we love it enough that we hate and abhor anything that is not true? Are lies of any kind ever a part of our speech?

Scriptures for Study: According to verse 165, what is a consequence of loving God's law?

JUNE 12

Loving God's Precepts and Testimonies

Consider how I love thy precepts: quicken me, O LORD, according to thy lovingkindness. (Ps. 119:159)
My soul hath kept thy testimonies; and I love them exceedingly. (v. 167)

THERE is a *third* synonym for God's Word David attaches to his **love** for that Word: **precepts** (21 times). The Hebrew here is *piqqûd* (6490H), a masculine noun meaning "precept, instruction." It is a poetic word, found only in the Psalms, always in the plural, and speaks of injunctions and moral obligations. It comes from a root that "expresses the idea that God is paying attention to how He wants things ordered."[247]

It should amaze us how church leaders today persist in doing things the way they choose, from creating whatever methods and ministries they deem fit to running the church like they would a corporation. Instead of opening Scripture to see how God wants things ordered, we do what pleases people. The first occurrence of **precepts** in this Psalm, in fact, says, "Thou hast commanded us to keep *thy* precepts diligently" (v. 4, emphasis added), underscoring that God wants things done His way, not ours.

It's not enough to read the Word, outline it, analyze it, exposit it, exegete it, or even memorize it. If we don't **love** it, all else is empty. It is our **love** for it that drives us to obedience and submission. When we really *love* Truth, it is impossible to compromise it, because anything that violates truth, however small, will be intolerable. "The more closely we cleave to God's precepts," Alexander Maclaren wrote, "the more shall we recoil from modes of thought and life which flout them."

Fourth and finally, David loved God's **testimonies**. Verse 167 is the final time David speaks of his **love** for the Word of God in this Psalm. The Hebrew is *ēdāh* (5713H), another feminine noun originally meaning a "testimony, witness, or warning sign." It eventually came to be used for a solemn testimony of the will of God, a sober and serious expression of God's standards for human behavior. Here we read not suggestions or optional proposals, rather God's absolute standards. Its first occurrence here is in verse 2: "Blessed are they that keep his testimonies," again showing blessing to those who conduct themselves according to God's standards. And, oh, how wondrously significant that the stone tablets containing the Ten Commandments are called God's "testimony" (Ex. 25:16; 31:18; 32:15)!

And so it is that David loved God's commandments, law, precepts, and testimonies. Such adoration permeated his heart and controlled his life. Such should be true of us. Whatever we adore in our lives is what will control us. When we truly love the Word of God, it alone will control our thinking, attitudes, actions, speech, desires, goals—in short, *everything*.

Scriptures for Study: What do the following verses declare about the writer's attitude toward God's word: Psalm 40:8; Romans 7:22?

JUNE 13

Delighting in God's Word

I will delight myself in thy statutes: I will not forget thy word. (Ps. 119:16)

TO further demonstrate his deep affection and adoration for God's Word, David not only uses the word "love" in Psalm 119, but he also uses **delight**. As we have seen, he uses "love" in conjunction with four of the eight synonyms for God's word in this psalm: commandments, law, precepts, and testimonies. In the present text, however, he uses still one more of those synonyms.

Statutes, which appears 21 times in this psalm, translates the Hebrew *ḥōq* (or *ḥuqqāh*, 2708H), which is derived from a verb that means "to cut, inscribe, or engrave." Oh, what a word this is! The old idiom "set in stone" illustrates it. God's statutes (or decrees) are engraved in stone, showing their permanence. Its first occurrence is in verse 5, where the psalmist says: "O that my ways were directed to keep thy statutes!" God's Word is not "up for grabs," not open for debate, not subject to reinterpretation for the times. *God's Word is set in stone!*

With that in mind, we then observe that there are actually three Hebrew words translated **delight** in this psalm. The first, which is here in our text, is *šā'a'* (8173H), which speaks of taking joy or enjoyment from something. The one in verse 24 (*ša'ašu'iym*, 8191H) is another form of that word used figuratively in the phrase "a pleasant plant" in Isaiah 5:7 to refer to God's pleasure in the people of Judah. It appears in this Psalm, in fact, several times (vv. 24, 77, 92, 143, 174).

A final word, however, is *ḥāpēṣ* (2654H), which indicates a stronger *emotional delight* than the others. Shechem, son of Hamor, for example, had an emotional **delight** in Jacob's daughter Dinah (Gen. 34:19). It appears also in Proverbs 31:13, where the Virtuous Woman "worketh willingly [i.e., with emotional delight] with her hands." (What an encouragement to Christian ladies today!)

It is this word David uses in verse 35: "Make me to go in the path of thy commandments; for therein do I delight." He took emotional **delight** in God's clear, definite, and authoritative "commandments." At one time or another we've all probably thought that God's commands are burdensome, but they are a delight to the godly believer.

> As the bird delights in the seed,
>   So upon Thy Word I feed.
> As the bee delights in the flower,
>   So do I long for the Word's power.
> As the deer pants for the water brook,
>   So upon Thy Word alone I look.
> As the miser delights in silver and gold,
>   So do I desire only Thy Word to hold.

Scriptures for Study: What do the following verses say about delight: Isaiah 58:13–14; Romans 7:22; 1 John 5:3?

JUNE 14

Loving God's Moral Law (1)

Thy word have I hid in mine heart, that I might not sin against thee. (Ps. 119:11)
O how love I thy law! (v. 97)

BUILDING on what we have considered in our last few studies, we turn to something even more specific, perhaps even a bit puzzling at first. David has encouraged us to love God's *law* and *commandments*, but how does this reconcile with our being under *grace*? Does living by grace mean we no longer serve the law?

It is a common misconception that there was no grace in the OT and no law in the NT. But law and grace exist in both. As Noah found grace in the eyes of the Lord (Gen. 6:8; cf. Ex. 33:12–17; Judg. 6:17; etc.), so "is the work of the law written in [our] hearts" (Rom. 2:15). As we have seen (Feb. 18), it is true that the aspect of the Mosaic system called "the judgments," which directed the social and civil life of Israel (Ex. 21:1—24:11), as well as the part called "the ordinances," which dictated the religious life of Israel (24:12—31:18), all pointed to Christ (Gal. 3:24–25) and ended with His fulfillment (Matt. 5:17). The Moral Law, however (the Ten Commandments), was written on men's heart from the beginning. As Genesis 26:5 makes clear, long before God gave the Mosaic Law, "Abraham obeyed [God's] voice, and kept [His] charge . . . commandments . . . statutes, and . . . laws" (cf. Job 23:12). Additionally, except for keeping the Sabbath, all the commandments are restated several times in the NT (cf. Rom. 13:9–10).[248]

The psalmist, therefore, tells us that he **hid** God's Word in his **heart**. **Hid** is *ṣāpan* (6845H), to hide, keep secret, to hide or conceal something of great value. **Heart** is *lēḇ* (3820H), which is used most often to refer to one's inner self and nature, including the intellect, emotions, and will, that is, the whole personality.

First, then, the Moral Law touches the *head*, the intellect. I once heard a preacher say long ago, "You might not be what you think you are, but *what* you think, you are." That is precisely the meaning of Proverbs 23:7: "For as he thinketh in his heart, so is he: Eat and drink, saith he to thee; but his heart is not with thee." Instead of *lēḇ*, "heart" is *nepeš* (5315H), which means breath or the act of breathing and figuratively refers to the inner being with its thoughts and emotions.

Even more significant is the Hebrew verb behind "thinketh" (*šā'ar*, 8176H), which appears only here in the entire OT and means "to calculate or to set a price on. The context here is that of misers who count the cost of everything their guests eat or drink. They find no enjoyment in their guests but only worry about the cost of it all."[249] And so it is that whatever we value, whatever we truly love, is what will monopolize our thinking. If we, therefore, think about the Ten Commandments, we will value them as "a chain of pearls to adorn us [and] our treasury to enrich us."[250]

Scriptures for Study: What do the following verses add to our thoughts today: Psalm 1:2; 37:31; 40:8; Job 22:22?

JUNE 15

Loving God's Moral Law (2)

Thy word have I hid in mine heart, that I might not sin against thee. (Ps. 119:11)
O how love I thy law! (v. 97)

THE *Law* by which God *rules* us, is as dear to Him as the *Gospel* by which He *saves* us," observed Puritan William Secker.[251] Ezekiel Hopkins likewise encouraged, "We find the same rules for our actions, the same duties required, the same sins forbidden in the Gospel as in the law."[252] God's Moral Law is called such because it reflects His own moral nature and, therefore, touches our entire being, first the *head*, the intellect.

Second, it touches the *heart*, the emotions. We use the word "heart" here as does our Western culture, as the seat of our emotions. "What is the sum of the Ten Commandments?" asked Thomas Watson.[253] Quoting Deuteronomy 6:5, his answer was to "love the LORD thy God with all thine heart, and with all thy soul, and with all thy might" (May 1–3). Think of it! If we say we love God, how can we not love His commandments? "If ye love me," Jesus said, "keep my commandments" (Jn. 14:15), and, "If ye keep my commandments, ye shall abide in my love" (15:10). To love God is to love His Law, and to love His Law is to love Him. There is no dichotomy here, rather a wondrous unity. As "righteousness and peace have kissed each other" (Ps. 85:10), law and love embrace at the Cross. "Man's law binds the hands only," Watson again observed, "God's law binds the heart."[254]

Third, the Moral Law touches the *hands*, that is, the will. What goes on in the head and heart is not theoretical; it is real and energizes actions. What the *head* cogitates, and where the *heart* meditates, the *hands* are sure to reciprocate.

Thankfully, this is as true of good as it is evil. David again teaches us here. He first declares, "The LORD rewarded me according to my righteousness; according to the cleanness of my hands hath he recompensed me." But why did God do so? David answers, "For I have kept the ways of the LORD, and have not wickedly departed from my God." Even more specifically he elaborates, "For all his judgments were before me, and I did not put away his statutes from me" (Ps. 18:20–22). Specifically, not only did David keep God's "statues" (June 13), but he also kept God's "ways." This is *derek* (1870H), which literally speaks of a "road" or "trodden path" and therefore metaphorically to a marked-out pattern of life, as Deuteronomy 8:6 commands: "Thou shalt keep the commandments [June 10] of the LORD thy God, to walk in his [patterns of life], and to fear him."

As we prepare to meditate on these commandments, let us realize that a desire to keep these moral mandates is proof positive of a regenerated life. By our very nature, none of us desires to obey God (Rom. 3:10–12). Such desire comes only by a transformed life. What does it mean to be a "new creature"? It means that "old things are passed away; behold, all things are become new" (2 Cor. 5:17).

Scriptures for Study: What do the following verses add to our thoughts today: Proverbs 2:1–5; 2:10–11?

JUNE 16

The Decalogue

[God] wrote upon the tables the words of the covenant, the ten commandments. (Ex. 34:28)

HAVE you ever wondered why most of **the ten commandments** are phrased in the negative? Why do they persist with that incessant, off-putting, "Thou shalt not"? The answer, of course, is that they presuppose man's naturally sinful condition, that "the heart is deceitful above all things, and desperately wicked" (Jer 17:9). Why have many in our day worked so diligently to remove **the ten commandments** from our courts of law? Simply because they do not want to face God's perfect religious, moral, and ethical standard, for it condemns them before court is even in session.

The Moral Law, therefore, stands forever as the very foundation of right behavior, that which we can never keep perfectly, since we are still in the flesh (Rom. 7), but ever strive to emulate. No one is (or ever has been) saved by keeping *any* law, including the Moral Law (Rom. 3:20; Gal. 3:11; cf. Matt. 19:16–26), but obedience of God's Word (Jn. 14:15, 23; 1 Jn. 2:1–5), which includes holiness of life (Eph. 4:24; 1 Thess. 4:3, 4, 7), is again proof positive of genuine salvation. In our fallen condition, the Law only *showed us* our sin and need for the Savior (Rom. 3:20; Gal. 3:19–25), but it now *serves us* by outlining how we are to live.

The ten **commandments** are referred to as such here in our text (and Deut. 10:4) using the Hebrew *dābār* (1697H), which means a word or speech and is a general term for God's revelation. This can be literally translated as "the ten words" (the Decalogue) because they are exactly what God said.

As is commonly observed, the Decalogue is divided into two parts. The first part consists of four "words" that address what man's relationship should be to the one true God. In turn, then, the first "word" brings us face-to-face with the *object* of worship, the second reveals the *manner* of worship, the third reinforces the *reverence* of worship, and the fourth specifies the *time* of worship. The second part of the Decalogue goes on to outline what our relationship should be to other men. We see there one "word" concerning family relationships and five "words" about community relationships.

To make all this even easier for us to assimilate, we are indebted to one commentator's wonderful summary of the Moral Law in ten actual words: "(1) religion, (2) worship, (3) reverence, (4) time, (5) authority, (6) life, (7) purity, (8) property, (9) tongue, and (10) contentment."[255] We will build on these in our next few studies, examining the same three principles for each: the OT *commandment*; the NT *counterpart*; and the combined *confrontation*.

My Dear Christian Friend, none of us has the ability to keep even one of God's commands, but, thankfully, God has promised: "I will put my spirit within you, and cause you to walk in my statutes . . . and do them" (Ezek. 36:27).

Scriptures for Study: To prepare for our study, read Exodus 20:1–26.

JUNE 17

The Law Concerning Religion

Thou shalt have no other gods before me. (Ex. 20:3)

HOW many religions are there? While some researchers count 21 major religions in the world, more broadly speaking, according to one research group, there are more than 4,200 religions, churches, denominations, religious bodies, faith groups, tribes, cultures, and movements.[256] While most in either category would claim to be "the one true religion," the God of the universe unapologetically declares of Himself: **Thou shalt have no other gods before me.**

First, the OT *commandment*. Having been in Egypt for 430 years (Ex. 12:41), the Israelites were quite familiar with polytheism (many gods) and paganism (the worship of idols). God's first and foremost command at the giving of His Law at Sinai, therefore, was that no other god was to be worshiped—*period*. The words **before me** are especially significant. This Hebrew expression is comprised of two words (*'al-pāniym*, 5921H/6440H), which can be rendered "no other gods before my face," or "in my presence," or even "in opposition to me." This is unambiguous; there are no gray areas. "The LORD God" (*Yāhweh/'Elōhiym*, v. 2) is the only true God, and He alone is to be worshipped.

Second, the NT *counterpart*. God's exclusiveness is reiterated many times in the NT. Jesus Himself, of course, declared to Satan, "Get thee hence, Satan: for it is written, Thou shalt worship the Lord thy God, and him only shalt thou serve" (Matt. 4:10). The Apostle Paul told the Corinthians, "We know that an idol is nothing in the world, and that there is none other God but one. For though there be that are called gods . . . there is but one God" (1 Cor. 8:4–6). And an angel instructed the Apostle John not to worship him but only to "worship God" (Rev. 22:9).

Third, the combined *confrontation*. "If we search our hearts with this 'candle of the Lord,' we shall find many an idol set up in their dark corners," wrote Alexander Maclaren, "and be startled to discover how much we need to bring ourselves to be judged and condemned by this commandment."[257] Why such a strong statement? Because idols are numerous and varied. While we tend to picture an idol as a stone or wooden image carved by an artisan in a primitive culture, an idol can be literally anything. The possibilities are endless, in fact. We can make idols of our country, car, boat, home, job, leisure activity, sports, furniture, clothing, books, yard, garden, pictures, art, collectibles, pets, or even a church ritual, church ordinance, church building, or particular Bible translation. And what idol is the greatest temptation of all? *Self*, when we (our feelings, views, opinions, etc.) become the chief focus. As one writer observes, "This suggests the logical possibility of over [313] million American religions, one for each of us."[258] An idol, then, can be anything we love *more than*, or even *as much* as, God, and that violates the very foundation of the Moral Law.

Scriptures for Study: What do the following verses tell us about this first commandment: Deuteronomy 6:14; Joshua 24:18–24; Psalms 73:25; 81:9?

JUNE 18

The Law Concerning Worship

Thou shalt not make unto thee any graven image or any likeness of any thing that is in heaven above, or that is in the earth beneath, or that is in the water under the earth. (Ex. 20:4)

STANDING beside the Moral Law's first mandate is the second. While "the first forbids us to have any other gods," observed G. Campbell Morgan, "the second forbids the creation of anything which is supposed to be a representation of Him, to assist man in worship."[259]

First, the OT *commandment*. Indeed, as we have noted (May 22), some Bible teachers insist that this commandment merely forbids art or other images of *false* gods, but the context makes the meaning clear. The first commandment commands us to worship God alone—"Thou shalt have no other gods before me" (v. 3)—but the second tells us to do so not by our own devices but only by His self-disclosure. Verse 5, in fact, goes on to detail how pagans make images of heavenly and earthly objects to represent their gods, but this must *never* be so of the True God.

Second, the NT *counterpart*. Of the many NT reinforcements of this command (including those cited yesterday), Acts 17:29 is among the most powerful: "Forasmuch then as we are the offspring of God, we ought not to think that the Godhead is like unto gold, or silver, or stone, graven by art and man's device." This verse is a conclusion to what has gone before it. We do not view God from the human perspective, such as making images of Him with our hands, rather we view Him from the divine perspective.

Especially pointed also is 1 John 5:21. Here, in one of the last verses of the NT to be penned, John commands *believers* (not unregenerate pagans): "Little children, keep yourselves from idols." "Keep" is *phulassō* (5442), "to keep watch, to guard," and was used of the garrison of a city guarding it against outside attack. This must have been a serious danger for John to end his letter with this thought.

Third, then, we see the combined *confrontation*. "Man is essentially an image-maker," wrote renowned Hebrew scholar Robert Girdlestone. "He seeks to make a visible representation even of God Himself, and gradually to transfer to the work of his own hands that reverence and dependence that properly belongs to the one living and true God."[260] That trait of man's nature, in fact, has been a perennial problem throughout history. From statues, to relics, to pictures of saints and even Jesus Himself, this pestilence has infected the Church. While several godly men have fought it through the ages (Eusebius of Caesarea, Jerome, Epiphanius, Augustine, John Calvin, J. C. Ryle, and others), the plague rages on.[261]

As our Lord Himself declared, "God is a Spirit: and they that worship him must worship [him] in spirit and in truth" (Jn. 4:24). And as G. Campbell Morgan again wisely submits, "The material cannot help the spiritual."

Scriptures for Study: What do verses 5 and 6 go on to add? 📖 Read Isaiah 40:18–26. What observations can you make?

JUNE 19

The Law Concerning Reverence

Thou shalt not take the name of the LORD thy God in vain; for the LORD will not hold him guiltless that taketh his name in vain. (Ex. 20:7)

CONTINUING what man's relationship should be to the one true God, man is commanded not to take God's **name in vain**, which is obviously closely connected with the first two commands. While disobeying the first one *banishes* God from the mind and the second *blemishes* our worship of Him, violating this third one *belittles* Him with irreverence.

First, the OT *commandment*. The Hebrew behind **in vain** (*sāw'*, 7723H) primarily means falsehood, emptiness, and vanity (futility). That latter sense, in fact, appears many times (e.g., Job 7:3; Pss. 60:11; 89:47; 127:1; Jer. 46:11; Hos. 12:11). In the present context, therefore, it seems best to understand this term in not using God's name in any false, empty, or futile way. As one Hebrew authority suggests, "The instruction is aimed at preserving reverential regard for the person of God; and thus *sāw'* might also be translated 'without due reverence.'"[262] As John Gill submits, we must not use God's name "in a light and trifling way, without any show of reverence of him, and affection to him." Albert Barnes adds that this also prohibits "any profane and idle utterance of the name of God."

Second, the NT *counterpart* strongly reinforces this principle. The very first instruction in the "Model Prayer" Jesus gave His disciples was, "After this manner therefore pray ye: Our Father which art in heaven, Hallowed be thy name" (Matt. 6:9). "Hallowed" translates *hagiazō* (37), to make clean, to render pure. In light of our study of God's name *'Elōhiym* (Jan. 14), as well as many other of His OT names,[263] this commands us to revere those names because they are reflections of His character, to say nothing that will in any way belittle Him or His name.

Third, the combined *confrontation*. Oh, how God's name is disrespected, demeaned, and disparaged in our day! It is used as an expletive, to pronounce a curse on someone, or to take an oath. The beloved J. Vernon McGee recounts one man who, after becoming a believer, made the statement, "When I was converted, I lost over half of my vocabulary!" Indeed, our Lord's name is used in so many flippant, careless, and thoughtless ways in our culture that it permeates every thought, word, and action. Even more tragic, Christians have been infected. (The expression, "Oh, my God!" or acronym "OMG" has become all too common even among believers.) Additionally, how little reverence there is even in our churches (cf. Feb. 1)!

It is also critical to note that the second and third commandments have judgment attached for violating them. Have not succeeding generations of Americans demonstrated that God has "visit[ed] the iniquity of the fathers upon the children" (v. 5)? We continue in our idolatry and the judgment continues to unfold. And how many of those continue to use God's name in vain, never thinking that God will rule them guilty of blasphemy?

Scriptures for Study: What does Leviticus 19:12 and 24:11–16 promise?

JUNE 20

The Law Concerning Time (1)

Remember the sabbath day, to keep it holy. Six days shalt thou labour, and do all thy work: But the seventh day is the sabbath of the LORD thy God: in it thou shalt not do any work . . . (Ex. 20:8–10)

IN light of the three foregoing principles of worship, it is not surprising that the proper time for worship would be addressed. "At regular intervals through all the days," wrote G. Campbell Morgan, "man is to turn wholly from that which is material to that which is spiritual."[264]

First, the OT *commandment.* **Sabbath** renders the Hebrew *šabbāṯ* (7676H), the root of which is verb *šābaṯ* (7673H), "to cease or rest." It first occurs in Genesis 2:2, where God "rested on the seventh day from all his work which he had made." That set the precedent that God desires His people to cease work (implying rest). Significantly, there was no prescribed Sabbath for man until it was instituted in our text (and prescribed in 16:23); there is, in fact, no indication that either the patriarchs in Genesis or Job (a contemporary of Abraham) observed the Sabbath.

Once instituted, however, this principle permeated OT revelation, appearing some 77 times. Why? While man needs rest, this is only secondary. The primary reason is in the word **remember**. This is *zāḵar* (2142H), which occurs some 238 times,[265] 57 of which are in the Psalms and means not only to remember but also "to think of or pay attention to." This underscores that *remembrance was a major aspect of worship* (e.g. Pss. 22:27; 45:17; 63:5–6; 77:11). Indeed, remembering all that God has done is to worship Him. One day each week was, therefore, to be kept **holy** (*qāḏaš*, 6942H), that is, set apart, set aside for worship. So critical is this fourth commandment, that the first three are fulfilled in man's relationship to God only by this one, in that man is both "a worker and a worshipper."[266]

Second, the NT *counterpart.* While there are some sincere believers who insist that the Sabbath is still in force and binding today, that is not the case. Yes, there are 60 occurrences of the word **Sabbath** in the NT (*sabbaton*, 4521), but all except one are in the Gospels and Acts and are used as historical reference, that is, something that occurred on a Sabbath day (e.g., Mk. 1:21). The only occurrence in the Epistles (Col. 2:16) is a rebuke of man-made religious traditions.

Do we, therefore, conclude that a time of worship is now unimportant? God forbid! While the *letter* of the Law (the Sabbath) is no longer in force, the *spirit* of that Law remains just as strong. The first day of the week, the day of our Lord's resurrection, became the Church's day for public worship (Jn. 20:19; Acts 20:7; 1 Cor. 16:2; Rev. 1:10). Church Fathers from the first two centuries—such as Justin Martyr, Barnabas, and Ignatius—also prove this beyond the slightest doubt.[267]

Oh, what a fulfillment the Lord's Day is! In the old economy, they worked *toward* their Holy Day; in the new we work *from* ours. And that day is not for *work*, much less one for *worldliness*, rather one for *worship*.

Scriptures for Study: Note the idea of remembrance in the psalms cited above.

JUNE 21

The Law Concerning Time (2)

Not forsaking the assembling of ourselves together, as the manner of some is;
but exhorting one another: and so much the more, as ye
see the day approaching. (Heb. 10:25)

IN his exposition of the Ten Commandments, Puritan Ezekiel Hopkins wrote of the Lord's Day: "God sanctifies it by *consecration*, we sanctify it by *devotion*. He hath set *it* apart for His worship; and, on it, we ought to set *ourselves* apart for His worship."[268]

Third, therefore, we should with our whole heart consider the combined *confrontation* the OT and NT mandates level at us. We live in a day of unprecedented abandonment of public worship in the Local Church, sadly, even by Christians themselves. It seems that church attendance is always the last consideration when anything else "comes up." It is rarely the overarching priority, and our text addresses this attitude in the strongest of terms.

(1) Notice the *rebuke*. **Assembling of ourselves together** is one word in the Greek (*episunagōgē*, 1997; cf. 2 Thes. 2:1) and is preceded by the definite article (**the**). This unique term emphasizes that **the** Christian congregation is just that, *the* gathering of Christian believers for the express purpose of worship, fellowship, and learning with Christ at the center. It is then the word **forsaking** (*egkataleipō*, 1459) that carries the devastating rebuke. While the root *leipō* means "to leave or forsake," *kataleipō* is stronger, as in "leave down, that is, leave behind or remaining." Adding the prefix *eg* (or *en*), "in, at, or by," further strengthens the word to its fullest: "to leave behind in any place or state . . . to leave in the lurch."[269] So strong is this word that it is used of Demas (Aug. 23), who had once been an active partner in ministry (Col. 4:14) but had then "forsaken" Paul (2 Tim. 4:10).

(2) Note also the *representatives*. **As the manner of some is** indicates that certain ones in the congregation had left the others in the lurch. While there are several possible theories as to why,[270] does that really matter? They had abandoned their spiritual siblings! Worse, the construction of the verb *egkataleipō* (**forsaking**) expresses continuous or repeated action. Like today, this had become a habit!

(3) Finally, consider the *reason* this is such a serious spiritual ailment: because **[we] see the day approaching**. Which day? Is it death, the last judgment, the destruction of Jerusalem, heightened persecution, Christ's Second Coming? We should rather ask again, does it matter? Whichever it was, it was **approaching** (*eggizō*, 1448, "to bring near, to be at hand"); it was just around the next corner. In light of that impending day, then, we should be **exhorting one another** (*parakaleō*, 3870), comforting, beseeching, admonishing, and even imploring one another in this area of faithfulness. Unfaithfulness in church attendance is a serious matter, and few things grieve the godly pastor's heart more deeply.

Scriptures for Study: How do the following verses challenge us in light of today's study: Matthew 25:13; 1 Corinthians 3:13; Ephesians 5:27?

JUNE 22

The Law Concerning Authority (1)

Honour thy father and thy mother: that thy days may be long upon the land which the LORD thy God giveth thee. (Ex. 20:12)

HAVING presented four "words" that address what man's relationship should be to Him, God turns to what our relationship should be to our fellow men. The first "word" concerns authority in the family. Some view it as a bridge, in fact, between the two categories. We agree.

First, the OT *commandment*. **Honour** is again the fascinating word *kāḇēḏ* (June 7), which demonstrates that parents "carry a lot of weight," that they are important, influential, and indispensable. How significant it is that this word is used of parents as it is of God, for they are His representatives in the home. Their offspring are, therefore, commanded to recognize that fact and to acknowledge it openly with the proper respect and obedience.

This honor is first given to the **father**. The Hebrew *'āḇ* (1H) "apparently is derived from such baby sounds as *abab*"[271] and includes the ideas of the head of a household, ancestor, patron of a class, benevolence, respect, and honor. Because it is also used of God as well as a human father, the place and importance of the latter is all the more pointed. **Mother** (*'ēm*, 517H) is a beautiful term that is used figuratively for Eve "because she was the mother of all living" (Gen. 3:20), of Deborah as "a mother in Israel" (Judg. 5:7), and of a city as mother of its inhabitants (Is. 50:1; Ezek. 16:44; Hos 2:2).[272]

So, to emphasize the importance of this parental pair, **father** and **mother** appear together some 100 times in Scripture. A dozen of these are in Proverbs alone, such as: "My son, hear the instruction of thy father, and forsake not the law of thy mother: For they shall be an ornament of grace unto thy head, and chains about thy neck" (1:8–9).

Second, the NT *counterpart*. The blazing NT enforcement of this fifth commandment appears, of course, in Ephesians 6:1–3, which presents a two-fold reminder. First, speaking directly to children, Paul commands the *action*, namely, *obedience*. "Obey" is *hupakouō* (5219), "to get under the authority of someone and listen." They are not just to "do what they are told" but are to listen and assimilate what they hear. Why? Because it "is right"; because there is nothing more foundational to human society than learning obedience.

But Paul goes on secondly to emphasize the *attitude* behind the action: *honor*. This is *timaō* (5091), "to estimate worth, hold in respect, honor, revere." To fail to honor parents is the same as saying they are worthless. But honoring them brings two blessings that will be generally true: *quality* of life ("it may be well with thee") and *quantity* of life ("you may live long on the earth"). Like obedience, if children do not learn respect for their parents, they will have none for anyone else.

Scriptures for Study: Read the following verses in Proverbs, noting what each adds to our study: 6:20–24; 10:1; 15:20; 19:26; 20:20; 23:22–25.

JUNE 23

The Law Concerning Authority (2)

Honour thy father and thy mother: that thy days may be long upon the land which the LORD thy God giveth thee. (Ex. 20:12)

"AS goes the home, so goes the nation," it has been *wisely* stated and *widely* demonstrated in the last several decades. Drug and alcohol abuse, sexual promiscuity, and many other plagues are pandemic. Even worse, the very things that would help solve the problems—morals, values, parental authority, corporal punishment, the Bible, and patriotism—have been thrown out and replaced with relativism, sexual liberation, alternate lifestyles, homosexual marriage, abortion, and contraceptives.

Dare I interject my fear that dividing our churches into age groups is not helping the situation? Is it not instructive that we do not find the 12-year-old Jesus in "Children's Temple" or "Junior Passover," rather we see Him with His parents at that great worship event (Luke 2:41–42)? Without exception, in fact, when we see God's people worshipping in Scripture, the family is together.[273] Even drawings in the catacombs demonstrate this biblical precedent.

Third, therefore, we once again should look to the combined *confrontation* of God's Moral Law as given in both the OT and NT. Let us consider the blessings that come with obeying this command of God:

(1) Honoring parents instills a deeper reverence for God. In 2 Timothy 3:1–5 we read Paul's terrible description of the sins of mankind in the last days. It is, indeed, significant that right in the middle of his list Paul says, "blasphemers, disobedient to parents, unthankful, unholy." Indeed, blasphemy of God and disrespect of parents are bedfellows. If one has no respect for parents, he will have no respect for God, and vice-versa. This places added responsibility upon parents. How will children learn love and reverence for God? By seeing it in the parents.

(2) Honoring parents promotes the right attitude toward law, government, and other adults. Any juvenile court judge will attest to the fact that where there is no respect for parents neither is there respect for the law. We would submit here that Christians really need to change their vocabulary. Parents should not have the attitude that they are "raising children." If one raises corn, for example, he will get corn. Likewise, if parents raise children, they will get children. (Are there not many 40-year-old children running around nowadays?) Rather, let our attitude be that we are raising future adults, future citizens, future godly Christians.

(3) Honoring parents passes on this heritage to the next generation. God has designed these principles to be passed on by precept and example to each new generation by the previous generation. God wants parents to teach their children these principles so they in turn can teach their children who will then teach their children, and so on. This practice will give us a lasting Christian heritage.[274]

Scriptures for Study: Read and prayerfully consider the verses listed in endnote 272 above.

JUNE 24

The Law Concerning Life

Thou shalt not kill. (Ex. 20:13)

HOW significant it is that this command appears here! It is the first one that speaks exclusively of our dealings with all other men in general. So, the worst possible sin to commit against another is murder. Why is murder an abomination to God (Prov. 6:17)? Because man is made in God's image, making murder a direct attack upon Him. So heinous is this crime that God instituted capital punishment (Gen. 9:6; cf. Matt. 26:52; Rom. 13:4; Rev. 13:10).

First, then, we observe the meaning of the OT *commandment*. This verse has been used by our nonresistance and pacifist brethren to teach that *all* killing is wrong. While we love these dear folks and certainly agree with their high view of the sanctity of life, both the Hebrew and Greek words that are used speak of murder, not *all* killing. (It is hard to explain why Jesus would instruct his disciples to buy a sword [Lk. 22:36] if He did not expect them to use it.)

Kill is the Hebrew *rāṣaḥ* (7523H), which while at times is used for an accidental killing (Num. 35:11; Josh. 20:3) or even death by means of an animal attack (Prov. 22:13), is used primarily to indicate premeditated murder (Deut. 5:17; Judg. 20:4; 1 Kings 21:19; Ps. 94:6; Jer. 7:9; Hos. 4:2; 6:9). If any doubt remains, it is completely erased by the Greek word used for "kill" (*phoneuō*, 5407) in Matthew 5:21: "Ye have heard that it was said by them of old time, Thou shalt not kill." This word is never used in any other way other than murder.[275] In fact, it appears in Romans 13:9—a direct reference to the sixth commandment—to parallel (and thereby clarify) the use of the Hebrew *rāṣaḥ* in our text.

Second, the NT *counterpart*. This command is repeated not only in Romans 13:9 (along with other "words" of the Moral Law) but also in James 2:11. Even more significant, however, is how our Lord Himself enhanced this prohibition. As noted above, during His Sermon on the Mount, Jesus cited the sixth commandment about murder (Matt. 5:21), but in the very next verse He added, "But I say unto you, That whosoever is angry with his brother without a cause shall be in danger of the judgment." Uncontrolled anger that could lead to murder—as in the idiom, "If looks could kill"—is as sinful as the act itself (cf. 1 Jn. 3:15).

Third, the combined *confrontation*. In addition to the applications already made, one that begs for recognition concerns the legalized murderers in our day who wear lab coats. As any honest person would admit, abortion, no matter what the reason, is premeditated murder. Inexplicably, however, not all Christians agree. One evangelical author, in fact, says that if "the fetus"—this is the term the pro-abortionist uses to escape the reality that we're talking about a human being—threatens the life of the mother, then it is the same as "a crazed madman threatening someone else with a revolver."[276] So much for the sanctity of life.

Scriptures for Study: What do the following verses say about the sanctity of life: Jeremiah 1:5; Judges 13:7; Pss. 127:3; 139:13–16; Luke 1:41, 44?

JUNE 25

The Law Concerning Purity

Thou shalt not commit adultery. (Ex. 20:14)

THROUGHOUT the Middle Ages, sexual love, even between spouses, was considered gross evil by the Roman Catholic Church, which then glorified celibacy. Eventually, in fact, it prohibited such activity on certain "holy days," ultimately totaling half the year![277] Thank God again for the Reformation! The Reformers, and the Puritans, recognized that "marriage is honourable in all, and the bed undefiled" (Heb. 13:4a). The second half of that verse, however, goes on to declare: "but whoremongers and adulterers God will judge."

First, then, we examine the OT *commandment*. It is significant, indeed, that right on the heels of the commandment that declares the *sanctity* of life is another that affirms the *sacredness* of marriage. Why? Because marriage is at the very foundation of the home and society itself, and nothing attacks marriage with more violence and wreaks more devastation than does **adultery**. That is precisely why it merited the death penalty under the Mosaic Law (Lev. 20:10).

For one thing, adultery *debases* the adulterer, making him a senseless animal who cannot control his urges (Jer. 5:8). It also *destroys* one's reputation, for "his reproach shall not be wiped away" (Prov. 6:32–33). It then *devastates* the marriage bond. Since marriage is a "covenant of companionship" (Mal. 2:14), sex within marriage is the "covenant cement"[278] that helps hold the marriage structure secure. This is one reason, in fact, why sex within marriage is required (1 Cor. 7:3, 5a). Adultery, then, destroys all this. Finally, adultery *dishonors* God, who created this union; we must always honor God with our bodies (1 Cor. 6:18–20).

Second, the NT *counterpart*. As with the sixth commandment, this one is not only reinforced in the NT (Rom. 13:9,10; 1 Cor. 6:9; Heb. 13:4; Jas. 2:11) but also enhanced. During His Sermon on the Mount, Jesus again cited the commandment but then added: "But I say unto you, That whosoever looketh on a woman to lust after her hath committed adultery with her already in his heart" (Matt. 5:27–28). "To lust is to look and to imagine the sexual possibilities."[279] In other words, to *lust* does not mean to *look*, rather it means to *linger*.

Third, the combined *confrontation*. We hardly need even mention the sex-saturated society we live in—that is a given—but we certainly need to face the reality that it has invaded the Church. Christian leaders have been caught in adultery and pornography addiction. Evangelicals are divided over the issues of homosexuality and even same-sex "marriage." Many Christians see no problem with couples living together outside of marriage and even make excuses for those caught in adultery and other sexual sin. So it is, then, "The Seventh Commandment requireth the preservation of our own and our neighbor's chastity, in heart, speech, and behavior" and forbids "all unchaste thoughts, words, and actions."[280]

Scriptures for Study: What is the price of sexual sin in the following verses: Proverbs 6:25–27; 1 Corinthians 6:9–10; James 1:14–15?

JUNE 26

The Law Concerning Property
Thou shalt not steal. (Ex. 20:15)

WE cannot help but be amazed that God's Moral Law addresses even the rights of personal property. While Socialism is nothing more than *pilfering*—it is a forced redistribution of what some have worked for to others who have not—God's law *protects* such property. What ludicrous folly was French anarchist Pierre-Joseph Proudhon's slogan (1840), "Property is theft!"

First, note the OT *commandment*. Running a close second behind lying, which is addressed in the ninth commandment, is stealing. It is a universal vice. "It is the smallest part of the thieves that are hung," Luther said. "If we're to hang them all, where shall we get rope enough?"[281] Indeed, to catalog all the ways one can steal would result in a long list. Such a listing is really not needed, however, simply because the definition of stealing is so simple. The Hebrew here (*gānaḇ*, 1589H), means "to take that which belongs to another without his consent or knowledge [and is] restricted to acts of theft done secretly."[282] Everyone knows what stealing is, however they might choose to justify it in any given situation.

Second, the NT *counterpart*. Not only is stealing included in Paul's listing of the commandments in Romans 13:9–10, but he reiterates in Ephesians 4:28a: "Let him that stole steal no more." The Greek behind both "stole" and "steal" is *kleptō* (2813, English, "kleptomania") and, like the Hebrew, pictures stealing by stealth, "the secrecy, craft, and cheating involved in the act."[283] Knowing that stealing, like lying and unrighteous anger (vv. 25–26), are among the easiest for Christians to fall back into, Paul challenged these believers not to live according to the culture.

Third, the combined *confrontation*. As serious as it is to steal from anyone, it is far worse to steal from God. As the last prophet of the OT recorded God's question to His people, "Will a man rob God? Yet ye have robbed me. But ye say, Wherein have we robbed thee? In tithes and offerings" (Mal. 3:8). The Israelites, of course, were required to tithe, that is, give ten percent of their income and goods for religious purpose. This practice actually preceded the Mosaic Law (Gen. 14:17–20; 28:22), but that system went on to prescribe several tithes, which, when totaled, amounted to about 23 percent (Lev. 27:30; Deut. 14).

NT Christian giving, however, transcends such pre-prescribed percentages: "Upon the first day of the week let every one of you lay by him in store, as God hath prospered him" (1 Cor. 16:2). "Prospered" (*euodoō*, 2137) literally means "to make good one's journey." What, then, is at the root of our giving? It is based upon the wonderful journey God has provided in Christ and flows from a thankful heart for all God has done (we will return to this theme on Dec. 1).

We can also rob God in the area of time. God has made us stewards of time (Eph. 5:15–17), so we must use it wisely, advantageously, and faithfully.

Scriptures for Study: What do the following passages say about theft: Leviticus 19:11, 13; 19:35–37; Deuteronomy 24:7; 1 Thessalonians 4:6?

JUNE 27

The Law Concerning the Tongue (1)

Thou shalt not bear false witness against thy neighbour. (Ex. 20:16)

LYING is, by far, the most prominent sin of mankind. It permeates our nature and society. Lying is often used to cover up other sins and is, far more than people realize, so *ingrained* in our being, and therefore so *imbedded* in our practical living, that it takes the very power of God to break its grip.

First, the OT *commandment*. Just as we should not take God's name in vain in our relationship to Him, neither should we sin in our speech in our associations with other people. The basic meaning of the Hebrew behind the word **false** (*šeqer*, 8267H) is a "lie, falsehood, or deception" and is "used of words or activities which are false in the sense that they are groundless, without basis in fact or reality."[284] The word **witness** in turn (*'ēḏ*, 5707H) reflects the idea of the ancient court of law, while **neighbour** (*rēa'*, 7453H) is a very broad term used of a lover (Hosea 3:1), a close friend (Deut. 13:6; Job 2:11), an acquaintance (Prov. 6:1), an adversary in court (Ex. 18:16), or even an enemy in combat (2 Sam. 2:16).[285]

With all this data gathered, the conclusion is apparent. Wherever it might be, whatever might be the situation, and whoever might be involved, God prohibits every type of falsehood. A lie is a lie, and it is forbidden—*period*. Why? Because it is **against [our] neighbour**, that is, another person. Mark it down: every lie is against someone; every lie hurts someone.

Second, the NT *counterpart*. The clearest NT reinforcement of this commandment appears in Ephesians 4:25: "Wherefore putting away lying, speak every man truth with his neighbour: for we are members one of another." There is no better way to define lying than to say it is "the antithesis of truth, *alētheia*,"[286] which is exactly the meaning of the Greek here (*pseudos*, 5579). As we have noted before, *alētheia* (225) is the real state of affairs, the way things really are, that which is reliable, constant, sure, and unchanging.[287] A lie, therefore, is *a statement that is contrary to fact offered with the intent to deceive*. As we will see, the ways to do this are many and varied.

While Paul's command here is a perfect reflection of the ninth commandment, he adds a deeper motive: all believers are members of the same body. To illustrate, do our eyes deliberately try to deceive the brain by sending false images? Does our brain try to deceive our feet into walking in the wrong direction? Of course not. If our body parts were constantly lying to one another, our body would soon destroy itself. Paul's point, then, is simply this: *lying is diametrically opposed to the doctrine of the Church*. There cannot possibly be *harmony* in the Church if there is not first *honesty* among the members. A lie, that is, *any* lie, regardless of its "shape or size," damages the whole body! We will continue these thoughts tomorrow by considering just how varied lies can be.

Scriptures for Study: What do the following verses say about lying: Ps. 119:29, 163; Proverbs 6:12; 12:22; Colossians 3:9?

JUNE 28

The Law Concerning the Tongue (2)

Thou shalt not bear false witness against thy neighbour. (Ex. 20:16)

"TO act the Cretan, is a proverb for to lie," an ancient axiom declared.[288] In the same way that to be "Corinthianized" meant that one had stooped to the grossest immorality and drunken debauchery common in Corinth, to be called a "Cretan" was the same as being called a liar, a term used even in the literature of the day. Paul, in fact, noted this by quoting the Cretan poet and reputed prophet Epimenides: "One of themselves, even a prophet of their own, said, The Cretans are alway[s] liars, evil beasts, slow bellies" (Titus 1:12). The word "always" indicates that this was not the exception but the rule, the general moral character, "the national sin" (John Gill) of the Cretans.

Third, then, we are faced with the combined *confrontation*. Fascinatingly, in the very same era as Epimenides but in a different part of the world, the prophet Jeremiah labored, and we see lying as a way of life even among God's chosen people. Jeremiah 5, in fact, is the most graphic biblical example of what exists in our society today. In the dark shadow of coming judgment, God sends Jeremiah rushing through the capital city Jerusalem seeking anyone who "executeth judgment, that seeketh the truth" and promises to "pardon" the sins of the entire nation if he can find *one person* (v. 1). But there was not a single one. Think of it! Not one person, whether rich or poor, whether citizen or leader (vv. 4–5), told the truth. Even though they mouthed the words "the LORD liveth," in reality "surely they [swore] falsely" (v. 2).

We can't help but wonder if God is asking of America today, "Are there any who tell the truth?" And we can't help but wonder what judgments are to come. As in Jeremiah's day, we are a generation of liars. We have no interest in, much less desire for, Truth. We weave, dodge, and duck the Truth like a boxer avoids being hit. Oh, let this not be true in our churches!

Now, just how varied is lying? This is perhaps answered as easily as looking at a thesaurus for synonyms. Consider these other words that reflect falsehood: fabrication, inaccuracy, misrepresentation, prevarication, deception, distortion, misinformation, or even idioms such as whopper, tall tale, or "fish story." To that list we could add: embellishing a story, cheating (because we're saying we did something on our own when we didn't), betraying a confidence, making excuses for wrong conduct, telling a half-truth, plagiarism, boasting, flattery, false humility, hypocrisy, false promises, and tragically much more.

The reason a lie is despicable is because it's a perversion of Truth. God created Truth, but when we lie we are trying to turn falsehood into Truth. How grotesque that is! That is why Paul commands that we "put away" (*apotithēmi*, 659, picturing taking off a soiled garment) all lying.

Scriptures for Study: Read Jeremiah 5. What observations can you make?

JUNE 29

The Law Concerning Contentment

Thou shalt not covet . . . (Ex. 20:17)

THE final "word" of the Decalogue is unique. While the other laws concerning our dealings with men address the externals of *conduct*, this one speaks to the internals of *character*. Instead of overt *acts*, it addresses covert *attitudes*. One or more of the preceding sins, in fact, will often spring from this seed.

First, the OT *commandment*. When used in the negative sense, the Hebrew (*ḥāmaḏ*, 2530H) speaks of passionate desire and lust. What does it mean to **covet**? It's not only wanting something, but rather wanting something someone else has, as the rest of our text clarifies: "your neighbor's . . . wife . . . manservant or maidservant . . . ox or donkey, or anything that belongs to your neighbor."

Second, the NT *counterpart*. Once again, the Apostle Paul enlarges on this sin in his letter to the Ephesian believers, challenging them not to allow sins such as fornication, uncleanness, or covetousness to overtake them (Eph. 5:3). "Covetousness" translates *pleonexia* (4124), "a greedy desire to have more," which is a good (and broader) definition of covetousness. As Puritan Thomas Watson submitted about this sin, it is "an insatiable desire of getting the world," and Augustine defined it as "to desire more than enough."[289]

In case we are tempted to think that covetousness is a "minor sin," Paul goes on to add a staggering addendum in verse 5: the "covetous man . . . is an idolater [and] hath [no] inheritance in the kingdom of Christ and of God" (he likewise wrote to the Colossians that "covetousness . . . is idolatry," Col. 3:5). Ephesus was an important city in the ancient world, not only because of its being the capitol of the Roman province of Asia Minor, as well as being its greatest commercial city—the "Gateway to Asia"—but also because it had become the religious center of pagan worship in all Asia. Ephesus was not only famous for the great temple of Diana (Artemis in Greek), one of the seven wonders of the ancient world, but was also known as the center of occult arts and practices. The Ephesian believers would have, therefore, been very much aware of what Paul was saying about no idolater being in God's kingdom. Just as idolatry was mentioned earlier in the Moral Law, we see it again here in all its severity and consequence. God simply will not tolerate any other gods! (We will return to this theme on Nov. 24.)

Third, the combined *confrontation*. What then is the cure for *covetousness*? There is only one: *contentment*. Covetousness is actually a theological issue, for it attacks God's sovereignty by saying that what He has provided is not enough. Contentment, however, says, "I am submitted to what *God* wants for me, not what *I* want for me." As Puritan Jeremiah Burroughs wrote, "I have a sufficient portion between Christ and my soul abundantly to satisfy me in every condition."[290]

Scriptures for Study: What do the following verses declare about today's theme: Philippians 4:11–12; Hebrews 13:5; James 4:1–3?

JUNE 30

Summary of the Moral Law

Jesus said ... Thou shalt love the Lord thy God with all thy heart, and with all thy soul, and with all thy mind. This is the first and great commandment. And the second is like unto it, Thou shalt love thy neighbour as thyself. On these two commandments hang all the law and the prophets.. (Matt. 22:37–40)

PURITAN Samuel Bolton masterfully summarizes the purpose and value of the Moral Law: "The law sends us to the gospel that we may be justified; and the gospel sends us to the law again to inquire what is our duty as those who are justified. . . . The *law* sends us to the *gospel* for our justification; the *gospel* sends us to the *law* to frame our way of life."[291] Even more masterfully, however, our Lord took the *Ten* Commandments and reduced them to only *two*.

The setting of our text, of course, is one of many times the religious leaders questioned Jesus with the purpose of trapping Him with His answer. The background of this incident was that over the centuries the rabbis had artificially systemized the Mosaic Law. They first divided it into the 613 commandments (ironically paralleling the 613 Hebrew letters in the Decalogue itself). They further organized these 613 into 248 that were positive (one for every part of the human body) and 365 that were negative (one for each day of the year). Finally, they then endlessly debated which laws were "heavy" (absolutely binding; e.g., Lk. 10:27) and "light" (less binding; e.g., Deut. 22:6). So, assuming Jesus would have His own system, this law-expert asked Him which law He thought was the greatest.

Instead of being dragged into a centuries old debate, however, our Lord went right to the Law itself! As noted in an earlier study (May 3), Jesus' response—**Thou shalt love the Lord thy God with all thy heart, and with all thy soul, and with all thy mind**—was part of the *Shema* ("hear"), which was recited twice daily (morning and evening) as a creed by devout Jews. That is the first and greatest all-encompassing command. At the very foundation of our relationship to God is our love for Him. If we love Him with our entire being (see May 1–3), then the farthest thoughts from our minds will be worshipping false gods, making images of the True God, taking His name in vain, or violating the prescribed day of worship.

The second greatest command encompasses all the relationships we have with others: **Thou shalt love thy neighbour as thyself.** If we truly love others, we will honor our parents (and all authority by extension), never murder, commit adultery, steal, lie, or covet. Think of it! Everything hangs on these two commandments.

Finally, it is extremely significant that Mark's account of this incident indicates that this scribe acknowledged Jesus' correct answer and told Him so, to which Jesus responded: "Thou art not far from the kingdom of God" (12:32–35). If such truth *registers* on the mind of an unrepentant scribe, should it not *resonate* in the heart of the godly believer?

Scriptures for Study: What do the following verses say about law and love: Romans 13:10; Galatians 5:14; James 2:8; 1 John 4:21?

JULY 1

Reading, Exhortation, and Doctrine

Till I come, give attendance to reading, to exhortation, to doctrine. (1 Tim. 4:13)

HERE in one of the Pastoral Epistles we encounter a verse that is among the most crucially important ones concerning the ministry of the Local Church. The Apostle Paul instructs Timothy, the pastor of the Church at Ephesus at the time, about the number one priority of the Church and its pastor.

We can say that with such confidence simply because of the words **give attendance**, which translate *prosechō* (4337), a nautical term for holding a ship in a direction, to sail onward. So what does Paul instruct Timothy to do? To hold his course. And which course is that? The Word of God. If, indeed, a church and its pastor love God and His Word, there will be this three-fold emphasis at the very core of the ministry. We will sail toward this harbor without deviation.

First, there will be the *declaration of the sacred Word*. There is actually some debate on precisely what **reading** refers to, whether Timothy's *personal* reading of Scripture or the *public* reading of Scripture in the Church. We submit it is the latter for three reasons, the first being that such public reading was the norm for the day. Because of the scarcity of manuscripts, the practice of reading and explaining Scripture in the synagogue (Acts 15:21; Lk. 4:16) was carried over into the Church (Col. 4:16; 1 Thes. 5:27). Second, since the other two principles in the verse are obviously carried on in public, so it would seem for this reading of Scripture. Third, this is all the more emphasized by the Greek definite article preceding all three of these principles: *the* **reading**, *the* **exhortation**, and *the* **doctrine**.

So, first and foremost, it is the public reading (and obvious exposition) of God's Word that should fill our churches. That should be our course. (Practically speaking, this has tragically become increasingly difficult in our day because of the plethora of translations that are in the pews.)

Second, there will be the *demand of submissive obedience*. **Exhortation** is *paraklēsis* (3874), an "admonition or encouragement for the purpose of strengthening and establishing the believer in the faith (see Rom. 15:4; Phil. 2:1; Heb. 12:5; 13:22)."[292] *Exhortation* simply applies the *exposition* that has come from reading (and obviously preaching) the Scripture and encourages our obedience.

Third, there will be the *delineation of systematic truth*. **Doctrine** is *didaskalia* (1319), which originally meant imparting information and later the teaching of skills. The fact that it (with other forms of the word) appears some 26 times in the Pastoral Epistles, coupled with the word *didachē* noted in a previous study (June 5), makes clear what the pastor's job is: he is to teach the truth of Scripture in a systematic fashion, applying this to the lives of God's people, and must never change that method (2 Tim. 4:2). The man who does that proves His love for God, His Word, and His people.

Scriptures for Study: What do the following verses say about the pastor's function: 1 Timothy 2:7; 3:2; 4:6, 16; 5:17; 2 Timothy 1:11; 3:16—4:4; Titus 1:9?

JULY 2

"It is Written" (1)

"... it is written ..." (Matt. 4:4; etc.)

WE plunge into the "deep end of the pool" today, that pool being Greek, the language of the NT. It is truly nothing less than fascinating. It is no wonder that God chose to use it to record His final messages to men, for it is the most precise of all earthly languages. It has tenses, voices, and moods that are alien to our weaker English tongue. It's for that very reason that the biblical languages (especially Greek) are so critical to the expositor. Without an understanding of what the text actually says, it is impossible to get to the full Truth. God chose to use such precision to present theological Truth clearly.

Much of Greek's exactitude is dramatically seen in its complex verbs, part of which lies in the verb tenses. A verb tense actually specifies two things: not only *time* but *aspect*, the latter, in fact, being the most critical. As one Greek grammar explains, "The basic genius of the Greek verb is not its ability to indicate *when* the action of the verb occurs (time), but *what type of action it describes* [aspect]."[293]

One such aspect is "continuous"—this is the *present tense*—which obviously means that the action of the verb is ongoing, continuing. "I am reading today's devotional," you could say. The second aspect a verb can possess is "neutral" (or "undefined"), which means the verb pictures a simple event without any process, as in the *aorist tense*, the simple past tense indicating completed action. So, after you finish today's meditation, you could say, "I read."

In case you are wondering the purpose of this boring grammar lesson, the reason is to get to the third aspect of a Greek verb, namely, *completed action with present effects* (or completed action with an emphasis on the resulting state of being). This is the *perfect tense*, which in a sense is a merging of the present and aorist. The perfect tense is actually extremely important, often expressing great theological truths. Without doubt the most important example, as well as the most important statement in Scripture, appears in John 19:30, when our Lord said from the cross, "It is finished." The aorist tense ("the work is done") would not be enough. Instead, the perfect tells us that the work of redemption was completed but also with the result of continuing consequence. That brings us to our theme.

One of the truly amazing words in the Greek NT is the verb *gegraptai*. The root *graphē* (1124) simply means "writing" (e.g., English "photograph"). In the perfect tense, however, the verb *graphō* ("to write," 1125) assumes extraordinary power and implications. While Scripture was written in the past, the resulting state of being *is* its continuing significance and applicability. **It** *is* **written**, therefore, is better than "It has been written." ("It stands written" might be even better.) As we will see, this word is perhaps the most powerful proof of the doctrine of the preservation of Scripture and causes our love for it to grow by leaps and bounds.

Scriptures for Study: What is being preserved in Matthew 4:4, 6, 7, and 10? We will study this in more detail tomorrow.

JULY 3

"It is Written" (2)

"... it is written..." (Matt. 4:4; etc.)

USING the precise grammatical structure of the Greek verb *gegraptai*, God has built into His Word the absolute assurance that not only were His exact words written down as He intended them, but also that the result would be a lasting effect. In short, He promises that *His Word will forever be preserved*.

As one noted Greek authority submits, "What is quoted as *gegraptai* is normative because it is guaranteed by the binding power of Yahweh."[294] In other words, the use of the perfect tense indicates that whatever Scripture says creates continually authoritative standards by God's power.

Now, if *gegraptai* (and the translation, **It is written**) appeared only occasionally, we might innocently overlook it or even be tempted to disregard its significance. But this word appears no less than 67 times in the Greek NT. These instances fall into four categories, the first being the largest.

First, it appears in reference to the OT Scriptures in 62 instances.[295] Among the most notable of these are the three occurrences during Jesus' temptation in Matthew 4:1–10. To each of Satan's allurements, our Lord responded with **It is written** followed by a quotation from Deuteronomy.[296] As one Greek scholar observes, "The full force of the Greek is, 'Even as it has been written and still stands written'—a mighty affirmation of the divine inspiration and authority of the OT Scriptures. This should be remembered when we read the simple English translation 'As it *is* written.' Emphasizing the 'is' will help bring this out [and indicates] the permanent state resulting from the action."[297] Likewise, in every other instance of *gegraptai*, the perfect tense unambiguously declares the preservation of the OT.

Second, *gegraptai* appears in reference to the NT Scriptures. While there is only a single example here, it is a powerful one: *"These are written*, that ye might believe that Jesus is the Christ, the Son of God; and that believing ye might have life through his name" (Jn. 20:31; emphasis added). The key question here is: What is the antecedent of "these"? At the very least it refers to all the things John has just recorded (and he could have written much more, v. 30). "These" could also refer to his three epistles, since the evidence indicates he wrote them at the same time. Further still, it is possible that "these" even includes the other three Gospel records, since John was the last to write. Whichever is correct, there is no doubt that John was referring not to Scripture penned *before* him but to Scripture being written *then* (i.e., *now* from John's perspective).[298]

Oh, how thrilling this is! We love not some collection of *dated precepts* from the *past* but rather *dynamic principles* for the *present*.

Scriptures for Study: *Gegraptai* appears 16 times in Romans. What does each of the following declare: 1:17 (cf. Hab. 2:4); 3:10 (cf. Ps. 14:1–3; 53:1–3); 9:13 (cf. Mal. 1:2–3); 10:15 (cf. Is. 52:7); 14:11 (cf. Is. 45:23; 49:18)?

JULY 4

"It is Written" (3)

". . . it is written . . ." (Matt. 4:4; etc.)

THE doctrine of the preservation of Scripture is grievously in decline these days, but Scripture itself could not be clearer on this truth: *gegraptai* is not only used in reference to the OT and NT but also in another startling way.

Third, it appears in reference to *all* of Scripture in two specific instances. The first is 1 Corinthians 4:6, where Paul tells those prideful, factious folks not to "think of men above that which is written." Matthew Poole puts the matter well: "All the church of Corinth, as well ministers as people, might learn to have humble opinions and thoughts of themselves, not to think of themselves above what, by the rules of God's word, was written in the OT they ought to think; or above what he had before written in this Epistle, or to the Romans" (Rom. 12:3).[299] Albert Barnes adds that it is also possible that this refers "to the general strain of Scripture, requiring the children of God to be modest and humble."[300] Expositor John Gill likewise agrees that this could refer to "the word of God in general."[301]

The second instance appears in Hebrews 10:7: "Then said I, Lo, I come (in the volume of the book it is written of me,) to do thy will, O God." "Volume" is *kephalis* (2777; from *kephalē*, 2776, a head) and refers to the "head," that is, the knob, of the wooden rod on which Hebrew manuscripts were rolled; so *kephalis* came to be used metaphorically to designate a roll or "volume."

But *which* volume is in view here? The answer lies in the verse that is actually quoted: "Then said I, Lo, I come: in the volume of the book it is written of me" (Ps. 40:7). In a clear messianic statement, Christ is declared as the theme of the entire "volume." Barnes comments: "Literally, 'in the roll of the book.' The phrase would most naturally denote the 'scroll of the law;' but it might include any volume or roll where a record or prophecy was made. In a large sense it would embrace all that had been written at the command of God at the time when this was supposed to be spoken. That is, as spoken by the Messiah, it would include all the books of the OT." Gill again adds, however, that this could, in fact, also refer to the entire "book of the Scriptures . . . in general." After all, Christ is the theme of the entire Scriptures, so His command "Search the scriptures; for in them ye think ye have eternal life: and they are they which testify of me" (Jn. 5:39) includes all of what the Scripture reveals of Him. Likewise, "beginning at Moses and all the prophets, [Christ] expounded unto [the disciples] in all the scriptures the things concerning himself" (Lk. 24:27), which again for us includes all Scripture.

This wondrous truth not only deepens our love for God's Word *quantitatively*, but it also confirms *qualitatively* that any approach to the text of Scripture that in any way discounts, disregards, or detracts from the doctrine of the preservation of Scripture is seriously flawed.

Scriptures for Study: Notice the fourth category of *gegraptai* in reference to the Lamb's Book of Life (Rev. 13:8; cf. 17:8).[302]

JULY 5

Bring the Book (1)

... bring the book ... (Neh. 8:1)

AMONG several biblical examples of God's people demonstrating their love and desire for God's Word, the scene in Nehemiah 8 is one of the most notable and dramatic. Having returned from 70 years of Babylonian exile and completing the reconstruction of the walls and gates of Jerusalem, the people gathered to hear the Word of God read and exposited.

First, they *recognized* the *sacredness* of the Word (v. 1). Demonstrating a unique unity, some 42,000 people "gathered as one man at the square which was in front of the Water Gate." This gate was so named because it led to the Gihon Spring in the Kidron Valley, but most notably, water is often used in Scripture as a picture of the Word of God (Jn. 15:3; Eph. 5:26; cf. Ps.119:9; Jn. 17:17) as it rinses, refreshes, and revives. It is also significant that while every other gate needed repair, this one needed none (cf. 3:26). No matter what attack is launched against God's Word, it remains unscathed. While Higher (Historical) Criticism attacks the Bible's historic accuracy and Lower (Textual) Criticism questions the authenticity of the text itself, this gate holds strong against every assault.

Most notable of all, however, is that the people "asked Ezra the scribe to **bring the book** of the law of Moses which the LORD had given to Israel." People nowadays ask for everything under the sun *except* the book, but these people did not want to hear Ezra's rhetoric, Nehemiah's stories, Zerubbabel's philosophy, or be entertained by a Jewish comedian. After 70 years in a pagan land, they wanted one thing only—the Word of God. Like the simplicity of a child who climbs up into the parent's lap and says, "Read to me," they pleaded, **Bring the book**. This is not bibliolatry, the worship of a *book*, rather it is the worship of the *One* who wrote it, for it is only there we learn about Him.

Second, they *realized* the *seriousness* of the Word (vv. 3–8). Instead of little snatches of Bible teaching, these people stood for several hours listening to the reading and exposition of God's Word. While today we keep our eyes on the clock to make sure we don't go "too long," time is irrelevant to the truly spiritual believer. Also, instead of *sitting* on padded pews or theater seats, they *stood* for hours because they were captivated by the Truth, underscoring that true believers are hungry for the Word of God. And again in contrast to our day, instead of an artsy, informal lectern (and often not even that), a large pulpit was built to elevate the Word over the people. This is, in fact, the first mention of such a podium in the Bible. It was large enough to hold not only Ezra but 13 others as well. Just as John Calvin replaced all the altars in the churches with pulpits, and just as Martyn Lloyd-Jones had the pulpit bolted to the floor at Westminster Chapel in London, that should likewise be the heart and hub of our churches today.

Scriptures for Study: Read Luke 4:14–21 (cf. Is. 61:1–2). Who was reading, what was the message, and what was the result?

JULY 6

Bring the Book (2)

... bring the book ... (Neh. 8:1)

CONTINUING our thoughts from yesterday, the people *realized* the *seriousness* of the Word (vv. 3–8), which they demonstrated by their rapt attention as it was read. Such a realization had two profound results.

One result was that they "they bowed their heads, and worshipped the LORD with their faces to the ground" (v. 6). As we observed in our study of worship (June 1–8), much of what passes for "worship" these days is simply man-centered and all about the *feelings* of the worshipper not *fidelity* to the Truth. Immersion in the Word, therefore, results in biblical worship.

Another result was that the people understood what was being read (v. 8). While this sounds obvious, there is a deeper truth here. As has been often noted by expositors, after 70 years in Babylon, Hebrew had been largely replaced by Aramaic as the spoken language. So, as the Word was read in Hebrew, Ezra and the others "gave the sense, and caused [the people] to understand the reading." Here is perhaps the most stunning illustration of expository preaching in Scripture. This need, in fact, is even more essential in our day because we are so far removed from Bible times in language, culture, and history. As J. Sidlow Baxter wrote, "Preaching . . . is the gravity center of the Christian pastorate."[303] By implication, without preaching we shift the weight of ministry and become unbalanced; our whole "center of gravity" shifts to something else. We would submit, in fact, that if systematic, in-depth preaching (preferably expository) is not this gravity center of a church's ministry, it is not a true NT church.

Third, God's people *remembered* the *security* of the Word (vv. 9–12). We again observe a two-fold truth. At the reading of the Word of God, "all the people wept." The Hebrew behind "wept" (*baḵāh*, 1058H) not only depicts weeping in general but also "bitter, intense weeping [and wailing] (1 Sam. 1:10; Is. 30:19; Jer. 22:10)" and is, in fact, "used to describe a penitent's weeping before the Lord (Deut. 1:45; Judg. 20:23; 2 Kings 22:19)."[304] Oh, the weeping that overwhelms the repentant sinner when the full measure and consequence of his sin descends with its crushing weight! The Israelites had much to weep about, having ignored the preaching of the prophets for decades and being taken into captivity for 70 years because of their rebellion and spiritual idolatry. Should we not likewise weep?

Once repentance comes, however, we can wipe away the tears and cast off the grief, "for the joy of the LORD is [our] strength" (v. 10). Don't be "grieved," the Levites announced, which enabled the people to go "their way" and celebrate "because they had understood the words that were declared unto them" (vv. 11–12). While most people today think the road to *happiness* is through *hedonism*, the true path is through *holiness*. Oh, the blessings and the bliss when we **bring the book**!

Scriptures for Study: What do the following verses in Psalm 119 teach us: 14, 16, 97, 103, 127, 171?

July 7

Bring the Book (3)

... bring the book ... (Neh. 8:1)

WHEN God's people returned to the land after their captivity, they *recognized* the *sacredness* of the Word, *realized* the *seriousness* of the Word, and *remembered* the *security* of the Word. These three in turn produced one additional spiritual reality.

Fourth, they *renewed* their *submission* to the Word (vv. 14–18). Verse 14 begins with the words "they found written in the law which the LORD had commanded," which encourages us that *diligence* leads to *discovery*. We learn little during our brief excursions in the Scripture. It is only when we take the time to plunge deep that we discover the riches that lie below the surface. As Paul declared, "The Spirit searcheth all things, yea, the deep things of God" (1 Cor. 2:10).

Specifically, then, as the Word was read that day, the people discovered something that had been lost a thousand years before. They learned "that the children of Israel should dwell in booths in the feast of the seventh month," that is, the Feast of the Tabernacles (or Booths). That feast, which began five days after Yom Kippur (the Day of Atonement), involved the Israelites presenting offerings for seven days while they lived in huts (booths) made of palm fronds and leafy tree branches to remember their journey in Canaan (Lev. 23:43). But while they had certainly observed the feast faithfully through the years, they had not actually built the booths since Joshua's day (v. 17) because doing so was inconvenient. They might very well have argued, as many do today, "Surely this practice is a non-essential as long as our hearts are right."

But the fact remained that "they found it written" and were renewed in their submission to and obedience of God's Word. And so they "[went] forth unto the mount, and fetch[ed] olive branches, and pine branches, and myrtle branches, and palm branches, and branches of thick trees, to make booths, as it is written" (v. 15). This challenges us, indeed, that the principles, precepts, and even precedents of Scripture are critical.

What then was the result of such renewed submission? "There was very great gladness" (v. 17). The Hebrew behind "gladness" (*śimḥah*, 8057H) refers to joy, rejoicing, gladness, pleasure, and celebration. Most of its some 90 occurrences "signify joy at several aspects of God's person and work," such as "joy in worship of Yahweh (v. 12; Is. 29:19; Jer. 33:11)" as well as one's joy in the Lord in general (Pss. 4:7; 30:11; 100:2).[305] So, just as the road to happiness is through holiness, as noted yesterday, the road to *celebration* is through *compliance*.

Ah, but did the submission and celebration last? Yes, but only for a time. The people again grew forgetful and fell into sin. They needed constant reminding. Oh, how critical it is that "the inward man [be] renewed day by day" (2 Cor. 4:16)!

Scriptures for Study: How do the following verses challenge us to renewal: Psalm 51:10; Isaiah 40:31; Romans 12:2; Ephesians 4:23?

JULY 8

Waiting Upon the LORD

They that wait upon the LORD shall renew their strength; they shall mount up with wings as eagles; they shall run, and not be weary; and they shall walk, and not faint. (Is. 40:31)

TO underscore the importance of yesterday's final thought about renewal, we turn today to a verse we listed in "Scriptures for Study." Because they were then captives in Babylon, Isaiah challenged the people with these words.

First, we see the *principle* that we are to **wait upon the LORD** (*Yāhweh*, see Jan. 21). The Hebrew behind **wait** (*qāwāh*, 6960H) means not only to *wait* but also to *look for* with eager anticipation and expectation. We wait upon God, for example, in confident expectation that He will deliver us from trials and oppression by the wicked (Pss. 27:14; 39:7; 40:1; Prov. 20:22; Isa. 25:9). Such waiting implies neither the passive idea of "let go and let God" nor sudden bursts of hyperactivity to "make things happen." Rather, it's forgetting what is behind, reaching forward to what is ahead, and straining on toward the goal (Phil. 3:12–14).

Second, we note the *promise* that if we wait upon the LORD, He will **renew [our] strength**. The Hebrew *ḥalap* (2498H), means to pass on, change, or renew and is used, for example, for the growth of grass (Ps. 90:5–6) and for the second growth of a tree (Job 14:7). If we are not waiting on Him, however, we cannot expect renewal. "He never promised the soaring strength of eagles so [we] could go on grunting in the sty of Babylon."[306]

Third, then, we see the *periods* during which we wait upon the LORD. The first period is during the easier times when we soar like **eagles**. It's easy to live for the Lord when all goes well, but it is also during such times that we must lean upon Him lest we become puffed up. It's at those times that we "put forth fresh feathers like the molting eagle," as this phrase can be translated. The second period is during the everyday difficulties of life, when we might not soar as eagles but will still **run** and not grow **weary** because we are resting in Him. The third period is during the serious problems and tragedies, when we will still be able to **walk** along without collapsing because we are trusting in His strength.

So, whether we are soaring, sprinting, or striding, "we faint not, [for] though our outward man perish, yet the inward man is renewed day by day" (2 Cor. 4:16). Each and every day is a new opportunity for spiritual invigoration, restoration, and transformation as we "grow in grace, and in the knowledge of our Lord and Saviour Jesus Christ" (2 Pet. 3:18).

> It's with the eagles we will sometimes soar;
> For renewed strength upon the Lord we wait;
> At times we'll run but not tire in the chore;
> At others we'll just walk but still not faint.

Scriptures for Study: How do the following verses encourage us: Psalm 27:14; Luke 18:1; 2 Corinthians 12:9–10; Galatians 6:9; and Hebrews 12:1?

JULY 9

Manna From Heaven (1)

This is the bread which the LORD hath given you to eat. (Ex. 16:15)

WE can only imagine the joy that overwhelmed the hungry children of Israel on that first morning when they discovered "a small round thing" lying on the ground and learned that it was food. So puzzled were they at first, however, that they said "manna," which actually transliterates the Hebrew *mān* (4478H) meaning "what is it?" A literal translation is: "And the sons of Israel see, and say one unto another, 'What is it?' for they have not known what it is" (YLT). Moses responded by telling them all they needed to know: **This is the bread which the LORD hath given you to eat.**

Appearing five times in the NT, the Greek *manna* (3131) also transliterates the Hebrew *mān*. The three most significant occurrences are in John 6, where Jesus responds to the Jews' demand for a sign to prove He was who He claimed to be; they even cited the miraculous manna as an example of what they wanted. But Jesus answered: "Moses gave you not that bread from heaven; but my Father giveth you the true bread from heaven. For the bread of God is he which cometh down from heaven, and giveth life unto the world" (vv. 32–33; cf. Rev. 2:17; see also Mar. 10). It is, therefore, by feeding upon *Christ*, and by extension His *Word*, that we have life and then continuous nourishment and growth. This double parallel is manifested in several ways, deepening our love and appreciation for both.

First, the manna was small and seemingly insignificant; it came with the morning dew and was certainly not a promising possibility for food (v. 14). Such was the case of our Lord, who was, just as Isaiah had prophesied, "despised and rejected of men" and not "[highly] esteemed" (Is. 53:3). During His three year earthly ministry, His character was impugned, His conduct was questioned, and His call was rejected. He was abused, abhorred, and abandoned. And nothing has changed. The masses today would scream "crucify Him" just as they did then. The same contempt is hurled at His Word. It is considered insignificant, irrelevant, and even ignominious. Ah, but while the world despises its only hope, we delight in our only help. While the world loathes Him, we love Him.

Second, the manna was plain looking, just a little round object lying on the ground. Likewise, Isaiah also wrote that Messiah would have no regal appearance, majestic looks, or any "beauty that we should desire him" (v. 2). So inconsequential was He that it was asked, "Can there any good thing come out of Nazareth?" (Jn. 1:46). The same attitudes prevail toward His Word. It is viewed as just another religious book, one full of dull philosophy, dated morality, disputable events, and even disreputable ethics. But again, while the world dismisses all this with a shrug, we embrace it with all our strength, for Jesus is "the Word [who] was made flesh, and dwelt among us" and is "full of grace and truth" (Jn. 1:14).

Scriptures for Study: Review our March 10 reading. How does it complement our study today?

JULY 10

Manna From Heaven (2)

This is the bread which the LORD hath given you to eat. (Ex. 16:15)

"CHRIST put his finger on the sore when he told [the people] they came like brute beasts to fill their belly," Calvin observed, "for they discover this gross disposition when they demand a Messiah by whom they are to be fed."[307] Indeed, they missed the whole point of the true manna from Heaven. They were *fixated* on the *world* around them instead of being *fascinated* by the *wonder* that was before them.

Third, the manna was easily accessible. Oh, how significant it is that the manna was not on a high mountain that demanded a daunting and dangerous climb to retrieve it. Neither was it hidden in the cracks and crevices of a deep gorge, requiring a painstaking and perilous search. Rather, all the people had to do was step out of their tents and there it was. Likewise, how accessible Jesus it! He is not on the mountaintop of intellectual pursuit or in the gorge of mystical enquiry. He is right in front of us. Just as He promised, "Come unto me, all ye that labour and are heavy laden, and I will give you rest" (Matt. 11:28), and, "If any man thirst, let him come unto me, and drink" (Jn. 7:37). When we step out of the tent of "self," there He is. The reason people do not come to Christ is not a question of His *accessibility*, but their own *accountability*. The same holds true of God's Word—it is right in front of us. All we have to do is open its pages and there find Truth, triumph, and tranquility. Flowing from this observation is another.

Fourth, the manna was lying on the ground. Yes, it was easily accessible, but it still demanded the humble act of stooping down to pick it up. We recall that Jesus Himself was "meek and lowly in heart" (Matt. 11:29) and "humbled himself" so far that He "became obedient unto death, even the death of the cross" (Phil. 2:8). So, because He asks nothing of us that He did not first do Himself, we must, therefore humble ourselves before God. Of all the evidences of men's depravity (Rom. 1:18–32), the total absence of humility is among the worst—"professing themselves to be wise, they became fools" (v. 22), have "changed the truth of God into a lie, and worshipped and served the creature more than the Creator" (v. 25), and are "proud" and "boast[ful]" (v. 30). This is true also of humbling ourselves before the absolute Truth of God's Word.

Fifth, the manna was adapted for all. "Gather of it every man according to his eating" (Ex. 16:16–18). Here was the ultimate "one size fits all." It met the need of every single person, regardless of age, gender, or size. Likewise, Jesus died for all His people without distinction of color, culture, or creed. His Word continues that wondrous work by teaching every truth, meeting every need, answering every question, and solving every dilemma. And just as each day's manna was for *that* day (v. 19), God's Word is needed *each* day.

Scriptures for Study: In 1 Corinthians 10:1–6, what is value of the Scripture record? 📖 How is Scripture profitable according to 2 Timothy 3:16–17?

JULY 11

Manna From Heaven (3)

This is the bread which the LORD hath given you to eat. (Ex. 16:15)

GOD'S feeding of His people in the wilderness is more than just a *story*; it is, in fact, a *promise:* God miraculously provides for His people.

Sixth, the manna came with the dew (vv. 13–14). We are reminded of Hosea 14:5, where God says, "I will be as the dew unto Israel." In the arid climate of the Holy Land, dew is especially heavy in the summer and early autumn and is therefore greatly valued for its refreshment (Ps. 133:3; Is. 18:4). Being careful of figurative language,[308] we cannot help but see a picture here of the Holy Spirit, God's very presence descending to enliven and empower. Our two-fold application underscores our Lord being conceived by the Holy Spirit (Matt. 1:18) and then His later promise that upon His departure He would send His indwelling Spirit to abide with us forever (Jn. 14:16) and then "teach [us] all things, and bring all things to [our] remembrance, whatsoever [He] said unto [us]" (v. 26; Apr. 13–19).

Seventh, the manna fell by miracle (v. 15). And what a miracle it was! Think of it! Tens of thousands of bushels of manna fell every day for 40 years. But as wondrous as that was, far greater was God's grace in the miracle of redemption. And the gift of God's Word is no less miraculous, for "holy men of God spake as they were moved [i.e. carried along] by the Holy Ghost" (2 Pet. 1:21).

Eighth, it was absolutely essential that the manna be collected early, before the hot mid-eastern sun melted it (v. 21). There was no place for the lazy person who wanted to sleep late and allow others to gather his food. This reminds us that our Lord's ordeal of purchasing our redemption began early. It also challenges us of how important it is that we seek God early (Ps. 63:1; Jan. 1).

Ninth, we must not overlook two negatives in this incident, the first being that when not used the manna bred worms and stank (v. 20). Some were lazy and tried to save some manna for the next day. Likewise, Christ and His Word must be sought every day. Again, it is critical that "the inward man [be] renewed day by day" (2 Cor. 4:16). As we are not fed by the memory of food, neither are we fed by yesterday's spiritual meal. So, while we all practice physical hygiene to avoid any offensive odor, how much more important is good "spiritual hygiene"?

Tenth and finally, how tragic, indeed, that the manna was eventually taken for granted, even loathed. Elsewhere we read that the people complained that all they had to eat was this manna (Num. 11:6). How ungrateful! But lest we be too quick to condemn, how often do we seek *substitutes* from the *world* in place of the *sustenance* of the *Word*? Instead of a place of *exposition*, we have turned our churches into places of *entertainment* and have replaced the nourishing bread of God's Word ("the staff of life," Mar. 10) with junk food.

Oh, dear Christian Friend, let us never lose our love for the Manna!

Scriptures for Study: Write down your own spiritual reflections from these studies on manna from heaven.

JULY 12

The Wilderness of Sin

...the wilderness of Sin ... the whole congregation of the children of Israel murmured ... (Ex. 16:1–2)

BEFORE leaving this scene of God's people in the wilderness, it's significant to note the name of that wilderness: **the wilderness of Sin**. This was a vast desert filled with sand, stone, and serpents between Elim and Mount Sinai in what is today Saudi Arabia. It's perhaps best identified as "an easily traveled plain along the shore of the Red Sea, since the terrain just inland is rugged," and the place where the people found themselves "exactly one month after departure from Raamses."[309] While it obviously does not *refer* to our English word "sin" (rather "Sinai"), it certainly does *reflect* it, as this incident vividly demonstrates.

First, the wilderness of sin was a place of *drought*. Having left Egypt a month before, it is probable that the provisions the people brought with them had steadily diminished and food was becoming a critical concern. An even greater concern later, however, was water (17:1). Generally speaking, one can live three to four weeks without food but only three or four *days* without water. Death lurks in the shadows of drought.

But far more serious than physical drought is spiritual drought. Its chief cause is leaving our love for the Lord and turning to other things, just as God's people did: "For my people have committed two evils; they have forsaken me the fountain of living waters, and hewed them out cisterns, broken cisterns, that can hold no water" (Jer. 2:13). Think of it! They abandoned the life-sustaining waters of God to serve dead idols (June 17).

Second, the wilderness of sin was a place of *dissent*. The desert was the ideal place for God to test His people, and they failed miserably. Instead of loving and trusting God, who had miraculously delivered them from Egypt and protected them in their journey, they absurdly pined for the seeming comfort of Egypt (vv. 3–4), forgetting all about how they had languished in slavery there. The Hebrew verb for **murmured** (*luîn* or *liyn*, 3885H) also means to grumble or howl, indicating very vocal opposition against God and His appointed leaders. God's people must be very careful how they treat and respond to the leaders God has given them.

Third, the wilderness of sin was a place of *disobedience*. Little did the people know that one day this repeated behavior, especially the refusal to enter the land at Kadesh-Barnea (Num. 13–14), would catch up with them and they would be sentenced to wandering in the wilderness for 40 years (15–19). Even Moses failed when after God instructed him to speak to the rock to bring water, he struck the rock twice in anger and cried to the people, in effect, "Must we bring water from this rock for you?" Such words implied human effort instead of God's power (20:2–13). Oh, let us not wander in **the wilderness of Sin**!

Scriptures for Study: What do the following verses tell us about spiritual drought: Psalms 1:2–3; 42:1–2; 63:1; 65:10–11?

July 13

The Right Affection

... seek those things which are above, where Christ sitteth on the right hand of God. Set your affection on things above, not on things on the earth. (Col. 3:1–2)

PURITAN Thomas Manton wrote, "Take a mirror and turn it toward Heaven, and there you shall see the reflection of Heaven, the clouds and things above. Turn it downward toward the earth, you shall see the reflection of the earth, trees, meadows, men. Just so does the soul receive a reflection from the things to which it is set. If the heart is set toward Heaven, that puts you into a heavenly frame. If you set your heart on earthly objects, you are a man of the earth!"[310] Indeed, our text declares what our affection should (and should not) be.

First, we *seek* heavenly things. The verb **seek** is *zēteō* (2212) and is in the present tense, indicating a willful and continuous striving after something, as did the merchant who looked for the perfect pearl (Matt. 13:45) and the woman who searched frantically for a lost coin (Luke 15:8). But what does Paul mean here by **things which are above**? This would be vague and nebulous, indeed, if it were not for the next phrase, which points us to **Christ**. We seek everything that pertains to Christ: His disposition, His devotion, His doctrine, and His duty. The aim of all that we seek is to please Him and bring Him glory.

Second, we *set our affection* on heavenly things. We can *look* for something but not necessarily *love* it. We can do things out of sheer *habit* but with no *heart*. **Set your affection** is one word in the Greek (*phroneō*, 5426) that means to have a mindset on something and involves the will, affections, and conscience. So, we don't just *seek* the things of Christ; we think them and even feel them. While **seek** marks the *practical exertion*, **set your affection** marks the *personal motivation*. Even though our feet are firmly planted on earth, our heads and hearts are in heaven. And where do such thoughts and feelings come from? Not from inner urges or mystic contemplation, but from Scripture alone. It is only there that we find **Christ**. "We set our minds upon things above, not by reposing in arm-chairs indulging in dreamy and mystical imaginings as to things that may be in heaven, but rather by setting our minds supremely upon Christ, and seeking in all things the furtherance of Heaven's interests."[311]

Third, we *shun* earthly things. The admonition to **set your affection . . . not on things on the earth** does not imply asceticism. It will do no good to lock yourself in a monastery, cutting yourself off from contact with the world, simply because the issue here is one of the heart, which is always with you. Paul speaks of attitudes, appetites, and aspirations. What do we *really* want in life? In what do you invest the majority of your time? What do you desire to accomplish more than anything else? What are your most valued investments? Are you pointing your "mirror" toward Heaven or earth?

Scriptures for Study: What do the following verses add to our study today: Romans 12:2; Philippians 4:8; 1 John 2:15–17?

JULY 14

What To Listen For In Scripture (1)

... the worlds were framed by the word of God ... (Heb. 11:3)

AMERICAN composer and conductor Aaron Copeland (1900–90) penned a fascinating book, *What to Listen for in Music*,[312] in which he masterfully explains the four elements of music. Who does not love and appreciate music at one level or another? Let us parallel this with what to listen for in Scripture, thereby deepening our love and appreciation for it.

The first element of music is *rhythm*, which can be simply defined as a regular, repeated pattern of sounds, as the simple metrical units of "ONE two, ONE two" illustrate. Most historians agree that much of early music was simply the beating of a drum. While that doesn't mean it's always good music, it is nonetheless the foundation. In fact, one biblical historian tells us that the early music of the Hebrews was "of a loud and piercing nature, emphasizing rhythm, and lacking sweetness."[313] Without rhythm there would be no music.

In our analogy, then, words form the foundation of Scripture. As our text declares, in fact, words are the foundation of *everything*. God called everything into existence with a **word**. As noted before, while *logos* often refers to a proclamation as a whole, that is, an entire discourse or speech, *rhēma*, which is used here, usually relates to individual words and utterances (Mar. 25, 28). While the atom is the physical building block of the universe, God's words are the spiritual ones. There are more than 807,000 words in the Bible. Words mean things, so every single one is important, and without them there can be no meaning. God's "word [as a whole, *logos*] is truth" (Jn. 17:17), so every individual word of that is crucial.

It is for that very reason that some translations of the Bible are woefully inadequate—they don't actually focus on the *words*. Instead of rendering the Greek and Hebrew words as closely as possible into the target language ("formal equivalence"), they simply express "the thought" of the author ("dynamic equivalence"). Instead of a word-for-word translation, this is a thought-for-thought "translation," which in reality amounts to little more than a paraphrase. The danger here is obvious and often disastrous. How can we know what the thought or meaning is unless we know exactly what God said? How can the words themselves not matter?

A dramatic example of this sad approach to Bible translation is the NIV's rendering of Ephesians 1:3–14, one of the most beautiful passages in Scripture. In a single Greek sentence, and with a minimum of words, Paul expresses several of the most profound truths in Scripture. The NIV, however, uses eight sentences, leaves out some words, and adds others. Out of 205 Greek words, in fact, 36 are not translated at all, and 87 of the English words have no backing from the Greek, nor are they warranted by the context for the sake of clarity. We submit that such a translation method does not reflect a true love and appreciation for God's *words*.

Scriptures for Study: What do the following verses declare about God's words: Psalm 12:6; 19:8; 119:130?

JULY 15

What To Listen For In Scripture (2)

... good doctrine ... (1 Tim. 4:6)

THE second element of music is *melody*, which can be defined as a rhythmically organized series of high and low tones which avoids unnecessary repetition and comes to a climactic and resolved end. Too much repetition of the same tones is not good music. Neither is ending on an open tone or chord.

Indeed, the adage is true: "Most people know a good melody when they hear it." People know what they like, what sounds good and what doesn't. The main point to remember about a melody is that it gives a song meaning. Rhythm provides little, if any, meaning; it's merely the foundation. It is the melody that is the key; it must exist and must not be overpowered or obscured by any other element of music.

For example, most of the music of the orient is dissonant and unresolved. Melody is non-existent, and there is no discernable beginning or end, which actually reflects the meaningless religious systems of the orient. Neither is some Jazz very good music. It's virtually impossible to score because it meanders wherever the performer feels like going. There is even Classical music that is not good music, such as the "12-tone row" developed by composer Arnold Schoenberg (1874–1951), which has little or no melody at all and is characterized by perpetual variation with no resolution.[314] Other Classical music is built on "fragmentation," the division of a musical theme (melody) into segments.

In our parallel, therefore, as we would listen to a melody in music, we read sentences in Scripture. Just as tones are arranged in a sequence to produce a beautiful melody, so are words arranged to express profound and complete doctrines. Further, the inspired sentences of Scripture always come to perfect resolution with no fragmentation or meandering variation.

So it is, then, that Paul encouraged Timothy to keep himself nourished with **good doctrine**. **Good** is *kalos* (2570; Mar. 13), which "expresses beauty as a harmonious completeness, balance, [and] proportion."[315] Doctrine is **good**, indeed. Oh, the flowing melodies of such "songs" as inspiration, justification, sanctification, and glorification! Oh, the symphonic themes that are introduced in the Doctrines of Sovereign Grace, which are then repeated again and again, coming finally to a glorious resolution! To dislike, decry, or deride doctrine, as is sadly common today, is as foolish as hating a beautiful melody.

Having summoned the musicians to play, Shakespeare's character Lorenzo says to his love Jessica, "How sweet the moonlight sleeps upon this bank. Here will we sit, and let the sounds of music creep in our ears; soft stillness, and the night become the touches of sweet harmony."[316] Oh, that this would be our attitude in listening to Scripture! It should be music to our ears!

Scriptures for Study: Read the following verses, noting what else Paul told pastors about doctrine: 1 Timothy 1:10; 4:16; 6:3; 2 Timothy 4:3; Titus 2:1, 7.

JULY 16

What To Listen For In Scripture (3)

... good doctrine ... (1 Tim. 4:6)

THE third element of music is *harmony*, which is truly fascinating. It actually did not appear until about the 9th-century. There are three kinds of harmony, only one of which we will mention here, since it is the best and the most widely accepted. "Harmonizing in thirds" (*faux-bourdon*, false bass) simply means playing the third or the sixth tone above or below the melody. For example, if one played the note "C" on a piano, the note a third up from that would be "E" and another third up would be "G" making the "C chord." Simply put, the purpose of harmony is to enhance the melody. Once again, the melody must not be obscured or overpowered. An example of such an assault on melody in Classical music would be Stravinsky's "Rites of Spring," which is full of atonality and dissonance caused by harmony run wild.

In our analogy, then, there are several things that add harmony to our reading and study of Scripture and thereby enhance the truths we are hearing. One, and by far the most important, is the *context*, that is, examining the *words* that surround the word in question, the *verses* that surround the verse, and the *basic theme of the book* where the verse appears. One example of the importance of the context appears in 1 Corinthians 9:27, where Paul writes about not becoming a castaway. While this is used by some to "prove" that believers can lose their salvation, the context clearly talks about rewards for Christian service, not salvation.

Another aspect of harmony is *history*, that is, an understanding of social customs, historical names and events, political climate and rulers, and even geographical references. Of countless examples, we are reminded of John 18:1, which simply records that on His way to the Garden of Gethsemane, Jesus crossed over the Brook Kidron. This appears at first to be a totally insignificant detail until we discover the historical background. At this time of the year (Passover), the Brook Kidron was filled with blood because the blood from thousands of lambs drained out of the back of the Temple right into it. How significant this must have been to our Lord as He was fully aware that He was the Lamb of God (Mar. 18–19)!

Consider also the historical significance of the term "body of this death" (Rom. 7:24), which Paul uses to graphically describe the believer's struggle with the flesh. A fascinating story is told of the ancient people near Tarsus, the city where Paul was born. Convicted murders were sentenced to an unimaginable execution. The corpse of the murdered person was tightly lashed to the murderer and remained there until the murderer himself died. In a few days, of course, the decay of the corpse would infect and kill the murderer. It is quite possible that Paul had this story in mind when he used this term.

Oh, what such harmony adds to the melody!

Scriptures for Study: What does Colossians 3:16 add to our thoughts today?

JULY 17

What To Listen For In Scripture (4)

I have not shunned to declare unto you all the counsel of God. (Act 20:27)

THE fourth and final element of music is *tone color* (or timbre), which can be defined as "that quality of sound produced by a particular medium of musical tone production [e.g., a voice or musical instrument]." In other words, "timbre in music is analogous to color in painting."[317] To illustrate, just as most people can immediately tell the difference between the colors of red and blue, most can just as easily discern the difference in tone of a violin and a trumpet (or in voice, a soprano and a bass).

There is a natural danger here, however. While each of us will like certain instruments, we will dislike others and be tempted to concentrate only on the former and avoid the latter. But the wise listener seeks to appreciate every instrument, realizing that the composer uses each one for a particular purpose. A melody could be played equally well on any one of a dozen instruments, but the composer "chooses the instrument with the tone color that best expresses the meaning behind his idea." A piccolo, for example, would hardly be appropriate to play the tune chosen for John Newton's great hymn, *Amazing Grace*, but what listener is not captivated when he hears it played on the bagpipes?

How does all this apply in our analogy of listening to Scripture? Simply that every theme in it, every "melody" along with its enhancing "harmony," expresses exactly what the Composer desired. Further, it is critical that we appreciate each of these, even though certain ones might appeal to us more than others.

Our text is part of Paul's farewell message to the Ephesian elders in Miletus. Among several exhortations, Paul challenged those pastors to do what he himself had done, to preach **all the counsel of God. Counsel** is *boulē* (1012), which means will, purpose, or intention; they were never to hold back any truths concerning God's purpose in the revelation of Christ but rather proclaim all of it. This obviously includes all the doctrines God has revealed since all biblical doctrines flow from the nature, character, and work of Christ.

So, while there are certain issues we would prefer not to deal with, such "melodies" must be "played." Likewise, we must be careful not to play only certain "songs" to the exclusion of all others. Some Bible teachers, for example, are so focused on eschatology and prophecy that they preach nothing else and build their entire ministry on this one subject. Still others avoid any "sad ballads" of rebuke or exhortation, which they call "negative preaching," and croon only happy little "tunes" that make people feel good.

What a blessing, indeed, music is! The more we listen to it, the more we love and appreciate it in whatever form it takes. How much more so is our affection and adoration of Scripture! It is the harmony of Heaven.

Scriptures for Study: What do the following verses add to our thoughts today: Matthew 28:20; John 14:26?

JULY 18

The Believer's Relationship to God's Word (1)

*... his delight [is] in the law of the LORD ... a tree planted by
the rivers of water ... (Ps. 1:2–3)*

THIS psalm has been called "The Preface" to the entire book of Psalms. In some respects, in fact, these six verses encapsulate the content of the whole collection. While verses 4–6 describe the *calamity* of the *ungodly*, verses 1–3 delineate the *character* of the *godly*. And at the very center of that character is the believer's relationship to God's Word.

First, we see the believer's *life* because he is **planted** in the Word. **Planted** is the interesting Hebrew word *sātal* (8362H). In all ten of its OT occurrences, it is used figuratively to describe either Israel or the righteous man as a tree or vine. More specifically, the word means "transplanted," as Israel is pictured as a transplanted tree in the parable of Ezekiel 17 (vv. 8, 10, 22–23). Because it has broken the treaty with Babylon and sought help from Egypt, it is uprooted and withers away. Since it obviously could not transplant itself, God would, therefore, take a tender shoot from the cedar and transplant it; this shoot is the Davidic line from which Messiah will come.

In like manner, we could not plant ourselves, rather God has transplanted us from the dead soil of the *world* into the living soil of the *Word*. Just as the root system of a tree goes deep into the earth and is firmly established in that spot, we too are deeply rooted in the Word, firmly established and unmovable in it. Further, our assurance comes simply from the fact that God has done it all.

Second, we note the believer's *location* because he is planted by the **rivers of water**. Significantly, the usual Hebrew word for **rivers** (*nāhār*, 5104H; e.g. Gen. 2:10) is not used here, rather it is *peleg* (6388H)—derived from *pālag* (6385H), to split or divide—and more precisely refers to a channel, canal, trench, brook, or branching-cut. This alludes to a common method of irrigation that is still used today, cutting streams and ditches to direct water from a river or lake. This was done, in fact, along the Nile River throughout Egypt, which explains its extraordinary fertility even in an extremely arid region where rainfall is rare (cf. Deut. 11:10).[318]

Further, as we have noted before (July 5), **water** is often used in Scripture as a picture of the Word of God (John 15:3; Eph. 5:26; cf. Ps. 119:9; Jn. 17:17). So, wherever we are, wherever God transplants us, He cuts the irrigating channel right to us to refresh and cleanse. As Paul wrote to the Ephesians, Christ "[sanctifies] and cleanse[s] [us] with the washing of water by the word" (Eph. 5:26).

Finally, we should not overlook that **rivers** is plural. As Spurgeon observes: "Even if one river should fail, he hath another. The rivers of pardon and the rivers of grace, the rivers of the promise and the rivers of the communion with Christ, are never-failing sources of supply."[319] Another adds, "The droughts that bring bleakness and barrenness to others do not affect [us]."[320]

Scriptures for Study: What does Isaiah 55:10–11 add to our thoughts today?

JULY 19

The Believer's Relationship to God's Word (2)

... his delight is in the law of the LORD ... [he] bringeth forth his fruit in his season; his leaf also shall not wither ... (Ps. 1:2–3)

IT is because the first two facets of our relationship to God's Word are true that there is a *third*: the believer's *labor* in the **fruit** he produces. While there might be bland, perhaps even blighted, trees in God's orchard, there are no completely barren ones. Just as fruit is proof positive of life in the tree, so is spiritual fruit in the life of the believer. In both cases, fruit is automatic. Both bear fruit because it is their nature to do so. Yes, there will be times when a tree will need pruning, perhaps even need treatment for disease, but it is still living and will bear its fruit **in [its] season**, that is, "at the proper time" (*ēṯ*, 6256H). "But what time is that?" we might ask. The time that God sovereignly wills. It is not our *effort* that produces fruit, but rather God's *energy*.

So what constitutes fruit in the Christian life? "The NT declares there are no less than five types of fruit: First, there is *witnessing for Christ* (Jn. 4:36; Rom. 1:13; 1 Cor. 16:15; Mark 1:17). While some teach that only *winning* people is fruit, just the *witnessing* itself is fruit. Second, there is *worship of God* (Heb. 13:15; Hosea 14:2, where 'calves' is *par*, 6499H, used figuratively for "fruit"). Third, there is *wholesome conduct* (Rom. 6:22; Col. 1:10; Phil. 1:10, 11). Fourth, there is *winsome character* (Gal. 5:22, 23), which is proof positive of true conversion. Fifth, there is *wealth-sharing with other Christians* (Rom. 15:28, 29; Phil. 4:16, 17)."[321]

Fourth, we observe the believer's *longevity* because **his leaf also shall not wither**. The Hebrew behind **wither** (*nāḇēl*, 5034H) is used often in the literal sense of the fading, drying up, and falling away of grass (Ps. 37:2), leaves (Is. 1:30), and flowers (28:1). It is also used figuratively in such verses as Exodus 18:18, where Jethro counsels Moses that he will surely just "wear away" if he tries to govern and judge the people by himself. But God's promise here is that this will never happen to the well-planted, well-watered believer.

As I write these words, in fact, I need only look out my office window for an illustration. Thousands of evergreens dot the mountains around our home in northwestern Colorado. It is now early October, so it won't be long until snow and cold descend at 6,400 feet above sea level. But those trees will remain "ever green." That is what God has promised us. No matter what foul weather comes, no matter what distress, disturbance, or difficulty arises, the believer is "ever green."

Further, David specifically mentions the **leaf**. While the trunk and branches of the tree are the *profession* of life, it's the leaves that are the *proof*. The former speaks the *words*, but the latter is the *witness*. Oh, what assurance of our security in Christ this gives us (Rom. 8:35–39)!

Scriptures for Study: Read John 15:1–6. What does this passage tell us about bearing fruit?

JULY 20

The Believer's Relationship to God's Word (3)

... his delight is in the law of the LORD; and in his law doth he meditate day and night; and whatsoever he doeth shall prosper. (Ps. 1:2–3)

AS we conclude our thoughts on the multi-faceted character of the believer's relationship to God's Word, we see a *fifth* aspect: the believer's *love* for the Word as manifested by his **delight** in it. While this psalm has no title, it is probably from David's pen.[322] If that is true, he uses the same Hebrew word here to declare what he does elsewhere (Ps. 119:35), namely, his emotional glee in God's Word (*chāpēsh*, 2654H; June 13). While the world looks for its merriment in this weekend's "big game," the latest block-buster movie, or the newest electronic gizmo, the godly Christian waits with breathless anticipation to learn another truth from God's Word. This leads immediately to something else.

Sixth, we see the believer's *learning* because **he meditate[s] day and night**. As we have noted before, the Hebrew behind **meditate** (*hāgāh*, 1897H) paints a picture of quiet and concentrated thought (review Jan. 5 and 6). But the psalmist goes deeper here. He adds that such thoughts are not to be limited to our morning "quiet time" or evening "vespers." Indeed not! **Day** (*yômām*, 3119H) speaks of daytime in general, that is, "during the day," and **night** (*laylāh*, 3915H) primarily describes the portion of time between sunset and sunrise (Gen. 1:5; cf. Ps. 136:9). In short, the godly believer's meditation is habitual. It's not during *a time* set *by* the clock, rather at *all times* continuing *around* the clock. Our meditation on God's Word should enter into and address every aspect of life. It is "interwoven with the business and converse of every day," wrote Matthew Henry, "and with the repose and slumbers of every night." While the world is "ever learning [but] never able to come to the knowledge of the truth" (2 Tim. 3:7), we already have the knowledge of the Truth and are ever learning more.

Seventh and finally, we note the believer's *lasting riches* in that **whatsoever he doeth shall prosper**. This phrase should not be twisted into support for modern health and wealth prosperity teaching, the so-called "name it and claim it" falsehood. It is obvious from the context that the primary idea is not *material* prosperity but rather *spiritual* prosperity, not the outward but the inward. As Charles Spurgeon well observed, "It is not outward prosperity which the Christian most desires and values; it is soul prosperity which he longs for."[323] Writing some 100 years earlier, John Gill likewise noted that this phrase refers "not so much [to] things temporal, for in these the good man does not always succeed, but in things spiritual; whatever he does in faith, from love, to the glory of God, and in the name of Christ, prospers."[324] How much grander it is when we think of prospering Christ and His Word and not ourselves!

Scriptures for Study: True prosperity is found in spiritual riches, not temporal wealth. Read Ephesians 1. How many spiritual riches do you find there?

July 21

Qualities of the Godly Man (1)

Fret not thyself because of evildoers . . . trust in the Lord . . . (Ps. 37:1–3)

PSALM 37 is another of David's striking works. Penned in his old age (v. 25), it addresses the age old conundrum about the *prosperity* of the wicked but the *pain* of the godly. The first 11 verses provide a wondrous summary of how we are to live by giving us five qualities of the godly man (or woman).

First, we see the godly man's *caution* in the words **fret not thyself because of evildoers** (v. 1). Interestingly, **fret not** is the only "negative" quality of the five, but it is listed first and is actually repeated twice more (vv. 7, 8). The Hebrew in all three cases is *ḥārāh* (2734H), which "is related to both a rare Aramaic root meaning to cause fire, and to an Arabic root meaning burning sensation in the throat."[325] Further, unlike other words for anger, "this one speaks of the original stirring up of the anger, as one would kindle a fire, and the heat that results from it."[326] The full force of this word is seen in its very first OT occurrence (Gen. 4:5), where Cain was angry at Abel, painting the graphic image of a fire being ignited in his heart and the horrific result.

It is easy to see from all this why David asserts his caution. It is probably safe to say that every believer has at one time or another felt at least a little "heated" at the seemingly unjust success of the wicked and the suffering of the righteous. But to do so is actually to criticize the sovereignty of God. He is sovereign over all things, including all men, whether they enjoy luster or endure lack. Further, David assures us that such prosperity is fleeting; the ungodly will be mowed down like grass in judgment, and their fame and fortune will wither to nothing (v. 2).

Second, we note the godly man's *confidence* because of his **trust in the Lord** (v. 3). The underlying sense of the Hebrew *bāṭaḥ* (982H), in fact, is "to have confidence in," and its many occurrences illustrate the plethora of things in which the ungodly put their confidence: military might (Deut. 28:52); human leaders (Jud. 9:26); friends (Ps. 41:9); wealth (Ps. 49:6); idols (Hab. 2:18); one's own righteousness (Ezek. 33:13), and even lies (Jer. 28:15).

Every one of those will ultimately and utterly fail us, so the godly man puts his confidence in God alone. "Faith cures fretting," Spurgeon encourages us. "Sight is cross-eyed, and views things only as they seem, hence her envy; faith has clearer optics to behold things as they really are, hence her peace."[327] Such trust, in turn, leads to doing **good**, demonstrating once again that true faith, genuine salvation, implicitly implies obedience (cf. Mar. 8). "True faith is actively obedient," Spurgeon observes again. "Doing good is a fine remedy for fretting. There is a joy in holy activity that drives away the rust of discontent." Finally, as a result, God promises, **thou shalt be fed [on truth]**, as it can be fully rendered. Truth is the food of faith, and our love of Truth is an insatiable appetite.

Scriptures for Study: What do each of the following verses say about **trust** (*bāṭaḥ*): Psalms 9:10; 21:7; 26:1; 44:6; 56:1; 91:2; 119:42?

JULY 22

Qualities of the Godly Man (2)

...delight...commit...rest... (Ps. 37:4–11)

FLOWING out of the first two qualities of the godly man in Psalm 37 are three others. *Third*, we observe the godly man's *cheerfulness* because of his **delight in the Lord** (v. 4). While the ungodly are *intoxicated* by the siren call of the flesh, the godly are *illuminated* by the serenade of the Word. The allurements of the world never satisfy, but when we delight in God, He will **give** us **the desires of** our **heart**. There is no danger here of the wrong wants or excess in the right ones, for our desires will match His.

Fourth, we note the godly man's *commitment* in the phrase **commit your way to the LORD** (v. 5). While this first appears to be redundant and already covered by "trust" (v. 3), **commit** actually goes deeper. It translates a fascinating Hebrew word (*gālal*, 1556H) that literally means "to roll," as in rolling a stone away from the mouth of a well (Gen. 29:8). We have all heard the old expression of letting something "roll off our back," and that is precisely the image here; we can let anything roll off *our* back and right on to *God's*. In fact, this was undoubtedly the image (and psalm, along with 55:22), that Peter had in mind when he wrote, "Casting all your care upon him; for he careth for you" (1 Pet. 5:7). We roll not just "the things we can't handle," rather *all* our worries upon Him whether they be devastating problems or just daily pressures. When we do this, as well as **trust** Him (v. 6; same word as in v. 3), **he shall bring it to pass**—He will work it all out for our good and His glory.

Fifth and finally, we see the godly man's *contentment* in the words **rest in the LORD, and wait patiently for him** (v. 7). French mathematician, physicist, inventor, writer, and Christian philosopher Blaise Pascal's (1623–62) often quoted observation—"I have discovered that all the unhappiness of men arises from one single fact, that they cannot stay quietly in their own chamber"[328]—is an insightful observation indeed. While obviously true in his day, is it not even more descriptive of our own? Seldom does anyone sit quietly anywhere for any reason.

David, however, goes far deeper. While he writes that we are to **rest** (*dāmam*, 1826H, to be silent, still, or motionless), he adds **in the LORD**. Just sitting still is not enough. Rather, we are silent and still before Him. "Be still, and know that I am God" (Ps. 46:10), an anonymous psalmist declares (Jan. 3).

Likewise, neither is it enough simply to **wait patiently**, David goes on to encourage, but to **wait patiently for [God]**. **Wait patiently** translates an interesting Hebrew word (*ḥûl*, 2342H) that means to whirl, shake, fear, dance, writhe, or grieve. It is used of shaking with fear (Jer. 5:22), worshiping in trembling awe (Ps. 96:9), or anxiously waiting, as it is here (cf. Gen. 8:10). So, no matter what rages and shakes around us, we wait on God in anticipation of what He will do.

Scriptures for Study: How do the following verses encourage you: Psalm 27:14; Proverbs 20:22; James 5:7–11? 📖 Review our January 3 reading.

The Rock and the Quarry

Hearken to me, ye that follow after righteousness, ye that seek the LORD: look unto the rock whence ye are hewn, and to the hole of the pit whence ye are digged. (Is. 51:1)

OUR text is one that has captivated this writer for many years. The historical setting, of course, is Isaiah's challenge to Israel to look back and remember where they came from. Using a simple metaphor, he declares that as stones are cut out of a rock and a quarry, the nation descended from Abraham and Sarah. It is the practical significance, however, that strikes us profoundly.

First, we must *listen* to God. **Hearken** (*sāma'*, 8085H) "basically means 'to hear with the ear' with several shades of meaning derived from it that generally denote *effective* hearing, that is, truly *listening*, paying attention, regarding, and obeying."[329] While many today say they love God, their failure to listen to Him and refusal to obey and **seek** His Word, reveals their empty profession.

Second, we should *look* to the **rock** from which we were carved. In September of 1501, 26-year-old Michelangelo was commissioned to fashion what would become the legendary sculpture *David* from an enormous block of second-hand marble, which had been left over from previous attempts and had deteriorated during 25 years of exposure to the elements. More than two years later, the 17-foot-tall, six-ton statue was complete, the work of genius; its exquisite artistry and stunning detail have awed admirers for centuries.

Ephesians 2:10 declares, "We are [God's] workmanship, created in Christ Jesus." As noted in our March 27 reading, "workmanship" (*poiēma*, 4161) refers to what is made or created. Another form, *poiētēs*, refers to one who makes something or to a work of art. In ancient Greek this referred to an author or poet. Our English word *poem*, in fact, is derived from *poiēma*. A Christian is, indeed, God's "masterpiece." Once a discarded "stony heart" (Ezek. 36:26), one worked on by others but abandoned, God has created a dazzling work of art whose testimony will confound a watching world.

Third, we ought to *linger* over the **pit** (quarry) from which we were dug. While Michelangelo lived to almost 89, he completed only about a dozen sculptures. This was not due to laziness but because of many lost years in quarrying the marble for his projects in the mountains of Pietrasanta and Carrara (where the piece for *David* had come). He actually had to build a road out of the quarry of Pietrasanta and transport his blocks on oxcarts.

God "brought [us] up also out of an horrible pit, out of the miry clay, and set [our] feet upon a rock, and established [our] goings" (Ps. 40:2). "Pit" (*bôr*, 953H) refers to rock-hewn reservoirs and wells, which when empty made perfect prisons (e.g., Joseph [Gen. 37:20ff] and Jeremiah [Jer. 38:6–7]). Only God could create a masterpiece that He quarried out of the pit of sin and the prison of spiritual death.

Scriptures for Study: What do the following verses declare: Psalms 61:2; 86:13; 142:7; Matthew 7:24–25?

JULY 24

The Glory of the Rainbow

I do set my bow in the cloud, and it shall be for a token of a covenant between me and the earth . . . (Gen. 9:13–16)

THE covenant concept is a dominant OT theme. The Hebrew always used for this idea (*beriyt*, 1285H) is a broad term covering several types of agreements, including a covenant between friends (1 Sam. 18:3) and rulers (1 Kings 5:12; "league"). The covenants, then, are the permanent, legal transactions God made with various individuals that also extended to their descendants. Scripture reveals several covenants: Noahic (Gen. 9:9–17), Abrahamic (12:1–3; 13:14–17; 17:1–22; and 22:16–18; cf. Gal. 3:8), Mosaic (Ex. 20:1–17; 21:1—31:18), Davidic (2 Sam. 7:4–17), and New (Jer. 31:31–32; Heb. 7:18–19, 22; 8:6–12).

The Noahic Covenant, then, which is spelled out in Genesis 9:8–17, where it is also named "the everlasting covenant" (v. 16), is God's unconditional promise that He will never again destroy the earth by flood, regardless of how wicked man becomes, and that He would continue to sustain the rhythms and balance of the earth for "perpetual generations" (v. 12). In other words, the Noahic Covenant will last forever and includes "every living creature of all flesh" (v. 15): humans, birds, beasts, and wild animals. God gave this covenant to Noah and "perpetual generations" for our peace of mind. Man could now enjoy life without worrying every time it started to rain that the world was going to be destroyed again.

It is also important to note that God uses the term "every living creature" four times in this passage (vv. 10, 12, 15, 16). We would probably miss the significance of this if it were not for the fact of Revelation 4:6–7, where the Apostle John sees a vision of the throne of God and four unusual "living creatures" before that throne worshipping God. Here, then, in these four categories, is the entire range of animal life on the earth, including: wild beasts, cattle, humans, and birds. This not only demonstrates that all living things bow before God's throne in worship but also that God is concerned with His creation and it is ever on His sovereign mind.

To seal this covenant with creation, God gave a sign, something He also did when making other covenants. The sign and seal of the Abrahamic Covenant, for example, was circumcision (Gen. 17:11; Rom. 4:9–12). Likewise, the weekly Sabbath was the sign of the Mosaic Covenant that God gave to racial Israel (Ex. 31:16–17).

So what was the sign God gave to all mankind and for all time that would remind them He would never destroy the earth again by a universal flood? *The rainbow* (vv. 13, 16). It is a perpetual, permanent, and palpable reminder of God's wondrous mercy and grace. It also deepens our love for Him and His Word because it assures us He will keep every covenant He has made. So, let us consider the sign, the significance, and the solemnity of the rainbow.[330]

Scriptures for Study: Read the entire passage on the Noahic Covenant (Gen. 9:9–17). What strikes you the most profoundly?

JULY 25

The Sign of the Rainbow (1)

I do set my bow in the cloud, and it shall be for a token of a covenant between me and the earth . . . (Gen. 9:13–16)

THE Hebrew word translated **bow** (or rainbow) is greatly significant, for it is the exact same word that also refers to the familiar weapon. In fact, of the 77 occurrences of the Hebrew *qesĕṭ* (7198H) in the OT, virtually all of them refer to the common weapon that shoots arrows (2 Kings 9:24) and is used by the hunter (Gen. 27:3) and the warrior (1 Sam. 31:3).

The bow is a truly ancient weapon, mentioned in Scripture for the first time in Genesis 21:20 (about 2000 BC) as being the weapon of choice of Ishmael, the son of Abraham and the Egyptian woman Hagar. Without doubt, however, it existed before that. It was the common long distance weapon (300–400 yards) of the Egyptians, Syrians (1 Kings 22:34), Philistines (1 Sam. 31:3), Elamites (Is. 22:6), Lydians (Jer. 46:9), and ultimately the Hebrews (2 Sam. 1:18), of which the Benjamites were experts (1 Chron. 8:40). The Septuagint uses the equivalent Greek word *toxon* (5115; e.g., Rev. 6:2).

Used figuratively, the bow symbolized victory (Ps 7:12) as well as falsehood and deceit (Ps. 64:3, 4; Hosea 7:16; Jer 9:3). It also pictured disease or calamity sent by God (Job 6:4; Ps. 38:2), and it is that concept that leads us to the other use of *qeshet*.

In contrast to the weapon, the three appearances of *qeshet* in Genesis 9:13–16 refer to a very different bow, which we might call "God's bow." After first using His "bow" to bring the calamity of the Flood in His "battle" with a wicked world, He then put away His bow, hanging it in the sky as a picture of peace. I was reminded here of old American westerns, where the hero would "hang up his guns" and be done with gun fights. God's bow hanging in the sky proclaimed to the world of that day, and for all time, that He would never destroy the earth again by a universal flood.

It is also important to notice that God said the rainbow was not only a reminder to *men*, but also a reminder to *Him* (v. 16): **I will look upon it, that I may remember the everlasting covenant.** This is obviously an anthropomorphism, that is, putting something in human terms so we can grasp it. It's not that God has to remember, for He is omniscient, but rather that this is just a further assurance that He is committed to keeping His promise.

My wife and I once shared the wonderful blessing of living in a house located on a hill overlooking a valley; we had the added fortune of seeing rainbows fairly regularly. Every one of them—whether partial, full, single, or double—was an unmistakable, undeniable, and unending guarantee that God keeps His promises without doubt, deviation, or dilution.

Scriptures for Study: What do the following verses say about God's promises: Deuteronomy 7:9; 1 Kings 8:23?

JULY 26

The Sign of the Rainbow (2)

I do set my bow in the cloud . . . (Gen. 9:13–16)

THE rainbow is a truly amazing and beautiful phenomenon, one that mesmerizes us every time it appears. Who can see a rainbow and not stop what they are doing and gaze upon it? Rain did not occur before the Flood, rather a mist watered the earth (Gen. 2:5–6). There are some teachers who believe the rainbow already existed before this time and that God just gave it a new significance; that view, in fact, actually comes from those who believe the Flood was only local, not universal. We lovingly disagree, however, and submit that the mist that watered the earth clearly implies entirely different atmospheric conditions, making it impossible for a rainbow to form. Additionally, the words, **I do set my bow in the cloud** (v. 13) seem to imply a new phenomenon that God initiates here for the first time.

It was the Flood, therefore, that brought a drastic atmospheric change, allowing falling water droplets to form, each of which acts as a prism. When sunlight enters a raindrop, the light is first refracted (bent) as it *enters* the surface of the raindrop, is then reflected off the *back* of the drop, and is refracted once again as it *leaves* the drop. This splits the sunlight into the varied colors of the optical spectrum. When conditions are right—which is when the angle of reflection between the sun, the drop of water, and our line of sight is between 40 and 42 degrees—we see this spectrum. It is most commonly listed in Isaac Newton's sevenfold order: red (inside), orange, yellow, green, blue, indigo and violet (outside). Newton was the first person to demonstrate that white light is composed of the light of all the colors of the rainbow. Newton's color list is also commonly remembered by the popular mnemonics "Roy G. Biv" and "Richard Of York Gave Battle In Vain."

As if one rainbow were not beautiful enough, at times a secondary one is formed outside the primary arc. This occurs when some light is reflected twice inside the raindrop before exiting. This causes the secondary rainbow to be fainter but still distinguishable when the observer is at 50 to 53 degrees. Amazingly, because of this mirroring effect inside the raindrop, the colors of this rainbow are in reverse order, with violet on the inside and red on the outside.

One kind of "sign" in the Bible is the miraculous kind, such as Jesus' miracles, which were to prove that His claims were true. The other type of sign is a symbol of spiritual truth. First, then, the rainbow was a sign to the *scarred*. Noah and his family had certainly been wounded by the events of the last 121 years, and so are we today by sundry things. God's promises are our assurance of healing. Second, it was a sign for the *scared*. There was undoubtedly fear about the future when they stepped off the ark, but God's promise was hanging in the sky. Third, it was a sign for the *servant*. There was (and now is) much to do, and God promises to aid us.

Scriptures for Study: How do the following verses comfort us: Philippians 4:6–4:7; Hebrew 4:16?

JULY 27

The Significance of the Rainbow (1)

I do set my bow in the cloud . . . (Gen. 9:13–16)

THE rainbow appears three more times in Scripture, once in the OT and twice in the NT. We see in these occurrences a three-fold significance that applies to the storms of life the believer will encounter.

First, Noah saw the rainbow *after* the storm. While a storm rages, it is difficult to think about anything else. Our foremost thoughts are simply finding shelter and hoping it doesn't do serious damage. Like Noah, we must wait until it's all over before seeing the sun again. It is then the rainbow reassures us that every storm is temporary and that no matter how much damage it does, it can always be worse.

God taught me this lesson early in life. When I was 15 years old, I was hospitalized with a life threatening illness. After two surgeries and several months of care, God delivered me from it, but, oh, what a time of learning it was. One of the encouragements my parents shared during that time, in fact, was, "Look around, son, and you will always see others worse off than you." How true that was at Riley Children's Hospital in Indianapolis! I saw many little ones far worse than I was and who would never be any better.

Second, Ezekiel saw the rainbow *during* the storm. Ezekiel 1–3 records the prophet's call, first describing the *visions* he saw (ch. 1) and then the *voice* he heard (chs. 2–3). No Scripture writer ever tried to describe God directly but did so using images the human mind could grasp. Ezekiel's visions of God began with a violent storm of horrendous wind and fiery lightning, demonstrating God's judgment power and blazing glory (1:4). Then came four "living creatures" (vv. 5–14), undoubtedly cherubs (9:3; 10:5, 15, 20), which are always symbolic of God's holy presence and unapproachability, as in their guarding God's glory in the Holy of Holies (Ex. 25:10–22; Ps 80:1). Next, beside each cherub was a wheel within a wheel (1:15–21), which seems to picture a chariot-throne that is in motion and moving toward judgment upon Jerusalem.

Finally, Ezekiel's fourth vision (1:22–28) included a "firmament" (an expanse) over the heads of the cherubs that dazzled like crystal, "the likeness of a throne," and the "likeness . . . of a man" on that throne, undoubtedly the pre-incarnate Son of God. It was then that a rainbow appeared, "the brightness" of which shown not in the semi-circle of a normal rainbow, rather "round about" (*sābîb*, 5439H, surrounding, all around), a complete eternal circle all around to "the likeness of the glory of the LORD" (v. 28).

Indeed, Ezekiel saw the rainbow *during* the storm, one unlike any other, to which his response was to "[fall] upon [his] face" in humble submission. Let us be reminded during the storms that come that God is on the throne and we are to submit to all He is doing.

Scriptures for Study: Read Romans 8:18, 28–30, 35–39. What do we learn here about "the storms of life"?

The Significance of the Rainbow (2)

I do set my bow in the cloud . . . (Gen. 9:13–16)

WHILE Noah saw the rainbow *after* the storm, and Ezekiel saw the rainbow *during* the storm, we see one other time when the bow appeared. Third, we see it *before* the storm, as revealed in the NT. Like Ezekiel, the Apostle John had a vision of the throne of God in heaven and wrote, "And he that sat [on the throne] was to look upon like a jasper and a sardine stone: and there was a rainbow round about the throne, in sight like unto an emerald" (Rev. 4:3). The Greek behind rainbow is *iris* (2463), which appears only here and in 10:1 and was used from the time of Homer for rainbow. In Classical Greek it refers to any bright halo surrounding an object, including the iris of the eye and the circle around the "eyes" of the peacock's feathers. This is, of course, the origin of our English word "iris" because of the numerous colors found among this family's 200–300 species of flowers.

Again like Ezekiel, John sees a rainbow *encircling* God's throne, announcing the completeness and perfection of God. This multi-colored bow is dominated by a soothing emerald green. As a symbol, then, of peace and God's faithfulness to His promises, this bow assures John *before* the coming horrendous judgments even start that there will be peace when it's all over.

Dear Christian Friend, all this reminds us that God is always faithful to His promises. Whether we see the rainbow *before*, *during*, or *after* the storm of trial, we are always assured of "the peace of God, which passeth all understanding, [which] shall keep [our] hearts and minds through Christ Jesus" (Phil 4:7).

In case we are tempted to think that God has made only a few promises, consider a moment just how many He really has made. We think first of what Peter calls "exceeding great and precious promises" (2 Pet. 1:4), which are all the salvation promises in Christ, such as: spiritual life (Rom. 8:9–13), resurrection life (Jn. 11:25; 1 Cor. 15:21–23), the Holy Spirit (Jn. 14:16; 14:26; 15:26; 16:7–8; Acts 2:33; Eph. 1:13), abundant grace (Rom. 5:15, 20; Eph. 1:7), joy (Ps. 132:16; Gal. 5:22), strength (Ps. 18:32; Is. 40:29–31), forgiveness (1 Jn. 1:9); guidance (Jn. 16:13), help (Is. 41:10, 13–14), instruction (Pss. 32:8; 34:11), wisdom (Prov. 2:6–8; Eph. 1:17–18; Jas. 1:5; 3:17), prayer (Prov. 15:29; 1 Jn. 5:14), provision (Matt. 6:33; Phil. 4:19), victory (1 Cor. 10:13), heaven (Jn. 14:1–3; 2 Pet. 3:13), eternal rewards (1 Tim. 4:8; Jas. 1:12), and the list goes on.

Second, however, in addition to all those and many more, prophecies and covenants are also promises, which adds hundreds more to the total. It has been calculated, in fact, that there are some 7,487 promises that God has made to man.[331] From the first promise (Gen. 3:15) to the last (Rev. 22:20), we can be absolutely assured that "he is faithful that promised" (Heb. 10:23).

Scriptures for Study: Take some time to read the verses cited today and rejoice in the promises of God.

JULY 29

The Solemnity of the Rainbow (1)

I do set my bow in the cloud . . . (Gen. 9:13–16)

IT is difficult, indeed, perhaps even impossible, for us today to fully fathom the solemnity of that moment when the first rainbow appeared. After what Noah and his family had been through, their first response upon exiting the ark was worship (Gen. 8:20), praising God for their deliverance from the incomprehensible destruction they had witnessed. It was then, on the heels of that worship, that God gave His promise and hung his assuring sign of that promise in the sky. Such solemnity provides us with at least three principles.

First, the rainbow is a *remembrance* of God's *power*. Every time we look at a rainbow, we remember the Flood and its unfathomable force. It is virtually automatic. And what is it that we remember, or at least *should* remember? We should remember that in His sovereign, omnipotent power God destroyed the earth because of sin. Because of His holy nature, God cannot tolerate sin. In a day when God is viewed as a tolerant grandfather sitting in His rocking chair throne and simply smiling understandingly at sin, men need to be told that God is a God of retribution and wrath, who will bring judgment on those who reject Him. As in those very days of Noah, God "shall not always strive with man" (Gen 6:3).

We also remember, however, not only God's power to execute *wrath*, but also His power to *save*. As He saved Noah and his family because they believed and obeyed what He said, He saves those today who receive Him as Savior and Lord.

This prompts us also to remember constantly God's wondrous grace. "Noah found grace in the eyes of the LORD" (Gen. 6:8). We find the phrase "found grace," in fact, 18 times in the OT. Lot "found grace" in God (19:19), as did Jacob (33:10), Joseph (39:4), and Moses (Ex. 33:12–13). Even in wrath there is grace, and we rejoice in it. No matter how *black* the night, no matter how *base* the sin, no matter how *bleak* the picture, God's grace is the light that pierces the darkness.

Further, not one of those men *earned* grace—he *found* it. "Found" is *māsā'* (4672H), to discover, find, or find out. The countless masses through the ages have tried to find salvation in themselves, their works, their belief system, and a plethora of other things. But salvation comes only by grace that is found in God alone. Noah was not spared because of His works; he was spared because of grace, to which he responded—again by grace—in faith and obedience. As we noted early in our daily readings (Feb. 16), when we meditate on grace, we step onto hallowed ground. No other word better epitomizes the Christian faith than does this one.

> Noah found grace in the eyes of the Lord
>   Grace that could not be merited or earned.
> He was delivered from God's wrathful sword,
>   For he believed the truth that others spurned.

Scriptures for Study: What observations can you make concerning grace in Exodus 33:12–17?

JULY 30

The Solemnity of the Rainbow (2)
I do set my bow in the cloud . . . (Gen. 9:13–16)

NOT only is the rainbow a *remembrance* of God's *power*, but *second*, it is a *reminder* of God's *purpose*. The appearance of the rainbow to Noah, Ezekiel, and the apostle John are all powerful reminders that God always has a purpose, even in the storms. As He revealed to the Apostle Paul, "We know that all things work together for good to them that love God, to them who are the called according to his purpose" (Rom. 8:28). Paul goes on in the next two verses to outline what theologians have called God's Golden Chain of Salvation: "For whom he did foreknow, he also did predestinate to be conformed to the image of his Son, that he might be the firstborn among many brethren. Moreover whom he did predestinate, them he also called: and whom he called, them he also justified: and whom he justified, them he also glorified."[332]

Just as our *salvation* is by God's sovereign purpose, all the *storms* that come our way are also by His sovereign purpose. Yes, storms will come. As Paul assured Timothy, "Yea, and all that will live godly in Christ Jesus shall suffer persecution" (2 Tim. 3:12), but there is a reason for it all. Peter reassures us: "That the trial of your faith, being much more precious than of gold that perisheth, though it be tried with fire, might be found unto praise and honour and glory at the appearing of Jesus Christ: Whom having not seen, ye love; in whom, though now ye see him not, yet believing, ye rejoice with joy unspeakable and full of glory" (1 Pet. 1:7–8).

Likewise, Paul adds: "For I reckon that the sufferings of this present time are not worthy to be compared with the glory which shall be revealed in us" (Rom. 8:18). That leads us to one other comforting principle.

Third and finally, the rainbow is a *reassurance* of God's *peace*. As we have seen, the rainbow assured Noah, and it now reassures us, that God is always faithful to His promises. Whether we see the rainbow *before*, *during*, or *after* the storm of trial, we are always assured of "the peace of God, which passeth all understanding, which shall keep our hearts and minds through Christ Jesus" (Phil 4:7). As Isaiah the prophet put it: "Thou wilt keep him in perfect peace, whose mind is stayed on thee: because he trusteth in thee" (Is. 26:3). Most important of all, our Lord assures us: "Peace I leave with you, my peace I give unto you: not as the world giveth, give I unto you. Let not your heart be troubled, neither let it be afraid" (Jn. 14:27).

So, dear Christian Friend, the next time you look at a rainbow, *remember*, be *reminded*, and be *reassured* of who God is and what He is doing. This gives new meaning to the old saying, "Keep looking up."

Scriptures for Study: What do the following verses tell us about the storms life will bring but also the rainbow we will be able to see: Romans 5:2–5; 2 Corinthians 4:15–17; Hebrews 10:36; 12:1 (cf. 11:1–40); James 1:3–4?

JULY 31

The Pilgrim's Journey (1)
... strangers ... pilgrims ... foreigners ... (Heb. 11:13; Eph. 2:19)

WE continue to see a steady decline in integrity, honesty, morality, and basic character in earthly society in general and in our American culture in particular. We see sin of every sort and those who will go to any lengths to justify it, and even defend it, as "normal." We have witnessed truly criminal regimes in government that have gone on virtually unabated and unchallenged. And the few voices that are raised in protest are quickly branded as intolerant, fanatical, politically incorrect, racist, and even worse.

In the shadow of all that, where does this put the child of God? What is our attitude to be? We submit that our attitude is expressed in our texts: just as Abraham, Isaac, and Jacob **were**, so are we **strangers and pilgrims on the earth** and are **fellowcitizens with the saints, and of the household of God**. Let us, therefore, consider two broad principles—the pilgrim's *journey* and the pilgrim's *life*—and thereby demonstrate where our love and true citizenship are.

Our well-known text in Hebrews relates directly to OT believers. The writer refers to several of these in the previous verses. He writes of *Abel* the first martyr, of *Enoch* who was translated and did not see death, of *Noah* who built the Ark for the saving of his house, of *Abraham* who went out, not knowing a destination, and of *Isaac* and *Jacob*, heirs with him of the same promise. He then amazingly summarizes, **These all died in faith, not having received the promises, but having seen them afar off and were persuaded of them, and embraced them, and confessed that they were strangers and pilgrims on the earth**. What a profound truth! Even though they never saw the promises fulfilled, they still said they were not part of this **earth**, rather **strangers and pilgrims** in it.

A pilgrim is one without a fixed habitation and who is journeying through a strange and foreign land. I can attest to that, having had the opportunity to minister in a foreign country. The first time I landed in that country, I was clueless as to where I was or where I was going. I was an alien who didn't speak the language or know the customs of the country. The only thing, in fact, that tied me to my homeland with any semblance of security was my passport, which I guarded with my very life.

Well, we as believers are, indeed, in a foreign land. Notice verse 14: "For they that say such things declare plainly that they seek a country." But this is equally true of all the people of God in every age of the world. These words therefore apply to us in a very real way. And what is our "Passport" to that country? What is it that ties us to our homeland? It is, of course, the Word of God. As we continue, we will trace many aspects of the pilgrim's journey. For now, let us each ask ourselves, "Where is my true homeland? Where do I feel most at home?"

Scripture for Study: What does Ephesians 3:6 call all those who are in Christ?

AUGUST 1

The Pilgrim's Journey (2)

... strangers ... pilgrims ... foreigners ... (Heb. 11:13; Eph. 2:19)

THE pilgrim's journey is a difficult, dangerous, and sometimes even a deadly one, but when we understand six aspects of this journey, it makes the day-to-day struggle easier.

First, the pilgrim *remembers* his original home. Abraham's, and by extension all his descendant's, original home was the city of destruction. It was there in the Ur of the Chaldees that he was born, educated, and lived (Gen. 11:28, 31; 15:7). It was there he followed the carnal life of the citizens. In this state he was far from God, far from peace, and far from safety. He was an alien without God, without Christ, without hope, "[a child] of wrath even as others."

Likewise, so were we. As Paul so vividly recalls in Ephesians 2:1–5, we were "dead in trespasses and sins," "walked according to the course of this world," lived by the dictates of "the lusts of our flesh," and "were by nature the children of wrath, even as others." As noted in a recent study, we should *look* to the rock from which we were carved and *linger* over the quarry from which we were dug (July 22). Such reminiscence will keep us on the right course.

Second, the pilgrim *recognizes* that his pilgrimage began through the influence of the Gospel on his heart. When the truth, God's revelation, came to him, his pain and peril were demonstrated. His hopeless condition was declared, his escape was denied, a better destination was revealed, and salvation, including present rest and future glory, was then detailed. Receiving the truth of the Gospel, he abandoned the city of guilt and death and fled for refuge to the only hope available. Likewise each one of us came to Christ by grace alone through faith alone. When we did, we left the land of destruction.

Third, the pilgrim *responds* by faith in God's testimony and sets his face towards the heavenly Zion. Abraham and the other Patriarchs believed God, and therefore set his heart to seek "a city which hath foundations, whose builder and maker is God" (Heb. 11:10). One commentator puts it well: "Why did Abraham hold such a light grip on real estate? Because . . . he did not have his heart set on present, material things, but on the eternal."[333]

This again pictures the NT believer. We too seek that heavenly city. Matthew 6:33 is the key to our understanding of this: "But seek ye first the kingdom of God, and his righteousness; and all these things [temporal needs] shall be added unto you." In contrast to the world's attitude that temporal needs are our whole life, God says the exact opposite: seek Me and the other things will not be a problem.

Scriptures for Study: What do the following verses declare about what awaits us in the future: John 14:2; Philippians 3:20; Revelation 21:2?

AUGUST 2

The Pilgrim's Journey (3)

... strangers ... pilgrims ... foreigners ... (Heb. 11:13; Eph. 2:19)

THE Christian pilgrim's journey is long, laborious, and often lonely, but there are several principles that ease the difficulty.

Fourth, the pilgrim *rejects* the possessions in the country through which he passes. As Paul wrote, "Set your affection on things above, not on things on the earth" (Col 3:2). The pilgrim's treasure is not here. His affections are placed on heavenly things. Possessions are not wrong in themselves, but they neither control us nor motivate us.

The phrase, "set your affection on," translates a single Greek verb (*phroneō*, 5426)—which is derived from *phrēn* (5424, "mind")—and means "to think, to have a mindset" and involves the will, affections, and conscience. Our Lord used it, for example, when He responded to Peter's objection about going to Jerusalem to suffer and die: "Get thee behind me, Satan: thou art an offence unto me: for thou savourest [*phroneō*] not the things that be of God, but those that be of men" (Matt. 16:23; cf. Mk. 8:33). The majority of its occurrences, however (26 out of 29), appear in Paul's letters and are equally pointed and powerful. To the Romans he wrote, "They that are after the flesh do mind [*phroneō*] the things of the flesh; but they that are after the Spirit the things of the Spirit" (8:5). More piercing yet, he wrote to the Philippians about those who are "the enemies of the cross of Christ: Whose end is destruction, whose God is their belly, and whose glory is in their shame, who mind [*phroneō*] earthly things" (3:19).

While we might tend to think that only the outwardly hostile critics of Christianity and those who deny its doctrines are "the enemies of the cross of Christ," we submit that there is something here that is much closer to home. As commentator Albert Barnes submits, "How many professing Christians are there who regard little else than worldly things!" Indeed, many are concerned only with fame, fortune, and fun. Christendom today is inundated with health and wealth, name-it-and-claim-it teachers, and our pulpits are populated by many who proclaim self-esteem and other man-centered, humanistic philosophies. We are compelled to agree with Barnes again: "These are the real enemies of the cross."[334]

In contrast, the true Christian pilgrim's mindset, will, and affections are set on heavenly things. He doesn't just *seek* such things, he *thinks* them. As an anonymous writer puts it, "He considers the world as the desert in the way to Canaan, the sea over which he crosses to the shores of glory."[335] He understands that "where [his] treasure is, there will [his] heart be also" (Lk. 12:34), and his treasure and heart are set on heaven. "If we send our money on ahead, then our affections will be weaned from the perishing things of this world."[336]

Scriptures for Study: What do the following verses declare: Matthew 6:19, 24; Proverbs 23:5; 1 John 2:15?

The Pilgrim's Journey (4)

... strangers ... pilgrims ... foreigners ... (Heb. 11:13; Eph. 2:19)

CONTINUING our thoughts on the true Christian pilgrim's journey, *fifth*, he *realizes* that he is often not even welcome in the country in which he travels. Here is a truth that becomes clearer every day.

Our text says Abraham, Isaac, and Jacob were **strangers and pilgrims on the earth**. **Strangers** is *xenoi* (singular *xenos*, 3581), which referred to a foreigner who did not belong to the community; it could also refer to a wanderer or a refugee. This was in direct contrast to *politēs* (4177, a "citizen" of the country), *epichōrios* (an "inhabitant" of the land), and *endēmos* (a "native" of the country). To the Greeks, a *xenos* was the same thing as a barbarian and was often regarded with hatred, suspicion, and contempt. They had virtually no rights, even by the standards of that day. This is, of course, where we get our English word *xenophobia*—a fear and hatred of strangers or foreigners or of anything that is strange or foreign.

They were also **pilgrims**; this is *parepidēmoi* (singular, *parepidēmos*, 3927), which refers to a stranger who doesn't just pass through but settles down, however briefly, either next to or among the native people. Paul uses a similar word for **foreigners** in Ephesians 2:19. This is *paroikos* (3941), a compound comprised of *para* (3844, by or alongside) and *oikos* (3624, house), so therefore, "by the house," "next to the house," or "one who has a house alongside others." This was a foreigner who lived beside the people of a country, one who was a neighbor that enjoyed the protection of the community (the natives) but one who had no citizen rights because his citizenship was elsewhere. He was a "resident alien," a licensed sojourner, one who paid an "alien tax" to live in the area without being naturalized. Yes, he lived *along side* the natives, lived *among* them, but he was not *one* of them. While he practiced the same culture to one extent or another, he was still a pilgrim, a foreigner, one who had merely temporary residence.[337]

Peter also used the term *parepidēmos* in his first epistle as he wrote "to the strangers [*parepidēmos*] scattered throughout Pontus, Galatia, Cappadocia, Asia, and Bithynia" (1 Pet. 1:1). In 2:11 he encouraged them "as strangers [*paroikos*] and pilgrims [*parepidēmos*]" to "abstain from fleshly lusts, which war against the soul." "Yes," Peter says in effect, "you live next door to these people, you are neighbors, but you will not live like they do."

So, it is clear that the true Christian will often feel out of place. As any foreigner, we speak a different language, we have different customs and lifestyle. Everything is different because we are not citizens. As a result, we will not only be misunderstood by the inhabitants here, but we will at times be disliked (or even despised).

Scriptures for Study: Read Ephesians 2:12–18. To what were we "aliens" and "strangers"? What has the blood of Christ accomplished?

August 4

The Pilgrim's Journey (5)

... strangers ... pilgrims ... foreigners ... (Heb. 11:13; Eph. 2:19)

THERE is one final aspect of the true Christian pilgrim's journey: *sixth*, he is *resolute* in his continual travel onward towards the city of habitation. He goes from place to place, from experience to experience, from dawn to dusk, from birth to old age in constant spiritual growth. He advances in knowledge, love, obedience, and holiness, and thus increases in heavenly mindedness. All he does here continually prepares him for an eternity in glory. True Christianity is progressive, deepening, and ever expanding.

As Paul declared of himself after 30 years of ministry (Phil. 3:12–14): "Not as though I had already attained, either were already perfect: but I follow after, if that I may apprehend that for which also I am apprehended of Christ Jesus. Brethren, I count not myself to have apprehended: but this one thing I do, forgetting those things which are behind, and reaching forth unto those things which are before, I press toward the mark for the prize of the high calling of God in Christ Jesus."

"Apprehend" (and "apprehended") translates *katalambanō* (2638), "to lay hold of, to seize with eagerness." Paul uses it here in reference to the ancient Olympic games. He is saying in essence, "While I am strenuously contending for the prize, ever eager to seize it, I have not yet attained it. I therefore continue to reach forth, to press toward, to pursue, to go after the prize of the knowledge of Christ."

Shakespeare's character Hamlet spoke of "the undiscovered country,"[338] that is, death with its fears and finality. In contrast, let us ponder:

The Discovered Country

It's now long ago since the poet spoke,
What he dubbed "the undiscovered country."
The picture was that of death's heavy yoke
And struggling with "to be or not to be."
The player pondered with terrible dread
That country lurking beyond the earth's shore.
Knowing no traveler returned once dead,
Terror did grip him at his very core.
But there's another realm he knew not of,
The "discovered country" where there's no fear.
It is with Jesus in Heaven above,
The kingdom of joy and eternal cheer.
    In that country is our citizenship,
    Forever with Him our companionship.

Scriptures for Study: How do the following verses encourage us: 2 Corinthians 4:17–18; 5:1; 2 Timothy 4:7–8?

AUGUST 5

The Pilgrim's Life (1)

... strangers ... pilgrims ... foreigners ... (Heb. 11:13; Eph. 2:19)

INSEPARABLY linked together are the pilgrim's *journey* and the pilgrim's *life*. Without the one, there cannot be the other. We turn now to the latter.

First, there is the pilgrim's *heart*, a renewed heart. He has been delivered from a love of sin and the world. He has received the "divine nature" (2 Pet. 1:4), which has made him a "new creature" in whom "old things are passed away" and "all things [have] become new" (2 Cor. 5:17). First and foremost, a man must be born *from* above, before he will live *for* it, and *follow* after it. He simply cannot make the journey without the heart of a pilgrim.

Second, there is the pilgrim's *head*. There must be the knowledge of what it means to be a pilgrim and how to walk in that way. The guide is the Word of God and that alone. Without it, we will be no better than the citizens of this earth, who are without any guide or authority. They depend upon how they feel at any given moment, what the latest self-help book says, or what is the latest philosophical or even political trend. God's Word is what must control our mind.

Third, there is the pilgrim's *heavenly spirit*. The Holy Spirit indwells the believer and imparts spiritual qualities: "the fruit of the Spirit is love, joy, peace, longsuffering, gentleness, goodness, faith, meekness, temperance" (Gal. 5:22–23).

Fourth and finally, there are the pilgrim's *heavy resources*. Even the resources of the pilgrim's life are vastly different from those of the country through which he travels. The country will have all kinds of seemingly powerful resources, but the pilgrim's are simple.

(1) He has his staff on which to lean. Anyone who has ever used a walking stick while hiking knows how valuable this simple tool is. And what is our staff? It is the promise that God's very presence shall go with us, and never, *never* leave us.

(2) His provisions are the bread and water given him from heaven. As Moses wrote to the nation of Israel (Deut. 8:3), " [God] humbled thee, and suffered thee to hunger, and fed thee with manna, which thou knewest not, neither did thy fathers know; that he might make thee know that man doth not live by bread only, but by every word that proceedeth out of the mouth of the LORD doth man live." And as Job declared, "Neither have I gone back from the commandment of his lips; I have esteemed the words of his mouth more than my necessary food" (23:12). Our provision, our manna, is the Word of God (July 9–11). People try to lean on everything under the sun, but we rely on the simple provision of the Word.

(3) Finally the pilgrim's raiment is that of the armor of God in Ephesians 6. *Truth* is the foundation garment; *righteousness* is our breastplate; the *gospel* is our sandals; *faith* is our shield; *salvation* is our helmet; the *Word of* God is our sword; and *prayer* is our empowering.[339]

Scriptures for Study: What do Ephesians 2:6 and Hebrews 10:34 declare?

AUGUST 6

The Pilgrim's Life (2)

... strangers ... pilgrims ... foreigners ... fellowcitizens ... (Heb. 11:13; Eph. 2:19)

DEAR Christian Friend, should not this world become more of an alien place to us each and every day? As wonderful as life is, it pales to insignificance in light of the fact that we are only temporary residents of this earth. We're just passing through. Our citizenship is in the Heavenly City. That is why Paul emphasizes that we are **fellowcitizens with the saints, and of the household of God. Fellowcitizens** is *sumpolitēs* (4847). The root *politēs* (4177) referred to a citizen, an inhabitant of a city, a freeman who had the rights of a citizen. Adding the prefix *sum* (4862, "together with") yields the idea of a citizenship "with others."

While it's nice to be fellow citizens with other like-minded Americans, it is immeasurably more important that we are fellow-citizens of Heaven. As Paul tells us, we are fellow citizens in **the household of God**, an extremely significant term. **Household** is *oikeios* (3609), which means "belonging to the house, member of the household." The word from which it is derived, *oikos* (3624, house, dwelling place), is truly ancient, going back 1600 years before Christ. Besides the literal idea of a house, it was also used in the metaphorical sense to denote the family, the property, and other similar concepts connected with the house itself. This makes Paul's point in our text wondrously clear—the Christian is a member of **the household of God**, His family, and enjoys the full fellowship of His house.

As Paul mentioned earlier in Ephesians 2:6, we are already "[sitting] together in heavenly places in Christ Jesus." Think of it! We are already there! Have you ever gone to a banquet and seen your name on a place card on a table, your place reserved as if you were already present? Likewise, everything in Heaven is already reserved for us. That is why our Lord said to His disciples, "I go to prepare a place for you" (Jn. 14:2). The table is set, our place card is positioned, and spiritually we are already there.

So, in light of *that* citizenship, how important is an earthly one? Sadly, while many preachers today put their emphasis on political reform and social change, we thank God for such stalwarts of the Truth as 17th-century English churchman Jeremy Taylor: "Faith is the Christian's foundation, hope is his anchor, death is his harbor, Christ is his pilot, and heaven is his country."[340]

Or as Vance Havner put it: "We are not citizens of this world trying to get to heaven; rather, we are citizens of heaven just trying to get through this world." We are already citizens of Heaven, our reservation has been confirmed, our place setting is on the table, and spiritually we are seated there. We are just trying to get through this foreign land on our way to our home country. So, with our "Passport" in hand, let that be our desire. When we are tempted to get caught up in the world's philosophies and politics, let us remember where our true citizenship is.

Scriptures for Study: What do Matthew 6:19–21 and Philippians 3:20 declare?

AUGUST 7

"What Saith the Scripture?"

... what saith the scripture? (Rom. 4:3; Gal. 4:30)

OF all the passions I have concerning Christian ministry, there is one that rises above them all and, in fact, drives them all and is the foundation for all ministry. Our texts declare that passion: **what saith the scripture?** In both verses, Paul is concerned with one thing only: what Scripture says on a particular subject. In the first instance (Rom. 4:3), he speaks of justification by faith and cites Abraham as the prime example. To emphasize his point, he quotes from Genesis 15:6. In the second instance (Gal. 4:30), he speaks again of justification by faith. Illustrating the principle that we are no longer under the Mosaic system but under grace (vv. 21–31), he again quotes from Genesis (21:10, 12).

Over and over again, we see Paul going to the OT Scriptures as His authority. He uses the phrase "it is written," for example, 30 times. Further, including all NT writers, we find this phrase a total of 62 times in the KJV (July 2–4). Similarly, "Scripture saith" appears six times. All this demonstrates the importance of the declarations of Scripture. Would that the phrase that characterized Christians today be: **what saith the Scripture?** How critical it is that we discern *everything*![341]

A dramatic illustration of this, which we borrow from A. W. Tozer, is when Moses asked his in-law Hobab to guide the Israelites through the wilderness, since he evidently knew much about that desert (Num. 10:29–32). Think of it! In spite of the fact that God promised that *He* would protect them (Ex. 23:20) and guide them (Num. 9:15–23), Moses mistakenly thought they needed someone else.

Now, please consider this: do we not see a plethora of "Hobabs" running the Church today? What is a Hobab? As Tozer so eloquently put it, "Hobab is anything gratuitously introduced into the holy work of God which does not have biblical authority for its existence." What is the ultimate danger in such Hobabs? "The more they trusted to Hobab, the less they trusted in God."[342]

The Church today is, indeed, trusting in a whole horde of Hobabs instead of God. She is trusting in countless tactics and techniques for success in ministry instead of the Holy Spirit empowered approach outlined in Scripture. She is captivated by and follows anything *new* and *novel*—a new ministry, a new method, a new idea, a new program, a new organization, even a new "missionary endeavor"—without considering it biblically, without ever testing either its *methodology* or even its *validity*, according to the Word of God. "No problem," it is argued, "if one fails, we'll just do more research and come up with another one."

Do we not see the deliberate denial of Scripture in such an attitude? It implicitly implies that Scripture's methods are not enough and must be supplemented by "whatever works." If **what saith the scripture?** was good enough for Paul, why isn't it for us? Do we *really* love God's Word?

Scriptures for Study: Read Psalm 19:7–9, the most concise statement on biblical sufficiency ever penned. What strikes you the most?

AUGUST 8

Live, Move, and Have Our Being

For in him we live, and move, and have our being; as certain also of your own poets have said, For we are also his offspring. (Acts 17:28)

TODAY we marvel at an amazing statement by the Apostle Paul. Its setting is his famous address on Mars Hill in the city of Athens during his second church planting journey. As with all good sermons, it reflects good homiletics. Framed by an introduction (vv. 22–23) and conclusion (vv. 29–30), Paul proclaims that God is the *source* of all things (v. 24), the *sustainer* of all things (v. 25), the *sovereign* over all things (v. 26), and as a result men should be *seekers* of God (vv. 27–28). In that fourth principle, we see first the *revelation* and then the *reasons*, the latter of which is our focus here.

First, God is our *energy*, for it is in Him we **live**. For the third time in our studies (cf. Mar. 5, 15) we encounter the Greek word *zaō* (2198), which speaks of vitality and active reality. What makes this statement, and the next two, so striking is their origin. As implied by the phrase, **as certain also of your own poets have said**, Paul actually quotes verbatim one of the Greek's greatest philosopher poets, Epimenides (600 BC). In one such poem, Minos, son of Zeus, lauds his father, declaring of him, "In thee we live and are moved, and have our being." Paul obviously does not agree with such a pagan idea, rather he uses the quotation as a springboard to declare the real Truth. **Live** underscores the spiritual reality that all our vitality, all our energy, comes from God alone. Every step we take, every breath we draw comes from God. "There needs not a positive act of [God's] wrath to destroy us," Puritan Matthew Henry observed; "if He suspend the positive acts of His goodness, we die of ourselves."[343]

Second, God is our *engagement*, for it is in Him we **move**. The Greek here is *kineō* (2795; English "kinetic"), "to set in motion, to stir." This takes the previous idea one step further. "We cannot stir a hand, or foot, or a tongue, but by him," Matthew Henry again submits; "as he is the first cause, so he is the first mover." While many athletes pride themselves in their abilities, it is God who by His mercy gives them the power to engage in it. Do we all not take for granted, in fact, even the simplest abilities to walk, pick up an object, and even engage in speech?

Third, God is our very *existence*, for it is in Him we **have our being**. This goes further yet—were it not for God we would not exist at all. The Greek *esmen* (2070) is used here, which is the present tense form of the simple verb *eimi* (1510; cf. Mar. 9), "to be, to have existence." While the philosopher Descartes is famous for coining the proposition, *Cogito ergo sum*, "I think, therefore I am" (or, "I am thinking, therefore I exist"), without God not one of us could speak a coherent word or even formulate a rational thought. Borrowing from another Greek poet, Aratus, Paul adds that we are all, in fact, whether believer or unbeliever, God's **offspring** in the general sense. What love and devotion should this instill in us?

Scriptures for Study: What do Job 12:10 and Colossians 1:17 declare?

AUGUST 9

"The Silent Dove in Distant Lands"

For thou hast delivered my soul from death: wilt not thou deliver my feet from falling, that I may walk before God in the light of the living? (Ps. 56:13)

THE setting of Psalm 56 is David's deep despair and flight into the Philistine city of Gath, ironically the hometown of Goliath, whom David had killed as a lad (1 Sam. 17). David was in imminent danger. The untranslated words in the inscription (*Jonath-elem-rechokim*) are a proper name perhaps best rendered as, "The Silent Dove in Distant Lands."[344] It is a sad picture of David (the innocent, uncomplaining dove; cf. 55:6) among enemies in a far off place. So David prays for three things. Verse 13 indicates that God answered all three requests and makes a fitting conclusion of the psalm and a wonderful application for us.

First, He *delivers* our *soul* (**thou hast delivered my soul from death**). As any fan of old American Westerns knows, when the bad guys have closed in, one of the good guys usually says, "They've got us surrounded!" That was David, surrounded by his enemies. But God **delivered** him. The Hebrew here (*nāṣal*, 5337H) indicates the power of one entity overcoming the power of another, underscoring the fact that it was God's work alone. David was powerless. Likewise, we were powerless in salvation and powerless still when we face the enemies of Christ now.

Second, He *directs* our *steps* (**deliver my feet from falling**). The word **falling** (*deḥiy*, 1762H) is a graphic one. It means "to pursue and cast down with the intent to harm" and in Arabic means "to drive."[345] It appears, for example, in Psalm 118:13, a Messianic Psalm in which the writer declares, "Thou hast thrust sore [*deḥiy*] at me that I might fall," picturing the violence that will be thrust upon Messiah. David uses it again in 62:3 to describe himself as a wall or fence that is tottering and about to fall because of the onslaught of the enemy.

But again, with no contribution from David, God did the delivering and directing. Likewise, as they did to David, the enemies of Christ will fight against us (v. 2), distort our words (v. 5), and lurk in ambush (v. 6). But God will give the victory when we love and trust Him and His Word (vv. 3, 10–12).

Third, He *demands* our *submission* (**walk before God in the light of the living**). David realized he had run ahead of God by going to Gath (1 Sam. 21:10–15), since God told him to go back to Judah (22:5), so he writes that from now on he will submit to God in all things, that his **walk** (conduct) will be in the realm of **the light of [life]** (cf. Jn. 8:12) in contrast to the realm of death and the world.

"In this short Psalm," Spurgeon wrote, "we have climbed from the ravenous jaws of the enemy into the light of Jehovah's presence, a path which only faith can tread."[346] Or, if we may submit, when comes the *violence* of the *foe*, we will rely upon the *victory* of *faith*. In Him the silent dove finds refuge.

Scriptures for Study: Read Psalm 34, the twin of 56. What observations can you make? How can you apply it to your Christian living.

AUGUST 10

Grounded or Moved?

If ye continue in the faith grounded and settled, and be not moved away from the hope of the gospel, which ye have heard, and which was preached . . . (Col. 1:23)

THE word **faith** here, of course, is a noun, not a verb. Paul is not referring to the act of believing rather **the** (definite article, Mar. 15) Christian **faith** itself, the body of revealed truth that constitutes Historical Evangelical Christianity. He encourages us with four attitudes we must have concerning that faith.

First, we are to be *steady*. To **continue** (*epimenō*, 1961) simply means to stay in one place, so in this context that place is the Christian **faith**. We don't jump in and out of the **faith** or move to another for awhile and then come back to this one later. We remain always in this one, in its doctrinal truths and godly living. An authentic believer never leaves **the faith**.

Second, we are to be *stable*. **Grounded** is especially profound. It is *themelioō* (2311), which in both Classical Greek and NT Greek means to lay the foundation of anything, such as a building. It comes from the root *thēma* (English "theme"), that which is laid down in the sense of being a fundamental.

Perhaps you have noticed how often the word "doctrine" has appeared in this book, about 60 times, in fact (e.g., June 5, July 1). That is not an accident, for it is the inevitable result of any sincere pursuit of biblical Truth. After all, the word "doctrine" appears no less than 45 times in the NT, 11 of which refer to Jesus' own emphasis, four to what the apostles declared in Acts, two specifically to the Apostle John, and most of the rest to the ministry of Paul. Why? Because it is the only thing that will ground us in the Truth (2 Tim. 4:2, etc.). Thomas Watson wrote, "It is the duty of Christians to be settled in the doctrine of faith. The best way for Christians to be settled is to be well grounded. . . . As feathers will be blown every way, so will feathery Christians"[347] (cf. Eph. 4:14–15; Titus 1:9).

Third, we are to be *settled*. Perhaps so there would be no mistaking his meaning, Paul adds this word, which is *hedraios* (1476), firm, unshakable, and stable. Oh, how we need stability in the shifting sands of our wobbly world!

Fourth, we are to be *steadfast*. The words **moved away** translate a single Greek word (*metakinō*, 3334), which is used metaphorically here to picture wavering. The danger was the wavering that is caused by false teachers and the danger of being seduced by them. Even more subtle, however, is what we often hear nowadays from those who say that such and such a thing "moved them." There are conferences, conventions, and even churches dedicated to "moving" people emotionally through music, motivational talks, and all manner of other things. We must, therefore be ever vigilant that we are **not moved away** from the faith, away from the doctrine in which we are **grounded** and **settled**. Let us each ask ourselves regularly, "Am I grounded or just moved?"

Scriptures for Study: How do the following verses encourage us: John 8:30–32; 1 Corinthians 15:58; Ephesians 3:17?

AUGUST 11

Trusting Horses and Chariots

But he shall not multiply horses to himself, nor cause the people to return to Egypt, to the end that he should multiply horses: forasmuch as the LORD hath said unto you, Ye shall henceforth return no more that way. (Deut. 17:16)
Some trust in chariots, and some in horses: but we will remember the name of the LORD our God. (Ps. 20:7)

WHY didn't God want His people to have horses and chariots? Because He wanted them to love and trust Him. But what do horses and chariots have to do with it? Our texts say much about this to God's people, both then and now.

First, God did not want them to *rely* upon their own *strength*. Who can forget that classic scene of the chariot race in the 1959 movie *Ben Hur*? It actually well illustrates the place those things had in the ancient world. Except for treading out grain for threshing (Is. 28:28), horses were not used in agriculture or traveling, rather for war (Job 39:19–25). Not only were they used as cavalry, but for pulling **chariots**, the ancient version of modern tanks. We can only imagine, for example, the terror that overwhelmed the Israelites when they saw Pharaoh's cavalry and 600 **chariots** pursuing them after leaving Egypt (Ex. 14:7, 9).

Anticipating that the people would one day want a king, God gave qualifications for such. He commanded that a king should **not multiply** *weapons* (**horses** and **chariots** for war), *wives* (for political alliances, v. 17a), or *wealth* (for power and influence, v. 17b). God wanted his leaders and His people to trust Him solely. Sadly, Solomon violated all three and David the last two (1 Kings 11:1–43).

Second, God did not want His people to *return* to their former *slavery*. Since Egypt was the primary source of horses, as demonstrated by Solomon's alliance with it (1 Kings 4:26; 10:26, 29; cf. Is. 31:1–3), such an act would **cause the people to return to Egypt**, the very place from which God had delivered them from bondage. Such a thing was unthinkable!

Third, God wanted His people to *remember* His *security*. Instead of depending upon the things the world offers, the **LORD** (*Yāhweh*, Jan. 21) wanted His people to remember and trust what He **said unto [them]** for their security. As the context goes on to say, it's the reading, writing, learning, and obeying God's Word that brings real security (vv. 18–20).

So how does all this apply? While some think this relates specifically to relying on today's military, we submit the application is more fundamental—after all, Christians are not likely to be attacked by a tank division. We submit that the deeper idea is spiritual, that being the world's attitudes, values, and resources. Are we relying upon human effort, ingenuity, rationalism, and methodology in our living and ministry? Or do we love and trust God's Word *solely* in all things?

Scriptures for Study: As God required a king to write out his own copy of the Law (Deut. 17:18), handwrite your own copy of various passages.

August 12

God's Handbook of Ethics

To know wisdom and instruction; to perceive the words of understanding; To receive the instruction of wisdom, justice, and judgment, and equity. (Prov. 1:2–3)

THE Book of Proverbs could be called *God's Handbook of Ethics*, meant especially for the young but certainly not exclusively for them. Simply put, it tells us the difference between the two polar opposites: wisdom and folly. The first two verses provide us with a three-fold summary of what this collection of ethics is about.

First, Proverbs is about *concentration*. **Know** is *yāḏa'* (3045H), to know relationally and experientially (Jan. 3). **Wisdom** (*ḥokmāh*, 2451H) refers to the skill, experience, shrewdness, and ability to make the right choices at the right times (Jan. 10). Further, **instruction** (*mûsār*, 4148H) refers to training that comes from discipline and even chastening. Such knowledge, then, does not come automatically or by osmosis. It requires concentrated thought, study, and discipline.

Second, Proverbs is about *comprehension*. **Perceive** well translates the Hebrew *biyn* (995H), which is more often rendered "understand" and "understanding" and carries other meanings such as: discern, observe, pay attention, be intelligent, and be discreet. *Biyn* is, therefore, much more than just gathering knowledge. It's about comprehending that knowledge and understanding how to use it.

The key idea of *biyn*, in fact, is "to discern, to distinguish between."[348] This, of course, immediately raises the question, "Distinguish between what and what?" The answer is equally obvious: wisdom and folly, right and wrong, Truth and error, and even precision and imprecision. Many today are fond of saying in most any situation, "Well, it's not really black and white; it's more of a gray area." But Scripture does not deal in gray areas, so it is absolutely essential that we discern from the two polar opposites in every situation.[349]

Third, Proverbs is about *captivation*. **Receive** (*lāqaḥ*, 3947H) is a broad term for taking or seizing something. Knowledge and wisdom come only through God's Word, so we must be ready to receive it, take it to ourselves, be captivated by it. Further, **instruction** is again *mûsār*, education that comes through discipline. Another common attitude of our day is that wisdom comes by mystical enlightenment. When we need wisdom, it is argued, we need only open our hearts, add a pinch of prayer, and God zaps us with wisdom. What a dreadful notion! Yes, God speaks in "a still small voice" (1 Kings 19:12), but that whisper will come via His Word (Jan. 4). And yes, if we lack wisdom, we are to ask God for it (Jas. 1:5), but again, He will give it through His Word.

I pray this short study will encourage you to go deeper. A good approach is to read one chapter a day and thereby go through the book in one month.[350]

Scriptures for Study: What do each of the following Proverbs encourage: 2:1–9; 4:5–7; 16:16?

AUGUST 13

Reflecting God's Glory

I beseech thee, shew me thy glory. (Ex. 33:18)

HERE is one of the most mystifying scenes in the Bible. Moses had witnessed God accomplish many staggering feats: miraculously deliver the people from Egypt by way of ten plagues, lead them by pillars of cloud and fire, part the Red Sea so they could cross on dry ground, and destroy the Egyptians at the close of that event. God even spoke to Moses privately and regularly.

But Moses wanted more and prayed: **I beseech thee, shew me thy glory**. What sanctified boldness! Was Moses presumptuous? Indeed not. We would submit that he was, on the contrary, passionate and perceptive. In his love for God, Moses understood better than anyone else what God's glory entails.

First, God's glory is *radiant*. Amazingly, God did not rebuke or refuse Moses' request, although He did, for Moses' own protection, put a limitation on what He showed him. God would not show His face to Moses, for no one can survive it (v. 20). Paul tells us that "the King of kings and Lord of lords . . . [dwells] in the light which no man can approach unto; whom no man hath seen, nor can see" (1 Tim. 6:16). Instead, He put Moses into a crevice in the rock (*neqārāh*, 5366H) to shelter him from His consuming radiance. One writer well describes, "Moses is to see the afterglow, which is a reliable indication of what the full splendor is to be."[351]

Second, God's glory is *representative*. It represents and comprises all that He is. God Himself adds in verse 19 that this incorporates three primary characteristics: **goodness** (*tûb* [2898H], from *tôb* [2896H], "good, pleasant, beneficial, precious, delightful, right, well-pleasing, fruitful, morally correct, proper, convenient"); **grace** (*ḥānan* [2603H], "to be gracious, considerate, show favor" and "depicts a heartfelt response by someone who has something to give to one who has a need"[352]); and **mercy** (*ḥesed* [2617H], "kindness and loyal love associated with a covenant relationship").

Third, God's glory is *reflective*. In a scene that is hard to imagine, we are told that when Moses came down from Mount Sinai, having been with God for 40 days and nights and holding the stone tablets with God's Law inscribed upon them, the skin of his face radiated light and the people were afraid to come near him (34:29–30). Think of it! Moses had seen only "the afterglow" of God's glory and now reflected only that, but even such a reflection was more than enough to startle the people and cause them to shrink away from God's holiness.

Do you reflect God? No, you cannot come before God as Moses did, but you certainly can through His Word. And because of the Holy Spirit's indwelling, you can reflect God's character so that others will see it and take notice. And just as the radiance faded from Moses' face when he was not with God, so will it be when you are away from His Word. At such times, we especially need "recharging."

Scriptures for Study: What do 2 Corinthians 3:18 and 4:6 add to our study today?

August 14

Our Response to Light

For God, who commanded the light to shine out of darkness, hath shined in our hearts, to give the light of the knowledge of the glory of God in the face of Jesus Christ. (2 Cor. 4:6)

BACK in our study of the names ascribed to our Lord in Scripture, we noted one of His great "I Am" statements: "I am the light of the world" (Jn. 8:12), which he declared while standing in the midst of four massive candleholders in the Temple treasury (Mar. 11). But how should we respond to that light? As with physical light, we can be either opaque, translucent, or transparent.

First, there are those who *obstruct* the light. Used literally, *opaque* (Latin *opācus*, shady or dark) refers to any object that blocks the light entirely, such as using a heavy curtain to prevent light from entering a room. This, of course, applies to the unbeliever, for Satan has "blinded the minds of them which believe not, lest the light of the glorious gospel of Christ . . . should shine unto them" (2 Cor. 4:4; cf. Jn. 3:19–21). Interestingly, opaque is also used metaphorically to mean hard to understand or unclear. This, too, depicts the unbeliever, who simply cannot understand spiritual things (1 Cor. 2:14; cf. Jn. 1:5).

Second, however, even the believer can *obscure* the light. The word *translucent* (Latin, *trānslūceō*, to shine through) applies here. A translucent object permits light to pass through but diffuses it so that objects on the other side cannot be seen clearly. Frosted window glass, for example, is translucent. Spiritually, then, while we *see* the light of God's Word, there are sadly those times when we allow it to be diffused so that we do not see it *clearly*.

One of the most common causes of this is our own preconceived ideas and presuppositions about a particular verse or doctrine, which prevents us from seeing clearly what Scripture is saying. This is the difference between what is called *exegesis* (literally, "to lead out of") and "eisegesis" ("to lead into"). While the former is a careful, objective examination of a text to see exactly what it says, the latter is the polar opposite, a subjective approach that reads into the text whatever the "interpreter" wants it to say. "Translucence" also occurs when we remove verses from their context or interpret them based upon ever-changing culture.

Third, we can *observe* the light in its full clarity and *obey* it in its entirety. This obviously is transparency. When we truly love God and His Word, we will allow nothing to obscure Him or it. We will regularly "clean the windows" so that we can clearly see our Lord's **face**. In light of yesterday's study, Paul makes reference to the incident with Moses in this letter (3:7, 13) and now sums up in our text. While the Israelites begged Moses to cover his face because they could not look on its brilliance, the enlightened believer has no such limitation. We see Jesus' face with full clarity in His Word and thereby have **knowledge of the glory of God.**

Scriptures for Study: What do Matthew 5:16 and 2 Corinthians 6:14 add to our study today?

AUGUST 15

Praying in Jesus' Name

And whatsoever ye shall ask in my name, that will I do, that the Father may be glorified in the Son. If ye shall ask any thing in my name, I will do it. (Jn. 14:13–14)

IN my early years of ministry, I taught in a Christian school. One of the students often commented that he didn't understand why we need to pray in Jesus' name, so he ended his prayers with, "In Jesus' name we pray, because we're supposed to, Amen." Thankfully, he came to understand the reasons why, but his earlier perplexity is actually shared by many.

Far worse, some think this phrase is simply a magic formula that ensures we will get what we pray for, even obligating God to give it, no matter what it is. It's hard to think for even a moment that such an attitude comes from a heart that truly loves God. Those who lovingly commune with Him will understand three reasons we pray in Jesus' name.

First, it means to pray in *accordance* with God's *purpose*. As our Lord made clear in "The Model Prayer," we pray in this manner: "Thy kingdom come. Thy will be done in earth, as it is in heaven" (Matt. 6:10). Every request we make must be consistent with God's will and the purposes of His kingdom. The Apostle John understood this principle: "If we ask any thing according to his will, he heareth us" (1 Jn. 5:14). I know of no uninspired writer who puts it as well as did Robert Law: "Prayer is a mighty instrument, not for getting man's will done in heaven, but for getting God's will done on earth."[353] Our Lord's words, **If ye shall ask any thing in my name, I will do it**, must not be divorced from His will and ways.

Second, praying in Jesus' name means to pray *admitting* our *poverty*. While the world (and sadly many in Christianity) believe in and live a life of *self-sufficiency*, the godly Christian's attitude is one of *Christ-dependency*. The latter is simply because of our spiritual poverty, recognizing that we have nothing in ourselves and depend upon Him to supply every need (Matt. 6:25–32; Phil. 4:19).

Third, praying in Jesus' name means to pray *acknowledging* God's *praise*. Once again, a misunderstanding of many is that prayer is primarily for our good, just getting things from God. I still recall a book on prayer I was required to read in Bible college in which the author insists that prayer is only about asking—it's not about praise, adoration, meditation, humiliation, or confession—just asking and nothing else.[354] But even the most cursory look at the seven Greek words used for prayer in the NT reveals several of its aspects, including intercession, supplication, requests, and giving of thanks.[355]

Our text, therefore, underscores the ultimate reason for prayer: we **ask . . . that the Father may be glorified in the Son** by the answer. We align our requests with the Father's own goal of glorifying His Son. To pray in Jesus' name is to concern ourselves with His person, His purposes, and His preeminence.

Scriptures for Study: What do the following verses tell us about prayer: John 15:7; 16:23, 26; 1 John 3:22; 5:14?

AUGUST 16

What Does It Mean to be a Christian? (1)

And the disciples were called Christians first in Antioch. (Acts 11:26)

WHAT does it mean to be a Christian? It is very enlightening to compare two dictionary definitions. Noah Webster was himself a dedicated believer, which prompted him to define "Christian" biblically in his 1828 dictionary not only as "a believer [and] professor of his belief in the religion of Christ," but to then add: "A real disciple of Christ; one who believes in the truth of the Christian religion, and studies to follow the example, and obey the precepts, of Christ; a believer in Christ who is characterized by real piety." In stark contrast, a modern Webster's simply reads "one who professes belief in the teachings of Jesus Christ." Oh, how Brother Noah has been watered down!

That does, indeed, underscore today's broad definition of "Christian." Many claim to be a Christian because they are moral, or they go to church, or they made "a profession of faith," or they "asked Jesus into their heart," or they "had an experience with God," or some other such claim. But Noah Webster understood what many today do not: just saying I am a Christian does not make it so.

What many also do not realize is that the term **Christian** was probably not originally meant as a compliment. On the contrary, the evidence indicates that it was a term used **first** in the city of **Antioch** as one of ridicule. While believers spoke of one another using the terms "brethren," "disciples," and "saints," non-believers used *Christianos* (5546, literally, "of the party of Christ") as a term of derision, much like "Nazarene" was used scornfully (cf. Jn. 1:45–46).

So, what does it mean to be a Christian? We would submit four principles that describe the true, biblical Christian.

First, being a Christian *commences* with reception of the *Cross*. The Cross is not a popular subject. It was a hideous and humiliating death meant for criminals (May 28), so for God to send His Son to such a death—as it is argued by some who even call themselves evangelicals—makes Christianity a "slaughterhouse religion" and even makes God a blood-thirsty barbarian. The Cross, they insist, was simply an example of sacrifice and servanthood that we should follow.

Such reinvention of the Christian Faith is, of course, gross apostasy. Jesus Himself unambiguously declared, "This is my blood of the new testament, which is shed for many for the remission of sins" (Matt. 26:28). Paul wrote that Christ was sent to be "a propitiation through faith in his blood" (Rom. 3:25). As we have noted before (Mar. 3), as far back as Genesis 3:15, in the shadow of the Fall, Jesus is in view. Satan would bruise Jesus' *heel* (cause Him to suffer), but Jesus would deliver the death blow to Satan's *head* at the Cross. From that moment forward, everything pointed to when Jesus would "save his people from their sins" (Matt. 1:21). Indeed, a Christian is one who first receives the Cross for salvation.

Scriptures for Study: What do the following verses say about the Cross: Ephesians 1:7; 5:2; 1 Peter 2:24; 3:18; 1 John 2:2?

AUGUST 17

What Does It Mean to be a Christian? (2)

And the disciples were called Christians first in Antioch. (Acts 11:26)

A Christian is one who first receives the Cross for salvation. Such "conversion," however, implicitly speaks of deeper realities.

Second, being a Christian *creates* transformed *character*. No verse speaks with more clarity on this truth than does 2 Corinthians 5:17: "Therefore if any man be in Christ, he is a new creature: old things are passed away; behold, all things are become new." There is a fascinating difference between two words that are used for "new" in the NT. One is *neos* (3501), which refers to something new in time, something that recently has come into existence, such as "new wine" (Matt. 9:17) and a "new lump" of leaven (1 Cor. 5:7).

The word used here, however, is *kainos* (2537), which refers to something new in quality, as it would be distinguished from something old and worn out, something that has never existed before. It is used, for example, to refer to the "new covenant" (Heb. 8:8) and the "new heavens" and "new earth" (2 Pet. 3:13). Much as he does here in our text, Paul used it again in reference to the "new man" we are in Christ (Eph. 4:24). In contrast, "old" is *archaios* (744, English "archaic"), which describes something that has existed for a long time, even reaching back to a beginning, whenever that beginning was.

Paul's intent, then, cannot be misunderstood. The old *passions* we were enslaved to, the old *practices* we indulged in, and the old *principles* we lived by are gone. Everything is new. "Regenerating grace creates a new world in the soul," wrote Matthew Henry; "all things are new; the renewed man acts from new principles, by new rules, with new ends, and in new company."

Paul's teaching here is not an isolated one. He uses the same Greek words for "new creature" again in Galatians 6:15. Likewise, in Ephesians 4:22–24, he details putting off the "old man" and putting on the "new man." "Putting off" (*apotithēmi*, 659) paints the graphic picture of changing clothes; as we would take off old worthless clothes and never use them again, we take off the old garments of sin and permanently put on the new garments Christ's righteousness.

Neither is this principle confined to the NT. The OT precedent appears several times in Ezekiel (11:19; 18:31; 36:26; cf. Is. 43:18–19). The prophet declared to people who were at the time (and prophetically are today) exiled in a foreign land because of their sin and rebellion: "I [God] will give them one heart, and I will put a new spirit within you; and I will take the stony heart out of their flesh, and will give them an heart of flesh."

Salvation is not *renovation*; it's not like a "fixer-upper" house. Salvation is *regeneration*; it is an entirely new dwelling filled with sparkling new furnishings, all of which have never existed before.

Scriptures for Study: Acts 19 records Paul's ministry in Ephesus. What changes occurred in people when they were converted?

AUGUST 18

What Does It Mean to be a Christian? (3)

And the disciples were called Christians first in Antioch. (Acts 11:26)

WHILE the definition of "Christian" is more and more blurred in our day, Scripture is not one bit ambiguous about it. Being a Christian not only *commences* with reception of the *Cross* and *creates* transformed *character*, but the final two principles are given special attention, for they are the two greatest evidences of true conversion to Christ.

Third, being a Christian *continues* with obedience to *Christ*. Decades before the so-called "Lordship Salvation" debate exploded into a firestorm, A. W. Tozer pointedly condemned "the widely-accepted concept that we humans can choose to accept Christ only because we need Him as Saviour and that we have the right to postpone our obedience to Him as Lord as long as we want to." Tozer rightly pointed out that we cannot divide or ignore the offices Christ holds and then drove home the clear Bible teaching: "The truth is that salvation apart from obedience is unknown in the sacred scriptures."[356]

That truth, in fact, simply could not be more clearly stated than did our Lord Himself: "If ye love me, keep my commandments. . . . If a man love me, he will keep my words: and my Father will love him, and we will come unto him, and make our abode with him. He that loveth me not keepeth not my sayings" (Jn. 14:15, 23, 24). God simply does not live in the person who habitually does not obey His Word. A true love for Christ immediately and fundamentally creates a desire to obey His Word. It is part of the transformation that occurs at conversion.

The Apostle John picked up on that truth and, therefore, wrote his first epistle as a test of true conversion. On this very point, he wrote: "And hereby we do know that we know him, if we keep his commandments. He that saith, I know him, and keepeth not his commandments, is a liar, and the truth is not in him. But whoso keepeth his word, in him verily is the love of God perfected: hereby know we that we are in him" (1 Jn. 2:3–5). So, no one "know[s]" Christ or is "in Christ" who does not keep His Word. Period. In fact, to say we know Christ but do not obey Him makes us a liar. Obedience is an "acid test" of genuine salvation. "There is no true knowledge of God and Christ" in such a mere professor of Christ, wrote John Gill; "nor is the truth of the *Gospel* in his heart, however it may be in his head; nor is the truth of *grace* in him, for each of these lead persons to obedience."[357]

Now, does this mean that we will keep God's Word perfectly? Of course not. We all grow at different rates and will have different struggles. What it does mean, however, is that our *inclination* is toward His Word and our *intention* is to obey it. "A world of confusion and disappointment results from trying to believe without obeying," Tozer wrote. "This puts us in the position of a bird trying to fly with one wing folded. We merely flap in a circle."[358]

Scriptures for Study: What do these OT verses add to our study: Psalm 119:4, 146; Proverbs 8:32; Ezekiel 36:27?

AUGUST 19

What Does It Mean to be a Christian? (4)

And the disciples were called Christians first in Antioch. (Acts 11:26)

IF the true meaning of being a Christian is not clear enough by now, Scripture provides us with one more principle that is perhaps the most definitive of all. *Fourth*, being a Christian *culminates* in godly *conduct*. In a society that is steeped in immorality, in a culture that is consumed by its own lusts, nothing more profoundly proclaims a transformed life than does godly behavior.

English Puritan Thomas Goodwin wrote more than 400 years ago, "We should keep up the name of 'saints' . . . for in these times it is to be feared that the name is out of use, because holiness itself is out of fashion."[359] Sadly, the same is true today. A "saint" is not a special category of Christian reserved for the few who have been officially "canonized" by the Roman Catholic Church. Such a false notion has not a single shred of biblical support. Paul used the term "saint" some 42 times in his epistles and *always* used it to refer to *all* Christians. But, as Goodwin stated, it has fallen out of use. Why? Not only because of Catholicism's perversion of the term, but also simply because holiness itself has fallen out of fashion.

That word "saint," in fact, is critical in understanding the true meaning of "Christian." It translates *hagios* (40), which is also rendered using the words "holy" (e.g., Eph. 1:4; 5:27; 1 Thess. 5:27) and "sanctification" (e.g., 1 Cor. 1:30; 1 Thess. 4:3–4; 2 Thess. 2:13). While in secular Greek it was used simply of a person who was devoted to a god, Paul elevated it far above that anemic idea to its own lofty level of meaning: "to set apart or be separate." Every Christian, then, is a saint, for he is now set apart from sin. As noted in an earlier study (Apr. 28), this does not mean we are *sinless*, but it does mean we sin *less*.

Why is this true? Simply because it is automatic; it is the result of conversion. As the psalmist declared, "the righteous LORD loveth righteousness" (Ps. 11:7; cf. 33:5) and again, "Thou lovest righteousness, and hatest wickedness" (45:7). Likewise, if we truly love God, we will love what He loves and hate what he hates.

The Apostle Paul made much of this principle. As also noted previously (Aug. 17), He commanded the Ephesians (and expected obedience) to take off the filthy garments of the "old man" and put on the pure garments of the "new man" (Eph. 4:22–32). To the Thessalonians, he wrote, "For this is the will of God, even your sanctification, that ye should abstain from fornication: That every one of you should know how to possess his vessel in sanctification and honour; For God hath not called us unto uncleanness, but unto holiness" (1 Thess. 4:3–4, 7). He then closed that letter with the words, "I charge you by the Lord that this epistle be read unto all the holy brethren" (5:27).

My Dear Christian Friend, while the term "Christian" doesn't mean much in the minds of most people today, it means much to our Lord.

Scriptures for Study: What do the following verses say about holiness: John 17:17–19; Romans 6:22; 1 Corinthians 5:9–11 and 6:9?

AUGUST 20

"Auditing" Christianity

But be ye doers of the word, and not hearers only, deceiving your own selves. (Jas. 1:22)

BEFORE leaving the principles of the last few days, let us ponder one more thought. I taught computer science, and a few Bible courses, at a local college for several years. At the beginning of each semester, students had to choose a grading option for the course. The "Letter Grade" option, of course, required them to do all the assigned work. In contrast, "Pass/Fail" meant they would do the work but would receive only a "P" or "F" at the end of the course, an easier option some chose if they did not plan on pursing a college degree. The "Audit" option, however, meant they could take the course only for whatever they wanted to get out of it and that no work was required of them.

That well illustrates James' very pointed statement in our text. **Hearers** translates a fascinating Greek word (*akroatēs*, 202), which was used of people who sat and listened to a singer or speaker simply for the pleasure of doing so with no responsibility attached. In other words, they "audited" the performance.

It is tragic, indeed, that there are some (if not many) in churches today who are simply "auditing" Christianity. Some shop around for a church that will entertain them and give them what they want. Others might actually be in a church that preaches the Truth, but they take little interest in it. They have no desire to obey it or implement it in their lives. As we have noted, such a persistent attitude indicates that such people are not true Christians, rather pretenders. Such people think they belong to God—perhaps because they made some vague, nebulous "profession" of faith at some point in their lives—when in reality they are not true believers.

What does James say about such auditors? He bluntly declares they are "deceiving [them]selves." **Deceiving**" (*paralogizomai*, 3884) means to reason alongside of, that is, to reason incorrectly, often including the idea of deliberate false reasoning for the purpose of deception. So, those who profess to be Christians but then hear the Word of God and persistently choose to disobey it, deliberately deceive themselves into believing they are true Christians when they are not.

I recently came across an old Scottish expression that struck me profoundly. It speaks of such false Christians as "sermon tasters who never tasted the grace of God." I was immediately reminded of big stores that offer free samples of food. Many "do church" the same way. They wander and browse, pick a sample or two, and then move on to the next attraction. They might even comment, "Mmm, that's pretty good," but nothing changes. They *taste* a little of God's *goodness*, but they are not *transformed* by His *grace*.

My Dear Christian Friend, let us each pray for our own continued commitment to God's Truth and solemnly warn those who only *profess* Christ but do not *possess* Him.

Scriptures for Study: What do the following verses say about deception: Galatians 6:3, 7; 2 Timothy 3:13?

AUGUST 21

A Famine In the Land (1)

Behold, the days come, saith the Lord GOD, that I will send a famine in the land, not a famine of bread, nor a thirst for water, but of hearing the words of the LORD. (Amos 8:11)

FAMINE is considered among the worst of natural disasters, and history records hundreds of horrific ones. One of the earliest recorded famines occurred in the Maya civilization (AD 800–1000) and was caused by a 200-year drought and resulted in millions of deaths. The Great Chinese Famine (1959–61), considered the worst famine in history, killed 20–43 million according to scholarly research. Much like the Soviet Famine of 1932–33, it was caused by Communist leaders who forced change upon the people: private ownership of land was outlawed, communal farming was implemented, and foolish new methods of planting were adopted. Death by starvation is both slow and painful.

Amos chapter 8, however, records a famine of far worse proportions. Amos (meaning "burden") lived in a time of stability, material prosperity, and expansion for both the northern (Israel) and southern (Judah) kingdoms. But such affluence brought with it many of the common "self" sins: self-sufficiency, self-centeredness, and self-indulgence. God called this shepherd and fruit farmer to deliver a message of both judgment and hope to Israel.

This chapter records the fourth in a series of five visions. God showed Amos "a basket of summer fruit," a symbol that Israel was overripe and could no longer be preserved. "The end is come upon my people of Israel," God declared; "I will not again pass by them any more" (vv. 1–2).

First, then, we note the *reason* for the famine. Immediately following the declaration of verse 2, we read the solemn summary of sin that would bring the famine. There was greed, oppression, and injustice. While they observed the feasts and sabbaths, it was all outward; inwardly they were dedicated only to making money.

The root of the problem, of course, went much deeper. The real cause of it all was the total absence of love for God and His Word (Deut. 6:5; Pss. 119:11; cf. v. 97; 37:31; 40:8). *That* is real famine! Mark it down: *if we do not love God's Word, we will soon ignore it and then quickly depart from it.*

Second, we read of the *reassurance* of the famine. The word **Behold** (*hinnēh*, 2009H) is an interjection that appears about 1,000 times in the OT and means look or see. Depending upon the context, it expresses strong feelings, surprise, hope, expectation, and certainty. In the present context, the latter idea is obvious, as the next principle demonstrates.

Third, the *Regulator* of the famine. **Lord** is *'Aḏōnāy* (136H), which speaks of dominion, possession, and sovereignty, and **GOD** is *Yāhweh* (3068H), the name He typically used when making covenants and giving promises to His people.[360] Indeed, "God said it, so that settles it" is an axiom we can count on.

Scriptures for Study: What can you observe in the verses referenced today?

AUGUST 22

A Famine In the Land (2)

Behold, the days come, saith the Lord GOD, that I will send a famine in the land, not a famine of bread, nor a thirst for water, but of hearing the words of the LORD. (Amos 8:11)

"THOSE that die by famine die by inches, and feel themselves die," wrote Puritan Matthew Henry.[361] That is true not only of physical famine but also the spiritual kind.

Fourth, Amos tells us of the *range* of the famine. The words **in the land** are a single word in the Hebrew (*'ereṣ*, 776H), which appears almost 2,500 times in the OT. While it obviously speaks here locally of the Promised Land (Gen. 12:7; 15:7; Josh. 1:2 ,4; etc.), it is also used at times to refer "to the whole earth under God's dominion (Gen. 1:1; 14:19; Ps.102:25)."[362]

The evidence of such worldwide famine is easy to see. The Bible was freely preached for centuries in North Africa and Asia, for example, but God sent a famine that continues to this day. The same thing is happening in Western Europe and, if theologian Walter Kaiser is correct (and we think he is), right here in America: "The famine of the Word continues in massive proportions in most places in North America."[363] The vast majority refuse to **[hear] the words of the LORD. Hearing** is *šāma'* (8085H), which means paying attention, regarding, and obeying.

We do, indeed, see such famine for God's Word everywhere we look, even in our churches. While the following is admittedly strong language, it is necessary for our day. We lovingly submit, a pastor who truly loves the Word of God will spend the majority of his ministry time studying and preparing to preach it. Shirking that number one responsibility (1 Tim. 3:2; 2 Tim. 4:1–4) demonstrates that he really does not love the Word and is part of the famine. Likewise, Christians who truly love the Word will also love the in-depth exposition of it. If they want something else, which is typical of our day, they do not love the Word at all, regardless of what they claim. A true love for God's Word produces the *preaching* of it, the *passion* for it, and the *practicing* of it.

Fifth and finally, we see the *results* of the famine: "And they shall wander from sea to sea, and from the north even to the east, they shall run to and fro to seek the word of the LORD, and shall not find it" (v. 12). "Wander" (*nûa'*, 5128H) refers to a displaced person, vagrant, or one who staggers in bewilderment. Is it any wonder that God takes away His Word from those who dilute it, despise it, and defame it? Whether one wanders from the Mediterranean to the Dead Sea, or from the Atlantic to the Pacific, there comes a time when God's Word will be hidden. Just like wisdom (Prov. 1:28), people will look for it but will not find it.

Oh, my Dear Reader, our day truly mirrors that of Israel's! Let us not continue in the same error. Let us treasure every opportunity to embrace God's Word.

Scriptures for Study: What do the following verses warn: Genesis 6:3; Jeremiah 14:12; and Ezekiel 8:18?

AUGUST 23

Demas

*For Demas hath forsaken me, having loved this present world,
and is departed unto Thessalonica. (2 Tim. 4:10a)*

THERE are many human failures in Scripture. Cain, of course, immediately comes to mind. Others include: Lot, Esau, Joseph's brothers, Achan, Sampson, King Saul, and the worst of all, Judas. Demas was another. We first meet him in Colossians 4:12–14, where he, Luke, and Epaphras are co-laborers with Paul in his church planting ministry. Paul mentioned him again as such in Philemon 24. Paul had undoubtedly trained Demas for ministry and expected him to carry it on faithfully. So what happened?

First, we see Demas' *desertion*: **Demas hath forsaken me**. Desertion is an attitude before it's an action. While one's body might be present, his heart can still be somewhere else. The Greek here is *egkataleipō* (1459), which we have seen before in Hebrews 10:25 concerning church attendance (June 21). So, as noted then, Demas left Paul "in the lurch"; he abandoned him and God's work.

Second, we note Demas' *defection*. To defect is to consciously change one's allegiance. Why did Demas do so? Because he **loved this present world** instead of loving the Lord. **Loved** is *agapaō* (25), the love of the will in contrast to a love of feelings and tender affection (*phileō*, 5368). Why did Demas defect? One possible explanation is that he was a true believer but simply feared the future. In this case, he was not tempted by riches, sinful behavior, or doctrinal apostasy, but rather just wanted to live longer and, therefore, sought safety elsewhere.

On the other hand, it is more probable that he was never a true believer. "If any man love the world, the love of the Father is not in him," John wrote (1 Jn. 2:15). In this case, Demas could have been a stony ground hearer in the Parable of the Sower (Matt. 13:5–7, 20–22; Nov. 13–15), who because of shallow soil appears to believe but withers away when the heat of "tribulation or persecution" arise. Or perhaps he was instead a thorny ground hearer, who again appears to believe but is choked by the "care of this world, and the deceitfulness of riches."

Third, then, we note Demas' *departure*: **departed unto Thessalonica**. It's quite possible that Thessalonica (modern Salonica) was his native land. It was the capitol of Macedonia and the epicenter of political and commercial activity. This undoubtedly led to the tradition that Demas became a priest of the Thessalonian idol gods. As John Gill notes, Epiphanius (c.315–403), Bishop of Salamis, a strong defender of orthodoxy and known for combating heresies, "places Demas among the [Gnostic] heretics Ebion and Cerinthus, as if he was one of them."[364]

What does the case of Demas teach us? We see once again that an authentic love for the Lord will be distinctive, dynamic, and never permanently diverted.

Scriptures for Study: What do these verses indicate about dedication: Luke 9:61–62; 14:26; 14:27; 14:33; 16:13; 17:32; and Philippians 2:21?

AUGUST 24

Love Not the World

Love not the world ... flesh ... eyes ... pride ... (1 Jn. 2:15–17)

IN light of yesterday's consideration of Demas, today's text immediately comes into focus. It is without doubt the key text on "worldliness" simply because the words **love not the world** indicate that this subject is far more about *attitude* than it is *action*. A person could be stranded alone on a desert island away from any contact with so-called worldly people and activities and still **love the world**. Likewise, a person might never lie, steal, or be immoral but still be worldly. It's all a matter of the heart. Puritan Thomas Watson wrote, "All the danger is when the water gets into the ship; so the fear is when the world gets into the heart."[365]

World, of course, is *kosmos* (2889), which, as we have noted before, is used in several ways in the NT (Feb. 22). In the present context (and in most of its 188 occurrences), it refers to the world system or order, that is, the attitudes, values, inclinations, philosophies, goals, drives, and purposes of society or culture. This system is in turn headed by Satan, the "prince of this world" (Jn. 12:31; 14:30; 16:11). **Love** is once again *agapaō* (25), the love from the will in contrast to a love from feelings and tender affection (*phileō*, 5368). So, love for the world is a measured choice, a willful turning away from the things of God's holy system and thereby toward the things of this satanic world system.

As Satan, therefore, works through his system, he uses three specific strategies. As many expositors observe, these are the same strategies he used against Eve in the Garden of Eden (Gen. 3), as well as the Lord Jesus in the wilderness (Matt. 4:1–11). Any sin we can name, in fact, fits into one of these categories.

First, there is the **lust of the flesh**. In general, **lust** (*epithumia*, 1939) in this context is strong evil cravings. **Flesh** (*sarx*, 4561), then, refers to craving bodily appetites that are out of control. Thirst, for example, is not sin, but drunkenness is. Second, while **flesh** pictures the baser appetites of human nature, **eyes** (*ophthalmos*, 3788) refers to the higher levels such as entertainments one can see and intellectual thoughts one can contemplate. Third, **pride** is *alazoneia* (212), which is derived from *alazōn* (213), who was in ancient times a wandering, vain, swaggering, and bragging charlatan and a favorite comedy character in Greek plays.

It is because of the origin and destructiveness of those devices that John issues the stern warning: **If any man love the world, the love of the Father is not in him**. We simply cannot love both the world and God. "No man can serve two masters," Jesus declared, "for either he will hate the one, and love the other; or else he will hold to the one, and despise the other. Ye cannot serve God and mammon" (Matt. 6:24). To love God, we must not be controlled by *sensation*, influenced by *sight*, or driven by *self*.

Scriptures for Study: What do the following verses say about our relationship with the world: 1 John 5:4–5; Romans 12:2; Colossians 3:1–2?

AUGUST 25

Friendship with the World

Ye adulterers and adulteresses, know ye not that the friendship of the world is enmity with God? whosoever therefore will be a friend of the world is the enemy of God. (Jas. 4:4)

AS if John's description of and warning about the world were not strong enough, James is even more pointed in the text before us. He speaks of **the friendship of the world**. **Friendship** is *philia* (5373), which appears only here in the NT and means to befriend, love, or kiss. It speaks of deep fondness that here "involves the adopting of the interests of the world to be one's own."[366]

First, loving the world is spiritual *adultery*. James calls worldly people **adulterers and adulteresses**—strong words, indeed! But it is also language that James' Jewish readers understood all too well. The prophets Ezekiel (16:32), Jeremiah (3:8), and Hosea (1:2) all used the same metaphor when rebuking Judah for her sins. God entered a covenant of spiritual marriage with Israel (Ezek. 16:8) but she committed adultery by worshipping false gods (Jer. 3:1–5; 3:20), thereby breaking the marriage contract (31:32).

The spiritual parallel is both striking and sobering. As Israel is the Wife of Jehovah, Christians are the Bride of Christ (Rom. 7:4; Rev. 21:9; cf. Eph. 5:25) and must, therefore, be faithful to Him. To have any affection for the world is to commit adultery.

Second, loving the world brings spiritual *antagonism*. So serious is such affection for the world that James writes that it is **enmity with God**. The Greek behind **enmity** (*echthra*, 2189) is a strong word that speaks of hostility and even hatred. Luke used it, for example, to describe the hatred Herod and Pilate had for each other (Lk. 23:12). Obviously, since a true Christian could never be God's enemy—we are, in fact, friends of our Lord (Jn. 15:15–16)—an enemy of God is one who is perpetually attached to the world. This does, however, serve nonetheless as a warning to believers. We must be very careful about any friendship with the world. Paul meant the same thing when he told the Corinthians not to be "carnal" (1 Cor. 3:1–4). The misnomer "carnal Christian" is not another category of "Christian," rather Paul told these believers to stop acting fleshly like the world.[367]

Third, loving the world results in spiritual *adversity*. The preceding verses detail two problems caused by friendship with the world. First, there is *disunity* with others (v. 1). A worldly spirit cannot help but bring conflict because everyone involved is concerned only about his own lust. Second, there is *distress* within ourselves (vv. 2–3), which includes uncontrolled desire, envy, and even murderous hatred. The problem, of course, is that we "have not because [we] ask not" God in prayer or because we ask with the wrong motive, "that [we] may consume it upon [our] lusts." The challenge is clear: do we love God or self?

Scriptures for Study: What will be the world's attitude toward the godly Christian according to John 15:19 and 17:14?

AUGUST 26

Achan

I saw ... coveted ... took ... [and] hid ... (Josh. 7:21)

AMONG the many tragic figures in Bible history listed a few days ago, Achan is one of the most significant. He dramatically illustrates the consequences of disregarding God's Word and yielding to temptation. Israel was defeated at Ai (their only defeat in Canaan), but the reason was a complete mystery at first. It seems that Joshua, in fact, actually blamed God (vv. 7–9), never stopping to think that if he had sought God's face *before* the battle (vv. 2–4), there would be no cause to do so after.

The root problem, of course, was Achan, whose name appropriately means "trouble." God had commanded His people to take no spoils of war from Jericho for themselves, for God alone had fought and won that battle, so all the spoils were His and were to be put in His treasury (6:17–21, 24). But what did Achan do?

First, he **saw**, the step of *discovery*. As a soldier in battle, there was obviously no way Achan could have prevented discovering the beautiful **Babylonian garment**—Babylon was famous for clothing interwoven with colorful pictures—and the small fortune of about five pounds of **silver** and one pound of **gold**. Looking at something and appreciating its beauty or value is not the problem.

Second, Achan **coveted**, the step of *desire*. Indeed, is it not the second look (our fixation) that lands us in trouble? Here, of course, is the key to the whole incident. "Thou shalt not covet . . . anything" (Ex. 20:17). Why is this included in God's Moral Law? Paul answers: covetousness is actually idolatry (Col. 3:5), as we have noted before (June 29). God simply will not tolerate any other gods!

James' epistle again comes into focus: "But every man is tempted, when he is drawn away of his own lust, and enticed" (1:14). "Drawn away" (*exelkō*, 1828) graphically pictures drawing, tugging, or compelling someone away from that which is good. Even more descriptive is "enticed" (*deleazō*, 1185), which pictures the idea of baiting a hook. Mark it down: *temptation is the urge to do evil with the promise of benefit*. All temptation carries with it something that appeals to the natural appetites, but the bait hides the consequences. So, "It is better to shun the bait than to struggle in the snare."[368]

Third, Achan **took**, the step of *disobedience*. What begins in the *heart* inevitably travels to the *hands*. Achan not only coveted (tenth commandment), but he also stole (the sixth), and worshiped another god (the first).

Fourth, Achan **hid**, the step of *deceit*. As Adam and Eve thought they could hide from God, so Achan thought he could get away with his sin by burying the loot under his tent. And in case we think our sin effects only us, let us remember that his entire family and possessions were destroyed. Indeed, it is better to shun the bait than to struggle in the snare.

Scriptures for Study: How do the following verses warn us: Numbers 32:23; Eccl. 12:14; Jeremiah 23:24; Amos 9:3?

AUGUST 27

The Christian's Place in the World

...out of...in...not of...into... (Jn. 17:6, 11, 14, 18)

IN the last few days, we have considered much about the world, most of which has admittedly, but necessarily, emphasized the negative. To close our thoughts, let us consider our Lord's own mostly positive words about our place in the world from John 17, His "High-Priestly Prayer."

First, we have been chosen **out of** the world: "I have manifested thy name unto the men which thou gavest me out of the world" (v. 6). Our Lord speaks here specifically of the disciples but also collectively of all the elect. Earlier in John's account, Jesus said: "I have chosen you out of the world" (15:19). In both verses, "out of" is *ek* (1537), a powerful little preposition that denotes separation from something even though still in it. Albert Barnes put it well: "I have, by choosing you to be my followers, separated you from their society, and placed you under the government of my holy laws."[369] That leads us right to another principle.

Second, while we have been chosen out of the world, we are still **in** the world: "I am no more in the world, but these are in the world" (v. 11). Jesus departed into Heaven but left His servants. This was not abandonment, as He promised to send His Spirit to abide with them (and us) forever (14:16; Apr. 13–16). As we will see in a moment, He has done so because He has much for us to do. But at the same time it means that we will face trials and tribulations in this world, even covert discrimination and overt persecution. As Jesus, therefore, earlier encouraged, "In the world ye shall have tribulation: but be of good cheer; I have overcome the world" (16:33). Yes, we are *in* the world, but we are not *alone* in the world.

Third, while we are **in** the world, we still must ever keep in mind that we are **not of** the world: "They are not of the world, even as I am not of the world" (vv. 14, 16). This is the very separation we have emphasized in previous studies. We are no longer part of the world system or victims of our culture. We live above both. We hear much about being "culturally *relevant*," but we submit that this is another term for "conformity." Being culturally relevant is to be a follower instead of a leader. Yes, we certainly must speak to the culture, but we must live above it. Instead of being "culturally relevant," the believer who truly loves His Lord is culturally *resistant*.

Fourth, we have been sent **into** the world: "I . . . sent them into the world" (v. 18). This reinforces the above. The idea in this little preposition (*eis*, 1519) is the exact opposite of *ek*; it pictures motion into a place or thing. Our Lord has sent us into the world and our culture not to coddle it, cower before it, or conform to it, but to preach Christ in it. Once our attitude toward the world is right, we are then ready to reach out to it with the only message that can transform it.

Scriptures for Study: How do the following verses encourage you: John 15:18–21 1 John 3:1–3?

AUGUST 28

A Life Motto

Trust in the LORD with all thine heart; and lean not unto thine own understanding. In all thy ways acknowledge him, and he shall direct thy paths. (Prov. 3:5–6)

UPON his departure from home, the great preacher A. T. Pierson's father gave him these verses as a life motto. Pierson testified 60 years later that "no important step has been taken in my life without looking to God for His guidance and never have I looked in vain."[370] Such a motto does, indeed, reflect a deep love for the Lord.

First, **Trust in the LORD** expresses our *confidence*. The Hebrew behind **trust** (*bāṭaḥ*, 982H) is a blessing, indeed. It doesn't carry the idea of "faith," rather, as one authority puts it, the "sense of well-being and security which results from having something or someone in whom to place confidence." The same writer goes on to detail how this word is never rendered in the Septuagint using the Greek *pisteuō* (Mar. 8), to believe in the intellectual and volitional sense. Rather, in the present positive sense of hopeful reliance upon God, it is translated using *elpizō* (1679, "to hope") to express the feeling of being safe or secure.[371]

Second, **with all thine heart** demonstrates our *commitment*. **Heart**, of course, is *lēb* (June 14), which is used most often to refer to one's inner self and nature, including the intellect, emotions, and will, that is, the whole personality. Our entire self, therefore, is confident in **the Lord**; there are no doubts.

Third, **and lean not unto thine own understanding** reflects our *conviction*. Sadly, this phrase is often interpreted to mean that we just sort of "let go and let God," that we in no way need to engage our mind and understanding. But remember, **the heart** is the whole personality, all of which must be engaged to live correctly. Nowhere, in fact, does Proverbs (or any other Scripture) say we should live mystically, rather we must constantly be learning and applying God's Word. So what is Solomon saying? Simply that we don't lean *only* on our understanding. "Self-confidence is like leaning on a broken reed," wrote Harry Ironside.[372]

Fourth, **in all thy ways acknowledge him** emphasizes our *concession*. **Acknowledge** is *yāda'* (3045H, Jan. 3), to know relationally and experientially. To really know God (as detailed in Part I of our daily studies), is to understand His attributes. In the present context, His omniscience, omnipotence, and sovereignty come into focus. We **trust** (have confidence) in His purpose and glory.

Fifth, **and he shall direct thy paths** accepts God's *control*. In this usage, the Hebrew behind **direct** (*yāšar*, 3474H) means "to make (a way) straight, i.e. direct and level and free from obstacles, as when preparing to receive a royal visitor."[373] Yes, there will be difficulties, but when we **trust** Him, He will clear them. Solomon wrote elsewhere, "A man's heart deviseth his way: but the LORD directeth his steps" (Prov. 16:9).

Scriptures for Study: What do the following verses encourage: Job 13:15; Proverbs 3:7; 28:6, 26?

AUGUST 29

Loving God and His People (1)

And this commandment have we from him, That he who loveth God love his brother also. (1 Jn. 4:21)

IT has been wisely said, "The most important thing a father can do for his children is to love their mother." If I may adapt that, I would submit, one of the most important things a Christian can do for God is to love His children. This truth is dramatically presented in 1 John. While John's *gospel* was written that men might *believe* on Christ and have life (Jn. 20:31), his first *epistle* was written that men might *know* they have that life (1 Jn. 5:13). It is for that reason that John records many tests of true Christian life, one of which is love for fellow believers.

First, we note the *precedent* in John 15:13: "Greater love hath no man than this, that a man lay down his life for his friends." Our Lord never asks us to do something He has not done first. He loved us so much that He died for us. While we could never equal that precedent, of course, the one aspect we can emulate is self-sacrifice, the willingness to deny ourselves for the sake of our brother.

Second, we recognize the *principle* in our text. What does our Lord's precedent say to us today who are so concerned about our feelings, preferences, and sensitivities, that such a thought would never occur to us? True love, however, lays down its life for another. Picking up on that truth and building on it, John wrote much about love for fellow believers in his first Epistle. In fact, he repeatedly mentions that *brotherly love is a major test of true Christianity*.

It's extremely significant that the word "commandment" (singular) appears seven times in John's first letter, the word "commandments" (plural) appears another seven, and each and every instance of the singular refers to the commandment to "love one another" (2:7–8; 3:23; 4:21). In other words, this singular commandment is crucial to the Christian faith. Our feelings are irrelevant. What matters is that we truly love one another. As we will see, in fact, if we do not love *each other*, we do not love *God*.

John expressed the need for love among the brethren earlier in the epistle (3:10; 3:14) but then reiterates it in our text with even more thundering force. He makes it crystal clear: if you say you love the *Lord*, but don't love your *brother*, it is a glaring contradiction. It is sad, indeed, and very troubling, to see bitterness, strife, criticism, petty rivalry, and discourtesy among professing believers.

J. C. Metcalfe astutely observed, "Do not Paul's pungent words in the first three verses of 1 Corinthians 13 need to be read again and again, and rigidly and honestly applied in our own lives? Experiences, gifts, soundness of knowledge, ministry, faith, charity, and even supreme sacrifice are swept aside, and love is enthroned alone."[374] Each of those practices are important, but without love none of them mean anything; they are vain, empty, and worthless.

Scriptures for Study: A striking illustration of the operation of love for the brethren appears in Acts 11. What observations can you make?

AUGUST 30

Loving God and His People (2)

If a man say, I love God, and hateth his brother, he is a liar: for he that loveth not his brother whom he hath seen, how can he love God whom he hath not seen? And this commandment have we from him, That he who loveth God love his brother also. (1 Jn. 4:20–21)

IN one of the most dramatic scenes in the history of English literature, Shakespeare depicts King Henry V standing before his men before the Battle of Agincourt in France (1415) speaking words of encouragement that rallied them together and carried them to victory. Among those words is the famous line: "We few, we happy few, we band of brothers."

The theme in all this, of course, is a martial philosophy, where unity and unit cohesion is absolutely critical for victory. This should strike us all profoundly because Christians are, indeed, in a war, and unity among this *band of brothers* (and obviously *sisters*) is crucial.

Third, therefore, we specify the *practice* of this principle. John's point in the first part of our text is that of empty profession, professing that which is not actually true in one's life. **If a man say, I love God**—there's the *profession*—but **hateth his brother**—there's the *reality*—**he is a liar.** Strong words, indeed. John doesn't say the man is embellishing or just mistaken, rather knowingly lying. Our orthodoxy can be impeccable, our doctrine even precise—we've plumbed every prophecy, expounded every truth, exegeted every verse—but we can still hate our Lord because we hate one of His people. John continues, **for he that loveth not his brother whom he hath seen, how can he love God whom he hath not seen?** In other words, if you can't love the one in front of you, you can't love the One above you. Finally John writes, **And this commandment have we from him, That he who loveth God love his brother also.** It's automatic.

It's interesting that at least six verses begin in a similar way, three using the phrase, "If we say" (1:6, 8, 10), and three opening with the words, "He that saith" (2:4, 6, 9). Love and hatred are incompatible; they are opposites. Again, to say we love God while we hate another believer is to speak a lie (2:9; 3:15). *There is no middle ground here.* As a "son of thunder" (Mk. 3:17), John was not a soft spoken milquetoast, rather he thundered out the truth that if we say we love God and really believe that we love Him, but at the same time hate another, we are deceived. If we say we love the Lord, and we know that we do not love Him, we are hypocrites and liars. Likewise, if we say we love God, but don't love other believers, that too is hypocrisy. Why? Because those believers are part of Christ. To mistreat a child of God is to mistreat the Lord Himself. Further, it is a direct attack on the Body of Christ because we are each members of that body (1 Cor. 12:12–27).

Scriptures for Study: What practical illustration does John offer of how to express our love for others in 3:17–18?

AUGUST 31

Loving God and His People (3)

And this commandment have we from him, That he who loveth God love his brother also. (1 Jn. 4:21)

IT is one thing to *say*, "Okay, I love my brother in Christ," but quite another to *show* it. Consider the love that Thomas Steward's brother William had for him. Thomas injured one of his eyes with a knife. A specialist decided that it should be removed to save the other. When the operation was over and he recovered from the anesthesia, it was discovered that the surgeon had blundered by removing the *good* eye, so rendering the young man totally blind. Undaunted, Thomas pursued his studies in law at McGill University in Montreal. He was able to do this only by the aid of his brother William, who read to him and accompanied him through all the different phases of college life. The blind brother came out at the head of his class, while the other came second.

How many of us would be willing to do that for a fellow Christian? How many of us are even willing to do something far less dramatic for a fellow believer? In short, *how many of us are willing to be second*? Are we willing to set ourselves aside for another?

Dear Christian Friend, we are, indeed, a *band of brothers* (and *sisters*). Are we acting like it? We close our thoughts with this encouragement and challenge from Theodore Epp, to which I could add nothing: "The love that we have for God is measured by the love that we have for other people. The closer we walk with God, the sweeter will be our love for others. Here is a good test: Select someone who is seemingly unlovable. Ask yourself, How can I get along with that person? How can I show my love to him? We might disagree with the person over issues or principles, but that need not affect our love for him or her. It is not necessary that we agree on all points with another person before we can love him. In fact, it is a greater expression of the life of Christ within us to show kindness and consideration to those with whom we disagree on certain things. This can indeed be a real test of our love for God. Our love for other people will prove how much we love the Savior. Seek to love the unlovable; this is the acid test of our love for God."[375]

📖 📖 📖

This brings us to the close of the second part of these daily meditations:

> I love you, Lord, in the depths of my soul,
> Worship in the recesses of my heart.
> I love your Word and give it full control,
> Loving not just You, but each body part.

Scriptures for Study: What do these Scriptures add to our study: Romans 12:9–10; 13:9–10; 1 Peter 3:8; 4:8.

PART III
Serving Our Lord

September
October
November
December

Serving My Lord

I want to serve my Lord in every way,
But not labor that is just outward show.
Rather service that's from the heart I pray
Will be the rule today and tomorrow.
May I serve Him each day not to please men
But solely for His honor and glory;
If serving here or across the ocean,
The greatest end is the Gospel Story.
In my service faithfulness is the key,
It is the one overarching command.
Whatever the strain or the difficulty,
I will by His grace meet every demand.
    When my life is over and my race run,
      I want only to hear the words, "Well done."

SEPTEMBER 1

What Is Christian Service? (1)

Not with eyeservice, as menpleasers; but as the servants of Christ, doing the will of God from the heart. (Eph. 6:6)

WHAT is Christian service? While that question might seem odd, it is one that must be asked. But why? After all, everyone knows what Christian service is. We serve Christ by faithful attendance at church, supporting it financially, teaching a Sunday School class, being a youth leader, evangelizing, or even doing something as mundane as mowing the church lawn.

We submit, however, that a Christian could do all those, and much more, but still not actually be serving Christ at all. Ponder it this way: when Jesus said, "No man can serve two masters, for either he will hate the one, and love the other; or else he will hold to the one, and despise the other. Ye cannot serve God and mammon" (Matt. 6:24), did He mean doing things for mammon? Did He mean evangelizing for mammon? Obviously not. He meant to be a lover of and submitted to mammon (*mammōnas*, 3126, material riches and possessions, not just money).[376] Likewise, terms such as "servants of sin" (Rom. 6:20), "serving divers lusts and pleasures" (Titus 3:3), and "the servants of corruption" (2 Pet. 2:19) mean being the willing and obedient subjects of sin, lusts, and corruption. We, then, are servants of Christ, loving Him and devoting ourselves to His lordship.[377] It is not just an issue of the *hands*, that is, *what* we are doing, rather it is matter of the *heart*, *why* we are doing it.

First, consider how Christian service is *defined*. **Servants** is *doulos* (1401), which is the most common NT Greek word for this principle and refers to "a slave, one who is in permanent relation of servitude to another [person], his will being altogether consumed in the will of the other."[378] A servant, in fact, is not only so out of *principle* but also because of *purchase*: "What? know ye not that your body is the temple of the Holy Ghost which is in you, which ye have of God, and ye are not your own? For ye are bought with a price: therefore glorify God in your body, and in your spirit, which are God's" (1 Cor. 6:19–20).

Another crucial NT word is *diakonia* (1248; e.g. Acts 6:4), which, along with other forms (*diakoneō* and *diakonos*) appears about 100 times and is variously translated "administration," "cared for," "minister," "servant," "serve," "service," "preparations," "relief," "support," and "deacon," among others. The root idea was "one who serves at table" (Acts 6:2) but probably included other menial tasks. That concept gradually broadened until it came to include any kind of service in the Church.

So, what is Christian service? Christian service (or ministry) is the result of a heart regenerated by the Holy Spirit and a will responsive to the Lordship of Christ that manifests itself in performing the outward duties God provides for us to do.

Scriptures for Study: Who is God calling "my servant" in Numbers 12:7 and 2 Samuel 7:8, and then "a servant" in Philippians 2:7?

SEPTEMBER 2

What Is Christian Service? (2)

Not with eyeservice, as menpleasers; but as the servants of Christ, doing the will of God from the heart. (Eph. 6:6)

SERVICE and work and activity; all are good and should be engaged in by every Christian," wrote A. W. Tozer. "But at the bottom of all these things, giving meaning to them, will be the inward habit of beholding God."[379]

Second, and going deeper, consider how Christian service is further *described*. Even more graphic than *doulos* and *diakonia*, Paul used *huperētēs* (5257), which literally means "under rower" and originally referred to the lowest galley slaves, the ones chained to their oar on the bottom tier of a ship. As he wrote to the Corinthians, "Let a man so account of us, as of the ministers [*huperētēs*] of Christ, and stewards of the mysteries of God" (1 Cor. 4:1). Just as the puffed up Christians in Corinth needed to be reminded of what a true minister is, we need reminding today. How many in "ministry" today consider themselves to be galley slaves?

Third, consider how Christian service should be *displayed*. First, our service should never demand *remuneration*. I shall not forget an incident a pastor once told me. He had brought in a young guest speaker who had asked for a certain amount of money when scheduling the meeting. The pastor assured him he would receive that amount. After the service, with the offering plates in hand, the pastor invited the speaker into his study, dumped the contents of the plates onto his desk, counted out the demanded price, and handed it to the speaker with a gentle rebuke: "If you hadn't demanded a price, all this would be yours." That impressed me deeply in years to come when my wife and I trusted the Lord from week to week in a four-year traveling ministry; there were some very challenging weeks, indeed, but several amazing ones. Sadly, demanding money for ministry is all too common nowadays for seminars, conferences, "ministry success programs," and more.

Second, neither should our service ever demand *recognition*. While our text deals specifically with the employer/employee relationship, Paul's point applies to all. We are not to serve for the purpose of **eyeservice, as menpleasers**. The most graphic definition of **menpleasers** (*anthropareskos*, 441) is "man-courting, i.e., fawning." Similarly, **eyeservice** (*ophthalmodouleia*, 3787) means that one serves only when someone else has their eye on him, only for the sake of appearance.

Oh, how unbiblical is the common term "full time Christian service"! It implies that some people—such as a pastor—are in full-time service, while others—those in the pew—are only "part-timers." But every Christian is to serve the Lord at all times. Whether playing an instrument in the church service, cleaning the church building, preparing the Lord's Supper, recording sermons, printing literature, developing and maintaining the church's website—the list is endless—we all are to be **doing the will of God from the heart**.

Scriptures for Study: What was Paul's command in 1 Corinthians 10:31? 📖 What did he command in Colossians 3:23?

SEPTEMBER 3

Complete Dedication (1)

I beseech you therefore, brethren, by the mercies of God, that ye present your bodies a living sacrifice, holy, acceptable unto God, which is your reasonable service. (Rom. 12:1)

OUR text is one of those in Scripture that can be called a "hinge pin," a point on which the whole of a particular matter turns. Our dedication to Christ (or lack thereof) dictates our growth and service. Sadly, many Christians are on a perpetual quest to get more *of* God and even more *from* God when they should be concerned about God getting all of them. What they actually miss here is that they already have *all* spiritual blessings in Christ (Eph. 1:3).

That is, in fact, the setting of our text. Paul writes **therefore . . . by the mercies of God**, which points back to the preceding 11 chapters of his letter. In this great doctrinal treatise, he explains the awe-inspiring **mercies** God has given us in Christ: salvation (1:16); propitiation and forgiveness of sin (3:25; 4:7–8); deliverance from sin's bondage (6:6, 18); reconciliation (5:10); justification (2:13; 3:4); Holy Spirit indwelling (8:9, 11); adoption (8:14–17); predestination (8:29); glorification (8:30); eternal life (5:21; 6:22–23); and resurrection (8:11).

Based upon all those **mercies** (and more!), Paul writes to all Christian **brethren**: **I beseech you**. In this context (as in some 40 others), *parakaleō* (**beseech**, 3870) means to plead with or implore. In light of the great truths he has explained, Paul pleads with the Roman believers to live a life that corresponds to those doctrinal realities. So, what does total dedication to Christ mean?

First, it *commences* with *presentation*. **Present** is *paristanō* (3936), to cause to stand near or before, to place at someone's disposal. It was used both in Classical Greek and in the Septuagint for bringing a sacrifice and laying it on the alter. Unlike a dead sacrifice, however, our **bodies** are a **living sacrifice**. God already has our souls, so He wants our bodies, that is, our attitudes, actions, affections, ambitions, and associations; in short, He wants our *all*.

Every person in the armed forces takes the well-known Oath of Enlistment.[380] Adapting that, should we not take a far more critical one? "I do solemnly promise that I will support and defend God's Truth against all enemies, internal and external; that I will bear true faith and allegiance to the same; and that I will obey the commands of the Lord Jesus Christ and the instructions of the leaders appointed over me, according to God's Holy Word. In Jesus name I pray, Amen."

Such a prayer, in fact, is our **reasonable service**. **Service** (*latreia*, 2999) refers to acts of worship and other religious service. **Reasonable** (*logikos*, 3050) has been interpreted variously: dedication and worship are the logical responses to the **mercies** God has given; or our worship is rationally, sensibly, mindfully performed; or such service is according to the Word of God.[381] In any case, the point is unchanged: we hand ourselves over to God completely to serve Him as He wills.

Scriptures for Study: What did Paul write on this subject earlier in Romans: 6:13, 16, and 19?

SEPTEMBER 4

Complete Dedication (2)

And be not conformed to this world . . . (Rom. 12:2a)

A couple of weeks before his 1961 inaugural address, John F. Kennedy delivered a speech to the Massachusetts Legislature where he laid out the four questions that sum up how history will ultimately judge those in public service: "were we truly men of courage . . . judgment . . . integrity . . . [and] dedication?" Of the later, he added, "devoted solely to serving the public good and the national interest." Tragically, in recent years, those qualities are very rare not only among public servants but also among many Christians in their service.

Second, dedication *consists* of *separation*: **be not conformed to this world**. Interestingly, **world** is not *kosmos* (Aug. 24), rather it is *aiōn* (165), an age or time period. **Conformed**, then, translates the fascinating word *suschēmatizō* (4964), a compound made from the root *schēmatizō*, to fashion, and *sun*, together with. The full idea, then, is to "not only conform to the external form, but to assume the form of something, to identify oneself essentially with someone else."[382] Further, this is "the act of an individual assuming an outward expression that does not come from within him, nor is it representative of his inner heart life."[383]

So, Paul's concern—and command, since **not** is an imperative—is that Christians not be fashioned and molded into the image of the age because this violates the very transformed character that results from becoming a Christian. One Greek expositor offers this fuller translation: "Stop assuming an outward expression which is patterned after this world, an expression which does not come from, nor is it representative of what you are in your inner being as a regenerated child of God."[384]

Among the gravest realities of the modern Church is that it has, in fact, become *modern*. Church services and programs *appeal* to the culture, *alter* the Gospel, and even *arouse* the flesh. Likewise, Christians allow themselves to be molded into thinking the way the world thinks. Just two simple examples are how many Christians actually believe abortion is sometimes acceptable and that it's even permissible for a couple to live together outside of marriage. From clothes, to speech, to habits, Christians are remolded into the image of the age. "The world is the devil's *lair* for sinners and his *lure* for the saints."[385]

Suschēmatizō appears in one other place in the NT and is no less powerful: "As obedient children, not fashioning yourselves [*suschēmatizō*] according to the former lusts in your ignorance" (1 Pet. 1:14). Part of being an obedient Christian, therefore, is not to be squeezed into the mold of this age. The godly, dedicated Christian thinks differently, believes differently, and lives differently. Dear Christian Friend, let us not be *tainted* by the world, rather *transformed* by the Word.

Scriptures for Study: What do the following occurrences of *aiōn* add to our study: Galatians 1:4 (world) Ephesians 2:2 (course); 6:12 (world)?

SEPTEMBER 5

Complete Dedication (3)

. . . but be ye transformed by the renewing of your mind . . . (Rom. 12:2b)

AFTER reading much about the selection and training of Navy SEALs (SEa, Air, and Land), I have come to believe that no other endeavor on earth (from an entirely human perspective) equals that dedication. Trainees learn quickly that, "The only easy day was yesterday," and three-fourths of those who start don't finish. Most notably, the one overarching characteristic of a SEAL is that he will never, *never* quit. What a challenge that is to the Christian who represents (and fights for) a far greater kingdom!

Third, then, dedication *continues* with *transformation*: **be ye transformed by the renewing of your mind. Transformed** is another one of those fascinating and descriptive NT words. It is *metamorphoō* (3339), from which we get our English word "metamorphosis" and means a total change in form and nature. As many have observed, there is no better example of this than the caterpillar that is transformed into a butterfly. At first it crawls slowly along the ground but ultimately flies gracefully in the air. After its transformation, it not only looks and acts differently, but it also even eats differently.

Of special significance is the fact that this same word is used for our Lord's transfiguration (Matt. 17:2; Mk. 9:2; Lk. 9:29). Luke 9:29, in fact, declares that "as he prayed, the fashion of his countenance was altered." The same is true of the believer. While we obviously are not transfigured as was our Lord, salvation brings with it a change of countenance. "We all, with open face beholding as in a glass the glory of the Lord," Paul wrote to the Corinthians, "are changed into the same image from glory to glory, even as by the Spirit of the Lord" (2 Cor. 3:18).

What a dramatic contrast! We are not to be *fashioned* rather *transformed*! Further, this transformation is not only an event at conversion but an ongoing process. The language Paul uses is striking. The verb is present tense, that is, continuing action. It is also in the passive voice. While the active voice would render this "Transform yourselves," the passive emphasizes, "Let yourselves be transformed." This is the work of God.

That does not mean, however, that we are disconnected from the process, that we just "let go and let God" as some teach. On the contrary, the verb is also an imperative, which commands us to do something, namely, **renewing** our minds. **Mind** is *nous* (3563), which refers to the intellect, understanding, reason, and thought. In a day when the vast majority of people are driven by feelings, emotions, "inner urges," and often just plain lust, the Christian lives according to the mind, the understating of spiritual Truth. And the only place we can go for such renewal is the Word of God.

Scriptures for Study: What do the following verses tell us about renewal: Ephesians 4:22–24; 3:10; Titus 3:5?

SEPTEMBER 6

Complete Dedication (4)

... that ye may prove what is that good, and acceptable, and perfect, will of God. (Rom. 12:2c)

FOURTH and finally, dedication *culminates* in *discrimination*. We use that word not in the negative sense of unfairly treating a person or group differently from other people or groups, rather in the positive sense, as Webster defines: "the ability to recognize the difference between things that are of good quality and those that are not."

The result of true dedication is that we will be able to discern God's will. **Prove** is *dokimazō* (1381), to "test, pronounce good, establish by trial." We discern God's will not by intuition, inner urges, or any other mystic method, rather by presenting ourselves to Him totally, separating ourselves from the philosophies of the age, and continually renewing our thinking by the Word of God. Paul then goes further by listing three characteristics of God's **will**:

(1) God's will is **good**. This is the wonderful Greek word *agathos* (18), which has a wide range of meanings, including: benevolent, profitable, useful, beneficial, excellent, virtuous, and suitable. Each of those is certainly true of God's will. (2) God's will is **acceptable**. This is *euarestos* (2101), well-pleasing. We all tend to think that by exercising our will, by choosing our own preferences, we will be pleased and satisfied. But let us ponder this: when we get to the end of our lives and look back, will it be our will or God's will that we regret? (3) God's will is **perfect**. *Teleios* (5046) is derived from *telos* (5056), which originally referred to the culminating point at which one stage ends and another begins and later the goal, the end, or completion. God's will, then, is complete, the greatest goal, the very best end.

In the movie *Ironweed*, Meryl Streep plays a ragged derelict who dies in a cheap hotel room. To prepare, she hugged a huge bag of ice cubes for more than half an hour. When the camera rolled, Jack Nicholson, her derelict friend, grieves beside her. But through take after take—and between takes, too—Meryl just lay there gray and cold. A frightened member of the crew whispered to the director, Hector Babenco, "What's going on? She's not breathing!" There was, in fact, no sign of life in Meryl's body. Babenco hesitated but let the scene proceed. But even after the shot was done and the set struck, Meryl continued to lie there, gray and still. Only after ten minutes had passed did she slowly emerge from the coma-like state into which she had deliberately sunk. In utter amazement, Babenco muttered, "Now *that* is an actress!"[386]

Total dedication does amaze people. How wonderful it would be for each of us if we were so dedicated to Christ that people say, "Now *that* is a Christian!"

Scriptures for Study: In the following verses, what other things are **good**: Romans 7:12; Ephesians 2:10; Philippians 1:6?

SEPTEMBER 7

The Christian Servant's Availability

Also I heard the voice of the Lord, saying, Whom shall I send, and who will go for us? Then said I, Here am I; send me. (Is. 6:8)

EVERY endeavor in life, whether a job, a profession, or even a relationship, requires certain abilities to accomplish successfully. What abilities are required for the Christian servant? Towering intellect? Magnetic personality? Masterful rhetoric? In our next few studies, let us examine several "abilities" every Christian servant needs to labor rightly for Christ. Today we consider *availability*.

First, we observe the *preparation*. In the opening verses of Isaiah 6, God gives the prophet a brief glimpse of His overwhelming holiness (Feb. 2) to prepare His servant for the call to the task of proclaiming judgment to His rebellious people. Isaiah's response to this overpowering vision was to become "undone" (v. 5). The Hebrew is *dāmāh* (1820H), to cease, to be silent, to destroy. John Calvin perhaps says it best: Isaiah "was so terrified by seeing God that he expected immediate destruction."[387] Isaiah goes on, in fact, to give the reason for his fear: "because I am a man of unclean lips, and I dwell in the midst of a people of unclean lips." Realizing his own sinfulness, Isaiah recognized his abject unworthiness.

This is the state every servant must enter if he wants to be used of God. Many today think they have much to offer God; they have their intelligence, cleverness, and talents and think themselves worthy, even invaluable. But they forget what Paul asked the Corinthians: "what hast thou that thou didst not receive? now if thou didst receive it, why dost thou glory, as if thou hadst not received it" (1 Cor. 4:7; cf. Jn. 3:27; Jas. 1:17)? All we have is from God; "He that glorieth, let him glory in the Lord" (1 Cor. 1:31, a shortened quotation of Jer. 9:23–24).

Second, we hear the *call*. Isaiah **heard the voice of the Lord, saying, Whom shall I send, and who will go for us?** While the plural pronoun **us** does not prove the Trinity, it certainly implies it (cf. Gen. 1:26; Jan. 14). God, in His triune perfection and purpose, calls his servants. **Whom shall I send?** does not imply that God didn't know if anyone would reply or only *hoped* someone would answer the call, rather He gives Isaiah the opportunity to serve. We have the same opportunity.

Third, we mark the *response*. Isaiah's immediate reply is striking: **Here am I; send me.** Calvin again submits, "So ready a reply shows how great is that cheerfulness which springs from faith." He who is unworthy and undone is also unhesitating and unswerving. That is a servant God can use.

Puritan Matthew Henry challenges us with a pointed admonition: "We must not say, 'I would go if I thought I should have success;' but, 'I will go, and leave the success to God. Here am I; send me.'" Sadly, many "ministries" today are success-oriented and will do virtually anything to achieve success. The biblical model, however, is that the One who *sends* is also the One who *succeeds*.

Scriptures for Study: How do the following verses challenge us about Christian service: Matthew 4:20–22; Acts 20:24?

SEPTEMBER 8

The Christian Servant's Reliability

Moreover it is required in stewards, that a man be found faithful. (1 Cor. 4:2)

THE second "ability" the Christian servant must have is *reliability*. Another word is *faithfulness*. This is, in fact, the overarching ability. There is no greater quality in a servant than this, for it drives everything else.

First, the servant's *rank*. "Servant" is not our only designation. Another is "steward." The Greek behind **stewards** is *oikonomos* (3623), which is comprised of *oikos* (3624; house) and *nemō* (to deal out, distribute, apportion). The parable of the Shrewd Manager (Lk. 16:1–13) well details the custom. While stewards were sometimes slaves (implied in Lk. 12:42), in this case, he was a freeman who had full charge of all his master's domestic affairs, including house, family, business, and children. He could even use the master's assets to full advantage but was also held responsible for how he did so. If he failed in his task, he was usually discharged immediately. (We'll return to this parable on Nov. 26.)

That perfectly describes what the Christian is to be. We should not say, "This is my house, my car, my money, and my children." All we have belongs to God. He entrusts us with it, and even allows us to use it, but it is His, and He will hold us accountable for what we do with it. We won't be *discharged* when we fail, but we can be *disciplined* (cf. Heb. 12:6). That leads to the key principle.

Second, the servant's *responsibility* is to be **faithful**. This is the Greek adjective *pistos* (4103). Not only has a Christian put his faith in Christ, but he is now one who is faithful, trustworthy, consistent, constant, and reliable. **Required** further emphasizes this essential truth: *real faith* results in *relentless fidelity*.

We can easily test ourselves using a simple acrostic of the word FAITHFUL. Are we faithful in our Fruitfulness? In general, there are three areas of fruitfulness: character (Gal. 5:22–23); conduct (Rom. 6:22; Phil. 1:11); and converts (Jn. 4:36; Rom. 1:13). Further, do we just "bear fruit" (Jn. 15:2a), "more fruit" (v. 2b), or "much fruit" (v. 5)? Are we faithful in our Affections? Do we "set [our] affection on things above . . . [or] things on the earth" (Col. 3:2)? Are we faithful in our Incentive? Is our motive self-glory or God's glory (1 Cor. 10:31)? Are we faithful in our Time? Do we "redeem" (Eph. 5:16) it or squander it? Are we faithful to the House of God (Heb. 10:25)? Are we faithful in our Finances, giving as God has "prospered" us (1 Cor. 16:2)? Are we faithful in our Uprightness, living by God's standards of morality (Ps. 143:10; 1 Pet. 1:15–16)? Are we faithful in our Labor, in all we do, because we know it is never "in vain" (1 Cor. 15:58)?

Third, the servant's *reputation*. **Found** is *heuriskōis* (2147), which when used figuratively, as it is here, means to gain perception or insight, to discover. What will others see when they look at us? Will they see a reputation for faithfulness? It's not our clever methods and popular programs that matter. It's our faithfulness.

Scriptures for Study: Meditate on the verses cited today and write down how each challenges you personally.

SEPTEMBER 9

The Christian Servant's Teachability

Understandest thou what thou readest? . . . How can I, except some man should guide me? (Acts 8:30–31)

THE third "ability" the Christian servant must have is *teachability*. An easy way to understand this principle is to observe its opposite. Those who do not have a teachable spirit talk far more than they listen, read very little, resent or retaliate against constructive criticism or correction, blame everyone else for their failure, and certainly won't ask a question when it might reveal their ignorance. In dramatic contrast, the story of the Ethiopian eunuch in Acts 8:26–39 is a wonderful example of how each of us should be.

First, a teachable spirit *recognizes* its own *emptiness*. Ethiopia refers not to the modern-day country, rather to ancient Nubia, south of Egypt in what is today Sudan. This man was an important official of Candace (a title, not a proper name), queen of the Ethiopians, and was in charge of all her treasure. While the Law prohibited eunuchs from entering the Lord's assembly (Deut. 23:1), he had nonetheless become a follower of Yahweh and had gone to Jerusalem to worship. But there was still an emptiness in his heart. Judaism of that day had degenerated so far that it was little more than a works-oriented religion. He was reading the book of Isaiah, undoubtedly from a scroll that would have been expensive and difficult for a Gentile to obtain. Specifically (v. 32), he was reading Isaiah 53:7–8 but did not understand it.

Second, a teachable spirit *responds* with *enquiry*. One version of an ancient far eastern story describes a young martial arts student who interrupted the master each time he introduced a new technique: "Oh, I know that. I do this when that happens." The master stopped talking, picked up a teapot, and began pouring tea into the student's cup. When the cup was full, however, the master continued pouring and the tea overflowed. "Stop!" the student shouted. "That's enough. My cup is full!" The master smiled and replied, "Yes, your cup is full, and I can teach you nothing until you empty your cup." Likewise, in response to Philip's question, the eunuch asked, **How can I, except some man should guide me?** A teachable spirit is aware of its limitations and lack of knowledge and humbly submits to those who can teach the needed Truth. It is also willing to change with more knowledge.

Third, a teachable spirit *rejoices* in its *enlightenment*. While some insist that verse 37 is not part of the original text, there is textual evidence that it is, but more importantly, it clearly belongs here "since it contains so clear a confession of faith required of persons to be baptized, which was used in the truly apostolic times."[388] So, with new knowledge and understanding, the eunuch believed the message and "went on his way rejoicing" (v. 39) in the truth that Jesus was the fulfillment of what Isaiah had spoken. A teachable spirit brings joy!

Scriptures for Study: What do the following verses tell us about a teachable spirit: Proverbs 2:2, 4; 3:7; 9:9; 1 Peter 5:5.

SEPTEMBER 10

The Christian Servant's Accountability

... every one of us shall give account of himself to God. (Rom. 14:12)

THE fourth "ability" the Christian servant must have is *accountability*. **Give account** is *logon dōsei*, a term commonly used to refer to a bookkeeper's ledger account.[389] In this context, Paul's point is that we each need to be concerned about our own ledger, not anyone else's. Building on that, we see several areas of accountability.

First, we are accountable for the *way* we live. This is the general principle of our text. Does not our culture grow more unaccountable every day? It seems that no one will take responsibility for his or her own actions—it's always someone else's fault. But **God** is keeping the "ledger," and every person will answer to Him. For the believer, this will be at the Judgment Seat of Christ (2 Cor. 5:10), where we will be rewarded for true service (1 Cor. 3:12–15; Rev. 22:12). For the unbeliever, however, only the Great White Throne Judgment awaits, where he will be cast forever into the lake of fire (Rev. 20:11–15).

Second, we are accountable for the *work* we do. As noted above (1 Cor. 3:12–15), true service is figuratively comprised of "gold, silver, [and] precious stones" because it is of lasting value, but everything else is "wood, hay, [and] stubble" because it is worthless and will be consumed. As Paul states earlier, "every man shall receive his own reward according to his own labour" (v. 8). While the context speaks specifically of preachers and teachers, there is an obvious application to all our labor, for as Jesus Himself declared: "behold, I come quickly; and my reward is with me, to give every man according as his work" (Rev. 22:12).

Third, we are accountable for the *words* we speak. Addressing the hardhearted, hateful, hypocritical religious leaders, Jesus said, "I say unto you, That every idle word that men shall speak, they shall give account thereof in the day of judgment" (Matt. 12:36). "Idle" translates *argos* (692), a compound comprised of *a* (1), without, and *ergon* (2041), work, and so literally, "not at work." Such words accomplish nothing. What a sobering thought! Think of it! Whether our words be vile and villainous, or just flippant and frivolous, we are accountable for them. Leaders are again especially accountable: "My brethren, be not many [teachers], knowing that we shall receive the greater condemnation" (Jas. 3:1; cf. Heb. 13:17).

Fourth, we are accountable for the *warning* we give. Once again to the religious leaders, Jesus said, "O generation of vipers, who hath warned you to flee from the wrath to come?" (Matt. 3:7). And as Paul again addressed the Corinthians, "For though I preach the gospel, I have nothing to glory of: for necessity is laid upon me; yea, woe is unto me, if I preach not the gospel!" (1 Cor. 9:16). Each of us is likewise responsible to warn this world of the wrath of God that is to come and proclaim Christ as the only Savior and Lord.

Scriptures for Study: What do these verses tell us about accountability: Ecclesiastes 12:14; Acts 20:26–27; Romans 2:16; 1 Peter 4:3–5?

SEPTEMBER 11

The Christian Servant's Adaptability

I am made all things to all men, that I might by all means save some. (1 Cor. 9:22)

THE fifth "ability" the Christian servant must have is *adaptability*. Tragically, few concepts have been more perverted than this one. Our text has been used, in fact, to turn many a local church into a circus, where "anything goes" since we must be **all things to all men**. To be consistent, however, we would be compelled to conclude, "We must become pornographers to appeal to pornographers" (or just insert any other behavior here). Since this is patently absurd, what exactly is Paul telling us in 1 Corinthians 9:19–23?

First, we must *recognize* the *message*, namely, the Gospel (v. 23). Our message must always be the pure Gospel of Jesus Christ. That cannot be allowed to be renegotiated or diluted in any way whatsoever, as it commonly is nowadays in culture-driven, people-centered churches. All that Paul did was so that the Gospel was presented unambiguously and uncompromisingly so that it would **save some**.

Second, we then *reconsider* the *method*. Did Paul adapt depending upon his audience? Of course, but *how* exactly did he adapt? Did he change, adjust, or revise the message? Did he package it in a way that made it more appealing to the "unchurched"? Was his approach pragmatic, where "the end justifies the means"? No. He merely "accommodated himself to the customs and habits of the people with whom he worked in order that he might gain a ready ear for the gospel. But never did he do anything which might compromise the truth of the gospel."[390]

Specifically, while he did not put himself back under the bondage of the Mosaic Law, Paul went ahead and observed its ceremonies if that opened a door to proclaiming the Gospel. When he was with Gentiles, however, he ignored the Mosaic system—although he never violated the Moral Law, which was a forerunner of "the law of Christ" (v. 21)—and he observed Gentile customs as long as it did not violate morality. He even condescended to the "weak" (v. 22), those who were slow to grasp the Gospel or were legalistic in their understanding, and repeated the message as many times as needed.

Third, let us *remember* the *model*. Our Lord Himself was the model for Paul's method. Jesus ate with tax collectors and sinners (Matt. 11:19), drank water given to him not only by a Samaritan but an immoral woman at Jacob's well (Jn. 4:9, 11, 27). He told the Pharisees to pay taxes to Caesar (Matt. 22:21). Yet, through it all, not a single syllable of the message of the Gospel changed.

So, while we can certainly *adapt* to our community, and even have a certain *appeal* to those we come in contact with, we must never *appease* anyone by compromising the Gospel message.

Scriptures for Study: What do the following verses add to our study: Romans 15:1; 1 Corinthians 10:33; 8:13?

SEPTEMBER 12

The Christian Servant's Trainability

Know ye not that they which run in a race run all, but one receiveth the prize? So run, that ye may obtain. (1 Cor. 9:24)

THE sixth "ability" the Christian servant must have is *trainability*. Our text, and the verses that follow (25–27), appear right on the heels of the passage we studied yesterday. While we examined teachability a few days ago, trainability goes deeper, for it demands even more effort and commitment.

First, we see *self-dedication*. Our text introduces an event the Corinthians knew very well. In addition to the Olympic games held in Rome, the Isthmian games were held in Corinth. The dedication of the athletes was obvious; they trained rigorously for ten months, the last month being spent right in Corinth under scrupulous supervision.

This is a critical lesson for every servant of God. Sadly, many are in positions of leadership, some even in the pastoral role, who are not adequately trained. Our Lord spent years training his disciples. Likewise, Paul invested years in training his co-workers and pastors, and that is precisely why he gave this model to Timothy: "And the things that thou hast heard of me among many witnesses, the same commit thou to faithful men, who shall be able to teach others also" (2 Tim. 2:2). Additionally, many Christians neither dedicate themselves to service nor listen to the training that comes from a strong pulpit ministry.

Second, we note *self-discipline*. The phrase "striveth for the mastery" (or "contend for the prize") in verse 25 translates a single Greek word, *agōnizomai* (75); the root *agōn* (73; English agony) means strife, contention, or strive for victory and referred specifically to the games. Further, "temperate" is *enkrateuomai* (1467) and means self-control. The ancient athletes had to practice self-control in many areas: when they slept, what they ate, and several other activities they engaged in. Everything revolved around the preparation for the games.

Here is another lesson for us. While athletes train with exceptional self-discipline in our day, many Christians do not, even though the race we are running is immeasurably more important. The ancients received little more than a pine wreath and great applause, but we are striving for that which is "incorruptible." Additionally, verse 26 switches images to the boxer or wrestler. "Shadow boxing" is not good training. We must constantly be engaged in the real fight.

Third, we make special note of *self-denial*. The phrase "I keep under" (or "buffet") in verse 27 is *hypōpiazō* (5299), which literally means "to strike under the eyes, beat the face black and blue, give a black eye."[391] Further, "bring it into subjection" (*doulagōgeō*, 1396) means "to make a servant." Are our bodies our slaves or are we slaves to our bodies? Each of us must be careful not to become a "castaway," that is, become disqualified for service.

Scriptures for Study: What observations can you make in these verses: Ephesians 6:12; Philippians 3:14; 1 Timothy 6:12; 2 Timothy 4:5, 7–8?

SEPTEMBER 13

The Christian Servant's Immovability

Therefore, my beloved brethren, be ye stedfast, unmoveable, always abounding in the work of the Lord, forasmuch as ye know that your labour is not in vain in the Lord. (1 Cor. 15:58)

THE seventh and final "ability" the Christian servant must have is *immovability*. By this we do not mean an inherent stubbornness that refuses to give an inch in an argument. Rather, this is steadfastness, staunchness, and single-mindedness in the things that matter.

First, we must be *unwavering*. **Stedfast** is *hedraios* (1476), a fascinating word from a root (*hedra*) that means chair or seat. It appears only two other times in the NT. Earlier in this letter, Paul encouraged his readers to be "stedfast in [their] heart" (7:37), and in Colossians 1:23 he commands us to "continue in the faith grounded and settled." Because the present context is about the resurrection, Paul tells us that we must be entirely settled on that historical reality, firmly seated in that doctrinal truth and everything that pertains to it, which, of course, implies the whole Gospel of Jesus Christ.

Second, we must be **unmovable**. This is *ametakinētos* (277), which appears only here in the NT. While similar to *hedraios*, it is even stronger, meaning absolutely motionless and utterly immobile; it "signifies an inability to move from [our] spiritual moorings."[392]

Oh, how that truth needs to be emphasized nowadays! As these words are being typed, even some of the most basic truths of Christianity are being reconsidered and renegotiated, doctrines such as not only the resurrection, but also justification by faith alone, the imputation of the righteousness of Christ, verbal inspiration, biblical sufficiency, and the list goes on. Never has there been a greater need for men to be **unmovable** than today. While we will be called narrow-minded, intolerant, and divisive, we must remain unmoved.

Third, we must be *unceasing*, **always abounding in the work of the Lord**. While we are **unmovable** on the inside, we are **abounding** (*perisseuō*, 4052, to be in excess, exceed in number or measure) on the outside. Pastors are *preaching*, God's people are *practicing*, and we all are *proclaiming* the Truth, the whole Truth, and nothing but the Truth.

Fourth, we must be *undiscourageable*. The added phrase, **forasmuch as ye know that your labour is not in vain in the Lord**, is an immeasurable encouragement. In the face of the world's resistance, rejection, and even ridicule, it is very easy to become discouraged. But Paul assures us there will be a resurrection and that all the claims of Christ are true. *Nothing* we do for our Lord is **in vain** (*kenos*, 2756, empty or hollow). It is all for His glory and our gain.

Scriptures for Study: How do the following verses encourage you: Galatians 6:9; Philippians 2:16; 1 Thessalonians 1:3; Hebrews 6:10; 2 Peter 3:17?

SEPTEMBER 14

Blameless

According as he hath chosen us in him before the foundation of the world, that we should be holy and without blame before him in love. (Eph. 1:4)

THE word "blameless" is often misunderstood. It does not mean sinless, rather, as Webster's 1828 dictionary defines it, "Without fault; innocent; guiltless; not meriting censure." The related term "above reproach" means that no valid criticism can be made. This can be used in a negative way, such as, "Some politicians behave as though they are above reproach," or in a positive way, such as, "A pastor must live blameless, above reproach" (cf. 1 Tim. 3:2). This principle actually involves two interrelated ideas in both the OT and NT.

First, blameless speaks of the *positional gain of salvation*. In the OT, any animal used in sacrifice had to be "without blemish" (Lev 1:3; 3:1, 6; 22:21; Num. 6:14). Anything less demonstrated a blatant disrespect for God (Mal. 1:6–14). Such violation also negated the purposeful imagery of the unblemished animal, which leads to the NT idea. There the "lamb without blemish and without spot" (1 Pet. 1:19) was none other that the Lord Jesus Christ Himself, "who through the eternal Spirit offered himself without spot to God" (Heb. 9:14). Positionally, then, salvation comes through "the Lamb of God, which taketh away the sin of the world (Jn. 1:29; Mar. 18–19). It is not earned by personal merit or good works, rather imputed to us by the death and resurrection of Christ (Col 1:22).

Second, blameless speaks of the *practical goodness for sanctification*. Flowing from the ritual sacrifice was the idea of moral blamelessness for the believer, who now could not rightly be accused of sin either before people or God (Pss. 15:2; 18:23). David, in fact, prayed, "Keep back thy servant also from presumptuous sins; let them not have dominion over me: then shall I be upright [or blameless], and I shall be innocent from the great transgression" (19:13).

Likewise, and even more significantly, the NT accentuates the moral uprightness of the believer. Our text tells us that the purpose of election on the human side is so that we will be and live holy. **Without blame** is *amōmos* (299), which is derived from the root *mōmos* (3470), "spot, blemish," and the prefix *a* (1), the "alpha-negative" that means "without." That is how we are to live—pure in attitude and action. The word indicates that a Christian lives above reproach; that is, no one can look at his life and see an unholy, ungodly life.

Peter also emphasizes this reality: "Beloved . . . be diligent that ye may be found of him in peace, without spot, and blameless" (2 Pet. 3:14). As a result of inward moral *character* there is outward moral *conduct*. While this is true of every godly believer, it is especially critical in those in spiritual leadership. That, in fact, is why it heads the list of the qualifications of a pastor in both NT passages that address those requirements (1 Tim. 3:2; Titus 1:6).

Scriptures for Study: What do the following verses say about blamelessness: Ephesians 5:27; Philippians 1:9–10; 2:14–15?

SEPTEMBER 15

Ship-Shape and Bristol Fashion

For though I be absent in the flesh, yet am I with you in the spirit, joying and beholding your order, and the stedfastness of your faith in Christ. (Col. 2:5)

THE title of today's meditation is a fascinating expression that transports us back to the days of the old sailing ships of Briton. "Ship-shape" has been around since the 17th-century but was merged with "Bristol Fashion" 200 years later. The port of Bristol lies in the southwestern portion of the UK where the Rivers Avon and Frome converge. At low tide, the harbor is too shallow to accommodate large ships, even those of the old sailing days. Amazingly, however, it has the second highest tidal range in the world, more than 40 feet. If a ship floated in on high tide and remained, it would be beached at low tide. Since the ship would tilt to one side as it settled on its keel, everything had to be stowed away or securely tied down to prevent utter chaos and cargo spoilage. While this problem was resolved in 1803 with the construction of the Floating Harbor, the expression remains to this day to indicate something that is in first-class order.

That is what God wants from us. The word **order** in our text (*taxis*, 5010) comes from a verb that means to arrange in order and was a military term that referred to an orderly array of soldiers. This was undoubtedly impressed upon Paul's mind as he observed Roman soldiers during his imprisonment.

First, then, there must be order in our *character*. It must be ship-shape, with nothing out of place. *Second*, there must be order in our *conduct*. This, too, must be in Bristol Fashion, with everything stowed away and tied down so that our testimony for Christ is not spoiled. As noted yesterday, we must be blameless.

Third, and as an extension of the others, there must be order in our *churches*. It is extremely significant that *taxis* also appears in 1 Corinthians 14:40: "Let all things be done decently and in order." The Corinthians had so confused and abused the spiritual gifts (as well as several other things) that there was chaos in the church. Sadly, the same disorder is standard fare in many churches today. Further, as A. W. Tozer well observed (60 years ago!): "Fiction, films, fun, frolic, religious entertainment, Hollywood ideals, big business techniques, and cheap, worldly philosophies now over-run the sanctuary. The grieved Holy Spirit broods over the chaos but no light breaks forth."[393]

Indeed, heavenly *realities* have been lowered to earthly *rabble*. The sacredness of the Church and God's Word have been replaced by little more than a carnival sideshow. Let us be challenged, then, that our *preaching* be orderly, as well-trained men exposit the Scriptures. Let our *praising* be orderly, as we worship in spirit and in truth. And let our *proclamation* be orderly, as we serve Christ according to biblical guidelines. Oh, let us keep it all ship-shape and Bristol fashion!

Scriptures for Study: How do these OT passages set the precedent for orderliness: 1 Chronicles 16:37–42; 2 Chronicles 29:35; Ezra 6:18?

SEPTEMBER 16

"Once More Unto the Breach" (1)

Put on the whole armour of God, that ye may be able to stand . . . [and] withstand in the evil day . . . (Eph. 6:11, 13)

IN my favorite Shakespeare play, the historically accurate *Henry V* (Aug. 30), Henry sails from England with a large fleet of warships, lands in France, and lays siege to the port city of Harfleur on the northern coast (very near, in fact, the shores where five centuries later the allies would land in Normandy). The cannons roar as the terrifying battle rages against the city walls. After rejecting King Charles' insulting offer to bring peace, the siege continues, ultimately leading to a staggering victory. As the English army prepares to storm the city, Henry's words ring out, the most famous lines being: "Once more unto the breach, dear friends, once more; Or close the wall up with our English dead."[394] Every Christian is also in a war, but this one is spiritual and far more significant and savage, for we, too, are called upon to go "once more unto the breach."

First, we *ready* our defense. **Stand against** is *stēnai pros* (2476/4314), a military expression that means to stand in front of with a view to holding a critical position, to hold one's ground. Further, **able** is *dunamai* (1410, Eng. "dynamic"), "that which overcomes resistance." By putting on God's armor, we are **able** to defeat any resistance Satan offers and overcome any obstacle he puts in our path, whether it be moral, spiritual, or even doctrinal. The idea here, then, is a primarily defensive tone, that we just face the enemy and hold our ground. This is further indicated by the fact that God has given us five pieces of *defensive* armor (vv. 14–17a) while giving only one *offensive* weapon, the sword (v. 17b).

Second, we *release* our offense. The word **withstand** (emphasis added) in verse 13 is different. While the root behind **stand** is *histēmi* (2476), **withstand** is *anthistēmi* (436), "to set oneself against, oppose, resist." This word is more offensive in tone, and is the same word used in James 4:7, "Resist the devil, and he will flee from you." So, not only must we be *defensive*, holding our present ground, but we must also be *offensive*, landing blows of our own on the enemy. Militarily speaking, no battle, no war, can be won by defense alone. God not only wants us to stand our ground, but He also wants us to resist and oppose using our only offensive weapon: the Word of God.

Third, we *rejoice* in our victory. The imagery in the context (vv. 10–18), of course, is that of the fully armored Roman soldier who goes victoriously into personal combat. Paul, therefore, assures us that we will not be defeated (vv. 11, 13), injured (v. 16), or humiliated (vs. 19–20).[395]

Oh, how we need men today who will, indeed, cry, "Once more unto the breach," and then lead the attack! Why? Because, as Shakespeare notes, "the game's afoot"! (We will note a momentous historical example tomorrow.)

Scriptures for Study: What do the following verses tell us about our spiritual battle: 2 Corinthians 4:4; 11:3, 13–15; 1 Peter 5:8?

SEPTEMBER 17

"Once More Unto the Breach" (2)

Put on the whole armour of God, that ye may be able to stand . . . [and] withstand in the evil day . . . (Eph. 6:11, 13)

TO illustrate yesterday's study, we turn to a pivotal historical incident.[396] Most Christians are totally unaware just how crucial the 4th-century was for Christianity. Arius, a parish priest in Alexandria, taught that Jesus was not coequal with God and was, in fact, a created being. Upon proclaiming his views concerning Christ's Deity in 313, Arius' teaching ignited controversy. By 318, the conflict had grown hostile and bitter. While Arius and his followers were condemned at a local church council in Alexandria in 321, the fight was far from over. False teaching is never so easily defeated. From Alexandria, their teaching (dubbed Arianism) spread all over Christendom.

More than 300 bishops gathered at the famous church-wide Council of Nicea in 325 to settle the controversy. For the sake of "unity," many were willing to compromise on the nature of Christ, but one man was not, a man whom God, in His eternal providence, strategically placed there for that very moment. Athanasius (293–373), a young 23-year-old theologian, also from Alexandria, fiercely debated Arius, a man 40 years his senior. It was, indeed, David taking on Goliath. In the end, Athanasius was triumphant, which led to the most basic of all the creeds of the Church, the Nicene Creed.[397]

But again, the war had only begun. While only three men (Arius and two followers) refused to sign the creed, many others who did sign still tolerated Arians, not wanting to call anyone a "heretic." Some even twisted the language of the Creed to say that Arianism really could fit into the wording. As a result, Athanasius was mercilessly persecuted. During his 46 years as bishop of Alexandria and his tireless and inflexible opposition to Arianism, he spent a total of 20 of those 46 years on the run, being exiled five times, usually because Arians were in political control, and enduring false charges that ranged from witchcraft to murder. It was because of all that, in fact, that the phrase *Athanasius contra mundum* (against the world) arose. He stood virtually alone against almost overwhelming defection from orthodoxy. It is not an exaggeration to say that were it not for Athanasius, who has been dubbed "The Father of Orthodoxy," we might all be Arians today.

Athanasius truly challenges us. He refused to compromise the Truth for any reason. He rejected such ideas that we have dubbed "Post-modernism," the "Emerging Church," "Post-evangelicals," and others. He would have grieved over popular platitudes, such as: "Christ unites us, but doctrine divides us." While most Christians today have never heard of Athanasius, he is one of the great illustrations of the *providence* of God, the *power* of truth, and the *perseverance* of courage. He was not afraid for a moment to go "once more unto the breach." Are we?

Scriptures for Study: What do these verses say about false teachers: Mark 13:22; Colossians 2:8; 1 Timothy 4:1–3; 2 Peter 2:1–3?

SEPTEMBER 18

Refined Gold

The fining pot is for silver, and the furnace for gold: but the LORD trieth the hearts. (Prov. 17:3)

GOD is always at work in the believer, making each one the servant He desires. As Paul told the godly Philippians, "Being confident of this very thing, that he which hath begun a good work in you will perform it until the day of Jesus Christ" (1:6). One way He does so is graphically illustrated in the refining of metals, which is actually mentioned many times in Scripture. While most such references are to the refining of **silver** (Prov. 25:4; Zech 13:9; Is. 48:10), a fascinating process to be sure, the refining of **gold** is especially significant.

First, we observe the *preparation*. Before it could be refined, gold ore first had to be crushed into pebbles and then ground into powder. This powder was spread onto a slightly inclined stone table and water was then poured over it. The comparatively heavier gold particles were left behind as the water washed away earthen materials. Here is the first striking parallel to how God works in the Christian servant. He must first "break us down," sometimes using discipline and chastising (Heb. 12:6), to separate what is vain from what is valuable. He then washes away the impurities "with the washing of water by the word" (Eph. 5:26). But the process is far from complete.

Second, we note the *procedure*. The next step was to gather the gold particles and place them in a crucible—a clay container that could withstand very high temperatures—and then heat them into a molten state for five days. As additional impurities rose to the top, they were skimmed off. The spiritual parallel here is again remarkable. The "heat" God uses to remove the remaining impurities in us are the trials and tribulations of life: **the LORD trieth the hearts**. While the Hebrew behind **trieth** (*baḥan*, 974H) means to try or prove and refers to any kind of test, it usually refers to God's testing of men. David declared that "The LORD trieth the righteous" (Ps. 11:5) and even goes on to request: "Search me, O God, and know my heart: try me, and know my thoughts" (Ps. 139:23). Job understood this long before David: "when he hath tried me, I shall come forth as gold" (23:10), and Peter understood it long after: "That the trial of your faith, being much more precious than of gold that perisheth, though it be tried with fire, might be found unto praise and honour and glory at the appearing of Jesus Christ" (1 Pet. 1:7).

Third, we see the *product*. How did the workman know the gold was pure? When he was able to see his face reflected clearly in the surface of the molten liquid. Likewise, we will come forth as gold when our Savior can see His face reflected in us. Additionally, gold is so malleable that a single ounce can be beaten into a sheet roughly 300 square feet, making it so thin that it appears transparent. We, too, are to be so malleable that He can shape us as He wills.

Scriptures for Study: What do the following verses add to our study today: Isaiah 64:8; 2 Timothy 2:21; James 1:12?

SEPTEMBER 19

Timothy (1)

But I trust in the Lord Jesus to send Timotheus shortly unto you . . . (Phil. 2:19–24)

AMONG the most outstanding examples in Scripture of a servant was Timothy, Paul's "dearly beloved son" in the faith (2 Tim. 1:2). The son of a Jewish mother (2 Tim. 1:5) and a pagan Gentile father (Acts 16:1, 3), Timothy was from Lystra in southern Galatia (modern Turkey) and was probably converted there during Paul's first church-planting journey (cf. Acts 14:6–23; 2 Tim. 3:10, 11). Because of the OT instruction he had received from his mother Eunice and grandmother Lois, both of whom were believers, Timothy already had a firm foundation in the truth, on which was built the superstructure during his many years of teaching from and labor with Paul. We learn much from Timothy through Paul's high recommendation of him to the Philippian believers.

First, we see that he was a *companion*. The Greek behind **likeminded** in verse 20 (*isopsuchos*, 2473) appears only here in the NT, but this single instance is striking. It is a compound comprised of *isos* (2470, equal) and *psuchē* (5590, soul) so literally means "equal-souled." Just how equal-souled Timothy was with Paul is underscored by the full phrase, **I have no man likeminded**, that is, there is no other man who is my equal, no other man who is not only on the "same page" with me, as the adage goes, but also on the exact same words on the page.

Think of it! Here was a man of God, a preacher, a theologian, who was perfectly in-sync with the Apostle Paul. He was in complete agreement on the nature of God, the character and work of Christ, the ministry of the Holy Spirit, the Doctrines of Grace, the correct philosophy of ministry, the work of discernment, and all else. Oh, that we, too, would be in-sync with the Apostle Paul!

Second, we note that Timothy was *caring*. Paul assured the Philippians that his trusted protégé and co-worker would **naturally care for [their] state** (v. 20). **Care** is another dramatic word in the original language. It is *merimnaō* (3309), which actually means anxious care, to be troubled. This word is used elsewhere in the negative sense of useless worry (e.g., Matt. 6:25–28; 10:19; Lk. 10:41), but Paul uses it here in the positive sense to demonstrate the deep concern the shepherd has for the sheep. He deeply cares about their **state**. This is *peri* (4012), meaning around or about (Eng. "perimeter"), so Timothy would care about everything in and around their lives. He would, in fact, do this **naturally** (*gnēsiōs*, 1104), that is, genuinely and sincerely. He was not in ministry for personal gain or professional recognition. He was there to serve God by serving God's people.

What a challenge this presents to us! As a shepherd does not drive the sheep but rather leads them, so pastors are to lead and care for God's people. So are parents to care for their children and each of us to care for one another.

Scriptures for Study: How do the following verses complement our study today: Philippians 2:2; John 10:13; 1 Corinthians 1:10?

SEPTEMBER 20

Timothy (2)

But I trust in the Lord Jesus to send Timotheus shortly unto you . . . (Phil. 2:19–24)

THE Apostle Paul's *third* recommendation of Timothy to the Philippian believers was that he was *courageous*. This principle is implied by Paul's observation of those with the opposite attitude: **For all seek their own, not the things which are Jesus Christ's** (v. 21). Seek is *zēteō* (2212), to seek after, look for, strive to find. Especially significant in this word is that the will is at the heart of the seeking (e.g., Matt. 13:45; 26:16; Lk. 15:8). While there were certainly those in Rome, as Paul mentions, who were preaching the Gospel, they were doing so with "envy and strife . . . [and] contention" (Phil. 1:15–16), that is, jealousy, contention, and rivalry. In short, they were preaching with selfish motives. But Timothy's willful, courageous, single-minded choice was to **seek Christ**.

Fourth, we see that Timothy was *confirmed*. Paul called upon his readers to recall: **ye know the proof of him** (v. 22). **Proof** translates a much neglected word in our own day, *dokimazō* (1381), to test, pronounce good, establish by trial. A related word, *dokimos* (1384), was originally used as a technical term for coins that were genuine. This underscores, of course, the principle of discernment. John used it, for example, in 1 John 4:1, where it's translated "try": "Beloved, believe not every spirit, but try the spirits whether they are of God: because many false prophets are gone out into the world." Timothy, therefore, had proven qualifications. So important was this that Paul would write to Timothy a few years later and list the very specific requirements for those in leadership (1 Tim. 3:1–14).

Fifth, we note that Timothy was *compliant*: **he hath served with me in the gospel**, Paul testified (v. 22). **Served** is *douleuō* (1398), to be in the position of a servant, to serve in subjection and obedience. Perhaps what should strike us most here, however, is the word **gospel**. This is that critical word *euaggelion* (2098, English "evangelism"), the good news. We are to serve the Gospel, not our own agendas, people's felt needs, cultural relevance, or anything else. "The gospel of Christ" alone "is the power of God unto salvation" (Rom. 1:16).

Sixth and finally, we rejoice in the fact that Timothy was *committed*, a fact that is implicitly implied in all five of the other features. Paul hoped to send Timothy immediately (v. 23) simply because he knew of Timothy's complete and unhesitating faithfulness to the task. We read elsewhere of Timothy, in fact, "For this cause have I sent unto you Timotheus, who is my beloved son, and faithful in the Lord, who shall bring you into remembrance of my ways which be in Christ, as I teach every where in every church" (1 Cor. 4:17).

Let us each examine ourselves and ask, "Am I the kind of servant Timothy was? Am I agenda-free and committed solely to the Gospel? Am I ready and willing to serve the Lord immediately anytime, anywhere?"

Scriptures for Study: What do the following verses tell us about commitment: Matthew 16:24; Luke 9:57–62; Luke 14:26?

SEPTEMBER 21

Epaphroditus (1)

Yet I supposed it necessary to send to you Epaphroditus . . . (Phil. 2:25-30)

ONE writer refers to Timothy and Epaphroditus in Philippians 2:19-30 as "a priceless pair," and they were, indeed.[398] In Timothy we have the pastoral side of faithful service, and with Epaphroditus we have the other side, that of a faithful Christian in the church. The name Epaphroditus was a very common one among the Romans and simply meant one devoted to Aphrodite (Venus to the Romans), the goddess of love and beauty. This man was one of those rare individuals who strike us as almost "super-human," but he really was no more than what any of us should be.

First, we read his *description*. While all we know of Epaphroditus is in this single passage, Paul's three-fold description tells us much. He first calls him **my brother**, indicating they were united in *brotherhood*. **Brother** is *adelphos* (80), which is an enormously significant word. It is a compound made from *delphus* (not in the NT), "a womb," and the prefix *a* (1). Not only is this prefix used as the "alpha negative," which makes a word mean the exact opposite,[399] it's also used in a "collative" manner, signifying unity.

The picture in *adelphos*, then, is "one born from the same womb." Originally, it referred to a physical brother (or sister with the feminine *adelphē*, 79). Later it came to refer to any near relative, such as a nephew or even a brother-in-law. Finally, there are several examples in the Septuagint where *adelphos* is used to refer even to fellow Israelites (e.g., Ex. 2:11; Lev. 19:17), showing a close relationship without any physical heritage. It was that very idea that was carried over into the NT. The idea of fellow Christians being brothers appears some 30 times in Acts and 130 times in Paul's epistles.[400] What is the significance of being a brother (or sister, 1 Cor. 7:15) in Christ?

(1) It means we have the same parentage. The Christian has been "born again" ("born from above," Jn. 3:3) and has been "born of God" (1 Jn. 3:9). We, therefore, have the same Father, the Sovereign God of the Universe. Paul often mentioned God being "*our* Father," that is, all Christians collectively (Rom. 1:7; Gal. 1:4; 1 Cor. 1:3; Eph. 1:2; etc.). (2) It shows a family relationship. In Romans 16:14 (and context) and 2 Timothy 4:21, Paul speaks collectively of several believers, wonderfully illustrating the family that every local church should be. (3) It shows closeness. So close is the relationship of Christian brothers that each would lay down his life for another (1 Jn. 3:16). (4) It means we have a future inheritance. All Christians have the same "riches of the glory of his inheritance in the saints" (Eph. 1:18).[401] Let us rejoice in the same description that was true of Epaphroditus.

Scriptures for Study: Who is spoken of as a brother in each of the following verses: 2 Corinthians 2:13; 2 Corinthians 8:22; Philemon 1:1.

SEPTEMBER 22

Epaphroditus (2)

Yet I supposed it necessary to send to you Epaphroditus . . . (Phil. 2:25–30)

IN his continuing *description* of Epaphroditus, Paul also notes that this dear brother was a **companion in labor**, demonstrating that they were united not only in *brotherhood* but also in *business*. We are reminded here of our Lord's words in the Temple when He was but 12 years old: "I must be about my Father's business" (Lk. 2:49). Likewise these two men were united in their labor of proclaiming the pure Gospel of Christ, just as we should be.

Finally, Paul says that Epaphroditus was a **fellowsoldier**, demonstrating that they were also united in *battle*. The Greek here (*systratiōtēs*, 4961) is a distinctively military term for "comrade-in-arms." As Paul told the Ephesian believers, we all are to put on "the whole armour of God" (Eph. 2:13–18), for we are, indeed, in a war against spiritual foes, those of false doctrine and its propagators.

Second, we notice Epaphroditus' *difficulty*. While laboring with Paul in Rome, Epaphroditus had contracted a serious, life-threatening illness. Why include this detail? Undoubtedly to underscore this dear servant's unselfish and uninterrupted labor even in the throes of suffering. It also teaches some doctrine, however. While some teachers insist there is "physical healing in the atonement," good heath is a right the Christian can claim, and sickness is a sure sign of God's chastening, Epaphroditus disproves all that. Here was an inarguably godly and committed Christian servant who, even in the midst of such selfless service, was plagued by an illness that had gone on for several months. This also completely undoes the "miraculous healing" claims of today's "faith healers." Just as Paul did not heal Timothy but prescribed "a little wine for thy stomach's sake and thine often infirmities" (1 Tim. 5:23), neither did he heal Epaphroditus. Such miraculous sign gifts, which were irrefutably temporary and always a sign to Jews to prove apostolic authenticity and authority, had already begun to fade.

Third, we marvel at Epaphroditus' *dedication*. As the previous observation makes plain, here was a truly dedicated servant of God. Paul called him a **messenger**. While this is the Greek *apostolos* (652), "apostle," it is used here not in the technical sense of one who was chosen specifically by Christ to be a witness of His life, teachings, death, and resurrection, rather it's used in the general sense of "one sent forth, a messenger, an ambassador." Paul also called Epaphroditus **one who ministered**, which translates the noun *leitourgos* (3011) and is comprised of *leitos*, meaning of the people, and *ergon* (2041), work. It was used in secular Greek of public officials who performed their public functions at their own expense, although the motive could have been out of vain glory or compulsion instead of patriotism. The godly Christian servant, however, serves out of pure motives and to God's glory, **not regarding his [own] life**.

Scriptures for Study: What else do we read about Epaphroditus in Philippians 4:18? 📖 How does this "priceless pair" encourage and challenge you?

SEPTEMBER 23

John the Baptist (1)

Among them that are born of women there hath not risen a greater than John the Baptist . . . (Matt. 11:11) . . . For he shall be great in the sight of the Lord . . . (Lk. 1:15–17)

THE following well summarizes the general attitude toward "greatness" that exists in our day: "Greatness is the quality that radiates from the inside out. It is who you are when you are honoring your values and living a life of purpose. In other words, when you are stepping into your true Self."[402] Note the personal pronouns "you" and "your" (used five times) and then the last word "Self." The world does, indeed, gauge greatness entirely by human attitude and achievement, whether it be in sports, business, politics, or entertainment. And what is the goal? With rare exception (if there are any), it is self-glory.

But God says something quite different. There are many in Scripture who we think of as great—Enoch, Noah, Melchizedek, Abraham, Joseph, Moses, David, Elijah, Elisha, Isaiah, Jeremiah, Peter, John, Paul, and many others. Likewise, we can think of many in history who we consider great: Athanasius, John Calvin, John Knox, William Tyndale, Charles Spurgeon, and others. But one stands above them all, one of whom Jesus Himself said was greater than all who had ever lived up to that point (and possibly even to this present day): **John the Baptist**.

First, we see his *personal* character. It is here we note the words **great** and **greater**. **Great** in our Luke text is *megas* (3173), which literally refers to something large or great in size, such as a stone (Matt. 27:60), a chasm (Luke 16:26), a river (Rev. 9:14), and so on. Metaphorically, then, it speaks of great in estimation, weight, or importance, such as a great commandment (Matt. 22:36, 38). **Greater** in our Matthew text, then, is *meizōn* (3187), which is actually the comparative of *megas*, meaning "greater than" or the "greatest among others." So, for John to be great **in the sight of the Lord** can only mean that John's character was beyond reproach, superior to that of anyone else in previous history.

The proof of this "greatness" was two-fold. Outwardly, his life was one of complete self-denial. This was reflected (Matt. 3:4) in his wardrobe of a camel's hair coat and leather belt, as well as his diet of locusts and wild honey and abstinence from wine (Lk. 1:15). He would be so preoccupied with the work God commissioned him to do that he would distance himself from virtually everything else. While Scripture certainly does not instruct us to go to the level John went, it does emphasize self-denial in our service. Self-denial is not necessarily *relinquishing* what we desire, rather the *renouncing* of our right to have it.

Further, inwardly, John was **filled with the Holy [Spirit]**, which was the source of the outward. Again, we will not equal John—he was **filled . . . even from his mother's womb**—but our service must also flow from the filling (the control) of the Holy Spirit (Apr. 8–10).

Scriptures for Study: What do the following verses say about self-denial: Luke 9:23–24; Titus 2:11–12; Hebrews 11:24–25?

SEPTEMBER 24

John the Baptist (2)

And he shall go before [Messiah] in the spirit and power of Elijah . . . And many of the children of Israel shall he turn to the Lord their God . . . (Lk. 1:15–17)

THROUGHOUT the centuries, Israel had gone through cycle after cycle of righteousness followed by rebellion, faith*ful*ness that turned to faith*less*ness. So deep did her apostasy become, that after Malachi's prophecy, there followed 400 years of God's silence. Not a single prophet arose, not a single miracle was performed, not a single revelation was given. But Malachi had also foretold that God would send a messenger who would herald the coming Messiah (3:1).

Second, therefore, we see John the Baptist's *position* as forerunner. **Go** (*proerchomai*, 4281) literally means to go before, and **before** (*enopion*, 1799) means in the presence of, in the sight of. Luke is literally saying, then, that John would "go forward in His [Messiah's] sight." John's entire purpose for existence was to prepare the path for Messiah, when he saw "Jesus coming unto him, and saith, Behold the Lamb of God, which taketh away the sin of the world" (Jn. 1:29). So powerful was his declaration that he resembled **the spirit and power of Elijah**, both of whom unflinchingly, uncompromisingly, and unendingly proclaimed the Truth.

Third, his *powerful* ministry. Neither John nor his ministry were popular. He did not preach personal fulfillment, health and wealth, self-esteem, relevance, or purpose (no other preacher in Scripture did either). Neither did John's message change depending upon his audience. All those methods are prominent today, and we are even told that we will not be effective unless we implement them.

But what do we see in John's case? Even in the face of strong opposition (Matt. 4:12; 14:1–10) and the fact that most would reject the message, **many of the children of Israel [did] he turn to the Lord their God**. The word **turn** translates *epistrephō* (1994), a compound comprised of *epi* (1909), to, and *strephō* (4762), to turn, and therefore to turn upon or toward. It was used literally in the sense of the physical movement of turning around, as when Jesus turned to see who had touched Him (Matt. 9:22). But it is used more often in the spiritual sense of turning from idolatry to the worship of the living God (1 Thess. 1:9), turning from spiritual darkness to light (Acts 26:18), and turning from sin to God in repentance and being converted (Matt. 13:15; Mk. 4:12; Acts 3:19; 9:35; 11:21; 14:15; 15:19; 26:20; 28:27; 2 Cor. 3:16; Jas. 5:19–20). John's message would affect entire families (**fathers** and **children**) and even some who had before stubbornly refused to believe (**the disobedient**).

Amazingly, after saying John was the greatest man who had ever lived, Jesus made the startling statement, "Notwithstanding he that is least in the kingdom of heaven is greater than he" (Matt. 11:11). True greatness is not about *what we do* but about *who we are*. We are Christians who are empowered for witness.

Scriptures for Study: Read Luke 3:7–14. What observations can you make about John's sermon?

SEPTEMBER 25

Making Disciples

Go ye therefore, and teach all nations . . . (Matt. 28:19–20)

VANCE Havner well said: "Evangelism is to Christianity what veins are to our bodies. You can cut Christianity anywhere and it will bleed evangelism. Evangelism is vascular. Talk about majoring on evangelism, you might as well talk about a doctor majoring on healing. That's our business."[403] As we have noted, just as Paul and Epaphroditus were united in their labor in the business of proclaiming the pure Gospel of Christ, so should we.

A key to understanding our serving the Lord is found in the words of our Lord Himself when He called His fisherman disciples: "Follow me, and I will make you fishers of men" (Matt. 4:19). Fish were a staple of life, and the vocation provided a vivid example. In fact, this imagery was not new; Greek and Roman philosophers had used it for centuries to describe the work of those who seek to "catch" others by teaching and argument (cf. Lk. 5:10). Wherever we go, wherever people are, we are to proclaim the gospel (Acts 1:8). To use another image, as literal sheep reproduce, so are we to do as spiritual sheep (Lk. 15:1–7). As we will note in subsequent studies, we are all witnesses of the Lord Jesus Christ (Acts 1:8). Our text is critical: **Go ye therefore, and teach all nations. . . . Teaching them to observe all things whatsoever I have commanded you.** The word **Go** is actually not a command; it's a present participle and means "going." The actual command is to "make disciples."

"Discipleship" is a term we hear used often these days but one that few people actually define. What exactly does "discipleship" or "discipling" mean? The word "teaching" in verse 20 is the familiar Greek word *didaskō* (1321), which speaks of systematic teaching. The word "teach" in verse 19, however, is *mathēteuō* (3100), which means not only to learn, but to become attached to one's teacher and to become his follower in doctrine and conduct of life. It's stronger than the similar word *manthanō* (3129; Matt. 11:29; 1 Tim. 5:4; 2 Tim. 3:14; etc), which means simply to learn without any attachment to the teacher. *Mathēteuō* appears, for example, in Acts 14:21, a critical verse in reference to Paul's ministry in Derbe: "And when they had preached the gospel to that city, and had taught many, they returned again to Lystra, and to Iconium, and Antioch."

So, true evangelism is far more than just proclaiming the Gospel; it is "making disciples," that is, *making followers* of Christ who are attached to Him and so obey Him in doctrine and conduct. Much "evangelism" today is just getting someone to repeat a prayer or "make a profession," however nebulous or self-defined it might be. But biblical evangelism is making committed followers of Christ. What is a disciple of Jesus? A true disciple is an open worshiper, an obedient worker, and an outspoken witness.

Scriptures for Study: In Acts 2:41–47, what are the characteristics of a disciple? 📖 Compare this study with September 11 on adaptability.

SEPTEMBER 26

The Believer's Commission (1)

But ye shall receive power, after that the Holy Ghost is come upon you: and ye shall be witnesses unto me both in Jerusalem, and in all Judaea, and in Samaria, and unto the uttermost part of the earth. (Acts 1:8)

WHEN we turn to Acts 1, we encounter the very words of our Lord Himself concerning the primary task we are to perform in our service for Him. The disciples asked a legitimate question: "Lord, wilt thou at this time restore again the kingdom to Israel?" (v. 6). As Jews, they were concerned whether Messiah would now, since He had risen from the grave, establish His literal, physical kingdom on earth as the prophets had repeatedly foretold.

While Jesus did not rebuke them, He did make it clear that this was not to be their concern right now: "It is not for you to know the times or the seasons, which the Father hath put in his own power" (v. 7). "Times" is *chronos* (5550; English, *chronometer*), which basically means "time, course of time, passage of time," or more precisely, "space of time whose duration is not as a rule precisely determined."[404] In contrast, "seasons" is *kairos* (2540), "a decisive or crucial place or point,"[405] such as a date.

Jesus' point was clear: it was not for them to know either the indefinite or the definite time of His establishing His earthly kingdom at His second coming to the earth. It was not that His kingdom is unimportant, rather there is another task that is for now *more* important. Until His return, He commissioned them to be **witnesses** of Him to the world. That is our task as well. While we have emphasized some of these principles before, they are worth repeating.

First, we note the *promise* of the commission: **ye shall receive power**. We are reminded here of our study of Jesus' promise of the coming *paraklētos* who would provide for the five basic needs of the believer (Apr. 11–30). As we discovered in that study, one of the those difficulties is society and how the Comforter "will reprove the world of sin, and of righteousness, and of judgment" (Apr. 23–25).

Second, then, we see the specific *power* of the commission: **the Holy Ghost**. Here is the fulfillment of the promise. "But when the Comforter is come, whom I will send unto you from the Father, even the Spirit of truth, which proceedeth from the Father, he shall testify of me: And ye also shall bear witness, because ye have been with me from the beginning" (Jn. 15:26–27). We must never get the "ye" before the "he" (Apr. 21). Only because of *His* power do *we* have power.

What is the nature of this **power**? It is *dunamis* (1411), which can be translated "that which overcomes resistance." What resistance? The domination of the world, the philosophy of pagans, and the traditions of religion (Apr. 25). Think of it! We possess the same power today as the disciples had then.

Scriptures for Study: What do the following verses tell us about **power**: Ephesians 3:20; 2 Thessalonians 1:11; 2 Timothy 1:7–8?

SEPTEMBER 27

The Believer's Commission (2)

But ye shall receive power, after that the Holy Ghost is come upon you: and ye shall be witnesses unto me both in Jerusalem, and in all Judaea, and in Samaria, and unto the uttermost part of the earth. (Acts 1:8)

THERE is a lot of misunderstanding about a call to Christian service," wrote Vance Havner. "Some are sitting around looking for signs in the sky, or waiting for a strange feeling within when they should be out in the harvest."[406] We have, indeed, been commissioned to such service.

Third, we note the *personnel* of the commission. As noted yesterday, there is first the "He" (the Holy Spirit) and then the "ye" (the believer). The Holy Spirit has made us **witnesses**. As we have noted before (May 9), this is *martus* (3144, English "martyr"), which was originally a legal term for one who gave solemn testimony and evidence in court.

Building on that, however, we see some encouraging applications of the legal aspect to our witnessing.[407] According to the Mosaic Law, for example, it was considered sinful for one to refuse to come forward as a witness if he did, in fact, have testimony to bear (Lev. 5:1). Likewise, how grievous it is if we do not give evidence of what we know. Also, according to the Talmud, no one could be a witness who had been paid to render this service. Neither do we witness with some ulterior motive. Also, those of low repute, such as, gamesters, usurers, and tax-gatherers, could not be witnesses. That is why we must be godly and blameless in our character and conduct lest we taint the message of Christ (Sept. 14).

Fourth, we see the *purpose* of the commission. The phrase **ye shall be witnesses unto me** can also be rendered "you shall be my witnesses." As we have noted before (Apr. 22), we *are* witnesses, whether positive or negative; we are either *pointing* others to Christ or *pushing* them away.

Fifth, we observe the *program* of the commission. Acts 1–7 *define* the infant church in **Jerusalem**, 8–12 *describe* the expanding church in **Judea and Samaria**, and 13–28 *detail* the advancing church **unto the uttermost part of the earth**. The same is true of our witness. We witness first at home, then to relatives and acquaintances, then on to those who are not particularly likeable, and finally to those we don't even know. While evangelistic meetings and crusades have their value, far more important are God's people who go out and witness one-on-one.

Puritan Richard Baxter boldly challenges us: "Oh, if you have the hearts of Christians, let them yearn towards your poor, ignorant, ungodly neighbors. Alas, there is but a step between them and death and hell. Have you hearts of rock that cannot pity men in such a case as this? Do you not care who is damned? If their houses were on fire, thou wouldst run and help them; and wilt thou not help them when their souls are almost at the fire of hell?"[408]

Scriptures for Study: What do these verses tell us concerning evangelism: Mark 16:15; Luke 24:46–49?

SEPTEMBER 28

Laborers in the Harvest

Then saith he unto his disciples, The harvest truly is plenteous, but the labourers are few; Pray ye therefore the Lord of the harvest, that he will send forth labourers into his harvest. (Matt. 9:37–38)

OUR text provides us with another graphic image of personal evangelism: we are **labourers** sent **into [God's] harvest**. Just as He emphasized on another occasion—"Lift up your eyes, and look on the fields; for they are white already to harvest" (Jn. 4:35)—our Lord uses familiar imagery to teach a critical truth.

First, we must understand the *nature* of the harvest. In the verses preceding our text, Jesus spoke of shepherding. As He went from place to place teaching, preaching, and healing, He "was moved with compassion on [the multitudes], because they fainted, and were scattered abroad, as sheep having no shepherd." With the same multitudes in view, He then changed His metaphor from the *flock* to the *field*. He depicted them as a field of precious ripe grain ready to harvest, unlike the Pharisees who saw them only as a commodity to exploit.

Second, we see the *need* for laborers. Herein lies the problem and the challenge—**the labourers are few**. While there is a *multitude* to proclaim the Gospel to, there is only a *minority* who proclaim it. The word **few**, in fact, is *oligos* (3641), from which we get our English word "oligarchy," a small group of people that controls a country, organization, or institution. This word also appears in 1 Peter 3:20 in reference to Noah and his family being the few who were delivered from the flood, as well as Matthew 22:14: "many are called but few are chosen."

This is, indeed, the sad reality. Our modern day multitudes are even greater than in Jesus' day, but still there are only a few who boldly proclaim the pure saving gospel. We are sometimes so consumed with our own concerns that witnessing for Christ is not even a thought. At other times we are too fearful to proclaim the truth lest we be accused of irrelevance or even intolerance.

Third, we should discern the *necessity* of the work. Why is this such a critical issue? Simply because of the message the words **his harvest** convey. The **harvest** metaphor is used throughout Scripture as a picture of judgment (e.g., Is. 17:10–11; Joel 3:11–14). Jesus Himself, in fact, used this metaphor in His parable of the wheat and tares latter in Mathew. He said first that the two plants are allowed to "grow together until the harvest" and then went on to explain that "just as the tares are gathered up and burned with fire, so shall it be at the end of the age" (Matt. 13:30, 40–42; cf. Rev. 14:14–20). It is that very reality of coming judgment upon the lost (Rom. 12:19; 2 Thess. 1:7–9) that should motivate us to be laborers in the field. Since we don't know who is among God's elect, we proclaim the Gospel to the multitudes and allow Him to separate the wheat from the tares.

Scriptures for Study: How do the following verses encourage us about our labor: 1 Corinthians 15:58; Galatians 6:9; Hebrews 6:10?

SEPTEMBER 29

How To Witness

There cometh a woman of Samaria to draw water: Jesus saith unto her, Give me to drink. (Jn. 4:7)

WHILE today's title might imply a *method*, that is not our intention. We merely turn to our Lord's encounter with a Samaritan woman (Jn. 4:1–42) as a perfect *model* for how to witness for Christ.

First, we simply *perceive* the contact. The first thing this incident demonstrates is that we don't have to force or manufacture opportunities to witness. They will occur in our everyday walk and will be easy to recognize. Jesus was weary from His journey and just stopped at a well for a drink. This was, of course, all according to God's sovereign providence, as will be the opportunities He gives us.

Such an approach also ignores prejudices and social barriers. Jesus' request for a drink of water from this woman was shocking. Not only was this a *Samaritan*—Jews who had intermarried with foreigners and lost their ethnic purity—but this was a *woman*—Jewish men did not speak with women (not even their wives) in public. Worse, this was an *immoral* woman, as is revealed later. This is further evident in that she came to this well at noon instead of the cool of the evening, as was the usual practice, and she traveled a significant distance when other sources of water were closer. All this avoided contact with other women and their inevitable scorn. Witnessing for Christ, however, ignores such things and reaches out to all those in "the fields . . . [that] are white already to harvest" (Jn. 4:35).

Second, we must *prove* the need. Since water was the relevant subject at hand, Jesus used it as means to generate interest and capture the woman's attention; He said God could give her "living water" that would ensure she would "never thirst" again and would "[spring] up into everlasting life" (vv. 10–14). It was from there, however, that He moved directly to confronting her lovingly with her sin. While that subject is avoided at all costs by those today who want to make Jesus more acceptable and salvation more palatable, any presentation of the Gospel that does not confront sin is not the Gospel at all. Sin is the problem, for it is the breaking of God's law.

Third, we then *proclaim* the Gospel. Once sin is acknowledged, as was the case here, the Gospel—the good news of what Christ accomplished in paying for that sin on the Cross—can then be presented. She acknowledged Him as Messiah (vv. 25, 29), and other Samaritans also believed not just because of what she said but because they heard Jesus for themselves (v. 42).

Fourth, we *partner* in the result. Again, verses 35–38 are about sowing and reaping. We are not alone in the process, nor can we take the credit for any of it. One might sow the seed that someone else harvests at a later time so we all can "rejoice together."

Scriptures for Study: Read Paul's counsel in 1 Corinthians 3:6–8. What does this teach us about evangelistic effort?

SEPTEMBER 30

Failing or Prevailing?

... Cast the net on the right side of the ship, and ye shall find ... (Jn. 21:6)

As any good storyteller ties up the "loose ends" of the story, John did that wonderfully with chapter 21 of his gospel. We have already examined Peter at some length (May 4–9), but before Jesus dealt with him specifically, He addressed seven of the apostles collectively (vv. 1–14).

First, we see men *failing*. What is immediately conspicuous here is the apostles were not where they were supposed to be. Instead of staying on the mountain where Jesus had told them to wait (Matt. 28:16), they went down to the Sea of Tiberius (i.e., Galilee) by Peter's suggestion. That first failing led directly to the second: they fished all night but caught absolutely nothing.

It is important to observe here that these men were experienced, professional fisherman. They knew what they were doing; they knew, for example, that the best time to fish the Sea of Galilee was at night. Being a fisherman, in fact, was a well-respected profession, making them all businessmen as well as tradesmen. So, to fail in this way was a blow to the ego. In this particular instance, though, there was a far more important lesson, a two-fold one in fact: they went back to the old life God had called them out of and were depending upon their own strength.

Sadly, we see much the same attitude in the Church today. With all our experience, we think we know what we are doing. We have created a plethora of programs and built a mountain of methods, but sooner or later every one of them becomes "old hat," or is no longer considered "relevant," and is cast off to make way for the next trend, and the process begins again. "Plans, rules, 'operations' and new methodological techniques absorb all [our] time and attention," wrote A. W. Tozer (in 1963!). "Apparently the idea that the Lord might have some instructions for [us] never so much as enters [our] heads."[409]

Second, then, we see Jesus *prevailing*. As the disciples drew near to shore, Jesus underscored their failure by asking, "Children, have ye any meat?" (v. 5), to which they confessed, "No." His next instruction was odd, indeed: **Cast the net on the right side of the ship, and ye shall find**. While not yet recognizing Jesus, they obeyed the authoritative voice of this stranger even though the instruction was patently ridiculous. They would have already tried that at some point during the night. But what was the result of doing it Jesus' way? All seven of them **were not able to draw [the net] for the multitude of fishes**.

This should again profoundly challenge us. Are we so busy doing things *our* way that we either cannot hear what the Lord says in His Word or just dismiss it as "irrelevant for our unique culture"? This story provides us with a principle I have cherished for most of my 43 years of ministry: If God's *people* will do God's *work* in God's *way*, they will receive God's *results* in God's *time* for God's *glory*.

Scriptures for Study: Read the similar incident in Luke 5:1–7, where Jesus originally called his disciples. What observations can you make?

OCTOBER 1

Champions of Faith

By faith . . . (Heb. 11:4)

AMONG the many thrilling studies I have undertaken in my years of ministry—the most notable have been Ephesians, Psalm 119, and the Doctrines of Grace—Hebrews 11 is also a favorite. It is because of the impact this chapter has had on my own life and ministry, a significant portion of this final section of our daily meditations is dedicated to it.

While it has often been called "The Faith Chapter," or "The Hall of Faith," we must be careful not to allow such clichés to detract from the power of this great chapter. This is not a series of Bible story summaries, rather it is the biblical record of the most powerful illustrations of faith in history. *It is the record of men and women who obediently acted solely on what God said without doubt or fear.*

A key to the full significance of this chapter is to recognize that these were not what the world calls "extraordinary people" or "special cases." If they were, they would be of little use as examples to us "ordinary folks." But they were just ordinary people (including their weaknesses and failures) who became *champions* for one reason only. A champion is a victor, a conqueror, and each of these individuals was just that simply because he or she believed what God said and obeyed. It is likewise God's desire that every believer be such a champion of faith.

The layout of the chapter is also significant. Verses 1–3 and 6 are the foundation on which the writer builds. Without them, the rest of the chapter would be far less powerful and practical. The remainder of the chapter describes eight qualities, or characteristics, of faith, each of which is demonstrated by one or more of the persons listed and introduced with the words **by faith**. Those qualities are the piety (Abel, v. 4), the pace (Enoch, v. 5), the performance (Noah, v. 7), the patience (Abraham, vv. 8–19), the power (the patriarchs, vv. 20–22), the perception (Moses, vv. 23–29), the prize-winning (Joshua and Rahab, vv. 30–31), and the proclamation (other champions, vv. 32–40) of faith. Additionally, we see the Perfect Pattern of Faith in 12:1–2, which is none other than our Lord Himself.

Oh, how we need a new emphasis upon biblical **faith**! As we will see, its meaning has been so obscured and redefined by contemporary thought that many Christians are completely unaware of its full implications. Worse, many of the sermons preached on faith also miss the mark. Not only are they shallow, but they also tend to emphasize faith as something exercised just for salvation, when in reality *faith is the key to living the Christian life*. It is a continuing reality that provides victory in everyday living. To "live by faith" means we do not "live by sight" (2 Cor. 5:7). Living by faith means we trust only in what God says and disregard the words of men in this world system. So, let us turn to this chapter not only to see faith *presented*, but also to see it *practiced*.

Scriptures for Study: What do the following verses tell us about faith: Acts 20:21; Galatians 5:6; Hebrews 10:22?

OCTOBER 2

The Meaning of Faith

Now faith is the substance of things hoped for, the evidence of things not seen. (Heb. 11:1)

PROBABLY the best way to describe [the] concept of modern theology is to say that it is faith in faith, rather than faith directed to an object which is actually there," Francis Schaeffer wrote. "Modern man cannot talk about the object of his faith, only about the faith itself. . . . [It] turns inward. In Christianity the value of faith depends upon the object towards which the faith is directed."[410]

Sadly, what has occurred since Schaeffer penned those words in 1968 is that the modern view of faith has taken over much of Christianity. We often hear such statements as "my faith," or "my faith helped me," or "I was so troubled that I lost my faith." Faith, then, is made to be its own object. But without an object, the entire concept of **faith** is incomplete and meaningless. What, then, *is* faith?

First, we must understand the *foundational definition* of faith. As we have noted before (Mar. 8), **faith** is not nebulous, not mere mental assent. The Greek verb *pisteuō* (4100), as well as the noun *pistis* (4102) that appears here, is very specific. They not only speak of trusting in and being firmly persuaded of something but also implicitly carry the idea of being committed to and obeying something. The crucial element of faith, then, is not the *act*, but the *object*.

Second, our text goes far deeper into a *fuller description* of faith. While a little awkward in English, *Young's Literal Translation* (YLT, 1898) renders our text well: "And faith is of things hoped for a confidence, of matters not seen a conviction." This provides us our two-fold portrait.

(1) Faith involves *confidence*. **Substance** is *hypostasis* (5287), which refers to that which stands under something else, that is, the foundation of something, the true essence and substance of it. Here, then, it describes the foundation, the very essence of faith as an absolute confidence that while we can't see something, we still know it's real and that it's ours. Faith is not "blind optimism" or "a leap into the dark" as many like to describe it. It is rather "a step into the light" because it is based upon the promise of God. True faith is living in a confidence that is so real that it gives absolute assurance. This is what we see in each of our "champions." They rested on the promises of God and lived in absolute confidence.

(2) Faith also includes *conviction*. This carries the previous thought one step deeper. **Evidence** (*elenchos*, 1650) simply means proof or persuasion, which also implies a response, an outward demonstration of the inward confidence. What is our proof? Not our faith, rather what God says, which we trust in implicitly and act upon immediately. As was true of each of our "champions," it is such faith that drives our service. So, putting it together, faith is *supreme confidence* in what God says and *settled conviction* that it will come to pass.

Scriptures for Study: What do these verses tell us about faith: Romans 8:24–25; 2 Corinthians 4:18; 1 Peter 1:8?

OCTOBER 3

The Majesty of Faith

For by [faith] the elders obtained a good report. (Heb. 11:2)

A great faith is like an oak that spreads its roots deep and is not easily blown down, Colossians 2:7," wrote Puritan pastor Thomas Watson. "A great faith is like the anchor or cable of a ship that holds it steady in the midst of storms. A Christian who is steeled with this heroic faith is settled in the mysteries of religion."[411]

Our text declares that the champions of faith listed in this chapter received a **good report** from God. This is *martureō* (3140; Apr. 22), to be a witness, cite evidence, or report the events. While we "bear witness" for Christ (Jn. 15:27; cf. Acts 1:8; Sept. 27), this verse declares the remarkable truth that God testifies of us! Think of it! He makes His approval known to those who trust Him. He blesses us, glorifies us, and lists us among the champions of faith.

The writer's use of *martureō*, in fact, is pivotal to this entire chapter. He uses it four more times (vv. 4 [twice], 5, 39). Further, he then uses the noun form *martus* (3144) in 12:1 to refer to the list of champions in chapter 11, calling them a "great cloud of witnesses." It is because God testified of them that they could testify of Him. In each case, we see that God approved of their lives and service.

We will examine 11:6 in more detail, but we should note one phrase now: "God is a rewarder of them that diligently seek him." God rewards our faith. What could be better than that? What could possibly be equal or be more majestic than God's approval and testimony of us? What else could possibly matter in comparison? Certainly not pleasure, profit, or possessions. Without faith, (confidence and conviction), there is no purpose, no truth, no absolutes, no peace, no meaning, no life, and no hope. Rather, as another Puritan, Thomas Adams, said, "It is the office of faith to believe what we do not see, and it shall be the reward of faith to see what we do believe."[412] Faith, in fact, Elisha Cole adds, is our "spiritual optic."[413]

Ponder one more thought today: have you ever noticed whose names are *absent* from this list of champions? Some who are listed, in fact, surprise us. After all, Rahab was a prostitute, and Sampson's shortcomings are legendary. But notice that while Abel is the very first name on the list, Adam is not here. How sad that there could be no **good report** of him. In fact, it is as if God pulled a veil over his spiritual life to hide it from our view. Surely, if there were anything praiseworthy about him after the Fall, it would have been mentioned here. But no, we read nothing in Scripture of his faith (or Eve's). They were undoubtedly believers (cf. Gen. 3:15), but as one commentator well puts it, "Adam's rebellion against his Maker was too great and too glaring to permit his name to be ever after mentioned with honor or respect."[414] How tragic it is that they never knew the majesty of faith!

Scriptures for Study: What other names can you note that are not listed with the Champions of Faith in this chapter and why?

OCTOBER 4

The Manifestation of Faith (1)

Through faith we understand that the worlds were framed by the word of God, so that things which are seen were not made of things which do appear. (Heb. 11:3)

THE remainder of Hebrews 11 provides a plethora of illustrations of faith, but this verse presents a very special one, one that uniquely and powerfully manifests faith, namely, believing the Genesis account of Creation.

First, we note our faith in the *means* of creation, which is, of course, **God** alone. Among the most disturbing developments in 21st-century Christianity has been the increasing denial of Genesis 1–3 as the literal and historical record of the creation events. More and more evangelicals have abandoned this in favor of the compromised position that the Genesis account does not prohibit the idea that there was some kind of evolutionary process.

The seriousness of such a compromise, however, cannot be overstated. If the opening chapters of Genesis are not literal and historical, several key doctrines of the Faith quite literally vanish. It affects the doctrine of Scripture itself, for example, since it goes to the issue of the Bible's infallibility and trustworthiness. If the Bible cannot be trusted in the first three chapters, what makes it trustworthy throughout the rest of the book? If it is just allegory, as some insist, how many other things in Scripture are also allegorical, and how can we tell the difference?

It also affects the doctrine of God; He is no longer the sole omnipotent Creator, rather the God of the Deist. It effects the doctrine of man, as well. If Adam and Eve were not real historical figures, then who is our real ancestor? Further, it affects the doctrine of sin. If Adam's fall was not a real event in history, then what is sin? Where did it come from? Who is to blame for it?

Of major significance is the doctrine of salvation, which is actually dependant upon the doctrine of Creation and a literal person named Adam. Twice in his epistles, Paul links our *salvation* in Christ with our *identification* in Adam. In other words, if we did not *fall* in *Adam*, we simply cannot be *redeemed* in *Christ*. Christ's position as the Head of the redeemed race exactly parallels Adam's position as the head of the fallen race (1 Cor. 15:21–22, 45; Rom. 5:12–21).

Equally significant, the doctrine of Christ is also affected. In the crucial "proto-evangelium" (first gospel) of Genesis 3:15, we read the first mention of the Redeemer who is to come. But if the story of the Fall is not historical fact but rather allegorical, how is it consistent to maintain that this prophecy is literal, not allegorical? How can the same incident be *both*?

Finally, since the concept of marriage comes right out of the creation account (Gen. 2:24), then the doctrine of marriage is meaningless if Adam and Eve weren't created just as Genesis records.

Our acceptance of this record, then, is a critical manifestation of our **faith**.

Scriptures for Study: Read 1 Corinthians 15:21–22, 45 and Romans 5:12–21. How would you explain their application to today's study?

The Manifestation of Faith (2)

Through faith we understand that the worlds were framed by the word of God, so that things which are seen were not made of things which do appear. (Heb. 11:3)

"IT is the nature of faith to believe God upon His bare Word," wrote Puritan John Trapp. "It *will* not be, saith sense; it *cannot* be, saith reason; [but] it *will* and *can* be, saith faith, for I have a promise for it."[415] That leads us to the other aspect of the manifestation of faith.

Second, we note our faith in the *method* of creation. Our text is the simple, direct, unambiguous declaration that God alone created all things out of nothing and did so by His Word alone.

This is exactly what we also read in the very first verse of the Bible: "In the beginning God created the heaven and the earth" (Gen. 1:1). Again, what a simple but enormously profound statement! No rationalistic explanations, no apologetic arguments, just a simple statement of fact. We would, therefore, submit: if we do not believe the Creation account as it is recorded here, then we do not believe the Bible. Period. We have failed the most important manifestation of faith there is. If we cannot believe the first chapter of the Book, in fact, how can we possibly believe any of the rest of it. Why? Because this is the statement of how everything began. If we don't believe that, there is not a single reason to believe anything else it says. *There simply is no better manifestation, no better proof, of our faith than the belief in the creation account as literal and historical.*

Notice carefully, in fact, what our text declares: it is only through **faith** that we **understand** the truth of Creation. Contrary to popular thought among many Christians today, creation is not a *scientific* issue; it is a *theological* issue. It's not about proofs and evidences; it's about believing what God said. Creation simply cannot be explained scientifically. Science didn't exist then and it doesn't help now.

Ponder this: There are several Christian apologists nowadays who present many scientific proofs for creation. While such "proofs" might be compelling when compared to evolution, what if none of them existed? What if they just weren't all that compelling after all? Would that make us doubt that the creation account is true? If so, we just failed the primary test of faith. What if we become so intimidated by the world that we create explanations such as the Gap Theory, the Day-Age Theory, or the Framework Hypothesis[416] so we can combine creation with science (which is exactly what has occurred)? We have failed the test.

So, we say again, understanding creation comes entirely by **faith**. We have faith in the Genesis account of creation simply because of what God has said. To try to explain it any other way is nothing but a fool's errand and will actually cripple our service for Him.

Scriptures for Study: What do the following verses say about creation: Genesis 2:1; Exodus 20:11; Psalm 33:6; John 1:1–3?

OCTOBER 6

Practical Faith

But without faith it is impossible to please him: for he that cometh to God must believe that he is, and that he is a rewarder of them that diligently seek him. (Heb. 11:6)

OSWALD Chambers has often been quoted: "Faith enables the believing soul to treat the future as present and the invisible as seen."[417] While that is most certainly true, how do we make it practical? Our text, of course, appears in the context of Enoch's faith, and we will meditate on him in a future study, but we should examine this verse now as it relates to the greater context of the whole chapter. Building upon what we have already seen, this verse goes deeper by providing us with four principles of practical faith.

First, we recognize the *impossibility*: **without faith it is impossible to please him**. This is first and foremost in putting our faith into practice. Some think they can please God by their religion, by performing various rituals, or practicing certain sacraments (cf. Gen. 4:1–7). Others think they can please God by their own good works and moral living (cf. Is. 64:6; Eph. 2:8–9; Titus 3:5). Still others think God will be pleased with them because of their nationality or family heritage, just as the Jews thought because they were descendents of Abraham (cf. Jn. 8:39–44). But there is no other way to please God than by believing what He says.

Second, we see the *inclination*: **he that cometh to God must believe that he is**. The word **is** translates *esti* (2076), a form of the word *eimi* (1510; Mar. 9), the usual word for existence. Paralleling the OT "I AM" (Ex. 3:14), Jesus used this word to refer to Himself as the "I Am." As noted yesterday, faith relies not on arguments or proofs, but simply on what God says. There is never enough evidence for the unbeliever.

Third, we feel the *intimacy*: **diligently seek him**. Not only must we believe that God *is*, but we must also seek and believe in the God who is holy, personal, loving, and gracious, the God who responds to those who come to Him. **Diligently seek** is the verb *ekzēteō* (1567), to seek out, search diligently, and is in the present tense. Practical faith, then, continually seeks God with full diligence. Our faith is constantly growing because it is based on the Word of God. The more diligent we grow in the Word, the deeper our faith and relationship become.

Fourth, we note the *incentive*: **he is a rewarder of them that diligently seek him**. While it is certainly enough for godly believers that God tells us to have faith, He adds an extra incentive by His grace—He adds reward. The greatest reward, of course, is our salvation and its assurance. As we will see in other verses, however, God has given us far more. Because of our faith, we will: receive God's approval (v. 4), one day be translated into God's presence (v. 5), receive guidance (v. 8–10), enjoy provision (vv. 24–26), and claim victory over difficulties (v. 30).

Such practical faith wonderfully equips us for service.

Scriptures for Study: What do these verses say about diligence: Psalm 119:10; Proverbs 8:17; Jeremiah 29:13; Matthew 6:33?

OCTOBER 7

Abel: The Piety of Faith (1)

By faith Abel offered unto God a more excellent sacrifice than Cain, by which he obtained witness that he was righteous, God testifying of his gifts: and by it he being dead yet speaketh. (Heb. 11:4)

TURNING to the list of champions in this great chapter, we emphasize again that these were not "larger than life" characters or a "special breed" of people. They were ordinary men and women who simply believed what God said and obeyed. They took God at His Word and did things exactly how He prescribed. Each of them encourages and challenges us to serve in the same way.

It is interesting to note four elements in each one of these examples: God *spoke* by His Word; each person was *stirred* in the heart; each then *submitted* in obedience; and God *spoke* again in approval. For each of our studies, we will condense those four elements into just three principles: the requirement, the response, and the result. Our first encounter, then, is Abel, who teaches us the *piety* of faith.

First, the *requirement*: **sacrifice**. Some Bible teachers insist that God rejected Cain's sacrifice because it was not blood. This is based primarily on viewing Genesis 3:21 as God teaching Adam that blood had to be shed for sin, knowledge that must have then been handed down to Cain and Abel. While we respect this view and its defenders, we humbly submit that it reads something into the text that is not actually stated there. The Hebrew, in fact, for the "offering" both men brought (Gen. 4:3–5) is *minḥāh* (4503H), which does not refer to blood at all (it's always used in Leviticus for bloodless sacrifice); nor did it have anything to do with sin or its atonement. It simply refers to the general idea of a gift. (We should also note that an offering of the fruits of the ground would in the future be prescribed under the Mosaic Law [e.g., Ex 23:16; 34:22].) **Sacrifice** in our text, then, is *thusia* (2378), which is used differently depending upon the context. So, the offering each man brought was appropriate to his vocation and could have been accepted equally as an expression of worship and gratitude to God for His bounty.

Second, the *response*: **Abel offered unto God a more excellent sacrifice than Cain**. The problem here was not in the *gift* but in the *giver*. It was not about *what* they brought but about the *way* they brought it. It wasn't about the outward, rather the inward. Cain's offering was not accepted because it wasn't the "first fruits" (the first and best) in contrast to Abel bringing the "firstlings" (Gen. 4:4; note also, **fat** is *ḥeleb* [2459H], which literally means "best"; e.g., Gen. 45:18, "fat of the land"). Most importantly, Abel's offering was by *faith alone*; Cain's was not. So, while **Cain** demonstrated *personal works*, **Abel** expressed *pious worship*.

How significant it is that this first example of faith is about worship! This underscores, indeed, that worship is God's primary requirement of man. Oh, yes, Cain, like many today, believed *in* God, but he did not *believe* God. True worship, as Abel illustrates, involves a real sacrifice and genuine faith.

Scriptures for Study: What does 1 John 3:12 tell us about Cain and Abel?

OCTOBER 8

Abel: The Piety of Faith (2)

By faith Abel offered unto God a more excellent sacrifice than Cain, by which he obtained witness that he was righteous, God testifying of his gifts: and by it he being dead yet speaketh. (Heb. 11:4)

CONTINUING our study, we go a little deeper into the *response* of **Cain** and **Abel**. While we examined worship in the second part of our daily readings on *loving* our Lord (June 1–8), we briefly consider it again because it's also an integral part of our *serving* Him.

(1) We must come to the place of worship. Some scholars speculate that an altar might very well have existed near the east side of the Garden of Eden where God had placed the cherubim to guard the entrance (Gen. 3:24). In any case, there obviously was a prescribed place simply because Cain and Abel knew where to find God's presence. Similarly, Christians today have a place of corporate worship. While it is certainly true that each of us is the temple of the Holy Spirit (1 Cor. 6:19–20) and can worship anywhere, Scripture repeatedly emphasizes the need for God's people to gather for worship (Acts 2:46–47; Heb. 10:25; June 5, 21).

(2) We must come at the proper time of worship. It is important to note the phrase "in process of time" in reference to when Cain and Abel brought their offerings (Gen. 4:3). This can also be literally rendered "at the end of days." Worship was, therefore, at the end of a certain period of time. Some view this as a reference to the Sabbath, the end of the week, the seventh day. But this assumes that the Sabbath had been established at this time for observance, which the text nowhere indicates (June 20). It far more likely refers to the end of the year (the same expression appears in Judges 11:4, where a year is clearly meant). This would have been the time of ingathering when an offering was made in thankfulness for the bounty God had given (cf. Ex. 23:16).[418] We, too, have a proper time of worship. The time of corporate worship is clearly specified in the NT as the first day of the week (Jn. 20:19; Acts 20:7; 1 Cor. 16:2; Rev. 1:10; June 20).

(3) We must come to worship in the right way. As noted yesterday, Cain and Abel were very different in the way they came to God. Cain was self-serving; Abel was God-exalting. Cain approached with works; Abel approached by faith. It is troubling, indeed, how many in our churches parallel Cain. They come to serve themselves, always looking for what the church can offer them. Many also think they can worship in whatever mode and with whatever method they choose. Also like Cain, when confronted with their sin, they get angry and even vengeful. Some (perhaps many) are not believers at all and are simply relying on their own works. "Forasmuch as this people draw near me with their mouth, and with their lips do honour me, but have removed their heart far from me" (Is. 29:13; cf. Matt. 15:8). The way of self-will, works, religion, and unbelief is "the way of Cain" (Jude 11).

Scriptures for Study: According to the texts referenced today, where did early Christians meet for worship?

OCTOBER 9

Abel: The Piety of Faith (3)

By faith Abel offered unto God a more excellent sacrifice than Cain, by which he obtained witness that he was righteous, God testifying of his gifts: and by it he being dead yet speaketh. (Heb. 11:4)

THE only similarity between Cain and Abel was that they had the same parents. In every other way possible, they were as different as night and day, light and darkness, works and faith.

Third, then, we see the *result*: because he **offered unto God a more excellent sacrifice than Cain . . . Abel . . . obtained witness that he was righteous**. John Calvin well summarizes **Cain**: "Cain conducted himself as hypocrites are accustomed to do; namely, that he wished to appease God, as one discharging a debt, by external sacrifices, without the least intention of dedicating himself to God."[419]

So, because God, of course, knew Cain's heart, He did not have "respect" for the offering he brought (Gen. 4:5). "Respect" is the Hebrew *šā'āh* (8159H), a verb that means to look at with interest but never with a casual or disinterested glance. In the present context, it means to look at with approval—God approved of Abel but not of Cain. The same idea appears in Isaiah 17:7–8, where "God says that the time is coming when a 'man will regard his maker' and no more have regard for the altars which his hands have made."[420] Tragically, instead of obeying God, Cain chose a religious act.

Oh, but what a wondrous difference we see in **Abel**! God accepted Abel's sacrifice because it was brought by faith. His sacrifice was **more excellent**, our text declares. This is one word in the Greek (*pleiōn*, 4119), which is used figuratively here to mean more, greater, higher, and to indicate worth, importance, and dignity. In light of the overall context of the book of Hebrews, we could translate this word as "better," for this is the key word in the book. Christ was better than the angels (1:4), He is a better hope (7:19), the better Mediator of a better covenant and better promises (8:6), Christians have a better country awaiting us, that is, heaven (11:16), and we also await a better resurrection (11:35).

Further, the result of Abel's faith was that he **obtained witness that he was righteous**. **Obtained witness** is again *martureō* (3140; Oct. 3), to be a witness, cite evidence, or report the events. God testified of Abel, and what evidence did He cite? Abel simply believed what God said. Even more significantly, God testified that Abel was **righteous**. Here is an early and wondrous illustration of justification by faith alone, a doctrine that is at the very core of biblical theology. Justification is the declarative act of God, as the Judge, whereby He declares that the demands of justice have been satisfied so that the sinner is no longer condemned. It is a declaration, not of *innocence*, but of *satisfaction*.[421] Think of it! God was satisfied with Abel. And while he is long **dead**, he still speaks to us today of living faith.

Scriptures for Study: In Hebrews 12:24, who and what speaks even "better things than that of Abel"?

OCTOBER 10

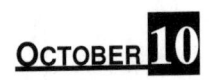

Enoch: The Pace of Faith (1)

Enoch walked with God ... (Gen. 5:22, 24)

GOD'S revelation is progressive. He reveals Truth to man one step at a time, and each new step builds upon the preceding ones. That principle is apparent with Abel and Enoch. While Abel shows us the *piety* of faith, he knew nothing of the *pace* of faith, that is, "keeping in step" with God as he walked with Him. While his parents enjoyed this, as they once walked with Him "in the garden in the cool of the day" (Gen. 3:8), this was unknown to Abel. Enoch, however, enjoyed this wondrous and forgotten reality.

First, we notice that the *requirement* for Enoch was different than that of Abel. While God required a *sacrifice* from Abel, He required *steadfastness* from Enoch. He wanted Enoch to have a closer relationship with Him, not just to *worship* Him but to *walk* with Him. **Walked** is *hālak* (1980), which literally refers simply to movement, such as a man walking (Gen. 12:9, "going"), an animal crawling (Lev. 11:27, "goeth"), or even the flowing of a river (Gen. 2:14, "goeth", first occurrence) or the tossing of the sea (Jonah 1:11, "wrought"). Figuratively, then, it pictures how a man "walks" in life, that is, how he conducts himself, how he lives. Such a man "[walks] not in the counsel of the ungodly" (Ps. 1:1)—that is, he does not take the advice, adopt the philosophies, and live by the standards of wickedness—rather he continually, consistently, and correctly obeys what God says.

Second, the *response*: What we notice immediately about our texts is the repetition of the phrase **Enoch walked with God**, which seems redundant. Why repeat it? Perhaps it was meant simply as a confirmation. We tend to think, however, that since repetition is sometimes used in Hebrew for emphasis, this phrase is repeated to dramatically demonstrate just how different Enoch was from the rest of society and how different was his departure from the earth (v. 24).

As many commentators observe, a striking feature about Enoch's walk with God is that it did not actually begin until after the birth of his son Methuselah (v. 22). By implication, it appears that before this Enoch was much like everyone else of that day. Perhaps he was not as bad as those described in Jude 14–15, but his life might very well have been one of tolerance and passive resignation. Some commentators suggest that he was involved in idolatry to one extent or another.

In any case, the change came. We are not told precisely why, but two reasons seem clearly implied. First, in the growing wickedness of that era before the Flood, we can easily imagine God showing Enoch the need to **[walk] with God**. It is possible, in fact, that God told him of the impending cataclysm that was coming. Second, we can likewise envision that God told Enoch what a father should be. As a result, Enoch spent the next 300 years **[walking]** with God. What precisely does that entail? We will go deeper tomorrow.

Scriptures for Study: What do these verses tell us about walking: Psalms 56:13; 86:11; Ps 128:1; Acts 9:31?

OCTOBER 11

Enoch: The Pace of Faith (2)

Enoch walked with God . . . (Gen. 5:22, 24)

GOING deeper into Enoch's *response* to God's requirement, in light of the meaning of **walked** noted yesterday—how we "walk" in life, how we conduct ourselves—we can observe four implications.

(1) Walking with God implies we are making the same *decisions*. In other words, every move we make is according to the will of God. Where do we find God's will? How does He lead? His Word, of course, reveals His will (Sept. 6). While many of us want to "put out a fleece" as Gideon did, he is actually the worst model of how to know God's will (Judg. 6:16, 36–40). God *told* Gideon His will, and that should have been enough (see Oct. 29–30 for a study of Gideon).

(2) Walking with God implies we are moving in the same *direction*. Jude 14–15 tell us that Enoch was a preacher whose message was, by faith, in total agreement with what God said about man's "ungodly" (which appears four times) condition. Do we likewise agree with God? Since "agreement" means "harmony of opinion" (Webster), it also implicitly implies an end to disharmony and controversy. So, to agree with God means we never oppose Him. It is very troubling to a pastor who has carefully studied, exposited, and applied a Scripture text only to hear his listeners say in rebellion, "I don't agree with that." Oh, how God wants our agreement! We cannot walk with Him without it. As the prophet asked rhetorically: "Can two walk together, except they be agreed?" (Amos 3:3).

(3) Walking with God implies we have the same *disposition*. Enoch was entirely disposed and inclined to trust God, but the wondrous truth here is such trust is mutual. Not only do we trust God, but He trusts us! With what has He trusted us? "Henceforth I call you not servants; for the servant knoweth not what his lord doeth: but I have called you friends; for all things that I have heard of my Father I have made known unto you" (Jn. 15:15). Jesus here marks a developmental change in His relationship with His disciples. No longer are they just slaves, but they are also friends. This does not negate them being slaves but rather transforms it into something better. Their *relationship* to the Savior was one of friendship, while their *responsibility* is servitude. He trusts us as friends who labor as servants.

(4) Walking with God implies we have the same *determination*. In other words, to walk with Him is to "keep step" with Him. We neither run ahead nor lag behind. Peter is probably our best illustration. On the night of our Lord's betrayal, Peter first *ran ahead*, grabbed a sword, and tried to "protect" his Lord. Later at Jesus' trial, however, Peter *lagged behind* as he followed "afar off." Neither did the children of Israel keep step with God. He wanted to escort them into the Promised Land, but they refused and so wandered in the wilderness for 40 years. Discouragement, defeat, and disaster will come if we don't keep step with God.

Scriptures for Study: What is God's will in each of the following: Romans 12:2; Ephesians 5:17–18; 1 Thessalonians 4:3–7; 5:18; 1 Peter 2:13–15?

OCTOBER 12

Enoch: The Pace of Faith (3)

Enoch walked with God . . . (Gen. 5:22, 24)
Walk in the Spirit . . . (Gal. 5:16a)

LET us go still deeper into Enoch's *response* to God's requirement. As we meditate on Enoch walking with God, we discover a profound application. While the OT precedent is walking with God, the deeper NT principle is walking in the Holy Spirit. **Walk in the Spirit**, Paul wrote to the Galatians.

Walk is *peripateō* (4043), a compound comprised of *peri* (4012), "about, around," and *pateō* (3961), "to walk," and so, "to walk about, to walk around, to walk concerning." When used figuratively, as it is here, it speaks of "conduct of life," that is, "how we walk about," how we conduct ourselves as we walk through life. The NT actually specifies several ways we are "to walk about."

(1) Walk in newness of life (Rom. 6:4). Because we are in Christ, all things that pertain to the old life are gone and everything now is new (2 Cor. 5:17). "Newness of life supposes newness of heart," wrote Matthew Henry, "for out of the heart are the issues of life, and there is no way to make the stream sweet but by making the spring so."[422]

(2) Walk by faith (2 Cor. 5:7). We must not be influenced by what we *see* but by what we *know*. "Faith is opposed to sight," Calvin wrote, "because it perceives those things that are hid from the view of men."[423] When God says it, that settles it.

(3) Walk honestly (Rom. 13:13). In a day of dishonesty and "gray areas," it is imperative that we live according to honesty and integrity.

(4) Walk in good works (Eph. 2:10). While they do not save us, as Paul makes clear in the two preceding verses, good works are the inevitable result of salvation.

(5) Walk in love (Eph. 5:2). As Christ loved us, we are to love one another and be concerned for each other's needs. This "should be the principle from which we act," Henry submits again, and "should direct the ends at which we aim."[424]

(6) Walk in wisdom (Col. 4:5). We must show those who are outside of Christ that we are driven by one thing alone. We must demonstrate that our wisdom is not of this world but is based solely upon God's Word (1 Cor. 1:18–20; 2:1–5, 13).

(7) Walk in Truth (2 Jn. 4). In a world that rejects absolutes and views all Truth, especially religious Truth, as relative, we must walk according to the Truth of God's Word alone as sufficient and authoritative. As Puritan William Gurnall observed, "News may come that Truth is sick, but never that it is dead."[425]

(8) Walk after His commandments (2 Jn. 6). We must not be influenced by the world's philosophies but by God's precepts.

In addition to those positives, there are some negatives. We must *not* walk after the flesh (Rom. 8:4), after the manner of men (1 Cor, 3:3), in craftiness (2 Cor. 4:2), by sight (5:7), in vanity (Eph. 4:17), or disorderly (2 Thes. 3:6).

My Dear Christian Friend, how is your walk?

Scriptures for Study: Read the texts cited today and record your observations.

OCTOBER 13

Enoch: The Pace of Faith (4)

By faith Enoch was translated that he should not see death; and was not found, because God had translated him: for before his translation he had this testimony, that he pleased God. (Heb. 11:5)

THE principles we observe in Enoch are, indeed, among the most blessed and encouraging in this entire chapter. We have noted the *requirement*, and the deeper *response*, but there is one more striking truth.

Third, the *result*, which is two-fold. First, we note the *unusual translation*. Both instances of **translated** are the verb *metatithēmi* (3346; **translation** is the feminine form *metathesis* [3331]). The root *tithēmi* (5087) means to set, place, or lay, and the prefix *meta* (3326) here denotes change of place or condition. The full idea, then, is, "To transpose, put in another place and hence to transport, transfer, [or] translate."[426] It also appears in 7:12 for the priesthood being transferred to Christ. So, in "the twinkling of an eye" (1 Cor. 15:52), God supernaturally transported Enoch from the earthly realm to the heavenly. Think of it! "God, out of an extraordinary grace and favor to [Enoch]," wrote Matthew Poole, "dispensed with the common sentence passed on the human seed in Adam."[427]

Second, we notice the *underlying truth*: **[Enoch] pleased God**. What a staggering statement! **Pleased** is *euaresteō* (2100), another compound word: the root *aréskō* (700), to please, and the prefix *eu* (2095), well. It is one thing to be *pleased*, but quite another to be *well* pleased, that is, to be gratified entirely and completely. Enoch lived in a day of great wickedness, a state that would eventually lead to the Flood. He was a light during those dark days, a light that shined through holy living and faithful proclamation of the Truth. Such faith (and faithfulness), which continued day after day for 300 years, pleased God, for as verse 6 reminds us, "without faith it is impossible to please [*euaresteō*]" Him.

The story has been told of the little girl who recounted the story of Enoch as she understood it: "Enoch used to take long walks with God, and one day they went a long way and God said, 'Enoch, you are far from home, and you had better go in with Me,' and he went in with Him." It seems that this story first appeared in Frederick Power's 1902 biography of William Kimbrough Pendleton (1817–1899), President of Bethany College. Power then applied it to Pendleton's death: "So simple was the home-going of the subject of these chronicles; such was his intimacy with God."[428]

Such should be our desire. One day God will translate each of us into His very presence. While some Christians believe in the Rapture (1 Thes. 4:13–18), others' view of future things does not include that. Whichever the case is, however, the underlying truth remains the same. Those who walk with God shall "in a moment, in the twinkling of an eye, at the last trump . . . be changed" (1 Cor. 15:52).

Scriptures for Study: How do the following verses add to our study today: Psalm 89:48; John 8:51–52?

OCTOBER 14

Noah: The Performance of Faith (1)

Make thee an ark ... (Gen. 6:14)
By faith Noah, being warned of God of things not seen as yet, moved with fear, prepared an ark to the saving of his house ... (Heb. 11:7)

MOST people, whether believer or unbeliever, have heard of Noah. Skeptics, of course, call his story legend, while true believers read his story as historic fact and recognize the Flood as the answer to geological questions that the skeptic prefers to credit to "millions of years." Deeper, however, Noah is among the most striking examples of faith in all of Scripture, and his story is not only a picture of salvation but also a portrait of service.

First, the *requirement*: **Make thee an ark**. Why did God command this? Genesis 6:5 describes the horrific state of the pre-flood civilization: "And GOD saw that the wickedness of man was great in the earth, and that every imagination of the thoughts of his heart was only evil continually." I am profoundly struck by that verse every time I read it. So deep was man in sin that every thought he had, every idea he entertained, every plan he made, was evil. Man was so corrupt that nothing he could think or do was pure. Sadly, our own day is closing in on that condition, and as Jesus Himself declares, "As the days of [Noah] were, so shall also the coming of the Son of man be" (Matt. 24:37).

God, therefore, **warned** (and "instructed," as the Greek *chrēmatizō* [5537] implies]) Noah concerning what was coming and told him to build an ark. But can we fathom the task God was actually giving Noah to perform? Even being conservative, if the cubit Noah used was only 17.5 inches (the smallest suggested by any authority), the ark was 437.5 feet long, 72.9 feet wide, and 43.75 feet high. To put it in perspective, that is one-and-a-half football fields in length, roughly one-half of that field in width, and about the height of a four-story building. Such a design made the ark virtually impossible to capsize; if turned at a 90 degree angle, it would automatically right itself. So, with three decks, its length and width yielded a total of 95,681 square feet of living space—this is the equivalent of 47 2,000 square feet houses—and its total volume was about 1,400,000 cubic feet. As Henry Morris reports, "The ark could have carried as many as 125,000 sheep-sized animals. Since there are not more than about 25,000 species of land animals known (mammals, birds, reptiles, amphibians), either living or extinct, and since the average size of such animals is certainly much less than that of a sheep, it is obvious that all the animals could easily have been stored in less than half the capacity of Noah's ark."[429]

What a task, indeed! And it took Noah 120 years to complete it. Likewise, God has given us a monumental task. While He hasn't told us to build an ark, He has nonetheless given us much to do.

Scriptures for Study: Read Genesis 6. What observations can you make and what strikes you the most profoundly?

OCTOBER 15

Noah: The Performance of Faith (2)

By faith Noah, being warned of God of things not seen as yet, moved with fear, prepared an ark to the saving of his house . . . (Heb. 11:7)

"WHERE reason cannot wade, there faith may swim," wrote Puritan Thomas Watson on the subject of the Trinity, adding that "the plumb line of reason is too short to fathom this mystery."[430] The same was true for Noah and his Ark.

Second, the *response*: **By faith Noah . . . prepared an ark**. Noah did three things in response to God's command.

(1) He *walked* with God. We find this description in Genesis 6:9, the same description, of course, we noted of Enoch. Both of these men walked with God in some very unique circumstances and for some very special results. As was true of Noah and Enoch, and what should be true of us now, is that we are making the same decision, moving in the same direction, have the same disposition, and possess the same determination.

(2) Noah *worked* in reverence. Putting yourself in Noah's place, how do you think you would have responded to God's command? Before you answer, consider how it sounded in that day. For one thing, it had never rained. Rain did not occur before the Flood, rather a mist watered the earth (Gen. 2:5–6). For another, there is no evidence of any large body of water near the building site. Neither would there have ever been a flood. Who of us would not have thought of some way (*any* way) to try to get out of doing something so unimaginably absurd?

Ah, but not Noah. We read not the slightest hint of protest, pretext, or procrastination. He simply did exactly what God said to do in the precise way He said to do it. We should also observe that if we compared our Bible to a giant sequoia tree, Noah possessed only a splinter of God's revelation. Sadly, many today can hear the Word preached, even examine it on a particular issue, but still say no to the will of God. But Noah had the barest morsel of revelation, and that was enough.

What a challenge this is to us that true faith does not question; it acts. Real faith does not argue, complain, or make excuses. True, biblical faith acts immediately on the Word of God. As we have seen, faith has a two-fold portrait: it involves both *confidence* and *conviction* (Oct. 2). Such was Noah. There are many faithful saints spoken of in Scripture, but in some ways Noah stands supreme as an example of unquestioning, unwavering, and undying faithfulness.

But there is something else. Noah labored in the reverence of spiritual devotion. **Moved with fear** is the single word *eulabeomai* (2125). As one Greek authority explains, "The true idea is pious care, a reverent circumspection with regard to things enjoined by God, and as yet unseen, yet confidently expected on the strength of God's Word."[431] Let us not *endure* our labor, rather *exult* in it.

Scriptures for Study: So important is Noah that he is mentioned many times in Scripture. How many can you find and what do they add to our study?

OCTOBER 16

Noah: The Performance of Faith (3)

By faith Noah, being warned of God of things not seen as yet, moved with fear, prepared an ark to the saving of his house; by the which he condemned the world, and became heir of the righteousness which is by faith. (Heb. 11:7)

CONCLUDING our thoughts on Noah's response to God's requirement, we not only see that He *walked* with God and *worked* in reverence, but his labor involved something else.

(3) He *warned* the world, which included two features. First, he *abandoned* the world. By standing for God, Noah simultaneously forsook the world. He left behind all that it had to offer and disregarded anything it had to say. Second, he then *admonished* (**condemned**) the world. His labor included declaring God's message of judgment to an unbelieving, ungodly world. Second Peter 2:5 calls Noah "a preacher of righteousness."

Every time I read the account of Noah, I think of what would have been expected of him by modern standards of "church ministry." He would have had to build several boats and then done anything to get people on one of them. He would have run an attendance contest, given away balloons with dinosaur pictures on them, put on a stage play, made people feel comfortable by appealing to their "felt needs," and then had a celebrity give his testimony. But Noah's ministry was not a pragmatic one; it was a biblical one. He just did it God's way, preaching righteousness for 120 years whether anyone believed or not. And no one did! Such "failure" nowadays is totally unacceptable and has caused many to change not only their method but even the message. Instead of believing what God says, we do whatever we think will get "results."

Why did Noah keep the same method and not change? Because he had faith in what God said. The performance of faith is to stand for righteousness, forsake this world, and warn unbelievers of judgment. We fear doing this because the world will call us foolish, naïve, and out of touch. Similar epithets were undoubtedly hurled at Noah, right up to the moment when water started pouring from the sky.

Third, the *result*: **became heir of the righteousness which is by faith**. An heir, of course, is one who receives something not because he earned it but simply because it was handed down by another. Noah could not earn righteousness, rather it was given to Him. And whose righteousness did he receive? The righteousness of Jesus Christ. Likewise, our inheritance is Christ (Eph. 1:11). We could not earn it, rather we could only inherit it by faith. Oh, what a picture the Ark is! Inside it was salvation, while outside was judgment. The waterproofing "pitch" is a further symbol. This is the Hebrew *kāpar* (3722H), the same basic word for "atonement." As pitch kept out the waters of judgment, so Christ's atoning blood keeps judgment from the sinner and makes him a saint and servant.

Scriptures for Study: What do the following verses declare: Romans 1:17; 3:22; 9:30; Galatians 5:5; Philippians 3:9?

OCTOBER 17

Abraham: The Patience of Faith (1)

By faith Abraham . . . (Heb. 11:8–19)

THE word "patriarch" is one of many English words transliterated directly from the Greek (*patriarchēs*, 3966) and refers to the father and founder of a family or tribe. It appears four times in reference to Abraham (Heb 7:4), the sons of Jacob (Acts 7:8–9), and David (Acts 2:29). The instance of David and other OT uses in the Septuagint (1 Chron. 24:31; 27:32; 2 Chron. 26:12) refer simply to the head of a family or tribe. While those who lived before the Flood (Adam to Noah) are technically patriarchs, it is the post-duluvian (after the flood) patriarchs that are prominent.

When we examine the patriarchs in the context of faith, one main theme comes to the forefront: *true faith is able to wait patiently for the fulfillment of God's promises in His time*. Did you get that? It is waiting for God to work in *His* time, not ours. Most of us are willing to wait for God as long as He moves "fast enough." But true faith waits even when we cannot see the fulfillment on the horizon. Further, true faith continues *working* faithfully while it's *waiting* patiently.

While there is much to examine in each of the patriarchs, we will major on Abraham, for as the father of the Jews, he was the ultimate example of faith to them. He is also, however, a great example to all believers. There are two basic ways to live: we can either live by *sight*, that is, base everything on what we can see, or we can live by *faith*, simply believing what God says even though we can't see it. Abraham, in the longest passage in Hebrews 11 on an individual character, does, indeed, take us deeper into what it means to live by faith.

First, the *requirement*. We read God's original statement of his covenant to Abraham in Genesis 12:1–3. By far, the most startling statement is the very first one: "Now the LORD had said unto Abram, Get thee out of thy country, and from thy kindred, and from thy father's house, unto a land that I will shew thee."

Have you ever pondered what God actually told Abram to do? Put yourself in his place for a moment. God told him to leave his homeland, his residence, and even his family without telling him where he was going, what kind of place it would be, or any other information on which to base the simplest commonsense decision. Oh yes, God made some "big promises," to use the term of the modern skeptic—"And I will make of thee a great nation, and I will bless thee, and make thy name great; and thou shalt be a blessing: And I will bless them that bless thee, and curse him that curseth thee: and in thee shall all families of the earth be blessed"—but where was the proof?

But that, of course, is what faith is all about; once again, it is *supreme confidence* in what God says and *settled conviction* that it will come to pass. "We do not live by *explanations*; we live by *promises*."[432]

Scriptures for Study: What does God promise in these verses: Isaiah 40:31; Romans 8:28? Philippians 4:19? Do you believe and act on those promises?

OCTOBER 18

Abraham: The Patience of Faith (2)
By faith Abraham . . . (Heb. 11:8–19)

WHEN we utter the name Abraham, we speak of one who simply believed and obeyed what God said with no proof whatsoever and one, in fact, who never actually saw the fulfillment of what was promised.

Second, then, we see the *response*. As a pilot looks at the gauges in front him to verify the status of his airplane, Hebrews 11:8–19 provides five gauges that enable us to monitor how we are walking by faith.

(1) The *exhortation* of faith. To understand the deep significance here, it is critical to consider Abram's background. His native home was Ur in Chaldea, which was in the general region called Mesopotamia near the mouth of the Euphrates River on its western bank, with canals that circled and bisected the city. The dominant feature of the city was the giant Ziggurat, a solid mass of brick work 200 by 150 and 50 feet high, which was referred to as the "Hill of Heaven" and "Mountain of God." The shrine of Nanna, the moon god and patron of the city, stood on top. Every aspect and activity of the city—its social, commercial, and economic life—revolved around this god and his consort Ningal.

Abraham was a sinful pagan just like his family and culture. Joshua 24:2 tells us that he was raised in a home that "served other gods," and there is nothing in the text that indicates that he was separated from that.[433] Puritan Matthew Henry puts it well: "Abraham . . . was bred up in idolatry, and lived long in it, till God by his grace snatched him as a brand out of that burning."

That leads us to the phrases **he was called** and **he went out** (v. 8). When God called Abram, what was his immediate response? *Obedience*, and that is the exhortation of faith Abraham provides us: *are we willing to leave Ur*? Are we willing to leave everything behind (Aug. 23–27) and follow our Lord completely?

As noted yesterday, God told Abram to leave everything he knew but did not tell him where he was going, and that is exactly how Abram responded: **he went out, not knowing whither he went**. Most of us are just fine with living by faith, that is, as long as we know *where* we are going and *how* we will get there. But that, of course, is not living by faith at all, rather it is living by sight (2 Cor. 5:7). Further, not only did Abram not know where he was going, but it also appears that he didn't really care where he was going. There was no objection, no argument, no excuses. All he knew was that God told him to leave Ur and would show him where to go in His own time. Are we likewise at peace with whatever God brings into our lives? "We are often called to leave worldly connections, interests, and comforts," Matthew Henry encouraged. "If heirs of Abraham's faith, we shall obey and go forth, though not knowing what may befall us; and we shall be found in the way of duty, looking for the performance of God's promises."

Scriptures for Study: What do the following verses tell us about Abraham: Genesis 15:1–6; 22:18?

OCTOBER 19

Abraham: The Patience of Faith (3)

By faith Abraham . . . (Heb. 11:8–19)

"ABRAHAM himself had no excellency which did not proceed from faith," wrote John Calvin. "By these two things—his promptness in obeying, and his perseverance—was Abraham's faith most clearly proved."[434]

(2) The *endurance* of faith. This second gauge of faith demonstrates that Abraham waited for God to work. He **sojourned in . . . a strange country, dwelling in [tents]**. Think of it! Abraham lived in a country, moving from place to place, where he owned not a single square foot of land. The land was his by *promise*, but not by *possession*, so he had to be *patient*. So patient was Abraham, in fact, that he never wavered even though he personally never witnessed the fulfillment of God's promise. As we have previously studied, we too are "strangers, pilgrims, and foreigners" (Heb. 11:13) in this world because our real home awaits in heaven (July 31–Aug. 6). While God doesn't require us to live in tents, which have always been a symbol of temporary residence for travelers, would we be willing to do so?

What is the secret of such patient endurance? Abraham **looked for a city which hath foundations, whose builder and maker is God** (v. 10). **Look for** is *ekdechomai* (1551), to await and expect, suggesting the idea of reaching out in readiness to receive something. Most significantly, the verb is in the imperfect tense, continuous action in the past, so Abraham continuously, patiently, and expectantly waited for God's promise in spite of disappointment. How important it is that we keep our eyes on the right object.

(3) The *energy* of faith. This third gauge of faith emphasizes that God can do the impossible. Most people are aware of Jesus' words, "If ye have faith as a grain of mustard seed, ye shall say unto this mountain, Remove hence to yonder place; and it shall remove; and nothing shall be impossible unto you" (Matt. 17:20). Sadly, however, that verse is often misinterpreted to mean that we can do anything as long as we have faith. In other words, faith itself is the energy. We see such ideas in the "power of positive thinking" psychology and "name it and claim it" prosperity teaching.

But as we have seen, the source of power is not faith, rather the source of power is God and His Word. So, if God actually told us to move a mountain, then we could most certainly do that by believing what He said. The setting of that verse, in fact, was the disciples' lack of faith to cast out a demon from a young boy, even though they had done so before (Mk. 6:13). The example in our text is further evidence (vv. 11–12). Could Abraham and Sarah "name it and claim it" and thereby conceive a child with their faith? Of course not. Rather it was all God's power, and they just believed what He said He would do. Once again, our faith is *always* in God's Word.

Scriptures for Study: What do the following verses tell us about little faith: Matthew 6:30; 8:26; 14:31; 16:8?

OCTOBER 20

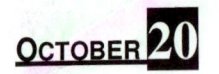

Abraham: The Patience of Faith (4)

By faith Abraham . . . (Heb. 11:8–19)

"AS fire is to the chemist, so is faith to the Christian," wrote Puritan Thomas Watson; "the chemist can do nothing without fire, so there is nothing done without faith."[435]

(4) The *expectation* of faith. The fourth gauge of faith emphasizes a state of mind and heart that never doubts or wavers. As we have noted, Abraham (and all the other patriarchs as well) never fully received the fulfillment of God's promises. This, however, must not be viewed as a gloomy negative but rather a glorious positive. It is once again a dramatic declaration that faith is *supreme confidence* in what God says and *settled conviction* that it will come to pass.

But the question immediately arises: "How could these men have such expectation and be so sure?" While we have already considered that they were content to be strangers and pilgrims on the earth, there is something else: they didn't *concentrate* on the present, rather they *contemplated* the future. Verse 13 also declares: **not having received the promises, but having seen them afar off**. Even though the fulfillment of the promises was *somewhere* in the future, that was enough. It was almost 500 years after Jacob died, in fact, that Israel entered the land that was promised, but to the patriarchs, God's Word was more than sufficient.

(5) The *evidence* of faith. The final gauge of faith is proving our faith through testing. What was Abraham's test? It was, of course, whether or not he was willing to give back to God the most precious thing in his life, his miracle son Isaac. Think of it! Abraham *received* Isaac by faith and then God demanded that he *relinquish* him on the same grounds. While Abraham knew that God would have to raise Isaac up from the dead (v. 19), he still did not know when that would take place and still had to endure the most unimaginable nightmare any parent could face by plunging a knife into his own child's chest.

The final gauge of our own faith is likewise the same. No, God is not going to ask us to take the life of our child, nor would He ever even condone it—here is just one of many reasons abortion is murder—but He will still test our faith by our willingness to make personal sacrifice for Him. What is He asking you to give?

Third, the *result*: **God was not ashamed to be called their God** (v. 16). What a result of faith! It would have been the easiest decision in the world for Abraham (and the other patriarchs) to have said, "Ah, these absurd promises are never going to be fulfilled. This stuff is impossible!" But he believed God, and God delighted in linking Abraham's name with His own. "They had acted in such a manner that it was fit that [God] should show toward them the character of a Benefactor, Protector, and Friend," wrote Albert Barnes.[436] Let that be true of our lives as well.

Scriptures for Study: How do the following verses encourage us: Romans 4:21; 8:24; 1 John 3:19?

OCTOBER 21

Isaac, Jacob, and Joseph: The Power of Faith

By faith Isaac . . . Jacob . . . Joseph . . . (Heb. 11:20–22)

THE underlying theme of the other Genesis patriarchs—Isaac, Jacob, and Joseph—is the power of faith. What power is this? It is the power of endurance that prevails all the way to the end. As verse 13 makes clear, all the patriarchs "died in faith, not having received the promises, but having seen them afar off, and were persuaded of them, and embraced them." True faith endures all the way to death. As has often been observed, "Faith sees the invisible, hears the inaudible, touches the intangible, and accomplishes the impossible,"[437] but if we may add, it also inherits the inconceivable.

First, the *requirement*, not surprisingly, was the same for Abraham's descendents as it was for him: just believe the promises of God. Abraham passed on to the next generation the covenant God had given him, which was then passed on again to the next, and the next after that. He has commanded the same from us. We must teach our children the Truth of God so they can in turn teach it to theirs!

Second, the *response*. Each subsequent patriarch knew implicitly what Paul would declare explicitly centuries later: "In hope of eternal life, which God, that cannot lie, promised before the world began" (Titus 1:2). Each, therefore, responded **by faith**. Because he believed the promises of God, **Isaac blessed Jacob and Esau concerning** those very **things** that were **to come** (v. 20). Likewise, because he believed, **Jacob** passed on the same blessing to both **the sons of Joseph** (Ephraim and Manasseh). Also, because he was deeply affected by the grace of God, "nothing was more natural than that the old man should lean reverently forward and incline his head upon the top of his staff, and adore the covenant faithfulness of his God."[438]

Joseph was inarguably the most impressive of all. If he would have had the "faith in faith" that is typical in our day, he would have without doubt "lost his faith" when his brothers sold him into slavery and when he was bombarded by the rank paganism of Egypt. But, on the contrary, his faith grew even deeper. Why? Because, once again, his roots were grounded in what God said. Period.

Third, the *result* was also the same as with Abraham. As noted yesterday, **God was not ashamed to be called their God** (v. 16). That is why God declared through Samuel, "Them that honor me I will honor" (1 Sam. 2:30). Just as nothing but faith can *please* God (Heb. 11:6), nothing but faith *honors* Him. He, therefore, honors those who honor Him by linking His name with theirs. He declares that He is, "The LORD God of your fathers, the God of Abraham, the God of Isaac, and the God of Jacob" (Ex. 3:15).

Oh, how the patriarchs encourage and challenge us! With far less *revelation* than we have, even in their failures they *rested* in God far more than we do.

Scriptures for Study: Can you find parallel passages for Exodus 3:15? What do they add to our study?

OCTOBER 22

Moses: The Perception of Faith (1)

By faith Moses . . . (Heb. 11:23–29)
God called unto him . . . Moses, Moses. (Ex.3:4a)

ONE contemporary, politically liberal personality well summed up much of American society when he said, "It used to be, everyone was entitled to their own opinion, but not their own facts. But that's not the case anymore. Facts matter not at all. Perception is everything. It's certainty."[439] Indeed, to most people today, "truth" (Mar. 15) is in the eye of the beholder, "wisdom" (Jan. 8, 10) is whatever works for you, and personal perception is all that matters.

Such philosophy, of course, can lead only to despair, disorder, and destruction, as has been demonstrated repeatedly in recent decades. The only place we will find truth, wisdom, and right perception is in the Word of God. Moses remarkably illustrates this; he did everything (well, almost everything) out of wisdom.

First, the *requirement*. To say that God required much from Moses is the height of understatement. We find the record of it in Exodus 3:1–10; verse 4 reads: "And when the LORD saw that he turned aside to see, God called unto him out of the midst of the bush, and said, Moses, Moses." As He always does, God once again spoke through His Word. And what did He require? He called Moses to challenge Pharaoh, demand that the Israelites be freed from bondage, and then lead some three million complaining people hundreds of miles back to the Promised Land they should never have left in the first place.

It is also striking that it was through Moses that God articulated the Moral Law, which while written on men's heart from the beginning (June 14), was for him written in stone so he could deliver it to the people. God's Word is the only source of wisdom, and there is no equal to the Ten Commandments. Oh, how different our culture would be if we all followed that rule of wisdom!

And so it is that Christians too are similarly called as was Moses. No, we are certainly not called to *do* what Moses *did*, but we are called to *have* what Moses *had*—wisdom. God wants us to "be filled with the knowledge of his will in all wisdom and spiritual understanding" (Col. 1:9) and to "walk in wisdom" (4:5). As noted in our study of Enoch (Oct. 12), our wisdom is not to be of this world but is to be based solely upon God's Word (1 Cor. 1:18–20; 2:1–5, 13).

Consider another challenging truth here. Of Moses' 120 years of life, the first 80 were invested in preparation for the final 40. During the first 40, he "learned in all the wisdom of the Egyptians" (Acts 7:22). In the second 40, however, on the "backside of the desert" (Midian in southern Arabia, the general area he would lead the Israelites to 40 years later), he learned how to listen, lead, and long-suffer, qualities that would serve him far better in the coming task. What is God doing in your life to prepare you to serve Him? What else might He have to do?

Scriptures for Study: Read Exodus 3:1–10. What strikes you the most profoundly in this passage?

OCTOBER 23

Moses: The Perception of Faith (2)

By faith Moses . . . (Heb. 11:23–29)
. . . And he said, here am I. (Ex. 3:4b)

NO other man in the annals of history had heaped upon him what was demanded of Moses. But by His mercy, God invested 80 years preparing Moses for the task before actually calling him to do it.

Second, the *response*: **here am I**. Moses' response to what God required was dramatic indeed. His wisdom and perception, which had grown through many years of service, manifested itself in two major principles.

(1) Moses *regarded* God's *Word*. Before we examine this specifically, it is essential to note that while Moses was certainly *available* (cf. Sept. 7), he was also *averse*. He offered no less than four excuses, in fact, why he should not be the one to perform this task. How often do we use the same excuses?

First, there was his question of *inadequacy*: "Who am I, that I should go unto Pharaoh, and that I should bring forth the children of Israel out of Egypt?" (Ex. 3:11). While in one respect this was a commendable attitude—none of us are worthy or qualified to serve God—it was still an excuse because when God calls us to serve He also equips us for the work (2 Cor. 3:5–6).

Second, there was Moses' question of *authenticity*. He was concerned that the people would deny his genuineness by asking, in effect, "What is the name of the One who sent you?" (Ex. 3:13). It is here we read that wondrous statement of God's essence: "Thus shalt thou say unto the children of Israel, I AM hath sent me unto you" (v. 14; Jan 14; cf. Mar. 9, 26). *That* is authenticity! We, too, can claim that the "I AM" has called and equipped us to serve.

Third, there was Moses' doubt about his *authority*. He feared that the people would simply dismiss his claims and deny his authority over them (Ex. 4:1). In modern parlance, the question is, "Who are you to tell us what to do?" In Moses' case, God performed a miracle to prove and seal Moses' authority (v. 3; Jews alone require signs, 1 Cor. 1:22). Such things are no longer needed today, however, because God's Word is final. He calls, qualifies, and equips church leaders (Acts 20:28; Eph. 4:11–16; 1 Tim. 3:1–13; Titus 1:7–9; Heb. 13:17).

Fourth, Moses' final doubt concerned his *insufficiency*. He was "not eloquent" and was "slow of speech" (Ex. 4:10). He was anything but a dynamic speaker, but God said, "I will be with thy mouth, and teach thee what thou shalt say" (v. 12). How tragic it is when people today prefer eloquence, expressiveness, and even entertainment, instead of truth. They want a "good communicator," even if what he communicates is weak or even false. They want a *pulpiteer*, not a *preacher*.

There is no mystery why Moses said, in effect, "Oh, Lord, please send someone else!" (Ex. 4:13). But he went nonetheless. Will we thus regard God's Word?

Scriptures for Study: How do the following verses encourage us: Matthew 10:19–20; John 14:26; Ephesians 6:19?

OCTOBER 24

Moses: The Perception of Faith (3)

By faith Moses . . . (Heb. 11:23–29)
. . . And he said, here am I. (Ex. 3:4b)

WHENEVER I think of Moses, I think of a man called to the impossible task of leading incorrigible people to an improbable goal. But he did it all by faith because he first regarded God's Word.

(2) Moses *rejected* the *world*. Martyred missionary Jim Elliot's immortal words apply here: "He is no fool who gives what he cannot keep to gain that which he cannot lose." Moses understood that long before Brother Elliot.

First, he rejected the world's *virtues* when he **refused to be called the son of Pharaoh's daughter** (Heb. 11:24). What a staggering decision! Moses was a prince in Egypt for 40 years. Egypt was at that time the wealthiest, most cultured, most advanced, most sophisticated society on earth. Moses himself was highly educated (cf. Acts 7:22), probably in the famed Heliopolis with its emphasis on the sun god Ra. To the world, all those things are *virtuous*, but Moses, who also knew Hebrew history and language from his mother, recognized their *vanity*. While the world would say, "Moses, you sacrificed *everything* for *nothing*," God says, "Moses, you sacrificed *nothing* for *everything*." Likewise, we will never know true wisdom if we depend upon the virtues of the world.

Second, Moses rejected the world's *vileness* when he chose **rather to suffer affliction with the people of God, than to enjoy the pleasures of sin for a season** (v. 25). Ancient Egyptian culture is fascinating in many ways. Its hieroglyphic writing, which dates from about 3000 BC and is composed of hundreds of symbols, baffled linguists for centuries and was deciphered only with the discovery of the Rosetta Stone (c.196 BC) in the 19th-century. Its literary works included funerary texts, letters, hymns, and poems. *The Story of Sinuhe*, written in Middle Egyptian, is considered a classic, its anonymous author being described as the "Egyptian Shakespeare." Socially, the Egyptians were immaculate in their hygiene and appearance, and they enjoyed leisure activities of games and music. Egyptian architecture, of course, is legendary and has mesmerized engineers for centuries.

Despite those fascinations, however, the Egyptians were also pagans to their core. Among Egypt's very complex polytheistic system, there was Isis, the mother goddess of health, marriage, and wisdom, whose worship later spread throughout the Greco-Roman world. Also preeminent were the sun god Ra and the creator god Amun, but there were many more, including the worship of individual animals that were believed to be manifestations of particular deities.

But Moses chose not the power, prestige, and pleasure of Egypt, but rather the abuse, attacks, and affliction his people suffered. That was the wise choice. Why? Because **the pleasures of sin** are only for **a season**; they're only temporary.

Scriptures for Study: What do these verses tell us about pleasure: Luke 12:19–20; James 5:5?

OCTOBER 25

Moses: The Perception of Faith (4)

By faith Moses . . . (Heb. 11:23–29)
. . . And he said, here am I. (Ex. 3:4b)

CONCLUDING our mediations on Moses' faith, not only did he reject the world's virtues and vileness, but he did likewise in two other ways.

Third, he rejected the world's *values*: **Esteeming the reproach of Christ greater riches than the treasures in Egypt: for he had respect unto the recompence of the reward** (v. 26). One of the marvels of ancient Egypt not mentioned yesterday was its wealth. It possessed, in fact, incalculable agricultural and mineral wealth. The rich fertile soil that resulted from annual flooding of the Nile River and the use of irrigation ditches and canals to water crops yielded immeasurable harvests. Egypt was also rich in building and decorative stone, copper and lead ores, gold, and semiprecious stones.

Oh, but what a difference there is between **treasures** and **riches**! While treasures will tarnish, riches will remain. Paul wrote of "the riches of [God's] grace" (Eph. 1:7). Both there and in our text **riches** is *ploutos* (4149, also wealth, goods). While the ancient Greek philosopher Plato (c. 427–347 BC) was a pagan, he had the right idea when he distinguished "material riches from true riches, which consist of wisdom, virtue, and culture."[440] True **riches** are not in *material* things but in *spiritual* things. As Moses recognized, who needs treasure when he has riches?

Fourth, Moses rejected the world's *vengeance*: **By faith he forsook Egypt, not fearing the wrath of the king** (v. 27). Moses didn't *sprint* out of Egypt in *fear*, rather he *strolled* out in *faith*. The vengeance of the king caused no concern in Moses whatsoever. Why? Because his courage flowed from his faith in what God said. Neither should we fear what the world can do to us.

Third, then, is the *result*. Following the same pattern, Moses not only regarded God's Word and rejected the world, he (and Israel) also received God's wealth.

(1) He received *redemption*. It was through faith that Moses **kept the Passover** (v. 28; cf. Ex. 11:5, Mar. 18). Likewise, the first and greatest aspect of our spiritual wealth is the redemption we have in Christ (Eph. 1:7).

(2) Moses received *renewal*. Verse 29 declares, **By faith they passed through the Red sea as by dry land**. What a renewing and revitalizing experience! Here was new life from certain death. God likewise wants our "inward man [to be] renewed day by day" (2 Cor. 4:16). "Renewed" is *anakainoō* (341), "to make new," not in the sense of moral change but that "each day [we are] . . . strengthened and lifted above all external pressures" by the Holy Spirit.[441]

(3) Moses received *riches*. This reiterates what we noted earlier in verse 26. Oh, let us read Ephesians 1 often and revel in that glorious list of the spiritual riches we have in Christ (cf. Matt. 6:18–21).

Scriptures for Study: How do the following verses encourage us: Job 21:13; Psalm 37:7, 9; Matthew 10:28; 2 Corinthians 5:7–8; James 5:1–3?

OCTOBER 26

Joshua: The Prize-Winning of Faith (1)

By faith the walls of Jericho fell down, after they were compassed about seven days. (Heb. 11:30)

TWO short verses in Hebrews 11 briefly mention two historical incidents but amazingly link the two seemingly contradictory champions involved: one a godly leader of Israel but the other a pagan harlot. From both, however, we learn the same lesson: the prize-winning of faith, that victory comes only when we obey the Word of God.

The book of Joshua is a record of the conquest of the land of Canaan and its later division among the tribes of Israel. The land was at that time inhabited by the Canaanites, a collection of various wicked and pagan peoples who were the descendents of Ham's son Canaan. God commanded His people to go in and simply take what He had given them. How significant it is that they are battling the Arab nations to this day! We look first, then, at Joshua.

First, the *requirement*: "The LORD said unto Joshua, See, I have given into thine hand Jericho, and the king thereof, and the mighty men of valour" (Josh. 6:2). Jericho ("Place of Fragrance") is the oldest city in the world; according to most archeologists, it dates to 5000–4000 BC (some even say 8000). At 846 feet below sea level, it is also the lowest city on earth. It was extremely significant in Joshua's day (1500–1400 BC), being the most important city in the Jordan valley (Num. 22:1; Num 34:15), a strategic juncture for caravans traveling east and west, and the strongest fortress in all of Canaan. Behind its massive walls, and with access to fresh water and storehouses of food, the citizens could rest with confidence.

With that backdrop, God told Joshua He would simply give this city into his hands—it was actually already his, in fact ("have given"). This was the fulfillment of God's promise to Abraham that He would give him and his descendants everything south to north from the Nile River in Egypt to Lebanon and everything west to east from the Mediterranean Sea to the Euphrates River (Gen. 15:18; Josh. 1:4). It was not the result of military might, brilliant strategy, or diplomatic negotiation. It came by God's power alone. All He demanded from His people at Jericho was a few symbolic acts and faith in His promise of the result.

As we have noted several times, but what still bears constant repetition, this is faith: the *supreme confidence* in what God says and *settled conviction* that it will come to pass. "How weak soever the believer finds himself, and how powerful soever he perceives his enemy to be," wrote Puritan David Dickson, "it is all one to him, he hath no more to do but to put faith on work, and to wait till God works."[442] That is what faith *pronounces*, and it is, as we will see in Joshua, what the godly believer *practices*.

Scriptures for Study: How do the following verses encourage us: 1 Corinthians 2:5; 2 Corinthians 10:3–5?

OCTOBER 27

Joshua: The Prize-Winning of Faith (2)

By faith the walls of Jericho fell down, after they were compassed about seven days. (Heb. 11:30)

WE have mentioned various Puritans several times on this magnificent topic of faith, for they understood it well. "Faith is the oil that feeds the lamp of hope," wrote Thomas Watson. He then added, "Faith and hope are two turtle-dove graces; take away one, and the other languishes."[443] Joshua understood that principle long before Watson did.

Second, the *response*. As we read the entire account (Josh. 6:1–20), we observe at least three aspects of Joshua's response.

(1) His *reasoning*. Joshua was a military man, and any military man, regardless of his rank, would look at this proposed "strategy" in horrified disbelief. It is easy to conceive that someone was thinking, "Let me get this straight. This is a double wall 30 feet high. The outer wall is six feet thick, the inner wall is 12 feet thick, there's a rubble-filled space between them of about 15 feet, they are linked together on top by houses, and all we're going to do is march around them and they will fall down. Brilliant!"

(2) His *realization*. While the human reasoning noted above would be the natural reaction, there is no suggestion whatsoever that anyone reacted that way. There is not the slightest hint of doubt, hesitation, or objection. As verses 6 and 7 indicate, Joshua obeyed God immediately and without question. This underscores a critical principle for us: nothing could be wiser than just doing what God says, regardless of how strange it might seem from the human perspective.

(3) His *recognition*. We would submit that there is a deeper meaning behind God's purpose in Jericho: the destruction of man's pride on both sides of the conflict. Not only was the pride of the people in Jericho shattered right along with their walls, but any pride the Israelites might have had in the victory was also crushed because their "battle" was only symbolic—the victory belonged to God alone. Likewise, let us *never* take *any* credit or glory for any work we do for God. It is not we who accomplish the work, rather it is God working through us.

Third, the *result* of Joshua's faith, of course, was overwhelming victory. While critics have scoffed at the possibility of marching around a city seven times in one day, Jericho was comparatively small, having a circumference of 656 yards and dimensions of 246 by 87 yards.[444] Also, since the city sits on a hill, the wall fell outward, dragging the inner wall and houses with it, the rubble thinning out as it went down the slope, thus enabling the Israelites to maneuver their way easily into the city.

Oh, the victory that is ours if we do things according to God's Word!

Scriptures for Study: Read the entire account of the battle at Jericho in Joshua 6. What observations can you make, and what strikes you the most profoundly?

OCTOBER 28

Rahab: The Prize-Winning of Faith

By faith the harlot Rahab perished not with them that believed not, when she had received the spies with peace. (Heb. 11:31)

OF all the Champions of Faith listed in Hebrews 11, the most unlikely, of course, was a pagan prostitute. The Amorites, in fact, were notoriously wicked. Rahab's house was on the wall (Josh. 2:15), probably near the front gate, a perfect spot to carry on her business. As noted yesterday, however, she was **by faith** part of the great victory at Jericho.

First, the *requirement*. The only thing God required of Rahab, or anyone else in Jericho for that matter, was belief. Everyone had heard of the exploits of the Israelites (Josh. 2:9–11). Their hearts, in fact, "did melt" in terror. Used literally, the Hebrew (*māsas*, 4549H) means to melt, dissolve, or breaking up and turning to water. Figuratively, then, it refers to "persons wasting away in sickness (Is. 10:18), of mountains breaking down (Isa. 34:3; Mic. 1:4), [or] persons' hearts 'melting,' losing courage," as it does here.[445] But *fear* is not *faith*. The same thing that was true then is still true today: men can be confronted with the truth, complete with ample evidence, and still reject it. Jesus did uncounted thousands of miracles, but there were only a few hundred people who believed in Him.

Second, the *response*. Rahab alone believed. Her confession of faith appears in Joshua 2:11: "the LORD your God, he is God in heaven above, and in earth beneath." A more amazing confession from a pagan is hard to imagine! Not only did she use the name "God"—this is *'Elōhiym* (430H), the Strong One who is to be feared and revered because of who He is (Jan. 14)—but more significantly she used "LORD." As we have seen before (Jan. 21), this is *Yāhweh* (3068H), God's personal "covenant name," which He used when making covenants and giving promises to His people. Rahab went on to confess God as sovereign Ruler of heaven and earth, thereby repudiating pagan myth and superstition.

The ultimate proof of Rahab's faith was her hiding the two spies, an act that would have without doubt brought death if she had been caught. Once again, true faith always results in an action. Much has been made of Rahab's lying to protect the two spies (vv. 4–5), but to do so misses the whole point of the story. No, God certainly did not bless her *lie*, rather He blessed her *faith*. That is the focus!

Third, the *result*. There are really two results of Rahab's faith. The first, of course, is that she and her family were miraculously *spared* the utter destruction of the city and its inhabitants (Josh. 6:21–23). Far more significant, however, Rahab was *honored*. Matthew 1:5 declares that she became an ancestor of Christ. She married Salmon, gave birth to Boaz, who then married Ruth, David's grandmother. Oh, what a result of simple faith in what God said!

Scriptures for Study: Read the entire account of Rahab in Joshua 2. What observations can you make, and what strikes you the most profoundly?

OCTOBER 29

Gideon: The Proclamation of Faith (1)

And what shall I more say? for the time would fail me to tell of Gedeon . . . (Heb. 11:32a)

WITH each subsequent example of faith in Hebrews 11, we have learned a little bit more about this key truth of Scripture. While the writer wanted to go on with his list, he admits that there would be no end to it. So, as a substitute, it is as if he is saying, "Time is too short for details, so let me just list a few more champions and leave the details to your own memory." These remaining examples demonstrate the *proclamation* of faith, that is, they were witnesses who testified of God with their lives. While we will look at verses 33–40 collectively, let us take the time to examine the seven examples in verse 32 in more detail. We look first at a fellow named Gideon (Judg. 6:11—7:25).

First, the *requirement*. To see the full significance here, it is important to introduce this man. While he became the fifth judge of Israel and eventually a "mighty man of valour" (6:12), he did not start out a champion. On the contrary, when we first meet him, he is a pathetic picture of unbelief.

The setting was that once again "the children of Israel did evil in the sight of the LORD: and the LORD delivered them into the hand of Midian seven years" (Judg. 6:1). The Midianites had so thoroughly prevailed that the people were driven into the hills to hide in ravines and caves. The foe had descended like a plague of locusts and devoured everything (vv. 3–5). So, as they usually did, "the children of Israel cried unto the LORD" (v. 6).

Our first glimpse of Gideon finds him "thresh[ing] wheat by [or in] the winepress, to hide it from the Midianites" (v. 11). The threshing floor was a level, hard-beaten plot in an open place near the field. The wine press consisted of two receptacles: an upper one where the grapes were trodden, and a lower that one received the juice. God called *this* man to lead? But it was worse than that!

Second, the *response*. Notice here the appalling "vocabulary of unbelief" (vv. 13, 15, 17).[446] We first hear Gideon gasp, "Oh my Lord," which demonstrates the *surprise* of unbelief. Why did he not expect God's deliverance? Next, "If the Lord be with us," expresses the *uncertainty* of unbelief. Why would he doubt? Then, "Why then is all this befallen us? and where be all his miracles which our fathers told us of"? epitomizes the *questioning* of unbelief. He knew that sin was the reason for the calamity. Why expect miracles when the people had turned to other gods? Next, "But now the LORD hath forsaken us" is the *complaint* of unbelief. And why would He not in view of their abject apostasy? Then comes another "oh," but a different one: "Oh my Lord, wherewith shall I save Israel?" which shows the *false humility* of unbelief. Gideon was going to accomplish nothing; the battle was God's. Finally, "show me a sign" is the *sign-seeking* of unbelief. He should have walked by faith not by sight. Let us expunge the vocabulary of unbelief!

Scriptures for Study: Read Judges 6, the first half of the account of Gideon. What observations can you make, and what strikes you the most profoundly?

OCTOBER 30

Gideon: The Proclamation of Faith (2)

And what shall I more say? for the time would fail me to tell of Gedeon . . . (Heb. 11:32a)

As we observed yesterday, Gideon's "vocabulary of unbelief" was tragic and disturbing. Continuing our thoughts on his response, what is the consequence of such unbelief? Mark it down: faith *energizes* while unbelief *paralyzes*. Short of having his spinal cord severed, Gideon could not have been more paralyzed. Unbelief hinders God's work in us and through us.

Further, what is the cause of such unbelief? It is simply this: looking at circumstances instead of looking at God. As someone has wittily put it, ten of the 12 spies Moses sent into Canaan were impressed by four "Gs"—they saw grapes, great cities, and giants, which made them feel like grasshoppers—but they forgot about the greatest "G" of all—*God*. Oh, how we need to keep our eyes *on Him*, not on what is going on *around us*.

Thankfully, after all his terror, turmoil, and tantrums, Gideon finally answered God's call (vv. 18–24), proclaiming his faith in the process. The proof of that, in fact, was even more striking than his prior apprehensions. First, he built an altar there unto the LORD, and called it Jehovahshalom" (v. 24), that is, "*Yāhweh* (is) Peace." Indeed, the peace of God wipes away fear.

Far more significantly, however, Gideon did something else that was an even more convincing proof of his faith: he tore down the altar to the pagan fertility god Baal, including the goddess Asherah ("grove" is *'ašērāh* [842H], the consort of Baal; cf. Judg. 3:7; 1 Kings 18:19; 2 Kings 23:4), that existed in his family's home (Judg. 6:24–30). This was a capital crime, punishable by death, so Gideon risked his life in doing this. While building the altar was evidence of his inward *surrender*, tearing down that idol was the first proof of his outward *service*. We all build idols because we're idolaters by nature, but the true child of God tears them down.

Third, the *result*. Verse 34 tells us that "the Spirit of the LORD came upon Gideon." That is an extraordinary statement. "Came upon" is *labaš* (3847H), which, when used literally, simply means "to clothe or put on clothing." Here, however, the figurative idea can be rendered, "The spirit of the Lord clothed itself [was clothed] with Gideon." In other words, "the Spirit of the Lord incarnated Himself in Gideon and thus empowered him from within."[447]

That explains how a man who was once *cowering* in *fear* in a winepress is now *conquering* in *faith* as he leads his band of brothers. While he started with 32,000 men, this was narrowed to 10,000 and finally to 300 to go against 135,000 Midianites. In modern military terms, this was a small battalion facing a field army, a thoroughly hopeless mismatch. To even consider such a thing, one would have to be either desperate or just insane. But it is God alone who gives victory to the remnant over the multitude. How? *By faith*!

Scriptures for Study: Read the rest of the account of Gideon in Judges 7–8. What observations can you make, and what strikes you the most profoundly?

OCTOBER 31

Remembering Reformation Day
... The just shall live by faith. (Rom. 1:17)

WE interrupt our "faith studies" to encourage a day of remembrance. It was on October 31, 1517 that Martin Luther nailed his 95 Theses on the church door in Wittenberg, an act that launched the Protestant Reformation. Luther had been through some enormous struggles, finally coming to understand that salvation is by grace alone through faith alone—not by merit, works, or any other human effort (Rom. 1:17; Eph. 2:8–9; etc.). He had also come to realize that *Scripture alone* was to be our sole authority.

It was in April 1521 that Luther was summoned to the final showdown at the Diet (assembly) in the city of Worms. The Roman Church requested that Emperor Charles V, himself a Roman Catholic, deal with the case of Luther, which he agreed to do. On that fateful day, the crowd that gathered was enormous, so huge, in fact, that it was difficult for Luther and his supporters to even reach the conference hall. Besides the Emperor, there were 206 high ranking officials, including dukes, archbishops, bishops, ambassadors, and papal nuncios. The diet began on April 17 with the brilliant Johann von Eck serving as the presiding officer. He asked Luther pointedly if he was the author of the numerous writings that had been placed on a table in the conference hall and then asked if he was willing to retract the doctrines in them that contradicted the accepted doctrines of the Church. Luther admitted he was the author but asked for some time for reflection before answering the other charge. After all, Luther knew that his answer might very well cost him his life, and we can only imagine the pressure he felt. After a night of much prayer, Luther was asked again in the crowded hall if he was willing to retract his teachings. To this he replied the now famous words:

"Unless I am convinced by Scripture and plain reason—I do not accept the authority of popes and councils, for they have contradicted each other—my conscience is captive to the Word of God. I cannot and I will not recant anything, for to go against conscience is neither right nor safe. Here I stand; I cannot do otherwise. God help me. Amen."

As in Luther's day, there is much in the Church today that not only is not *based* on Scripture, but much of which even *contradicts* Scripture. In my humble view, in fact, the key to Luther's statement is that to go against a conscience that is "captive to the Word of God . . . is *neither right nor safe*," for that is precisely what is happening today. The Church is simply not captive to Scripture, not driven by God's Word *alone*.[448]

So, let us honestly reflect: Isn't all this a little bit more worthy of consideration and celebration than the other significance of October 31? Which one is on your mind today?

Scriptures for Study: What do the following verses tell us to remember: Psalm 77:11; Luke 17:32; Hebrews 13:7; Revelation 2:5?

NOVEMBER 1

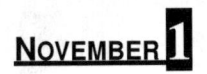

Barak: The Proclamation of Faith

... for the time would fail me to tell of ... Barak ... (Heb. 11:32b)

JUDGES chapter 4 opens with the familiar refrain, "And the children of Israel again did evil in the sight of the LORD." This time God appointed a woman as a judge, a very unique and special case, indeed. Because male leadership was always the norm, it is obvious that there was not a single man worthy of leading in this situation. While some insist that Deborah's case justifies women in leadership today, this is inarguably incorrect. Not a single woman ever served as a priest, was an OT author, or had an ongoing proclamation or teaching ministry. The NT is clearer still; there is *spiritual equality* between men and women (Gal. 3:28), but there are also *differing roles* (e.g. 1 Tim. 2:12; 3:1–7; etc).[449] Deborah's role, then, was only in the judicial sense, for she declined to lead the military campaign against the Canaanites, deferring instead to the man who is now our focus: Barak, who did proclaim his faith but not without some trepidation.

First, the *requirement*. God's requirement of Barak came by way of Deborah. He was to take 10,000 men and set a trap for Sisera's troops near Mount Tabor, where the Lord would give the victory near the Kishon River. Like Joshua at Jericho, the victory was assured—it was already won, in fact. All Barak and his men really had to do was just show up.

Second, the *response*. Sadly, instead of acting like Joshua, Barak at first reflected the same lack of faith that Gideon had. Instead of immediately obeying and getting on with the job, he negotiated. He wanted some kind of security, so he demanded that Deborah, God's representative, go with him (4:7).

Now, from a purely human perspective, Barak's fear was understandable. While the superiority of the enemy in the Gideon incident was one of numbers, the superiority here was primarily one of weaponry. Sisera's forces consisted of 900 chariots. A chariot was a mobile firing platform. Firepower could be quickly rushed wherever it was needed. The Canaanite version had a three-man crew, one driver and two weapons men. Even more significant was the chariot's shock value; like modern tanks, it could be used as a spearhead to cut a swathe through the ranks of the enemy. Even worse, these chariots were made of iron, which was far superior to the bronze weapons of the Israelites.

But mark it down: *fear* and *faith* are both a choice. We must decide which one we will allow to rule. Making *demands* of God is the same as *denying* Him. The only weapon we need is God's Word (cf. Eph. 6:17).

Third, the *result*. Sisera, of course, relied upon his chariots, but he didn't count on God sending torrential rain during the June–September dry season and the resulting flooding of the Kishon River that turned the area into a quagmire. Oh, if we would just trust God's Word!

Scriptures for Study: Read the entire account in Judges 4:1—5:31. What observations can you make, and what strikes you the most profoundly?

NOVEMBER 2

Samson: The Proclamation of Faith

... for the time would fail me to tell of ... Samson ... (Heb. 11:32c)

WE come to one of the most enigmatic characters in Scripture. Samson was a man *set apart* for God from birth but was never truly *submitted* until his death. Here was a man who was prideful from the beginning but humbled like no other at the end. And, oh, how *mighty* he was with men, but what a *weakling* with women!

First, the *requirement*. Israel had been in subjugation to the Philistines for 40 years. Sadly, however, there is no indication that they even once cried out to God for deliverance. They had grown complacent, content, and even comfortable under pagan rule; they actually resented Samson upsetting the *status quo* between them and the Philistines. So God had to intervene and deliver them from themselves. Through his parents, God said Samson would deliver His people but also demanded that he be set apart according to the Nazarite vow—he was never to drink wine, touch a dead body, or cut his hair.

Second, the *response*. We can only imagine Samson's wild youth, for when we start reading about him, we see him violate two of the three requirements: he got drunk and touched a lion's carcass. We also see his flawed character: he was proud and arrogant, disrespected his parents by marrying a Philistine woman against their counsel, had no control over his tongue, lied frequently, and lost his temper. And then, of course, there was that whole business with Delilah!

This begs the question: how on earth could God use a fellow like Samson and include him in a list of the faithful? But before we get too harsh in our criticism, each of us should first ask: "Do I not also do such things, or at least other things, that violate God's clear principles about commitment, character, and conduct?"

In spite of much wasted opportunity, we are drawn to Samson's prayer at the end, his proclamation of faith: "O Lord GOD, remember me, I pray thee, and strengthen me, I pray thee, only this once, O God, that I may be at once avenged of the Philistines for my two eyes." Here we note three of God's greatest names: "Lord" is *Aḏōnāy* (136H), which speaks of His dominion, possession, and sovereignty; "GOD" is *Yāhweh* (3068H; Jan. 21), His "covenant name"; and "God" is *'Elōhiym* (430H), the Strong One who is to be feared and revered because of who He is. *Finally*, a prayer of repentance and trust pours from Samson's lips.

Third, the *result*. There was, predictably, a negative result. In keeping with 1 John 2:15–16, as a result of the lust of the flesh, Samson lost his strength, as the result of his lust of the eyes, he was blinded, and as a result of the pride of life, he was the most humiliated of slaves. But there was also the positive: he died for his God, bringing judgment upon as many as 3,000 Philistines. Samson serves as a warning for each of us to be one of the *faithful*, not one of the *failures*.

Scriptures for Study: Read Samson's full story in Judges 13–16. What observations can you make, and what strikes you the most profoundly?

NOVEMBER 3

Jephthah: The Proclamation of Faith

... for the time would fail me to tell of ... Jephthah ... (Heb. 11:32d)

THE 1976 film *Rocky* is considered by many to be a contemporary classic. The story is certainly a classic one: a rags-to-riches tale of an uneducated but kind-hearted working class club boxer who gets a shot at the world heavyweight championship. Well, the next champion in our Hebrews 11 list is that kind of story, although the ending is not a "happily-ever-after" one.

First, the *requirement*. We read Jephthah's story in Judges 11–12. Born of his father Gilead and a harlot, he was later banished from his home because of that illegitimacy. With no inheritance, then, he went into Tob, a district of Syria, where he led a band of raiders who fought against the Ammonites (descendents of Lot), who had oppressed the Israelites for 18 years because of their idolatry. Gaining fame from this, Israel's leaders approached him to lead all their forces against Ammon, which was, of course, God's will.

Second, the *response*. Jephthah's reply was a striking proclamation of faith: "If ye bring me home again to fight against the children of Ammon, and the LORD deliver them before me, shall I be your head?" (v. 9). Not only did he use this opportunity to be installed as Israel's God-appointed leader, but he unequivocally recognized "the LORD" (*Yāhweh* (3068H; Jan. 21) as the One who would alone give victory. While there have been many opportunists who entered "ministry" for their own ends, Jephthah was a true man of faith who wanted to serve God and give Him the glory.

Not all was positive, however. Jephthah did something else that was abundantly foolish. He made a vow to the Lord that if He would give the victory over the Ammonites, then Jephthah would sacrifice to the Lord the first thing that came out of his house when he returned home (vv. 31–32). It was common in that day to make vows to one's god, but making bargains with the True and Living God is not only unnecessary but also unwise.

Third, the *result*. God did, indeed, give the victory, but when Jephthah's only child, a daughter, was the first person to come out of the house upon his return, the folly of his vow hit with full force. This incident has generated debate. Some have tried to soften it to mean a "living sacrifice" in perpetual virginity, but the evidence leans heavily toward the meaning of a literal "burnt offering."

Whichever view one holds, however, the lesson to be learned here remains unchanged. We must simply believe God, and not make bargains with Him. Jephthah was seriously tainted by his culture and fell back upon superstition and human wisdom. We must constantly guard against the ever-present tendency to do the same. Sadly, we have secularized worship, pragmatized ministry, and humanized evangelism. Let us be *marked* by the *Word* not *marred* by the *world*.

Scriptures for Study: Read Jephthah's full story in Judges 11–12. What observations can you make, and what strikes you the most profoundly?

NOVEMBER 4

David: The Proclamation of Faith

... for the time would fail me to tell of ... David ... (Heb. 11:32e)

AS Mathew Henry observed of David, "Few ever met with greater trials, and few ever discovered a more lively faith." How true! The most striking description of David, though, was that he was a man after God's own heart (1 Sam. 13:14; Acts 13:22). What does that mean? We would submit two features. In his *doctrine*, David desired God's will in all things. Unlike Saul, he paid scrupulous attention to God's Word and never tried to alter it to suit himself or the situation. In his *duty*, David mimicked God as a shepherd (Pss. 23; cf. 78:72), again unlike Saul, who was never anything but a selfish king.

First, then, we see the *requirement*. David was actually anointed three times: the first, performed by Samuel, symbolized God's choosing and ordaining him (1 Sam. 16:3); the second recognized David as king of Judah (2 Sam. 2:4–7); and the third recognized him as king over all Israel, thereby uniting all 12 tribes (5:3). As with all His other "champions," God simply required that David believe and obey.

Second, the *response*. As one reads David's story, it becomes apparent that the idea of doubting God or lacking faith never once even occurred to him. Pivotal, of course, was his encounter with Goliath. Sadly, David's victory here is often allegorized into meaning that we can "defeat all the giants" that come into our lives, which misses the point entirely. The key truth was David's motive of God's glory. In one of the greatest statements in Scripture, he bravely (and with incredulous disgust!) said: "who is this uncircumcised Philistine, that he should defy the armies of the living God?" (1 Sam. 17:26). While the Israelites preferred *fear*, David proclaimed *faith*. Both are a willful choice. Oh, that we would live by this motive!

David went on, in fact, to proclaim his faith repeatedly. By faith, he endured Saul's relentless attacks, and instead of raising his hand against "the Lord's anointed" (1 Sam. 24:6), he waited on God to place him on the throne. By faith, he subdued God's enemies and expanded the kingdom in every direction (2 Sam. 8). By faith, he believed God's covenant with him (2 Sam. 7; cf. 23:5), so much so that he drew up blueprints for the temple and began stockpiling materials for it (1 Chron. 28:11–19; 29:1–5) even though he would never actually see it built.

Third, the *result*. No less than four times we read that the Lord was "with" David (1 Sam. 16:18; 18:12, 14, 28). The Hebrew here (*'im*, 5973H) indicates "something done together or in common with," including the concepts of "fellowship, companionship, and common experiences."[450] David did, indeed, have something in common with God and a companionship that was truly unique. Why? Because he believed God. Was David perfect? Certainly not. His failures with Bathsheba and Uriah are notorious, but those make him even more of an example for us. We will also fail in various ways, but true faith will endure and be blessed.

Scriptures for Study: Read the full story of David and Goliath in 1 Samuel 17. What observations can you make, and what strikes you the most profoundly?

NOVEMBER 5

Samuel: The Proclamation of Faith

... for the time would fail me to tell of ... Samuel ... (Heb. 11:32f)

THE next proclaimer of faith in our list is Samuel, who was both the last judge and the first prophet of Israel. The job of a prophet, in fact, was to do just that: proclaim God's Word to those who didn't want to hear it. It is extremely significant that Samuel and the prophets are listed here among warriors. A prophet was, indeed, one who waged war; while it was not war against an outward enemy, it was war against the greater inward foe of rebellion.

First, the *requirement*. Even though Samuel's parents devoted him to the Lord before he was born, and while he had lived in the Temple since he was weaned (which usually occurred at three years of age), God still had to make His requirement known to the lad personally. He did precisely that when the boy was only some 12 years old: "the Lord called Samuel" (1 Sam. 3:4), and, oh, what a task He had for him to do! God's Word was rare in those days, and His revelation was not widely known (v. 1). This was probably because there was no one who was willing to make himself wholeheartedly available. But there was now one who was ready to serve completely and tell people what they needed to hear.

Second, the *response*: "Here am I" (vv. 4, 6, 8). What an astounding proclamation of faith coming from one so young! It demonstrates how alert and attentive Samuel was. He thought Eli was calling him, however, so in verse 10 "the LORD came, and stood, and called as at other times, Samuel, Samuel," to which "Samuel answered, Speak; for thy servant heareth."

Oh, how God wants this response from us all! "Heareth" is *sāma'* (8085H), "to hear with the ear" but with several shades of meaning that denote *effective* hearing, that is, truly *listening*. Ideas included in this word are paying attention, regarding, and obeying. It appears repeatedly to indicate obedience to God. We are told to "hear the word of the LORD" (e.g., Isa. 66:5; Jer. 22:29), "hear [His] voice" (Isa. 28:23), "[hearken] unto counsel" (Prov. 12:15), and obey His law and "commandments" (Isa. 42:24; Neh. 9:16). Take a moment to read Deuteronomy 6:4–9. As we have noted before (May 3), these verses comprise the "Shema," the basic confession of faith of Judaism recited both morning and evening. As with dozens of other illustrations, Samuel proves that true faith always indicates obedience.

Third, the *result* is also striking: "Samuel grew, and the LORD was with him, and did let none of his words fall to the ground [i.e., go unfulfilled]. And all Israel ... knew that Samuel was established to be a prophet of the LORD" (1 Sam. 3:19–20). Unlike today's self-appointed (and false) prophets, whose predictions are often wrong, a true prophet of God was *always* right (Deut. 18:22). Anyone today whose words do not match the clear teaching of Scripture should be exposed as a false teacher, and sadly, there are many.

Scriptures for Study: Read Samuel's early history in 1 Samuel 2–3. What observations can you make, and what strikes you the most profoundly?

NOVEMBER 6

The Prophets: The Proclamation of Faith

... for the time would fail me to tell of ... the prophets. (Heb. 11:32g)

AS Israel's first prophet, Samuel not only set the precedent, but he also "set the bar high," as the saying goes.

First, the *requirement*. The Greek behind "prophet" (*prophētēs*, 4396) indicates one who, along with proclaiming truth already revealed (implied in Acts 13:1), also speaks immediately of the Holy Spirit, that is, speaking under the direct inspiration of the Holy Spirit.[451] Since our text refers back to OT prophets, however, it is the Hebrew *nāḇiy'* (5030H) that is critical. While there has been debate as to the meaning of the Hebrew noun, it is likely that it comes from the Akkadian root *nabû*, "to call," and therefore refers to one who is called by God to announce His words[452] (e.g., Ex. 7:1–2). A prophet, then, is called by God to act in His place and pass on His words. While Scripture does not record God's call of every prophet, it does record several using *nāḇiy'*, including: Jeremiah (1:5; cf. vv. 1–10), Ezekiel (2:5; cf. vv. 1–4), and Haggai (1:1–3, 12).[453]

Second, the *response*. In each case, God's *call* was answered, His *command* obeyed, and His *communication* proclaimed. Going deeper, we discover that the prophets proclaimed four distinct aspects of God's truth.

(1) The prophets *announced* great doctrines. It is amazing, indeed, that most NT doctrines have their basis in OT theology. From sin, to salvation, to service, the NT is *enfolded* in the OT, while the OT is *unfolded* in the NT. While some theological truths (e.g., the Church) are foreign to the OT, most NT subjects are rooted in the Old, such as: God's nature, creation, man, morality, sin, redemption, justification, sanctification, worship, wisdom, truth, and the list goes on.

(2) The prophets *annunciated* warnings about sin. Reflecting His character as a merciful and gracious God, we never see Him execute judgment without first warning man about sin and rebellion. Over and over again the prophets urged the people to repent of their sin lest God's wrath descend.

(3) The prophets *articulated* comfort. Again reflecting His character, God comforts, encourages, and blesses those who do repent, obey, and follow Him. The final chapters of Isaiah, for example, are filled with such notes of confidence.

(4) The prophets *anticipated* future events. The greatest of these events, of course, was the coming of Messiah (Is. 9:1–7; 53: Jer. 23:5, 6; Micah 5:2; etc.). They also spoke of national and international events, both near (such as returning to the land) and far (such as the Millennial Kingdom).

Third, the *result* of all this was that God used these men to proclaim His truth. While the office of prophet no longer exists (simply because it's not needed), every Christian is to proclaim the truth, especially to those who do not want to hear it.

Scriptures for Study: What were the functions of the prophet in each of the following verses: Isaiah 40:1–2; 58:1; Ezekiel 3:17; 18:30?

NOVEMBER 7

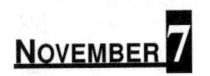

Other Champions: The Proclamation of Faith
Who through faith . . . (Heb. 11:33–40)

WHILE the author has neither time nor space to list as many champions as he would like, he alludes to many others by his descriptive language. Every statement the author made, in fact, would have "rang a bell" in the minds of his readers.

Verse 33 mostly looks back on those in verse 32,[454] but "stopped the mouths of lions" obviously refers to Daniel, as we find a similar expression in Daniel 6:22. "Quenched the violence of fire" without doubt refers to that vivid miracle of Shadrach, Meshach, and Abed-nego in the fiery furnace (Dan. 3:19–28). "Escaped the edge of the sword" points us back to Elijah's escape from Ahab's wrath (1 Kings 19:1–18), as well as Elisha, who thwarted assassination (2 Kings 6). "Out of weakness were made strong" speaks of Hezekiah's miraculous healing and added longevity (2 Kings 20:1–7). "Waxed valiant in fight" and "turned to flight the armies of the aliens" both bring to mind several pictures, such as Gideon (Judg. 7:21) and Barak (4:15), and David once again (1 Sam. 7:51). "Women received their dead raised to life again" refers to two specific cases: the widow of Zarephath, whose child Elijah brought back to life (1 Kings 17), and the Shunamite woman, for whom Elisha did the same (2 Kings 4).

The writer then turns to the extra-biblical record of the Maccabean Age, the 400 years between the testaments. Many were "tortured," which is the Greek *tumpanizō* (English "tympani"), a large drum-like device upon which the victim was stretched and beaten with clubs; such did "not [accept] deliverance" by recanting their faith. "Others had trial of cruel mockings and scourgings, yea, moreover of bonds and imprisonment": Hanani was imprisoned by Asa (2 Chron. 16:7–10), Micaiah was imprisoned by Ahab (1 Kings 22:13–28), Jeremiah was imprisoned and put in stocks by Pashur (Jer. 20:1–3) and was beaten and imprisoned again by Zedekiah (37:1–16). Still others were "stoned," such as Zechariah (2 Chron. 24:20–22) and Jeremiah according to Jewish tradition, as well as "sawn asunder," as tradition also says about Isaiah by the order of Manasseh.

The writer then seems quickly to add others who "were tempted, were slain with the sword: they wandered about in sheepskins and goatskins; being destitute, afflicted, tormented; (Of whom the world was not worthy:) they wandered in deserts, and in mountains, and in dens and caves of the earth."

What did they all have in common? They all "obtained a good report through faith" even though they "received not the promise" in this life (v. 39). "Good report" is *martureō* (3140; Apr. 21), which speaks of a witness giving solemn testimony of what he knows and offering evidence. All these proclaimed the Truth by unwavering faith, and we must do the same.

Scriptures for Study: Who is your favorite Champion of Faith? Why? What biblical reason(s) can you cite?

NOVEMBER 8

The Perfect Pattern of Faith (1)
... Looking unto Jesus ... (Heb. 12:1–2)

NO study of Hebrews 11 would be complete without a look at the first two verses of chapter 12. This is true, of course, because of the word **wherefore** (i.e., "therefore"), which introduces the final conclusion to all that has been said about faith. Some insist that the thrust of these verses is the **race** that we now **run** in light of the preceding examples of faith. While that is certainly in view as an application, that is not the main thrust. The primary focus is our **looking unto Jesus** as not only the source and object of faith, but also the Perfect Pattern of Faith. Three principles flow from these two verses.

First, the *challenge*, which is two-fold. (1) Before any runner can successfully, or even efficiently, run a race, he must first **lay aside every weight**. **Weight** is *ogkos* (3591), which appears only here in the NT and refers to a mass, bulk, burden, or impediment. While this obviously refers to such obstacles as pride, worldliness, anger, lust, and so forth, it also refers to things that are not necessarily evil, but in some way still hinder us. There is no rule, for example, that prevents a runner from wearing lead weights on his ankles when running the 100-yard dash, but he would obviously never consider doing so. That is the first challenge to us. A weight is something that hinders our progress, diverts our attention, takes our mind off the Lord and His Word, dampens our enthusiasm for spiritual things, or takes us away from the right priorities.

(2) Even more striking, the next phrase tells us we must also lay aside **the sin which doth so easily beset us**. This obviously does not refer again to "weights"—that would be redundant. Nor does it speak of sin in general. The Greek construction refers to *one specific sin*. This is clear because of the definite article (**the**) and the singular noun **sin**. So which sin is the most entangling one? Chapter 11 provides the answer. The whole chapter defines, describes, and details the principle of *faith*, so the most entrapping sin of all is *unbelief*. When we lack faith, fail to lean upon God's promises, or doubt His Word, such unbelief entangles our feet, trips us up, and we fall in defeat.

It is also important to understand the phrase **we also are compassed about with so great a cloud of witnesses**. Some interpret this to mean that the "champions" of chapter 11 are spectators who are watching and encouraging us as we **run** our **race**. Some go so far to say that our loved ones in heaven are also watching us with interest. Scripture, however, nowhere supports such an idea. **Witnesses** is again *martus* (3144; May 9, Sept. 27), a legal term for one who gave solemn testimony and evidence in court. No, these are not spectators of *our* race, rather "former contestants" in *the* race. Sadly then, as we've seen, even some of those were guilty of weights and unbelief. We must, therefore, be ever vigilant.

Scriptures for Study: What do the following verses add to our study: 1 Timothy 6:10; 2 Timothy 2:4; 1 Peter 2:1; 4:2?

NOVEMBER 9

The Perfect Pattern of Faith (2)

... Looking unto Jesus ... (Heb. 12:1–2)

EACH of those mentioned in Hebrews 11 displayed some single aspect of the life of faith," A. W. Pink observed, "but in the Saviour they were all combined in their consummate excellence. . . . [So] our Lord is to be 'looked to,' as the Perfect Pattern of Faith for us to follow."[455]

Second, the *commitment*: **let us run with patience the race that is set before us**. It is significant that Paul used this metaphor several times (cf. 1 Cor. 9:24–27; Phil. 2:16; 3:14; 2 Tim. 2:5; 4:17), which is one of several reasons many believe Paul was the writer.[456] So why use a footrace as a metaphor for the Christian life? Simply because the Christian life is a life of endurance.

Some preachers look at this metaphor and conclude that if Paul were living today he would probably be an avid sports fan and even follow his favorite teams. We respectfully submit, however, that not only does such an idea run counter to the pride that drives virtually all athletics, but more basic than that, it misses the real point of the metaphor. It's quite possible, in fact, that this **race** metaphor was based, at least in part, upon the legend of Pheidippides, a Greek messenger who ran the 25 miles from Marathon, Greece to Athens in 490 BC to deliver news of a military victory against the Persians in the Battle of Marathon (that was, of course, the basis for the modern marathon event). So strenuous was that run, as the legend goes, that Pheidippides died immediately after delivering the news.

That does, indeed, picture the Christian life. It is not a 100-yard dash or even the longer one-mile run. It is a long, exhausting "marathon" that demands discipline, training, and unwavering commitment. **Race**, in fact, is *agōn* (73; English "agony"), which means "strife, contention, [a] contest for victory."[457] Further, **patience** is *hupomonē* (5281), to remain under, that is, to stay behind, stand one's ground, survive, remain steadfast.

Third, the *comfort*, of course, is found in **looking unto Jesus**. As we have noted before (Mar. 21), **looking** is *aphoraō* (872), which means not just to look upon something with understanding but to look *away* from everything else; we are, therefore, "Looking away unto Jesus." As we have also seen, **author** is *archēgos* (747), which means not only originator and founder, but also leader, chief, and prince. Not only is our Lord the cause of our faith but also the chief example. Further, He is the **finisher** (*teleiōtēs*, 5051), the completer, the perfecter of our faith. Not one of the examples in chapter 11 was perfect: Enoch lived in mediocrity for 60 years, Noah got drunk, Abraham was impatient, Moses disobeyed, Sampson was an utter mess, David committed adultery and even murder, and on it goes. We are not told to imitate a single one of them, rather only to imitate the Perfect Pattern, to **[look] away unto Jesus**.

Scriptures for Study: What do the following verses add to our study: John 17:1–4; Philippians 1:6; Hebrews 2:10; 5:9?

NOVEMBER 10

Add To Your Faith (1)
... add to your faith ... (2 Pet. 1:5–7)

"FAITH is a journey, not a destination,"[458] wrote A. W. Tozer. Faith is not an end in itself. While it is, of course, at the foundation of the Christian life, there is a structure that must then be built upon that groundwork.

This principle is nowhere better stated than in our text. In verse 1, Peter first reminds his readers of their "like precious faith." The words "like precious" translate *isotimos* (2472), which appears only here in the NT and is a compound comprised of *isos* (2470), "equal in quantity or quality," and *timē* (G5092), "held as of a great price." What a grand truth! Every single Christian possesses the exact same priceless gift, the gift of faith (cf. Eph. 2:8–9). Peter goes on in verses 2–4 to further remind them of the wondrous character of this faith: "all things that pertain unto life and godliness . . . exceeding great and precious promises . . . [and] the divine nature."

But Peter does not end the matter there. On the contrary, he then underscores that there is much that follows. In verse 5, he writes, **And beside this**. The Greek here (*kai auto touto*) has been variously translated: "and this same also"; "and for this very reason"; "for this very cause." **Add to your faith**, Peter goes on to write. **Add** is *epichorēgeō* (2023), another compound from *epi* (1909), upon, and *chorēgeō* (5524), to furnish, and so, "to furnish upon, that is, besides, in addition, to supply further, to add more unto."[459] *Chorēgeō*, in fact, is derived from *chorēgos* (English, "chorus"), which originally referred to the chorus leader of the ancient Greek tragedies who supplied everything the group needed. Peter's point is unmistakable. Every true believer is to **[give] all diligence** to fully supply his faith by adding seven specific spiritual characteristics. "Faith ought not to be naked or empty," Calvin observed; "these are its inseparable companions."

First, there is **virtue**. This is *aretē* (703), which was strongly rooted in Greek philosophy. Among the Classical writers, it was a very broad term that spoke of excellence of any kind, such as mental excellence, moral quality, or physical power. Especially to the Stoics it spoke of the highest good of humanity. While Peter uses this word two other times (1:3; 1 Pet. 2:9), the only other NT writer who did so, and him only once, was Paul (Phil. 4:8).[460] Similar to Paul, who tells us that we are to "think" on things that are virtuous, Peter adds that we must **add** moral excellence to our **faith**. The life of faith, then, is not nebulous, and certainly not riotous, rather it is virtuous. It is a life of moral magnificence.

Second, there is **knowledge**. We have encountered this principle many times, for as Peter later writes, "But grow in grace, and in the knowledge of our Lord and Saviour Jesus Christ. To him be glory both now and for ever. Amen" (3:18).

Scriptures for Study: What do the following verses say about knowledge: Ephesians 1:18; 5:17; Philippians 1:9; Colossians 1:9?

NOVEMBER 11

Add To Your Faith (2)

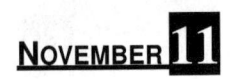

... add to your faith ... (2 Pet. 1:5–7)

PETER "does not just mean that we mechanically add each one of these to the one that has gone before," wrote Martyn Lloyd-Jones of our text; "what he is concerned about is that there shall be a perfect whole, a perfect balance, that the chorus of the play shall be fitted out."[461]

Third, we are to add **temperance** to our faith. The key to the Greek here (*enkrateia*, 1466) is the root *krat*, which denotes power or lordship (e.g., a "plutocrat" is a person whose power derives from his wealth). Thus, Peter speaks of one having dominion over self. It was used of athletes, for example (as Paul does in 1 Cor. 9:25), who must abstain from rich foods and sexual activity so they can focus all their strength on their training. Philo (25 BC–AD 50), the famous Hellenistic Jewish philosopher, regarded this very highly and related it "to food, sex, and the use of the tongue."[462] In contrast to false teachers, who are often easy to identify because of their lack of such traits, true faith generates self-control.

Fourth, we are to add **patience** to our faith. As mentioned yesterday, this is again *hupomonē* (5281), to remain under and steadfast. In Classical Greek, it was "used frequently in military contexts," meaning to dig in and hold ground.[463] That latter idea, in fact, demonstrates that this is not a word of passive endurance, rather one of "energetic resistance to hostile power."[464] It is not just staying where we are but also looking forward to where we are going.

Fifth, we are to add **godliness** to our faith. This word (*eusebeia*, 2150) literally means "well-directed reverence,"[465] and speaks of devoutness and devotion. The pagans used it for their gods—Paul even made reference to this in Athens (Acts 17:23)—but the NT writers sanctified it by applying it to the One True God. It is an inward holy *worship* that is then manifested in an outward holy *walk*.

Sixth, we are to add **brotherly kindness** to our faith. Like the city in Pennsylvania, this is *philadelphia* (5360), which is comprised of *phileō* (5368), "tender affection," and *adelphos* (80), "a brother." As Matthew Poole observed, "This is joined to godliness, to show that it is in vain to pretend to true religion and yet be destitute of brotherly love." That is why Matthew Henry wrote, "A tender affection to all our fellow Christians, children of the same Father, servants of the same Master, members of the same family, travelers to the same country, and heirs of the same inheritance, and therefore are . . . loved with a pure heart fervently."

Seventh and finally, we are to add **charity** to our faith. In addition to the "tender affection of *phileō*, the word here, of course, is *agapē* (26), a willful, sacrificial love for believers and even unbelievers. As we close our study of faith, we see with unmistakable clarity that faith is not *vague*, rather it is *vital*.

Scriptures for Study: What do the following verses say about these characteristics: Romans 12:10; 1 Timothy 4:7–8; James 1:3–4; 1 Corinthians 13:1–8.

NOVEMBER 12

The Paradox of Parables

Therefore speak I to them in parables: because they seeing see not; and hearing they hear not, neither do they understand. (Matt. 13:13)

WHO doesn't like a good story? From the characters, to the setting, to the plot, to the conflict, and finally to the resolution, we all are captivated by the unfolding of a good yarn. A very special kind of story, however, is the parable. While parables appear in the OT (e.g., 2 Sam. 12:1–4), our Lord was certainly the Master of it. As has been observed, in fact, about one-third of Jesus' teaching was couched in parables.

Parables transliterates *parabolē* (3850), which literally means a placing side by side and, therefore, a comparison or similarity, an analogy. In other words, it is "a short story under which something else is figured or in which the fictitious is used to represent and illustrate the real."[466] But, as the disciples asked, why use parables (Matt. 13:10)? Why not just be literal and clear? Why be abstract? Why not just say what you mean? The answer is that parables are designed to make the hearer think, but herein lies a paradox, a seemingly contradictory two-fold purpose.

First, they were meant to *reveal* truth to those who *desired* it. As Jesus said in verse 11, "It is given unto you to know the mysteries of the kingdom of heaven." Parables actually illustrate great truths about salvation, obedience, service, the Church, prayer, evangelism, and more. As we will note tomorrow, the specific truth mentioned in Matthew 13 is the Kingdom of Heaven.

Second, however, parables were meant to *conceal* truth from those who *defied* it. Our Lord said that those who are not spiritually inclined would not **understand** His parables. The Greek (*suniēmi*, 4920) refers to "the assembling of individual facts into an organized whole, as collecting the pieces of a puzzle and putting them together."[467] In other words, then, those who did not want the truth would be unable to "put the pieces together" from the stories Jesus told, unable to comprehend the fuller meaning He was conveying. He was actually presenting deep truths that demanded deep thinking, but the majority just couldn't get it.

Ponder this: Is it not probable that if our Lord were here today He would speak in parables? Are not most people totally disinterested in knowing absolute Truth? Are there not even many professing believers who actually abhor doctrine and deep Bible preaching and teaching? Are there not many books written about "loving God" and having a "relationship with Jesus" but never exposit Scripture? Are not mysticism, feelings, and "impressions" elevated above God's Word?

The parables are both mirrors and windows: as mirrors, they reflect what we *are*; as windows, they enable us to see what we *should be*. So, let us desire the deeper things of God's Word by meditating on several of our Lord's parables. (You are encouraged to read each parable first before each daily study.)

Scriptures for Study: Read the parable in 2 Samuel 12:1–4. Who is telling it, to whom is it being told, and what is its point?

NOVEMBER 13

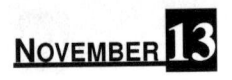

The Parable of the Sower (1)

... Behold, a sower went forth to sow ... (Matt. 13:3–9; 18–23)

THE parable of the sower is among the most well known of our Lord's parables and serves as a model for all the others. This is actually the first parable in a series about the nature of the "Kingdom of Heaven." This term (used only by Matthew) and "Kingdom of God" (used by the other gospel writers) both refer to the same thing: the sphere of God's dominion over His people.[468] While that is presently God's rule over the hearts of believers (Luke 17:21), it will be fully realized in the literal, earthly Millennial Kingdom (Rev. 20:4–6).

It is very instructive to note that while the other kingdom parables begin with the words, "The kingdom of heaven is likened unto," this one does not. The reason is immediately apparent when we begin reading: it outlines how the kingdom begins, that is, who is part of the kingdom and who is not. Understanding this parable is exceedingly helpful to the Christian servant who faithfully proclaims the Gospel. As countless expositors have noted, it consists of three elements.

First, there is the *seed*, which is the Word of God. Oh, that we would always begin, continue, and end right here! It is in Scripture alone (*sola Scriptura*) that we find Christ (who *is* the Word), salvation, and absolute Truth. This seed is not philosophy, politics, social change, prosperity, purpose, or self-esteem. It is the pure, unadulterated Christ of the Cross. If we are not proclaiming that, or if we are touting anything else, every syllable we utter is empty and powerless.

Further, we must scatter the seed. Just as the farmer does not dig a single hole and pour all the seed into it but scatters it throughout the field, we must spread the Gospel everywhere we go. Further still, we must sow *all* the seed. While this is especially true of preachers, who are commanded to preach and teach not just selected subjects but rather "all the counsel of God" (Acts 20:27), every Christian should be "speaking the truth in love" (Eph. 4:15), whatever it is and wherever it is required. Finally, this seed is perfect; as we will see, only the soils are different.

Second, there is the *sower*. I for one cannot speak highly enough of farmers. They are truly an amazing breed. First, they are *dedicated*, totally committed to a daunting task. We must likewise be devoted to an even more difficult task, speaking the Truth in a culture that denies it. Second, farmers are *discerning*, selecting the proper times and conditions to plant. We must do the same in sowing God's Word. Third, farmers are *diligent*, ever conscientious as those who must give an account for their labors. We, too, will give an account for our sowing. Fourth, farmers are *durable*, ever persevering no matter what difficulties arise. We also must remain stable and secure when we face the obstacles and discouragements that will come. The encouragement, however, is that we are responsible only for sowing; God brings the results (1 Cor. 3:7). Sowing is not about our human methodologies, rather the simple scattering of the seed.

Scriptures for Study: What does 1 Peter 1:23–25 add to our study today?

NOVEMBER 14

The Parable of the Sower (2)

... Behold, a sower went forth to sow ... (Matt. 13:3–9; 18–23)

UNLIKE an allegory, which is a complex metaphor with multiple characters and actions that all have a hidden meaning, a parable is a simple short story that has one main point and a single primary application. While this parable is unique in its three emphases, there is still a primary point.

Third, there are the *soils*. As noted yesterday, the seed is the Word of God and is always exactly the same. The soils on which the seed lands, however, are very different, indeed, and are the central emphasis of the parable. These diverse soils—people in Jesus' day immediately understood the images—perfectly describe the four types of hearers and the way each responds to the proclamation of the Gospel.

(1) The *Surface* Hearer is pictured by the "seeds [that] fell by the way side, and the fowls came and devoured them up" (v. 4). The paths that ran between the fields in Galilee were packed down and hardened by those who traveled them. When a seed hit such a path during planting, it simply could not penetrate and take any root at all. Birds quickly gobbled down the exposed seed, and any seed they missed was "trodden down" under the feet of the next passerby (Lk. 8:5).

When this person hears the Word, it hits the surface and stays there. It simply cannot penetrate because of how hardened to spiritual things the person has become. He doesn't "understand" the truth (v. 19; *suniēmi*; see Nov. 10) simply because he has been hardened by the countless "feet" that have walked on his "path," the feet of the humanist, the relativist, the evolutionist, the so-called atheist, and many others. To this person, in fact, the Gospel is utter foolishness (1 Cor. 1:18). The birds picture Satan and his tools—such as pride, skepticism, false teachers, and more—to snatch away the seed lest it fall in a small crack in the path and take root. We will encounter many of this kind of hearer in our witness for Christ.

(2) The *Shallow* Hearer is pictured by the seed that "fell upon stony places" (vv. 5–6). This was a shallow layer of soil that rested on top of the unseen limestone layer beneath. This was very deceptive. The seed would take root more quickly than other seed and the plants would actually look healthier. But because the roots could not penetrate the rocky layer, they remained shallow (which meant little water), so when the sun got hot, the plants withered away.

Oh, how many hearers there are like this! They hear the truth and immediately receive it with joy, but the roots are shallow (vv. 20–21). Shallow evangelism, shallow preaching, shallow profession, and more contribute to a situation that is all too common. Emotion, experience, and zealousness have replaced true conviction of sin, repentance, and transformation. Ironically, the rock beneath this soil is even harder than the road. When difficulties arise because of the Word, the Word is quickly rejected. We must make the true Gospel clear to such hearers.

Scriptures for Study: What do 2 Corinthians 4:4 and Hebrews 10:29 tell us about the unbeliever?

NOVEMBER 15

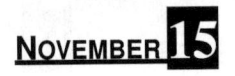

The Parable of the Sower (3)

... Behold, a sower went forth to sow ... (Matt. 13:3–9; 18–23)

COMMON to folk tales and other story telling is "the rule of three," such as the recurrence of three in the tale of Goldilocks and the Three Bears. We see this in the parables as well, such as three responses in the parable of the talents, three travelers on the Jericho Road, and the three elements in this parable (the seed, sower, and soils), and again, the soils are the primary application.

(3) The *Strangled* Hearer is pictured by the seeds that "fell among thorns; and the thorns sprung up, and choked them" (v. 7). No farmer ever has to plant weeds. Even ground that looks good can be infested with the seeds of destruction. While the good seed does take root, it is starved of nutrients, robbed of moisture, and choked by lack of space.

This hearer, therefore, is choked, and in typical "rule of three" fashion, Luke's account—"choked with cares and riches and pleasures of this life" (8:14)—notes three specific types of "weeds." First, there is the *domination* of the world. "Cares" is *merimna* (3308), which speaks of anxiety that disrupts the mind. The many interests and concerns of life (though legitimate in themselves) can so occupy the mind that thoughts of the Word are suffocated. Second, there is the *deceitfulness* of "riches." Oh, how many people think that wealth will make them happy and content! But that is a deception. Such an attitude is never satisfied and always wants more. Such obsession chokes any thought of the Word. Third, there is the *desire* for other things, the "pleasures of this life." Again, enjoying life is not sinful—God has given us "richly all things to enjoy" (1 Tim. 6:17)—but when that becomes the focus, as was true of the Rich Young Ruler (Matt. 19:16–22), it strangles everything else. As we proclaim the Gospel, we will encounter this hearer often in our culture of possessions and pleasure.

(4) The *Steadfast* Hearer is pictured by the seeds that "fell into good ground" (v. 8). This soil is soft, loose, deep, rich, moist, and free from the impediments of the other types. This, then, is the one who "hears" the Word (v. 23) and "understands" (*suniēmi*; see Nov. 10). So, in contrast to the rebellious mind of the surface hearer, the emotional mind of the shallow hearer, and the crowded mind of the strangled hearer, here we see the transformed mind (cf. 2 Cor. 5:17).

Further, as proof of life, the seed that grows in this soil inevitably reproduces itself through its fruit, for where there is no fruit there is no life (Jn. 15:2). Whether it is the highest degree of fruitfulness ("hundredfold"), the intermediate ("sixty"), or the lowest ("thirty"), a true hearer of the Word is also a doer of the Word (Jas. 1:22). This must also be our emphasis as we witness to others. Today's easy-believeism—Christianity without the cross, salvation without repentance, and life without obedience—is not the biblical Gospel.

Scriptures for Study: Read John 15:1–8. What principles of fruitfulness can you observe?

NOVEMBER 16

The Parable of the Good Samaritan (1)

... But a certain Samaritan ... had compassion ... (Lk. 10:25–37)

HERE is another of our Lord's most famous parables. Even literary critics have considered it one of the best stories ever told and the perfect model for the short story.

Sadly, some have severely damaged this magnificent story by turning it into an allegory. Origen, for example, viewed every element of the story as having a symbolic meaning: the victim as Adam; Jerusalem as paradise; Jericho as the world; the thieves as man's hostile influences; the victim's wounds as sins; the priest as the Law; the Levite as the Prophets; the Good Samaritan as Christ; the donkey as Christ's body carrying fallen man; the inn as the Church; the two denarii as the knowledge of the Father and the Son; and the return of the Good Samaritan as Christ's Second Coming.[469] Such so-called interpretation is tragic because it misses the simple point of the story. While allegory views the parable as teaching salvation, it does no such thing; its emphases are self-denial, sacrifice, compassion, and benevolence. These become blazingly clear when we study the people in this classic story, for the best stories are character-driven.

First, the **lawyer** saw a *problem* to *argue*. The occasion of our Lord's parable was His response to a challenging question from a **lawyer** (*nomikos*, 3544), an expert in the Mosaic Law. While some view the lawyer's question as possibly sincere, the language strongly indicates that it was meant to provoke an argument. The word **behold** and the abruptness of the lawyer standing up imply that he rudely interrupted Jesus. Further, **tempted** (*ekpeirazō*, 1598) means "to put to the test"; as did other critics, this man was testing Jesus to see if He would agree with or contradict the Law. While the lawyer quoted the Law in verse 27 (Deut. 6:5; Lev. 19:18), he went on in verse 29 to try to **justify** himself with that very Law and then asked the academic and argumentative question, **Who is my neighbor?** Such people do not want *answers*; they just want *argument*.

There is a very important lesson here. Christian "apologetics" are enormously popular nowadays. It is common for Christians to debate atheists, evolutionists, cultists, and so forth in open forums. The Greek *apologia* (627; e.g., Acts 22:1; 26:1; 1 Pet. 3:15), however, simply does not imply such an idea. It was originally used as a legal term for an attorney presenting a defense for his client, but such a defense of God's Truth involves simply *declaring* it, not *debating* it. Is it not significant that there is no church office of "apologist" in Scripture? As did our Lord, we are simply to proclaim the Truth, not argue and debate it (1 Cor. 2:1–5). Our arguments and "evidences" are not compelling, rather it is "the gospel of Christ" alone that "is the power of God unto salvation" (Rom. 1:16).

Scriptures for Study: Review our April 23 study, including the "Scriptures for Study." Do you have any additional observations?

NOVEMBER **17**

The Parable of the Good Samaritan (2)
... But a certain Samaritan ... had compassion ... (Lk. 10:25–37)

"THERE is no new thing under the sun," Solomon wrote (Ecc. 1:9), and the parable before us is irrefutable proof. The same greed, violence, racial bigotry, and indifference exist today as they did then.

Second, the **thieves** saw *prey* to *attack*. Unlike *kleptēs* (2812), which means to steal in secret (e.g., Judas, Jn. 12:6), *lēstēs* (3207) goes beyond just theft to include violence (e.g., the **thieves** at the crucifixion, Matt. 27:38). Jericho (Oct. 26) was located about 15 miles east northeast of Jerusalem but also about 3,400 feet lower in elevation and 846 feet below sea level. The steep, rocky, mountainous road between them was uninhabited in places and infested with robbers, who could easily hide in such terrain. Since the road was well traveled—many of the travelers were temple workers—it provided a "target-rich environment" for such evil.

Such predators obviously did not see a *person* on the road that day; they saw only *prey*. There is another lesson for us here. While a true Christian would not physically attack an innocent person, we can certainly do so just as devastatingly in another way: verbally with gossip ("talebearer" in Prov. 11:13; 18:7–8; 20:19), slander ("backbiters" in Rom. 1:30 and "backbitings" in 2 Cor. 12:20), and other uncontrolled and damaging speech, as James addresses at length (Jas. 3:1–12).

James, in fact, paints several graphic pictures of all this. In verses 3–4, he describes the tongue's *power* to *direct*, illustrating with the bit in a horse's mouth and the rudder of a ship. In verses 5–8, he describes the tongue's *proclivity* to *devastate*, illustrating with a raging fire and a subtle poison. Finally, in verses 9–12, he describes the tongue's *propensity* to *discrepancy*, illustrating with a fountain that flows with both sweet and bitter water and a fig tree that produces different fruit.

The 18th-century expositor, theologian, and pastor John Gill (1697–1771) was one of the historic giants of the faith, a true champion. His biographer, however, recounts how several ladies in the congregation "became very critical of Gill. Sometimes it was Gill's attention to his wife, at other times it was their pastor's old-fashioned appearance in the pulpit and the fact that he kept to the tradition of wearing a wig and adorning his neck with very long bibs as a sign of his office. These bibs really angered one lady member who decided to turn her anger into action. Armed with a pair of scissors, she asked her pastor if she could do him a good turn. Receiving an affirmative answer, the determined lady took hold of Gill's bibs and with a snip of her scissors shortened them by a good length. Now it was Gill's turn. He asked the lady if he could do her a reciprocal favour. The lady agreed and Gill asked for her scissors. On taking them in his hand, he told his sister that the length of something in her possession had been a cause of concern for some time. Would the lady kindly stretch out her tongue!"[470]

Scriptures for Study: Read the verses cited today. What observations can you make? How does all this encourage and challenge you?

NOVEMBER 18

The Parable of the Good Samaritan (3)

... But a certain Samaritan ... had compassion ... (Lk. 10:25–37)

SEPARATING our relationship with God from our interaction with people is a staggering contradiction. While the first four commandments of the Moral Law speak of our relationship to God, the other six address our relationship to our fellowman (June 16). There is no divorcing one category from the other. This is vividly illustrated by two other characters in Jesus' story.

Third, the **priest** and the **Levite** saw a *predicament* to *avoid*. Of all the characters in this story, the **priest** would have actually been the one most likely to aid a fellow Jew. After all, a priest represented man to God. He was the mediator, offering sacrifices, prayers, and praise to God on behalf of the people (Mar. 29). By definition, a priest was a servant. He would have known the command of Leviticus 19:34: "the stranger that dwelleth with you shall be unto you as one born among you, and thou shalt love him as thyself." He should have, therefore, ran to meet the need of this victim. Likewise, the **Levite**, one who assisted the priests, would have also known the Law's command to show mercy to those in need.

Here, then, were fellow Jews who would not come to the aid of one of their own, **who passed by on the other side** of the road in total indifference to a dying man. Why? Perhaps they felt they had already done their part for God by serving in the Temple, or they feared the robbers still lurked nearby, or they would have been ceremonially unclean if the man turned out to be dead and they touched the body.

In the end, however, the *reason* is irrelevant because the *cause* was an unregenerate heart. This, of course, is what James also confronts in his epistle using virtually identical imagery: "If a brother or sister be naked, and destitute of daily food, And one of you say unto them, Depart in peace, be ye warmed and filled; notwithstanding ye give them not those things which are needful to the body; what doth it profit? Even so faith, if it hath not works, is dead, being alone" (2:15–17).

Once again there is a lesson here for believers. Do we ever get too busy to help someone in real need? Do we rationalize that someone else will do it? This leads us right to another character in this drama.

Fourth, the **inn host** saw a *patron* to *attend*. The **inn** of that day was not like today's Hilton or Marriott. On the contrary, while one could pay for lodging and meager meals, the public inn was little more than a brothel and even a hangout for robbers. Likewise, innkeepers were "invariably untruthful, dishonest and oppressive."[471] All this man saw, then, was just another paying customer who he would attend to only because he was being paid to do so. While we certainly recognize that he had a business to run, nowhere do we read of an ounce of compassion.

This character provides yet another lesson for us. We must be ever careful not to serve simply because it's our job, because we are getting paid for it, or because it is expected of us.

Scriptures for Study: What does James 4:17 warn and how does it apply?

NOVEMBER 19

The Parable of the Good Samaritan (4)

... But a certain Samaritan ... had compassion ... (Lk. 10:25–37)

HAVE you ever thought about the victim in this story, perhaps even putting yourself in his place? Imagine if this were a real incident. Perhaps he was conscious after the attack and saw those who passed by. Perhaps he reached out a hand in a plea for help or even had enough strength to speak and beg those passersby for aid. How does one turn his back on the life or death needs of a fellow human being?

Fifth, only the **Samaritan** saw a *person* to *assist*. A Samaritan! While the priest would have been the most likely one to aid a fellow Jew, a Samaritan was by far the most *un*likely. When the northern tribes of Israel were taken into Assyrian captivity in 722 BC (the monarch Sargon, who took his name from the famous Sargon of Accad, claimed to have taken 27,290 captives), it inevitably led to their intermarrying with pagans, which then produced children of mixed blood. These were the Samaritans, who established their own priesthood, temple, and ceremonies. The result was a genetic hatred between the Jews and the Samaritans. Part of a Pharisee's morning prayer, in fact, was to thank God he was not born a Gentile, woman, or Samaritan. In this Samaritan, however, we see three characteristics.

(1) *Sympathy*—**he had compassion on him** (v. 33). The Greek (*splagchnizomai*, 4697) goes much deeper than mere pity, rather "to feel deeply or viscerally."[472] The same word is used in 15:20 for the father's compassion for his prodigal son and several times of our Lord as He looked upon lost sinners (Matt. 9:36; 14:14; 15:32; 18:27). This kind of sympathy flows from one who thinks of others instead of himself. If a Samaritan could have this for a Jew, what does that say about our attitude toward a fellow believer (or even a stranger) in need?

(2) *Service*. Verse 34 describes the Samaritan disinfecting (with the **wine**), soothing, salving (with the **oil**), and bandaging the **wounds**, putting the man on his **own beast** (probably a donkey), taking him to an **inn**, and caring for him. Perhaps he even kept a vigil throughout the night, regularly checking on him. Here is true service, service that neither requires, nor even expects, anything in return.

(3) *Sacrifice* (v. 35). The Samaritan could have easily, and perhaps even justifiably, left the next morning without another thought for the man. After all, he had without doubt saved the man's life and done much to contribute to his recovery. But, no, he gave the innkeeper **two pence** (denarii), which was two day's wages for a common laborer, enough to pay for several weeks room and board. Still further, he promised more, if needed, when he returned.

The story ends with Jesus asking, in effect, "So who was the real neighbor to this man?" and then adding, **Go, and do thou likewise** (vv. 36–37). **Likewise** indeed! Only a transformed believer can (and must) love like that.

Scriptures for Study: What does the Apostle John tell us in the following verses: 1 John 3:16–18; 3:23–24; 4:11?

NOVEMBER 20

The Parable of the Talents (1)

... Well done, thou good and faithful servant ... [or] ... Thou wicked and slothful servant ... (Matt. 25:14–30)

AS one writer observes, while the reference "in the Parable of the Ten Virgins" (vv. 1–13) is to our *personal state*, in 'The Talents' it is to the *personal work* of the Disciples."[473] In other words, the former is about *waiting* for the Master to come, the latter about *working* until He arrives. Still further, we see the inward *attitude* in one that motivates the outward *action* in the other. The above extract from our text, therefore, challenges each of us to examine our Christian service, for we will one day give an account for it.

First, we acknowledge the *commission* we are given (vv. 14–15). Our story opens with a **man** of obvious wealth who is going on a journey of long duration and an unknown time of return. He entrusts his **servants** with his wealth so that they might use it wisely.

The parallel is obvious. The wealthy man pictures our Lord, who has departed into Heaven and whose return time is unknown. In His absence, He has entrusted His wealth to us to use for His gain and glory. **Talent** transliterates *talanton* (5007), which refers not to coinage but to weight. The talent was about 75 pounds, so a talent of silver—**money** in verse 18 is *argurion* [694], "a piece of silver"— was 20 years wages for a common worker.

Our English word **talent**, then, is "a metaphorical application of" *talanton* borrowed from this parable.[474] Our Lord has entrusted us with great wealth. He has entrusted us with natural abilities, spiritual gifts, financial resources, and other "talents," all of which actually belong to *Him* not us. "Every good gift and every perfect gift is from above, and cometh down from the Father of lights" (Jas 1:17). We are, therefore, to invest all that He has entrusted us with for the furtherance of His interests, not our own.

Especially significant is that each servant was given a different level of responsibility: to **one he gave five talents, to another two, and to another one; according to his several ability**. Likewise, in His sovereign purpose, God entrusts each one of us with different "talents" (His endowments) according to our abilities (natural strengths). Each of us will also have different opportunities to use what God has given us.

Like the two faithful servants in the story, a true servant of the Master will desire to faithfully use the "talents" He has given. Whether one receives the enormous responsibility of **five talents** (e.g., pastors and other leaders) or the lesser responsibility of **two talents** or even **one** (e.g., Christians of various levels of growth and ability), the true child of God will produce results that glorify God and Christ's Kingdom.

Scriptures for Study: What do the following Scriptures add to our study: 1 Corinthians 3:5–9; 4:2; 12:4?

NOVEMBER 21

The Parable of the Talents (2)

... Well done, thou good and faithful servant ... [or] ... Thou wicked and slothful servant ... (Matt. 25:14–30)

ANYTHING whereby we may glorify God is 'a talent,'" wrote J. C. Ryle. "Our gifts, influence, money, knowledge, health, strength, time, senses, reason, intellect, memory, affections, privileges as members of Christ's Church, advantages as possessors of the Bible—all are talents."[475] And let us be reminded that all these belong to God who has simply entrusted them to us.

Second, we examine the *character* we reflect (vv. 16–18). The response of these three servants falls into only two categories. The first two servants vividly demonstrate faithfulness. As we have noted before (Sept. 8), there is no greater quality in a servant than faithfulness, for it drives everything else. The faithfulness of these servants is evident in that the first servant **went and traded**. The Greek construction of **went** can be translated "having gone" showing immediacy—he didn't know how long his master would be gone, so he didn't waste a minute—and **traded** (*ergazomai*, 2038, "work," "labor," "make gains by trading") implies not a one-time transaction but ongoing business activity. As a result, the servant doubled the amount his master had entrusted him with. While the second servant was entrusted with less than the first, he was equally faithful and also doubled the amount. Such faithfulness does, indeed, reflect exemplary character.

In contrast to such faithfulness, the second category, of course, is unfaithfulness, which was true of the third servant. It was common to bury valuables in ancient times for security, but the master did not want his servants simply to *protect* his assets, rather he wanted them to *proliferate* those resources.

Let us ponder a moment on what motivated the actions of these servants. Did greed motivate the first two? Obviously not, for it wasn't their money. Did selfishness motivate the third servant? No, for the same reason. Was it rather fear of failure or just simply laziness? Perhaps one or both of those were part of it. We would submit, however, an underlying motive in both cases: while the first two loved their master, the third did not. True love drives us to do what is best for others and do what pleases them. A lack of love (perhaps even hatred in this case) drives us to do nothing. We will make excuses for our actions, as this servant did, instead of simply admitting our lack of love.

It has been debated whether the unfaithful servant pictures an unbeliever or simply the nominal Christian who fails to use what God has given. In the end, however, the result is the same. Those who love the Lord will be faithful in using the "talents" and opportunities He has given. Those who don't love Him will just bury them.

Scriptures for Study: How do the following verses encourage you: Galatians 6:9–10; Colossians 4:17; Hebrews 6:10–11; 1 Peter 4:10?

NOVEMBER 22

The Parable of the Talents (3)

... Well done, thou good and faithful servant ... [or] ... Thou wicked and slothful servant ... (Matt. 25:14–30)

GOD gives "talents" to each one of His servants *sovereignly* for His purpose, *suitably* for our abilities, *sufficiently* for our use, and *specifically* for our accountability.

Third, then, we realize the *consequence* we face (vv. 19–27). The first thing on the master's agenda when he returned was to settle up with his servants. Perhaps he thought, "How did they handle what I left them? Was my confidence in them well-founded?" Upon hearing the report of the first two servants—note in the word **behold** the servants' excitement to show the master what they accomplished for him—the master responded with a three-fold *commendation*.

(1) There was *praise*: **Well done, thou good and faithful servant**. Once again, we see the key principle for a servant: faithfulness (Sept. 8), a relentless fidelity to the concerns of the Master. And it is faithfulness alone that God blesses. It's not about the methods we develop, the programs we start, the organizations we found, or the success we report. It's all about faithfulness. (2) There was a *promotion*: **thou hast been faithful over a few things, I will make thee ruler over many things**. Do you see what happened? Servants were promoted to rulers! (3) There was *pleasure*: **enter thou into the joy of thy lord**. As we have noted before (May 31), **joy** is *chara* (5479), which means "gladness and rejoicing" and goes infinitely beyond mere human feelings of happiness. This is not the fleeting pleasures (plural) of the world, rather the eternal pleasure (singular) of Heaven.

In contrast to the faithful, the master had nothing but condemnation for the unfaithful, who not only invented an excuse for his failure by accusing the master of being **hard** (*skleros*, 4642, harsh, stern, severe, or offensive) but also lied about the master's character by charging him with dishonesty. If he really thought that, he could have at least put the money in the bank to draw some interest. As noted yesterday, the real problem here was lack of love for the master. This challenges each of us to examine our heart whether we truly love the Master and then admit the excuses we make (and the other people we blame) for our lack of faithfulness.

Fourth, the *celebration* we enjoy (vv. 28–30). These closing verses again underscore a contrast: the faithful receive even more resources and opportunities for service, while the unfaithful lose the resources and opportunities they already have. For the former there is *rejoicing*, but for the latter there is only *regret*.

As we close our meditations on this parable, let us be reminded once again that all this is about the Master's resources, not ours. He entrusts them to us, we invest them, and He gets the glory. Oh, my Dear Christian Friend, let us all strive simply to one day hear, **Well done**. That alone will be enough.

Scriptures for Study: What do the following verses tell us about our labor: 1 Corinthians 15:58; 2 Corinthians 5:9; Colossians 1:29?

NOVEMBER 23

The Parable of the Faithful Servant

Who then is a faithful and wise servant . . . ? (Matt. 24:45–51)

EARLIER in His Olivet Discourse, our Lord emphasized a principle He reiterated throughout His ministry: *true belief* is exhibited by *transformed behavior*. Just as true salvation is demonstrated by godly living, true service is verified by laboring until the Lord returns. He, therefore, asks, in effect, "Who is the genuine servant?" a question each of us must answer.

First, we note the *description* of the true **servant** (*doulos*, Sept. 1). There are three characteristics of the authentic servant. First, of course, he is **faithful**. At the risk of repetition, it simply cannot be stated too often that faithfulness is the key to all Christian service. The least gifted servant who is faithful is incalculably more valuable than the most gifted one who cannot be trusted implicitly. While the world's philosophy is success, God's is faithfulness. Second, the true servant is **wise**. The Greek here is not the common *sophia* (4678, Jan. 8), rather *phronēsis* (5428), which basically meant a "way of thinking, frame of mind, intelligence, good sense" but often had the fuller idea of "discernment and judicious insight."[476] It was being able to see beyond just the knowledge of a thing, to see how that thing applied and how it was practical. While the world desires the spectacular, the authentic servant discerns the practical. Third, such a servant is the right kind of **ruler** (*kathistēmi*, 2525, to set in office, to appoint as a ruler). Whether a pastor, a husband, a father, an employer, or "just" a Christian, we all are to lead rightly by word and deed.

Second, we rejoice in the *delight* the true servant receives. **Blessed is that servant** (v. 46), Jesus declared. **Blessed** is *makarios* (3107), which means far more than "happiness" as is commonly taught. It speaks of true contentment, "possessing the favor of God," and "is equivalent to having God's Kingdom within one's heart."[477] **Doing** (*poieō*, 4160), then, is a present participle indicating continuous action, not periodic service, rather a *continual* **doing**. Faithfulness once again is the key. Oh, what reward there is for faithful service!

Third, we see the *distinction* between a true and false servant. In striking contrast, our Lord lists three characteristics of the counterfeit servant. He is *unfaithful*. He neglects his responsibilities because the master **delayeth his coming**. True faithfulness, however, is confirmed when no one is looking. The counterfeit is also *unkind*. He beats **his fellowservants**. This would include not only physical but verbal abuse. Sadly, there are many today who claim to be "Christian" but prove they are not because of their attacks upon those who actually stand for the Truth. Finally, the counterfeit is also *unruly* as he goes **to eat and drink with the drunken**, thereby erasing any remaining doubt as to his true character and the judgment that awaits (vv. 50–51). This parable is a sobering warning about how we are living and serving as we are waiting.

Scriptures for Study: How does 2 Timothy 4:6–8 encourage us?

NOVEMBER 24

The Parable of the Rich Fool (1)

... Thou fool ... So is he that layeth up treasure for himself, and is not rich toward God. (Lk. 12:13–21)

MONEY plays a crucial role in society. Since it is a necessary commodity, we think much about it: how to get it, guard it, and grow it. Our Lord recognized this and as a result, about one-third of his nearly 40 parables address money either directly or indirectly.

Contrary to some thinking, money is not evil, rather the *love* of it is "the root of all [kinds of] evil" (1 Tim. 6:10) or "a root of all the evils."[478] It's significant, indeed, that this does not say "the love of the sword" (or the modern equivalent "the gun") or any other object on earth is this root, rather the love of money. Now, like all objects, money is morally neutral. That is why even wealth is not evil (Deut. 8:18; 1 Tim. 6:17; cf. Job 1:3; Gen. 13:2; 26:13; 30:43; Ruth 2:1; Matt. 27:57). Neither is it evil to invest (Matt. 25:27), save (Prov. 21:20; 30:25), or do financial planning (Prov. 27:23–24). What matters, however, is the place we give money and what we do with it. The parable before us is a powerful one about greed and priorities, and it has much to say about our Christian service.

First, we read Jesus' *warning* (v. 15). The preamble of the parable (vv. 13–14) consisted of a certain man who asked Jesus to settle an inheritance dispute between him and his brother. Rabbis often settled such matters, but Jesus wanted no part of such argument because it was driven by nothing but greed. He, therefore, warned: **beware of covetousness**. The Greek *pleonexia* (4124) means "greedy desire to have more," a good definition of the English **covetousness**.

Covetousness is, indeed, a greatly "ignored sin," one that few people consider being very serious at all. But this, of course, overlooks (no doubt deliberately) the appearance of this prohibition in God's Moral Law: "Thou shalt not covet" (Ex. 20:17; June 29). So serious is it, in fact, that Paul included it in a list of horrific sins: "Mortify therefore your members which are upon the earth; fornication, uncleanness, inordinate affection, evil concupiscence, and covetousness, which is idolatry" (Col. 3:5). Why does Paul call covetousness "idolatry," that is, the worship of a false god? Puritan Henry Smith well answers: "Covetousness is called idolatry, which is worse than infidelity, for it is less rebellion not to honor the king, than to set up another king against him."[479] Whatever object we covet, it is that object that we put in God's place, the one we now worship, adore, and desire.

Oh, how on guard we must be here! Whether it be pleasure, possessions, power, popularity, or prestige, we must banish covetousness. We cannot serve God when we are serving *another* god. To adapt an old saying, whatever we covet is like seawater: the more we drink, the thirstier we become, and in the end it will destroy us. As Jesus went on to say, in effect, life is more than possessions.

Scriptures for Study: Read 1 Timothy 6:6–10. What observations can you make? What strikes you the most profoundly?

NOVEMBER 25

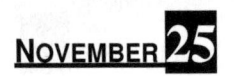

The Parable of the Rich Fool (2)

... Thou fool ... So is he that layeth up treasure for himself, and is not rich toward God. (Lk. 12:13–21)

HAVING noted Jesus' *warning*, we turn to the parable itself. When we do, one feature jumps off the page. As the old play on words goes, this man had "I (not 'eye') trouble." The personal pronouns "I" and "my" appear no less than 11 times in the span of three verses (17–19, KJV). As is common in our own day, it was all about him, which is at the core of covetousness.

Second, then, we should take careful note of the rich man's *wantonness* (vv. 16–20). The parable begins with no implied wrong; the farmer simply had a bumper crop (**brought forth plentifully** is *euphoreō*, 2164, to bear well, yield abundantly; English "euphoria"). The story immediately takes a turn, however. Again, as the pronouns demonstrate, the man thought of no one but himself. Instead of sharing the surplus, which would have cost him very little, he tore down *his* barns to build *his* bigger barns to store *his* grain for *his* use.

As if that were not bad enough, the man smugly added that he would now retire to a life of ease and hedonism. This was precisely the philosophy of the ancient Epicureans, named after their materialistic founder Epicurus around 307 BC. Materialism is a philosophy that views matter as the only reality in the world, denies the existence of God and the soul, and thereby considers material possessions and physical comfort as all there is. This is also the philosophy of many today, not just the rich but from every class. They live for the weekends so they can party and play, accumulate possessions to make them happy, and disregard anything spiritual. Sadly, even some Christians have been lured into some of this.

Our Lord's summation of such a philosophy is both blunt and brutal: **Thou fool, this night thy soul shall be required of thee**. **Fool** is *aphrōn* (878), "without reason . . . senseless, foolish, stupid, without reflection or intelligence, acting rashly."[480] There is no greater folly than materialism, for when the materialist dies, he has less than nothing.

Third, we consider the *wisdom* (v. 21): **So is he that layeth up treasure for himself, and is not rich toward God**. While the materialist faces only *ruin*, the godly enjoys true *riches*. **Rich toward God** is the key principle here. **Toward** is the little Greek preposition *eis* (1519), which primarily denotes motion into or toward a place or thing. To be rich toward God, then, means we place our resources into Him and into the things that concern His Kingdom and emphasizes spiritual enrichment over sensual enjoyment. As our Lord declared elsewhere, let us lay up treasures in heaven, not on the earth (Mat 6:19–21). Let us likewise invest our time and money in ministry here, for the returns are eternal.

Scriptures for Study: Read Matthew 6:19–34. What observations can you make? What strikes you the most profoundly?

NOVEMBER 26

The Parable of the Shrewd Manager (1)

... No servant can serve two masters ... Ye cannot serve God and mammon. (Lk. 16:1–13)

BEFORE us today is a parable that is often misunderstood. Also known as the Parable of the Unfaithful Steward, it appears at first glance to actually commend dishonesty. As we will see tomorrow, however, that is not what our Lord was commending.

First, we consider the *parable*. As we have noted before (Sept. 8), a steward had full charge of all his master's domestic affairs, even to the point of using his assets. Since this entailed the master's total trust, a steward was "on his own." In this case, however, the steward mismanaged the funds and **wasted** them. While some commentators accuse him of embezzlement, **wasted** does not imply that at this point (*diaskorpizō*, 1287, to scatter, disperse, or squander). When the master heard of this, he called the steward in for an explanation, but none could be offered. This also demonstrates that no embezzlement is implied at this point, for if there had been, the master would have launched legal action. Still he dismissed the steward for his abject failure.

Now, before we criticize this man too hastily and harshly, we should consider how we also sometimes fail miserably in our stewardship. How about the stewardship of our *treasures*? While tithing (the giving of ten percent) is often considered a "good place to start," this is not the NT standard. On the contrary, we are to give "as God hath prospered" us (1 Cor. 16:2). "Prospered" is *euodoō* (2137), "to prosper, make good one's journey." This does not imply a fixed amount, rather it is based upon the wondrous journey God has provided in Christ.

Consider also the stewardship of our *time*. Paul addresses this most profoundly in his exhortation, "Redeeming the time, because the days are evil" (Eph. 5:16). "Redeeming" is *exagorazō* (1805), "to buy up"; we are to "buy up" all our time and devote it God, to consider each and every moment as an opportunity for growth, service, and witness. The fool *wastes* time, but the wise man *invests* it.

Finally, think again about your "*talents*," as we recently studied (Nov. 20–22). Every ability you have, every gift and skill, is from God. We must, therefore, use every one of them to *spread* the Gospel, *support* other believers, and *share* our resources with those in need. "The Macedonians first gave themselves, then service and substance [2 Cor. 8:1–5]," wrote Vance Havner. "Have you ever put yourself on God's collection plate?"[481]

Like the steward in this parable, we too will one day give an account of our stewardship (Rom. 14:10–12). Will we hear our Lord's commendation, "Well done," or will we stand with regret at how we wasted His resources?

Scriptures for Study: What does 1 Corinthians 3:13–15 tell us about our future accountability?

NOVEMBER 27

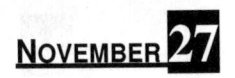

The Parable of the Shrewd Manager (2)

... No servant can serve two masters ... Ye cannot serve God and mammon. (Lk. 16:1–13)

AS our Lord continues His parable, we learn about the steward's reaction to his dismissal. Deeply concerned with how he would now make a living—he was incapable of physical labor and was ashamed at the thought of begging—he came up with a creative solution. To ingratiate himself to his master's debtors, the now unemployed steward, who still had access to the accounts, drastically lowered what the debtors actually owed. By appearing to be unusually gracious, he ensured his future needs of an income, a residence, and an almost legendary status in the community. In short, he bought friends.

What was the master's reaction to this? With all the celebration and praise of both himself and the manager that was no doubt going on, the master didn't dare reverse what had been done. His reputation would have been ruined. So, making the best of a bad situation, he had to compliment the manager on his creativeness; he **commended** him because he had done **wisely** (*phronimōs*, 5430), that is, shrewdly and advantageously. The same word is used of the "wise" man who built his house on the rock in expectation of a future storm (Matt. 7:24) and the five "wise" virgins who brought extra oil in anticipation of future need (25:1–13). I was reminded here of the Banco Central heist in Brazil in 2006, one of the most creative in history. The thieves were able to steal almost $70 million dollars by working for months digging a tunnel more than 250 feet long to arrive below the bank. We certainly don't praise the *crime*, but we do acknowledge the *cleverness*.

Second, we note the *principles*. Our Lord goes on to apply His parable with three lessons about our stewardship. In regard to others, we *seek* heavenly friends (v. 9). Unlike the steward in the parable who bought earthly friends, we use **mammon** (*mammōnas*, 3126, material riches; Sept. 1) to finance evangelism and thereby "purchase" heavenly friends.

In regard to ourselves, then, we *secure* eternal investments (vv. 10–12). When we realize that we are owners of nothing but rather stewards of everything, it transforms our outlook. Our Lord tests us in these verses. If we are **faithful in that which is least** (earthly money), we will be **faithful also in much**; if **therefore** we remain **faithful in the unrighteous mammon**, God **will commit to [our] trust true** spiritual **riches**, both now and in Christ's future kingdom.

Finally, in regard to God, we are *single-minded* (v. 13). **No servant can serve two masters**, Jesus concluded; we **cannot serve God and mammon**. Loving one master automatically drives us away from the other. They are mutually exclusive with nothing in common. We must, therefore, be single-mindedly set upon God and use the resources He lends us for His glory and others' good.

Scriptures for Study: What does Proverbs 6:6–8 encourage us to do? How, then, does 23:5 warn us?

NOVEMBER 28

The Parable of the Laborers in the Vineyard

... So the last shall be first, and the first last ... (Matt. 20:1–16)

WE address another parable today that has sparked debate. Some view it as speaking of salvation, but it's hard to imagine Jesus using the earning of money to picture earning salvation. Others view it as earning rewards for service, but the problem here is that unlike all the workers who received the same pay, not all of us will receive the same reward (1 Cor. 3:8). Still others have come up with strange interpretations, such as, Jesus distinguishing Jews from Gentiles, that is, Jews being called first and Gentiles later.

The simplest way to understand this parable, however, is to note its straightforward emphasis on having the right attitude in our service. We can test ourselves by asking three questions.

First, what is my *virtue* in service? Peter's question to Jesus in 19:27 demonstrates a typical attitude: "[Unlike the rich young ruler] we have forsaken all, and followed thee; what shall we have therefore?" Nowadays we would ask, "What's in it for me?" This attitude is reflected dramatically by the early workers (v. 2) who insisted on a contract before they went to work, while the later workers, in contrast, simply trusted the owner to give them what was right (v. 4). We too should serve without making deals with God, trusting instead in His sovereign plan and purpose (v. 15).

Second, what is my *view* of other workers? At the end of the day, as was customary, the workers were paid for their labor. The early workers watched as the later ones were paid a full day's wage for part-time work, undoubtedly thinking this meant they would receive even more because they actually worked a full day. Much to their shock, however, they received the contracted wages. They voiced their discontent by *bragging* on how hard *they* had worked and *belittling* what the *others* had done.

Peter made the same mistake of looking at others not only here but elsewhere. After Jesus recommissioned him (May 5–9) and foretold his martyrdom, Peter saw John coming toward them and asked, "Lord, and what shall this man do?" Jesus' answer was a rebuke, "What is that to thee? follow thou me" (Jn. 21:18–22). In other words, in effect, "Stop looking at others, and keep your eyes on Me." Much of our failure and ineffectiveness in service comes by concentrating on (and even competing with) others. But those who desire to be **first** will be **last**.

Third, what are my *values* in service? As we have noted, Jesus mentioned money often in His parables, and here it tests motive. Sadly, much so-called ministry today is not real ministry because it's driven by money. An earmark of false teachers is they are in it for the money (2 Pet. 2:1–3), but the danger for us all is service driven by a desire for *remuneration* and *recognition* (Sept 2).

Scriptures for Study: How do these verses encourage us in our service: Ephesians 6:8 and Hebrews 6:10?

NOVEMBER 29

The Parable of the Unprofitable Servant

... unprofitable servants: we have done that which was our duty to do. (Lk. 17:7–10)

WE live in a day of a growing "entitlement" mentality, the attitude by which one thinks something is owed to them simply because of who they are or, even more basic, just by life in general. Sadly, this attitude has even overtaken some Christians and churches. The parable before us, however, underscores that no one, especially God, owes us anything. It rebukes any notion of self-importance. Why? Because we are **servants** (*doulos*, Sept. 1).

First, a servant labors *unlimitedly* (vv. 7–8). This servant was a busy fellow, indeed. He had spent the entire day plowing and cultivating fields (*arotriaō*, 722), or tending sheep (*poimainō*, 4165), or perhaps both. Who wouldn't want to come home after that and **sit down to [eat]**? But his day was far from over. The master came first, so the servant fixed his supper and served it to him, which undoubtedly included cleanup afterwards as well. A servant's needs always come last, and he can expect one duty after another to be placed upon him.

Second, a servant labors *unselfishly* (v. 8). As we read this parable, we are tempted to think that the master was being selfish, but there is no hint of this in the servant. If there had been, he actually would have been guilty of selfishness, thinking only of himself, not of the master who alone deserved the service.

Third, a servant labors *unthanked* (v. 9). There are many thankless jobs in our society: farmers, teachers, soldiers, police officers, and firefighters (forgive me if I missed some, which proves the point). Now, I'm not advocating that we not thank these people; on the contrary, we should do so as often as possible. But a lack of thanks goes with the job. Such people do not serve because they want thanks; they serve because there is a need.

Herein lies a strong challenge to every Christian **servant**. Sadly, we have all been guilty of expecting thanks for what we did. When we do that, however, we actually cease to serve at all. If we do something under the guise of "serving the Lord," but expect thanks or recognition, we are merely satisfying ourselves.

Fourth, a servant labors *unreservedly* (v. 10). We do everything that is **commanded** of us simply because it is our **duty** as servants. **Duty** is *opheilō* (3784), to owe, be indebted, be under obligation.

Fifth, a servant labors *unprofitably*. **Unprofitable** is *achreios* (888), which appears only here and Matthew 25:40 of servants that are worthless, useless, and good-for-nothing. In ourselves, "that is, in [our] flesh dwelleth no good thing," Paul wrote (Rom. 7:18), but Christ makes us "able ministers" (2 Cor. 3:6). God does not *need* us, but He has chosen to *use* us and will one day exalt us (1 Pet. 5:6).

My Dear Christian Friend, let us each be a beacon in our entitlement culture that no one owes us anything, rather we owe our Lord everything.

Scriptures for Study: How do the following verse challenges us: Luke 14:11; 18:14; James 4:10?

NOVEMBER 30

The Parable of the Unmerciful Servant

... Shouldest not thou also have had compassion on thy fellowservant, even as I had pity on thee? ... (Matt. 18:21–35)

OUR final parable is about one of the most detestable characters in all of literature. The story was prompted by Peter's question about how often he should forgive his brother. Rabbinic teaching dictated that the offended party had to forgive only three times, so Peter probably felt quite magnanimous and even spiritually attuned to Jesus' teaching when he submitted **seven times**.

Jesus' answer of **seventy times seven**, however, undoubtedly startled Peter. This does not imply that we carry a notebook with us to keep track of those who offend us until we hit 490 and then unleash our wrath on 491! His point, obviously, was that a true forgiving spirit does not keep score. He then told the story.

First, this servant was *dishonest*. While settling financial matters with his servants, a king found one (probably a tax collecting official) in the hopeless debt of **ten thousand talents**. Since a talent was about 75 pounds of either gold or silver, this was 750,000 pounds! As historical records indicate, the taxes collected in Palestine at this time amounted to about 800 talents a year, so this embezzling servant had stolen more than twelve years worth of taxes, tens of millions of dollars.

The servant's dishonesty did not stop there, however. When confronted with his crime and the threat of being sold into slavery, along with his entire family, he promised to repay it all, knowing all the while that such a debt could never be repaid. It would have taken a working man of that day 200,000 years to repay such a debt. This, of course, was Jesus' whole point. We are all sinners and owe God an unpayable debt. It is His grace alone that could forgive the unforgivable, and it is Christ alone who could pay the unpayable.

Second, this servant was *despicable*. The second servant is a clear picture of a fellow believer and how he was mistreated. While the first man was forgiven an unpayable debt, he refused to forgive his fellow servant of what was in comparison a microscopic pittance (100 days wages)—this might even have been a loan taken from stolen funds. His hypocrisy is even more graphically demonstrated by his ignoring the other man's plea, which consisted of the very same words he had used to the king: **Have patience with me, and I will pay thee all**. While such appalling behavior is hard to imagine, we have all been guilty of just such conduct when we fail to forgive a fellow believer for *any* offence. Why? Because whatever it is, it's infinitesimal compared to what God has forgiven us.

Third, this servant was *disciplined*. Other servants who were disgusted by this scene reported it to the king, who was outraged and severely chastised the servant. "He that demands mercy, and shows none, ruins the bridge over which he himself is to pass," wrote Puritan Thomas Adams.[482] We hurt only ourselves.

Scriptures for Study: What do the following verses tell us about our treatment of fellow believers: Ephesians 4:26, 4:31–32; 1 Peter 3:8–9?

DECEMBER 1

Grace Giving (1)

... Upon the first day of the week let every one of you lay by him in store, as God hath prospered him ... (1 Cor. 16:1–2)

SADLY, because of the abuses of money by false teachers (2 Pet. 2:1–3) and even the misuses and mismanagement of it by true believers and churches, this is a touchy issue. But we dare not ignore this subject any more than we would ignore a marital problem simply because it is a sensitive area. Giving, in fact, is a crucial aspect of Christian living. While we considered in an earlier study that giving is one aspect of *loving* our Lord (June 26), we go deeper here to recognize it also as an integral part of our *serving* Him. The text before us is one of two key NT passages on Christian giving, the other being 2 Corinthians 8–9. In the tradition of journalism and other information gathering professions, let us first approach this crucial subject using the classic "five Ws and one H."

First, there is the *who* of giving. With the words **let every one of you lay by him in store**, Paul makes clear that every believer is to give to the work of God. The matter is not about age, social status, or even economic standing, rather it is all inclusive. This is, in fact, one of the most important lessons we can teach our children, a lesson they will carry with them throughout their lives. Even those who are not well off financially are to give. That is precisely the lesson we learn from the widow and her two mites (Mk. 12:41–44). A "mite" (*lepton*, 3016) was the smallest bronze Jewish coin in circulation. These two *lepta*, then, were worth a whopping 1/64 of a Roman denarius (a laborer's daily wage). While the rich gave out of their surplus, she gave all she had. Likewise, if we do not give when we have a *pittance*, we will not give when we have *plenty*.

Second, there is the *what* of giving. What amount should we give? It is amazing, indeed, that the almost universal and automatic response to that question is, "Oh, I should tithe my ten percent." *Tithing*, however, had nothing whatsoever to do with *giving*. Several tithes were prescribed by the Mosaic Law, which totaled about 23 percent. Ten percent was given for the Levites (Lev. 27:30) because they received no land inheritance or other means of support, another ten percent was set aside to sustain the national feasts and holidays (Deut. 14), and an additional tithe was collected each third year for a benevolence fund (14:28–29). Again, these were not freewill offerings, but rather taxes to operate the government, just as Christians are required to pay their taxes (Rom. 13:6).

While even the OT had "freewill offerings" (e.g. Lev. 22:18, 21), the NT standard is far superior. We give as God has **prospered** us (*euodoō*, June 26). This is "grace giving," giving not because we *have* to but because we *want* to. Tithing was by *law*, giving is by *grace*. "Grace giving" means that we give to God in proportion to what He has given us. It's an issue not of the *wallet* but of the *heart*.

Scriptures for Study: What example of giving do we read about in 2 Corinthians 8:1–3?

DECEMBER 2

Grace Giving (2)

... Upon the first day of the week let every one of you lay by him in store, as God hath prospered him ... (1 Cor. 16:1–2)

AS John Calvin commented on our text, "If a heathen poet [Seneca] could say, 'What riches you give away, those alone you shall always have,' how much more ought that consideration to have influence among us, who are not dependent on the gratitude of men, but have God to look to?"[483]

Third, there is the *when* of giving. **Upon the first day of the week**, Paul wrote. Oh, how wondrous every Lord's Day is! It is the day observed by the Early Church (Jn. 20:19; Acts 20:7; Rev. 1:10) and is still the day we should gather for worship and equipping for service (cf. Eph. 4:11–12). So, not only did they meet each Lord's Day (June 20), but one aspect of that worship was giving. This encourages us to do likewise.

Fourth, there is the *where* of giving. In addition to the above, the phrase **lay by him in store** underscores the fact that the Local Church is where God's people are to give. The imagery of the ancient "treasury" could not be clearer. **In store** translates the graphic Greek word *thēsauros* (2344). It was common practice, in both pagan and Jewish culture, to have a treasury right in the religious temple where gifts and taxes were stored. This treasury was called the *thēsauros*, "treasury, treasure box, storehouse." That meaning makes perfect sense of our English *thesaurus*—a "treasury of words." Paul instructed the Corinthians, therefore, to bring their gifts to the "storehouse," the place they met each Lord's Day, so those gifts could be managed and distributed from there.

While not a popular view nowadays, there's no other place spoken of in Scripture for giving than the Local Church, with the exception of giving to someone who is in need (James 2:15–17). Literally thousands of parachurch organizations (faith-based organizations that carry out their mission independent of local church oversight) siphon off millions of dollars (and other currencies) from local churches, many of which suffer serious financial strain. While many argue that there are both pros and cons to such organizations, when we weigh them according to Scripture alone, the cons are far weightier than the pros. God wants His people to support the Local Church, the organization *He* founded.

Fifth, there is the *why* of giving. There are two reasons for our giving. First, it *praises* God for what He has given. Again, this is an act of worship. Second, our giving *provides* for the needs of God's people. Paul specifically mentioned **the collection for the [poor] saints** in Jerusalem. This is not only about benevolence and meeting the needs of fellow believers, but also it enables the church to carry on all aspects of its ministry. While giving is not a gauge of spirituality, spirituality does, in fact, produce a giving spirit.

Scriptures for Study: What do the following verses say about our giving: Galatians 6:10; James 2:15–17; and 1 John 3:17?

DECEMBER 3

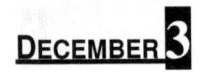

Grace Giving (3)

... the grace of God bestowed on the churches of Macedonia ... (2 Cor. 8:1–3)

"SOME of us are like the Dead Sea," wrote Oswald Chambers, "always taking in but never giving out, because we are not rightly related to the Lord Jesus."[484] Today we consider one other principle of giving.

Sixth, there is the *how* of giving. In his second letter to the Corinthians, Paul encouraged them again to give. Amazingly, he used **the** dreadfully poor **churches of Macedonia** (Philippi, Thessalonica, and Berea in northern Greece), as prime examples of how to give.

(1) We are to give *graciously*. When we truly meditate on **the grace of God bestowed on** us, how can we not be motivated to give according to such grace? Grace not only *delivered* us, but it now also *drives* us. "These Macedonians had been saved by grace," wrote Harry Ironside, "and now the rich grace of giving is bestowed upon them. Giving is a grace."[485]

(2) We are to give *transcendingly*. Grace giving lives above difficulty. The phrase **great trial of affliction** demonstrates that the Macedonians lived above *pressure*. **Great** is *polus* (4183, much), **trial** is *dokime* (1382, approved or tried), and **affliction** is *thlipsis* (2347, to crush, press, or compress). The image is graphic: the Macedonians lived under tremendous spiritual pressure that tried their faith. They also lived above *poverty* (*ptōcheia*, 4432), which refers to a beggar, someone completely destitute, such as Lazarus (Lk. 16:20; cf. Mk. 12:42–43; Rom. 15:26). "Here we have a metaphor taken from exhausted vessels," John Calvin again observed, "as though he had said, that the Macedonians had been emptied, so that they had now reached the bottom."[486]

None of this deterred the Macedonians from giving. They did not fall into the age old trap, "Oh, if only I had more money so I could give," because if we do not give when we have little, we will not give when we have much.[487] They understood what Paul wrote to one of those very churches: "But my God shall supply all your need according to his riches in glory by Christ Jesus" (Phil. 4:19).

(3) We are to give *joyfully*. Even in the shadow of abusive pressure and abject poverty, the Macedonians gave not grudgingly, resentfully, or even dutifully, rather out of utter **joy**. The Greek is *chara* (5479), which means "gladness and rejoicing" and goes infinitely beyond mere human feelings of happiness or exuberance. In Scripture, especially in Paul's epistles, we see the paradox that real joy is found even in the midst of pain, suffering, and affliction.

Their joy, in fact, was in **abundance**. This is *perisseia* (4050), which denotes a surplus, a superabundant fullness. What accounts for such joy? This comes not by looking at the surrounding circumstances, but by keeping our eyes fixed upon the sufficiency of Christ.

Scriptures for Study: What did Paul write earlier in this letter (6:10) about giving? 📖 What do we then read in Acts 2:45?

DECEMBER 4

Grace Giving (4)

... the grace of God bestowed on the churches of Macedonia ... (2 Cor. 8:1–3)

"OUR gifts are not to be measured by the amount we contribute," Charles Spurgeon once preached, "but by the surplus we keep in our hand."[488]

(4) We are to give *generously*. In addition to what he already wrote, Paul added the astounding words that the deep poverty of the Macedonians **abounded unto the riches of their liberality**, thereby painting another graphic picture. **Abounded** is *perisseuō* (4052), the verb form of the noun *perisseia* noted yesterday for **abundance** and means to be in excess, exceed in number or measure. It's used elsewhere, for example, to express abounding love (1 Thess. 3:12), hope (Rom. 15:13), and grace (Rom 5:15; 2 Cor. 9:8; Eph. 1:7–8). **Riches**, then, is *ploutos* (4149, English "plutonic"), which even Plato recognized as being more than material wealth; he actually distinguished "material riches from true riches which consist of wisdom, virtue, and culture."[489] Paul repeatedly emphasized that true wealth consists of spiritual riches (Eph. 1:7, 18; 2:7; 3:8, 16; etc.).

Finally, Paul adds the word **liberality**; this is *haplotēs* (572), which carried a numerical meaning of "single" in contrast to "double" (*diplous*, 1362). In the ethical sense, it meant straightness, openness, speaking without a hidden meaning. This developed into the NT usage of sincerity, without duplicity, and "uncomplicated simplicity."[490] The picture is complete. We are to give excessively of both the material and spiritual riches we have without any hidden agenda or duplicitous motive. God gave us the work we do so we can give to the work He does.

(5) We are to give *proportionately*. The Macedonians gave according to their **power** (*dunamis*, 1411; Apr. 22, 25; Sept. 26), that is, their strength or ability to overcome resistance. Again, as he wrote in his first letter, Paul reemphasizes that no set amount is required, such as a tithe, rather we give according to how God has prospered us and according to what we have, not what we don't have (v. 12).

(6) We are to give *sacrificially*. Continuing the previous thought, the Macedonians then gave **beyond their power**, that is, over and above their ability; in other words, they sacrificed to give more. With the same godly thinking of Spurgeon, Harry Ironside wrote, "He estimates our gifts, not by the amount we give, but by the amount we have left. If a man is a millionaire and gives a thousand dollars, that does not count as much as one who has an income of a dollar a day and gives a dime."[491] How selfless are we in our giving?

(7) We are to give *voluntarily*. In contrast to cults that demand their followers to give, godly Christians are **willing of themselves**. **Willing** is *authaeretos* (830; cf. v. 17, the only other NT occurrence), which speaks not only of volition but also spontaneity. Once again, it's not about tithing; it's all about "grace giving."

Scriptures for Study: Read the rest of 2 Corinthians 8 and 9. What other principles of giving can you identify?

DECEMBER 5

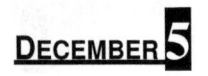

The Blessedness of Giving

... It is more blessed to give than to receive (Acts 20:35)

THE words of our text are truly unique, for while Paul tells the Ephesian elders to **remember the words of the Lord Jesus**, these are the only words our Lord spoke during His earthly ministry that do not appear in any of the four Gospels. Not everything that Jesus said or did is recorded in Scripture (Jn. 20:35; 21:25), which makes this verse all the more significant.

Just as Paul would later write to the Ephesians—"Let him that stole steal no more: let him labor, working with his hands the thing which is good, that he may have to give to him that needeth (Eph. 4:28)—Jesus' words were greatly needed in Ephesus. That city was among the most pagan cities of the day. One of the seven wonders of the ancient world was the great temple of Diana (or Artemis in Greek), and its ministers accumulated enormous wealth. In striking contrast, Paul speaks of Christ's ministers toiling with their own hands (20:34) and then adds Jesus' climactic words, **It is more blessed to give than to receive**. As we have noted (Nov. 23), **blessed** is *makarios* (3107), which speaks of contentment, and "is equivalent to having God's Kingdom within one's heart."[492]

First, it is more *praiseworthy* to give. People are praised, honored, and admired for their success, but how much more laudable it is to give. We are again reminded of Jesus' commendation of the widow who gave all she had.

Second, it is more *pleasurable* to give. We all enjoy receiving a gift, but when we give we also receive—we receive the joy of knowing that our gift brought help and joy to someone else. Again, as *makarios* indicates, there is true contentment in giving. "Folks who are always going around with an open hand, hoping you will give them something, are not happy people," Harry Ironside observed. "The happy ones are those who give to others."[493]

Third, it is more *profitable* to give. Blessings are like seeds; both are designed to produce more of the same. An old epitaph, reportedly engraved on the tombstone of 19th-century nobleman Robert of Doncaster at his request, reads: "What I kept I lost; what I gave I kept."

Fourth, it is more *pious* to give. True piety speaks of devoutness and godliness. We think first of God the Father, "who giveth us richly all things to enjoy" (1 Tim. 6:17). It is in His very nature to give. We think, then, of our Lord and Savior, whose whole life and ministry was about giving. "The grace of our Lord Jesus Christ, that, though he was rich, yet for [our] sakes he became poor, that [we] through his poverty might be rich" (2 Cor. 8:9). Finally, we consider also the Holy Spirit, who gives us regeneration (Jn. 3:5–8), comfort (April 11–12), spiritual gifts (1 Cor. 12:8), and much more. Think of it: to give is to imitate God!

Scriptures for Study: What do the following verses say about giving: Proverbs 19:17; Philippians 4:17?

DECEMBER 6

Whom Will You Serve?

... choose you this day whom ye will serve ... (Josh. 24:14–15)

THE text before us today demonstrates that every one of us will choose who we intend to serve. Contrary to popular belief, there is no such thing as "non-committal." We will choose one or we will choose another.

Serve is *'ābad* (5647H), a verb that appears almost 300 times in the OT and speaks of labor either on one's own behalf (Gen. 2:5; 4:2; Isa. 19:9) or for another person (Gen. 29:15; Exod. 1:14). It appears seven times in these two verses and a total of 18 times in the chapter. Joshua makes clear that the people must choose who they will serve. There were four choices then and four choices now.

First, there was the *cultic* choice of the Mesopotamian gods (**the gods which your fathers served**). Nimrod, the grandson of Ham and great-grandson of Noah, founded the cities of Babel (Babylon, Gen. 10:10–11). Semiramis, Nimrod's wife, became the first high priestess of idolatry, and Babylon became the mother of all pagan religion (Rev. 17:5). Throughout history such religions have practiced every unspeakable perversion known to man. Israel repeatedly fell into such idolatry, but there is little difference in our own day. There are cults that are religious, social, and economic, and every person chooses a god to serve.

Second, there was the *comfortable* choice of **Egypt**. We are immediately reminded here of the Israelites' complaint to Moses: "Is not this the word that we did tell thee in Egypt, saying, Let us alone, that we may serve the Egyptians? For it had been better for us to serve the Egyptians, than that we should die in the wilderness" (Ex. 14:12). Forgetting they were slaves in Egypt, they actually preferred the illusion of comfort they thought it afforded. We live in a culture of comfort in our day. While there is nothing wrong with a nice house, modern conveniences, and entertainment, we must never become slaves to them.

Third, there was the *contemporary* choice of the **Amorites in whose land they** currently lived. The gods of the Amorites, such as Molech, were horrific; worship involved temple prostitution and infant sacrifice. But the Israelites chose to be a part of it all, to be relevant to the culture, to blend in with everyone else. We see the same today. In the name of "cultural relevance," some Christians compromise Truth and morality. We even have our own version of "Molech," as we sacrifice millions of babies through abortion to the gods of selfishness and convenience.

Fourth, there was the *Christian* choice of the true God (**LORD**). Of course, they were not "Christians" in that day, but they worshipped the same LORD nonetheless. LORD is once again *Yāhweh* (Jan. 21), God's covenant name. All His covenants pointed to the coming Messiah. So, **choose you this day whom ye will serve**. It's all or nothing. Let us "put away . . . the strange gods which are among [us] and incline [our] heart unto the LORD God" (v. 23).

Scriptures for Study: What does God command in Exodus 23:24 and 32–33?

DECEMBER 7

Attachment To God's House (1)

One thing have I desired of the LORD, that will I seek after; that I may dwell in the house of the LORD all the days of my life, to behold the beauty of the LORD, and to enquire in his temple. (Ps. 27:4)

WE have previously considered the importance of attendance to the Local Church in our section on loving the Lord (June 21), but we return to this theme one last time simply because of just how crucial it really is, for it is also a part of our service for Him. In light of that previous study, and if I may be so bold, there is something seriously amiss with the Christian who does not desire such attendance and make it a priority of life. David himself challenges us with his testimony. Of the many outstanding qualities we see in David, only his love for God's Word (Pss. 19; 119) equaled his passionate attachment to God's house.

First, we see the *place* of his attachment: **the house of the LORD**. This is the place David longed to be more than anywhere else. When driven into exile, it wasn't his possessions, power, or position that David missed; rather it was God and the "sanctuary" (Ps. 63:1–2), that is, God's presence in the tabernacle, the place of prayer and public worship, David longed for.

Yes, this was OT, but there is most certainly a NT parallel. As the Apostle Paul wrote to the Ephesians, "In whom ye also are builded together for an habitation [*katoikētērion*, 2732, dwelling place] of God through the Spirit" (2:22). Going deeper with the Corinthians, at one point he showed them that *individually* every Christian is indwelt by the Holy Spirit (1 Cor. 6:19). Even before that, however, Paul told them that they were indwelt *collectively*, that is, the Holy Spirit dwells not only in each Christian, but He dwells in the entire assembly, the Church as a whole (3:16–17). It is extremely important that we understand that the Holy Spirit not only makes His earthly sanctuary in the *Christian*, but that He also makes His earthly sanctuary in the *Church*, that is, the Universal Church, the Body of Christ.

Does this principle have any practical application to the *Local* Church? Some answer with a resounding "No!" Many insist, "Where we meet is not a 'sanctuary' because the Spirit indwells the believer who is the real 'sanctuary;' rather, we all meet in the 'auditorium,' or what we just dubbed our new building, our 'multipurpose facility.' Calling it the 'sanctuary' is too narrow, too rigid, too formal."

We would lovingly submit, however, it is this very attitude that has helped destroy the spirit of reverence and true worship in many churches. Tragically, as A. W. Tozer once observed, today's church has been turned into "a religious theater."[494] God designed the Local Church to be a reflection of the Universal Church. Both are the dwelling place of God's presence, so both should manifest reverence and worship. This should be the place where we want to be.

Scriptures for Study: Review our June 21 reading. 📖 What do the following verses in Psalms say about **the house of the LORD**: 23:6; 122:1; 92:13?

DECEMBER 8

Attachment To God's House (2)

One thing have I desired of the LORD, that will I seek after; that I may dwell in the house of the LORD all the days of my life, to behold the beauty of the LORD, and to enquire in his temple. (Ps. 27:4)

PURITAN Richard Baxter wrote, "[God's] *tabernacles* served to shew His power, His *courts* showed His majesty, and His *altars* showed His deity. His *house* serves to shew them all . . . His praise and glory is the sum of all."[495]

Second, the *point* of David's attachment: **dwell in the house of the LORD**. Dwell is *yāšab* (3427H), which also means "to inhabit, endure, or stay." Significantly, the Septuagint renders *yāšab* here (and elsewhere) with the Greek *katoikeō* (2730), "to inhabit a house." The clear truth in all this, then, is permanence, continually dwelling in one place. This leads to another principle.

Third, the *period* of his attachment: **all the days of my life**. There was no better place on earth to David than God's house, and it was there he wanted to spend every day. Likewise, what better place is there to be today each time the church meets? What could possibly be more important?

Fourth, the *purpose* of his attachment: **to behold the beauty of the LORD, and to enquire in his temple**. While in popular thinking the Church is wholly people-centered, David was there not for Himself but for God alone. How significant it is that David worshipped in the days before Solomon built the actual **temple**, when the place of worship was just a tent. But it was still beautiful to him. What a contrast that is to the building we think we need to have! Further, this was the place David came **to enquire** (*bāqar*, 1239H), to investigate and consider the things of God. That is what preaching does today.

Fifth, the *pre-eminence* of his attachment: **One thing**. For David, this came *above* everything else and *before* everything else. Oh, how often some flimsy excuse keeps us from our attendance in God's House! Should not this **one thing** overrule everything else?

Sixth, the *perseverance* of his attachment: **I seek after**. This was not just some wish David made, not just a preference over several other options, but rather a desire he actively pursued. "Holy desires must lead to resolute action," Spurgeon wrote. "The old proverb says, 'Wishers and woulders are never good housekeepers,' and 'wishing never fills a sack.' Desires are seeds which must be sown in the good soil of activity or they will yield no harvest."[496]

Seventh, the *prayer* of his attachment: **I desired of the LORD**. Desired is *šā'al* (7592H), one of several words used for prayer in the OT. It simply means "to ask something of someone," whether one is just asking a question (Gen. 32:17), making a simple request (Judg. 5:25), or even begging (Prov. 20:4). This entire verse, then, is David's prayer. Is it ours? Do we ask Him to help us make it our priority?

Scriptures for Study: What do the following verses in Psalms add to our study: 26:8; 65:4; 84:4, 10?

December 9

Reasons For Church Attendance (1)

... not forsaking the assembling of ourselves together ... (Heb. 10:25)

BEFORE we leave this subject, I would share my pastor's heart, for this is not a minor concern. It is, in fact, an extremely serious matter that every true pastor is burdened by. Commenting on our text, R. Kent Hughes shares his pastor's heart when he writes: "People have a thousand reasons to stay away from church. This is not a new problem. The early Jewish church had had a fall-off in attendance due to persecution, ostracism, apostasy, and arrogance. Today persecution and ostracism may not be our experience, but people find many other reasons to absent themselves from worship, not the least of which is laziness. But de-churched Christians have always been an aberration, as Cyprian, Augustine, Luther, Calvin, and the various classic confessions repeatedly affirm."[497]

Pastor John Gill was equally candid: "This evil practice arises sometimes from a vain conceit of being in no need of ordinances, and from an over love of the world."[498] Commentator and professor E. Schuyler English also effectively "meddles" into the life of such Christians: "Point out a man or a woman who does not desire communion with other Christians, and you are pointing to one whose spiritual condition is low and whose testimony for Christ is weak indeed."[499] Still another writes: "One of the first indications of a lack of love toward God and the neighbor is for a Christian to stay away from the worship services. He forsakes the communal obligations of attending these meetings and displays the symptoms of selfishness and self-centeredness."[500]

Speaking from my own heart, in all my four decades plus of ministry, I have never quite gotten past this oddity. I just don't understand it. I have seen countless things come before church, proving that such attendance is not only not the priority but also is flippantly considered as "no big deal." I've seen Christians abandon church for any number of reasons. I could make a list, but such a list would go on *ad infinitum*. It would be far better if we each examine ourselves to see where our priority lies. One I can't resist mentioning, however, is the lady I once heard say, "Oh, I can't be at church tonight because I'm getting my hair done."

If I may also say again from my heart, I lovingly submit that there is something very troubling with the Christian whose priority is not faithful, consistent attendance in the Local Church. I know that might sound intolerant—or even that most terrible of words, "legalistic"—but such nonchalance about unfaithfulness is a staggering contradiction. What can possibly be more important than our attendance in the Local Church, where we worship, fellowship, and receive the essential nourishment of God's Word?

I would, therefore, offer seven reasons for **not forsaking the assembling of ourselves together, as the manner of some is**.

Scriptures for Study: What do we read about the Early Church in the following verses: Acts 2:1, 42, 46–47; 20:7?

Reasons For Church Attendance (2)

... not forsaking the assembling of ourselves together ... (Heb. 10:25)

IN addition to the many verses that unambiguously assume regular attendance in the Local Church (Acts 2:42; 20:7; 1 Cor. 5:4; 11:17, 18, 20; 14:23; 16:2), this is the clearest statement of the mandate itself (June 21). But why is this so critically important? We would submit seven reasons.

First, to obey Christ. This should be enough. While there will certainly be times of illness, the yearly vacation, or the unforeseen emergency that keeps us away from church, these are the few exceptions that establish the consistent rule.[501]

Second, to praise and worship our God. This, too, we have noted several times. While the common attitude today is that the Local Church is a place for the "unchurched," entertainment, and the meeting of "felt needs," all that is foreign to and the antithesis of Scripture. This is the place God's people meet for corporate worship. Once again, it's not about us; it's about God (June 1–2).

Third, to hear the Word of God. The primary reason the office gifts were given (Eph. 4:11) was "for the perfecting of the saints, for the work of the ministry, for the edifying of the body of Christ" (v. 12). Faithful attendance is, therefore, essential for consistent growth in biblical knowledge and application. "Perfecting" translates is *katartismos* (2677), which appears only here in the NT and means "to put in order, restore, furnish, prepare, equip," and that is the job of called, qualified, trained, and ordained leaders.

Consider David once again: "Behold, I have longed after thy precepts" (Ps. 119:40a). In stark contrast to the common dismissing of church today, David's use of the words "longed after" are most instructive. The Hebrew *tā'ab* (8373) appears only twice in the OT, both in Psalm 119. David declares in verse 174, "I have longed for thy salvation, O LORD; and thy law is my delight." A derivative (*ta'abâ*, 8365) occurs once more back in verse 20: "My soul breaketh for the longing that it hath unto thy judgments at all times." This word speaks of an intense hunger, and David was broken hearted when deprived of God's Word. How many of us are broken hearted when we can't be under the preaching and teaching of the Word? Mark it down: the consistent, truly committed Christian is one who has an insatiable appetite for God's Word.

Let us ponder this a moment very practically. As soldiers are trained as a combat unit at a specific training facility, so are Christians. What would be the result if soldiers were as unfaithful to their training sessions as some Christians are to the church? What would that do to the quality of the unit in both combat readiness and morale? Likewise, we are in a war, and we are not only *required* to be in training, but we should also *want* such training because of the ferocity of the war.

To illustrate another way, what if we were as unfaithful to our daily job as we are to the local church? How long would we be employed?

Scriptures for Study: What are your thoughts on the verses cited today?

DECEMBER 11

Reasons For Church Attendance (3)

... not forsaking the assembling of ourselves together ... (Heb. 10:25)

THERE is a *fourth* reason for **not forsaking the assembling of ourselves together, as the manner of some is**: your own personal edification. This reason, in fact, is critical. Returning to Ephesians 4:11–12, our Lord gave the office gifts not only "for the perfecting of the saints, for the work of the ministry," but also "for the edifying of the body of Christ." The Greek *oikodomē* (3619), and other forms, is a compound comprised of *oikos*, "house or dwelling," and *dōma*, "to build." While the entire body of Christ is obviously in view here, individuals comprise that body, so each is vital to the structure, which in turn can obviously be applied to the Local Church. No single building material is isolated from the rest in building a literal house; none is meant to stand alone. Likewise, it is vital that every believer be present for God's preparation of them and their subsequent use in the spiritual building.

I read of a pastor who visited a man who wasn't attending church very faithfully. It was a cold winter day, so they warmed themselves by a fire as they talked. "My friend, I don't see you at church on the Lord's Day," the pastor said. "You seem to come only when it's convenient, or only when you feel like you need to come. You miss so very often. I wish you'd come all the time." The man didn't seem to be getting the message, so the pastor said, "Let me show you something." He then took the tongs from beside the fireplace, pulled open the screen, and began to separate all the coals so that none of them were touching each other. In a matter of moments, the blazing coals had all died out. "My friend," he said, "that is what's happening in your life. As soon as you isolate yourself, the fire goes out."

Pastor and commentator Lloyd J. Ogilvie puts it still another way: "We Christians are like short-lived radioactive isotopes; we have a very short half-life. Get us away from the worship of God with other saints and our radioactivity dissipates quickly and we lose our effective radiance."[502]

Fifth, to encourage your pastor. There are few things that discourage and grieve a pastor more than seeing Christians who are sporadic in their attendance. Scripture calls him a shepherd, and like a literal shepherd he wonders where in the world his sheep are when they are absent from the fold. He is concerned because those sheep need nourishment but have wandered from the rich pasture where the food is waiting. He is concerned because there are predators just waiting for such a moment to pick off a wandering sheep that is oblivious to the danger. The biblical pastor spends the majority of his time in the Word so he can feed those sheep. So when they don't care to show up to hear what God has laid on his heart, it grieves his spirit. Ponder it this way: what hostess would not be upset if she spent the whole day preparing a meal but the invited guests didn't bother to show up?

Scriptures for Study: How do the following verses encourage you: Colossians 3:16; 1 Thessalonians 5:12–13; Hebrews 13:17?

DECEMBER 12

Reasons For Church Attendance (4)

... not forsaking the assembling of ourselves together ... (Heb. 10:25)

MY Dear Christian Friend, I pray these studies on faithful attendance have not appeared as my scolding you, rather their entire purpose has been to encourage you with this vitally important priority.

Sixth, to encourage other believers. Many people feel they can worship God by being out in nature or by viewing a church service on television. But what of other believers? What about the other Christian soldiers in our company? Just as literal soldiers depend upon one another, so do we. We encourage each other in spiritual combat. We love and protect each other. Those who just shrug this off by not "showing up" discourage the others who do. Consider this often quoted statement by Martin Luther: "At home, in my own house, there is no warmth or vigor in me, but in the church when the multitude is gathered together a fire is kindled in my heart and it breaks its way through."

Seventh and finally, to be a testimony to others. I am again grieved when I see Christians forsake their responsibility of church attendance in such a way that unbelievers see it. I have seen many other things take precedence even though unbelievers at those times knew that the Christians involved missed church to be there. What message does that send? How is this a testimony of our commitment and love for Christ? Is our faith and spiritual life important only when it is convenient and doesn't interfere with our schedule? Is our church life just a satellite that revolves around everything else, or does everything else revolve around it? What is really at the core of our "universe"?

As our text once again declares, **exhorting one another: and so much the more, as ye see the day approaching.** Which day is approaching? The views vary,[503] but the point is that whichever event is in view, that event is **approaching**. This is the Greek *eggizō* (1448), "to bring near, to be at hand." Today we might say, "It's just around the next corner." In light of that impending day, then, we should be **exhorting one another** (*parakaleō*, 3870), that is, comforting, beseeching, admonishing, and even imploring one another in this area of faithfulness to the assembly. As one commentator submits: "To neglect Christian meetings is to give up the encouragement and help of other Christians. We gather together to share our faith and to strengthen one another in the Lord. As we get closer to the day when Christ will return, we will face many spiritual struggles, and even times of persecution. Anti-Christian forces will grow in strength. Difficulties should never be excuses for missing church services. Rather, as difficulties arise, we should make an even greater effort to be faithful in attendance."[504]

Dear Christian Friend, is there any doubt as to the enormous importance of faithful attendance in the Local Church?

Scriptures for Study: Review these studies and reflect on the impact they have had on your heart.

DECEMBER 13

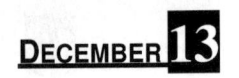

Well Doing

And let us not be weary in well doing: for in due season we shall reap, if we faint not. (Gal. 6:9)

WHILE Paul had thoroughly grounded the Galatians in the doctrine of justification by faith alone, the Judaizers had infiltrated those churches and turned them away from the simplicity of the Gospel (Feb. 19). The purpose of his stern letter was to bring them back to the Truth.

First, we note here the *engagement*. As with most of his letters, Paul spent the first half on *doctrine* and the second on *duty*. In chapter 6 he emphasizes that the life of liberty apart from the Law nonetheless requires sacrificial service. **Well doing** is also two words in the Greek: **doing** is *poieō* (4160), which also means to make or produce, and the adjective **well** (*kalos*, 2570) is a broad and comprehensive concept that speaks of beauty, excellence, and high quality. All this is, therefore, far more than just "doing our duty" or feeling the need to do at least "a little something" for someone in need. It is actually accomplishing something with excellence and the highest quality we can.

Second, the *exhortation*: **let us not be weary in well doing. Weary** is *ekkakeō* (1573), a vivid word that means "to turn out to be a coward, to lose one's courage, to faint or despond in view of trial,"[505] or even stronger, "to be utterly spiritless."[506] It's one thing to be *discouraged*, but quite another to faint in *despondency*. What is Paul's challenge? He tells us not to get dreary, not to sink into depression, not to become so dispirited that we just quit.

But, oh, how easy it is to become **weary**! Let us not minimize that. When we see the wicked flourish and then, on top of that, see little result from our doing good in our lives, the lives of others, and our evangelism, it is easy to throw up our hands and say, "Oh, why even bother!" What causes such weariness? Sometimes it's simply because of the wrong motivation. Is our **doing** for God's glory or our own? At other times it's simply because we are **doing** in our own strength and methods, not depending upon the Lord and His method. Like the Galatians, we are apt to begin in the Spirit but then seek to finish in the flesh (3:3). So, how do we prevent such weariness?

Third, the *endurance*: **for in due season we shall reap, if we faint not**. As every farmer knows, we cannot sow and reap on the same day. It takes time, cultivation, and patience. We just keep sowing and allow God to bring the harvest, even if in some cases we never see it. We are reminded of Paul's challenge to the Corinthians, "I have planted, Apollos watered; but God gave the increase. So then neither is he that planteth any thing, neither he that watereth; but God that giveth the increase. Now he that planteth and he that watereth are one: and every man shall receive his own reward according to his own labour" (1 Cor. 3:6–8).

Scriptures for Study: How do the following verses encourage us: Luke 18:1; 2 Corinthians 4:1, 16? 📖 You might want to review our July 8 reading.

DECEMBER 14

Ministering to One Another (1)

God is not unrighteous to forget your work and labour of love, which ye have shewed toward his name, in that ye have ministered to the saints, and do minister. (Heb. 6:10)

THE verse before us today assures us that God will bless our caring for one another and encourages us to continue it. **Minister** is *diakoneō* (1247), which, as we have noted before (Sept. 1), referred basically to "one who serves at table," but probably included other menial tasks. That concept gradually broadened until it came to include any kind of service in the Church.

Pastors have been called "ministers" for a long time. A pastor, in fact, is often viewed as the fellow who is supposed to do everything in the church, from preaching, to hospital visiting, to mowing the church lawn. But all believers are ministers, servants (e.g., Gal. 5:13), and are to attend to the needs of one another.

What makes this all the more wondrous is that when we serve one another, we automatically serve Christ. In closing His Olivet Discourse, Jesus said that when He returns, He will usher His sheep into His Kingdom, which He "prepared for [them] from the foundation of the world." He went on to list His reasons: they fed Him when He was hungry, gave Him drink when He was thirsty, welcomed Him when He was a stranger, clothed Him when His clothes were worn out, visited Him when He was ill, and comforted Him when he was in prison. When His sheep voice confusion—they didn't even exist when He walked the earth so they couldn't possibly have done any of these things—He explains, "Inasmuch as ye have done it unto one of the least of these my brethren, ye have done it unto me" (Matt. 25:33–40). Now, this does not imply salvation by works, rather it demonstrates that there is a "sacred union among the children of God," as Calvin put it, and so these are the things we now do simply because of our transformation in Christ.

And so it is, then, that we all **work and labour** for one another. **Work** (*ergon*, 2041), is a general word for an act, deed, or employment, but **labor** is the more graphic *kopos* (2873), which means "exertion and toil," "the process of becoming tired," and the "consequent fatigue and exhaustion."[507] Peter used this word, for example, when he told the Lord that he and his companions "toiled" all night fishing and had caught nothing (Lk. 5:5). It is also used to describe the pastor's responsibility to "labour [to the point of exhaustion] in the word and doctrine" (1 Tim. 5:17), since his primary function is to preach and teach (cf. 3:2). Paul also used this to describe four people in the Roman church who labored tirelessly and sacrificially for Christ: Mary, Tryphena, Tryphosa, and Persis (Rom. 16:6, 12).

With this in mind, how can we practically minister to one another? It is encouraging, indeed, that God has not left us to our own opinions here, rather He has provided specific ways we can serve. By turning to several verses that use the term "one another," we discover no less than 12 ways we can minister.

Scriptures for Study: What do the following verses add to our study today: Mark 9:41; Galatians 5:13; 1 John 3:18?

DECEMBER 15

Ministering to One Another (2)

... ye have ministered to the saints, and do minister. (Heb. 6:10)

"IS it nothing for a man to be employed in comforting, relieving, and supporting others?" asked Puritan William Bridge. "This is so great a service that the very angels are employed therein." How, then, can we do this? By observing the many instances of the words "one another" in the NT.

First, we love one another. While noted in our studies of loving the Lord (Aug. 29–31), it is here at the core of our serving Him. As John declared, "For this is the message that ye heard from the beginning, that we should love one another" (1 Jn. 3:11; cf. 2:7–8; 3:23; 4:21; Jn. 15:12). All the other instances of "one another," in fact, flow from this. "Freely we serve because we freely love."[508]

Second, we prefer one another: "Be kindly affectioned one to another with brotherly love; in honour preferring one another" (Rom. 12:10). "Preferring" is *proēgeomai* (4285), which is comprised of *pro*, before, and *hēgeomai*, to lead the way and so, therefore, to take the lead in honoring one another. In other words, "Instead of contending for superiority," wrote Matthew Henry, "let us be forward to give to others the pre-eminence." Paul wrote his own commentary on this verse in Philippians 2:3–4, "Let nothing be done through strife or vainglory; but in lowliness of mind let each esteem other better than themselves. Look not every man on his own things, but every man also on the things of others."

Sadly, we all often do the exact opposite. We think of ourselves first and foremost in any situation. We serve only when we know we will be recognized and even elevated over others. But that is not how love and true service function. We go to the front of the line not to *receive* honor for ourselves, but rather to lead the way in *recognizing* honor in others.

Third, we receive one another: "Wherefore receive ye one another, as Christ also received us to the glory of God" (Rom. 15:7). Here is a profound follow-up from the previous principle. "Receive" translates *proslambanō* (4355), which here literally means "to receive to oneself, admit to one's society and fellowship, receive and treat with kindness."[509]

People do all kinds of things for "acceptance" nowadays, and others in turn demand certain things before they will accept the ones in question. University fraternities, for example, demand certain actions and behavior (which are often mean-spirited and wicked) from "pledges" before they are accepted into membership (tragically, this occurs even in some Christian institutions). At other times we reject those who do not agree with us on some minor (not *major*, but *minor*) point of doctrine or practice.

What, then, is the basis of our acceptance? One thing and one only: "as Christ also received us to the glory of God." That is more than enough reason.

Scriptures for Study: Paul used this word earlier in Romans 14:1–3. What observations can you make here?

DECEMBER 16

Ministering to One Another (3)

. . . ye have ministered to the saints, and do minister. (Heb. 6:10)

"IN matters of equity between man and man," wrote theologian, logician, and hymn writer, Isaac Watts, "our Savior has taught us to put my neighbor in place of myself, and myself in place of my neighbor."[510]

Fourth, we admonish one another: "And I myself also am persuaded of you, my brethren, that ye also are full of goodness, filled with all knowledge, able also to admonish one another" (Rom. 15:14). This "one another" comes right on the heels of and is a fitting sequel to "receive one another" (v. 7), which we considered yesterday. "Admonish" is the verb *noutheteō* (3560), which appears eight additional times in the NT and is filled with meaning. It combines *nous* (3563), mind, and *tithēmi* (5087), to place. It is, therefore, placing before the mind, that is, imparting understanding, laying on the heart, setting right, reminding, and warning.

There is a huge emphasis on counseling nowadays, which actually takes one of three forms. The first is the totally secular approach of psychology, which is, in all its many varieties, completely humanistic and contrary to God and His Word. Another is foundationally the same but adds some Scripture so it can call itself "Christian." The result is a staggering contradiction that ultimately denies biblical sufficiency. Tragically, this approach is epidemic in Christendom today. The third type is true *biblical* counseling and is the only one we find sanctioned in Scripture simply because it is the only one that relies solely and completely on God's Word. It doesn't rely upon *techniques*, rather upon *Truth*.

What we see before us, then, is the latter type. Long before there were seminars, training courses, and certified counselors, there were Christians who were so *saturated* in the Truth, so *solemnly* obedient, so *spiritually* attuned, that they were competent to admonish one another. "Experts" today say that even pastors are not qualified to counsel, much less lay Christians, and that only those who are specially trained and licensed are competent. But we cannot help but wonder how Paul, or even Jesus Himself, was ever effective in ministry without being certified.

We also hear much today about "psychological problems," but again, Scripture does not support this concept. Whatever problem arises in a person, it is either *physical* or *spiritual*; there is nothing in between. As an earthly physician can care for the former, only the Divine Physician can cure the latter.

So, while there will be times when more serious problems arise that demand pastoral attention, every Christian should be "competent to counsel" those who desire it and seek it. Obviously, it must not be done self-righteously or judgmentally, nor should it involve "rebuke" (this is pastoral only: 1 Tim. 5:20; 2 Tim. 4:2; Titus 1:13; 2:15). Rather it is an opportunity to humbly remind another of the Truth and warn them of consequences.

Scriptures for Study: What do you observe in these other instances of *noutheteō*: Colossians 3:16; 1 Thessalonians 5:14 ("warn"); 2 Thessalonians 3:15.

December 17

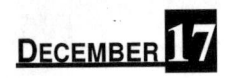

Ministering to One Another (4)

... ye have ministered to the saints, and do minister. (Heb. 6:10)

FIFTH, Paul tells us that we minister when we bear one another's burdens: "Bear ye one another's burdens, and so fulfil the law of Christ. . . . For every man shall bear his own burden" (Gal. 6:2, 5). At first glance these verses seem absurdly contradictory, but a deeper look wipes away any doubt because the two instances of the word "burden" are two different Greek words. While some view these as interchangeable, there seems to be, in fact, a subtle difference, especially since Paul uses both in such close proximity.

In verse 5, "burden" is *phortion* (5413), which is singular and denotes a load, even a ship's cargo, but also one that can be "carried by an animal or man."[511] It was also used to "designate the pack usually carried by a marching soldier"[512] and for "a child in a mother's womb."[513] Our Lord used this very word when He said, "Take my yoke upon you, and learn of me; for I am meek and lowly in heart: and ye shall find rest unto your souls. For my yoke is easy, and my burden is light" (Matt. 11:29–30). So, every Christian must bear his own load in his Christian living, but Jesus assures us it will be light enough to carry without collapse.

"Burdens" in verse 2, however, is *baros* (922). In Classical Greek it literally referred to a crushing weight or physical burden but was more significantly used in the figurative sense of stress, oppression, dejection, and misery. It's used in Acts 15:28–29, where it was decided at the Jerusalem Council not to put any "burden" of the Mosaic Law on Gentiles except to "abstain from meats offered to idols, and from blood, and from things strangled, and from fornication." In the present context, then, it is the weight of sin that had "overtaken" certain believers (v. 1). *Baros* is also in the plural denoting the further oppressiveness of more than one load.

We are, therefore, to help "bear" (*bastazō*, 941, to raise upon a basis, support, carry) such overpowering spiritual burdens of a fellow believer. This means we prop him up, help him get back on his feet, and carry him along until he is strong enough to continue. In so doing, we "fulfil the law of Christ," the law of love. As we have noted, all these "one anothers" flow from love.

Sixth, and right in line with our previous principle, we comfort one another: "Wherefore comfort one another with these words" (1 Thess. 4:18). "Comfort" is *parakaleō* (3870), to call to one's side to aid; the noun form is *paraklētos*, which as we have studied (April 4–30) is used of the Holy Spirit (The Comforter) and Christ (The Advocate). Used here the verb speaks of consoling, encouraging, and comforting. The context speaks specifically of comforting those who have lost believing loved ones by assuring them they will be reunited. There will be times when we all need comforting from the Word of God in trials and troubles, and all of us are to be "comforters" as the Holy Spirit enables.

Scriptures for Study: What encouragement does Paul add earlier in 1 Thessalonians: 3:2, 7; 5:11.

DECEMBER 18

Ministering to One Another (5)

... ye have ministered to the saints, and do minister. (Heb. 6:10)

"ONE good deed is more worth than a thousand brilliant theories," wrote Charles Spurgeon. "Let us not wait for large opportunities, or for a different kind of work, but do just the things we 'find to do' day by day."[514]

Seventh, we minister when we forebear one another: "forbearing one another in love" (Eph. 4:2). The context of this verse is unity. Christian unity has been a perennial problem since the early days of Christianity. As early as Acts 6, unity was threatened. Additionally, in almost every one of Paul's Epistles there is something about unity. Paul commanded believers here "to keep the unity of the Spirit in the bond of peace." "Keep" is *tēreō* (5083), which is derived from *tēros* (a warden or guard) and means to keep an eye on, watch over, observe attentively, and even guard protectively. Notice that we are not told to *create* unity. When we try, we inevitably create instead compromise, tolerance, uniformity, or other false unity. Rather, we guard the unity Christ created.

Paul lists four ways that we guard Christian unity, one of which is "forbearing one another in love." Interestingly, while we might think that to speak of "love" would be enough, Paul knew it wouldn't be because he understood human nature, so he adds that we are also to be "forbearing one another." This is *anechomai* (430), "to hold one's self upright, to bear, to endure." This is the same word Paul uses in 2 Timothy 4:3 to describe people who will not "endure [put up with] sound doctrine" but will seek teachers who will tickle their ears. The idea here, then, is that sometimes we just put up with each other, that we bear with each other in misunderstandings, problems, and conflicts, that we love each other and sacrifice ourselves for others anyway. This doesn't mean we just put up with it but still boil within, rather we forbear in love. Without this kind of love and forbearing, unity will be destroyed and God's work right along with it.

Eighth, right on the heels of the above, Paul went on to write that we forgive one another: "And be ye kind one to another, tenderhearted, forgiving one another, even as God for Christ's sake hath forgiven you" (Eph. 4:32). Instead of the usual word for forgiveness (*aphesis*, 859, "release, pardon, or cancellation"), the word here is *charizomai* (5483), the root of which is *charis*, grace (Feb. 16), and means showing favor, graciously giving to someone. In other words, true forgiveness is treating the offender graciously, responding to unkindness with kindness.

Oh, but that person wronged me," we argue, "he hurt me, he insulted me!" But let us consider what *we* did to the Savior, but He forgave us according to His grace. We live in a day when raw feelings drive people's actions. Should we, therefore, *deny* our feelings? Indeed not, we should *deal* with them; they should be controlled by a mind that is driven by God's Word.

Scriptures for Study: What do the following verses add to our study today: Romans 12:20–21; 1 Corinthians 13:7?

December 19

Ministering to One Another (6)

... ye have ministered to the saints, and do minister. (Heb. 6:10)

NINTH, Paul tells us another way we minister is when we edify one another: "Let us therefore follow after the things which make for peace, and things wherewith one may edify another" (Rom. 14:19). "Edify" is *oikodomē* (3619), which we recently considered (Dec. 11). When we are with each other, either privately or corporately, we should build each other up with our actions and speech.

Tenth, we are to exhort one another: "And let us consider one another to provoke unto love and to good works: Not forsaking the assembling of ourselves together, as the manner of some is; but exhorting one another: and so much the more, as ye see the day approaching" (Heb. 10:24–25). While the Greek behind "provoke" (*paroxusmos*, 3948) means "irritate" in other contexts (Acts 15:39; 17:16; 1 Cor. 13:5), its meaning here is the neutral sense of stimulating or stirring up (English *paroxysm*, meaning excitement or impulse). We should stir up each other's spiritual affections. "Exhorting," then, (*parakaleō*, 3870), as we have noted (June 21, Dec. 12; cf. July 1), means comforting, beseeching, admonishing, and even imploring one another to be faithful. As with admonition (Dec. 16), we don't do this self-righteously or judgmentally but rather in humble love.

Eleventh, we are to confess our sins to one another: "Confess your faults one to another" (Jas. 5:16a). "Faults" is *paraptōma* (3900), which is variously translated elsewhere as "trespass" (Matt. 6:14–15; 2 Cor. 5:19), "sins" (Eph. 1:7; 2:5), and "offense" (Rom. 4:25; 5:15–20). It is a deviation from uprightness and truth, the committing of a fault. So, when we sin against someone, we don't make an excuse, we don't blame someone else, rather we "confess" it, that is, we admit it as the sin it is (*exomologeō*, 1843, to agree openly, to acknowledge).

Twelfth and finally, and as the capstone of all the others, we are to pray for one another: "pray one for another" (Jas. 5:16b). We have mentioned prayer many times throughout our studies (e.g., Aug. 15), and one of the most critical aspects of prayer is intercessory prayer, praying for others. Not only must pastors pray for those he leads (May 24), but it is essential that believers pray for each other as well. Is it not difficult to be unforgiving, unaffectionate, unkind, unreceptive, and unforbearing of someone when we are praying for them? The context, of course, speaks of prayer for healing the sick (v. 14), but there are many other needs. Further, we should pray for all kinds of people (1 Tim. 2:1), including: the spiritual lives of our friends (Job 42:8), government leaders (1 Tim. 2:2), Christian leaders (Phil. 1:19), and even our enemies (Jer. 29:7) and persecutors (Matt. 5:44).

Dear Christian Friend, let us again be encouraged in all this to serve our Lord by serving "one another." As always, God will bless our faithfulness.

Scriptures for Study: What do the following verses say about edification: Romans 15:2; Ephesians 4:29; 1 Timothy 1:4?

DECEMBER 20

Exalting Christ

... God also hath highly exalted him ... (Phil. 2:9)

PHILIPPIANS 2:5–11 has been called "The Great Parabola of Scripture." A parabola is an arc, where you start at a low point, go up to the highest point, and then come back down. When you shoot an arrow, for example, or hit a golf ball, it arcs up into the air, reaches its highest point, and comes back down, thus following the path of a parabola. In our Lord's case, however, it is reversed: He started at the highest point (heaven, vv. 5–6), descended to the lowest point (earth, vv. 7–8) to die on the Cross for our sins, and returned to the highest point where He is exalted in glory (vv. 9–11).

This passage is, indeed, among the most glorious in the NT. As Handley C. G. Moule wrote of this passage: "it is the most conspicuous and magnificent of the dogmatic utterances of the New Testament."[515] For Paul himself, it is the most comprehensive and moving statement he ever wrote about Jesus. It sweeps us along from Christ's *inherent* glory in eternity past, to His *incarnate* purpose on earth, to His *infinite* exaltation in eternity future.

The idea of exaltation, in fact, is at the core of the passage. The words **highly exalted** in verse 9 translate *huperupsoō* (5251). The root *hupsoō* simply means "to elevate," but the prefix *huper* (5228) intensifies it dramatically. It means "over, above, or beyond," so the full idea in **highly exalted** is "to elevate above others, raise to the highest position." This is the only place in the NT, in fact, the Greek word appears.

This truth is of particular importance at this time of the year, the so-called Christmas Season. There are, indeed, masses of people (even Christians) who say that Jesus is "the reason for the season" and claim to make Him the center of this time of year while their actions (and even attitudes) say something very different. Of all the times of the year, this should be one when Christ alone is **highly exalted**, but instead many other things are in the forefront, while He is merely a footnote among the festivities or merely an honorable mention.

Again, the critical nature of this passage cannot be overemphasized. R. C. H. Lenski used a Latin term in calling this "a great *sedes doctrinae*,"[516] that is, a seat (or base) of doctrine, a term used of clear passages of Scripture that treat individual doctrines and hence are proof passages for that doctrine. Indeed, this passage is a mini-course in Christology. It teaches the divinity of Christ, his eternal preexistence, his equality with God the Father, his incarnation, his full humanity, his voluntary death on the cross, the certainty of his victory over evil, and the eternalness of his reign.

In our next few studies, we will see in this passage how Christ is exalted in three areas: His *person*; His *purpose*; and His *position*.

Scriptures for Study: In preparation for our study, meditate on Philippians 2:5–11 and write down your own observations.

DECEMBER 21

Exalting Christ's Person

... Christ Jesus ... (Phil. 2:5–8a)

IN Philippians 2:5–11, we see Christ exalted first in His *person*. Verse 5 sets the stage. The context (vv. 1–4) speaks of the unity of God's people and the humility each should demonstrate. The greatest example of this, of course, and the one we should emulate, is **Christ Jesus**. It is no accident that Paul uses that great Messianic title (see Mar. 2 and 3 for these two words).

There are two other words here that are absolutely essential in understanding the person of **Christ Jesus**: **form** (v. 6) and **fashion** (v. 8). To the causal reader they appear to be just synonyms, but they are in reality very different. **Form** is *morphe* (3444), which refers to the inward essential nature of a person that never changes. It is used here both of Jesus as God in verse 6—**the form [nature] of God**—and as a servant in verse 7—**the form [nature] of a servant**. This is among the strongest statements in Scripture of the deity of Christ. This word unambiguously states that no one could be in the *form* (nature) of God if He were not, in fact, *God*. In contrast, the word **fashion** is *schema* (4976), which refers to outward shape or appearance that can change from time to time. A human being, for example, is *morphe* in **form** (nature), but in his or her *schema*, the **fashion** (appearance) can be an infant, toddler, adolescent, or adult.

To further underscore our Lord's deity, Paul says that Jesus is **equal with God** (v. 6). **Equal** is *isos* (2470), which means alike in quantity, quality, or dignity. This is, in fact, where we get the mathematical term "isosceles triangle," one that has two sides of equal length. Paul goes on to add that **Christ Jesus** was also the quintessential example of a **servant**, as He took on the **form** of a servant. But he adds something else: Jesus **was made in the likeness of men** (v. 7). **Likeness** is another term that is essential for the proper understanding of the incarnation of Christ. It is *homoiōma* (3667), which means shape, similitude, or resemblance, that which is made like something else. Jesus was not a phantom, a close copy, or a clone. He was in every way human. He had human appearance, personality (intellect, emotion, and will), and physical needs. He was, in fact, "in all points tempted like as we are, yet without sin" (Heb. 4:15). He was what man was (and was supposed to remain) in the Garden of Eden.

What an exalting of **Christ Jesus** this is! He was both fully God and fully human. The teaching that insists Jesus emptied Himself of His deity is gross apostasy and exposes an unregenerate heart (Jn. 8:24). Paul places the two realties side-by-side: *morphe theou* (**form of God**) and *morphe doulos* (**form of a servant**). As one commentator well says: "Christ's incarnation was not an emptying of Himself of His deity, but a clothing of Himself in humanity—in order to be a servant."[517]

Scriptures for Study: How is Christ exalted in each of the following verses: John 17:5; 1 Timothy 3:16; Titus 2:13; Hebrews 1:3, 6, 8; 13:8?

DECEMBER 22

Exalting Christ's Purpose

. . . he humbled himself, and became obedient unto death, even the death of the cross. (Phil. 2:8b)

THE word **cross** appears 26 times in the NT. The culmination of all four Gospel records of our Lord's life, of course, is His death on the Cross. As one commentator astutely points out, in fact, each one devotes much if its content to the last week of His life: two-fifths of Matthew; three-fifths of Mark; one-third of Luke; and almost one-half of John.[518]

Further, the Cross is the central theme of all Scripture, even the OT. Everything in the sacrifices foreshadowed the Cross. Further, as Jesus Himself reminded the disciples on the road to Emmaus, all this was foretold long ago (Luke 24:25–27). Beginning even in Genesis 3:15, in fact, the Cross was in view as God declared: "I will put enmity between thee and the woman, and between thy seed and her seed; it shall bruise thy head, and thou shalt bruise his heel." One prophet after another proclaimed what was to come, such as: Isaiah (7:14; 9:6), Daniel (9:24–26), and Zechariah (13:7).

As we have noted before, however, the cross is not a popular subject in human thinking (Aug. 16). So, how, then, is Christ exalted in this kind of death? The answer is because **he humbled himself**. Humbled is *tapeinoō* (5013), to bring low, abase, or humiliate. The very idea of belittling and humiliating oneself is abhorrent to all of us. No human who understood the agony, humiliation, and stigma of crucifixion would choose such a death for himself. *So, to voluntarily choose to be crucified was actually a supernatural act.*

What an example this is for us! Do you understand? Do you realize that choosing to humble yourself is a "supernatural choice"? We live in an age of "self." Everything is driven by personal feelings and wants, sadly, even among professing Christians. Like the Greeks and the Romans, the last thing anyone chooses in our day is humility. Our Lord Himself, however, declared: "whosoever shall exalt himself shall be abased; and he that shall humble himself shall be exalted" (Matt. 23:12). Our Lord also uses *tapeinoō* here. Later in this letter to the Philippians (4:12), Paul wrote: "I know . . . how to be abased," which is again *tapeinoō*. How did Paul know this? Because his example was Christ Himself. Peter also used the same word when he wrote: "God resisteth the proud, and giveth grace to the humble. Humble yourselves therefore under the mighty hand of God, that he may exalt you in due time" (1 Pet. 5:5–6). Peter of all people understood the supernatural change that must come before one can be humble. James likewise used this word: "Humble yourselves in the sight of the Lord, and he shall lift you up" (4:10).

So, let us, indeed, exalt our Lord in His purpose!

Scriptures for Study: Read the passages cited today. How do they encourage and challenge you?

DECEMBER 23

Exalting Christ's Position (1)

... God hath highly exalted him ... (Phil. 2:9–11)

TO illustrate once again "The Great Parabola of Scripture," one commentator outlines Philippians 2:5–11 this way: the Sovereign (v. 6); the Servant (v. 7); the Sacrifice (v. 8); and finally the Sovereign again (vv. 9–11).[519] So, as the arc of "The Great Parabola of Scripture" returns to Heaven, we see our Sovereign Savior exalted above all else. There is no passage of Scripture that better declares the exaltation of our Lord than do the opening verses of Hebrews (1:2–3, 6, 8). We also cannot help but be reminded of John's vision of heaven in Revelation 5:11–12. We see, therefore, four features of this exaltation in our text.

First, the *root* of his exaltation (2:9a). **Wherefore** obviously refers back to verses 5–8. In the shadow of our Lord's horrendous humiliation, the Father brought Him back to heaven in magnificent exaltation. While the natural man exalts himself, true *exaltation* comes only through *humiliation*. Again, the full idea in **highly exalted** (*huperupsoō*, 5251) is "to elevate above others, raise to the highest position." The *Servant* has now returned to His rightful place as *Sovereign*. He who was *mocked* has now returned to His *magnificence*. He who was *crucified* has now been *coronated*. As Paul wrote to the Ephesians: "[The Father] raised [Christ] from the dead, and set him at his own right hand in the heavenly places, Far above all principality, and power, and might, and dominion, and every name that is named, not only in this world, but also in that which is to come: And hath put all things under his feet, and gave him to be the head over all things to the church, Which is his body, the fulness of him that filleth all in all" (1:20–23).

Second, we see the *right* of his exaltation (2:9b). Here is a staggering truth. As I meditated upon this, I was a bit overwhelmed. What **name** (*onoma*, 3686, "name, title, character, reputation") is Paul referring to here? What **name** has the Father **given** (*charizomai*, 5483, graciously, wholeheartedly bestowed) to the Son? We have studied many of His names and titles: Jesus; Christ; The Son of God; The Son of Man; The Only Begotten; I Am; The Bread of Life; The Light of the World; The Door; The Good Shepherd; The Resurrection and the Life; The Way, The Truth, The Life; The Vine; The Alpha and Omega; The Lamb of God; The Cornerstone; The Prince and Perfecter of Faith; The Savior; The Bridegroom; The Carpenter; and The Word (see Mar. 2–Apr. 2).

So which **name** does Paul mean? The answer does not come immediately. Whatever this name is, however, it **is above** [superior in rank, dignity, and worth to] **every** other **name**. It excels all others known to human language in its character, dignity, honor, power, and position. This name, as we will see, places Christ in His rightful place. That leads us, then, immediately to our third feature, which we will examine tomorrow.

Scriptures for Study: Read Hebrew2:1–8 and Revelation 5:11–12. How do these passages bless your heart?

DECEMBER 24

Exalting Christ's Position (2)

... God hath highly exalted him ... that Jesus Christ is Lord (Phil. 2:9–11)

THE *third* feature of our Lord's exaltation in our text is the *response* to his exaltation (2:10–11a). Verse 10 provides another clue to the **name which is above every name**. At this name, every single **knee** in the universe will **bow**. This will be the fulfillment, in fact, of Isaiah 45:22–23: "Look unto me, and be ye saved, all the ends of the earth: for I am God, and there is none else. I have sworn by myself, the word is gone out of my mouth in righteousness, and shall not return, That unto me every knee shall bow, every tongue shall swear."

Paul expounds on that very truth by specifying three classes of beings who will bow before Messiah. First, those **in heaven** will bow, which includes all the redeemed saints who are already there as well as the 10,000 times 10,000 angels who are there (Rev. 4:8–11; 5:8–12). Second, those **in earth** will bow, which includes both believers and unbelievers who are still on this planet. Third, those **under the earth** will bow, which includes the exact opposite of those **in heaven**; these are the unbelievers and fallen angels who are now in hell awaiting final judgment and eternal punishment.

But Paul is not done. Not only will all creatures **bow** before this name, but **every tongue** will also **confess** it. **Tongue** is *glossa* (1100), which refers to human language. So, every single individual, whatever his or her language or ethnicity, will **confess** Christ. **Confess** (*exomologeō*, 1843) is an intensified form of *homologeō* (3670), which literally means to say the same words. So, every individual will admit the Truth, will actually agree with God on who Christ is. Think of it! Every being in the universe, in one way or another, will bow before Christ and acknowledge exactly who He is. The believer will do it *freely* in adoration, while the unbeliever will be *forced* to do it even in his rebellion and condemnation.

Paul finally reaches the climax to which he has been building. What is the **name** that is above all others? At what name will all creatures **bow** and **confess**? It is not **Jesus**, as wonderful as that name is. This was actually a common name and implied no superiority. The name, of course, is **Lord**.

The significance of this word cannot be overemphasized. This great title, **Lord** (*kurios*, 2962) was the number one confession of the Early Church, the title of majesty, authority, honor, and sovereignty. As Peter declared: "Therefore let all the house of Israel know assuredly, that God hath made that same Jesus, whom ye have crucified, both Lord and Christ" (Acts 2:36). Paul elsewhere proclaimed the essential doctrine of the Lordship of Christ in salvation: "If thou shalt confess with thy mouth the Lord Jesus, and shalt believe in thine heart that God hath raised him from the dead, thou shalt be saved" (Rom. 10:9). The Lordship of Christ is, indeed, a critical doctrine of Scripture, so we will conclude that thought tomorrow.

Scriptures for Study: What do each of the following verses declare about Christ's Lordship: Luke 2:11; John 13:13; John 20:28; Acts 2:36; Acts 10:36?

DECEMBER 25

Exalting Christ's Position (3)

... God hath highly exalted him ... that Jesus Christ is Lord ... (Phil. 2:9–11)

CONTRARY to popular teaching, salvation doesn't come first and then lordship later when we decide to obey. One who does not acknowledge Jesus as ruling Lord who he now desires to follow and obey is not a true believer. In fact, because the natural man will never submit to the Lordship of Christ, Paul reminded the Corinthians, "No man can say that Jesus is the Lord, but by the Holy Ghost" (1 Cor. 12:3). Later he added, "If any man love not the Lord Jesus Christ, let him be Anathema Maranatha" (16:22). "Maranatha" is two Aramaic words (*maran atha*) that mean "our Lord has come" and intensifies "Anathema" (devoted to destruction), pointing to the approaching judgment by that very **Lord** when He returns. Those who do not recognize Him as **Lord**, right along with "Jesus" (Savior) and "Christ" (Anointed Messiah) is cursed. Is it any wonder that Jesus is called **Lord** more than *700 times*, 92 of which are in the book of Acts where He is called "Savior" only twice? **Lord** (sovereignty and rule) is what He is all about! This name, in fact, will be further expanded: "And he hath on his vesture and on his thigh a name written, KING OF KINGS, AND LORD OF LORDS" (Rev. 19:16). It is grievous, indeed, that the so-called Lordship Salvation Debate arose back in the 1980s (cf. Aug. 18). Without Lordship there is no salvation, and denying this fact is horrific error. It attacks the very foundation of salvation.

Fourth and finally, then, we note the *reason* for his exaltation (2:11b). As with everything else, the reason for all this is **the glory of God the Father**. That dear pastor and expositor James Montgomery Boice offers us this little masterpiece: "This is not true of any honor given to humans. If you glorify human beings, you dishonor God. You do so if you exalt yourself or your merits as a means of salvation, or exalt human beings as mediators between yourself and God, as saints who win God's favor for you, or exalt human wisdom as that which is ultimately able to solve the world's problems, or place your hopes for the future in psychiatry, science, systems of world government, or whatever it may be. If you exalt the ability of mankind in any of those ways, you dishonor God, who declares that all of our works are tainted by sin and that we will never solve our own problems or the problems of others except by turning to Christ and depending upon his power to do it. *The only way to honor God is to give honor to Jesus Christ.*"[520]

My Dear Christian Friend, I pray this encourages us in how we should respond *when* our Lord's name is dishonored and in whatever *way* it is dishonored. Let us exalt Christ *alone* on this day. Let us not give Him just lip service. Let us not focus just on the *child* in a *manger* but primarily on the *Christ* of *majesty*.

Scriptures for Study: Take some time today to exalt Christ alone with these verses: John 5:22–27; Acts 2:32–36; 5:31; Romans 14:9–11; Ephesians 1:20–23; Hebrews 2:9; 12:2; 1 Peter 1:21. How have these six studies on exalting Christ encouraged you?

DECEMBER 26

Christian Evidences (1)
... your work of faith, and labour of love ... (1Thes. 1:3)

NO church is perfect, the church at Thessalonica included, but it was nonetheless a model church in many ways. Yes, persecution called for a challenge to continue standing firm (1:2–10; 2:13–16), the pagan culture prompted Paul's concern about new believers falling back into immorality (4:1–8), and there was some misunderstanding about the end times (4:13—5:11), but none of that negated Timothy's glowing report to Paul (3:6–9). Additionally, Paul wrote of his thankfulness for this church no less than three times (1:2; 2:13; 3:9). Appropriately, then, Paul begins this first letter with a list of evidences that these Christians didn't just *profess* Christ but that they *possessed* Him (1:3–10). As we draw our daily studies to a close, these proofs encourage us one more time with our own profession and possession of faith.

First, there was *production* because they had a working faith: **work of faith** (v. 3a; May 12). Paul tells us first that our *works* are tied to our *faith*, for "faith without works is dead" (Jas. 2:17). Faith and works are two sides of the same salvation coin. A dead faith is merely an intellectual experience, an *affirmation* with no *action*, just *words* without *works*. This was not theory to James, for he offered a practical illustration (vv. 15–16). He asked, in effect, "If a fellow believer comes to your door in need of clothing and food but you just respond with, 'Have a nice day, and I'll pray for you,' how is that a product of true faith?" Works do not *procure* salvation but salvation *produces* works.

I once read of a godly mother who consistently taught her little daughter lessons of faith and trust, especially that God is always near so there is no reason to be afraid. After tucking the child in one night, the mother turned out the light and went downstairs. A thunderstorm arose accompanied by a typical blinding flash of lighting and deafening crash of thunder. "Mama, come get me!" the little one cried. Finding her in tears, the mother said, "Hasn't mama told you that God is with you." "Yes," she replied, "but I just needed someone that's got skin on them." Likewise, those in need require servants who have skin on them.

Second, there was *affection* because they had a laboring love: **labour of love** (v. 3b). As works are tied to faith, *labor* is tied to *love*. "God will not forget your work and labour of love" (Heb. 6:10). We can certainly serve without loving, but we cannot love without serving. Is the only reason we serve because the pastor asks us to? Do we do it just because it's expected of us? Do we do it only because we will be recognized for it? Not the Thessalonians. They not only had "ministered to the saints," but they were still doing so, and they did it all not only because of their affection for the Lord and desire to please Him, but because of their affection for "the saints." God never forgets this kind of service.

Scriptures for Study: How do the following verses confirm today's study: Romans 12:13; 15:25–27; 1 John 3:14–18?

DECEMBER 27

Christian Evidences (2)

... patience of hope ... gospel came ... in word [and] power ... (1Thes. 1:3, 5)

THE Thessalonian believers were dear to the Apostle Paul. Each one understood God's sovereign "election" (v. 4) of them in eternity past based solely upon His purpose, grace, and love "to the praise of the glory of His grace" (Eph. 1:4, 6) and apart from any action or merit of their own (2:8–9).[521] In the rest of this passage, Paul lists the evidences of such a staggering salvation.

Third, there was *continuation* because they had a persevering hope (v. 3c): **patience of hope**. Once again, as works are tied to faith, and labor is tied to love, we now see that *patience* is tied to our *hope*. We can only be patient in trials and tribulations because our **hope** (that is, certainty, *elpis*, 1689) is in Christ. The only reason we can be patient in anything is that we are looking way beyond the circumstances to our position in Christ.

First Corinthians 16:13 comes to mind: "Watch ye, stand fast in the faith, quit you like men, be strong." Paul's pointed admonition first says to *wake up*. "Watch" is *grēgoreuō* (1127), to be awake, refrain from sleep. Enemies surround us, so we must be vigilant. We must then *stand up*, that is, "stand fast" (*stekō*, 4739). In a day when few are standing unapologetically for the Truth, we need to stand firm. We must also *man up*, or as they say out West, "cowboy up." "Quit you like men" (*andrizō*, 407) literally means "to behave oneself with the wisdom and courage of a man, as opposed to a babe or child in Christ, to behave courageously."[522] Oh, how this is needed today! Finally, we must *build up*. "Be strong" (*krataioō*, 2901) means just that, to make strong and grow stronger.

After ten months of war, Winston Churchill said of Great Britain's monumental struggle against Hitler in 1941, "Surely from this period of ten months this is the lesson: never give in, never give in, never, never, never, never in nothing, great or small, large or petty—never give in except to convictions of honour and good sense. Never yield to force; never yield to the apparently overwhelming might of the enemy."[523] How much more this kind of continuation of commitment is needed in the Church today! What an evidence that is! It is always too soon to quit.

Fourth, there was *absorption* because they had been under powerful preaching (v. 5). Paul wrote here that the **gospel came** to them first by the **word**. Unlike the charlatans of the day, who fleeced the people using pleasing rhetoric and philosophy, Paul preached the unadulterated Gospel. So absorbed were they in it, in fact, that they never lost that fervor (2:13). It was not the Word **only**, however; it came **also** in the **power** (*dunamis*, 1411[524]) of **the Holy Ghost**. Only He can energize the Word in our hearts. Such preaching not only came **in much assurance** (*plērophoria*, 4136, full conviction) in Paul's heart, but it also created assurance in theirs. Such absorption in God's Word is proof positive of true conversion.

Scriptures for Study: What does 1 Corinthians 2:4–5 add to our study today?

DECEMBER 28

Christian Evidences (3)

And ye became followers of us, and of the Lord, having received the word in much affliction, with joy of the Holy Ghost. (1Thes. 1:6)

CHARLES Spurgeon told the story of a servant girl whose pastor asked her, "What evidence can you give of your conversion?" Among other proofs, she gave this one: "Now, sir, I always sweep under the mats."[525] Such a sense of doing right leads us to another Christian evidence.

Fifth, there was *reception* because of their obedience to the Word (v. 6a): **And ye became followers of us, and of the Lord, having received the word in much affliction**. **Followers** translates the fascinating Greek word *mimētēs* (3402), from which we get our English word mimic. As Aristotle observed, at the beginning of civilization man learned skills by mimicking animals. Weaving and spinning were learned from spiders, for example, and house building was learned from birds. Plays, paintings, sculptures, and poetry were merely "imitations of reality." Even an actor was called a *mimos* (a "mimer").

Paul's use of it here and elsewhere (see *Scriptures for Study*) is enormously significant. In every case, we are challenged to mimic what is good and godly. People today, and sadly even some Christians, mimic athletes, entertainers, world leaders, military figures, and the like, but the Christian is to mimic God, copy His attributes, attitudes, and actions.

Here, then, is a key Christian evidence: obedience to God's Word. **Received** is *dechomai* (1209), which means to receive to oneself, to welcome and so metaphorically to approve and embrace. As we have noted several times, obedience of God's Word (Jn. 14:15, 23; 1 Jn. 2:1–5) is proof positive of genuine salvation. Spurgeon again wonderfully observed, "Obedience is faith incarnate."[526]

Sixth, there was *jubilation* because of their transcendent joy (v. 6b): **with joy of the Holy Ghost**. As we have also noted before (May 31), true **joy** (*chara*, 5479, "gladness and rejoicing") goes far beyond circumstances. Joy is an absolute, even under the great pressure of **affliction**, that is, persecution (*thlipsis*, 2347, to crush, press, compress, squeeze; cf. 2 Cor. 2:4; Phil. 1:16).

Spurgeon once again encourages us: "There is a quiet, rippling rill of intense comfort in a Christian's heart, even when he is cast down and tried. . . . I know that there are many who, like myself, understand what deep depression of spirit means, but yet we would not change our lot for all the mirth of fools or pomp of kings! Our joy no man takes from us—we are singing pilgrims—though the way is rough. Amid the ashes of our pains live the sparks of our joys, ready to flame up when the breath of the Spirit sweetly blows on them. Our latent happiness is a choicer heritage than the sinner's riotous glee."[527] What a great Christian evidence!

Scriptures for Study: What are we to mimic in each of the following verses: 1 Corinthians 4:16; 1 Thessalonians 2:14; Hebrews 6:12; 1 Peter 3:13?

DECEMBER 29

Christian Evidences (4)

... ye were ensamples ... [and] sounded out the word of the Lord ... (1 Thes. 1:7–8)

THE Bible knows nothing of salvation apart from obedience," wrote A. W. Tozer. "[It] recognizes no faith that does not lead to obedience. Faith and obedience are forever joined and each one is without value when separated from the other."[528] This leads to another Christian evidence.

Seventh, there was *confirmation* because of their right behavior (v. 7): **So that ye were ensamples to all that believe in Macedonia and Achaia.** Here is another particularly significant principle. **Ensamples** translates *tupos* (5179), from which we get our English word "type" and literally means "to strike with repeated strokes." From that came the idea of an image, impression, or mark created by such repeated strokes. Figuratively, then, "a type is a model of some reality which was yet to appear, a prototype of that which was yet to be developed and evolved."[529] Joseph, for example, was a type, a model, of Christ as the rejected kinsman who becomes their Savior (Gen. 37:1–50:26; Acts 7:9–14). Likewise, the deliverance of the Israelites from Egypt was a type, a picture of redemption.

"Typology" can certainly be abused, such as forcing types into virtual allegory, a practice adopted by early Church Fathers Origen, Ambrose, and Jerome. Examples include reading significance into the cords and pins of the tabernacle, each pillar of the temple, and even the 153 fish that the disciples caught on the night the risen Lord appeared to them.

Our text, however, is a wondrously accurate picture, indeed. The Thessalonians became exact duplicates, "dead ringers," for right behavior. Others needed only to look at them to know how to live godly. We also must be such "types." Such confirmation is a powerful Christian evidence.

Eighth, there was *proclamation* because of their strong witness (v. 8): **For from you sounded out the word of the Lord not only in Macedonia and Achaia, but also in every place your faith to God-ward is spread abroad; so that we need not to speak any thing.** What a statement! The words **sounded out** are a single word in the Greek, *exēcheō* (1837), which is the origin of our English word "echo." Appearing only here, it literally means "to sound out," implying "a loud, unmistakable proclamation."[530] In extra biblical literature, it was used for a loud clap of thunder or a blaring trumpet. Further, the verb is in the perfect tense (completed action with emphasis on the result), which pictures a continuation, a reverberation, an "echo" of the sound. A powerful Christian evidence, then, is being a "trumpeter" of the Gospel. Biblical evangelism is not so much about *citywide crusades*, but rather *committed crusaders* whose consistent witness for Christ echoes through their communities (Sept. 27).

Scriptures for Study: What do these verses say about pastors: Titus 2:7; 1 Peter 5:3? 📖 What does Romans 10:14–18 tell us about evangelism?

DECEMBER 30

Christian Evidences (5)

... ye turned to God from idols to serve the living and true God ... [and] wait for his Son from heaven ... (1 Thes. 1:9–10)

THE elect of God are easy to spot, easy to distinguish from the world of unbelievers, because they exhibit indisputable evidence of the salvation God has wrought in them. Our text provides two final Christian evidences.

Ninth, there was *transformation* because of their changed allegiance: **For they themselves shew of us what manner of entering in we had unto you, and how ye turned to God from idols to serve the living and true God** (v. 9). As we have observed several times, Scripture declares that salvation is a total transformation of life (e.g. Aug. 17; Sept. 5).

The Thessalonians dramatically demonstrated this truth beyond the tiniest tinge of doubt. As all Gentile cities of the day, Thessalonica was thoroughly pagan, and its inhabitants practiced many immoral acts as part of their religious worship. Those who came to Christ, however, **turned to God from idols to serve the living and true God.** Turned is *epistrephō* (1994), which is comprised of *epi* (1909, to) and *strephō* (4762, to turn) and so "to turn upon, or toward." It appears often as physically "turning around" (e.g., Matt. 9:22; Mk. 5:30; Lk. 17:4; Acts 9:40; Rev. 1:12). Like our text, Acts 14:15 speaks of turning from idolatry to worship the living God, and 26:18 speaks similarly of those who turn from darkness to light. All this underscores further the idea of turning to God in repentance (Acts 3:19; 9:35; 26:20; 2 Cor. 3:16). Such an "about-face," a turning in the opposite direction, is the clear meaning of true salvation and an evidence of its authenticity. "Another proof of the conquest of a soul for Christ will be found in *a real change of life,*" Spurgeon wrote. "If the man does not live differently from what he did before, both at home and abroad, his repentance needs to be repented of, and his conversion is a fiction."[531]

Tenth and finally, there was *anticipation* because of their waiting for Jesus' return: **And to wait for his Son from heaven, whom he raised from the dead, even Jesus, which delivered us from the wrath to come** (v. 10). Christ's return is a major theme in both of Paul's letters to these believers.[532] Therefore, the capstone of these Christian evidences is waiting for that glorious event. **Wait** is *anamenō* (362), "waiting with patience and confident expectancy."[533] Unlike some of the Thessalonians who used Jesus' return as an excuse to quit working (cf. 2 Thes. 3:10) and become busybodies, true anticipation of that event will keep us busily serving right up to that moment. We rejoice with Puritan Thomas Adams: "[He] that rose from the clods, we expect from the clouds."[534]

Let us, therefore, be as the Thessalonians, for "they were elect, exemplary, enthusiastic, and expectant."[535]

Scriptures for Study: What do the following verses declare about Jesus' return: Acts 1:11; Philippians 3:20; 1 Thessalonians 4:16–17; 2 Peter 3:12, 14?

DECEMBER 31

Knowing, Loving, and Serving

... I love thee ... Feed my lambs. (Jn. 21:15)

A fitting close to our year of devotional studies is again Jesus' recommissioning of Peter in John 21:15–17 (May 5–9). Few knew, loved, and served our Lord as Peter did, so he will help us with our final review.

First, we have *meditated* on *knowing* the Lord. As we have noted, Peter was, indeed, our Lord's "little shadow." With rare exception, wherever Jesus was, there was Peter also. He shared in every aspect of his Master's life and knew Him better than anyone else. Why? We would submit first that he wanted to *know more*. Observing every action and hanging on every word, Peter was the proverbial sponge that absorbed it all. Further, we suggest that Peter wanted to *think deeper*. Perhaps he thought back to the time when Jesus told him to "launch out into the deep, and let down your nets for a draught" (Lk. 5:4) and applied that to going deeper in every aspect of life. Finally, we propose that Peter wanted to *do right*. If knowing and thinking do not lead to doing, it is all empty. Peter wonderfully encourages us, then, to know our Lord ever better. "That I may know him" (Phil. 3:10) Paul reminds us again (Feb. 25–27). And if we are tempted to think that none of this is "practical," as we often hear today, let us consider this challenge: "Once you become aware that the main business that you are here for is to know God, most of life's problems fall into place of their own accord."[536]

Second, we have *matured* in our *loving* the Lord. I never tire of this scene of Peter with Jesus. His three-fold question, Peter's three-fold admission, and Jesus' three-fold recommission comprise the perfect test for all those who say, "Oh, yes, I love Jesus." In a very real sense, in fact, our love for the Lord has been at the core of *all* our daily studies. Without a deep love for Him, knowing is nothing but *mental exercise* and serving is nothing more than *mechanical exertion*. It is our love for Him that is the *motivating energy* that gives it all meaning. As Peter's love grew deeper from a *phileō* affection to an *agapaō* application, so have we grown in our understanding of the primacy of love for Christ. We love God not because "we have fallen in love with Him," as today's expression goes, but because we willfully love Him with a conscious, committed, and compliant adoration.

Third, we have *measured* our *serving* of the Lord. With full knowledge that he would die a martyr's death (Jn. 21:18–19), Peter served His Lord with fervor, fortitude, and faithfulness. Church tradition indicates that he was crucified under Nero's reign. All the Apostles, in fact, except John, as well as countless servants since, died for Christ's sake. It has been wisely said that we never get a second chance to make a first *impression*, but we submit that we do have every chance to make a lasting *impact*. Peter made such a measured impact. So should we.

Oh, my Dear Christian Friend, get to know your Lord further, so you can love Him deeper, and then serve Him better.

Scriptures for Study: Meditate today on John 14:15–24.

Postscript

"What think ye of Christ?" (Matt. 22:42)

    C – Cross
    H – Hope
    R – Redemption
    I – Inheritance
    S – Salvation
    T – Truth
    O – Obedience
    S – Sanctification

A Final Thought

Cast thine eyes which way thou wilt and thou shalt hardly look upon anything but Christ. Jesus hath taken the name of that thing upon Himself. Is it day? and dost thou behold the sun? He is called the Sun of Righteousness. Or is it night? and dost thou behold the stars? He is called a Star, "There shall come a Star out of Jacob." Or is it morning? He is called "the bright Morning Star." Or is it noon? and dost thou behold clear light all the world over? He is "that light that lighteth every man that cometh into the world." Come nearer; if thou lookest upon the earth, and takest a view of the creatures about thee, dost thou see the sheep? "As a sheep before her shearer is dumb." Or seest thou a lamb? "Behold the Lamb of God." Seest thou a shepherd watching over his flock? "I am the Good Shepherd." Or seest thou a fountain, waters, rivers? He is a Fountain. Or seest thou a tree good for food, or a flower? He is "the Tree of Life, and the Lilly of the Valley, and the Rose of Sharon." Art thou adorning thyself, and taking a view of thy garments? "Put ye on the Lord Jesus Christ." Art thou eating meat, and taking a view of what thou hast on thy table? He is the Bread of God; the true Bread from Heaven; the Bread of Life.[537]

—Puritan Isaac Ambrose

Selected Bibliography

Archer, Gleason; Harris, Laird; Waltke, Bruce. *Theological, Wordbook of the Old Testament (TWOT)*. Chicago: Moody Bible Institute, 1980.

Baker, Warren; Carpenter, Eugene. *The Complete Word Study Dictionary: Old Testament*. Chattanooga: AMG Publishers, 2003.

Barclay, William. *New Testament Words*. Louisville: Westminster John Knox Press, 1964, 1974.

Barnes, Albert. *Barnes Notes on the Bible* (electronic edition, public domain).

Bartlett, John, *Bartlett's Familiar Quotations*, 16th Edition (New York: Little, Brown, and Company, 1992, 2002).

Baxter, J. Sidlow. *Explore the Book*, Complete in One Volume (Zondervan, 1960).

Brown, Colin (general editor). *The New International Dictionary of New Testament Theology* (4 vol.). Grand Rapids: Zondervan, 1975.

Charnock, Stephen. *The Existence and Attributes of God*. Baker Books reprint of 1853 edition, 1996. We would also recommend Daniel Chamberlin's excellent book, *A Portrait of God*, a 177-page summary of Charnock's classic (CreateSpace, 2011).

Gill, John. *The New John Gill's Exposition of the Entire Bible*. Modernised and adapted for the computer by Larry Pierce of *The Online Bible*. Originally completed in 1766.

Girdlestone, Robert Baker. *Girdlestone's Synonyms of the Old Testament*. Reprint; Grand Rapids: Baker Book House, 1983.

Kittel, Gerhard (Ed.). *Theological Dictionary of the New Testament (TDNT)*, 10 Vols. Grand Rapids: Eerdmans, 1964; reprinted 2006.

———. *Theological Dictionary of the New Testament: Abridged in One Volume* by Geoffrey W. Bromiley ("Little Kittel"). Grand Rapids: Eerdmans, 1985.

Morris, Henry. *The Defender's Study Bible*. Grand Rapids: World Publishing, 1995.

Packer, J. I. *Knowing God*, 20th Anniversary Edition. Downers Grove: Intervarsity Press, 1973.

Robertson, A. T. *Word Pictures in the Greek New Testament*. Electronic edition, public domain.

Thayer, Joseph. *Thayer's Greek-English Lexicon of the New Testament*. Grand Rapids: Associated Publishers and Authors, Inc., nd.

Thomas, I. D. E. (Editor). *A Puritan Golden Treasury*. Carlisle, PA: Banner of Truth, 1975, 1989.

Tozer, A. W. *The Knowledge of the Holy*. New York: HarperCollins Publishers, 1961.

———. *God Tells the Man Who Cares*. Camp Hill, PA: Christian Publications, 1992.

———. *Of God and Men*. Camp Hill, PA: Christian Publications, 1995.

———. *The Price of Neglect*. Camp Hill, PA: Christian Publications, n.d.

———. *The Pursuit of God*. Camp Hill, PA: Christian Publications, 1948.

———. *The Tozer Pulpit* (2 Vol.). Camp Hill, PA: Christian Publications, 1994.

Trench, Richard. *Synonyms of the New Testament*. Peabody, MA: Hendrickson, 2000.

Vincent, M. R. *Word Studies in the New Testament*. Public domain, electronic edition.

Vine, W. E. *An Expository Dictionary of New Testament Words*. Old Tappan, NJ: Fleming H. Revell Company, 1966. Electronic edition, Logos Research Systems.

Watson, J. D. *A Hebrew Word for the Day: Key Words from the Old Testament*. Chattanooga: AMG Publishers, 2010.

———. *A Word for the Day: Key Words from the New Testament*. Chattanooga: AMG Publishers, 2006.

———. *The Doctrines of Grace from the Lips of our Lord: A Study in the Gospel of John*. Eugene, OR: Wipf & Stock, 2012.

———. *Salvation Is of the Lord: An Exposition of the Doctrines of Grace By a Former Arminian*. Meeker, CO: Sola Scriptura Publications, 2015.

———. *Truth on Tough Texts: Expositions of Challenging Scripture Passages*. Meeker, CO: Sola Scriptura Publications, 2012.

———. *Upon this Rock: Studies in Church History and Their Application*. Meeker, CO: Sola Scriptura Publications, 2012.

———. *Winds of Doctrine: A Survey of Contemporary Theology*. Meeker, CO: Sola Scriptura Publications, 2014.

Watson, Thomas. *A Body of Divinity*. Carlisle, PA: Banner of Truth Trust, 1890, 1992.

———. *The Sermons of Thomas Watson* (originally titled *Discourses on Important and Interesting Subjects*, 1829). Soli Deo Gloria Publications reprint, 1990.

———. *The Ten Commandments*. Carlisle, PA: Banner of Truth Trust, 1890, 1992.

Wuest, Kenneth. *Word Studies in the Greek New Testament* (electronic edition). Grand Rapids: Eerdmans, 1966.

Zodhiates, Spiros, et. al. *The Complete Word Study Dictionary*. Chattanooga: AMG Publishers, 1992, electronic edition.

Main Text Index

Genesis
1:1 1/14
5:22, 24 10/10–12
6:6 1/29
6:8 2/16
6:14 10/14
9:13–16 7/24–30

Exodus
3:4 10/22–25
16:1–2 7/12
16:15 7/9–11
20:3 6/17
20:4 6/18
20:7 6/19
20:8–10 6/20
20:12 6/22–23
20:13 6/24
20:14 6/25
20:15 6/26
20:16 6/27–28
20:17 6/29
32:1 5/22–24
33:18 8/13
34:28 6/16

Leviticus
19:2 2/6–7

Deuteronomy
6:5 5/1–2
6:5–7 5/3
12:32 6/3–4
17:16 8/11
18:15–18 3/28

Joshua
7:21 8/26
24:14–15 12/6

2 Samuel
9:7 1/2

1 Kings
19:1–12 1/4

1 Chronicles
29:11–12 1/21, 1/22

Nehemiah
8 7/5–7

Psalms
1:2–3 7/18–20
5:12 2/10–11
11:6 2/9
14:1 1/13
20:7 8/11
27:4 12/7–8
33:9 3/26
37:1–3 7/21
37:4–11 7/22
46:10 1/3
50:23 6/7
56:13 8/9
62:11 1/18
63:1 1/1
89:14 2/8
95:3 1/25
95:6 6/2
103:8 2/12–15
104:34 1/5–6, 6/8
119:11 6/14–15
119:16 6/13
119:47–48 6/10
119:97 6/11, 6/14–15
119:132 6/9
119:159 6/12
119:167 6/12
139:7–12 1/30–2/1
145:17 2/8

Proverbs
1:2–3 8/12
2:5 1/9
3:5–6 8/28
17:3 9/18
24:3–4 1/10

Isaiah
6:3 2/2–5
6:8 9/7
40:31 7/8
51:1 7/23

Daniel
7:13 3/6

Amos
8:11 8/21–22

Malachi
3:6 1/26

Matthew
1:21 3/2–3
4:4 7/2–4
9:15 3/24
9:37–38 9/28
13:3–9; 18–23 11/13–15
13:13 11/12
16:16 3/4–5
18:21–35 11/30
20:1–16 11/28
21:37 6/1
22:37–40 6/30
24:45–51 11/23
25:14–30 11/20–22
26:37 5/18
26:75 5/4
28:19–20 9/25

Mark
3:14 5/17
6:3 3/27
12:30 5/1–2

Luke
1:15–17 9/23–14
2:43 5/20–21
10:1 5/16
10:25–37 11/16–19
12:13–21 11/24–25
16:1–13 11/26–27
17:7–10 11/29

John
1:1 3/25
1:14 3/7–8
1:18 3/7–8
1:29 3/18–19
1:36 3/18
1:38 3/1
1:41 3/31
3:16 2/22–24, 3/17–18
3:18 3/17

4:7   9/29
6:2   5/15
6:35   3/10
6:44   5/26
6:67–68   5/14
8:12   3/11
8:58   3/9
10:7, 9   3/12
10:11, 14   3/13
10:18   5/28
10:29   5/29
11:25–26   3/14
14:6   3/15, 5/25, 5/27
14:13–14   8/15
14:16   4/4–7, 4/11–16
14:26   4/17–19
15:1,5   3/16
15:13   5/30
15:26–27   4/20–22
16:7–11   4/23–25
16:22   5/31
17:6,11,14,18   8/27
21:6   9/30
21:15   12/31
21:15–17   5/5–9

Acts
1:8   9/26–27
2:42   6/5–6
8:30–31   9/9
11:26   8/16–19
13:23   3/22
15:18   1/16
17:28   8/8
20:27   7/17
20:35   12/5

Romans
1:17   10/31
3:20   2/18
4:3   8/7
6   3/26
7   3/27
8   3/28
11:33   1/11–12
12:1–2   9/3–6
14:12   9/10

1 Corinthians
4:2   9/8
2:15   4/3
9:22   9/11
9:24   9/12

13:13   5/12–13
15:58   9/13
16:1–2   12/1–2

2 Corinthians
4:6   8/14
8:1–3   12/3–4

Galatians
2:20   5/19
3:1   2/19
4:30   8/7
5:13   2/20
5:16   10/12
6:9   12/13

Ephesians
1:4   9/14
1:11   1/23–24
2:19   7/31–8/8
2:20   3/20
5:18   4/8–10
6:6   9/1–2
6:11,13   9/16–17

Philippians
2:5–11   12/20–25
2:19–24   9/19–20
2:25–30   9/21–22
3:10   2/25–28

Colossians
1:9–10   1/7–8
1:23   8/10
2:5   9/15
2:7   2/29
3:1–2   7/13

1 Thessalonians
1:3–10   12/26–30

1 Timothy
4:6   7/15–16
4:13   7/1

2 Timothy
4:10   8/23

Titus
2:11   2/17

Hebrews
1:3   1/19

4:14   3/29
6:10   12/14–19
10:25   6/21, 12/9–12
11:2   10/3
11:3   7/14, 10/4–5
11:4   10/1–2, 10/7–9
11:5   10/13
11:6   10/6
11:7   10/14–16
11:8–19   10/17–20
11:13   7/31–8/6
11:20–22   10/21
11:23–29   10/22–25
11:30   10/26–27
11:31   10/28
11:32   10/29–30, 11/1–6
11:33–40   11/7
12:1–2   3/21, 11/8–9
12:2   3/21

James
1:17   1/27, 1/28
1:22   8/20
4:4   8/25

1 Peter
1:2   1/17
1:8   5/10

2 Peter
1:5–7   11/10–11

1 John
2:1   4/26–30
2:15–17   8/24
3:20   1/15
4:8   2/21
4:9   3/7–8
4:21   8/29–31

Jude
1   1/20
25   3/23

Revelation
2:1–7   5/11
19:16   3/30
22:16   4/1–2
22:13   3/17

About the Author

DR. J. D. "Doc" Watson (ThD, DRE) entered the ministry in 1974, serving in several capacities including 35 years in the pastorate, 30 of which at Grace Bible Church in Meeker, Colorado. He also speaks at Bible Conferences and other venues.

In addition to his other published books, he continues to write and edit the bi-monthly publication *Truth on Tough Texts*. His driving passion is the exposition of the Word of God as the sole and sufficient authority in all matters. This is demonstrated in no better way than in his 3-1/2 year (500,000 word) exposition of the Epistle to the Ephesians, which he hopes to publish in 2017.

Dr. Watson also serves on the board of On Target Ministry (www.ontargetministry.org), which is committed to providing Bible education to national pastors overseas. He has had the opportunity to serve in this capacity at the Haiti Bible Institute, which was founded by OTM in 2009. He likewise serves on the board of the Institute for Biblical Textual Studies, which is committed to defending the Traditional Text of the New Testament. He has also contributed articles to other publications, including a weekly column in his local newspaper based upon his pulpit ministry.

The other loves of his life are his wife, Debbie (since 1974), his son, Paul (since 1988), his daughter-in-law Celeste (since 2013), his church family (since 1986), and his favorite hobby, golf (since 1968).

📖 Books by the Author 📖

A passion for writing has led to several books by the author, several of which are already available while others are scheduled for publication in the near future. His books have been published by three publishers. See our website (www.TheScriptureAlone.com) or the blog above for detailed descriptions, contents, sample chapters, and endorsements.

Now Available

Truth on Tough Texts: Expositions of Challenging Scripture Passages

Upon This Rock: Studies in Church History and Their Application

Seek Him Early: Daily Devotional Studies on Knowing, Loving, and Serving Our Lord Jesus Christ

Salvation is of the Lord: An Exposition of the Doctrines of Grace by a Former Arminian

Sovereign Grace Pulpit: The Doctrines of Grace from the Sermons of Charles Haddon Spurgeon (Complied and Edited)

Winds of Doctrine: A Survey of Contemporary Theology

The Forgotten Tozer: A. W. Tozer's Challenge to Today's Church

A Taste of Heaven on Earth: Marriage and Family in Ephesians 5:18—6:4

A Light Unto My Path: An Exposition of Psalm 119

The Swan Song of the Old Shepherd: An Exposition of Psalm 23

The Doctrines of Grace from the Lips of Our Lord: A Study in the Gospel of John (Wipf & Stock Publishers)

A Word for the Day: Key Words from the New Testament (AMG Publishers)

A Hebrew Word for the Day: Key Words from the Old Testament (AMG)

We Preach Christ: The Bible Story (booklet)

Future Titles

The Christian's Wealth and Walk: An Expository Commentary on Ephesians (2 volumes) (early 2019)

Church History in the Light of Scripture: Exercising Discernment in Christian History

Contending for the Faith: An Expository Commentary on Jude

The Seven Churches of the 21st Century: An Exposition of Revelation 2 & 3

Kurios Iēsous Christos: An Epic Poem of the Life of the Lord Jesus Christ

Sonnets for the Savior: A Collection Dedicated to His Glory

Soli Deo Gloria

Greek Pronunciation Guide

Single Vowel Sounds

Name	Transliteration	Pronunciation
alpha	*a*	a in father
bēta	*b*	b in baboon
gamma	*g*	g in gag
delta	*d*	d in dawdle
epsilon	*e*	e in egg
zēta	*z*	z in zoo
ēta	*ē*	a in gate
thēta	*th*	th in thug
iōta	*i*	i in picnic
kappa	*k*	k in kumquat
lambda	*l*	l in lump
mu	*m*	m in mud
nu	*n*	n in nonsense
xi	*x*	x in vex
omicron	*o*	ough in ought
pi	*p*	p in pepper
rho	*r*	r in rarity
sigma	*s*	s in success
tau	*t*	t in tight
upsilon	*u*	u in full
phi	*ph*	ph in phosphorus
chi	*ch*	ch in German ach, ich
psi	*ps*	ps in tipsy
ōmega	*ō*	o in oaf

Double Vowel (Diphthong) Sounds

Name	Transliteration	Pronunciation
alpha+iōta	*ai*	as in hair
alpha+upsilon	*au*	as in waft or lava
epsilon+iōta	*ei*	as in see
epsilon+upsilon	*eu*	as effort or every
ēta+upsilon	*ēu*	as in reef or sleeve
omicron+iōta	*oi*	as in see
omicron+upsilon	*ou*	as in group
upsilon+iōta	*ui*	as in see

Consonant Combinations

Name	Transliteration	Pronunciation
gamma+gamma	*gg*	as in go
gamma+kappa	*hk*	as in go
gamma+chi	*gch*	as in ghost

Hebrew Pronunciation Guide

Hebrew Consonants

Hebrew Name	Transliteration	Phonetic Sound	Example
Aleph	ʾ	Silent	Similar to *h* in honor
Beth	B	b	as in boy
Veth	$\underline{b}$	v	as in vat
Gimel	G	g	as in get
Gimel	$\underline{g}$	g	as in get
Daleth	D	d	as in do
Daleth	$\underline{d}$	d	as in do
Hē	H	h	as in hat
Waw	W	w	as in wait
Zayin	Z	z	as in zip
Cheth	Ḥ	ch	Similar to *ch* in the German *ach*
Teth	Ṭ	t	as in time
Yodh	Y	y	as in you
Kaph	K	k	as in kit
Chaph	$\underline{k}$	ch	Similar to *ch* in the German *ach*
Lamedh	L	l	as in lit
Mem	M	m	as in move
Nun	N	n	as in not
Samekh	S	s	as in see
Ayin	ʿ	Silent	Similar to *h* in honor
Pē	P	p	as in put
Phē	$\underline{p}$	f	as in phone
Tsadde	Ṣ	ts	as in wits
Qoph	Q	q	as in Qatar
Resh	R	r	as in run
Sin	Ś	s	as in see
Shin	Š	sh	as in ship
Taw	T	t	as in time
Thaw	$\underline{t}$	th	as in this

Hebrew Vowels

Name	Transliteration	Sound
Shewa (Silent)	Not transliterated or pronounced	
Shewa (Vocal)	e	u as in but
Pathah	a	a as in lad
Hateph Pathah	a	a as in lad
Qamets	$\bar{a}$	a as in car
Hateph Qamets	$\bar{a}$	a as in car
Sere	$\bar{e}$	ey as in prey
Sere Yodh	$\bar{e}y$	ey as in prey
Seghol	e	e as in set
Hateph Seghol	e	e as in set
Hiriq Yodh	iy	i as in machine
Hiriq	i	i as in pin
Qamets Qatan	o	o as in hop
Holem	$\bar{o}$	o as in go
Holem Waw	$\hat{o}$	o as in go
Qubbuts	u	u as in put
Shureq	$\hat{u}$	u as in tune

NOTES

[1] We would here recommend E. A. Johnston's biography, *J. Sidlow Baxter: A Heart Awake* (Baker Books, 2005).

[2] Originally three volumes: *A New Call to Holiness*; *His Deeper Work in Us*; and *Our High Calling* (Zondervan).

[3] As another writer well observes, in our electronic media culture, "We scan for information, but we do not appreciate literary craftsmanship" (T. David Gordon, *Why Johnny Can't Preach: The Media Have Shaped the Messengers* [P & R Publishing, 2009], 49).

[4] Sadly, this book went out of print many years ago. We have, however, been granted the privilege of republishing it electronically on our website: www.TheScriptureAlone.com. Our sincere thanks to our dear Christian brother, William Ross of Scotland, the member of Dr. Baxter's family who retains the rights to his books.

[5] While Davidic authorship of this Psalm has been debated, I lean that way mainly for stylistic reasons. It is much the same tone as 63:1–11, the title of which is specific (description of the enemies, etc.; cf. 23:1–6; 26:1–12). As Spurgeon put it, "It smells of the son of Jesse" (*The Treasury of David*).

[6] For a deeper study, see chapter 44, "The King and Mephibosheth," in the author's *Truth on Tough Texts*, 433–441.

[7] Tozer, *The Knowledge of the Holy*, vii. For an in-depth study of Tozer and his contemporary thought, see the author's, *The Forgotten Tozer: A.W. Tozer's Challenge to Today's Church* (Sola Scriptura Publications, 2013).

[8] Thomas Watson, "How We May Read the Scriptures With Most Spiritual Profit" (Direction IX).

[9] A *kōan* is a story, dialogue, question, or statement.

[10] Both Hebrew word studies adapted form the author's, *A Hebrew Word for the Day*, 6, 71.

[11] Zodhiates, *Word Study Dictionary*, entry #G3191.

[12] Vincent, *Word Studies*, comment on 1 Tim. 4:15.

[13] For deeper study of Psalm 119, see the author's, *A Light Unto My Path: An Exposition of Psalm 119* (Sola Scriptura Publications, 2013).

[14] E.g., Albert Barnes, John Gill, Mathew Henry, Matthew Poole, Charles Spurgeon, etc.

[15] *John Gill's Exposition of the Entire Bible* (electronic edition).

[16] Thomas, *A Puritan Golden Treasury* (Banner of Truth, 1975, 1989), 183.

[17] *The Treasury of David* (electronic edition, public domain), note on Ps. 104:34.

[18] For a study of the words in this verse, see the author's, *A Word for the Day*, 32–34, 133, 145, 218–224.

[19] Tozer, *The Knowledge of the Holy*, 2. See also the author's, *The Forgotten Tozer: A.W. Tozer's Challenge to Today's Church* (Sola Scriptura Publications, 2013).

[20] Thomas, *Puritan Golden Treasury*, 163.

[21] The first meaning is from Aristotle and the second from Zodhiates, *Word Study Dictionary*, entry #G4678

[22] It is also used in this way in the Septuagint (Ex. 15:5; Neh. 9:11; Zech. 10:11).

[23] Bartlett, *Familiar Quotations*, 1, 711. This is in turn documented from Carlos P. Romulo, *I saw the Fall of the Philippines* (1942).

[24] Charnock, *Discourses Upon the Existence and Attributes of God*, Vol. 1, 25.

[25] For a study of the names of God in the OT, see the author's *A Hebrew Word for the Day*, 7–31.

[26] Many use this verse to teach the idea that God's election is based *solely* upon His foreknowledge that we would believe. In other words, it is insisted that "foreknowledge" simply means "precognition," that God simply knew who would believe and elected them accordingly. But as I have written elsewhere:

"It is, however, a fact of the language that that is not what the Greek *proginoskō* ('foreknowledge') means. To argue otherwise is foolish. The root *proginoskō* means 'to know by experience' and is practically synonymous with love and intimacy. Joseph, for example, 'did not know' Mary before Jesus was born, that is, they had not yet been physically intimate (Matt. 1:25). The prefix *pro*, when used of time, adds the ideas of before, earlier than, or prior to. The fact that it does not mean precognition is beyond all doubt when we read another verse in this same chapter, one often either overlooked or ignored: '[Christ] verily was foreordained [*proginoskō*] before the foundation of the world, but was manifest in these last times for you' (v. 20). Obviously this doesn't mean that God simply foresaw that Christ would be manifested. Rather, He was, as we are, foreordained and foreknown by an intimate relationship before the foundation of the world. In other words, foreknowledge is not to *foresee* but to '*fore-love.*' This is exactly what we see when we read what God said to Jeremiah: 'Before I formed thee in the belly I *knew* thee; and before thou camest forth out of the womb I sanctified thee, and I *ordained* thee a prophet unto the nations' (Jer. 1:5, emphasis added). What a thought that is! Christ knew us in the elective and saving sense before we even existed" *(The Doctrines of Grace from the Lips of Our Lord*, 97–98; for a more detailed study, see *Salvation Is of the Lord*, 114–118).

[27] Charles Spurgeon once said of this fact, "What two shepherds for the flock! Men of such most extraordinary gifts and graces were seldom if ever united in one pastorate."

[28] Watson, *Body of Divinity*, 58–59.

[29] His actual words reportedly were: "In every block of marble I see a statue as plain as though it stood before me, shaped and perfect in attitude and in action. I have only to hew away the rough walls that imprison the lovely apparition to reveal it to the other eyes as mine see it."

[30] William Hendriksen, *New Testament Commentary: Galatians, Ephesians, Philippians, Colossians, Philemon* (Baker Academic, 2007), note on Col. 1:17.

[31] *Bartlett's Familiar Quotations*, 79.

[32] According to the *Encyclopedia Judaica*. For a deeper study of this word and its compounds, see the author's *A Hebrew Word for the Day*, 8–21.

[33] R. C. Sproul, Ligonier Ministries via the Internet.

[34] Henry Thiessen, *Introductory Lectures in Systematic Theology* (Eerdmans, 1949), 128. I must take exception to the Revised Edition of this work (1979), as the quoted statement has sadly been removed. While the Revised Edition has some merit, the original is to be preferred in my respectful opinion. Charles Hodge is virtually identical: "Sovereignty is not a property of the divine nature, but a prerogative arising out

of the perfections of the Supreme Being" (*Systematic Theology* [Eerdmans, 1989 reprint], Vol. 1, 440).

[35] Westminster (III.1): "God from all eternity, did, by the most wise and holy counsel of His own will, freely, and unchangeably ordain whatsoever comes to pass (Eph. 1:11, Rom. 11:33, Heb. 6:17, Rom. 9:15,18); yet so, as thereby neither is God the author of sin, (James 1:13,17, 1 John 1:5) nor is violence offered to the will of the creatures; nor is the liberty or contingency of second causes taken away, but rather established (Acts 2:23, Matt. 17:12, Acts 4:27–28, John 19:11, Prov. 16:33)."

[36] Warren W. Wiersbe, *From Worry To Worship* (Back To The Bible, 1983). I would also recommend D. Martyn Lloyd-Jones' *From Fear To Faith* (InterVarsity, 1983).

[37] Arthur W. Pink, *The Sovereignty of God* (Baker, 1930, 1992), 21.

[38] Donald Gray Barnhouse, *Romans* (Eerdmans, 1983), Vol. 2, 340–341.

[39] Jonathan Edwards, *The Works of Jonathan Edwards*, "Sermon on Romans 9:18" (Banner of Truth Trust), Vol. II, 854.

[40] Watson, *Body of Divinity*, 66.

[41] Warren Wiersbe, *The Wiersbe Bible Commentary: NT* (Colorado Springs: David C. Cook, 2007), comment on James 1:17.

[42] Charnock, *Existence and Attributes of God*, Vol. I, 349.

[43] *Ibid*.

[44] *Ibid*, 360.

[45] Girdlestone, *Synonyms of the OT*, 103–104.

[46] Taken from the author's *A Hebrew Word for the Day*, 220.

[47] Watson, *Body of Divinity*, 69.

[48] Emory H. Bancroft, *Christian Theology* (Zondervan, 1925, 1949), 25.

[49] William Evans, *The Great Doctrines of the Bible* (Moody Press, 1912, 1974), 33.

[50] Watson, *Body of Divinity*, 53

[51] Charnock, *Existence and Attributes of God*, Vol. I, 366–367

[52] *The Treasury of David*, comment on Ps. 139:7.

[53] Watson, *Body of Divinity*, 82.

[54] *Keil & Delitzsch Commentary on the Old Testament* (public domain, electronic edition), note on Is. 6:3.

[55] This beloved term was introduced to me in 1971 by the headmaster of Heritage Christian School (Indianapolis, IN), Mr. R. James Weaver (M.Ed.), in the first Bible doctrine class of my life. It has stuck with me ever since.

[56] Charnock, *The Existence and Attributes Of God*, Vol. II, 112–13.

[57] Evans, *The Great Doctrines of the Bible*, 40 (emphasis added).

[58] "*Abba* (5) is actually from the Aramaic '*ab* (2H). While the Greek *patēr* (3962) is usually used to translate *abba*, *abba* itself appears three times in the NT (Mark 14:36; Rom. 8:15; Gal. 4:6). It was used among Jews as the familiar term children used for their fathers, and is used even today in Hebrew speaking families, not only by small children but by adult sons and daughters. An unfortunate English equivalent that has been popularized today is 'Daddy.' This term has taken on a too sentimental tone and has given way to a somewhat 'buddy-buddy' relationship with God. More precisely it means, 'my father,' 'Father, my Father,' or 'Dear Father,' which emphasize the necessity of reverence. Historically, in fact, the childish word (*daddy*) receded" (Watson, *A Word for the Day*, 4).

[59] *Matthew Henry's Commentary on the Whole Bible* (electronic edition, public domain).

[60] Tozer, *God Tells the Man Who Cares*, 12.

[61] It is also argued, "God was also protecting the health of His people by prohibiting meat that was likely to transmit disease in days when there was little or no refrigeration and the use of antibiotics in animal husbandry was unknown." We humbly submit, however, that is logically flawed. Does this mean that these meats were still prohibited up to the day refrigeration and antibiotics were invented? Does God's truth rely upon man's inventions? Also, contrary to popular opinion, cooking does not necessarily remove the impurities present in such meat, such as *trichinella spiralis*, for example, just one of the some 18 worms found in hogs. These facts, and many others, are clearly and quite easily demonstrated scientifically and medically. To argue otherwise, we lovingly submit, is simply foolish.

[62] Many medical authorities today say that eating pork is a prime cause of cancer, blood disease, liver troubles, tumors, and the like. On this subject, we recommend J. Sidlow Baxter, *Our High Calling* (Zondervan, 1967), 157. His discussion is short (141–160) but excellent. Additionally, Dr. Russell J. Thomsen, a medical doctor, makes some very good comments in his book, *Medical Wisdom From The Bible* (Spire Books, Fleming H, Revell Co., 1974), 98–103.

[63] *TWOT*, entry #1879.

[64] For a deeper study, see the author's *A Hebrew Word for the Day* (52).

[65] Watson, *Body of Divinity*, 90.

[66] While these words appear in the screenplay and movie *Tora! Tora! Tora!*, some observers doubt that Yamamoto said these exact words. They do not appear, for example, in *The Reluctant Admiral*, the definitive biography of Yamamoto in English by Agawa Hiroyu (1979). This biography does relate, however, that "Yamamoto alone" (while his staff was celebrating) spent the day after Pearl Harbor "sunk in apparent depression." It's a fact that he was upset by the bungling of the Foreign Ministry that led to the attack happening while the countries were technically at peace, thus making the incident an unprovoked sneak attack that would certainly enrage the enemy. The biography also reports a letter to Ogata Taketora (Jan. 9, 1942) in which Yamamoto wrote, "A military man can scarcely pride himself on having 'smitten a sleeping enemy'; in fact, to have it pointed out is more a matter of shame" (285).

[67] Brown, *NIDNTT*, vol. III, 354.

[68] *Thayer's Lexicon*, entry #1342.

[69] Watson, *Body of Divinity*, 92.

[70] Joseph Exell, (ed.), *The Biblical Illustrator, Psalms* (Baker, 1967), 278.

[71] For a deeper study, see the author's *A Hebrew Word for the Day* (96, 98).

[72] For a deeper study, see the author's *A Word for the Day* (86).

[73] Thomas, *Puritan Golden Treasury*, 189.

[74] *All Things for Good* (originally, *A Divine Cordial*, 1663) (Banner of Truth, 1986, 2011), 18.

[75] Watson, *Body of Divinity*, 94 (emphasis added).

[76] Watson, *Body of Divinity*, 97.

[77] Watson, *Sermons*, 508.

[78] Watson, *Body of Divinity*, 98–99.

[79] Thomas, *Puritan Golden Treasury*, 112.
[80] For a deeper study of these Hebrew and Greek words, see the author's *A Hebrew Word for the Day* (97–98) and *A Word for the Day* (44–45).
[81] *TWOT*, #694.
[82] Thayer, #5485
[83] Brown, *NIDNTT*, Vol. 2, p. 115.
[84] N. H. Snaith, *The Distinctive Ideas of the Old Testament* (London: The Epworth Press, 1944), 128.
[85] Thomas, *Puritan Golden Treasury*, 128.
[86] Harry Ironside, *Expository Messages on The Epistle to the Galatians* (Neptune, NJ: Lozeaux Brothers, 1978), 130–132.
[87] J. Sidlow Baxter, *Majesty: The God You Should Know* (Here's Life Publishers, 1984), 131.
[88] Packer, *Knowing God*, 111.
[89] "Little Kittel," 7.
[90] Tozer, *Knowledge of the Holy*, 104.
[91] For the fuller explanation of these nine usages, see the author's *The Doctrines of Grace from the Lips of Our Lord* (50–53), or *Salvation Is of the Lord* (182–190).
[92] Thomas, *Puritan Golden Treasury*, 122.
[93] *Luther's Explanatory Notes on the Gospels* (public domain, electronic edition).
[94] Watson, *Body of Divinity*, 196.
[95] "Little Kittel," 1118.
[96] Charnock, Vol. II, 449 (emphasis added).
[97] We would here recommend John MacArthur's excellent "harmony" of the Gospels, *One Perfect Life* (Thomas Nelson, 2012), a blending of the four Gospels into one chronological narrative with the addition of explanatory notes.
[98] Thomas, *Puritan Golden Treasury*, 163.
[99] Tozer, *Pursuit of God*, 16.
[100] "The word dung is *skubalon* (4657). Sadly, every modern translation misses the depth of this word by rendering it refuse (ASV), rubbish (NASB, ESV, NIV, NKJV), garbage (NLT), or even trash (NCV). But *skubalon* goes even further than those somewhat milder images. It's an extremely coarse, ugly, and repulsive word that also referred to excrement, and the AV correctly captures that image. Paul considered everything in this world as nothing more than the most repulsive thing he could think of in comparison to knowing the Lord Jesus Christ" (Watson, *A Word for the Day*, 194).
[101] For a study of these seven Greek words and related principles of prayer, see the author's *A Word for the Day*, 149–152.
[102] Brown, *NIDNTT*, Vol. 3, 530.
[103] *Romeo and Juliet*, II.2.43–44.
[104] Willem A. Van Gemeren, ed., *New International Dictionary of Old Testament Theology and Exegesis* (Zondervan, 1997), #H9005.
[105] For a deeper study of the Hebrew for "Name" and the names of God in the OT, see the author's *A Hebrew Word for the Day* (3–4, 7–30).
[106] Zodhiates, *Word Study Dictionary*, #G810.

[107] This is true because the grammatical construction is that of the "genitive case," which primarily indicates possession or source and often includes the English word "of" in the translation.

[108] Other examples include Zodhiates, *Word Study Dictionary* (#G5207): "'Son of peace' meaning friendly, giving one's benediction, receiving someone hospitably (Lk.10:6). 'Sons of the day' (a.t.) meaning enlightened with true knowledge (1Thes. 5:5). 'Son of consolation' (Acts 4:36). 'Sons of light' means enlightened with the true light (Lk. 16:8; Jn. 12:36; 1 Thes. 5:5, the opposite of sons of this world or of this age, meaning devoted to the philosophy of this age or this world [Lk. 16:8; 20:34]). 'Sons of disobedience' meaning the disobedient (Eph. 2:2; 5:6; Col. 3:6). . . . 'sons of the resurrection' (Lk. 20:36; author's translation) meaning partakers in it; 'sons of the prophets and the covenant' (Acts 3:25, author's translation) meaning to whom the prophecies and the covenant appertain). 'Son of perdition' meaning devoted to destruction (Jn.17:12). 'Son of hell,' meaning deserving everlasting punishment (Matt. 23:15)."

[109] J. Oliver Buswell, *A Systematic Theology of the Christian Religion* (Zondervan, 1962), Vol. 1, 105.

[110] Watson, *A Word for the Day*, 294; see more detail on these words there.

[111] Buswell, *Systematic Theology*, Vol. 1, 105.

[112] Zodhiates, *Word Study Dictionary*, #G444.

[113] John F. Walvoord and Roy B. Zuck, *The Bible Knowledge Commentary* (Scripture Press Publications, Inc., 1983, 1985), comment on Jn. 3:16.

[114] *Wuest's Expanded Translation* (Eerdmans, 1961).

For a deeper study of "only begotten," including grammatical and historical evidence for this translation, see chapter 45, "The 'Only Begotten' Son," in the author's *Truth on Tough Texts*, 442–49. This article also reprinted in the author's *The Doctrines of Grace from the Lips of Our Lord*.

Briefly, some translators weaken this verse with the translation "only Son" (RSV, ESV) or "one and only Son" (NIV). But this is a serious error because Christ is not the only Son of God. All believers, in fact, are sons and daughters of God. Jesus was the only physically born (begotten) Son of God. All others have been "adopted" into God's family. Before salvation, we were children of the Devil (Jn. 8:44), but by trusting in Christ, we were "adopted" (placed into) the family of God (Jn. 1:12; Eph. 1:5; etc.). This distinction is critically important.

[115] WCF, Chapter VIII, section II, with an identical statement in the *London Baptist Confession of 1689*.

[116] Inclusivism is the teaching that, although salvation comes through Jesus, it is not necessary to possess specific knowledge concerning Jesus as Savior. Other religions, in fact, can be vehicles of salvation for people who never heard of Jesus Christ, but "finally" (ultimately) are included because of their sincerity and positive response to general revelation. One could, for example, look at the beauty of the Rocky Mountains as they drive through Estes Park, "see God in it all," and therefore go to heaven. Examples of modern inclusivists include: Clark Pinnock, Billy Graham, and C. S. Lewis. For a more detailed explanation and examples, see the author's, *Upon This Rock*, 102–103.

[117] "The fact that 'to believe' is 'to obey,' as in the OT, is particularly emphasized in Heb. 11. Here the *pisteuein* [faith] of OT characters has in some instances the more

or less explicit sense of obedience. . . . Paul in particular stresses the element of obedience in faith. For him *pistis* [faith] is indeed *hupakon* [obey] as comparison of Rom. 1:5, 8; 1 Thes. 1:8 with Rom. 15:18; 16:19, or 2 Cor. 10:5 with 10:15 shows. Faith is for Paul to *hupakouein tō euangeilō* [literally, 'obedient to the good news'], Rom. 10:16. To refuse to believe is not to obey the righteousness which the Gospel offers by faith, Rom. 10:3. . . . He coins the combination *hupakon pisteuō* [literally, 'obedience of faith'], Rom. 1:5" (*TDNT*, Vol. VI, 205).

[118] Jacob Neusner, *The Mishnah: A New Translation* (Yale University Press, 1988), Sukkah 5:2–4.

[119] For more detail concerning this scene in the Temple, as well as the Greek words *phōs*, *skotos*, and *kosmos*, see the author's *A Word for the Day* (68, 167–68, 226)

[120] *Thura* (2374) referred to a common door, such as, a house door, the "outer door" that led from the street to the courtyard, the door of a walled sheepfold, the door of a single room or prison cell, the gate of a city, and even the rough-cut door of a cave or sepulcher.

[121] *The Treasury of David*, comment on Psalm 23:1.

[122] Brown, *NIDNTT*, Vol. 2, 98.

[123] See the much more detailed discussion of this wondrous truth in the author's *The Doctrines of Grace from the Lips of Our Lord* (42–46), or *Salvation Is of the Lord* (162–68).

[124] John Gill, *Exposition of the Entire Bible*, comment on John 11:26.

[125] A. T. Robertson, *Grammar of the Greek New Testament in the Light of Historical Research* (Hodder & Stoughton, 1919), 756.

[126] For a deeper study of the Greek word *alētheia*, see the author's *A Word for the Day* (32–34)

[127] Adapted from Thomas a Kempis: "Without the way there is no going; without the truth there is no knowing; without the life there is no living" (*Imitation of Christ*, iii., 56).

[128] Brown, *NIDNTT*, Vol. 3, p. 224.

[129] Quotation in text by, and table below adapted from, the observation of Simon Kistemaker, *New Testament Commentary: Exposition of the Book of Revelation* (Baker Academic, 2001, 2007), 583–84.

Similarities Between Revelation 1 and 22

1:1	22:6
God gave Jesus [his revelation] to show his servants what must soon take place by sending his angel.	the Lord God has sent his angel to show his servants what must soon take place.
1:3	**22:7, 10**
Blessed are the ones who hear the words of this prophecy and who heed the things written in it. For the time is near.	Blessed is the one who keeps the words of the prophecy of this book. For the time is near.

1:8, 17	22:13
I am the Alpha and the Omega the First and the Last.	I am the Alpha and the Omega the First and the Last.
1:1	**22:16**
And he made it known by sending his angel to his servant John who testified.	I, Jesus, have sent my angel to you to testify these things in the churches.

[130] R. C. H. Lenski, *Commentary on the New Testament: Galatians, Ephesians, Philippians* (Hendrickson Publishers, 1937, 2001), 454.

[131] For a deeper examination of this metaphor in Eph. 2:20–21, see the author's *A Word for the Day* (191–93).

[132] Zodhiates, *Word Study Dictionary*, #G747.

[133] Zodhiates, *Word Study Dictionary*, #G5051.

[134] William Hendriksen, *New Testament Commentary: Exposition of the Gospel According to Luke* (Baker Academic, 1978, 2007), 152.

[135] William Moister, *Missionary Anecdotes* (London: Wesleyan Conference Office, 1875), 229.

[136] See the author's *A Taste of Heaven on Earth: Marriage and Family in Ephesians 5:18–6:4* (Sola Scriptura Publications, 2013).

[137] Kittel, Vol. II, 237.

[138] Brown, *NIDNTT*, Vol. 2, 606.

[139] For a fuller exposition of John 1:1–3, see the author's *The Doctrines of Grace from the Lips of our Lord*, 3-9). Parts of today's meditation were adapted from those pages.

[140] Brown, *NIDNTT*, Vol. 3, 1081.

[141] Zodhiates, *Word Study Dictionary*, entry #G3004.

[142] We take more than 3,500 English idioms for granted. Some common ones include: "killing time," "throw in the towel," "kick the bucket," "dig your heels in," and "paint yourself into a corner." Hebrew has its own idioms, hundreds of them. For example, *be'arba enayim* literally means "with four eyes," indicating meeting face-to-face, as in, "The two men met with four eyes."

[143] "Carpenter" is *tektōn* (5045), which actually implies more than just a carpenter. In secular Greek, it was used not only of a craftsman or builder in wood but also stone and metal and was also used in the same ways in the Septuagint (2 Sam. 5:11; 2 Kings 12:11; Is. 40:20; 1 Sam. 13:19; 1 Kings 7:14). It is very likely, then, that Jesus was not just a carpenter but also a mason and a smith. As one writer submits, Jesus might very well have fit the modern titles of "general contractor or builder" (David A. Croteau, *Urban Legends of the New Testament* [B&H Publishing, 2015], 25).

[144] Modern translations, and the Greek text behind them, omit the word "rule" (*kanōn*) and the words that follow based solely upon only four Greek manuscripts, which the critics, as always, dogmatically assert are superior because they are older, even though thousands of others disagree. The manuscript evidence for the Traditional Text reading, which the AV translation reflects, is overwhelming. The reading, in fact, is clearly awkward if these words are omitted.

[145] See also: Ezek. 1:3; Dan. 9:2; Hos. 1:1 ; Joel 1:1; Jonah 1:1; Mic. 1:1; Zeph. 1:1; Hag. 1:1; Zech. 1:1; Mal. 1:1.

[146] Brown, *NIDNTT*, Vol. 3, 1121.

[147] Greek *monarchos*; from *mono* (one) and *archē* (rule, authority, dominion, power).

[148] Henry Thiessen, *Lectures in Systematic Theology* (Eerdmans, 1949), 303.

[149] Brown, *NIDNTT*, Vol. 3, 689, 693, 706.

[150] Charles C. Ryrie, *Basic Theology* (Victor Books, 1986), 343.

[151] "Who Is the Holy Spirit?" in *How to Be Filled With the Holy Spirit* (cited from *A Treasury of A. W. Tozer A Treasury of A. W. Tozer* [Baker, 1980], 290).

[152] More specifically, "Pantheism" is an apostate view of God, found in the religion of India, for example, which affirms that there is no God apart from nature, and that everything in nature is a part or manifestation of God. In other words, God is all, and all is God.

[153] For a detailed study of this key doctrine, see the author's, *A Taste of Heaven on Earth: Marriage and Family in Ephesians 5:18–6:4* (Sola Scriptura Publications, 2013), 13–31. This detailed exposition is also contained in Volume 2 of the author's, *The Christian's Wealth and Walk: An Expository Commentary on Ephesians* (Sola Scriptura Publications, 2017).

[154] Wuest.

[155] Cited by A. W. Tozer, *The Tozer Pulpit*, Vol. 1, Book 2, 61.

[156] Harry Ironside, *In the Heavenlies: Practical Expository Addresses on the Epistle to the Ephesians* (Loizeaux Brothers, 1937), 269 (emphasis added).

[157] Brown, *NIDNTT*, Vol. 3, 109.

[158] Zodhiates, *Word Study Dictionary*, 1283.

[159] Brown, *NIDNTT*, Vol. 1, 474.

[160] Arthur W. Pink, *Exposition of the Gospel of John* (Zondervan), 778.

[161] Jamison, Fausset, and Brown, *A Commentary: Critical, Experiential, and Practical*, 3 vols. (Eerdmans Publishing Company, reprint 1993) Vol. 3, 435.

[162] Pink, 778. His actual comment is: "The Holy Spirit would comfort, or strengthen in a variety of respects: consolation when they were cast down, grace when they were weak or timid, guidance when they were perplexed, etc."

[163] For a detailed study of this doctrine, see chapter 22, "The Sealing of the Holy Spirit," in the author's, *Truth on Tough Texts*, 220–33. This doctrine is also detailed in the author's, *The Christian's Wealth and Walk: An Expository Commentary on Ephesians*, Vol. 1 (Sola Scriptura Publications, 2017), 1:13–14.

[164] Baxter, *Explore the Book*, Vol. 6, 328. While the text reads "closet Friend," I once heard Baxter say "bosom friend" instead. Baxter probably borrowed these lines from Frederick Lucian Hosmer's poem, "The Indwelling God," which reads: "And be thy daily Friend."

[165] Tozer, *Of God and Men*, 38. For a detailed analysis of Tozer's work, see the author's book, *The Forgotten Tozer*.

[166] The words in the Greek can be neuter in gender as in the KJV translation, or they can be masculine as in the NASB ("combining spiritual thoughts with spiritual words") and the NIV ("expressing spiritual truths with spiritual words").

[167] Vance Havner, *Pepper and Salt* (Fleming H. Revell, 1966; reprinted by Baker, 1983), 18.

[168] Trench, *Synonyms*, 29, 30.
[169] *Calvin's Commentaries: Ephesians* (public domain, electronic edition), comment on Eph. 5:11.
[170] Brown, *NIDNTT*, Vol. 1, 73. Also, for a more detailed study of this verse, see chapter 20 ("What Is the Old Man") in the author's *Truth on Tough Texts*, 203–09.
[171] J. Sidlow Baxter, *A New Call to Holiness* (1967, 1973), 98. In my humble opinion, Baxter's trilogy on the Christian doctrine of sanctification is unequalled. The other two volumes are: *His Deeper Work In Us*, and *Our High Calling* (Zondervan). These were also republished in a one volume edition: *Christian Holiness Restudied and Restated* (Zondervan, 1977).
[172] Brown, *TNIDNTT*, Vol. 3, 719.
[173] This quotation has been disputed, since proof is unclear. Whether true or not, however, the principle itself is no less accurate.
[174] This paragraph adapted from the author's *A Word for the Day*, 71.
[175] Gila Manolson, *Head to Heart* (Targum, 2002). She goes on to define it, however, in an equally dreadful fashion: "Love is the attachment that results from deeply appreciating another's goodness."
[176] Vine, *Expository Dictionary*, "Love (To)" entry.
[177] *Morning and Evening*, June 5 evening reading.
[178] *Hamlet*, I.2.2.
[179] Matthew Henry, *A Church in the House, or Family Religion* (public domain, Internet Archive [https://archive.org/details/churchinhouseorf00henr]), 18–20.
[180] William Hendricksen, *New Testament Commentary* (Baker), comment on Matt. 26:51.
[181] John MacArthur, *A Tale of Two Sorrows*, a sermon on Matthew 26:1—27:10 (GTY 141, 2012).
[182] Some view the word "these" as referring to the boats, nets, and other objects connected with the fishing trade. Jesus is, therefore calling Peter to turn his back on his former life and be committed fully to Him. We humbly submit, however, that this seems unlikely. In light of Peter's boast in Matthew 26:33—"Though all men shall be offended because of thee, yet will I never be offended"—it makes far more sense that Jesus is asking if he still had that attitude, if he still thought his love and commitment was greater than all the others. This is, in fact, the view of the vast majority of commentators.
[183] From William Cowper's hymn, *Hark, My Soul, It Is The Lord!* (1768).
[184] *In Tenderness He Sought Me*, W. Spencer Walton (1894).
[185] Avot 5:16. *The Torah* was what the Jews called "The Law," the first five books of the Old Testament. Questions arose concerning the meanings of these laws, so over the years an oral law called "the tradition of the elders" developed. That tradition was put into written form around A.D. 200 and was called *The Mishnah*, which means "repetition," as much of Jewish education was based on repetition, and was actually a principle part of what was called the "Talmud," the commentaries that were written on the Law.
[186] Thomas Watson, *All Things for Good* (Banner of Truth, 1986; first published in 1663 as *A Divine Cordial*), 68.
[187] Ibid, 69 (emphasis added).

[188] First uttered by the Roman poet Sextus Propertius (50 BC–16 BC). *Elegies*, xxxiii, 43 (Latin: *Semper in absentes felicior aestus amantes.*).

[189] For a detailed study, see the author's, *The Seven Churches of the 21st Century: An Exposition of Revelation 2 & 3* (2018).

[190] Brown, Vol. 3, 230.

[191] For a more detailed examination of this and related issues, see the author's *Truth on Tough Texts* (33–46) and *Winds of Doctrine* (53–77).

[192] Thomas Watson, *The Ten Commandments* (Banner of Truth reprint, 1981; originally published as part of *A Body of Practical Divinity*, 1692), 74.

[193] These studies were sparked by a message I heard by a dear brother I knew back in the 1980s, Pastor Chester Martin. While he submitted the "five levels" and developed them, all the material here is my own.

[194] Tom Carted, ed., *2,200 Quotations from the Writings of Charles H. Spurgeon* (Baker, 1988), 216.

[195] Tozer, *Tozer Pulpit*, I.1.46.

[196] There is a textual note here worthy of mention. Some Greek manuscripts read 72 instead of 70. While some scholars insist that the manuscript evidence is evenly divided, that is an odd statement when you collate the data. The support for 72 is: P75, Codex B (Vaticanus), D (Bezae), 0181, most of the Old Latin manuscripts, the Sinaitic Syriac, the Curetonian Syriac, the Sahidic, and a single Bohairic manuscript. Among the Church Fathers, it appears in some manuscripts of Origen (d. 254 AD) and in Adamantius (c. 300–350 AD). The support for 70, however, is demonstrably stronger: Aleph (Sinaiticus), A, C, L, W, Theta Psi family 1 (1, 118, 131, 209, 1582), family 13 (13, 69, 124, 174, 230, 346, 543, 788, 826, 828, 983, 1689, 1709), and the majority of extant manuscripts. Additionally, it is supported by the Syriac Peshitta, the Syriac Harclean, and the Bohairic. It is also supported by quotations in the Church Fathers including Irenaeus (2nd-century), Clement (c. 95), and Tertullian (c. 220). The entire issue revolves around the presence of a second occurrence of the Greek *duo* ("two") in the manuscripts that read 72. Including the extra *duo* with *hebdomekonta* ("twenty") yields the 72 reading. This is easily explained by viewing it as a copying error.

In addition to that internal evidence, there is ample external evidence, as 70 was inarguably a pivotal number for the Jews. This was the number of the nations mentioned in Genesis 10, the number of the family of Jacob that came into Egypt (Gen. 46:27), the number of elders that Moses appointed to aid him (Num. 11:16, 11:25), and the number that comprised the Sanhedrin, the ruling council of the nation. As Albert Barnes concludes: "It is not improbable that our Saviour appointed this number with reference to the fact that it so often occurred among the Jews, or after the example of Moses, who appointed seventy to aid him in his work."

If that data is not sufficient, it is also significant that several modern translations that are actually based on the Critical Text read "seventy" (NASB, HCSB, NRSV) instead of "seventy-two" (NIV, ESV, CEV, NLT). Why? It seems obvious that the translators recognized the overwhelming evidence.

Now, many ask at this point, "What difference does it really make?" We actually hear this question quite often when it comes to such textual matters. We submit, however, that this is not only a very odd question but also an extremely troubling one. *What difference does it make?* We submit that it makes a great deal of difference. The very historical accuracy of Scripture—that is, the doctrine of infallibility itself—is at stake here. Also at stake is the doctrine of the verbal, plenary inspiration of Scripture. Did the Holy Spirit move the author (2 Pet. 1:21) to write "seventy" or "seventy-two"? Both cannot be correct, so it most certainly makes a difference which one.

[197] See John Gill, *Exposition of the Entire Bible* (Lk. 10:1), for a list that some believe is an accurate summary of those 70 witnesses.

[198] While a few men in the NT were called "apostles" who did not actually possess the strict qualifications—James (Gal. 1:19), Barnabas (Acts 14:14), possibly Silas and Timothy (1 Thess. 2:6), and possibly Apollos (1 Cor. 4:6, 9)—in each context the title seems an honorary one because of each man's association with Paul and because each did the work of an apostle but did not hold the office of apostle. Far too much emphasis has been placed on this unofficial meaning of the word apostle. Some today go so far as to say that the office still exists in a more or less "general sense."

[199] Wuest, *Word Studies*, comment on Mark 3:14.

[200] Vance Havner, *Pepper 'n' Salt* (Baker, 1983 reprint), 25.

[201] Robertson, *Word Pictures*, comment on Acts 11:25.

[202] Watson, *The Ten Commandments* (Banner of Truth Trust, 1965; originally published 1692), 59–60.

[203] For a more detailed study of these issues, see chapter 43, "The Pestilence of Idolatry," in the author's *Truth on Tough Texts*, 421–432.

[204] *Commentaries*, comment on Ex. 32:1.

[205] H. I Hester, *The Heart of Hebrew History* (William Jewell Press, 1949), 123.

[206] Alexander Maclaren, *Maclaren's Expositions of Holy Scripture* (public domain, electronic edition), comment on Ex. 32:1–8.

[207] *The Complete Pulpit Commentary* (public domain), homily by J. Orr on Ex. 32:5.

[208] Archibald G. Brown, a sermon titled: "The Devil's Mission of Amusement: The Church's Task–Entertainment or Evangelization?" Available on many Internet websites. This should be required reading of every Christian leader in our day.

[209] *Barnes' Notes on the Bible* (public domain, electronic edition), note on Judg. 2:11.

[210] https://www.barna.org/barna-update/article/5-barna-update/67-americans-are-most-likely-to-base-truth-on-feelings#.U0SCWfldVDU.

[211] I am indebted to my friend and fellow author, JD Wetterling, and his wonderful little book, *No One: When Jesus Says It, He Means It* (Christian Focus, 2006). While my approach and outline are very different, as well as are two of the six verses that are addressed (because of the Greek *oudeis*), his little book was a blessing and encouragement when putting together the present studies.

[212] For a deeper study of *helkuō*, see the author's *Salvation Is of the Lord* (201, 223).

[213] Spiritual Science Research Foundation (www.spiritualresearchfoundation.org).

[214] Calvin (*Commentaries*): "This is an explanation of the former statement', for he is the way, because he leads us to the Father, and he is the truth and the life, because in him we perceive the Father."

[215] Hypovolemic shock is an emergency condition in which severe blood and fluid loss make the heart unable to pump enough blood to the body. This type of shock can cause many organs to stop functioning.

[216] J. C. Ryle, *Expository Thoughts on the Gospels: John* (public domain), Vol. 1.

[217] For an exposition of this debated passage, see chapter 19, "What Does 'Fall Away' Mean?" in the author's *Truth On Tough Texts*, 195–202.
[218] Brown, *NIDNTT*, Vol. 1, 481–82.
[219] Watson, *Sermons*, 42.
[220] Recounted in *Windows on the Word: Illustrations from Our Daily Bread* (Radio Bible Class, 1984), 91–92.
[221] Zodhiates, *Word Study Dictionary*, #G2347.
[222] Thomas, *Puritan Golden Treasury*, 159.
[223] Watson, *Sermons*, 619.
[224] Zodhiates, *Word Study Dictionary*, #H7812.
[225] As I have written elsewhere, while the Reformers did, indeed, come out of Catholicism, they did not come out far enough (see the author's, *Upon This Rock*, 59–70). Just two examples are Luther's view of the Lord's Supper and Zwingli's retaining the practice of infant baptism. There were actually two reasons the Reformers failed to come out far enough. First, instead of throwing out everything, opening their Bible, and completely starting over from scratch, they chose to just modify existing beliefs as long as those beliefs were not explicitly rejected in Scripture. Second, there was a predilection toward mysticism in that day, which especially affected the Lord's Supper. (These issues are also covered in more detail in his upcoming works, *"In Remembrance of Me"* and *Church History In the Light of Scripture*).
[226] See the author's, *Upon This Rock*, 59–70.
[227] Watson, *Sermons*, 410.
[228] *Westminster*, 1646 (21.1); *London*, 1689 (22.1).
[229] Jeremiah Burroughs, *Gospel-Worship* (London: Peter Cole, 1650), 9–10 (emphasis added).
[230] John Gill, *Exposition of the Entire Bible*, comment on Mark 7:6.
[231] Wuest, *Word Studies*, comment on Philippians 2:1.
[232] For a detailed study of this and related texts, see two chapters in the author's, *Truth on Tough Texts*: chapter 3, "How Often Should the Lord's Supper Be Observed?" and chapter 50, "The Lord's Supper: Memorial or More?"
[233] Except Paul singing in prison (Acts 16:25).
[234] A. W. Tozer, *The Price of Neglect* (Christian Publications, n.d.), 16.
[235] Watson, *Body of Divinity*, 7.
[236] These five studies (June 9–13) were adapted from the author's, *A Light Unto My Path: An Exposition of Psalm 119* (Sola Scriptura Publications, 2012).
[237] Vine, *Expository Dictionary*, entry "Love (To)."
[238] *The Treasury of David*, comment on Psalm 138:2.
[239] Henry Morris, *The Defender's Study Bible* (World Publishing, 1995), comment on Ps. 138:2.
[240] John Gill, *Exposition of the Entire Bible*, comment on Psalm 119:48.
[241] *Matthew Henry's Commentary on the Whole Bible*, comment on Psalm 119:48.
[242] Charles Bridges, *Exposition of Psalm 119* (Banner of Truth, 1994; originally published 1827), 20.
[243] *TWOT*, #2255.
[244] Thomas, *Puritan Golden Treasury*, 184.
[245] A. F. Kirkpatrick (Editor), *The Book of Psalms* (University Press, 1906), 700.

[246] C. H. Mackintosh, *Short Papers*, Section 6.
[247] Zodhiates, *Word Study Dictionary*, #H6490.
[248] To summarize what the following studies present: Having no other gods (Ex. 20:3; Deut. 5:7; Matt. 4:10; Acts 5:29; 1 Cor. 8:4–6); making no idols or images (Ex. 20:4–6; Deut. 5:8–10; Acts 17:29–31; 1 Cor. 8:4–6; 10:14; Col. 3:5; 1 Jn. 5:21); not profaning God's name (Ex. 20:7; Deut. 5:11; Jas. 5:12); setting aside a day of worship (Ex. 20:8–11; Deut. 5:12–15); Jn. 20:19; Acts 20:7; 1 Cor. 16:2; Rev. 1:10); honoring one's father and mother (Ex. 20:12; Deut. 5:16; Eph. 6:1–3; Col. 3:20); not murdering (Ex. 20:13; Deut. 5:17; Rom. 13:9, 10; Jas. 2:11); not committing adultery (Ex. 20:14; Deut. 5:19; Rom. 13:9,10; 1 Cor. 6:9; Heb. 13:4; Jas. 2:11); not stealing (Ex. 20:15; Deut. 5:19; Rom. 13:9, 10; Eph. 4:28); not lying (Ex. 20:16; Deut. 5:20; Eph. 4:25,31; Col. 3:9; Tit. 3:2); not coveting (Ex. 20:17; Deut. 5:21; Rom. 7:7; 13:9; Eph. 5:3–5; Heb. 13:5 Jas. 4:1–3).
[249] Zodhiates, *Word Study Dictionary*, #H8176.
[250] Watson, *Ten Commandments*, 14.
[251] Thomas, *Puritan Golden Treasury*, 165 (emphasis Secker's).
[252] *The Works of Ezekiel Hopkins*, 3 Vols. (Philadelphia: Leighton Publications, 1863), Vol. 1, 251.
[253] Watson, *Ten Commandments*, 6.
[254] Ibid, 45.
[255] John F. Walvoord and Roy B. Zuck, *The Bible Knowledge Commentary*, comment on Ex. 20:1–2. Our subsequent studies build upon these "ten words," but the content is my own.
[256] http://johnwindbell.hubpages.com/hub/How-many-Religions-are-there, and http://www.adherents.com/.
[257] *Maclaren's Expositions of Holy Scripture*, comment on Ex. 20:3.
[258] Robert Bellah, et al., *Habits of the Heart* (Harper & Row, 1985), 221.
[259] G. Campbell Morgan, *The Ten Commandments* (The Bible Institute Colportage Association of Chicago, 1901), 25–26.
[260] Girdlestone, *Synonyms of the OT*, 328.
[261] For a deeper study of the biblical and historical issues mentioned here, see chapter 43, "The Pestilence of Idolatry," in the author's, *Truth on Tough Texts*, 421–32.
[262] Stephen D. Renn, (Ed.), *Expository Dictionary of Bible Words* (Hendrickson Publishers), 2005.
[263] For a study of the names of God in the OT, see the author's *A Hebrew Word for the Day*, 7–31.
[264] G. Campbell Morgan, *The Ten Commandments* (Baker, 1974), 44.
[265] *Zākar* is at times used of God (e.g., Jer. 23:36). This, of course, does not mean he can forget as would we and must consciously try to remember. Rather it refers to fulfilling His word, acting in a fashion consistent with His promise.
[266] Morgan, *Ten Commandments*, 46.
[267] The following is from the author's *A Hebrew Word for the Day* (77, 382):
"Justin Martyr described a typical worship service of his day: 'And on the day called Sunday, all who live in cities or in the country gather together to one place, and the memoirs of the apostles or the writings of the prophets are read, as long as time permits; then, when the reader has ceased, the president verbally instructs, and

exhorts to the imitation of these **good** things. Then we all rise together and pray, and, as we before said, when our prayer is ended, bread and wine and water are brought, and the president in like manner offers prayers and thanksgivings, according to his ability, and the people assent, saying Amen.'

"*The Epistle of Barnabas* 15:8–9 (AD 100): 'Finally, [the Lord] says to them: 'I cannot bear your new moons and Sabbaths' [Isa. 1:13]. . . . This is why we spend the eighth day in celebration, the day on which Jesus both rose from the dead and, after appearing again, ascended into heaven.' (J. B. Lightfoot and J. R. Harmer [translators], *The Apostolic Fathers*, Second Edition [Baker Books, 1989], 183.)

"*The Letters of Ignatius: To Magnesians* 8:1–9:1 (107): 'Do not be deceived by strange doctrines or antiquated myths, since they are worthless. For if we continue to live in accordance with Judaism, we admit that we have not received grace. . . . If, then, those who had lived in antiquated practices came to newness of hope, no longer keeping the Sabbath but living in accordance to the Lord's Day, on which our life also arose through him and his death.' (Lightfoot, 95). It is incontrovertible fact that the early church meant on the first day of the week."

[268] *The Works of Ezekiel Hopkins*, Vol. 1, 374 (emphasis added).

[269] Zodhiates, *Word Study Dictionary*, #G1459.

[270] See chapter 37, "Forsaking the Assembly," in the author's *Truth on Tough Texts* for an in-depth study of our text. Briefly, on the current point:

"There have been several theories offered as to what this reason was. Perhaps they didn't think it was important, perhaps it was due to apostasy, or perhaps they simply had no interest in it. One strong possibility was that they were dissatisfied with other church members. While the congregations were mostly Jewish, there would have been at least some Gentiles, since the 'middle wall of partition' between them had been 'broken down' by Christ (Eph. 2:14). The Jews had always been exclusive, however, and despised other nations. It's quite possible that, as Calvin puts it, 'the Gentiles were a new and unwonted addition to the Church,' causing many to forsake attendance altogether. Another strong possibility—and we think it possible that more than one of these reasons existed—was they simply feared persecution. Persecution is referred to, in fact, further down in the passage (vv. 32–39; 12:4). It is reasonable to assume that this applied even to meetings in house churches, as the Romans, like all dictatorships, were suspicious of private meetings."

[271] *TWOT*, #4. We would also note that *'ab* (2H) is the Aramaic form, the basis for the NT usage of *abba* (5), which appears three times (Mk. 14:36; Rom. 8:15; Gal. 4:6). For a more detailed study of all these words, see the author's *A Word for the Day* (4) and *A Hebrew Word for the Day* (29).

[272] See *TWOT*, #115.

[273] Lev. 23:3, 14; Deut 29:10–13; Josh. 8:35; 2 Chron. 20:13; Neh. 12:43; Joel 2:15–16; Matt. 18:1–5; Mk. 10:13–14; Lk. 2:41–42; Acts 2:46; 20:20.

[274] For an in-depth study of the family, see the author's, *A Taste of Heaven on Earth: Marriage and the Family in Ephesians 5:18–6:4* (Sola Scriptura Publications, 2012).

[275] Matt. 19:18; 23:31, 35; Mk. 10:19; Lk. 18:20; Rom. 13:9; Jas. 2:11; 4:2; 5:6. See also the Septuagint: Ex. 20:15; Deut. 4:42; 5:17.

[276] David Broughton Knox, *Not By Bread Alone: God's Word on Present Issues* (Banner of Truth, 1989), 119.

[277] Leland Ryken, *Worldly Saints: The Puritans as They Really Were* (Zondervan, 1986), 40, 41.
[278] Pastor Tim Keller as cited in Philip Graham Ryken, *Preaching the Word: Exodus* (Crossway, 2005), electronic edition, comment on Ex. 20:14.
[279] Ibid, Ryken.
[280] *The Westminster Shorter Catechism*, Answer 71 and Answer 72.
[281] Cited in Alexander Maclaren, *Maclaren's Expositions of Holy Scripture* (public domain, electronic edition), comment on Ex. 20:15.
[282] *TWOT*, #364.
[283] Brown, *NIDNTT*, Vol. 2, 377.
[284] *TWOT*, #2461a.
[285] Zodhiates, *Word Study Dictionary*, #H7453.
[286] Brown, *NIDNTT*, Vol. 2, 470.
[287] For a deeper study of the Greek word *alētheia*, see the author's *A Word for the Day* (32–34).
[288] Albert Barnes: "Thus the scholiast says, *paroimia esti to kretizein epi tou pseudesthai*, to act the Cretan, is a proverb for to lie."
[289] Watson, *Ten Commandments*, 174.
[290] Jeremiah Burroughs, *The Rare Jewel of Christian Contentment* (1648; reprint Banner of Truth, 1964), 18.
[291] Samuel Bolton, *The True Bounds of Christian Freedom* (1645; reprint Banner of Truth, 1964), 71, 72 (emphasis added).
[292] Zodhiates, *Word Study Dictionary*, #G3874.
[293] William D. Mounce, *Basics of Biblical Greek Grammar* (Zondervan, 1993, 2003), 126 (emphasis in the original; "aspect" added).
[294] Kittel, *TDNT*, Vol. I, 747.
[295] Matt. 2:5; 4:4, 6, 7, 10; 11:10; 21:13; 26:24, 31; Mk. 1:2; 7:6; 9: 12, 13, 11:17; 14:21, 27; Lk. 2:23; 3:4; 4:4, 8, 10; 7:27; 10:26; 19:46; 24:46; Jn. 8:17; Acts 1:20; 7:42; 13:33; 15:15(16); 23:5; Rom. 1:17; 2:24; 3:4, 10; 4:17; 8:36; 9:13, 33; 10:15; 11:8, 26; 12:19; 14:11; 15:3, 9, 21; 1 Cor. 1:19, 31; 2:9; 3:19; 9:9; 10:7; 14:21; 15:45; 2 Cor. 8:15; 9:9; Gal. 3:10, 13; 4:22, 27; 1 Pet. 1:16.
[296] Verse 4 (Deut. 8:3), verse 7 (6:16), and verse 10 (6:13).
[297] Ralph Earle, *Word Meanings in the New Testament* (Hendrickson, 1974, 1986), comments on the perfect tense in Mk. 1:2 and Matt. 4:4.
[298] One other crucial point, in fact, that Greek grammarians make in regard to the perfect tense is, as Daniel Wallace puts it, the existing results of the past action are "in relation to the time of the speaker" (*Greek Grammar Beyond the Basics: An Exegetical Syntax of the New Testament* [Zondervan, 1996], 576). This is obviously important enough when a NT writer is referring back to the OT, but it is even more significant when the writer is referring to what is being written *now*. In other words, the writer is no longer looking back and saying the results of the action *then* are continuing till *now*, rather he is looking forward and saying that the effects of the action *now* are going to continue in the *future*.
[299] *Matthew Poole's Commentary* (public domain, electronic edition), 1 Cor. 4:6.
[300] *Barnes Notes on the Bible* (public domain, electronic edition), 1 Cor. 4:6.
[301] *Gill's Exposition of the Entire Bible* (public domain, electronic edition), 1 Cor. 4:6.

[302] While these obviously do not relate directly to Scripture, they do underscore the significance of the perfect tense. The negative particle (*ov*, "not") indicates full and complete negation, so when coupled with the perfect tense underscores the continuing lost state of those not in the Lamb's Book. As one commentator writes: "The negation of the perfect tense emphasizes a permanent state of affairs; the name does not stand (or remain) written" (Robert Thomas, *Revelation 8–22: An Exegetical Commentary* [Moody, 1996], 164).

[303] J. Sidlow Baxter, *Rethinking Our Priorities* (Zondervan, 1974), 245.

[304] Zodhiates, *Word Study Dictionary*, #H1058.

[305] Stephen Renn (Ed.), *Expository Dictionary of Bible Words* (Hendrickson, 2005), under the "Joy, Joyful" entry.

[306] Raymond C. Ortlund, Jr. (R. Kent Hughes, Ed.), *Preaching the Word: Isaiah* (Crossway, 2005), electronic edition, comment on Is. 40:31.

[307] *Commentaries*, comment on John 6:31.

[308] Warren Wiersbe wisely cautions: "Biblical images must be studied carefully and identified accurately, for the same image may be used with different meanings in different contexts. The dew is a case in point. In Hosea 6:4, it represents the fleeting religious devotion of the hypocrites, while in 13:3, it symbolizes the transiency of the people who think they're so secure. Both Jesus and Satan are represented by the lion (Rev. 5:5; 1 Pet. 5:8)." (*The Wiersbe Bible Commentary: OT* [David C. Cook, 2007], comment on Hosea 14:5–8 (1406).

[309] Leon J. Wood, *A Survey of Israel's History*, Revised and Enlarged (Zondervan, 1970, 1986), 112.

[310] Cited by Charles Spurgeon, *Flowers from a Puritan's Garden*, 1883.

[311] *F. B. Hole Commentary on the NT and Selected Books of the OT* (public domain, electronic edition), comment on Col. 3:2.

[312] Aaron Copeland, *What to Listen for in Music* (McGraw-Hill, 1939, 1957). The studies here refer to pages 31–67 of the Mentor Books edition (paperback) from New American Library.

[313] Elmer Mould, *Essentials of Bible History* (New York: Ronald Press, 1939, 1951).

[314] Each octave on a piano has five black keys and seven white keys, so there are twelve pitches in an octave. The most fundamental rule of 12-tone music is that once a note has been used, it cannot be used again until the other eleven pitch tones are used, even if you play in a different octave. This makes resolution impossible.

[315] Zodhiates, *Word Study Dictionary*, #G2570.

[316] *The Merchant of Venice*, Act V, Scene 1.

[317] This and the further description of tone color adapted from Copeland, *What to Listen for in Music*, 56–57.

[318] One particularly fascinating example is "Joseph's Canal" south of Cairo (*Bahr Yussef*, "the waterway of Joseph"), which parallels the Nile and is still in use today. Under Joseph's authority as administrator under Pharaoh, it was built to combat the infamous famine of his day.

[319] *Treasury of David*, comment on Ps. 1:3.

[320] John Phillips, *Exploring the Psalms* (Loizeaux Brothers, 1988), Vol. 1, 19.

[321] From the author's *A Hebrew Word for the Day* (261). For a more detailed discussion of each of these principles, see his *A Word for the Day* (231–35).

[322] As some have suggested, since the title "The Psalms of David" was prefixed to the whole book, this seems to indicate the author of this first psalm in the series. This is reasonable in light of the second psalm—while also without a title it is ascribed to David in Acts 4:25—and many that follow.

[323] *Treasury of David*, comment on Ps. 1:3.

[324] *Gill's Exposition of the Entire Bible*, comment on Ps. 1:3.

[325] *TWOT*, #736.

[326] From the author's *A Hebrew Word for the Day* (208).

[327] *Treasury of David*, comment on Ps. 37:3.

[328] *Pensées (Thoughts)*, Section II, The Misery of Man Without God, #139.

[329] From the author's *A Hebrew Word for the Day* (151).

[330] The following six studies (July 24–29) were adapted and expanded from the author's *A Hebrew Word for the Day* (275–78).

[331] See Herbert Lockyer's *All the Promises of the Bible* (Zondervan, 1962), 10.

[332] See the author's *Salvation Is of the Lord*.

[333] William MacDonald, *Believer's Bible Commentary*, comment on Heb. 11:10.

[334] *Barnes Notes on the Bible*, comment on Phil. 3:19.

[335] Parts of these studies were adapted and greatly expanded from an outline by an unknown author in William E. Ketchem (Compiler/Editor), *Funeral Sermons and Outline Addresses: An Aid for Pastors* (New York: Harper and Brothers, 1899), 178–183.

[336] William MacDonald, *Believer's Bible Commentary*, comment on Lk. 12:34.

[337] Preceding word studies and today's "Scriptures for Study" taken from the author's *A Word for the Day*, 337.

[338] *Hamlet*, III.1.80.

[339] For a detailed exposition of "The Armor of God" in Ephesians 6, see Vol. 2 of the author's, *The Christian's Wealth and Walk: An Expository Commentary on Ephesians* (Sola Scriptura Publications, 2017).

[340] Joseph S. Exell (ed.), *The Biblical Illustrator, The Psalms* (London: James Nisbet & Co., 1886), 405.

[341] For a deeper study of discernment, see chapter 6, "Where Has Our Discernment Gone?" in the author's *Truth On Tough Texts* (65–85)

[342] *The Price of Neglect*, 20–21. For a detailed analysis of Tozer's work, see also the author's, *The Forgotten Tozer*.

[343] *Matthew Henry's Commentary on the Whole Bible*, comment on Acts 17:28.

[344] Albert Barnes writes, "In the expression in the title 'upon Jonath-elem-rechokim,' the first word (*Jonath*) means a 'dove,' a favorite emblem of suffering innocence; and the second (*êlem*) means 'silence,' dumbness, sometimes put for uncomplaining submission; and the third (*râchôqiym*) means 'distant' or 'remote,' agreeing here with places or persons, probably the latter, in which sense it is applicable to the Philistines, as aliens in blood and religion from the Hebrews. Thus understood, the whole title is an enigmatical description of David as an innocent and uncomplaining sufferer among strangers." Barnes goes on to report other renderings that have been offered.

[345] *TWOT*, #420.

[346] *Treasury of David*, comment on Ps. 56:13.

[347] Watson, *A Body of Divinity*, 1.

[348] "The background idea of the verb is to 'discern,' and this lies behind the [derivatives, such as] . . . the preposition *bên* 'between.' The combination of these words, 'discern between,' is used in 1 Kings 3:9, 'That I may discern between good and evil.' *Biyn* includes the concept of distinguishment that leads to understanding" (*TWOT*, #239).

[349] For a deeper study of discernment, see chapter 6, "Where Has Our Discernment Gone?" in the author's *Truth On Tough Texts* (65–85)

[350] We would recommend Warren Wiersbe's, *Be Skillful (Proverbs): God's Guidebook to Wise Living* (David C. Cook, 2010), a wonderfully readable and practical exposition (as are all his "BE Series" expositions).

[351] Hywel R. Jones, Professor Emeritus of Practical Theology at Westminster Seminary California. Cited in William MacDonald, *Believer's Bible Commentary*, comment on Ex. 33:18–23.

[352] *TWOT*, #694.

[353] Robert Law, *The Tests of Life: A Study of the First Epistle of St. John* (Edinburgh: T. & T. Clark, 1909), 304.

[354] John R. Rice wrote, "Prayer is not praise, adoration, meditation, humiliation nor confession, but asking. . . . Praise is not prayer, and prayer is not praise. Prayer is asking. . . . Adoration is not prayer, and prayer is not adoration. Prayer is always asking. It is not anything else but asking" (*Prayer—Asking and Receiving* [Muphreesboro, TN: Sword of the Lord, 1942], 29).

[355] For a study of the seven words for prayer see the author's, *A Word for the Day: Key Words of the New Testament* (AMG Publishers, 2006), 149–50.

[356] Tozer, *The Tozer Pulpit (I Call It Heresy)*, Vol. 2, 20–32. For a detailed analysis of Tozer's work, see also the author's, *The Forgotten Tozer*.

[357] Gill, *Exposition of the Entire Bible*, comment on 1 Jn. 2:5 (emphasis added).

[358] A "Tozer-gram," cited in James L. Snyder, *In Pursuit of God: The Life of A. W. Tozer* (Christian Publications, 1991), 100.

[359] Thomas, *Puritan Golden Treasury*, 49.

[360] For a study of the names of God in the OT, see the author's *A Hebrew Word for the Day*, 7–31.

[361] *Matthew Henry's Commentary on the Whole Bible*, comment on Ps. 59:8–17.

[362] Zodhiates, *Word Study Dictionary*, entry #H776.

[363] Walter C. Kaiser, Jr., *Revive Us Again* (Broadman & Holman, 1999), 166.

[364] Gill, *Exposition of the Entire Bible*, comment on 2 Tim. 4:10. Others, such as Thomas Watson (*The Lord's Prayer* [Banner of Truth, 1989 reprint], 204) also cite Dorotheus, bishop of Tyre (c.255–362) on this point.

[365] Thomas, *Puritan Golden Treasury*, 313.

[366] Zodhiates, *Word Study Dictionary*, entry #G5373.

[367] For a deeper study of this misnomer, see chapter 28, "Is There a 'Carnal Christian'?" in the author's, *Truth On Tough Texts*, 274–81.

[368] The author once heard this statement by Ravi Zacharias.

[369] Barnes, *Notes on the Bible*, comment on Jn. 15:19.

[370] Delavan Leonard Pierson, *A. T. Pierson: A Biography* (London: James Nisbet & Co., 1912; Reprinted, Greeley CO: Chambers College Press, 2013), 30.

[371] *TWOT*, #233.
[372] Harry Ironside, *Proverbs* (Electronic edition), comment on Prov. 3:5–6.
[373] *TWOT*, #930.
[374] Cited in Paul R. Van Gorder, *In the Family: Studies in First John* (Radio Bible Class, 1978), 140–41.
[375] Theodore Epp, *Tests of Faith: Studies in the Epistles of John* (Back to the Bible, 1957), 88.
[376] *Mammōnas* does not mean just "money" as some modern translations weakly render it. "In rabbinic writings, it means not merely money in the strict sense but a man's possessions, everything that has value equivalent to money, and even all that he possesses apart from his body and life" (Brown, *NIDNTT*, Vol. 2, 837).
[377] The preceding sparked by a thought from Arthur W. Pink in his article, "Christian Service" (Public Domain, 1947).
[378] Zodhiates, *Word Study Dictionary*, #G1401.
[379] Tozer, *Pursuit of God*, 96.
[380] "I do solemnly swear (or affirm) that I will support and defend the Constitution of the United States against all enemies, foreign and domestic; that I will bear true faith and allegiance to the same; and that I will obey the orders of the President of the United States and the orders of the officers appointed over me, according to regulations and the Uniform Code of Military Justice. So help me God." Officers take a similar one.
[381] We lean toward the first interpretation. John Gill wrote: "It is agreeably to reason, and especially as sanctified, that men who have their beings from God, and are upheld in them by him, and are followed with the bounties of Providence; and especially who are made new creatures, and are blessed by him with all spiritual blessings in Christ, that they should give up themselves to him, and cheerfully serve him in their day and generation" (*Exposition of the Entire Bible*). Or as Isaac Watts' great hymn declares: "Love so amazing, so divine, demands my heart, my life, my all."
[382] Brown, *NIDNTT*, Vol. 1, 708–10.
[383] Wuest, *Word Studies*, comment on Romans 12:2.
[384] Ibid.
[385] John Phillips, *Exploring Romans* (Moody Press, 1969), 186.
[386] As reported in the December 1987 issue of *Life* magazine. (Disclaimer: Use of this illustration is not an endorsement of either the movie or the actors.)
[387] *Calvin's Commentaries*, comment on Is. 6:5.
[388] John Gill, *Exposition of the Entire Bible*, comment on Acts 8:37. As Gill explains, "This whole verse is wanting in the Alexandrian copy, and in five of Beza's copies, and in the Syriac and Ethiopic versions; but stands in the Vulgate Latin and Arabic versions, and in the Complutensian edition; and, as Beza observes, ought by no means to be expunged, since it contains so clear a confession of faith required of persons to be baptized, which was used in the truly apostolic times."
[389] Robertson, *Word Pictures*, comment on Rom. 14:10–12.
[390] William Macdonald, *Believer's Bible Commentary*, comment on 1 Cor. 9:19–22.
[391] Zodhiatus, *Expository Dictionary*, entry #G5299.
[392] Simon J. Kistemaker, *Baker's New Testament Commentary*, comment on 1 Cor. 15:58.

[393] Tozer, *God Tells the Man Who Cares*, 145.

[394] *Henry V*, III.1.1–8, 27–34.

[395] For a detailed exposition of "The Armor of God" in Ephesians 6, see Vol. 2 of the author's, *The Christian's Wealth and Walk: An Expository Commentary on Ephesians* (Sola Scriptura Publications, 2019).

[396] See the author's more detailed recounting of several historical figures in chapters 10 and 11 in *Upon This Rock*, 137–160. Our September 16 and 17 studies were adapted from those pages.

[397] In part, it reads: "We believe in . . . one Lord Jesus Christ, the only-begotten Son of God, begotten of the Father before all worlds; God of God, Light of Light, very God of very God; begotten, not made, being of one substance with the Father . . ."

[398] Warren Wiersbe, *The Wiersbe Bible Commentary: NT* (David C. Cook, 2007), comment on Phil. 2:19–30.

[399] For example, *karpos* (2590) means "fruit," while *akarpos* (175) means "without fruit, fruitless, barren." Likewise, the root *mōmos* (3470) means "spot, blemish" but with the prefix added, *amōmos* (299) means "without blemish; spotless; free from faultiness."

[400] Kittel, Vol. I, 145.

[401] The preceding adapted from the word study of *adelphos* in the author's *A Word for the Day*, 333.

[402] Leadership Coach, Bonnie Flatt: http://bonnieflatt.com/.

[403] Preaching at the Moody Bible Institute's Founder's Week in 1974.

[404] Brown, *NIDNTT*, Vol. 3, 839.

[405] Kittel, *TDNT*, Vol. III, 455.

[406] Dennis Hester (compiler), *The Vance Havner Notebook* (Baker, 1989), 44.

[407] *International Standard Bible Encyclopedia* (public domain, electronic edition), "Witness" entry.

[408] Thomas, *Puritan Golden Treasury*, 92–93.

[409] A. W. Tozer, *God Tells the Man Who Cares*, 168–69.

[410] Francis Schaeffer, *The God Who Is There* in *The Complete Works of Francis A. Schaeffer Trilogy* (Crossway, 1982), Vol. 1, 64–65.

[411] Thomas Watson, *Mischief of Sin* (Soli Deo Gloria, 1994; first published 1671), 151.

[412] Thomas, *Puritan Golden Treasury*, 103.

[413] Ibid.

[414] *Adam Clarke's Commentary* (public domain), comment on Heb. 11:2.

[415] Thomas, *Puritan Golden Treasury*, 103 (emphasis added).

[416] The Gap Theory was created for the sole purpose of fitting the geological ages into the Bible, teaching that Genesis 1:1 indicates complete creation, while 1:2 and what follows is the *re*creation after a "gap" of millions of years between the two verses. Similarly, the Day Age Theory teaches that each "day" of Creation consisted of millions of years, which again allows for the geological ages. Finally, because of the parallelism of the "days" of creation, the Framework Hypothesis looks at the Genesis account basically as poetry. Days 1, 2, and 3 describe the *formation* of the world, while 4, 5, and 6 answer to each of those with the *filling* of the world (e.g., Day 1, darkness, light, paralleled with Day 4, heavenly light-bearers). So, it is argued, the

biblical account is nothing more than a framework that should overlay our scientific understanding of origins.

[417] China Inland Mission.

[418] John Gill, *Exposition of the Entire Bible*, here cites the view of Aben Ezra (Abraham ibn Ezra, 1089–1167), one of the most distinguished Jewish rabbis of the Middle Ages. He was a poet, grammarian, and commentator.

[419] *Commentaries*, comment on Gen. 4:5.

[420] *TWOT*, entry #2429.

[421] See the author's, *Salvation Is of the Lord*, 120–22. In part:

"In its bare essence, justification is a legal (or forensic) term. It means 'to declare or pronounce righteous and just, not symbolically but actually.' Justification does not imply that there is no guilt. On the contrary, we are worthy of death. We who were once under condemnation are now declared to be righteous because of Christ. Justification is the declarative act of God, as the Judge, whereby He declares that the demands of justice have been satisfied so that the sinner is no longer condemned. In the strict sense of the word, justification does not *make* us righteous, nor does it change our behavior, for these are accomplished by *regeneration* and *sanctification* While all three of these work together, they are still distinct. On the other hand, justification is more than just pardoning the sinner, as a judge would pardon a criminal. Again, justification is a declaration, not of *innocence*, but of *satisfaction*."

[422] *Matthew Henry's Commentary on the Whole Bible*, comment on Rom. 6:4.

[423] *Commentaries*, comment on 2 Cor. 5:7.

[424] *Matthew Henry's Commentary*, comment on Eph. 5:2.

[425] William Gurnall in Thomas, *Puritan Golden Treasure*, 299.

[426] Zodhiates, *Word Study Dictionary*, #G3346.

[427] *Matthew Poole's Commentary on the Holy Bible*, comment on Heb. 11:5.

[428] Frederick Dunglison Power, *Life of William Kimbrough Pendleton: LL.D., President of Bethany College* (St. Louis: Christian Publishing Company, 1902), 484.

[429] Morris, *Defender's Study Bible*, note on Gen. 6:15.

[430] Watson, *Body of Divinity*, 112.

[431] Vincent, *Word Studies*, comment on Heb. 11:7.

[432] As noted on Jan. 24, Warren W. Wiersbe, *From Worry To Worship* (Back To The Bible, 1983). I would also recommend D. Martyn Lloyd-Jones' *From Fear To Faith* (InterVarsity, 1983).

[433] A minority of commentators submit that Abraham was not a pagan and remained separate from that culture. There is nothing in the text, however, that warrants such a view. The whole idea of God's calling him pictures salvation.

[434] *Commentaries*, comment on Heb. 11:8.

[435] Watson, *Body of Divinity*, 176.

[436] *Barnes' Notes on the Bible*, comment on Heb. 11:16.

[437] This has been credited to Charles Spurgeon.

[438] *Barnes' Notes on the Bible*, comment on Heb. 11:21.

[439] John Colbert (comedian, writer, producer, actor, media critic, and television host), A.V. Club interview, Jan. 25, 2006.

[440] Cited in Brown, *NIDNTT*, Vol. 3, 840–841, based on the writings of Aristotle (*Politics*, 1, 9, 1256b–1258a, 8; 2, 9, 1269a, 34f) and Plato (*Republic* 7, 521a; 8, 547b; *Phaedo* 279c).

[441] Kittel, *TDNT*, Vol. III, 452.

[442] Thomas, *Puritan Golden Treasury*, 103.

[443] Watson, *Sermons*, 401.

[444] Marten H. Woudstra, *The Book of Joshua, New International Commentary on the Old Testament* (Eerdmans, 1981), 109. Woudstra gives the measurements in meters: "600 meters and dimension of 225 by 80 meters."

[445] Zodhiates, *Word Study Dictionary*, #H4549.

[446] Our thanks to J. Sidlow Baxter for this descriptive term, *Explore the Book*, Vol. 2, 21–22.

[447] Vine, *Expository Dictionary*, "(To) Cloth" entry.

[448] For more on the Reformation, see the author's book, *Upon This Rock*.

[449] For a more detailed discussion, see chapter 27, "What Does the Scripture Say About Women Teachers?" in the author's *Truth On Tough Texts*, 266–73.

[450] Zodhiates, *Word Study Dictionary*, #H5973 and *TWOT* #1640b.

[451] Zodhiates writes, "In the NT *prophētēs* corresponds to the person who in the OT spoke under divine influence and inspiration. This included the foretelling future events or the exhorting, reproving, and threatening of individuals or nations as the ambassador of God and the interpreter of His will to men (Ezek. 2). Hence the prophet spoke not his own thoughts but what he received from God, retaining, however, his own consciousness and self–possession (Ex. 7:1; 2 Pet. 1:20, 21; especially 1 Cor. 14:32). . . . In Eph. 2:20; 3:5, the prophets, named side by side with the Apostles (meaning the Eleven and those who were commissioned by Jesus directly) as the foundation of the NT church, are to be understood as exclusively NT prophets. They are listed in Eph. 4:11 between apostles and evangelists (see 1 Cor. 12:28). NT prophets were for the Christian church what OT prophets were for Israel. They maintained intact the immediate connection between the church and the God of their salvation. They were messengers or communicators. Such prophets were not ordained in local churches nor do they have successors" (*Word Study Dictionary*, #G4396).

[452] *TWOT*, #1277, summarizes: "Actually the views of the derivation are four. 1) From an Arabic root, *naba'a*, 'to announce,' hence 'spokesman' (Cornill, Koenig, Eiselen, G. A. Smith). 2) From a Hebrew root, *nābā'*, softened from *nāba'* 'to bubble up,' hence pour forth words (Gesenius, von Orelli, Kuenen, Girdlestone, Oehler). 3) From an Akkadian root *nabû* 'to call,' hence one who is called [by God] (Albright, Rowley, Meek, Scott), hence one who felt called of God; 4) From an unknown Semitic root (A. B. Davidson, Koehler and Baumgartner, BDB, E. J. Young, Heinisch.) The latter view is favored by Hobart E. Freeman in his excellent book (*An Introduction to the Old Testament Prophets*, Moody, 1968, 37–39). This paragraph is a very brief summary of Freeman's treatment."

[453] Word studies adapted from the author's *A Word for the Day* (180) and *A Hebrew Word for the Day* (130).

[454] "Subdued kingdoms" refers to David; Josephus, in fact, used this term to refer to David. "Wrought righteousness" is also reminiscent of David (2 Sam. 7:15) as well as Samuel (1 Sam. 12:3–4). And it is David once again who "obtained promises" (2 Samuel 7:12–16).

[455] Arthur W. Pink, *An Exposition of the First Epistle of John* (public domain), comment on 1 Jn. 2:6.
[456] For a study of the authorship of Hebrews, see the author's "Does the Authorship of Hebrews Matter?" in *Truth on Tough Texts*, 86–98.
[457] Zodhiates, *Word Study Dictionary*, #G73.
[458] A. W. Tozer, *Born After Midnight* (Christian Publications, n.d), 15.
[459] Zodhiates, *Word Study Dictionary*, #G2023.
[460] See the author's *A Word for Day* (222) for more on this word as Paul used it.
[461] Martyn Lloyd-Jones, *Expository Sermons on 2 Peter* (Banner of Truth, 1983), 26.
[462] Kittel, *TDNT*, Vol. II, 341.
[463] Brown, *NIDNTT*, Vol. 2, 772.
[464] Kittel, *TDNT*, Vol. IV, 582.
[465] Zodhiates, *Word Study Dictionary*, #G2150.
[466] Zodhiates, *Word Study Dictionary*, #G3850.
[467] Zodhiates, *Word Study Dictionary*, #G4920.
[468] From the author's *Truth On Tough Texts* (427–28): "Various Bible teachers have made a huge issue of this by insisting they are distinct. I am convinced, however, that there is no difference in these terms. Here's why.

"During the Intertestament Period—the 400 years between the events of the OT and the NT—the Jewish people developed a superstitious fear of using God's name. Because they believed it was too holy, they didn't use the covenant name of God (Yahweh or Jehovah, indicated by the word LORD (note the small capital letters) in most English Bibles. As a result, they substituted other words for the name of God, and 'heaven' became a common substitute. By NT times, in fact, that practice was so ingrained that the Jewish people instantly understood any reference to the kingdom of *heaven* as a reference to the kingdom of *God*.

"Again, while some Bible teachers insist these two terms speak of two different things, they simply do not. Matthew is the *only* writer who uses Kingdom of Heaven" (32 times) because his audience was Jewish and would have been offended by the term *God*. While I do believe in certain distinctions in Scripture, I am convinced that this one has been needlessly manufactured. Scripture simply does not say they are different.

"Parallel accounts in the other Gospels prove this beyond any doubt. Matthew 4:17, for example, recounts that Jesus preached, 'Repent: for the kingdom of *heaven* [*ouranos*] is at hand,' while Mark's account (1:15) of the same scene states that Jesus preached, 'The kingdom of *God* [*theos*] is at hand: repent ye, and believe the gospel.' If these terms refer to two totally different things, then the inescapable conclusion is that either Matthew or Mark misspoke. Likewise, in the Beatitudes, Matthew records Jesus saying: 'Blessed are the poor in spirit: for theirs is the kingdom of *heaven* [*ouranos*]' (5:3), while Luke's account reads, 'Blessed be ye poor: for yours is the kingdom of *God* [*theos*]' (6:20). If I may be so blunt, arguing over these terms is just silly and even counterproductive.

"So, to what do these refer? Both refer to the sphere of God's dominion over His people. While presently that is God's rule over the hearts of believers (Luke 17:21), it will be fully realized in the literal, earthly millennial kingdom (Rev. 20:4–6)."
[469] Origen, *Homily* 34.3, Joseph T. Lienhard, trans., *Origen: Homilies on Luke, Fragments on Luke* (1996), 138.

[470] George M. Ella, *John Gill: And the Cause of God and Truth* (Durham, England: Go Publications, 1995), 190.
[471] *International Standard Bible Encyclopedia* (public domain).
[472] Zodhiates, *Word Study Dictionary*, #G4697.
[473] Alfred Edersheim, *The Life and Times of Jesus the Messiah*, New Updated Edition (Hendrickson, 1993), 791 (emphasis in the original).
[474] Noah Webster's 1828 *Dictionary of American English* (public domain).
[475] *Expository Thoughts on the Gospels: St. Matthew* (Cambridge: James Clarke, 1974), 336–37 ("our" removed from each item in list to shorten the quote).
[476] Brown, *NIDNTT*, Vol. 2, 616.
[477] Zodhiates, *Word Study Dictionary*, #3107. See the author's deeper discussion of *makarios* and two related words ("hope" and "joy") in *A Word for the Day*, 12–14.
[478] *Young's Literal Translation* (YLT).
[479] Thomas, *Puritan Golden Treasury*, 68.
[480] Thayer, *Lexicon of the New Testament*, entry #40. See the author's deeper discussion of *aphrōn* and the related word *anoētos* (453) in *A Word for the Day*, 92–93.
[481] Vance Havner, *Seasonings* (Fleming H. Revell, 1970), 54
[482] Thomas, *Puritan Golden Treasury*, 112.
[483] *Commentaries*.
[484] Oswald Chambers, *My Utmost for His Highest* (Discovery House, 1963), from September 7 reading.
[485] Harry Ironside, *Addresses on the Second Epistle to the Corinthians* (Loizeau Brothers, 1939, 1958), 194.
[486] *Commentaries*.
[487] The late Robert Bearss, a dear pastor and friend, enjoyed telling this story: "The Sunday School teacher asked her class of 10-year-olds, 'Who would give a million dollars to the missionaries?' Immediately every hand enthusiastically shot up into the air. 'Well,' she continued, 'Who would give a thousand dollars to the missionaries?' Again, every hand was eagerly raised. 'Now,' she continued again, 'Who would give a dollar to the missionaries?' Once again, every hand was raised with great excitement, except for one boy, who instead, scowled and gripped his pants pocket. 'Johnny,' the teacher asked, 'Why didn't you raise your hand this time?' 'Well, you see,' stammered Johnny, 'I *have* a dollar.'"
[488] *Metropolitan Tabernacle Pulpit*, sermon #2234, "The Best Donation (2 Cor. 8:5)."
[489] Cited in Brown, *NIDNTT*, Vol. 3, 840–841, based on the writings of Aristotle (*Politics*, 1, 9, 1256b–1258a, 8; 2, 9, 1269a, 34f) and Plato (*Republic* 7, 521a; 8, 547b; *Phaedo* 279c).
[490] Brown, *NIDNTT*, Vol. 3, 572.
[491] Harry Ironside, *Addresses on the Second Epistle to the Corinthian* (Loizeau Brothers), comment on 8:1–3.
[492] Zodhiates, *Word Study Dictionary*, #3107. See the author's deeper discussion of *makarios* and two related words ("hope" and "joy") in *A Word for the Day*, 12–14.
[493] Harry Ironside, *Addresses on Acts* (Loizeau Brothers, 1939, 1958), comment on 20:35.
[494] A. W. Tozer, *Whatever Happened to Worship?* (Christian Publications, 1995), 97.

[495] Thomas, *Puritan Golden Treasury*, 54 (emphasis in the original, but quotation slightly compressed).

[496] *Treasury of David*, comment on Ps. 27:4.

[497] R. Kent Hughes, *Preaching the Word: Hebrews, Volume 2, An Anchor For The Soul* (Crossway Books, 1993), electronic edition.

[498] Gill, *Exposition of the Old and New Testaments*, comment on Heb. 10:25.

[499] E. Schuyler English, *Studies in the Epistle to the Hebrews* (Findlay, OH: Dunham Publishing Company, 1955), 315.

[500] William Hendrickson and Simon Kistemaker, *Baker's New Testament Commentary* (Baker, 1984), electronic edition, comment on Heb. 10:25.

[501] Latin, *exceptio probat regulum*. The often used expression "the exception proves the rule" is imprecise, "leading the unwary to think that any self-respecting rules must have an exception. What is meant is that the existence of an exception to a rule provides an opportunity to test the validity of a rule: Finding an exception to a rule enables us to define the rule more precisely, confirming its applicability to those items truly covered by the rule" (Eugene Ehrlich, *Amo, Amas, Amat and More* [Harper and Row, Hudson Group, 1985], 121).

[502] Lloyd J. Ogilvie (Ed.), *The Preacher's Commentary* (Thomas Nelson, 1982–1992), electronic edition, note on Heb. 10:25.

[503] Death, the last judgment, the destruction of Jerusalem, heightened persecution, or Christ's Second Coming.

[504] *Life Application Study Bible*.

[505] Zodhiates, *Word Study Dictionary*, #G1573.

[506] Thayer, *Lexicon*, #1573.

[507] Brown, *NIDNTT*, Vol. 1, p. 262.

[508] John Milton, *Paradise Lost*, Book V, Line 538.

[509] Zodhiates, *Word Study Dictionary*, #G4355.

[510] Isaac Watts, *Logic: Or, The Right Use of Reason* (Boston: John West and Company, 1809), 162.

[511] Brown, *NIDNTT*, Vol. 1, 260.

[512] *Bible Knowledge Commentary*.

[513] Kittel, *TDNT*, Vol. IX, 84.

[514] *Morning and Evening*, November 26, Morning.

[515] *Philippian Studies: Lessons in Faith and Love* (London: Hodder and Stoughton, 1897), 97.

[516] R.C.H. Lenski, *Commentary on the New Testament: Galatians, Ephesians, Philippians* (Hendrickson, 2001), 769.

[517] John Philipps, *Exploring Ephesians and Philippians: An Expository Commentary* (Kregal, 1995), 81.

[518] James Montgomery Boice, *Philippians* (Baker, 1971, 2000, electronic edition), comment on Phil. 2:8.

[519] Lehman Strauss, *Devotional Studies In Philippians* (Loizeaux, 1959), 111–116.

[520] James Montgomery Boice, *Philippians* (Baker, 2000), 139–40 (emphasis added).

[521] See the author's *Salvation Is of the Lord*. For a short, basic presentation, see his *The Doctrines of Grace From the Lips of our Lord*.

[522] Zodhiates, *Word Study Dictionary*, #G407.

[523] Address at Harrow School, October 29, 1941 (*Bartlett's Familiar Quotations*).
Famous also were Churchill's words on August 20, 1940, during the Battle of Britain: "Never in the field of human conflict has so much been owed by so many to so few." He meant that the whole population (so many) owed an unpayable debt to so few (the RAF pilots) who saved England from Hitler. In the spirit of such dedication, let us adapt that statement: *Never in the realm of spiritual conflict has so much been owed by so many to a single one.*

As one historian adds, however, Churchill "was not able to include the scientists as a crucial part of those 'few' because they made their contributions in the secret war of code breaking and surveillance. Without them Britain surely would have gone down. . . . Their contribution gave the British radar superiority, critical to the RAF. With radar, the RAF knew about each incoming wave of bombers without wasting fuel and flying time scouting for them. Radar gave them a [15–20] minute warning when Germans were approaching the English coast as well as relatively accurate prediction as to the size of formation and direction of flight. Thus, radar was the source of victory—the first time electronic devices were the decisive factor in a battle" (Stephen E. Ambrose and C. L. Sulzberger, *American Heritage History of World War II* [Viking Adult; Rev Sub edition, 1997], 79).

[524] See Apr. 22, 25; Sept. 26; and Dec. 4.
[525] Sermon #2406, "An Appeal to Children of Godly Parents," March 31, 1895.
[526] *My Sermon Notes*, (public domain), Vol. 4, 215.
[527] Sermon #1652, "The Singing Pilgrim."
[528] A. W. Tozer, *Paths To Power* (Christian Publications, n.d.), 24–25.
[529] Zodhiates, *Word Study Dictionary*, entry #G5179.
[530] Vincent, *Words Studies*, comment in 1 Thes. 1:8.
[531] *The Soul Winner* (Revell, 1895), 28 (emphasis in the original).
[532] See 2:17, 19; 3:13; 4:15–17; 5:8, 23; 2 Thess. 3:6–12.
[533] Vine, *Expository Dictionary*, "Wait" entry.
[534] Thomas, *Puritan Golden Treasury*, 48.
[535] Warren Wiersbe, *The Wiersbe Bible Commentary: NT* (David C. Cook, 2007), comment on 1 Thes. 1:9–10.
[536] Packer, *Knowing God*, 34.
[537] Cited in R. A. Bertram (compiler) *A Homiletic Encyclopaedia of Illustrations in Theology and Morals: A Handbook of Practical Divinity and a Commentary on Holy Scripture*, Fourth Edition (London: R. D. Dickinson, 1880).

Made in the USA
Middletown, DE
28 May 2024